한국의 토익 수험자 여러분께,

토익 시험은 세계적인 직무 영어능력 평가 시험으로, 지난 40여 년간 비즈니스 현장에서 필요한 영어능력 평가의 기준을 제시해 왔습니다. 토익 시험 및 토익스피킹, 토익라이팅 시험은 세계에서 가장 널리 통용되는 영어능력 검증 시험으로, 160여 개국 14,000여 기관이 토익 성적을 의사결정에 활용하고 있습니다.

YBM은 한국의 토익 시험을 주관하는 ETS 독점 계약사입니다.

ETS는 한국 수험자들의 효과적인 토익 학습을 돕고자 YBM을 통하여 'ETS 토익 공식 교재'를 독점 출간하고 있습니다. 또한 'ETS 토익 공식 교재' 시리즈에 기출문항을 제공해 한국의 다른 교재들에 수록된 기출을 복제하거나 변형한 문항으로 인하여 발생할 수 있는 수험자들의 혼동을 방지하고 있습니다.

복제 및 변형 문항들은 토익 시험의 출제의도를 벗어날 수 있기 때문에 기출문항을 수록한 'ETS 토익 공식 교재'만큼 시험에 잘 대비할 수 없습니다.

'ETS 토익 공식 교재'를 통하여 수험자 여러분의 영어 소통을 위한 노력에 큰 성취가 있기를 바랍니다.

감사합니다.

Dear TOEIC Test Takers in Korea,

The TOEIC program is the global leader in English-language assessment for the workplace. It has set the standard for assessing English-language skills needed in the workplace for more than 40 years. The TOEIC tests are the most widely used English language assessments around the world, with 14,000+ organizations across more than 160 countries trusting TOEIC scores to make decisions.

YBM is the ETS Country Master Distributor for the TOEIC program in Korea and so is the exclusive distributor for TOEIC Korea.

To support effective learning for TOEIC test-takers in Korea, ETS has authorized YBM to publish the only Official TOEIC prep books in Korea. These books contain actual TOEIC items to help prevent confusion among Korean test-takers that might be caused by other prep book publishers' use of reproduced or paraphrased items.

Reproduced or paraphrased items may fail to reflect the intent of actual TOEIC items and so will not prepare test-takers as well as the actual items contained in the ETS TOEIC Official prep books published by YBM.

We hope that these ETS TOEIC Official prep books enable you, as test-takers, to achieve great success in your efforts to communicate effectively in English.

Thank you.

입문부터 실전까지 수준별 학습을 통해 최단기 목표점수 달성!

ETS TOEIC® 공식수험서
스마트 학습 지원

구글플레이, 앱스토어에서
ETS 토익기출 수험서 다운로드

구글플레이   앱스토어

ETS 토익 모바일 학습 플랫폼!
ETS® 토익기출 수험서 [어플]

교재 학습 지원
1. 교재 해설 강의
2. LC 음원 MP3
3. 교재/부록 모의고사 채점 및 분석
4. 단어 암기장

부가 서비스
1. 데일리 학습(토익 기출문제 풀이)
2. 토익 최신 경향 무료 특강
3. 토익 타이머

모의고사 결과 분석
1. 파트별/문항별 정답률
2. 파트별/유형별 취약점 리포트
3. 전체 응시자 점수 분포도

ETS TOEIC 공식카페 ▼

etstoeicbook.co.kr

ETS 토익 학습 전용 온라인 커뮤니티!
ETS TOEIC® Book [공식카페]

강사진의 학습 지원   토익 대표강사들의 학습 지원과 멘토링

교재 학습관 운영   교재별 학습게시판을 통해 무료 동영상 강의 등 학습 지원

학습 콘텐츠 제공   토익 학습 콘텐츠와 정기시험 예비특강 업데이트

---

www.ybmbooks.com에서도 무료 MP3를 다운로드 받을 수 있습니다.

RC

All New

토익 정기시험
실전 1

1000

토익 정기시험
실전❶ 1000
RC

발행인 허문호
발행처 YBM

편집 이태경, 이혜진, 박효민, 오유진
디자인 강상문, 이미화, 이현숙
마케팅 정연철, 박천산, 고영노, 김동진, 박찬경, 김윤하

초판인쇄 2023년 6월 12일
3쇄발행 2024년 1월 2일

신고일자 1964년 3월 28일
신고번호 제 300-1964-3호
주소 서울시 종로구 종로 104
전화 (02) 2000-0515 [구입문의] / (02) 2000-0383 [내용문의]
팩스 (02) 2285-1523
홈페이지 www.ybmbooks.com

ISBN 978-89-17-23932-4

RC

All New
토익®
정기시험
실전 1

실전 1

1000

PREFACE

Dear test taker,

Welcome to the new ETS® TOEIC® 정기시험 실전 1000 Vol.1. Now more than ever, English proficiency is a key to success in our increasingly globalized world. Whether you want to clearly communicate with friends and work colleagues, efficiently interpret business documents, or easily navigate international travel, this test preparation book has been designed to help you meet your English-language goals through the TOEIC test.

The ETS® TOEIC® 정기시험 실전 1000 Vol.1 is unique among test preparation materials. This book contains TOEIC practice tests created by the same team of English-language experts at ETS who develop the actual TOEIC Tests. These practice tests go through the same rigorous review process as the ones you will encounter on test day. There is no better resource to use as you prepare to take the TOEIC test.

The ETS® TOEIC® 정기시험 실전 1000 Vol.1 includes the following key features:

- Nine complete practice test forms and one actual test
- New TOEIC questions of the same quality and difficulty level as those in actual TOEIC test forms
- Specific explanations to help learners prepare for the test

By using this test preparation book, you can be confident that you will be studying authentic materials that will help you to build both your English skills and your familiarity with the test structure and question types. It is one of the best resources available to help you maximize your TOEIC test score and demonstrate to the world what you can do.

Thank you for choosing to use the ETS® TOEIC® 정기시험 실전 1000 Vol.1 for your test-preparation needs. We wish you all the best in your language-learning journey.

최신 실전문제
전격 공개!

'출제기관이 독점 제공한' 실전문제가 담긴 유일한 교재!

이 책에는 정기시험 실전문제 9세트와 기출문제 1세트가 수록되어 있다.
최신 ETS 실전문제로 실전 감각을 키워 시험에 확실하게 대비하자!

핵심 포인트를 꿰뚫는 명쾌한 해설!

최신 출제 경향을 가장 정확하게 알 수 있는 실전문제를 풀고
출제포인트가 보이는 명쾌한 해설로 토익을 정복해 보자!

'ETS가 제공하는' 표준 점수 환산표!

출제기관 ETS가 독점 제공하는 표준 점수 환산표를 수록했다.
채점 후 환산표를 통해 자신의 실력이 어느 정도인지 가늠해 보자!

TOEIC 소개

Test of English for International Communication(국제적 의사소통을 위한 영어 시험)의 약자로, 영어가 모국어가 아닌 사람들이 일상생활 또는 비즈니스 현장에서 꼭 필요한 실용적 영어 구사 능력을 갖추었는가를 평가하는 시험이다.

시험 구성

구성	PART	유형		문항 수	시간	배점
Listening	Part 1	사진 묘사		6	45분	495점
	Part 2	질의응답		25		
	Part 3	짧은 대화		39		
	Part 4	짧은 담화		30		
Reading	Part 5	단문 빈칸 채우기		30	75분	495점
	Part 6	장문 빈칸 채우기		16		
	Part 7	독해	단일 지문	29		
			이중 지문	10		
			삼중 지문	15		
Total	**7 Parts**			**200문항**	**120분**	**990점**

평가 항목

LC	RC
단문을 듣고 이해하는 능력	읽은 글을 통해 추론해 생각할 수 있는 능력
짧은 대화체 문장을 듣고 이해하는 능력	장문에서 특정한 정보를 찾을 수 있는 능력
비교적 긴 대화체에서 주고받은 내용을 파악할 수 있는 능력	글의 목적, 주제, 의도 등을 파악하는 능력
장문에서 핵심이 되는 정보를 파악할 수 있는 능력	뜻이 유사한 단어들의 정확한 용례를 파악하는 능력
구나 문장에서 화자의 목적이나 함축된 의미를 이해하는 능력	문장 구조를 제대로 파악하는지, 문장에서 필요한 품사, 어구 등을 찾는 능력

※ 성적표에는 전체 수험자의 평균과 해당 수험자가 받은 성적이 백분율로 표기되어 있다.

수험 정보

시험 접수 방법

한국 토익 위원회 사이트(www.toeic.co.kr)에서 시험일 약 2개월 전부터
온라인으로 접수 가능

시험장 준비물

신분증	규정 신분증만 가능 (주민등록증, 운전면허증, 기간 만료 전의 여권, 공무원증)
필기구	연필, 지우개 (볼펜이나 사인펜은 사용 금지)

시험 진행 시간

09:20	입실 (9:50 이후 입실 불가)
09:30 ~ 09:45	답안지 작성에 관한 오리엔테이션
09:45 ~ 09:50	휴식
09:50 ~ 10:05	신분증 확인
10:05 ~ 10:10	문제지 배부 및 파본 확인
10:10 ~ 10:55	듣기 평가 (LISTENING TEST)
10:55 ~ 12:10	독해 평가 (READING TEST)

TOEIC 성적 확인

시험일로부터 약 10-11일 후, 인터넷과 ARS(060-800-0515)로 성적을 확인할 수 있다.
TOEIC 성적표는 우편이나 온라인으로 발급받을 수 있다(시험 접수 시 양자택일).
우편으로 발급받을 경우는 성적 발표 후 대략 일주일이 소요되며, 온라인 발급을 선택하면
유효기간 내에 홈페이지에서 본인이 직접 1회에 한해 무료 출력할 수 있다. TOEIC 성적은
시험일로부터 2년간 유효하다.

토익 점수

TOEIC 점수는 듣기 영역(LC)과 읽기 영역(RC)을 합계한 점수로 5점 단위로 구성되며 총점은
990점이다. TOEIC 성적은 각 문제 유형의 난이도에 따른 점수 환산표에 의해 결정된다.

토익 경향 분석

PART 1 사진 묘사 Photographs

총 6문제

1인 등장 사진

주어는 He/She, A man/woman 등이며 주로 앞부분에 나온다.

2인 이상 등장 사진

주어는 They, Some men/women/people, One of the men/women 등이며 주로 중간 부분에 나온다.

사물/배경 사진

주어는 A car, Some chairs 등이며 주로 뒷부분에 나온다.

사람 또는 사물 중심 사진

주어가 일부는 사람, 일부는 사물이며 주로 뒷부분에 나온다.

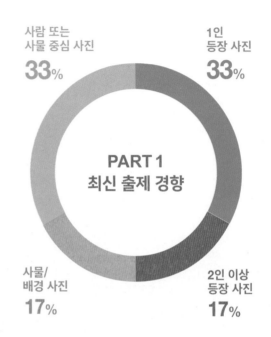

사람 또는 사물 중심 사진 **33**%

1인 등장 사진 **33**%

PART 1 최신 출제 경향

사물/배경 사진 **17**%

2인 이상 등장 사진 **17**%

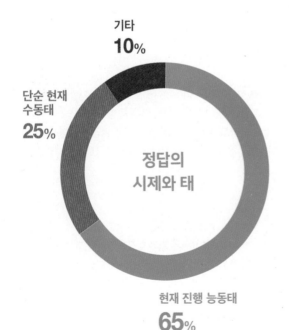

기타 **10**%

단순 현재 수동태 **25**%

정답의 시제와 태

현재 진행 능동태 **65**%

현재 진행 능동태

<is/are + 현재분사> 형태이며 주로 사람이 주어이다.

단순 현재 수동태

<is/are + 과거분사> 형태이며 주로 사물이 주어이다.

기타

<is/are + being + 과거분사> 형태의 현재 진행 수동태, <has/have + been + 과거분사> 형태의 현재 완료 수동태, '타동사 + 목적어' 형태의 단순 현재 능동태, There is/are와 같은 단순 현재도 나온다.

PART 2 질의응답 Question-Response

평서문
질문이 아니라 객관적인 사실이나 화자의 의견
등을 나타내는 문장이다.

의문사 의문문
각 의문사마다 1~2개씩 나온다. 의문사가
단독으로 나오기도 하지만 What time ~?,
How long ~?, Which room ~? 등에서처럼
다른 명사나 형용사와 같이 나오기도 한다.

명령문
동사원형이나 Please 등으로 시작한다.

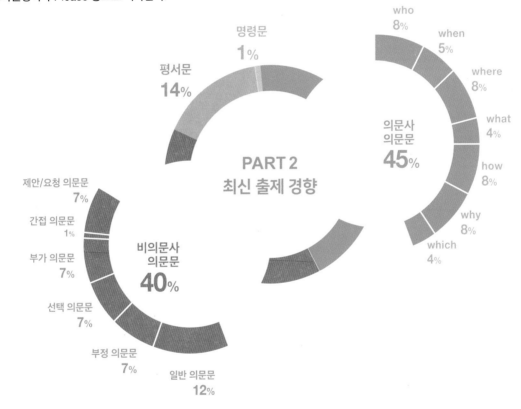

PART 2 최신 출제 경향

- 명령문 1%
- 평서문 14%
- 제안/요청 의문문 7%
- 간접 의문문 1%
- 부가 의문문 7%
- 선택 의문문 7%
- 부정 의문문 7%
- 일반 의문문 12%
- 비의문사 의문문 40%
- 의문사 의문문 45%
  - who 8%
  - when 5%
  - where 8%
  - what 4%
  - how 8%
  - why 8%
  - which 4%

비의문사 의문문
일반(Yes/No) 의문문 적게 나올 때는 한두 개, 많이 나올 때는 서너 개씩 나오는 편이다.
부정 의문문 Don't you ~?, Isn't he ~? 등으로 시작하는 문장이며 일반 긍정 의문문보다는 약간 더 적게 나온다.
선택 의문문 A or B 형태로 나오며 A와 B의 형태가 단어, 구, 절일 수 있다. 구나 절일 경우 문장이 길어져서 어려워진다.
부가 의문문 ~ don't you?, ~ isn't he? 등으로 끝나는 문장이며, 일반 부정 의문문과 비슷하다고 볼 수 있다.
간접 의문문 의문사가 문장 처음 부분이 아니라 문장 중간에 들어 있다.
제안/요청 의문문 정보를 얻기보다는 상대방의 도움이나 동의 등을 얻기 위한 목적이 일반적이다.

PART 3 짧은 대화 Short Conversations

- 3인 대화의 경우 남자 화자 두 명과 여자 화자 한 명 또는 남자 화자 한 명과 여자 화자 두 명이 나온다. 따라서 문제에서는 2인 대화에서와 달리 the man이나 the woman이 아니라 the men이나 the women 또는 특정한 이름이 언급될 수 있다.

- 대화 & 시각 정보는 항상 파트의 뒷부분에 나온다.

- 시각 정보의 유형으로 chart, map, floor plan, schedule, table, weather forecast, directory, list, invoice, receipt, sign, packing slip 등 다양한 자료가 골고루 나온다.

PART 3 대화의 유형
2인 대화 & 시각 정보 23%
2인 대화 63%
3인 대화 14%

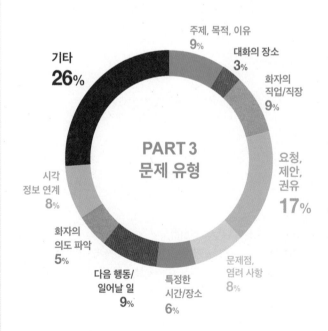

PART 3 문제 유형
기타 26%
주제, 목적, 이유 9%
대화의 장소 3%
화자의 직업/직장 9%
요청, 제안, 권유 17%
문제점, 염려 사항 8%
특정한 시간/장소 6%
다음 행동/ 일어날 일 9%
화자의 의도 파악 5%
시각 정보 연계 8%

- 주제, 목적, 이유, 대화의 장소, 화자의 직업/직장 등과 관련된 문제는 주로 대화의 첫 번째 문제로 나오며 다음 행동/일어날 일 등과 관련된 문제는 주로 대화의 세 번째 문제로 나온다.

- 화자의 의도 파악 문제는 주로 2인 대화에 나오지만, 가끔 3인 대화에 나오기도 한다. 시각 정보 연계 대화에는 나오지 않고 있다.

- Part 3에서 화자의 의도 파악 문제는 2개가 나오고 시각 정보 연계 문제는 3개가 나온다.

PART 4 짧은 담화 Short Talks

총 10담화문 30문제 (지문당 3문제)

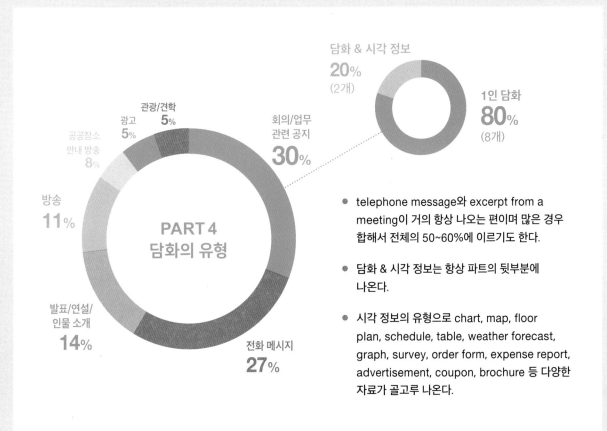

담화 & 시각 정보
20%
(2개)

1인 담화
80%
(8개)

관광/견학 5%
광고 5%
공공장소 안내 방송 8%
회의/업무 관련 공지 30%
방송 11%

PART 4
담화의 유형

발표/연설/ 인물 소개 14%

전화 메시지 27%

- telephone message와 excerpt from a meeting이 거의 항상 나오는 편이며 많은 경우 합해서 전체의 50~60%에 이르기도 한다.

- 담화 & 시각 정보는 항상 파트의 뒷부분에 나온다.

- 시각 정보의 유형으로 chart, map, floor plan, schedule, table, weather forecast, graph, survey, order form, expense report, advertisement, coupon, brochure 등 다양한 자료가 골고루 나온다.

- 문제 유형은 기본적으로 Part 3과 거의 비슷하다.

- 주제, 목적, 이유, 담화의 장소, 화자의 직업/직장 등과 관련된 문제는 주로 담화의 첫 번째 문제로 나오며 다음 행동/일어날 일 등과 관련된 문제는 주로 담화의 세 번째 문제로 나온다.

- Part 4에서 화자의 의도 파악 문제는 3개가 나오고 시각 정보 연계 문제는 2개가 나온다.

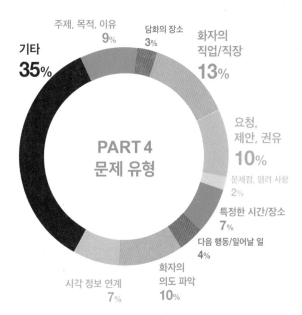

주제, 목적, 이유 9%
담화의 장소 3%
기타 35%
화자의 직업/직장 13%

PART 4
문제 유형

요청, 제안, 권유 10%
문제점, 염려 사항 2%
특정한 시간/장소 7%
다음 행동/일어날 일 4%

시각 정보 연계 7%
화자의 의도 파악 10%

문법 문제

시제와 대명사와 관련된 문법 문제가 2개씩, 한정사와 분사와 관련된 문법 문제가 1개씩 나온다. 시제 문제의 경우 능동태/수동태나 수의 일치와 연계되기도 한다. 그 밖에 한정사, 능동태/수동태, 부정사, 동명사 등과 관련된 문법 문제가 나온다.

어휘 문제

동사, 명사, 형용사, 부사와 관련된 어휘 문제가 각각 2~3개씩 골고루 나온다. 전치사 어휘 문제는 3개씩 꾸준히 나오지만, 접속사나 어구와 관련된 어휘 문제는 나오지 않을 때도 있고 3개가 나올 때도 있다.

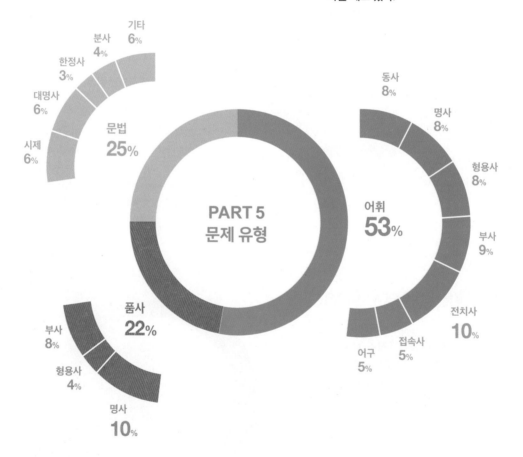

품사 문제

명사와 부사와 관련된 품사 문제가 2~3개씩 나오며, 형용사와 관련된 품사 문제가 상대적으로 적은 편이다.

PART 6 장문 빈칸 채우기 Text Completion

총 4지문 16문제 (지문당 4문제)

한 지문에 4문제가 나오며 평균적으로 어휘 문제가 2개, 품사나 문법 문제가 1개, 문맥에 맞는 문장 고르기 문제가 1개 들어간다. 문맥에 맞는 문장 고르기 문제를 제외하면 문제 유형은 기본적으로 파트 5와 거의 비슷하다.

어휘 문제

동사, 명사, 부사, 어구와 관련된 어휘 문제는 매번 1~2개씩 나온다. 부사 어휘 문제의 경우 therefore(그러므로)나 however(하지만)처럼 문맥의 흐름을 자연스럽게 연결해 주는 부사가 자주 나온다.

문맥에 맞는 문장 고르기

문맥에 맞는 문장 고르기 문제는 지문당 한 문제씩 나오는데, 나오는 위치의 확률은 4문제 중 두 번째 문제, 세 번째 문제, 네 번째 문제, 첫 번째 문제 순으로 높다.

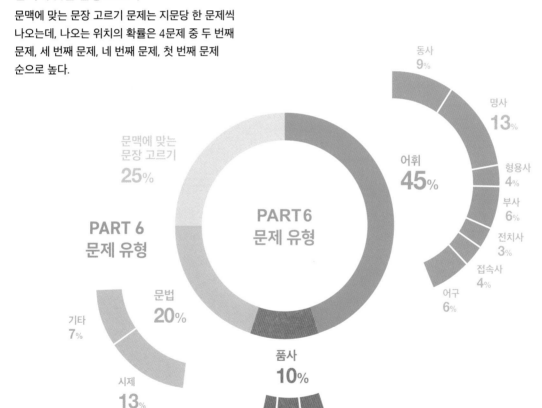

문맥에 맞는 문장 고르기 25%

PART 6 문제 유형

PART 6 문제 유형

문법 20%

기타 7%

시제 13%

동사 9%

명사 13%

어휘 45%

형용사 4%

부사 6%

전치사 3%

접속사 4%

어구 6%

품사 10%

부사 2% 형용사 4% 명사 4%

문법 문제

문맥의 흐름과 밀접하게 관련이 있는 시제 문제가 2개 정도 나오며, 능동태/수동태나 수의 일치와 연계되기도 한다. 그 밖에 대명사, 능동태/수동태, 부정사, 접속사/전치사 등과 관련된 문법 문제가 나온다.

품사 문제

명사나 형용사 문제가 부사 문제보다 좀 더 자주 나온다.

지문 유형	지문당 문제 수	지문 개수	비중 %
단일 지문	2문항	4개	약 15%
	3문항	3개	약 16%
	4문항	3개	약 22%
이중 지문	5문항	2개	약 19%
삼중 지문	5문항	3개	약 28%

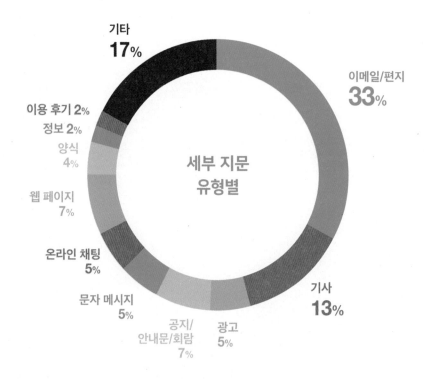

세부 지문 유형별

기타 17%
이메일/편지 33%
기사 13%
이용 후기 2%
정보 2%
양식 4%
웹 페이지 7%
온라인 채팅 5%
문자 메시지 5%
공지/안내문/회람 7%
광고 5%

● 이메일/편지, 기사 유형 지문은 거의 항상 나오는 편이며 많은 경우 합해서 전체의 50~60%에 이르기도 한다.

● 기타 지문 유형으로 agenda, brochure, comment card, coupon, flyer, instructions, invitation, invoice, list, menu, page from a catalog, policy statement, report, schedule, survey, voucher 등 다양한 자료가 골고루 나온다.

(이중 지문과 삼중 지문 속의 지문들을 모두 낱개로 계산함 – 총 23지문)

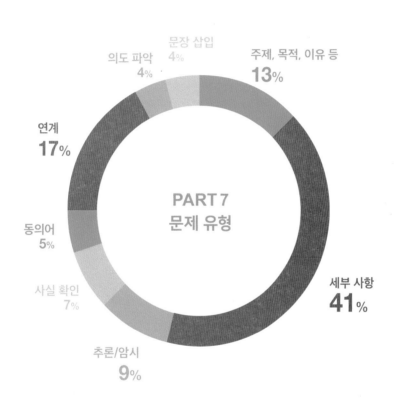

의도 파악
4%

문장 삽입
4%

주제, 목적, 이유 등
13%

연계
17%

PART 7
문제 유형

세부 사항
41%

동의어
5%

사실 확인
7%

추론/암시
9%

- 동의어 문제는 주로 이중 지문이나 삼중 지문에 나온다.
- 연계 문제는 일반적으로 이중 지문에서 한 문제, 삼중 지문에서 두 문제가 나온다.
- 의도 파악 문제는 문자 메시지(text-message chain)나 온라인 채팅(online chat discussion) 지문에서
  출제되며 두 문제가 나온다.
- 문장 삽입 문제는 주로 기사, 이메일, 편지, 회람 지문에서 출제되며 두 문제가 나온다.

점수 환산표 및 산출법

점수 환산표 이 책에 수록된 각 Test를 풀고 난 후, 맞은 개수를 세어 점수를 환산해 보세요.

LISTENING Raw Score (맞은 개수)	LISTENING Scaled Score (환산 점수)	READING Raw Score (맞은 개수)	READING Scaled Score (환산 점수)
96-100	475-495	96-100	460-495
91-95	435-495	91-95	425-490
86-90	405-470	86-90	400-465
81-85	370-450	81-85	375-440
76-80	345-420	76-80	340-415
71-75	320-390	71-75	310-390
66-70	290-360	66-70	285-370
61-65	265-335	61-65	255-340
56-60	240-310	56-60	230-310
51-55	215-280	51-55	200-275
46-50	190-255	46-50	170-245
41-45	160-230	41-45	140-215
36-40	130-205	36-40	115-180
31-35	105-175	31-35	95-150
26-30	85-145	26-30	75-120
21-25	60-115	21-25	60-95
16-20	30-90	16-20	45-75
11-15	5-70	11-15	30-55
6-10	5-60	6-10	10-40
1-5	5-50	1-5	5-30
0	5-35	0	5-15

점수 산출 방법 아래의 방식으로 점수를 산출할 수 있다.

STEP 1

자신의 답안을 수록된 정답과 대조하여 채점한다. 각 Section의 맞은 개수가 본인의 Section별 '실제 점수(통계 처리하기 전의 점수, raw score)'이다. Listening Test와 Reading Test의 정답 수를 세어, 자신의 실제 점수를 아래의 해당란에 기록한다.

	맞은 개수	환산 점수대
LISTENING		
READING		
총점		

Section별 실제 점수가 그대로 Section별 TOEIC 점수가 되는 것은 아니다. TOEIC은 시행할 때마다 별도로 특정한 통계 처리 방법을 사용하며 이러한 실제 점수를 환산 점수(converted[scaled] score)로 전환하게 된다. 이렇게 전환함으로써, 매번 시행될 때마다 문제는 달라지지만 그 점수가 갖는 의미는 같아지게 된다. 예를 들어 어느 한 시험에서 총점 550점의 성적을 받는 실력이라면 다른 시험에서도 거의 550점대의 성적을 받게 되는 것이다.

STEP 2

실제 점수를 위 표에 기록한 후 왼쪽 페이지의 점수 환산표를 보도록 한다. TOEIC이 시행될 때마다 대개 이와 비슷한 형태의 표가 작성되는데, 여기 제시된 환산표는 본 교재에 수록된 Test용으로 개발된 것이다. 이 표를 사용하여 자신의 실제 점수를 환산 점수로 전환하도록 한다. 즉, 예를 들어 Listening Test의 실제 정답 수가 61~65개이면 환산 점수는 265점에서 335점 사이가 된다. 여기서 실제 정답 수가 61개이면 환산 점수가 265점이고, 65개이면 환산 점수가 335점 임을 의미하는 것은 아니다. 본 책의 Test를 위해 작성된 이 점수 환산표가 자신의 영어 실력이 어느 정도인지 대략적으로 파악하는 데 도움이 되긴 하지만, 이 표가 실제 TOEIC 성적 산출에 그대로 사용된 적은 없다는 사실을 밝혀 둔다.

토익˚ 정기시험
실전 ❶ 1000
RC

토익˚ 정기시험
실전 ❶ 1000
RC

실전 TEST

01

READING TEST

In the Reading test, you will read a variety of texts and answer several different types of reading comprehension questions. The entire Reading test will last 75 minutes. There are three parts, and directions are given for each part. You are encouraged to answer as many questions as possible within the time allowed.

You must mark your answers on the separate answer sheet. Do not write your answers in your test book.

PART 5

Directions: A word or phrase is missing in each of the sentences below. Four answer choices are given below each sentence. Select the best answer to complete the sentence. Then mark the letter (A), (B), (C), or (D) on your answer sheet.

---

101. When she held her last meeting, Ms. Toba ------- her sales staff to perform even better next quarter.

   (A) encourage
   (B) is encouraging
   (C) encouraged
   (D) was encouraged

102. All staff have been informed ------- the proposed partnership with ERI Finance.

   (A) for
   (B) about
   (C) to
   (D) at

103. On Friday, Mr. Nakamura will discuss ------- ideas for supporting busy waiters.

   (A) his
   (B) him
   (C) himself
   (D) he

104. The Forestry Commission was created to ------- the state's natural resources and wildlife.

   (A) allow
   (B) manage
   (C) succeed
   (D) finish

105. By following established guidelines, construction workers will be able to complete their tasks -------.

   (A) safety
   (B) safe
   (C) safeness
   (D) safely

106. With her numerous credentials, Dr. Kwan is highly ------- to teach medieval history at Maston University.

   (A) arranged
   (B) ready
   (C) available
   (D) qualified

107. ------- at the annual technology conference is mandatory for all engineers at the Treemont Corporation.

   (A) Attendance
   (B) Attend
   (C) Attends
   (D) Attended

108. The café ------- features poets, folk singers, and drama groups on its stage.

   (A) tightly
   (B) occasionally
   (C) vaguely
   (D) realistically

109. Before the seminar began, attendees were assured ------- all scheduled presenters would appear.

(A) who
(B) around
(C) that
(D) therefore

110. Forever Pet has been a leader in bringing new products, ------- Fun Bone and Chew Right, to the market.

(A) however
(B) furthermore
(C) as if
(D) such as

111. Ms. Turner is in charge of ------- the organization of records in the human services department.

(A) improve
(B) improved
(C) improving
(D) improvement

112. Sheefon Bank clients always receive an e-mail or text ------- following any change to their account password.

(A) issue
(B) alert
(C) claim
(D) member

113. A drop in consumer demand has led to a ------- decrease in the production of large pickup trucks.

(A) remark
(B) remarked
(C) remarking
(D) remarkable

114. After coating the potatoes in flour and spices, chefs should place them ------- into the deep fryer.

(A) rarely
(B) honestly
(C) doubtfully
(D) directly

115. Several banks have released applications that allow ------- customers to pay bills easily by phone.

(A) their
(B) they
(C) them
(D) themselves

116. The personnel department will ------- only those applicants who have five or more years of experience for the position.

(A) participate
(B) consider
(C) grant
(D) make

117. Employees of Belfore Electronics Ltd. are ------- involved in community-assistance programs.

(A) active
(B) actively
(C) activate
(D) activity

118. The executives at Macalter Equipment decided they would not ------- the contract without major changes.

(A) renew
(B) consume
(C) identify
(D) resemble

119. Wet suits are made with a ------- layer of rubber that traps heat and keeps divers warm.

(A) protect
(B) protects
(C) protective
(D) protectively

120. Newcamp Services managers will meet to discuss the proposed ------- of three smaller branches into one large branch.

(A) security
(B) bracket
(C) connector
(D) merger

GO ON TO THE NEXT PAGE

121. At Yarzen Technology, clients' records are ------- and can only be accessed by a small group of fund managers.

(A) confide
(B) confidential
(C) confidentially
(D) confidentiality

122. The featured panel at the NHJ Medical Conference will discuss recent ------- in online health-care services.

(A) memories
(B) varieties
(C) trends
(D) rehearsals

123. All of Millville's restaurants ------- several times a year by the city health department.

(A) inspect
(B) inspected
(C) are inspecting
(D) are inspected

124. Sweet Sunlight Bakery has steadily built a ------- base of customers with its delicious cookies and cakes.

(A) brief
(B) loyal
(C) strict
(D) careful

125. According to financial analysts, ------- in medical technology companies are expected to increase in value.

(A) invest
(B) investing
(C) invested
(D) investments

126. The city's harbor is ------- to container ships and fishing vessels of all sizes.

(A) accessible
(B) formal
(C) reasonable
(D) likely

127. Maya's Dancewear expanded its advertising markets, and sales have ------- increased.

(A) controlling
(B) consequently
(C) beneath
(D) even though

128. Dobson Ice Cream will not introduce any new flavors ------- the customer survey results are analyzed.

(A) around
(B) until
(C) despite
(D) past

129. The renovated company gym ------- with free weights and exercise machines.

(A) will equip
(B) to equip
(C) has been equipped
(D) is equipping

130. ------- driving their cars, workers who travel to the town center should use the bus lines.

(A) Because of
(B) Instead of
(C) Whenever
(D) Although

PART 6

Directions: Read the texts that follow. A word, phrase, or sentence is missing in parts of each text. Four answer choices for each question are given below the text. Select the best answer to complete the text. Then mark the letter (A), (B), (C), or (D) on your answer sheet.

Questions 131-134 refer to the following article.

Local Barbershop Wins State Competition

By Miranda Warren

MALENDA COUNTY (January 12)—Pat and Kenny's Barbershop, ------- at 3949 Grand Street, has
131.
been named the best barbershop in the state by the Barber and Hairdresser's Coalition. The

criteria for selection include reputation, affordability, professionalism, and accreditations.

------- .
132.

Founders and owners Kenneth Webber and Patrick Miller have been best friends since

childhood. ------- opened the shop 34 years ago. ------- the shop retains its old-fashioned charm,
133. **134.**
the barbers have mastered the latest styles, not just the more traditional ones. People of all ages

seeking a haircut or a new style should try Pat and Kenny's Barbershop.

---

131. (A) locate
(B) located
(C) locates
(D) location

132. (A) The results will be announced later
this month.
(B) We are proud to serve our community
with excellence.
(C) Pat and Kenny's shop excelled in all
four categories.
(D) Please call in advance to schedule an
appointment.

133. (A) I
(B) We
(C) They
(D) He

134. (A) While
(B) Despite
(C) Even
(D) Yet

GO ON TO THE NEXT PAGE

Gasgo Propane Tank Exchange

You have chosen a safe and ------- way to obtain fuel for your stoves, grills, heaters, fireplaces, or
                                    135.

other devices. Simply follow the directions ------- .
                                              136.

When your tank runs out of propane, take it to our store and leave it on one of the clearly marked

green shelves outside the store. ------- . Then, pay the cashier inside the store for a fresh tank of
                                   137.

propane. Next, the cashier or another staff member will accompany you to the outdoor exchange

area. The staff person will give you a full tank to take home and provide help if you have multiple

tanks to carry. Follow the instructions on the tank to connect it to your device.

Be sure to visit us again when you need a ------- .
                                            138.

135. (A) economy
    (B) economics
    (C) economize
    (D) economical

136. (A) below
    (B) finally
    (C) sometimes
    (D) hourly

137. (A) Come again very soon.
    (B) It is warmer in the store.
    (C) Do not take it inside.
    (D) The tank is prefilled.

138. (A) model
    (B) version
    (C) heater
    (D) replacement

Questions 139-142 refer to the following e-mail.

To: Technicarn Enterprises Customers
From: Technicarn Enterprises Customer Service
Date: 10 September
Subject: Serving You

Dear Valued Customer:

We want your ------- with Technicarn Enterprises to be easy and enjoyable. To that end, we are
     139.

pleased to announce our newly designed Web site, with enhanced customer-friendly features.

Our new Web site provides answers to your questions 24 hours a day, every day of the year.

On our home page, you can get information about system setup, or you can troubleshoot by

visiting ------- the Internet Issues or TV and Streaming Issues pages. ------- , you can find
   140.   **141.**

detailed information concerning account management, access, billing, and payment.

------- . Please explore the new Web site at your earliest convenience:
142.

www.technicarnenterprises.com. As always, thank you for allowing us to serve you.

Best regards,

The Technicarn Enterprises Customer Service Team

---

139. (A) experience
    (B) experienced
    (C) experiencing
    (D) experiential

140. (A) either
    (B) both
    (C) rather
    (D) each

141. (A) Therefore
    (B) Regardless
    (C) For example
    (D) Moreover

142. (A) We also need to inform you that your
        payment is five days past due.
    (B) We recommend that you purchase all
        related accessories in our retail store.
    (C) If you get an error message, disconnect
        from the Internet and try again.
    (D) If you cannot find what you need online,
        simply call our support number.

GO ON TO THE NEXT PAGE

Garner City Transport Cares About the Environment

Beginning May 1, the sale and use of paper tickets and transit passes will be ------- on all Garner

143.
City Transport bus and subway lines. This change applies to single-ride tickets ------- to weekly

144.
and monthly passes. Eliminating paper benefits the environment and leads to less litter.

Riders can download the free Garner City Transport app. With the app, they can add money their
accounts, purchase tickets, plan ------- , and track arrival and departure times.

145.

Alternatively, passengers can purchase a rechargeable transit card at any station. ------- . Value

146.
can be added to the card via the Garner City Transport Web site at www.garnercitytransport.org.

---

143. (A) enlarged
(B) discontinued
(C) accessible
(D) refreshed

144. (A) sharing
(B) but
(C) except
(D) as well as

145. (A) routes
(B) responses
(C) software
(D) careers

146. (A) People often use credit cards to
purchase meals during the flight.
(B) Many people like public transportation
because it is inexpensive.
(C) The durable cards are made from
recycled materials.
(D) There was a small price increase last
month.

PART 7

Directions: In this part you will read a selection of texts, such as magazine and newspaper articles, e-mails, and instant messages. Each text or set of texts is followed by several questions. Select the best answer for each question and mark the letter (A), (B), (C), or (D) on your answer sheet.

Questions 147-148 refer to the following advertisement.

Harbis Stationery Store Clearance Sale Prices indicated are for in-store purchases only. 500 Pinstone Street / SHEFFIELD / S12HN	
Seasonal items	
Box of ten preprinted seasonal cards (25% off)	£ 8.99
Box of five customizable seasonal cards or invitations (50% off)	£ 11.99
All school supplies 10% off	
Box of 24 pens	£ 1.79
Desk lamp	£ 19.99
Wireless mouse	£ 17.99
Backpack	£ 29.99
Visit Harbis Stationery at www.harbisstationery.uk	

147. What is indicated about Harbis Stationery Store?

   (A) It provides materials for students.
   (B) It has stores in multiple locations.
   (C) It is celebrating an anniversary.
   (D) It provides free shipping for online orders.

148. What item is discounted by the greatest percentage?

   (A) Box of ten cards
   (B) Box of five invitations
   (C) Wireless mouse
   (D) Desk lamp

GO ON TO THE NEXT PAGE

To:	Wenbin Peng <wpeng@chenconstruction.com>
From:	Toshi Auto Group <cs@toshiautogroup.com>
Date:	February 26
Subject:	Your leased vehicle

Dear Mr. Peng:

As you know, Toshi Auto Group handles all the service needs for cars leased by employees of Chen Construction. According to our records, you took possession of your leased car on March 1 of last year. Your car is now due for its required annual service and maintenance check. To book your appointment, please call us at (215) 555-0109 or visit us online at www.toshiautogroup.com/serviceappointments.

Sincerely,

Toshi Auto Group
Customer Service

149. What is the purpose of the e-mail?

(A) To inquire about leasing a vehicle
(B) To inform a customer of required car maintenance
(C) To announce the release of a new car
(D) To register a used car for an extended warranty

150. What is indicated about Chen Construction?

(A) It performs the servicing of its company vehicles.
(B) It has a new project beginning March 1.
(C) It provides leased cars to some employees.
(D) It will soon begin a construction project for Toshi Auto Group.

Questions 151-153 refer to the following article.

LONDON (2 February)—On Thursday, Tillford Press announced the launch of its new imprint, Tillford Exalt. This new line will feature books promoting healthy lifestyles, memoirs with uplifting messages, and volumes that provide guidance for special occasions such as birthdays and weddings. Tillford Exalt will also publish calendars and greeting cards that complement the main products.

Already contracted to write memoirs are the award-winning actress Alexia Leoz, London-based conductor and composer Seung-Hyun Bae, and celebrity cook Lain Lai. Ms. Lai's story of her life and career will be the first to be launched. It is set for release in December.

Tillford vice president Frederick Bissett said the company saw a need for books that celebrated accomplishments and life events from multiple perspectives. "We wanted authors from a wide variety of cultural backgrounds, and we think we're off to a great start," he said. He noted that Tillford Exalt's authors were not always famous; the books will be exploring their beginnings, their everyday lives, their first jobs, their marriages and families—as well as their achievements.

Tillford Press is based in Manchester. It has offices in New York, Toronto, and Sydney, but its publications are sold throughout the world.

151. What is the main purpose of the article?

(A) To promote a new line of cookware
(B) To advertise an orchestra concert
(C) To announce a new series of books
(D) To provide a calendar of local events

152. What is planned for December?

(A) An awards ceremony
(B) The publication of a life story
(C) The release of a new album
(D) The launch of a celebrity's restaurant

153. What does Frederick Bissett emphasize about Tillford Exalt?

(A) Its record-breaking sales
(B) Its roots in Manchester
(C) Its focus on fiction and poetry
(D) Its broad range of authors

GO ON TO THE NEXT PAGE

Questions 154-155 refer to the following text-message chain.

Greg Skagen (8:58 A.M.) Hi, Brenda. I'm here in the warehouse. All of my trainees have arrived, but I noticed the power door at Loading Dock B is acting up.

Brenda Sadauskas (8:59 A.M.) Again?

Greg Skagen (8:59 A.M.) When I push the button to open it, it raises all the way up but then drops back down to the closed position after about 30 seconds.

Brenda Sadauskas (9:00 A.M.) I'll come down with the maintenance technicians. Why don't you bring your trainees to my area? You can teach them how to create shipping labels and then have them pack and label this morning's shipments.

Greg Skagen (9:02 A.M.) Yes, that works.

Brenda Sadauskas (9:03 A.M.) Thanks. Then you could show them the loading dock operations in the afternoon.

154. What problem does Mr. Skagen mention?

(A) Some new employees are absent.
(B) Some boxes are incorrectly labeled.
(C) A package delivery is delayed.
(D) An access door is malfunctioning.

155. At 9:02 A.M., what does Mr. Skagen most likely mean when he writes, "Yes, that works"?

(A) An electrician has arrived at a work site.
(B) Some equipment is operating smoothly.
(C) Trainees can help with some shipments.
(D) Ms. Sadauskas is well suited for her job.

SERVICE REQUEST FORM

Complete all fields and deliver to Technology Services (room 412).

Requester Name: Elenora Deckow

Requester Office: Room 718

Requester Phone: Ext. 5709

Service Location: Room 500

Service Type (choose one):

☐ Cleaning   ☒ Repair   ☐ Installation/Setup   ☐ Other

Description of Request

There is a problem with the television audio. When I played an online video, the image was fine, but I could not hear anything. I checked all the settings, and I was able to hear the same video on other televisions with no problem. I'm supposed to deliver a product demonstration for a client in room 500 next Monday, so I would greatly appreciate it if the issue can be fixed by this Friday.

---

156. Why was the form submitted?

(A) An image is not displaying clearly.
(B) A projector needs to be set up.
(C) Audio is not functioning properly.
(D) A microphone needs to be repaired.

157. What is Ms. Deckow planning to do next week?

(A) Visit a client site
(B) Deliver a product
(C) Create an online video
(D) Give a presentation

Ella Glatt (11:34 A.M.)
Hi. I know this is a busy day, but I wanted to know whether anyone from the finance team could come to the marketing meeting.

Stef Goldberg (11:35 A.M.)
Hi, Ella. I wish I could, but it starts at 2:00. I need to be at a different meeting at 2:30.

Ella Glatt (11:36 A.M.)
Oh, right. I forgot you were going to the executive board meeting.

Daniel Seidal (11:36 A.M.)
I'm also supposed to go to the 2:30 meeting. Is it essential that one of us attend the marketing meeting?

Ella Glatt (11:37 A.M.)
Well, it would be helpful to have someone from the finance department there, at least for 15 minutes or so.

Bill Iverman (11:38 A.M.)
The quarterly reports just came in, and Daniel, Stef, and I need to review them by the end of the day.

Ella Glatt (11:39 A.M.)
You all have plenty to do.

Daniel Seidal (11:41 A.M.)
That's true! But I could come from 2:00 to 2:15. That's all I can commit to.

Ella Glatt (11:43 A.M.)
Sounds great. We just need one of you to clarify a few quick points about the budget for the next advertising campaign.

158. At what time will the executive board meeting begin?

(A) 2:00 P.M.
(B) 2:15 P.M.
(C) 2:30 P.M.
(D) 3:00 P.M.

159. In what area does Mr. Iverman most likely work?

(A) Marketing
(B) Finance
(C) Advertising
(D) Executive management

160. Why does Ms. Glatt want a colleague to attend a meeting?

(A) To summarize a previous meeting
(B) To explain a promotional campaign
(C) To provide information about a budget
(D) To review recently approved documents

161. At 11:43 A.M., what does Ms. Glatt most likely mean when she writes, "Sounds great"?

(A) She accepts Mr. Seidal's offer.
(B) She agrees that Mr. Iverman should attend the meeting at 3:00 P.M.
(C) She is pleased with the proposed budget.
(D) She is happy that a project has been completed.

GO ON TO THE NEXT PAGE

To:	amal.abboud@bunzifoundation.org
From:	maria_mcfarland@myemail.com
Date:	Thursday, August 22
Subject:	Project Coordinator Position
Attachment:	📎 résumé_m.mcfarland.pdf

Dear Mr. Abboud,

My friend Josiah Wilkins told me that you are seeking a project coordinator for your company. I have a degree in business administration and am attaching my résumé as I think I am an excellent fit for your needs. As you will see, I have experience using several cloud-based project-management programs. Furthermore, my organizational skills enable me to coordinate multiple activities simultaneously, and I can convey expectations clearly to team members involved in each phase of a project.

My current role as project coordinator for an international engineering firm, where I have worked for the past five years, has also afforded me ample experience managing teams, schedules, and budgets. While I enjoy the kind of work I do, it has become clear to me that I need motivation from a strong mission. The goal of your company to create sustainable housing projects is something that I strongly support and would be delighted to work on.

Through my work and volunteer activities, I have spent many months abroad in various countries throughout Asia and the Middle East. This seems particularly relevant to mention, as I am comfortable leading geographically and culturally diverse teams.

Thank you for your attention, and I look forward to speaking with you soon.

Kind regards,

Maria McFarland

162. What does Ms. McFarland mention about Mr. Wilkins?

(A) He informed her of a job opening.
(B) He will require a professional reference.
(C) He would make a good business partner.
(D) He is considering resigning from his position.

163. The word "convey" in paragraph 1, line 5, is closest in meaning to

(A) transport
(B) communicate
(C) recommend
(D) adapt

164. Why does Ms. McFarland want to leave her current position?

(A) She wants a higher salary for her efforts.
(B) She wants to work with a more experienced team.
(C) She wants more opportunities for advancement.
(D) She wants a role that inspires her more.

165. Why does Ms. McFarland mention her travels?

(A) To request a placement in a particular country
(B) To discuss how she came to acquire strategic industry contacts
(C) To explain how she became aware of certain world issues
(D) To emphasize her experience with people of different backgrounds

GO ON TO THE NEXT PAGE

https://trexdale.com/aboutus

About Our Company

Trexdale Supply specializes in designing, producing, and installing furniture for all types of scientific laboratories. We provide a range of fully assembled cabinets, workstations, benches, and more, all made exclusively at our production facility in Dallas, Texas. Our lab furniture is available in a wide variety of sizes and configurations to match the needs of any research application.

Our business offers products as well as design-consulting services. For start-up labs, we have a team of consulting specialists available to evaluate your facility's specific needs and assist you in arranging your space and choosing the most suitable furniture. Recently, for example, we were chosen by a major producer of biofuels to provide expert help in changing the layout of a research laboratory to maximize available space. As a result of this project, this client has realized substantial savings by reducing energy usage in the lab.

Please visit the "Lab Planning" section of this Web site if you are interested in learning more about building or renovating a laboratory facility. There, you can fill out an interest form to contact one of our consultants about your next project.

166. What does Trexdale Supply make?

(A) Medical supplies
(B) Farming equipment
(C) Cabinets and furniture
(D) Glass laboratory equipment

167. What did Trexdale Supply do in a recent project?

(A) It reorganized a client's laboratory.
(B) It converted its vehicles to use biofuels.
(C) It expanded staffing at its production facility.
(D) It helped a client organize a trade show.

168. What method of communicating with Trexdale Supply is mentioned?

(A) By e-mail
(B) By phone
(C) By instant message
(D) By an online form

Questions 169-171 refer to the following job advertisement.

PRODUCT DEMONSTRATORS NEEDED!

Are you outgoing and enthusiastic? — [1] —. Do you enjoy talking to all types of people? Put your personality and communication skills to work! — [2] —. BBD Staffing is seeking to hire in-store product demonstrators to promote our clients' merchandise to shoppers. — [3] —. As a member of our team, you will demonstrate a wide range of small kitchen appliances and tools in grocery stores and other retail venues.

For some products, you will be required to prepare simple recipes. You will also need to answer shoppers' questions. Thus, it is essential that you can become familiar with clients' products and provide key information to consumers. Because many of the demonstrations require working with food, candidates must have a Professional Food Handler certificate. — [4] —.

To apply, upload a video of no more than one minute in length telling us why you would be a successful product demonstrator at www.bbdstaffing.com/applications.

---

169. What work experience would best qualify a candidate for the position?

(A) Cook
(B) Cashier
(C) Interior designer
(D) Event planner

170. According to the advertisement, what should people interested in applying do next?

(A) Respond to a survey
(B) Arrange for an interview
(C) Submit a recording
(D) Provide references

171. In which of the positions marked [1], [2], [3], and [4] does the following sentence best belong?

"Many of the world's best-known brands rely on our product demonstrators to generate positive impressions of their products."

(A) [1]
(B) [2]
(C) [3]
(D) [4]

GO ON TO THE NEXT PAGE

Gorman Unveils Newest Smartphone Model

LONDON (20 April)—Gorman Mobile unveiled its newest smartphone to an eager reception at the annual Technobrit Conference. The Pro Phone 4, which includes 512 GB of storage, a 7-inch screen display, and an optional stylus pen, will hit the shelves on 11 June. Unlike its predecessor—the Pro Phone 3—it features a larger screen, an ultrawide camera lens, and 8K-resolution filming capability.

— [1] —. The £999 starting price is £100 more than that of the previous model. Add-ons, such as the stylus pen, protective case, and wireless headphones, cost an additional £39, £59, and £79, respectively.

Gorman Product Manager Ian Hill doesn't believe the price increase will dissuade customers. — [2] —.

"The Pro Phone 4 is a game changer in terms of its picture quality and sleek design," said Hill. "Improvements were based on direct customer feedback, which cited the poor camera functionality as the biggest drawback of prior models. Our clients spoke, and we listened and adapted accordingly." — [3] —.

One similarity that the Pro Phone 4 has with previous models is the charger. Going against the trend of competing wireless companies, Gorman is instead focusing on convenience.

"We want to afford our customers the ability to reuse elements of the other Gorman devices they've already purchased," said Hill. "Why add to the overload of cables already in circulation?" — [4] —.

172. What is the purpose of the article?

(A) To promote a technology show
(B) To introduce a product
(C) To interview smartphone users
(D) To announce a recall of a device

173. How much do the Gorman Pro Phone 4 wireless headphones cost?

(A) £39
(B) £59
(C) £79
(D) £100

174. What does the Pro Phone 4 have in common with prior models?

(A) The screen size
(B) The camera resolution
(C) The price
(D) The charger

175. In which of the positions marked [1], [2], [3], and [4] does the following sentence best belong?

"These upgrades do come at a cost."

(A) [1]
(B) [2]
(C) [3]
(D) [4]

GO ON TO THE NEXT PAGE

WORK ORDER: 7549

Requester:	Xi, Gina
Date Entered:	Wednesday, 9 April
Date Due:	Thursday, 10 April
Type:	Technology end-user request
Summary:	Voice-mail security settings
Technician Assigned:	Arnold, Sam
Computer Workstation ID:	HYS31

Description:

Is it possible to remove the new layers of security on my voice mail in the new phone system? I really don't want to use a password, and I certainly don't want to change it every month. I don't need a high degree of security because my work is not confidential. If someone else gained access to my messages, it wouldn't do much harm.

To:	Gina Xi
From:	Sam Arnold
Date:	Thursday, 10 April
Subject:	Tech support request 7549

Hello, Ms. Xi,

This is in reference to your work order 7549 related to the new phone system. I am happy to help you with that. I understand that you do not feel that a high degree of security is needed for your voice-mail settings, but the new system does require you to have a password to retrieve your voice mail. However, company policy allows me to change the settings for employees who do not work with confidential material. I can update the security settings so that you do not have to reset the password on a regular basis.

I want to make sure that you understand the risk involved with a lower level of security. Anyone who gains access to your voice-mail account can do more than simply listen to your messages. They would be able to delete messages, change your greeting, or change your password so that you would lose access to your own voice mail (at least until someone here at IT could override the password change). If you still feel comfortable with that level of risk, let me know, and I will change the settings so that your password never expires.

Sam Arnold

Tech Support Associate

176. What does Ms. Xi's request indicate about the company?

(A) It provides mobile phones to some employees.
(B) Its employees value confidentiality.
(C) It has recently changed its phone system.
(D) It offers technology training to employees.

177. In the e-mail, the word "regular" in paragraph 1, line 6, is closest in meaning to

(A) periodic
(B) orderly
(C) customary
(D) legitimate

178. Where did Mr. Arnold learn about the details of Ms. Xi's request?

(A) In a weekly managers' meeting
(B) In a work order
(C) In a phone call
(D) In a personal voice mail

179. How does Mr. Arnold try to satisfy Ms. Xi's request?

(A) By agreeing to everything Ms. Xi asked for
(B) By resetting the password on Ms. Xi's phone
(C) By referring the matter to another technician
(D) By proposing to fulfill only part of Ms. Xi's request

180. What does Mr. Arnold ask Ms. Xi to do?

(A) Make the needed changes to her voice-mail system
(B) Attend training about the new voice-mail system
(C) Confirm that she wants him to change her voice-mail system
(D) Provide a clear description of the problem with her voice-mail system

GO ON TO THE NEXT PAGE

```
╔══════════════════════════════ *E-mail* ══════════════════════════════╗

     To:        Linda Hanshu

     From:      Cliff Merson

     Subject:   Lighting Issue

     Date:      September 4, 10:12 A.M.
```

Hi, Ms. Hanshu:

I want to check on the issue we discussed about lighting in the latest chapter of *Titan Adventure*. In past versions of the game, getting the reflections and lighting in green and blue areas correct has been a particular challenge, and it was a problem that kept arising. As the new release, *Neptune's Voyage*, is primarily an underwater adventure, addressing this problem is crucial. You said you would take charge of this, and I hope to hear that you have found a solution to the problem. The team was hoping to have one last rendering of the lighting for the game by October 10 for a preliminary run-through. Will the final version of the lighting be ready by then?

All other aspects of the game are on schedule. Please send me an update about the lighting at your earliest convenience.

Regards,

Cliff Merson
Project Manager, Rimerko Games

Review of *Titan Adventure: Neptune's Voyage*

By Leo Weber, April 1

This new installment of *Titan Adventure* will surprise and delight both new players and old aficionados long familiar with the series. Though open-world formats have been widespread in recent years, *Neptune's Voyage* brings something new to the format. By stripping down instructional guides, the game gives users the opportunity to discover new areas and devices. In *Neptune's Voyage*, you wake up as Thetis, a dolphin that is tasked with rescuing Neptune from an underwater cave. Users then climb, run, ride, sail, and fly through the world of the game, encountering new towns, ruins, and other creatures along the way. Some of these creatures will be familiar to longtime fans, but there is plenty of novelty as well. This newest version also corrects the green and blue image rendering that was sometimes a problem in earlier installments of *Titan Adventure*.

Neptune's Voyage launches May 5 on Rimerko Clutch and FS5. It is available in English, Korean, Japanese, French, and Spanish.

181. In the e-mail, what is suggested about Mr. Merson?

(A) He coordinates a game development team.
(B) He is convinced that *Titan Adventure* is overpriced.
(C) He is a new employee at Rimerko Games.
(D) He will leave on a business trip on October 10.

182. In the review, what is indicated about *Neptune's Voyage* ?

(A) It is a major competitor of *Titan Adventure*.
(B) It features an open-world format.
(C) It is the first video game in a series.
(D) It is Rimerko's most challenging game.

183. What can be concluded about Ms. Hanshu?

(A) She wrote the script for *Neptune's Voyage*.
(B) She successfully addressed Mr. Merson's concern.
(C) She won an award for game design.
(D) She is a project manager.

184. What does Mr. Weber find exciting about *Neptune's Voyage* ?

(A) It has players act in the role of Neptune.
(B) It uses lighting to show players where to navigate.
(C) It introduces a completely new set of characters.
(D) It lets players explore new features without guidance.

185. When will *Neptune's Voyage* be available?

(A) On September 4
(B) On October 10
(C) On April 1
(D) On May 5

GO ON TO THE NEXT PAGE

Questions 186-190 refer to the following schedule, e-mail, and job advertisement.

Wonder Ridge Radio Broadcast Schedule, Monday–Friday

6 A.M.–Noon	Noon–4 P.M.	4 P.M.–7 P.M.	7 P.M.–10 P.M.
COFFEE BREAK	**AFTERNOON JAZZ**	**FOLK FRENZY**	**JOSIE'S JOINT**
Local news and interviews with community members	Music from traditional jazz to jazz fusion	Folk music from around the world	Modern sounds selected by our station's own music director
Host: Felice Finney	Host: Malachi Mzee	Host: Penny Ariza	Host: Josie Jones

---

E-mail

To:	feedback@wonderridgeradio.org
From:	pfabre@sendmail.net
Subject:	My new radio station!
Date:	October 22

To the folks at Wonder Ridge Radio:

As I was driving last week, I got tired of listening to sports talk and turned the dial. Suddenly, my car was filled with a song that I hadn't heard in many years. It was traditional music from France, where my grandmother was born. She used to play that song when I was a child. I never expected to hear it on the radio here in Wonder Ridge. Thanks for this experience and for all your great programs.

Your new fan,

Pierre Fabre

Wonder Ridge Radio Job Opening: Programming Assistant

Posted November 2

Job Description

The programming assistant reports to the director of programming and supports the radio station by performing a variety of research and communication functions. This role is an entry-level, part-time position.

Responsibilities

- Conducting background research on interviewees

- Keeping up-to-date on news and news makers in order to suggest potential topics and guests for on-air interviews

- Updating the station's Web site and program host biography pages

- Using scheduling software to update the broadcast schedule

- Communicating with listeners, especially via e-mail and social media

To apply, e-mail a résumé and cover letter to hiring@wonderridgeradio.org.

---

186. According to the schedule, who is Ms. Jones?

(A) The advertising manager at a radio station
(B) The host of a community news program
(C) The music director at Wonder Ridge Radio
(D) The host of a sports radio program

187. What is the purpose of the e-mail?

(A) To express praise for the radio station
(B) To ask about job opportunities
(C) To request more sports talk show programming
(D) To inquire about the name of a song

188. When did Mr. Fabre most likely first listen to Wonder Ridge Radio?

(A) Between 6 A.M. and noon
(B) Between noon and 4 P.M.
(C) Between 4 P.M. and 7 P.M.
(D) Between 7 P.M. and 10 P.M.

189. What does the job advertisement suggest applicants must have?

(A) A willingness to travel
(B) Familiarity with computers
(C) A degree in communications
(D) Extensive experience in the radio industry

190. What radio program will probably receive the most support from the programming assistant?

(A) *Coffee Break*
(B) *Afternoon Jazz*
(C) *Folk Frenzy*
(D) *Josie's Joint*

Instructions for Requesting Records

Thank you for your interest in official records and documents maintained by the City of Abilene. To file a request for public information, please follow these steps.

1. Create an account in the Records Center Web portal. Currently, all requests must be made through the portal.

2. Use the drop-down menu to locate the department from which you are seeking information and submit your request. You will receive a confirmation e-mail with a reference number.

3. The department staff will locate the requested records and contact you when they are available. You can have the records delivered to you, or you can pick them up in person. If you prefer to pick them up in person, you must make an appointment with the department staff.

4. If there are any fees associated with your request, you will receive an itemized statement detailing the services provided and the charges for those specific services.

E-Mail Message

To:	Joo-Hee Park <jhpark@coa.net>
From:	Keith Brandenberg <kbrandenberg@mailcurrent.com>
Date:	May 3
Subject:	RE: Reference number W2486

Dear Ms. Park,

Thank you for confirming that my documents are available. I would like to pick them up in person as soon as possible. Do you have any appointments available this week?

I have a question about the fee. Apparently, I am being charged $300 for my documents. I do not understand why the fee is so high, and there was no explanation included in your e-mail. I have requested records several times in the past in my role with RJ Environmental Engineering and have never paid such a high fee. In this case, I am only requesting two maps of the city's underground pipelines, which will inform our firm's current work advising the city on wastewater management.

Please clarify the fee for me, and let me know if I can pick up my documents this week. Thank you.

Best regards,

Keith Brandenberg

City of Abilene Administrative Building

Visitors must sign in prior to entering this facility. Please enter your name and the room you will visit in the logbook.

First-Floor Directory:
IT Services – Room 100
Parks and Recreation – Room 101
Transportation – Room 102
Wastewater – Room 103

191. What do the instructions indicate about records requests?

(A) They can be made only on certain days.
(B) They can be made only online.
(C) They can be filed only by authorized personnel.
(D) They can be filed only after a fee is paid.

192. According to the e-mail, how does Mr. Brandenberg plan to use some public information?

(A) To add information to a Web portal
(B) To help his company advise the city
(C) To identify an accounting error
(D) To learn how an agency is structured

193. What does the sign indicate visitors must do before entering a building?

(A) Go through a security screening
(B) Get a parking permit
(C) Present some identification
(D) Sign a logbook

194. What was Mr. Brandenberg expecting to receive?

(A) An itemized statement of fees
(B) A letter from his company
(C) A phone call from a city official
(D) A password for the Web portal

195. What room will Mr. Brandenberg most likely visit?

(A) Room 100
(B) Room 101
(C) Room 102
(D) Room 103

GO ON TO THE NEXT PAGE

Questions 196-200 refer to the following review and e-mails.

Famous Actor, First Book

LONDON (25 February)—Fans of Simon Eklund will be delighted with his autobiography, *The Theatre Lights Dimmed*, the first book he has written in his storied career as an actor. It provides wonderful insight into his career, starting with his first roles in cinema in his native Sweden, moving into his work in France and Italy, and finishing with his recent theatre work in the U.K.

In his book, Mr. Eklund dedicates a fair amount of text to discussing his mentor, Charles Gunnarsson, who helped him develop his skills early on in Stockholm. He also describes the difficulty of transitioning into different types of roles, especially from comedic to dramatic acting. He includes several funny anecdotes about his first attempts at acting onstage here in London. He describes them as disastrous, but anyone who saw his recent performance in *Life and Games* would say just the opposite.

Mr. Eklund has long been a captivating actor on stage and screen, and now he is a thoroughly engaging author.

—Uma Joshi

To:	Edith Hocking
From:	Uma Joshi
Date:	2 March
Subject:	RE: Opportunity

Dear Edith,

Thank you for agreeing to arrange an interview with Mr. Eklund for me. I think this will be a great follow-up to my recent piece.

In a helpful coincidence, I will be visiting his home country next month to address a journalists' convention. I am the featured speaker and will discuss the benefits of diversity in journalism. I'm sure we can set up something with Mr. Eklund just before or after my speech.

Best,

Uma Joshi
Arts and Culture Editor
Top News U.K.

E-mail

To:	Uma Joshi <ujoshi@topnews.co.uk>
From:	Maria Cazalla <mcazalla@zephyrmail.se>
Date:	20 March
Subject:	RE: Information

Dear Ms. Joshi,

We are all very excited about your interview next month with Mr. Eklund. He enjoys all your writing for *Top News U.K.*—the news stories, interviews, and, of course, your recent article about *The Theatre Lights Dimmed*!

I just wanted to finalize a few details with you. We have arranged transportation for you from your hotel to Mr. Eklund's house and then back to the hotel. Please let me know how many people there will be in your group, because Mr. Eklund would like you all to stay for lunch.

Sincerely,

Maria Cazalla

196. What does the review mention about Mr. Eklund?

(A) He enjoys his work as a director.
(B) He has been a mentor to many young people.
(C) He is a well-known actor.
(D) He has written many books.

197. Where most likely will Ms. Joshi meet Mr. Eklund?

(A) In Sweden
(B) In France
(C) In Italy
(D) In the United Kingdom

198. According to the first e-mail, what is one reason Ms. Joshi will travel in April?

(A) To go on a vacation
(B) To interview for a new job
(C) To attend an international film festival
(D) To speak at a conference

199. What is the purpose of the second e-mail?

(A) To reserve a hotel room
(B) To confirm meeting arrangements
(C) To discuss an idea for a movie
(D) To ask for transportation

200. What can be concluded about Mr. Eklund?

(A) He hopes to write for a British news site.
(B) He just hired a new assistant.
(C) He was pleased with Ms. Joshi's review of his book.
(D) He frequently cooks special meals.

Stop! This is the end of the test. If you finish before time is called, you may go back to Parts 5, 6, and 7 and check your work.

토익 정기시험
실전 ❶ 1000
RC

실전 TEST

02

PART 5

Directions: A word or phrase is missing in each of the sentences below. Four answer choices are given below each sentence. Select the best answer to complete the sentence. Then mark the letter (A), (B), (C), or (D) on your answer sheet.

---

101. Last week, three staff members ------- at the local library's book sale.

(A) volunteer
(B) voluntary
(C) volunteered
(D) volunteering

102. In April, prices are expected to drop ------- 20 percent.

(A) with
(B) on
(C) since
(D) by

103. The project management software allows staff to handle many tasks by -------.

(A) themselves
(B) them
(C) they
(D) theirs

104. Local manufacturers have ------- shipping times by hiring external shipping companies.

(A) attempted
(B) reduced
(C) weakened
(D) finished

105. Gramwell Corporation may charge an ------- fee for last month's work.

(A) add
(B) adding
(C) additionally
(D) additional

106. Ms. Kang prefers to complete ------- current project before transferring to the finance department.

(A) herself
(B) she
(C) her
(D) hers

107. There are ------- criteria that must be met for a password to be changed successfully.

(A) specific
(B) to specify
(C) specify
(D) specifies

108. To assist the costume designers in preparing for the film, fabric samples can be sent to the ------- designer.

(A) leader
(B) leads
(C) led
(D) lead

109. The product presentation has been fully rehearsed, so it can be ------- any day next week.

(A) film
(B) filmed
(C) films
(D) to film

110. The new logo is part of a comprehensive effort to ------- the brand's identity and appeal to younger consumers.

(A) remind
(B) refer
(C) refresh
(D) repeat

111. The latest sport utility vehicle from Bondon Automotive can carry eight people ------- .

(A) comfortable
(B) comfort
(C) comfortably
(D) comforting

112. ------- deciding to replace the food-service provider, the management team conducted a survey of all employees.

(A) Before
(B) Unless
(C) Whether
(D) Except

113. Although Mr. Cho was ------- about transferring to the Houston office, he is now working there confidently and productively.

(A) hesitate
(B) hesitant
(C) hesitation
(D) hesitated

114. The personnel office should be contacted about unpaid leave ------- supervisors cannot approve it.

(A) as
(B) either
(C) like
(D) instead

115. Yesterday the board voted to ------- with discussions about acquiring Atlasburg Financial.

(A) proceed
(B) proceeded
(C) proceeding
(D) proceeds

116. Robles Corporation encourages employees to work toward a ------- goal, rather than pursuing individual interests.

(A) common
(B) regular
(C) usual
(D) plain

117. The ------- in the brochure are an accurate representation of what guests staying at the resort can expect to find.

(A) image
(B) images
(C) imaged
(D) imaging

118. Current employees interested in the new managerial position should ------- about the internal hiring process.

(A) provide
(B) inquire
(C) evaluate
(D) control

119. Colleagues in the accounting department consider the matter closed and ------- cannot provide more input.

(A) large
(B) consequently
(C) very
(D) anyone

120. The CEO hopes that the consultant's advice will ultimately ------- higher profits for the company.

(A) yield
(B) submit
(C) invent
(D) resolve

GO ON TO THE NEXT PAGE

121. A team of experts is reviewing the contract from a financial ------- so please do not share it with the client yet.

(A) perspective
(B) belief
(C) movement
(D) proportion

122. To prevent noise that is distracting to performers, the lobby gift shop is ------- open during performances.

(A) almost
(B) even
(C) never
(D) soon

123. Zuper Brite lightbulbs ------- reduce energy consumption when compared with standard incandescent lightbulbs.

(A) great
(B) greater
(C) greatest
(D) greatly

124. The airport's proposed ------- project will include two remodeled terminals and an updated transportation system.

(A) encouragement
(B) modernization
(C) assistant
(D) importance

125. Market Research is the ------- of the company concerned with better understanding our clients' needs.

(A) divisional
(B) divisible
(C) division
(D) divide

126. Mr. Tanaka was so pleased by the quarterly performance report ------- he canceled the weekly updates.

(A) in case
(B) which
(C) that
(D) seldom

127. Quincycom's price increase is justifiable ------- there is an improvement in the quality of the Internet service we receive.

(A) whereas
(B) likewise
(C) because of
(D) only if

128. The chart attached to this e-mail presents a ------- of Vivasyco's latest smartphone with a model from Eustace Tech.

(A) comparison
(B) pronouncement
(C) guideline
(D) publicity

129. It is the catering director's ------- to inform the chef of the intended menu well in advance of the event.

(A) obliged
(B) obligated
(C) obligatory
(D) obligation

130. Given her experience in health care, Ms. Chung is ------- well suited to manage the company's wellness program.

(A) formerly
(B) expectantly
(C) particularly
(D) avoidably

PART 6

Directions: Read the texts that follow. A word, phrase, or sentence is missing in parts of each text. Four answer choices for each question are given below the text. Select the best answer to complete the text. Then mark the letter (A), (B), (C), or (D) on your answer sheet.

Questions 131-134 refer to the following product description.

Sanberg Industries: Big Angle Television Wall Mount

The Big Angle Television Wall Mount is perfect for mounting televisions from 40 inches to 75 inches in size as measured diagonally across the screen. The mount connects easily to your wall, ------- freeing your tabletops and saving space. The ------- mount comes with a 25-inch arm that
131.   132.
bends in multiple directions so you can enjoy watching television from anywhere in the room. Plus, it has vertical and horizontal tilt capabilities, so your television can be placed ------- in the position
133.
you like. ------- .
134.

---

131. (A) due to
(B) so that
(C) although
(D) thereby

132. (A) mysterious
(B) flexible
(C) skillful
(D) limited

133. (A) exact
(B) exacting
(C) exactly
(D) exacted

134. (A) Like all products by Sanberg Industries, it also comes with a five-year guarantee.
(B) Your inquiry about your Sanberg product will be addressed within two business days.
(C) We are grateful that you have worked for Sanberg Industries for so many years.
(D) High-definition televisions offer an improved viewing experience.

GO ON TO THE NEXT PAGE

To: minjunlee@alto.com
From: contest@asianaturemag.org
Date: 7 September
Subject: Tenth annual contest

Asia Nature magazine wants to thank you for your ------- . Your participation in our tenth annual
135.

amateur photography contest is appreciated. Each photograph we receive is judged by our panel

of experts. ------- . Their works have been displayed in galleries around the world.
136.

Asia Nature magazine depends on people like you who care about the environment and

------- nature's beauty. We ask that you visit our Web site and make a contribution today.
137.

Without ------- readers like you, we would not be able to continue our work.
138.

135. (A) subscription
(B) letter
(C) submission
(D) article

136. (A) Photographing nature is a difficult
skill to learn.
(B) Every reader of our magazine
knows that wildlife is precious.
(C) *Asia Nature* magazine has been
published for fourteen years.
(D) These professionals are among
the best in their field.

137. (A) value
(B) values
(C) valuable
(D) valued

138. (A) crowded
(B) accidental
(C) generous
(D) light

New Italian Food Shop Opening Soon

CALGARY (28 March)—This Saturday marks the grand opening of Calgary's latest Italian specialty food shop. Salerno's Italian Food will sell its own brand of fresh pastas and sauces ------- imported goods. The shop is located on the corner of Macall Avenue and Arnhem Street.
139.

------- . This small part of Calgary is becoming a very popular place to go for gourmet food. Leo
140.

Sarri, the store's owner, was ------- the chef at Milano's. He is looking forward to Saturday and
141.

says he is thrilled to be entering the ------- world for the first time.
142.

139. (A) even though
(B) in order to
(C) in spite of
(D) as well as

141. (A) efficiently
(B) later
(C) previously
(D) especially

140. (A) The weather on Saturday is expected to be beautiful.
(B) This area is already home to several bakeries, bistros, and coffee shops.
(C) Fresh pastas and sauces are superior to mass-produced ones.
(D) We will soon learn what consumers think of the products that Salerno's offers.

142. (A) retail
(B) education
(C) shipping
(D) travel

GO ON TO THE NEXT PAGE

Experienced Machinist Wanted

Caliphar Tech Industries is seeking experienced machinists ------- problems, set up and operate
143.

machinery, and troubleshoot machines in our main production plant. ------- . Examples of the
144.

equipment we make include pumps and fans for various industries.

Caliphar Tech Industries features a fast-paced work environment with tight deadlines. We need

team players who can work together ------- pressure. We offer ------- salaries and excellent
145.   146.

benefits. Contact humanresources@caliphartechindustries.com.

143. (A) analyze
(B) analyzer
(C) analyzing
(D) to analyze

144. (A) Send specifications for your project to our
production director.
(B) Our factory manufactures components used
in industrial equipment.
(C) We hope you enjoy the tour of our innovative
manufacturing plant.
(D) Congratulations on being hired by Caliphar
Tech Industries.

145. (A) along
(B) under
(C) beyond
(D) for

146. (A) compete
(B) competition
(C) competitive
(D) competed

PART 7

Directions: In this part you will read a selection of texts, such as magazine and newspaper articles, e-mails, and instant messages. Each text or set of texts is followed by several questions. Select the best answer for each question and mark the letter (A), (B), (C), or (D) on your answer sheet.

Questions 147-148 refer to the following advertisement.

Uncle Pete's Marionette Theater Presents
Moose Lake
March 27–May 7

Ever since the founding of Uncle Pete's Marionette Theater, our adaptation of the well-known ballet *Moose Lake* has been one of our most beloved shows. Our 100 handcrafted marionettes will take you on a thrilling adventure into the world of *Moose Lake*.

As our skilled puppeteers pull the strings and make the puppets move, you will cheer for Maria and the Moose Prince. You may be unhappy with the Lizard King and his minions. You will be enthralled by the Drifting Dragonflies!

Uncle Pete's version of *Moose Lake* has been delighting viewers of all ages for more than 30 years. Shows sell out every year, so get your tickets today.

Tickets are available at the box office, 521 Perry Avenue, Fenton.

---

147. What is being advertised?

(A) A lake cruise
(B) A puppet show
(C) A string quartet
(D) An adventure park

148. What is Uncle Pete's version of *Moose Lake* based on?

(A) A classic children's book
(B) A popular film
(C) A video game
(D) A dance performance

GO ON TO THE NEXT PAGE

Clean House Janitorial Services

Copper County's trustworthy and efficient cleaning solution since 1972

NEW CUSTOMER PROMOTION
*Copper County residents ONLY

Save 15%
on your first year of home cleanings!
*Carpet-cleaning service NOT included

Call 916-555-0137 today for details and to schedule your first service.

Offer valid through December 31

149. What is indicated about Clean House Janitorial Services?

(A) It was founded in 1972.
(B) It specializes in office cleaning.
(C) It offers a discount on carpet cleaning.
(D) It prefers online communication.

150. Who in Copper County may use the coupon?

(A) Any large retail store
(B) New customers
(C) Returning customers
(D) Any resident

Pierre Gitane
26 Bent Tree Lane
Charlotte, NC 28804
April 15

Dear Mr. Gitane,

This letter is to inform you that you are due for your semiannual dental care visit. Go to our Web site and fill out a form to request an appointment. Or if you prefer, call us at (704) 555-0138 to reach one of our receptionists.

We are happy to announce that we now offer teeth whitening and invisible braces to improve your smile. Please let us know if you are interested in one or both of these services.

We look forward to hearing from you soon.

All best,

Sarah Hamadi

Sarah Hamadi
Office manager, Red Street Dental Care

151. Why did Mr. Gitane receive the letter?
    (A) He just got a new dentist.
    (B) It is time for a routine checkup.
    (C) Red Street Dental Care is requesting his feedback.
    (D) He was dissatisfied with his last visit.

152. What does the letter state about the teeth-whitening service?
    (A) It costs about the same as invisible braces.
    (B) It was not available at Red Street Dental Care until recently.
    (C) It takes up to six months to obtain the desired results.
    (D) It is not covered by dental insurance plans.

GO ON TO THE NEXT PAGE

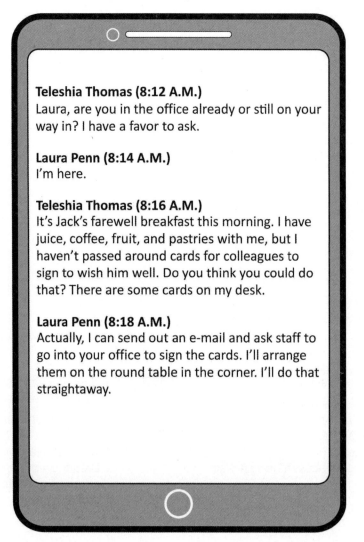

153. At 8:14 A.M., what does Ms. Penn most likely mean when she writes, "I'm here"?

(A) She is paying attention.
(B) She is in the same room as Ms. Thomas.
(C) She is waiting for Ms. Thomas to arrive.
(D) She is already at the office.

154. What will Ms. Penn most likely do next?

(A) Give a presentation
(B) Postpone a meeting
(C) Put cards on a table
(D) Arrange seats in a staff room

Questions 155-157 refer to the following menu.

History

Welcome to the historic H. G. Walsh Building and North Riverview Restaurant! Constructed by H. G. Walsh in 1897, the building served as Astoria's post office until 1942. It has subsequently been a general store, a boutique, and a family-run restaurant serving up fresh seafood. Over the past century, the building's second floor has been used for private parties, such as birthdays and weddings.

Facing a potential demolition in the late 1970s, the building was purchased by its current owners, Henry and Juana Thomason, in 1981. Subsequent investment and extensive renovation helped save the H. G. Walsh Building, and in 1996 it gained status on the National Register of Historic Places. With its stunning views of the Columbia River and an extensive seasonal menu, the H. G. Walsh Building has become a prime destination for visitors to Oregon's Pacific coast.

Fall Menu

Seafood chowder | Cup: $5, Bowl: $8
Cream-based with clams, shrimp, and mussels

Fish and chips | Cod: $12, Halibut: $15
Three pieces breaded in a buttermilk batter

Grilled salmon | $20
Served with lemon-garlic sauce and a side salad

Bok choy | $12
Pan-seared in a garlic-ginger oyster sauce and served over rice noodles

Chef's salad | $11
Mixed greens tossed with toasted almonds, blue cheese dressing, and avocado

---

155. The word "served" in paragraph 1, line 2, is closest in meaning to

(A) supplied
(B) delivered
(C) presented
(D) functioned

156. What is suggested about the H. G. Walsh Building?

(A) It is a one-floor building.
(B) It is located on the waterfront.
(C) It is located next to a post office.
(D) It has remained largely unchanged.

157. What can be purchased for less than $10?

(A) Seafood chowder
(B) Fish and chips
(C) Bok choy
(D) Chefs salad

GO ON TO THE NEXT PAGE

Headquarters Teams Help Out in Stores

Hannen has operated one of the largest chains of department stores in the Southwest since 1962. The In-Store Project, launched on February 7, is a new initiative from the Hannen Department Store corporate operations team. Following recommendations from employees at various levels, the initiative was developed to allow company headquarters to better understand the day-to-day operations at the individual store level.

The In-Store Project places employees from the corporate headquarters in stores, where they are paired with store employees to work typical shifts. This allows both types of Hannen employees to ask questions and learn about one another's work. So far, the initiative has led to a greater understanding among store employees of the decisions made at the corporate level and a greater understanding among headquarters employees on how corporate plans are implemented.

Hannen plans to complete store visits within the next two months and conduct repeat visits annually.

158. Why did the company start the project?

(A) It is a current trend among large companies.
(B) The parent company required it.
(C) It was suggested by some employees.
(D) Some customers requested it.

159. What does the project involve?

(A) Store employees visiting other department store chains
(B) Interns being hired to receive on-the-job training
(C) Corporate employees temporarily working in stores
(D) Teams of employees working to redesign stores

160. What does the article indicate about the future of the project?

(A) The company plans to do it again each year.
(B) The company plans to expand it to other stores it owns.
(C) It is being discontinued because it has been unsuccessful.
(D) It will not be completed because it is too expensive.

KARLINGA BEACH
(December 4)—More resources need to be allocated to promote cultural tourism to the region, officials from the Karlinga Beach Tourism Department (KBTD) concluded at a planning meeting held yesterday. The department also drafted a new marketing campaign, titled "Connect with Karlinga Beach," that will highlight the region's rich history and culture. "Everyone agreed that, moving forward, we should focus less on advertising traditional beach activities and more on new eco-friendly tourist activities," said Tourism Director Arnold Bhatt.

During the meeting, Mr. Bhatt gave a presentation in which he analyzed the results from an online questionnaire designed by students from the region's university. Respondents included both local residents and tourists. In one key result, more than 80 percent of all respondents agreed that there should be more emphasis on promoting eco-friendly tourism. In another finding, more than 75 percent of surveyed tourists indicated they would like to see a wider selection of locally sourced, organic food options. "For me, the tourists' response was unexpected," said Mr. Bhatt. "But, looking at the full picture, it makes sense, as there are many family farms on the land near the beach."

The insights from the survey are welcome news for Kathy Li, who operates the KLP Organic Farm. Its grocery store, located on the farm property, is stocked year-round with fresh, seasonal, organically grown produce. In the future, if tourist visits increase, Ms. Li plans to offer prepared foods and beverages.

161. What is the main purpose of the article?

(A) To announce recent personnel changes
(B) To outline proposed marketing plans
(C) To explain a decrease in local tourism
(D) To encourage participation in a survey

162. What is indicated about Karlinga Beach?

(A) It has a short tourism season.
(B) It offers inexpensive accommodations.
(C) It is accessed mostly by ferry.
(D) It is close to a university.

163. According to the article, what is true about Mr. Bhatt?

(A) He was surprised by a survey result.
(B) He changed the design of a questionnaire.
(C) He is concerned about a region losing farmland.
(D) He wants to increase attendance at public meetings.

164. What is mentioned about KLP Organic Farm?

(A) It offers free tours to hotel guests.
(B) It publishes its own newsletter.
(C) It recently opened a restaurant.
(D) It sells fruits and vegetables on-site.

GO ON TO THE NEXT PAGE

Treks Auto

Keeping your vehicle running smoothly demands getting the job done right. Leave yours in the hands of the professionals at Treks Auto, and always be sure you're getting exactly what you need and nothing that you don't. — [1] —. Our repair shop has been based in Leeds ever since Tony Reker opened his first garage in 1963. — [2] —. For three generations, our family-run business has been proud to serve the West Yorkshire community with fair pricing and a commitment to honest service.

— [3] —. Treks Auto offers a variety of oil-change packages. Each package includes a complimentary tyre-pressure check, tyre rotation, fluid fill-up, standard oil filter, five-litre oil change, and brake inspection. Choose from the oil options listed below. — [4] —.

Synthetic Blend	High Mileage	Full Synthetic
£25	£40	£50
Recommended for vehicles with fewer than 125,000 miles or under ten years old.	Best for vehicles with more than 125,000 miles or over ten years old.	Ideal for vehicles with more than 125,000 miles and with special manufacturer-recommended maintenance needs.

165. What is indicated about Treks Auto?

(A) It is based in London.
(B) It was started in 1983.
(C) It is focused on great customer service.
(D) It has been a family-run business for five generations.

166. What is indicated about the oil-change packages?

(A) They all cost the same.
(B) They each include free brake-pad replacement.
(C) Only one of the packages offers a fluid fill-up.
(D) They are based on the number of miles a vehicle has been driven.

167. In which of the positions marked [1], [2], [3] and [4] does the following sentence best belong?

"Ask any of our service technicians if you are unsure of the best one for your car."

(A) [1]
(B) [2]
(C) [3]
(D) [4]

New Addition to Shadeside Plaza

BIRCH CITY (November 12)—Design Glory, a jewelry business operated by lifelong Birch City resident Tamara Banda, has set up a brick-and-mortar store in the city's Shadeside Plaza shopping area. — [1] —. Ms. Banda said the shop, which opened on November 9, features her entire line of handmade jewelry along with a selection of beautiful natural crystals that can become the centerpiece of any room.

Ms. Banda emphasizes that she sets her jewelry brand apart from others by offering handmade designs at price points that won't break a budget. To keep her overhead costs in check, she says she sources materials creatively from a variety of local metal suppliers. — [2] —. Although managing the store, which is open Tuesday through Saturday from 11:00 A.M. to 5:00 P.M., will occupy much of her time, Ms. Banda said she still intends to operate booths at regional arts festivals. — [3] —. She will also continue to serve on the planning committee for the annual art show at Central Arts University, where she learned her jewelry-making techniques.

The idea of opening a physical store came to Ms. Banda when a friend, Brad Machado, told her of his positive experience in operating his retail bookshop on the opposite side of Shadeside Plaza from where Design Glory is now. — [4] —. The shopping area, he said, benefits from the heavy foot traffic nearby.

168. What is indicated about Design Glory?

(A) It had a delayed opening date.
(B) It sells decorative stones.
(C) It has weekly craft demonstrations.
(D) It is closed on Saturdays.

169. What does Ms. Banda say is special about her jewelry?

(A) It is designed by local students.
(B) It looks old-fashioned.
(C) It is affordable.
(D) It is lightweight.

170. Who is Mr. Machado?

(A) A property developer
(B) A metal supplier
(C) A photographer
(D) A bookseller

171. In which of the positions marked [1], [2], [3] and [4] does the following sentence best belong?

"She noted as well that she will be participating in the City Art Museum's craft fair next month."

(A) [1]
(B) [2]
(C) [3]
(D) [4]

GO ON TO THE NEXT PAGE

Questions 172-175 refer to the following text-message chain.

Sandra Kyle (8:19 A.M.)
Good morning. I'm on my way but running late because of a lane closure on Roseway Boulevard. It's all backed up, and the bus is barely moving.

Lucas Bodin (8:20 A.M.)
Sounds terrible!

Sandra Kyle (8:21 A.M.)
I'm supposed to take notes at our 8:30 A.M. meeting. Could one of you please fill in for me until I arrive?

Carolina Mata (8:23 A.M.)
Wait, haven't you heard? The meeting was moved to Thursday.

Sandra Kyle (8:24 A.M.)
Really? What a relief.

Carolina Mata (8:26 A.M.)
Mr. Chang is in Portsville meeting with the client about the final design for the new warehouse building. He won't be back until tomorrow.

Sandra Kyle (8:27 A.M.)
Yes, I heard he was going to Portsville.

Lucas Bodin (8:30 A.M.)
The client requested some last-minute changes, so Mr. Chang is away longer than expected. Hopefully the changes are minor, because we're already over the allocated budget.

Carolina Mata (8:33 A.M.)
We will get an update at the Thursday meeting. Hopefully it's good news.

172. Why does Ms. Kyle expect to be late for work?

(A) The bus is slow because of poor weather.
(B) The bus is stuck in traffic.
(C) She missed the bus.
(D) The bus arrived late at her stop.

173. Why was the meeting postponed?

(A) A colleague is out of the office.
(B) The client needs more time to prepare.
(C) Mr. Bodin has a scheduling conflict.
(D) Ms. Mata needs to prepare an update.

174. At 8:24 A.M., what does Ms. Kyle most likely mean when she writes, "Really"?

(A) She is disappointed by certain designs.
(B) She disagrees with the decision.
(C) She is surprised by Ms. Mata's comment.
(D) She already heard the news.

175. What is indicated about the project?

(A) It is more expensive than planned.
(B) It has some technical difficulties.
(C) It has been poorly managed.
(D) It cannot be completed on time.

GO ON TO THE NEXT PAGE

Thompson and Groves

The law firm of Thompson and Groves is seeking a dedicated assistant to join our established environmental litigation team.

This assistant will work on a wide range of legal services, such as
- investigating evidence related to cases being prepared for court;
- preparing exhibits, charts, and diagrams to display information; and
- communicating with clients and keeping files updated.

The best candidate for this position
- is self-directed, responsible, and capable of juggling many projects at once; and
- has strong communication, organization, and computer skills.

To apply, e-mail your résumé to Julia Powell (in human resources), julia.powell@thompsonandgroves.com, by May 25. Interviews will be conducted at the beginning of June, and our selection will be made in early July.

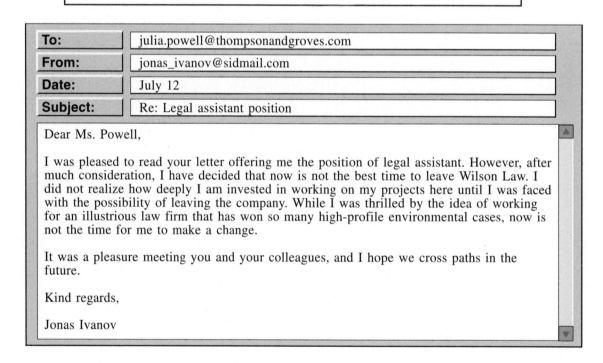

To:	julia.powell@thompsonandgroves.com
From:	jonas_ivanov@sidmail.com
Date:	July 12
Subject:	Re: Legal assistant position

Dear Ms. Powell,

I was pleased to read your letter offering me the position of legal assistant. However, after much consideration, I have decided that now is not the best time to leave Wilson Law. I did not realize how deeply I am invested in working on my projects here until I was faced with the possibility of leaving the company. While I was thrilled by the idea of working for an illustrious law firm that has won so many high-profile environmental cases, now is not the time for me to make a change.

It was a pleasure meeting you and your colleagues, and I hope we cross paths in the future.

Kind regards,

Jonas Ivanov

176. What is included in the job advertisement?

- (A) A brief history of the Thompson and Groves law firm
- (B) Directions to a company's office
- (C) A description of the job's pay and benefits
- (D) A description of the ideal applicant

177. What most likely is one of Ms. Powell's job responsibilities?

- (A) Preparing exhibits and charts
- (B) Updating computer files
- (C) Hiring new employees
- (D) Writing about environmental issues

178. What does Mr. Ivanov indicate in his e-mail?

- (A) He has changed his career goals.
- (B) He has decided to stay at his present job.
- (C) He has decided to retire.
- (D) He will apply for a different job.

179. What does the e-mail mention about the Thompson and Groves law firm?

- (A) It is well-known for its successes.
- (B) It will be moving to a larger space.
- (C) It no longer specializes in environmental issues.
- (D) It will be hosting an international conference.

180. What is suggested about Mr. Ivanov?

- (A) He received a promotion in May.
- (B) He met with Ms. Powell in June.
- (C) He and Ms. Powell have a mutual friend.
- (D) He has just completed a certification program.

GO ON TO THE NEXT PAGE

MEMO

To: Kildare Recreation Centre Staff
From: Madeline Byrne
Date: 11 April
Subject: Daily Passes

As discussed in April's staff meeting, we are considering raising the cost of daily passes from €5 to €9. The exact increase will be decided in our May meeting. This change is expected to bring in an extra €5,000 over the next year, which we will use toward the cost of replacing our outdoor running track. With the increased revenue from the fee change, we will be close to the €7,000 needed for the improvement.

I realize that the outdoor running season is short, and I know that in our meeting, some staff members wanted to consider other uses for the money. The possibilities of using the funds for a remodeled reception area, a new floor for the dance studio, or more flat-screen televisions throughout the centre were raised. However, the board of directors thought it would be wiser to focus on the improvement most frequently requested by our members. The upgrades suggested by the staff fall into the €1,000–€2,000 range, and we hope to be able to consider them in the coming years.

NOTICE
Kildare Recreation Centre Visitors

Effective 1 June, the cost of a daily pass for nonmembers will be €8. This modest increase will allow us to provide visitors with a much better outdoor running track. The cost of monthly and annual memberships has not changed. Please visit the registration office during regular business hours to discuss membership-related issues.

181. What is the purpose of the memo?
    (A) To announce an increase in membership numbers
    (B) To explain how certain funds will be used
    (C) To describe tasks to be done for an event
    (D) To solicit donations for a project

182. What did the staff do at the April meeting?
    (A) They designed a survey for recreation center members.
    (B) They objected to a price increase.
    (C) They proposed upgrades to a recreation center.
    (D) They considered moving a reception area.

183. According to the memo, what do the recreation center members most frequently ask for?
    (A) A remodeled reception area
    (B) A new dance studio floor
    (C) Additional flat-screen televisions
    (D) An improved outdoor running track

184. In the notice, the word "modest" in paragraph 1, line 2, is closest in meaning to
    (A) shy
    (B) modern
    (C) creative
    (D) small

185. What is true about the new fee for daily passes for nonmembers?
    (A) It is less than what was originally considered.
    (B) It will be effective starting May 1.
    (C) It can be paid online.
    (D) It was approved at a June meeting.

GO ON TO THE NEXT PAGE

E-mail

To:	jsantos@coloniamenor.com
From:	markash@amtrcorp.com
Date:	September 4
Subject:	Job tip

Hello, Juan,

It was nice to see you again at the Tech Writers' Conference in Mexico City. You mentioned that your cousin Carlos Cruz wants to find a product design job here in Dallas. Well, the company I work for, AMTR Corporation, is about to post a job for a junior industrial designer, which might interest him. So far, the company has announced the opening only to current employees, but next week it will appear on the company Web site. The salary is good, and there may not be any qualified candidates in-house. Please let him know about this opportunity.

Heide Markas

---

https://www.amtrcorp.com

AMTR Corporation   HOME   ABOUT   **CAREERS**   CONTACT   BLOG

Current Opportunities

Junior Industrial Designer: This is a full-time position developing and improving the full range of products manufactured by AMTR Corporation in Dallas, Texas.

Sample Job Duties:
- Design consumer and office supply products, including personal computers, tablets, copiers, and printers
- Collaborate with design team and colleagues from engineering, marketing, and manufacturing departments to develop new products
- Improve sustainability efforts by promoting the use of recycled, recyclable, and reusable materials

Qualifications:
- Understanding of design principles, theories, and concepts
- Ability to analyze and apply customer feedback
- Proven analytical and problem-solving skills
- Experience in creating sketches, storyboards, models, and prototypes
- Bachelor's or master's degree in industrial design

```
*E-mail*
```

To:	Carlos Cruz <ccruz@bmail.com>
From:	Pamela Wang <wangp@amtrcorp.com>
Date:	November 11
Subject:	Job Application

Dear Mr. Cruz,

Thank you for submitting your application for junior industrial designer to AMTR Corporation. Our hiring committee has reviewed your application and determined that you meet the qualifications for the position. We will contact you shortly to schedule an initial interview. Interviews will be held on-site at our Dallas headquarters during the first two weeks of December. In the meantime, you will receive a request for professional references via e-mail. Please respond to the request as soon as you receive it.

Cordially,

Pamela Wang
Human Resources Specialist
AMTR Corporation

---

186. What is the purpose of the first e-mail?

(A) To share information about a new job opening
(B) To ask whether a company is hiring new staff
(C) To learn whether a colleague will attend an upcoming conference
(D) To congratulate someone for getting a new job

187. What does the company that Ms. Markas works for produce?

(A) Guides for creating Web sites
(B) Operating manuals for passenger airplanes
(C) Transportation system maps
(D) Office equipment

188. What is explained in the second e-mail?

(A) The procedure for submitting an application
(B) What applicants can expect during an interview
(C) The next steps of the hiring process
(D) AMTR Corporation's expectations for designers

189. What will AMTR Corporation do during the first two weeks of December?

(A) Move its headquarters to Dallas
(B) Begin reviewing applications
(C) Send out professional references
(D) Perform the first round of interviews

190. What is most likely true about Mr. Cruz?

(A) He will begin the job in November.
(B) He has a degree in industrial design.
(C) He has relocated to Dallas.
(D) He recently interviewed for a new job.

GO ON TO THE NEXT PAGE

Shingle Town Roofing
Color Options

Choose from our many colors of high-quality, affordable shingles
for a long-lasting, beautiful roof.

Color	Product Number
Lawnwood Blue	(#302)
Charcoal Bliss	(#702)
Foxwood Gray	(#704)
Mission Gray	(#707)
Cedarwood	(#203)
Hickory Nut	(#209)
Brick Red	(#505)

Joanne Westley
8021 Daffodil Lane
Herndon, Virginia 22090

Dear Ms. Westley,

This is to confirm our agreement to replace your roof in Herndon, Virginia, on
August 4. As discussed, we will be using our exclusive Prime Technology System with
Hickory Nut color shingles. The Prime Technology System is guaranteed to keep
your house dry and has a ten-year warranty for labor and materials.

Our crew will arrive at 8:30 A.M. We have received your deposit and signed contract.
The remainder of the charge is due upon completion of the job. Please contact us if
you have any questions.

Martin Sage

Martin Sage, customer service representative
Shingle Town Roofing

| **Shingle Town Roofing: Installation Schedule for August 1–7** | | | | | | |
| Note to installation crew: Be sure to confirm the job location and the required materials. | | | | | | |
Sunday	**Monday**	**Tuesday**	**Wednesday**	**Thursday**	**Friday**	**Saturday**
1	2 Harris residence (#702)	3 Landsford Apartments E-3 (#505)	4 Westley residence (#209)	5 Kendelwood Motel (#302)	6 Hopewell Gardens (#704)	7 Hopewell Gardens (#704)

191. What is the purpose of the letter?

(A) To get a cost estimate for a new roof
(B) To request a deposit for a job
(C) To ask a contractor to do a project
(D) To finalize a business arrangement

192. What does Mr. Sage indicate about the Prime Technology System?

(A) It requires a separate fee for the ten-year warranty.
(B) It prevents water from leaking into a house.
(C) It is available for only certain types of shingles.
(D) It requires a large crew to install.

193. Where is a shingles installation scheduled to take place on August 3?

(A) At the Harris residence
(B) At Landsford Apartments
(C) At Kendelwood Motel
(D) At Hopewell Gardens

194. What color shingles will the crew be installing at Kendelwood Motel?

(A) Lawnwood Blue
(B) Charcoal Bliss
(C) Mission Gray
(D) Brick Red

195. When will Shingle Town Roofing do work at 8021 Daffodil Lane?

(A) On Monday
(B) On Tuesday
(C) On Wednesday
(D) On Thursday

GO ON TO THE NEXT PAGE

https://carinasolutions.com/home

Home **Services** **Contact Us** **Reviews**

Carina Solutions
The Best Software Option for Hotel Management

We will help you manage all aspects of your hotel. Whether you need help with your reservation system, managing staff, or improving your advertising and online presence, our software will work for you!

Here are just a few of the tasks our software can do.
- Manage online bookings and payments
- Track staff hours and vacation time
- Promote your hotel on top booking Web sites
- Manage property maintenance

Contact us today to begin using the trial version of our software completely free for three months. More information about the pricing and features of the Premier software version can be found on the Services page of our Web site.

---

https://carinasolutions.com/reviews

Home **Services** **Contact Us** **Reviews**

My trial version of the Carina Solutions hotel management software expires tomorrow, and I have to decide whether to purchase the Premier version or search for something better.

I have two main concerns.

1. The reservations module does not allow you to keep information about repeat guests on file. This forces staff to reenter repeat customers' information manually, which wastes time.

2. The software offers full functionality only when accessed on a desktop computer, which is unfortunate because I do almost everything on my mobile phone. The interface should be the same no matter what device you use.

—Submitted by Susan Yan

https://carinasolutions.com/reviews_response

| Home | Services | Contact Us | Reviews |

Dear Ms. Yan,

Good news! We have updated some features of Carina Solutions since you began your trial subscription. There is now an automatic rebooking feature that you can use to register repeat guests, cutting down on manual data entry.

Additionally, you should know that one of the differences between the trial version and the Premier version is that the interfaces are the same across all devices.

Remember, Carina Solutions hotel management software is more than just a booking tool. Learning about all the features in the Premier version can help you fill your hotel with happy customers. Make sure to visit carinasolutions.com to see our instructional videos.

Marcus Feldman
Carina Solutions representative

196. According to the Web page, what is true about the maker of Carina Solutions software?

(A) It makes products for the transportation industry.
(B) It makes two versions of its software.
(C) Travelers use its products to find discounted hotel prices.
(D) Its products are not yet available for sale.

197. What is implied about Ms. Yan?

(A) She has been using Carina Solutions for nearly three months.
(B) She was referred to Carina Solutions by another client.
(C) She plans to stay at a hotel during her next trip.
(D) She works for a software company.

198. What is Ms. Yan's concern about hotel guest information?

(A) It cannot be downloaded easily.
(B) The system does not protect it with a secure password.
(C) She cannot enter corrections to misspelled names or addresses.
(D) It must be entered every time a guest makes a reservation.

199. What does Mr. Feldman indicate about the company's videos?

(A) They contain information about interesting places to visit.
(B) They are available for guests to view in their hotel rooms.
(C) They describe many ways that the company's software can be used.
(D) They were created by the company very recently.

200. What is suggested about the Premier version of Carina Solutions software?

(A) It must be updated every three months.
(B) It addresses Ms. Yan's second concern.
(C) Optional features can be added for a fee.
(D) Ms. Yan may contact Mr. Feldman to receive a discount coupon.

Stop! This is the end of the test. If you finish before time is called, you may go back to Parts 5, 6, and 7 and check your work.

토익 정기시험
실전 ❶1000
RC

실전 TEST

03

In the Reading test, you will read a variety of texts and answer several different types of reading comprehension questions. The entire Reading test will last 75 minutes. There are three parts, and directions are given for each part. You are encouraged to answer as many questions as possible within the time allowed.

You must mark your answers on the separate answer sheet. Do not write your answers in your test book.

PART 5

Directions: A word or phrase is missing in each of the sentences below. Four answer choices are given below each sentence. Select the best answer to complete the sentence. Then mark the letter (A), (B), (C), or (D) on your answer sheet.

101. Video game designers need a broad ------- of computer programming.

(A) knowledge
(B) known
(C) knowing
(D) know

102. Concerning the item that was lost in transit, we will take responsibility for ------- .

(A) it
(B) its
(C) its own
(D) itself

103. The Springly Energy marketing team is working hard ------- our latest products.

(A) promote
(B) to promote
(C) promoted
(D) were promoting

104. The job advertisement lists several ------- needed to be considered for an interview.

(A) specialists
(B) qualifications
(C) engagements
(D) assortments

105. When the contract is signed and received, it will become ------- immediately.

(A) effective
(B) effect
(C) effected
(D) effectively

106. It is unlikely that a policy change could have ------- the financial challenge that the construction company faced.

(A) shared
(B) banned
(C) forbidden
(D) prevented

107. Barsan Photo is ------- that their latest printer will not be available before the start of the third quarter.

(A) acknowledge
(B) acknowledges
(C) acknowledging
(D) acknowledgement

108. Thanks to the new system we installed, all lights and other devices turn on ------- when you enter the office.

(A) heavily
(B) seriously
(C) automatically
(D) furiously

109. ------- the high demand for apartments, the study says single detached homes will be the most popular dwelling in five years.

(A) Despite
(B) Apparently
(C) As expected
(D) In contrast

110. The process for estimating our yearly expenses is -------, so we can start planning staffing for next year.

(A) careless
(B) full
(C) entire
(D) complete

111. As of June 26, only one ------- had called to request space at the trade show.

(A) exhibitor
(B) exhibit
(C) exhibition
(D) exhibiting

112. To keep costs ------- an established budget, the owner decided to reduce the size of the garage to be constructed.

(A) into
(B) over
(C) within
(D) beside

113. The outdoor sales event was a great success ------- the cold and rainy weather.

(A) in spite of
(B) provided that
(C) although
(D) unless

114. No ------- of Mr. Hanson's book would be complete without mentioning his insightful analysis of the world of business blogs.

(A) finish
(B) summary
(C) composition
(D) organization

115. Updating the product line that buyers have complained about will send an obvious ------- to our valued customers.

(A) messaging
(B) messenger
(C) message
(D) messaged

116. The Internet will ------- be a crucial part of the economy for the foreseeable future.

(A) concisely
(B) perfectly
(C) currently
(D) undoubtedly

117. The management team required little ------- before deciding to promote Ms. Yang.

(A) deliberation
(B) deliberate
(C) deliberated
(D) deliberately

118. The human resources office is adopting a more ------- policy that would give employees additional vacation days.

(A) generous
(B) collaborative
(C) severe
(D) regional

119. Mr. Greaves will speak to our suppliers about ------- handling of the transportation situation.

(A) they
(B) their
(C) them
(D) these

120. This is only a preliminary list of job candidates, so interviewers should ------- the possibility of last-minute additions.

(A) wait
(B) decide
(C) expect
(D) figure

GO ON TO THE NEXT PAGE

121. Market conditions were ------- enough last year for us to make several new acquisitions.

(A) favor
(B) favorite
(C) favorably
(D) favorable

122. Web advertising is smart in the sense that it can be highly specific and target a market ------- great accuracy.

(A) near
(B) during
(C) between
(D) with

123. The library director requests that staff obtain ------- in instructional technology to better support the library's educational programs.

(A) certification
(B) certified
(C) certifiable
(D) certifier

124. ------- existing products, which are designed for people with technical expertise, this new program should appeal to a wider audience.

(A) Before
(B) Instead of
(C) Unlike
(D) While

125. Some functions of our Web team are to identify problems with applications and then ------- fixes.

(A) priority
(B) prioritize
(C) prioritized
(D) prioritization

126. This partnership ------- a great opportunity for us at Stolant Tech to broaden our inventory of available software.

(A) corresponds
(B) represents
(C) appreciates
(D) intends

127. We will need to delay the start of the advertising campaign because the relevant contracts have only been ------- completed.

(A) part
(B) parted
(C) partial
(D) partially

128. ------- much of the accounting staff will be on vacation next week, the ones remaining in the office will be very busy.

(A) Until
(B) Except for
(C) Because
(D) Due to

129. ------- sending multiple e-mails to share ideas and reach a decision, the team leader called a one-hour meeting to discuss the issue.

(A) As a result
(B) In order to
(C) The same as
(D) Rather than

130. Applicants for the position of flight attendant at Joyous Airlines need to ------- a calm sense of authority at all times.

(A) estimate
(B) appear
(C) involve
(D) project

PART 6

Directions: Read the texts that follow. A word, phrase, or sentence is missing in parts of each text. Four answer choices for each question are given below the text. Select the best answer to complete the text. Then mark the letter (A), (B), (C), or (D) on your answer sheet.

Questions 131-134 refer to the following notice.

Darway City Park Project Updates

Darway City Park management strives to keep all visitor trails ------- while improvement projects
131.
are underway. Currently, crews are trimming vegetation around directional signs along the park's

Woodmor bike path, so cyclists should ride carefully in this area. Note that ------- possible,
132.
renovation work is scheduled to take place during off-peak times because fewer people use the

park then. New informational signs that highlight specific features of the surrounding natural

environment will also be installed along sections of the trail. ------- . This phase of the project will
133.
be completed next month, and there is expected to be little ------- to park users as it progresses.
134.
The city's Department of Parks makes every effort to avoid trail closures and detours during work

projects.

131. (A) open
(B) noticeable
(C) practical
(D) genuine

132. (A) frequently
(B) considering
(C) whenever
(D) moreover

133. (A) They are intended to increase
visitors' enjoyment of the park.
(B) They are designed to
communicate these updated
regulations.
(C) Visitors especially enjoy using the
park café and other amenities.
(D) Planting new trees requires proper
planning and site selection.

134. (A) supplement
(B) reduction
(C) implementation
(D) disruption

GO ON TO THE NEXT PAGE

Questions 135-138 refer to the following e-mail.

From: McGuckin, Edward
To: All Summer Guests
Sent: Wednesday, May 15, 8:02 A.M.
Subject: Enjoying local beaches

We look forward to your visit to the Grand Hotel at Miracle Beach! The town council has recently passed an ordinance requiring that beachgoers pay for ------- to the local beaches. We know how
           135.
important free beach entry has been for our guests. ------- , we have arranged for beach passes
           136.
to be available for you—free of charge. All you have to do is ask for the pass when you check in and return the pass when you check out.

Please be advised that municipal beach-patrol staff members will be walking along the beach ------- to check for passes such as the ones we are providing. ------- . Make sure to get your
137.   **138.**
pass and avoid the possible penalty.

135. (A) accessing
(B) access
(C) accessory
(D) accessed

136. (A) Nevertheless
(B) Otherwise
(C) However
(D) Therefore

137. (A) regular
(B) regularly
(C) regulate
(D) regulation

138. (A) Take all personal belongings with you when you leave the beach.
(B) Sadly, having to pay for the beach is a growing phenomenon nationwide.
(C) A fine will be imposed on anyone who has not secured passes for local beaches.
(D) We will also provide beach towels for any guest who asks for one.

Questions 139-142 refer to the following e-mail.

From: Eun-Mi Park
To: All Employees at the New Korea Financial Group (NKFG)
Subject: Workplace Improvements
Date: March 12

As part of our commitment to providing a comfortable environment for our employees,

maintenance work will begin this week with the goal of ------- individual work spaces. The work
                                                              139.

will proceed in stages. First, new carpeting will be installed tomorrow in each office and cubicle.

To help ensure that this project ------- smoothly, please remove all personal items from the floor
                                   140.

in your work area before you leave today. ------- , open metal bookcases will be replaced later in
                                           141.

the week with state-of-the-art, high-density plastic bookshelves with sliding doors. We are

confident that these initiatives will improve the appearance of work spaces throughout the

company. ------- . Thank you in advance for your understanding and cooperation.
         142.

139. (A) combining
     (B) enhancing
     (C) cleaning
     (D) reassigning

140. (A) running
     (B) runs
     (C) ran
     (D) to run

141. (A) For example
     (B) Normally
     (C) Next
     (D) In summary

142. (A) We regret any inconvenience these measures
         may cause this week.
     (B) We are proud of the financial services we
         provide to our loyal customers.
     (C) The metal bookshelves were installed only five
         years ago.
     (D) Books are always welcome at local charities.

GO ON TO THE NEXT PAGE

The Newly Renovated Clairmont Cinema

By Sara Langly

BRISTOL (12 September)—After six months, the Clairmont Cinema has finally reopened. Since the owners were ------- about their plans, filmgoers were not sure what to expect when the doors
143.
opened last night. The biggest change is that there are now three theatres inside the complex

instead of just one. ------- . On the one hand, filmgoers now have access to more of the
144.
independent films that Clairmont Cinema has long been proud of offering. On the other hand,

these films are showing on very small screens. ------- , I felt like I was at home watching television.
145.
Still, the multiple offerings are fantastic, as is the new refreshment stand, so I encourage all film

lovers to discover for ------- what the new Clairmont Cinema has to offer.
146.

143. (A) vague
(B) flexible
(C) joyful
(D) encouraging

145. (A) Instead
(B) Regardless
(C) In conclusion
(D) In fact

144. (A) This has advantages and disadvantages.
(B) A large number of filmgoers came to the reopening.
(C) Big changes are often difficult but necessary.
(D) The owners will likely enjoy significant profits.

146. (A) them
(B) oneself
(C) themselves
(D) itself

PART 7

Directions: In this part you will read a selection of texts, such as magazine and newspaper articles, e-mails, and instant messages. Each text or set of texts is followed by several questions. Select the best answer for each question and mark the letter (A), (B), (C), or (D) on your answer sheet.

Questions 147-148 refer to the following notice.

Dear Neighbor,

Now that the long, cold winter is just behind us, we would love to invite you to help us improve the newly established Moon Township Community Garden. The township committee acquired the land where the community pool used to be located, and we hope to create on this land an area for families to come and enjoy the green space in our beautiful town. We will have volunteers on hand during the weekends for the remainder of the month to assist families with arranging and planting the flowers, shrubs, and trees of their choice. We hope you participate in decorating our beautiful community garden!

Sincerely,
Moon Township Committee for Green Spaces

147. During which season of the year was the notice most likely written?

(A) Winter
(B) Spring
(C) Summer
(D) Autumn

148. What are families encouraged to do?

(A) Use a community pool
(B) Purchase flowers
(C) Vote for township committee members
(D) Help to plant a garden

GO ON TO THE NEXT PAGE

Sparkling Creek Coffeehouse & Grill
Gift Certificate

Presented to: Natasha Tucker

Amount: $75

From: Hua Xie

Message: Thank you for your help with my article.
You did a great job editing!

Authorized by: Jenny Lenox

149. Why was Ms. Tucker given a gift certificate?

(A) To acknowledge good work at a restaurant
(B) To express gratitude for help that was provided
(C) To authorize a reward
(D) To repay a loan

150. Who most likely is Ms. Lenox?

(A) An employee at a restaurant
(B) A friend of Ms. Tucker's
(C) An editor
(D) Ms. Xie's assistant

Questions 151-152 refer to the following checklist.

Welcome E-mail

☐ Warmly welcome new staff to our team

☐ Include dates for training sessions

☐ Include daily training schedule (as attachment)

☐ Provide phone numbers of mentors

☐ Create list of documents to bring

Onboarding

☐ Announce start dates

☐ Include information about social gathering to welcome new hires and allow them to meet company leaders

☐ Contact the Technology Team to create e-mail accounts

☐ Prepare new ID badges and keys

☐ Prepare benefits packages (health insurance and retirement)

☐ Personally meet new hires upon their arrival

---

151. What is the purpose of the checklist?

(A) To announce a new e-mail system
(B) To prepare for new employees
(C) To assist people who are leaving a company
(D) To notify trainers of a schedule

152. What is one goal of the social gathering?

(A) To meet managers
(B) To learn about benefits
(C) To receive identification documents
(D) To begin training exercises

GO ON TO THE NEXT PAGE

Questions 153-154 refer to the following text-message chain.

Lucy O'Malley (1:36 P.M.)
I am at the office, but I can't find the Miller file anywhere.

Stanley Hamstead (1:37 P.M.)
Did you check in the future projects file cabinet?

Lucy O'Malley (1:39 P.M.)
No luck. Any other ideas?

Stanley Hamstead (1:40 P.M.)
I bet it is in Charles Wada's office. Check on his desk and let me know.

Lucy O'Malley (1:47 P.M.)
Got it! How would you like me to get this to you?

Stanley Hamstead (1:48 P.M.)
Would it be too much to ask you to deliver it?
We need the original documents with signatures.
Please get here as soon as you can.

Lucy O'Malley (1:50 P.M.)
Not a problem. I'll take a taxi.

153. At 1:39 P.M., what does Ms. O'Malley most likely mean when she writes, "No luck"?

(A) She does not support a future project.
(B) She is unsure where a coworker's office is.
(C) She was unable to find something.
(D) She needs more instruction from Mr. Wada.

154. What will Ms. O'Malley probably do next?

(A) E-mail some documents
(B) Call a courier service
(C) Deliver some documents herself
(D) Contact Mr. Wada

Fetler Airlines Tarmac Delay Contingency Plan

Onboard departure delays are situations we do our best to avoid. On rare occasions, weather, visibility, airport conditions, or other circumstances cause unavoidable ground delays. In these cases, if the delay lasts more than 60 minutes, we will provide complimentary snacks and beverages. If the delay continues for more than two hours (for domestic flights) or three hours (for international flights), the aircraft will return to the gate, and passengers can get off the plane. Passengers will receive notifications at the gate every 30 minutes regarding the status of the delay. These notifications will include the reasons for the delay and whether further amenities will be available such as meal or hotel vouchers.

---

155. What is the purpose of the notice?

(A) To apologize for a flight delay
(B) To list in-flight beverage options
(C) To describe flight safety procedures
(D) To explain an airline policy

156. In what situation will passengers be provided free refreshments?

(A) If the flight is delayed more than one hour
(B) If the flight is canceled due to poor visibility
(C) If the flight is more than two hours long
(D) If the plane temporarily returns to the gate

157. The word "status" in paragraph 1, line 7, is closest in meaning to

(A) rank
(B) lateness
(C) condition
(D) supervisor

GO ON TO THE NEXT PAGE

Questions 158-160 refer to the following article.

MARIGOLD CITY (11 May)—The Marigold City Council has received a draft of the plans to build a new sports arena in outer Marigold. The arena, which will host both sporting events and concerts, will be built on the site of the former Marigold Furniture Factory. The building has remained empty since Marigold Furniture moved production to another location over five years ago.

The arena's designers now need to send the construction plans to the city's planning commission for acceptance. Building can begin once the plans, and any revisions, are accepted. Construction is expected to start early next year and take approximately two years.

158. The word "draft" in paragraph 1, line 2, is closest in meaning to

(A) wind
(B) cost
(C) version
(D) change

159. What will the new structure replace?

(A) An empty lot
(B) A city park
(C) An unused building
(D) A shopping mall

160. According to the article, what is the next step in a process?

(A) Construction of the new structure will begin.
(B) Plans will be presented for approval.
(C) The construction company will seek investors.
(D) Residents will vote on the plan.

United Kingdom's Top-Selling Paint Just Got Better

More Choices for Jasmine Leaf Paint

Jasmine Leaf Paint has been the number one selling house paint for the last five years in a row. — [1] —. But being the best seller is not enough for us. — [2] —. That's why we are bringing you additional ways to make your home more beautiful!

Our specially blended Blendex Formula interior paint and primer are prized for their stain resistance, excellent coverage, low-odour formula, ease of cleanup, and lifetime guarantee. In addition, we are now offering our paints in cans of five different sizes. And you can now get our paints in five beautiful finishes: flat, eggshell, satin, semigloss, and high gloss. — [3] —.

If you want rich, long-lasting, beautiful walls and ceilings inside your home, ask for Jasmine Leaf Paint at a quality paint store near you. — [4] —.

161. For whom is the advertisement primarily intended?

(A) Landscapers
(B) Paint store owners
(C) Art students
(D) Homeowners

162. What is new about Jasmine Leaf Paint?

(A) It is now stain resistant.
(B) It now features a lifetime guarantee.
(C) It is now thicker.
(D) It is now available in more sizes.

163. In which of the positions marked [1], [2], [3], and [4] does the following sentence best belong?

"This all means more convenient options for you."

(A) [1]
(B) [2]
(C) [3]
(D) [4]

FOR IMMEDIATE RELEASE

Contact: Lily Kwan, lkwan@itamitheater.com

SEATTLE (April 10)—Following the recent announcement that Artistic Director Lucas Freeland has stepped down, the Itami Theater Board of Directors has appointed Xu Li as the interim artistic director. — [1] —. Ms. Li has been at Itami for ten years, serving as director of new play development.

Ms. Li has been pivotal in Itami's artistic direction. — [2] —. She will continue to guide the play selection for next season. "I am honored that the board trusts me to carry forward the work that the entire team at Itami Theater has established," said Ms. Li. "I am excited to work with our dedicated staff, everyone from stagehands to costume designers, to build a thrilling season next year." In addition to overseeing the development of new plays for the theater, Ms. Li is a director. — [3] —. Later this season, she will direct *Forest Creatures*, written by the award-winning playwright May Nunes.

"Ms. Li is a wise choice to serve as Itami's interim artistic director," says Executive Director John Stojanowski. "Her deep theatrical knowledge will help Itami Theater continue its artistic endeavors after the departure of Mr. Freeland and during the search for a permanent artistic director." — [4] —. The board of directors is committed to taking its time in its search for a permanent artistic director. The board is pursuing candidates from across the country and expects the hiring process to take six to nine months.

164. What is suggested about the Itami Theater?

(A) It focuses on new playwrights.
(B) It is searching for a new costume designer.
(C) It is building a second stage.
(D) It has operated for over ten years.

165. What is indicated about Ms. Li?

(A) She has written many plays.
(B) She is new to Itami Theater.
(C) She performs different roles in her current job.
(D) She is hiring new actors.

166. What is indicated about the hiring process for a permanent artistic director?

(A) It should be completed within nine months.
(B) Interviews will be conducted in six months.
(C) Only local job candidates will be considered.
(D) Successful candidates will have directing experience.

167. In which of the positions marked [1], [2], [3], and [4] does the following sentence best belong?

"She has directed the plays *Summer and Fall and Love and Other Adventures in the Snow*."

(A) [1]
(B) [2]
(C) [3]
(D) [4]

Meeting Minutes—August 10

In attendance: Miguel Luna, Jennifer Lin, Amal Taylor, Vladimir Ikram, Nevena Ivanova

Amal Taylor, the product manager, opened the meeting. She reported that our new line of herbal teas will be on local store shelves and in restaurants starting September 25. The initial launch includes three flavors: peppermint, lemon ginger, and hibiscus flower. More varieties are expected to be added next year.

Next, Miguel Luna shared his prototypes of the tea boxes and discussed the sustainability of the materials used to produce them. The colorful designs received positive feedback from meeting attendees.

After that, Jennifer Lin provided a brief overview of the marketing budget for the product launch. Funds are currently limited to one advertising campaign. For more detailed information about the marketing budget, contact Ms. Lin directly.

Finally, Vladimir Ikram led a discussion about advertising options. Radio advertisements have been successful in the past and are cheaper than television. Digital advertisements were also considered. The final decision was to start with print advertisements in *The Southtown Times*.

The next meeting will be on August 17.

---

168. What does the company intend to do in the future?

(A) Open a series of tea shops
(B) Expand its product line
(C) Develop beverages other than tea
(D) Replace the current tea varieties

169. Who most likely is Mr. Luna?

(A) A shipping clerk
(B) A factory supervisor
(C) A store owner
(D) A packaging designer

170. Who can provide information about the marketing budget?

(A) Ms. Lin
(B) Ms. Taylor
(C) Mr. Ikram
(D) Ms. Ivanova

171. Where will the products initially be advertised?

(A) In a newspaper
(B) In an online magazine
(C) On the radio
(D) On social media

GO ON TO THE NEXT PAGE

Joanne Matos (11:45 A.M.)
Tuyet and Jim, do you know where I can find that big signboard—the one that we usually post at the entrance to advertise when we're having a sale inside?

Tuyet Nguyen (11:58 A.M.)
I haven't seen it lately. Why?

Joanne Matos (11:59 A.M.)
I'm setting up for this afternoon's party under the tent out in the café courtyard, and I want to have seating information posted for people as they arrive.

Tuyet Nguyen (12:01 P.M.)
Jim likely has it. He usually sets things up for those sales. But I think he's gone for the day.

Jim Thomas (12:02 P.M.)
No, I'm not! I'm out making a delivery right now, but I'll be back soon. You can find the signboard in the alcove just inside our building's delivery entrance. Just put it back when you're done so that I can find it the next time I need it.

Joanne Matos (12:04 P.M.)
No problem. Thanks!

172. Why did Ms. Matos begin the text-message chain?

(A) She needs help locating something.
(B) She is wondering what time Mr. Thomas will arrive.
(C) She wants to know why the tent is up today.
(D) She wants help putting up decorations.

173. What will happen this afternoon?

(A) There will be an outdoor event.
(B) There will be a sale.
(C) Ms. Nguyen will order a signboard.
(D) Mr. Thomas will deliver an additional tent.

174. Where is Mr. Thomas most likely texting from?

(A) The tent
(B) The building entrance
(C) His home
(D) A delivery site

175. At 12:04 P.M., what does Ms. Matos most likely mean when she writes, "No problem"?

(A) She will probably be finished soon.
(B) She will meet Mr. Thomas at the entrance.
(C) She will return an item to its original location.
(D) She understands Ms. Nguyen's explanation.

GO ON TO THE NEXT PAGE

Central Art Museum

Upcoming Special Exhibits

Worldwide Fashion
November 1–28
Discover how clothing and accessories have changed throughout time in various parts of the world. See clothing samples, historical items, and sketches.

Jeffrey Lamb: Naturalist
December 1–29
Scientist Jeffrey Lamb spent his life studying and taking pictures of wildlife on six continents. See photos of animals and landscapes from the researcher's personal collection, taken during his forty-year career.

Humans in Art
January 1–29
This collection of paintings and sculptures from dozens of artists, past and present, shows us the many ways artists can depict a human subject. Works from both famous and relatively unknown artists are included here.

Everyday Art
February 1–26
A variety of handmade items are on display in this exhibit showing art in everyday life. From handmade quilts to furniture, see these household items in a whole new way.

Review of Central Art Museum
Reviewer: Mary Walsh
Stars: ★ ★ ★ ★ ★

I recommend the Central Art Museum to anyone interested in not only art but history as well. I've made two trips to the museum recently. My first trip was with my school's photography club. We only saw the special exhibit featuring photography, but I left wanting to see the rest of the museum. I returned a few days later and had the chance to walk through the entire museum. Each exhibit was different but full of interesting pieces. Be sure to stop at the interactive room near the gift shop for a hands-on experience. During my first trip, the room had cameras with fun backgrounds. Visitors took pictures of themselves, and for a small fee, I got a printout of myself as if I were holding a flag on the moon! Like the special exhibits, the activities at the interactive room change every month, so you will always find something new and interesting to do.

176. According to the schedule, what would a visitor most likely see at the first special exhibit?

(A) Shoes
(B) Furniture
(C) Radios
(D) Paintings

177. What is indicated about the special exhibit in February?

(A) It includes mostly paintings done by local artists.
(B) It will end before the other exhibits listed on the Web site.
(C) Visitors may see items similar to those that they have in their homes.
(D) It has returned to the museum after a popular earlier appearance.

178. Why did Ms. Walsh go to the museum a second time?

(A) She wanted to take more photographs.
(B) She wanted to see more of the museum.
(C) She accidentally left an item at the museum.
(D) She got a discount on a ticket.

179. What does Ms. Walsh recommend that readers do?

(A) Take a guided tour of the museum
(B) Call the museum for more information
(C) Buy something at the museum gift shop
(D) Participate in an activity at the museum

180. What exhibit did Ms. Walsh visit on the first trip to the museum?

(A) Worldwide Fashion
(B) Jeffrey Lamb: Naturalist
(C) Humans in Art
(D) Everyday Art

GO ON TO THE NEXT PAGE

Home Improvement Supply - Materials Overview

Countertops	Cabinets	Flooring
Ceramic tile	Golden oak	Hardwood
Stainless steel	Dark redwood	Vinyl
Marble - premium	Black walnut	Stone
Granite - premium	Synthetic laminate	Concrete

See the product catalog for the complete range of styles and colors. Contact a sales representative for pricing. Order delivery is usually 7—10 business days.

Note: Black walnut cabinets and hardwood flooring are local products fabricated by small regional manufacturers. Please allow a minimum of three weeks to fulfill orders.

Modern Styles
Your Remodeling Experts

Client Intake Form

Client Name: Theresa Dellman	**Phone:** 555-0130

Desired completion date: April 21

Project description: Commercial ☐ Residential ☒

Client wants a complete remodel within three weeks, including new countertops, cabinets, flooring, and appliances (refrigerator, dishwasher, stove, oven).

Client preferences:

- Countertops: black granite
- Cabinets: Client kept samples and will let me know by the April 3 deadline for ordering.
- Flooring: Client will let me know by April 3.

Notes:
Ten percent off coupon to be applied to materials purchase. Not valid on premium materials.
Project contract and deposit were received on April 1.

181. According to the product information, where can customers see examples of all products?

(A) On a Web site
(B) In a product catalog
(C) In a store
(D) In a newspaper advertisement

182. Who most likely completed the form?

(A) An appliance repair person
(B) A restaurant chef
(C) A design store representative
(D) A cooking instructor

183. According to the form, what does the client need to provide?

(A) A signature on the contract
(B) Approval for work to begin
(C) Proof of homeowner's insurance
(D) Decisions on two types of materials

184. What material will probably NOT be used to make the cabinets for the project?

(A) Golden oak
(B) Dark redwood
(C) Black walnut
(D) Synthetic laminate

185. What is indicated about the marble and granite?

(A) They are not eligible for a discount offer.
(B) They are no longer being manufactured.
(C) They are produced in limited colors.
(D) They are very popular with customers.

GO ON TO THE NEXT PAGE

Alexandria's Restaurant Showcase

June 5 — Alexandria's Restaurant Showcase is back! From July 8 to July 25, participating restaurants in the Alexandria area will offer set menus at discounted prices. As in past years, restaurants can offer a two-course lunch menu for $15, a two-course dinner menu for $20, or a three-course dinner menu for $30. Both customers and restaurant owners love the showcase. Food enthusiasts try new options at a lower cost, and restaurants report it's the time of year when dining areas are at their fullest.

Alexandria had its first restaurant showcase 15 years ago. It was modeled on a similar showcase in the beach town of Willmar. Originally, only eight restaurants participated. Since then, the showcase has grown, adding more restaurants and extending the number of days each year. This year, there will be 40 participating restaurants—about 70 percent of all the restaurants in Alexandria. Those looking to book a table should act fast. Some restaurants require reservations, and the most popular places book up quickly. To see the list of participating restaurants and make a reservation, visit www.alexandriarestaurants.com/showcase.

---

https://www.alexandriarestaurants.com/showcase/reservations

Showing search results for: **Center City Neighborhood**

Claire's
French food
Serving lunch and 3-course dinner
Open Tuesday–Sunday
Call (703) 555-0102 to make a reservation.

Fresh Fish Grill
Seafood
Serving lunch and 3-course dinner
Open Monday–Sunday
Call (703) 555-0195 to make a reservation.

Jin-Yi's House
Korean food
Serving 2-course dinner
Open Wednesday–Saturday
Call (703) 555-0198 to make a reservation.

Roberto's Pizzeria
Italian food
Serving lunch only
Open Tuesday–Sunday
No reservations necessary

https://www.foodreviews.com/alexandria/freshfishgrill

Nori Sato

I highly recommend Fresh Fish Grill. It was my first time eating there, and not only was the food excellent, but the staff was welcoming and efficient. I had some clients in town and was lucky enough to get a reservation on the last day of the restaurant showcase. We all really enjoyed the experience. I would gladly take clients there again.

186. What does the article mention about Alexandria's Restaurant Showcase?

(A) Every restaurant in Alexandria participates.
(B) Restaurants are open seven days a week.
(C) It is the busiest time of year for restaurants.
(D) Restaurants are open only for dinner.

187. What is indicated about Alexandria's first Restaurant Showcase?

(A) It took place eight years ago.
(B) It had 40 participating restaurants.
(C) It took place before a similar showcase began in Willmar.
(D) It had a shorter duration than this year's restaurant showcase.

188. What is true of all the restaurants on the Web page?

(A) They are open on Mondays.
(B) They serve the same type of food.
(C) They require a reservation.
(D) They are in the same neighborhood.

189. How much does it cost to eat at Roberto's Pizzeria during Alexandria's Restaurant Showcase?

(A) $8
(B) $15
(C) $20
(D) $30

190. What is suggested about Ms. Sato?

(A) She went to Fresh Fish Grill on July 25.
(B) She went to Fresh Fish Grill with her family.
(C) She has dined at the Fresh Fish Grill many times.
(D) She knows the owner of Fresh Fish Grill.

Student Activities Coordinator
Rollervy University
Maynard, MA 01754

Responsibilities:
- Promotes involvement in campus extracurricular activities such as student government, arts, theater, cultural organizations, volunteer groups, and athletic club teams
- Updates the Rollervy University student activities Web site and manages all social media
- Coordinates student outings to local sporting and cultural events in the Boston metropolitan area
- Addresses inquiries by answering phones, responding to e-mails, and greeting walk-in visitors

To apply, write your cover letter in an e-mail, attach your résumé, and send it to the Human Resources Manager, at jobs@rollervy.edu. Please address the following:

- What relevant job experience do you have?
- Why do you believe you are a good fit for the position?
- What are your professional strengths?
- In which areas could you improve?

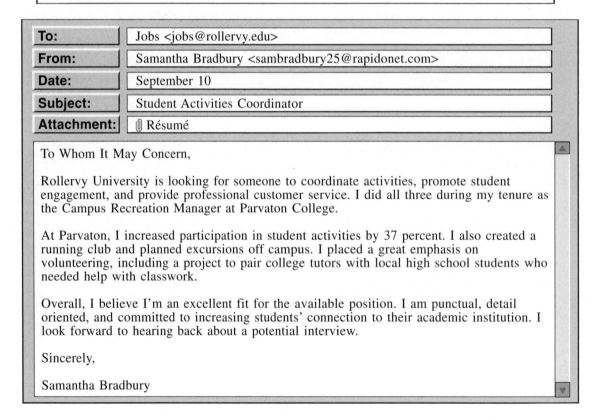

To:	Jobs <jobs@rollervy.edu>
From:	Samantha Bradbury <sambradbury25@rapidonet.com>
Date:	September 10
Subject:	Student Activities Coordinator
Attachment:	📎 Résumé

To Whom It May Concern,

Rollervy University is looking for someone to coordinate activities, promote student engagement, and provide professional customer service. I did all three during my tenure as the Campus Recreation Manager at Parvaton College.

At Parvaton, I increased participation in student activities by 37 percent. I also created a running club and planned excursions off campus. I placed a great emphasis on volunteering, including a project to pair college tutors with local high school students who needed help with classwork.

Overall, I believe I'm an excellent fit for the available position. I am punctual, detail oriented, and committed to increasing students' connection to their academic institution. I look forward to hearing back about a potential interview.

Sincerely,

Samantha Bradbury

```
┌─────────────────────────────────────────────────────────────┐
│                         *E-mail*                            │
├─────────────────────────────────────────────────────────────┤
│  To:       │ Samantha Bradbury <sambradbury25@rapidonet.com> │
│  From:     │ Lisa Cooper <jobs@rollervy.edu>                 │
│  Date:     │ October 2                                       │
│  Subject:  │ Interview                                       │
└─────────────────────────────────────────────────────────────┘
```

Dear Samantha,

I am writing to check on your availability to interview for the Student Activities Coordinator position. Your preliminary interview would be conducted virtually. If selected for the next round, your second interview would be in person at the Rollervy University main campus. If you are still interested, please respond and let me know if you are free at 9 A.M. on either October 8 or October 9.

Kind regards,

Lisa Cooper

191. According to the job advertisement, what is one responsibility of the Student Activities Coordinator?

(A) Help students with difficult assignments
(B) Inform students about local events
(C) Train students to give presentations
(D) Lead workshops about Web site development

192. According to the first e-mail, what is one way that Ms. Bradbury promoted student engagement?

(A) She volunteered at a local recreation center.
(B) She participated in several cultural excursions.
(C) She recruited high school students to be tutors.
(D) She started a sports group.

193. What information did Ms. Bradbury leave out of her cover letter?

(A) Her relevant job experience
(B) Her interest in the position
(C) Her professional strengths
(D) Her areas for improvement

194. What does the second e-mail indicate about the hiring process?

(A) Every applicant must fill in a form online.
(B) Applicants should submit two reference letters.
(C) Some applicants will have an in-person interview.
(D) Applicants with four-year degrees are preferred.

195. Who most likely is Ms. Cooper?

(A) The Human Resources Manager
(B) An office assistant
(C) A university admissions counselor
(D) The Student Activities Coordinator

GO ON TO THE NEXT PAGE

To:	Celeste O'Brien
From:	Monica Cheung
Date:	October 15
Subject:	Mobile phone reimbursement policy

Dear Ms. O'Brien,

As the Assistant Director of Accounting, I am writing about the policy regarding mobile phone expenses. Many Ferd Data Services employees use their personal mobile phones for business calls. To get reimbursed, they must submit a form every month. Ferd then pays up to 30 percent of the phone bill. My department confirms each employee's calculations and then schedules payments that vary every month.

Some companies have moved to a flat-rate model, whereby all employees who qualify receive a fixed amount each month (e.g., $20). No staff time is required for monthly processing; the allowance is automatically included in each paycheck.

I hope that, as head of Human Resources, you will consider adopting a policy like this.

Sincerely,

Monica Cheung

Ferd Data Services
MEETING AGENDA

Location: Online
Date: October 24
Time: 3:00 P.M.
Host: Celeste O'Brien, Vice President, Human Resources
Attendees: Human Resources Managers; Finance Managers; Department Heads

OBJECTIVES:
1. Consider issues with the current mobile phone reimbursement program
2. Review other options along with advantages and disadvantages
3. Select a new reimbursement model, if appropriate

OPTIONS:
1. Continue to reimburse employees for up to 30 percent of their business mobile phone use
2. Provide a flat monthly amount to employees who qualify; employees with high costs can submit requests for additional compensation
3. Provide qualified employees with mobile phones for business use

Ferd Data Services Employee Policies

Mobile Phone Reimbursement Policy
Revised October 30

Employees who work remotely and/or travel for business purposes should be reimbursed for business use of mobile phones. Three options are available:
- Employees who qualify will receive a mobile phone allowance of $20 per month, regardless of actual expenses. To enroll in the program, employees must submit a Mobile Phone Allowance form with their supervisor's signature. The $20 allowance will be applied to each month's paycheck.
- Employees with large charges may submit actual expenses to receive additional reimbursement.
- Managers and executives may opt for a company mobile phone, which is for business use only.

196. What is the purpose of the e-mail?

    (A) To describe patterns of employee behavior
    (B) To suggest updates to certain technology
    (C) To consider replacing a vendor
    (D) To request a revision to a reimbursement policy

197. According to the e-mail, who is Ms. Cheung?

    (A) A telemarketer
    (B) A member of the accounting team
    (C) A human resources specialist
    (D) An electronics engineer

198. What did Ms. O'Brien do after receiving Ms. Cheung's e-mail?

    (A) She invited Ms. Cheung to a meeting.
    (B) She rejected Ms. Cheung's suggestion but proposed alternatives.
    (C) She collaborated with other company leaders to address an issue.
    (D) She transferred to a different department.

199. According to the policy, who qualifies to receive a company mobile phone?

    (A) Ferd Data Services managers and executives only
    (B) All Ferd Data Services employees who work from home
    (C) Employees who travel for business purposes
    (D) Employees who submit a monthly form

200. What best describes the result of the meeting on October 24?

    (A) Attendees agreed to continue following the original procedures.
    (B) Attendees decided to collect more information before making a decision.
    (C) Attendees decided to adopt some of the options discussed.
    (D) Attendees completed a survey about mobile phone use.

Stop! This is the end of the test. If you finish before time is called, you may go back to Parts 5, 6, and 7 and check your work.

토익 정기시험
실전 ❶1000
RC

실전 TEST

04

READING TEST

In the Reading test, you will read a variety of texts and answer several different types of reading comprehension questions. The entire Reading test will last 75 minutes. There are three parts, and directions are given for each part. You are encouraged to answer as many questions as possible within the time allowed.

You must mark your answers on the separate answer sheet. Do not write your answers in your test book.

PART 5

Directions: A word or phrase is missing in each of the sentences below. Four answer choices are given below each sentence. Select the best answer to complete the sentence. Then mark the letter (A), (B), (C), or (D) on your answer sheet.

101. After software updates, our customers report significant ------- in both speed and reliability.

(A) improvable
(B) improvements
(C) improves
(D) improved

102. McNeal Unlimited's market profile was finished before the due date listed ------- the project plan.

(A) in
(B) about
(C) until
(D) along

103. Employees can take up to two weeks off at a time as long as ------- requests are approved in advance.

(A) they
(B) their
(C) themselves
(D) them

104. Service representatives are responsible for being the ------- contact for each of our clients.

(A) small
(B) most
(C) abundant
(D) primary

105. The ------- of the fund-raiser was due to bad weather, so the event will be rescheduled for next weekend.

(A) cancellation
(B) cancel
(C) canceled
(D) canceler

106. AVB Education's online courses help users master many computer skills more ------- than other learning methods do.

(A) nearly
(B) lightly
(C) previously
(D) effectively

107. The ------- of several celebrities at the Sasaki Museum attracted local residents seeking photographs.

(A) presenter
(B) presented
(C) presence
(D) presentable

108. The committee enthusiastically ------- the theater company's grant application because it encourages community participation.

(A) approved
(B) caused
(C) affected
(D) practiced

109. Mr. Ibrahim told the management team that preparation for the annual shareholders' meeting was going ------- as planned.

(A) preciseness
(B) precise
(C) precision
(D) precisely

110. Aryxco's shipping costs vary based upon the destination and the weight ------- the package.

(A) as
(B) along
(C) between
(D) of

111. The health records of our clients are stored on a ------- server that is accessible only to authorized users.

(A) secure
(B) securing
(C) securely
(D) secureness

112. Before we sign a contract with the heating company, we must confirm that its proposal meets our installation -------.

(A) customers
(B) businesses
(C) requirements
(D) volunteers

113. The area ------- the new Furniture Vine headquarters is covered by dense forest.

(A) among
(B) happening
(C) foreseeable
(D) surrounding

114. The firm's top analysts expect that the acquisition of Valuwest, Inc., will lead to a ------- future for shareholders.

(A) prosperous
(B) voluntary
(C) sizable
(D) calculating

115. Upon reviewing the draft of the agreement, the lead lawyer will notify Ms. Gwan's team ------- any concerns.

(A) regarding
(B) afterward
(C) toward
(D) as soon as

116. Following a two-year break, the Grear Institute is once again ------- career-building workshops for health-care workers.

(A) informing
(B) providing
(C) passing
(D) deciding

117. The Cedar Lake Hotel adjusted its ------- prices in an attempt to increase its share of the growing market.

(A) competed
(B) competition
(C) competitor
(D) competitive

118. Operating hours of Big Midwest Cafés are subject to local ------- enforced by the city in which the café is located.

(A) fragments
(B) equalities
(C) regulations
(D) categories

119. The legal department ------- revisions to the amendment last week, and Ms. Koehler sent it to the corporate group for review.

(A) completed
(B) completes
(C) will complete
(D) is completing

120. Ms. Arriata asked all ------- in yesterday's Productivity and Technology workshop to send in their questionnaires.

(A) activities
(B) objectives
(C) participants
(D) schedules

TEST 4

GO ON TO THE NEXT PAGE

121. Consumers noted that Sunnyside Chocolates taste ------- different from all other chocolates.

(A) distinguish
(B) distinguishably
(C) to distinguish
(D) distinguishing

122. With bicycling becoming more popular than ever, the city council plans to ------- the number of bicycle lanes on city streets.

(A) generate
(B) invent
(C) expand
(D) organize

123. Claston Industry's guidelines help ensure that equipment ordered from all suppliers ------- safety standards.

(A) meets
(B) meeting
(C) to meet
(D) was met

124. Though Ms. Daiyu ------- handles customer inquiries, Mr. Mei takes over when she gets a special assignment from her manager.

(A) never
(B) almost
(C) deeply
(D) usually

125. Opportunities for growth cannot ------- by Aksika Medical without a careful analysis of the costs and benefits.

(A) pursue
(B) be pursued
(C) pursuing
(D) to pursue

126. Mayson Technology not only leads its competitors in revenue ------- in award-winning innovations.

(A) but also
(B) so that
(C) and
(D) yet

127. Our presentation will provide an overview of ------- the theoretical and the practical aspects of machine learning.

(A) each
(B) any
(C) such
(D) both

128. The responsibilities of new assembly-line supervisors at the Streamline Auto Plant increase ------- as they gain more experience.

(A) diligently
(B) completely
(C) progressively
(D) cooperatively

129. Although unforeseen factors initially ------- the construction of the wind farm, it opened on schedule.

(A) complicate
(B) complicated
(C) are complicating
(D) be complicated

130. ------- Haruto sees an opportunity for professional development, he is sure to take advantage of it.

(A) Even though
(B) Owing to
(C) Whenever
(D) Whereas

PART 6

Directions: Read the texts that follow. A word, phrase, or sentence is missing in parts of each text. Four answer choices for each question are given below the text. Select the best answer to complete the text. Then mark the letter (A), (B), (C), or (D) on your answer sheet.

Questions 131-134 refer to the following Web page.

Evergreen Mountains Scenic Railway

The Evergreen Mountains Scenic Railway has reopened after a yearlong renovation project. First built over a century ago, the railway is one of the oldest in the nation. The recent closure was necessary to make extensive upgrades to the aging tracks and train cars. ------- , renovations were
131.
made to the historic station.

Sightseers on the railway will enjoy a trip through the Evergreen Forest as they ------- to the top of
132.
Walden Mountain. Here the train will make an hour-long stop for visitors to tour the new visitor center or ------- enjoy the views from the highest mountain in the region. The return trip takes
133.
a different route back to the station. ------- . Tickets for this amazing journey are available online.
134.

131. (A) Additionally
(B) However
(C) Nevertheless
(D) For example

132. (A) ride
(B) riding
(C) rides
(D) ridden

133. (A) simple
(B) simplest
(C) simplify
(D) simply

134. (A) The renovations took longer than expected.
(B) Walden Mountain is the tallest of the Evergreen Mountains.
(C) Other nearby mountains do not have tourist attractions.
(D) The entire trip takes approximately 2.5 hours.

GO ON TO THE NEXT PAGE

To: Marcus Witt <mwitt@bmail.com>
From: Julie Mendell <contracts@nevycorp.com>
Date: 1 June
Subject: Your contract with Nevy
Attachment: Renewal form

Dear Mr. Witt:

Greetings from the Nevy Corporation. I hope this message finds you well.

As I mentioned on our recent call, we are conducting a review of our current ------- . This **135.** includes your agency. ------- the difficult year, we have been impressed with your agency's **136.** professionalism and positive results. ------- . Please sign the attached document and return it to **137.** us at your earliest convenience.

We ------- forward to strengthening our relationship with you and your team. If you have any **138.** questions or concerns, please let us know.

Sincerely,

Julie Mendell
Partner Relations Manager

---

135. (A) versions
(B) contests
(C) equipment
(D) partnerships

136. (A) Although
(B) Despite
(C) Instead
(D) Since

137. (A) Therefore, we would like to extend your contract for another two years.
(B) Unfortunately, we were unable to reach you in time.
(C) Please confirm your contact details at your earliest convenience.
(D) We certainly understand the concerns you raised when we last spoke.

138. (A) were looking
(B) would look
(C) looked
(D) look

Questions 139-142 refer to the following advertisement.

Save Big at Buelo Fitness!

At Buelo Fitness, we seek to improve the physical and mental well-being of all Carver residents.

Since the gym is locally owned, ------- will give you the attention and guidance you need to
139.

maximize your fitness. ------- another year comes to an end, why not get in shape?
140.

------- . But you must act fast! These limited-time deals are only valid through December 31.
141.

The Buelo Bundle consists of fifteen classes within three months for just $100. The Buelo

Unlimited package is just $10 for the first month, and then $100 per month thereafter. It requires a

six-month ------- .
142.

TEST
4

139. (A) we
(B) one
(C) they
(D) mine

140. (A) As
(B) During
(C) Beyond
(D) Following

141. (A) Call us if you have any questions.
(B) Check out these positive reviews from
customers.
(C) We are offering two special deals to help
you begin.
(D) Exercise should be combined with healthy
eating habits.

142. (A) lease
(B) development
(C) opportunity
(D) commitment

GO ON TO THE NEXT PAGE

To: jliu@lle.com
From: customersupport@gerdenbank.com
Subject: Service Fee
Date: 27 May, 10:34 A.M.

Dear Ms. Liu,

------- an error in our internal computer processing system, a service fee was incorrectly deducted
  143.

from your savings account on 23 May. This error has been fixed, and a refund was posted to your

account on 25 May. You ------- this deposit on your next statement under the description "Fee
                       144.

adjustment."

We apologize if this has resulted in any ------- . Please contact us if you have any concerns
                                         145.

regarding this issue. ------- .
                      146.

Sincerely,

Jennifer Ayers
Customer Support
Gerden Bank

143. (A) In fact
     (B) Because of
     (C) In reply to
     (D) Except for

144. (A) found
     (B) were finding
     (C) will find
     (D) have found

145. (A) confusion
     (B) satisfaction
     (C) explanation
     (D) calculation

146. (A) We just added 280 new customers
         to our base.
     (B) Please let us know whether you
         want to open a checking account.
     (C) Gerden Bank has an important
         message for our customers.
     (D) As always, thank you for choosing
         Gerden Bank.

PART 7

Directions: In this part you will read a selection of texts, such as magazine and newspaper articles, e-mails, and instant messages. Each text or set of texts is followed by several questions. Select the best answer for each question and mark the letter (A), (B), (C), or (D) on your answer sheet.

Questions 147-148 refer to the following memo.

MEMO

To: All Staff
From: Amaya Sodhi
Subject: Online Portal
Date: 22 August

The online portal is now up and running. To use it, patients must first obtain an activation number from a staff member here. Patients will then be able to register to access their records, get lab results, and book appointments.

We had also planned to launch a payment option within the portal. However, the Web developers are still dealing with issues with the billing system. As a result, that part of the system will be implemented at a later time.

It will take some time for all of us to learn how to work with the portal. If you have any questions, please contact Marie at extension 244.

---

147. Where most likely does Ms. Sodhi work?

(A) At a hotel
(B) At a medical office
(C) At a credit card company
(D) At an employment agency

148. What has been delayed?

(A) A software update
(B) The hiring of new employees
(C) The delivery of information to Marie
(D) An online payment system

GO ON TO THE NEXT PAGE

Welcome to the
Mirjana Springs Hotel
in Dubrovnik.

The network password for complimentary Web access is "**Mirjanawifi.**" It is offered throughout the hotel.

For hotel-related requests, please contact the front desk. For information on local attractions and tourist excursions, please see Ms. Novak in our recreation office.

We hope you enjoy your stay!

Room #: 1296	**Check-in:** May 23
Guest: Devon Tolga	**Checkout:** May 25
Clerk: Malina Babic	**Arrival time:** 8:23 P.M.

149. What is indicated about Internet access at the Mirjana Springs Hotel?

(A) It does not require a password.
(B) It is not very reliable in the evening.
(C) It is not available in room 1296.
(D) Guests do not have to pay for it.

150. What is indicated about Ms. Novak?

(A) She works at the front desk.
(B) She will check out on May 25.
(C) She helps set up sightseeing trips.
(D) She is Ms. Babic's supervisor.

Mini-pure: Portable Air Purifier

Mountain Clear Air, a leader in air purifying devices, introduces Mini-pure, the first portable air purifier of its kind. Developed by leading environmentalists and engineers, Mini-pure cleans air by using negative ions! Plus, it's small and convenient, so you can take it with you wherever you go.

- Environmentally friendly and effective
- Fits easily into a purse or briefcase
- Reduces pollutants and allergens
- Charges quickly with any standard phone charger
- For use at home, in the office, or anywhere

Find out more at Minipureairclean.com.

TEST 4

151. For whom is the advertisement most likely intended?

(A) Medical engineers
(B) Hotel operators
(C) Environmental specialists
(D) Everyday consumers

152. What is NOT indicated about the air purifier?

(A) Its size
(B) Its purpose
(C) Its cost
(D) Its power source

GO ON TO THE NEXT PAGE

Jim Szymanski (9:42 A.M.)
Bev, I want to give you a heads-up. There's a broken water valve at the Eastbury Student Apartments. The water there will be shut off for 2 hours.

Bev Munoz (9:43 A.M.)
No problem. We can wash our hands at the Carlton Apartments after we finish this job.

Jim Szymanski (9:44 A.M.)
Right. We'll be doing the same thing this morning as we did last time. We'll enter each apartment unit and vacuum out the filter in the wall air conditioner. Any filter that looks too dusty should be replaced. Also, we should clear out debris from the vents.

Bev Munoz (9:46 A.M.)
Got it. Will all the apartments be unoccupied?

Jim Szymanski (9:47 A.M.)
The students are on school holiday. But you may want to knock on the doors just in case.

Bev Munoz (9:48 A.M.)
OK. I can handle Building A because I'm parked nearby. You could work on Building B. The work will go more quickly that way, and we'll have time for an afternoon lunch break.

Jim Szymanski (9:49 A.M.)
Exactly. Let me know if you need anything else this morning.

---

153. What will Mr. Szymanski and Ms. Munoz do this morning?

(A) Remove litter from parking areas
(B) Service some air conditioners
(C) Repair broken water pipes
(D) Install kitchen appliances

154. At 9:47 A.M., what does Mr. Szymanski imply when he writes, "The students are on school holiday"?

(A) Parking will be easy to find.
(B) No students live in Building A.
(C) The apartments should be vacant.
(D) Students often make their own repairs.

Questions 155-157 refer to the following e-mail.

To:	Larisa M. Lee
From:	Minnich Furniture
Subject:	Furniture Sale Ends Friday
Date:	Wednesday, 28 August

Minnich Furniture Seasonal Sale!
Last three days for up to 50% savings. Shop for:

Sectionals **Sofas** **Lamps** **Bedroom sets**

Over 1,000 items on sale. Hurry! Inventory is going fast!
Shop online at www.minnichfurniture.com

- Limited quantities of certain items are available. Limit 2 sale items per customer.
- Offer applies to Internet orders only. Additional cost for shipping.
- Returns must be initiated within 30 days.
- See Web site for full details and photos of all offerings.

155. Who most likely is Ms. Lee?

(A) A potential customer
(B) A sales representative
(C) An interior designer
(D) A warehouse employee

156. How can purchases be made from Minnich Furniture?

(A) By shopping at one of several retail stores in the area
(B) By visiting the central warehouse
(C) By phoning the call center
(D) By placing an online order

157. What is indicated in the e-mail?

(A) The sale will end in 30 days.
(B) Returns of discounted items are not allowed.
(C) Customers can buy only two items at sale price.
(D) Only 1,000 items are left in stock.

GO ON TO THE NEXT PAGE

Questions 158-161 refer to the following letter.

Johan Krueger
Xolani Publishing
291 Waring Road
Pretoria 0002 South Africa

16 June

Nadja Abdi, Office Manager
64 Kenda Avenue
Nairobi 00606 Kenya

Dear Ms. Abdi,

Thank you for requesting a free trial issue of *Modern Style Magazine*. Enclosed is your complimentary issue. Businesses like yours benefit greatly from our magazine service. Did you know that patients typically wait up to twenty minutes before their checkup or cleaning? Having magazines to read helps the wait time pass quickly.

Ready to order a full subscription? Return the enclosed card and get 20 percent off the newsstand price. As a bonus, we will include a copy of our annual review issue at no extra charge.

Sincerely,

Johan Krueger
Johan Krueger, Xolani Publishing

P.S. We publish magazines for a variety of readers worldwide, including popular titles such as *Sports Today*, *Home Repair Journal*, and *Budget Traveler Monthly*. As a business, you can request a complimentary trial issue of any title in our catalogue. Just visit our Web site today!

158. What type of business does Ms. Abdi most likely manage?

(A) A hair salon
(B) A dental clinic
(C) A coffee shop
(D) A law firm

159. The word "pass" in paragraph 1, line 4, is closest in meaning to

(A) cross
(B) happen
(C) elapse
(D) overlook

160. What is indicated about Xolani Publishing?

(A) Its products appeal to people with various interests.
(B) It mainly publishes academic journals.
(C) Its customer base is limited to South Africa.
(D) It sells mostly digital subscriptions.

161. What is NOT offered to Ms. Abdi in the letter?

(A) A free trial issue of another magazine
(B) A discounted subscription rate
(C) A bonus for referring new subscribers
(D) A free issue of *Modern Style Magazine*

Questions 162-165 refer to the following press release.

FOR IMMEDIATE RELEASE

Contact: Roberto Barboza
351 922 555 965

LISBON (18 June)—This year's International Candy Conference will be held in Lisbon, Portugal, at the Vil de Maitros Convention Center near the Bibb Bubblegum factory. Thousands of candy industry specialists from around the world are expected to attend the event on 8–10 September. — [1] —.

Amanda Bibb, CEO of Bibb Bubblegum, takes the chewing gum industry very seriously. — [2] —. As the company's fourth-generation CEO, she proudly shares, "My family is excited to sponsor this event and thrilled to be the first chewing gum company ever to host the International Candy Conference!" Ms. Bibb is also especially pleased that the candy conference will be in Portugal this year. — [3] —. "Bibb Bubblegum started with a tiny shop near Lisbon. While our main factory is local, we now sell our gum in seven countries. We hope this event will bring attention and revenue to our community as well as to the international bubblegum market."

For more information about the International Candy Conference and for tours of the Bibb Bubblegum factory, contact Roberto Barboza at 351 922 555 965 or visit www.BibbBubblegum.com. — [4] —.

---

162. What is the main purpose of the press release?

(A) To explain the history of the candy industry
(B) To announce the expansion of a gum company
(C) To introduce the CEO of a new business
(D) To promote a conference and its sponsor

163. What is indicated about the Bibb Bubblegum company?

(A) It allows visitors to tour its facility.
(B) Its headquarters are in Lisbon.
(C) It is a new candy business in Portugal.
(D) It offers more flavors than other gum companies do.

164. Who most likely is Mr. Barboza?

(A) A shop owner
(B) A company representative
(C) A newspaper writer
(D) A travel agent

165. In which of the positions marked [1], [2], [3], and [4] does the following sentence best belong?

"That number now will likely include many gum manufacturers, as Bibb Bubblegum will host this year's event."

(A) [1]
(B) [2]
(C) [3]
(D) [4]

GO ON TO THE NEXT PAGE

Your upgraded Impala card is in the mail!

At Impala Credit Union, your safety and convenience are paramount. That is why we are introducing contactless technology for all our member credit and debit cards. With this new development, you will no longer have to swipe or insert your card in a chip reader at checkout. In fact, you will not even need to remove your card from a physical wallet; simply hold it near a point of sale for it to be read!

There are a few important things to keep in mind. First, your current card will be deactivated on October 31. You may continue to use it until that time.

Second, the upgraded card may arrive before your current one expires. Once you activate the new card, the old one will automatically be deactivated and no longer be valid for use. You will need to manually activate your new card by following the instructions on the attached sticker.

Third, your contactless technology card will have a new card number, expiration date, and security number. When activating, you will be prompted to choose a PIN (personal identification number). The PIN from your current card will not automatically transfer over. Be sure to update your card on file for all preferred online retailers and app subscriptions to ensure continued access.

We hope that you enjoy your new card. For any questions regarding your contactless technology Impala card, feel free to contact customer service at **1-610-555-0168**.

---

166. What is the purpose of the notice?

(A) To request customer feedback
(B) To alert customers of credit card fraud
(C) To inform customers of a new payment method
(D) To announce a change in billing policies

167. What is indicated about the new Impala card?

(A) It will be valid for use as of October 31.
(B) It does not need to be removed from a wallet for use.
(C) It cannot be used for app subscriptions.
(D) It will contain the same identification information as the old card.

168. What do customers need to do when activating their new card?

(A) Select a PIN
(B) Cancel their current card
(C) Enter the security number
(D) Transfer outstanding balances

Questions 169-172 refer to the following online chat.

Frieda Jung (9:16 A.M.) I have to be out of the office starting on Wednesday until next Monday. I need to present a funding request at the regional legislature office. Would you both feel comfortable giving the presentation about the new Riverwalk to the urban development committee on Friday?

Cassie Alswith (9:18 A.M.) I think we could handle that. Right, Austin?

Austin Everett (9:20 A.M.) Definitely. I'm not sure how available you will be, Ms. Jung, but we could send you an overview of the presentation on Thursday if you'd like.

Frieda Jung (9:22 A.M.) I don't think that's necessary. Please be sure to highlight the revenue that we think will be brought into the region by the new businesses, as well as the positive environmental impacts our research group noted.

Austin Everett (9:23 A.M.) Got it. We will make sure to do that.

Cassie Alswith (9:25 A.M.) Would it be okay if I submit the weekly progress report on Monday instead of Friday? That way I'll have a little more time to prepare for the presentation.

Frieda Jung (9:26 A.M.) Yes, that's a good idea.

Cassie Alswith (9:26 A.M.) Great. Thank you!

Frieda Jung (9:27 A.M.) I might not respond to e-mail as frequently while I'm gone, but feel free to call me or text me if there's anything urgent that comes up.

169. Why will Ms. Jung be out of the office?

(A) She is interviewing for a different job.
(B) She has another work obligation.
(C) She is taking time off for personal reasons.
(D) She has a doctor's appointment.

170. At 9:22 A.M., what does Ms. Jung most likely mean when she writes, "I don't think that's necessary"?

(A) She is frustrated with Mr. Everett.
(B) She is confident in the abilities of Mr. Everett and Ms. Alswith.
(C) She does not enjoy reading e-mails.
(D) She thinks the meeting should be canceled.

171. What is indicated about the Riverwalk?

(A) It will likely bring extra business to the area.
(B) It is located in the center of the city.
(C) Ms. Alswith is skeptical about its benefits.
(D) The construction on it has progressed quickly.

172. What is suggested about Ms. Alswith's report?

(A) It has never been submitted late.
(B) It will be submitted to the legislature office.
(C) It is submitted every Friday.
(D) It must be reviewed by Mr. Everett on Monday.

GO ON TO THE NEXT PAGE

Westmouth Financial Services
1311 Paul Street
Exeter EX8 9YJ, United Kingdom

14 July

Dear Ms. Tartal,

I am writing to notify you of some upcoming changes regarding your retirement investment account at Westmouth Financial. — [1] —. Firstly, as you may already know, your primary financial services advisor, Felix Reardon, is retiring next month. — [2] —. I have over fifteen years of experience working in personal finance and have worked at Westmouth Financial for three of those years, helping over 25 clients meet their retirement goals through savvy financial planning. I am excited to help you continue this journey.

Secondly, I would like to schedule a time to meet or talk with you about your current portfolio. — [3] —. We could meet in person or just have a simple phone or video chat, but it would be good for us to touch base to plan your investment strategy for the next ten years as you are nearing your retirement. Along those lines, I specifically wanted to see if you were interested in shifting some of your funds into more stable assets like bonds and annuities. — [4] —. I usually recommend shifting into these safer options as you get closer to retirement. Please feel free to call me or send an e-mail so we can arrange a time to talk. Thanks, and I look forward to speaking more.

Sincerely,

Rita Hidayat

Rita Hidayat, Account Manager

173. What is indicated about Ms. Hidayat?

(A) Personal finance is her second career.
(B) She has been in her current role for three years.
(C) She was Mr. Reardon's mentor.
(D) She retired fifteen years ago.

174. What is suggested about Ms. Tartal's financial portfolio?

(A) It does not have a great deal of value.
(B) Mr. Reardon did not manage it well.
(C) Ms. Tartal expected it to perform better.
(D) It has several risky assets.

175. In which of the positions marked [1], [2], [3], and [4] does the following sentence best belong?

"Therefore, I will be taking over the management of your account."

(A) [1]
(B) [2]
(C) [3]
(D) [4]

GO ON TO THE NEXT PAGE

Questions 176-180 refer to the following article and survey.

New Home for Theatre Group

AUCKLAND (11 July)—The south end of Darby Street is dominated by the imposing Victorian building that formerly held the main branch of Pacific Trade Bank. That building is now the home of the Cornata Theatre Company. After a grand-opening ceremony on Tuesday, tours of the new theatre were given to attendees.

The debut show is *Relax*, a comedy by Mi-Sun Yeo about a popular tourist site. Performances are scheduled to begin on Saturday, 16 July, and run until the end of the month.

According to Noah Larkins, the artistic director of the Cornata Theatre Company,

"talk-backs" will immediately follow every performance. Talk-backs allow the director and cast members to share their thoughts about the play, and audience members can ask them questions. "We want to be part of the artistic communities in both Auckland and the larger community around us," said Mr. Larkins.

The building houses a main stage theatre that seats approximately 325 people and a smaller studio theatre upstairs. The company will also offer acting classes for children and adults. For more information or to buy tickets, visit the company's Web page at www.cornatatheatre.nz.

Thank you for attending *Relax*. Please take a few moments to tell us about your experience.

Name and e-mail address: Julia Cruz <jcruz@northwing.nz>

1. How would you rate the performance you saw?
   Excellent _X_   Good ___   Fair ___   Did not enjoy ___

2. How would you rate your overall theatre experience?
   Excellent ___   Good _X_   Fair ___   Did not enjoy ___

3. How did you hear about us? (Check all that apply.)
   Print advertisement _X_   Social media _X_   Television ___   E-mail ___

Comments: The play was a fascinating story, and the acting was brilliant. I'm delighted to be a subscribing member of the theatre this season. If all the shows are this good, I'll be very happy. There did seem to be a problem with the concession stand. There was a long line for food and drinks, and it did not move very quickly.

176. What is the purpose of the article?

(A) To examine the history that a play is based on
(B) To attract participation from amateur actors
(C) To announce the opening of an arts venue
(D) To advertise a service for tourists

177. Who is Ms. Yeo?

(A) A playwright
(B) A banker
(C) A department head
(D) A director of tourism

178. What does the article mention about the building on Darby Street?

(A) It contains apartments for many families.
(B) It was once a bank.
(C) It is the oldest building on the street.
(D) It offers a community jobs program.

179. What is suggested about Ms. Cruz?

(A) She heard about a theater from an e-mail.
(B) She enjoyed the food and drinks offered.
(C) She did not think the acting was very good.
(D) She saw the first play performed in a new theater.

180. What does Ms. Cruz indicate in the survey?

(A) She recently moved to Auckland.
(B) She works at a nearby restaurant.
(C) She is a season subscriber.
(D) She stopped at a theater after shopping.

GO ON TO THE NEXT PAGE

Blendora Coffee
Item 16: Creamy Vanilla Blendelicious

Steps	
1. Pour espresso	Use dark roast or decaf. For small drinks, add 1 shot. For medium drinks, add 2 shots. For large drinks, add 3 shots.
2. Pour milk	For regular drinks, use whole milk. When customers request a light drink, use nonfat milk.
3. Add flavor	Use vanilla powder. For small drinks, add 2 scoops. For medium drinks, add 3 scoops. For large drinks, add 4 scoops.
4. Add ice	Use the markings on the ice scoop for small, medium, and large drinks.
5. Blend	Press the orange button on the blender. The texture should be creamy.
6. Finish and serve	Pour into a plastic cup. For regular drinks, top with whipped cream and use a domed lid. For light drinks, do not top with whipped cream and use a flat lid.
7. Clean up	Rinse blender cover and metal blender cup. Wipe the counter.

Blendora Coffee Barista Training

Trainee: Matt Molinelli
Trainer: Kuniko Osawa
Date: June 17

Drink: Creamy Vanilla Blendelicious (Light) Size: ☐ Small ☑ Medium ☐ Large

Rate the quality of the finished beverage.
☐ Perfect ☐ Very Good ☑ Good ☐ Acceptable ☐ Unacceptable

What errors did the trainee make?
Mr. Molinelli measured correctly for a medium beverage, and he used nonfat milk. However, he did everything else according to the regular recipe, not the light one.

Comments: Mr. Molinelli was adept at using his hands, and he kept a smile on his face. Once he memorizes the recipes, he will be an excellent barista.

181. Who are the instructions meant for?

(A) Dishwashers at a restaurant
(B) New employees at a coffee shop
(C) Customers placing an order
(D) Restaurant equipment manufacturers

182. According to the instructions, what is true of the Creamy Vanilla Blendelicious?

(A) It is available in two sizes only.
(B) It is served hot.
(C) It is not available in decaf.
(D) It is sometimes served with a flat lid.

183. How many scoops of vanilla powder did Mr. Molinelli use?

(A) One
(B) Two
(C) Three
(D) Four

184. What did Mr. Molinelli do wrong?

(A) He put whipped cream on the drink.
(B) He used the wrong type of milk.
(C) He used only one shot of espresso.
(D) He washed the blender without using soap.

185. What does Ms. Osawa suggest about Mr. Molinelli in the form?

(A) He asked her for help to make the drink.
(B) He presented a friendly appearance.
(C) He had never used a blender before.
(D) He has an excellent memory.

GO ON TO THE NEXT PAGE

Dialed-In: The Web Site for Professional Connections

Quentin Rines **Dialed-In Code number:** 04404782	**Position wanted:** Director of Commercial Lending

Experience:
Assistant Manager, Commercial Lending
First Bank of Barbados
Three years, three months (present position)

Loan Officer
First Bank of Barbados
Three years, eight months

Teller
First Bank of Barbados
1 year, two months

To:	Quentin Rines <qrines@islandlink.bb>
From:	Rozella Huy <rozella.huy@ventana.com>
Date:	14 November
Subject:	Job offer

Dear Mr. Rines:

On behalf of all staff here at Ventana Bank, I want to say how pleased we were to meet you last week. We appreciate that you were able to spend so much time with us discussing your background and plans for the future. We are pleased to offer you the position of director of commercial lending. The position will be based in our George Town location on the Cayman Islands. Should you accept the position, you will receive the pay and benefits described during the interview process, as well as a relocation reimbursement of USD $1,000.

Please let us know whether you accept the offer by 29 November and inform us of your preferred start date. We hope to have the position filled by mid-December.

Congratulations on being selected. We look forward to welcoming you to our team.

Sincerely,

Rozella Huy
President, Ventana Bank

```
┌─────────────────────────────────────────────────────────────┐
│ ═══════════════════════  *E-mail*  ═══════════════════════  │
├─────────────────────────────────────────────────────────────┤
│  To:       Tomas Melville <tmelville@homenetwork.bb>        │
│  From:     Quentin Rines <qrines@islandlink.bb>             │
│  Date:     14 November                                      │
│  Subject:  New position                                     │
├─────────────────────────────────────────────────────────────┤
│  Mr. Melville,                                              │
│                                                             │
│  I just received the job offer from Ventana Bank that we    │
│  discussed on Monday. They are meeting my salary request    │
│  and offering me money for relocating too.                  │
│                                                             │
│  This has been my goal ever since you hired me as a teller, │
│  right out of college. But now that I have been offered my  │
│  dream job, I am having doubts. The new location seems so   │
│  far away. I would rarely get to see my parents and my      │
│  siblings.                                                  │
│                                                             │
│  I would welcome your help in this matter. Could we get     │
│  together in the next few days for lunch or coffee? As you  │
│  know, I have always valued your input, and I have missed   │
│  our lunchtime conversations since you retired.             │
│                                                             │
│  Quentin                                                    │
│                                                             │
└─────────────────────────────────────────────────────────────┘
```

TEST 4

186. According to the online profile, what is Mr. Rines's current job?

(A) Director
(B) Assistant manager
(C) Loan officer
(D) Teller

187. What is indicated about Mr. Rines in the first e-mail?

(A) He was offered $1,000 to help pay for moving.
(B) He worked with Ms. Huy at First Bank of Barbados.
(C) He plans to go on a short trip to the Cayman Islands.
(D) He recently opened an account at Ventana Bank.

188. What is Mr. Rines's concern about the position?

(A) It pays less than advertised.
(B) It requires him to move to the Cayman Islands.
(C) It requires him to start before he is ready.
(D) It seems to be more demanding than he originally thought.

189. According to the second e-mail, why does Mr. Rines want to meet with Mr. Melville?

(A) To offer him a job
(B) To request a loan
(C) To ask for advice
(D) To thank him for his help

190. What is suggested about Mr. Melville?

(A) He lives in George Town.
(B) He contacted Mr. Rines using the Dialed-In Web site.
(C) He is a friend of Ms. Huy's.
(D) He once worked at First Bank of Barbados.

GO ON TO THE NEXT PAGE

The Mayan Joy Cocoa Process
From our organic fields to your kitchen table!

| 1. We plant and cultivate the seeds following ancient traditions. | 2. We dry, clean, and prepare the seeds naturally. | 3. We toast the cocoa beans and remove the shells by hand. | 4. We grind the shelled beans to produce 100% pure cocoa powder. | 5. YOU enjoy our Mexican cocoa, a rich, sensational, delicious superfood! |

Mayan Joy Cocoa
Av Tulum Plaza Galerias
Cancun, Quintana Roo 97655
Mexico

March 24

James Grigio
39 Lansford Lane
Valley Falls, Kansas 66088
United States

Mayan Joy Cocoa Representative:

When I was recently in Mexico, I purchased a block of your fine cocoa. It was the best I ever had! I did some research on your products, and I was very impressed with your process. I especially appreciate that your workers take care to remove the shells from the beans by hand.

I would like to purchase some more to make my own chocolates at home. Please send me information and pricing. I would prefer to purchase a one-pound block of pure, unsweetened Yucatan cocoa. I will be sweetening the candy myself, so I am not looking for sweetened cocoa.

Thank you.

James Grigio
James Grigio

Mayan Joy Cocoa Products Chart

House Blend	Artisan Block	Block Gift	Mountain Bag
Half-pound bag $25	1 pound $40	2 pounds $98	1 pound $65
Item: D-23	Item: C-100	Item: C-200	Item: M-42
Rich, bittersweet, blended powder	Pure cocoa from the Yucatan	Pure cocoa from the Yucatan	Mountain grown in the highlands of Guatemala
Ready for making steamy, frothy, hot drinks	Perfect for drinks, cooking, baking, and confections	Beautifully displayed in a handcrafted wooden gift box	Unsweetened cocoa in bag designed with artwork from Guatemala
Cocoa, white and brown sugar, cinnamon, ancho, allspice, anise, and cayenne	100% pure cocoa in block form	100% pure cocoa in block form	100% pure cocoa in block form

191. Based on the process chart, what is done to the seeds immediately after they are cultivated?

(A) They are made into a beverage.
(B) They are ground into powder.
(C) They are toasted.
(D) They are dried.

192. What does Mr. Grigio indicate in the letter?

(A) He lives in Cancun, Quintana Roo.
(B) He grows natural cocoa.
(C) He owns a chocolate shop.
(D) He bought cocoa in Mexico.

193. What step in Mayan Joy Cocoa's process does Mr. Grigio praise?

(A) Step 1
(B) Step 2
(C) Step 3
(D) Step 4

194. What is true about the Mayan Joy Block Gift?

(A) It is the only product that comes in a decorated container.
(B) It is the only product that is from the Yucatan.
(C) It is larger than the other products from Mayan Joy.
(D) It contains more added sugar than the other Mayan Joy products.

195. What product will Mr. Grigio most likely purchase?

(A) House Blend
(B) Artisan Block
(C) Block Gift
(D) Mountain Bag

GO ON TO THE NEXT PAGE

Customer Survey Feedback Report

Generated for: Floorsy, Inc.
Conducted by: Gwyneth Gupta
Medallion Marketing Consultants

	Completely Unsatisfied	Somewhat Unsatisfied	Neutral	Somewhat Satisfied	Very Satisfied
Overall customer experience	☐	☐	■	☐	☐
Customer service	☐	■	☐	☐	☐
Product options	☐	☐	■	☐	☐
Product value	☐	☐	☐	■	☐
Web site organization	☐	☐	☐	☐	■

Comments: The results of Medallion's survey are compiled above. We had 923 responses. There are several areas where Floorsy could improve its services to grow the business. First, customers had issues getting adequate customer service—this was due to slow e-mail response times, especially when making changes to orders. Medallion recommends investing in a chat window for the Web site and training customer representatives to use it. Customers enjoyed the Web site, and the chat feature would allow customers to get immediate service.

One general comment stood out regarding product options. Customers appreciated the wide variety of low-pile carpets with short fibers. They appreciated their high durability for areas where people frequently walk. However, they were also interested in thicker shag rugs for lounge areas like living rooms.

Floorsy Discount Coupon

Thank you for responding to our customer survey!
As a reward for your support, get 20% off your next online purchase from May 1 to 31!

Enter the code **REWARD20** at checkout.

Note: Floorsy.com offers free shipping and handling on all orders.

Thank You For Your Order

Dear Mr. Lindsay,

Thank you for your phone order. The following items from your order #104850 have been delivered.

Hendesia Low-Pile Rug in Ruby Red (6 x 9)	x 1	$180.00
Verenia Shag Rug in Blue (6 x 9)	x 1	$250.00

Subtotal	$430.00
Discount	$86.00 (Code: REWARD20)
Total	**$344.00**

Paid in full

As a growing business, we take all reviews and comments seriously. Please visit www.floorsy.com/comments to submit a review, and receive 10% off your next purchase.

If you need assistance with your purchase, please e-mail customerservice@floorsy.com.

196. What is indicated in the report?

(A) Customers found the Web site easy to navigate.
(B) Customers think the products are too expensive.
(C) Customer service representatives received high marks.
(D) Customers rarely communicate by e-mail.

197. What is one recommendation Ms. Gupta makes in the report?

(A) To hire more interior designers
(B) To lower the price of the rugs
(C) To change the returns policy
(D) To spend more money on customer support

198. According to the coupon, what is true about Floorsy?

(A) It rarely has sales.
(B) It ships items at no extra cost.
(C) It does not offer gift cards.
(D) Its Web site is poorly organized.

199. What can be concluded about Floorsy?

(A) It has fully redesigned its Web site.
(B) It has offered Ms. Gupta a management position.
(C) It has added shag rugs to its product offerings.
(D) It has hired additional customer representatives.

200. What is most likely true about Mr. Lindsay?

(A) He spoke to Ms. Gupta about his order.
(B) He was somewhat unsatisfied with the rugs.
(C) He sent an e-mail to change his order.
(D) He submitted responses to the customer survey.

Stop! This is the end of the test. If you finish before time is called, you may go back to Parts 5, 6, and 7 and check your work.

토익 정기시험
실전 ❶1000
RC

실전 TEST

05

READING TEST

In the Reading test, you will read a variety of texts and answer several different types of reading comprehension questions. The entire Reading test will last 75 minutes. There are three parts, and directions are given for each part. You are encouraged to answer as many questions as possible within the time allowed.

You must mark your answers on the separate answer sheet. Do not write your answers in your test book.

PART 5

Directions: A word or phrase is missing in each of the sentences below. Four answer choices are given below each sentence. Select the best answer to complete the sentence. Then mark the letter (A), (B), (C), or (D) on your answer sheet.

101. Pering Township ------- enough money to build a new library next year.

(A) raised
(B) convinced
(C) observed
(D) tackled

102. ------- ground floor café is popular with building residents.

(A) Our
(B) Ourselves
(C) Ours
(D) Us

103. The additional training will help you become more ------- with RNV Laboratory's procedures.

(A) primary
(B) brief
(C) familiar
(D) deep

104. Reviews of employee performance are conducted ------- a quarterly basis.

(A) to
(B) against
(C) on
(D) with

105. Concert venues routinely record ------- to evaluate the success of their marketing campaigns.

(A) attendance
(B) attendant
(C) attended
(D) attending

106. The new contract must be signed and returned ------- any work can begin.

(A) before
(B) provided that
(C) as far as
(D) unless

107. The park's maps ------- the difficulty level of each hiking trail.

(A) explaining
(B) explain
(C) to be explained
(D) to explain

108. Braley's Deli prides itself on its fresh ingredients and ------- customer service.

(A) rapid
(B) occasional
(C) expected
(D) proposed

109. The next technology coordination team meeting will be held ------- teleconference at 3:00 P.M. tomorrow.

(A) by
(B) of
(C) in
(D) for

110. Weiss Landscaping has a ------- grasp on its client base because of its excellent customer service.

(A) firm
(B) firmest
(C) firmly
(D) firming

111. We add funds to our savings account ------- we can to ensure we have money on hand for unexpected expenses.

(A) either
(B) even so
(C) whenever
(D) whereas

112. Last year's model of Rulster's electric vehicle ------- at a significant discount.

(A) offers
(B) offered
(C) was offering
(D) is being offered

113. Freight trains are Choman Transport's ------- method of shipping materials if time is not an important factor.

(A) valuable
(B) taken
(C) preferred
(D) plain

114. In order to respond to customer concerns, the sales department has collected all the ------- that has been sent.

(A) correspond
(B) corresponded
(C) corresponding
(D) correspondence

115. Festival officials stored items that were left behind after the event until they could determine ------- owned them.

(A) who
(B) theirs
(C) whose
(D) that

116. Even though there were problems with traffic last year, officials have again ------- to hold the parade in the city center.

(A) updated
(B) controlled
(C) decided
(D) advanced

117. We will make arrangements for Ms. Tanaka's ------- once we finalize the schedule for her tour of our corporate headquarters.

(A) arrive
(B) arrives
(C) arrival
(D) arrived

118. Given the benefits it will provide, members of the community were ------- excited about the proposal for a new shopping center.

(A) responsibly
(B) popularly
(C) mistakenly
(D) understandably

119. Ultra Star Construction gained ------- savings by purchasing materials from different suppliers.

(A) substance
(B) substantial
(C) substantiate
(D) substantially

120. Research project managers at Envira Hospital often hire external ------- with extensive experience in their fields.

(A) patients
(B) contenders
(C) characters
(D) consultants

GO ON TO THE NEXT PAGE

121. Ms. Kwan reported that she is ------- finished with her report pending receipt of final client reviews.

(A) too
(B) more
(C) almost
(D) often

122. Based on sales reports from the past three months, the ------- seems to be that our newest products are gaining popularity.

(A) aim
(B) trend
(C) offer
(D) style

123. Newport Hills Property Developers are hiring ------- contractors to build a state-of-the-art water filtration system.

(A) qualified
(B) qualification
(C) qualify
(D) qualifies

124. ------- to *Alpine Climber* magazine include Karl Saenz and Holli Bergits, two of Europe's best photographers.

(A) Buyers
(B) Novelists
(C) Passengers
(D) Contributors

125. Notes on the ------- of the merger of LN Bank and East Way Bank will be included in the meeting minutes.

(A) financially
(B) financing
(C) financial
(D) financed

126. Ms. Ahmad asked that we complete our assignments ------- so that she can include them in her monthly budget report today.

(A) prompt
(B) prompted
(C) promptly
(D) prompting

127. The new operations manager was surprised that the directors wanted cost estimates even for minor tasks ------- labeling.

(A) apart
(B) at least
(C) in full
(D) such as

128. After additional research, Mr. Haines has ------- his report on the prevalence of migratory birds in the region.

(A) estimated
(B) revised
(C) inflicted
(D) advised

129. According to the publisher, Clark Lee's book is selling well ------- a few recent negative reviews.

(A) except
(B) despite
(C) even if
(D) as soon as

130. Employees in the Kano Insurance personnel department must be able to analyze every application -------.

(A) objects
(B) objectives
(C) objecting
(D) objectively

Directions: Read the texts that follow. A word, phrase, or sentence is missing in parts of each text. Four answer choices for each question are given below the text. Select the best answer to complete the text. Then mark the letter (A), (B), (C), or (D) on your answer sheet.

Questions 131-134 refer to the following article.

Major Expansion for Local Biotech Startup

Medicatenet, a leading biotechnology company, ------- yesterday that it has raised $200 million in
131.

venture capital from investors. It plans to use those ------- to install cutting-edge technology
132.

involving machine learning to develop new medicines. The investment will enable Medicatenet to

triple its workforce ------- the next twelve months. ------- .
133.   134.

131. (A) announce
(B) announced
(C) announcement
(D) to announce

132. (A) funds
(B) laboratories
(C) parts
(D) teams

133. (A) between
(B) about
(C) at
(D) over

134. (A) With great fanfare, Medicatenet
has published the results of a
five-year study.
(B) Most therapies are developed in a
trial-and-error process.
(C) Medicatenet is just one of several
leading biotechnology
companies.
(D) To accommodate this increase,
the company has signed a lease
to expand into a new facility in
Norwalk.

GO ON TO THE NEXT PAGE

Questions 135-138 refer to the following e-mail.

From: Valeria Sanchez <vsanchez@mellowbayresort.com>
To: Seo-Jun Hak <seo-junhak2390@amail.com>
Subject: Arrival at Mellow Bay Resort
Date: June 4

Dear Mr. Hak,

Your stay at Mellow Bay Resort is coming soon! The check-in time is between 3:00 P.M. and 8:00 P.M. Please call us at (305) 555-0125 if you plan to arrive before or after these hours. Your room may be given to another guest if you arrive after 8:00 P.M. without ------- .
135.

When checking in, you will receive complimentary tickets for the breakfast buffet, ------- is located down the hall from the lobby. You may also want to make dinner reservations
136.
at Lookout Restaurant on the top floor of the hotel with ------- views of the ocean and town.
137.
Also be sure to stop at our guest services desk for information about local attractions.

------- . There is so much in the bay area to explore! We look forward to welcoming you as our
138.
guest.

Best regards,

Valeria

135. (A) notice
(B) choice
(C) appearance
(D) luggage

136. (A) how
(B) why
(C) when
(D) which

137. (A) sturdy
(B) recent
(C) spectacular
(D) faithful

138. (A) Guests used to receive a discount on one item at the gift shop on the first floor.
(B) We can help you with plans to enjoy scuba diving, sailing, or other activities.
(C) Every room has a cable television connection with access to popular movies.
(D) Guests can sometimes check in to the hotel early with no additional charge.

January 17

Kenji Davis
26 Peartree Lane
Baltimore, MD 21205

Dear Mr. Davis,

It was a pleasure to talk with you at the Annual Model Train Show in Baltimore earlier this month.
I ------- by the high quality of the antique trains that you had on display.
    139.

You mentioned that you might want to sell several sets of antique trains. Faremount Antique

Auctions would be an ideal ------- for you. Twice a year we hold an online auction of antique
                         140.

toys that attracts bids from model train collectors from around the world. Our most recent

auction was in November. ------- . I believe you will find that items in our auction sold for higher
                        141.

prices ------- similar items did at other sites.
     142.

Our next auction will be held May 21–22. Let me know if you are interested in participating.

Sincerely,

Justine Garcia, Faremount Antique Auctions

139. (A) impress
 (B) impressed
 (C) was impressed
 (D) was impressing

140. (A) basis
 (B) marketplace
 (C) foundation
 (D) career

141. (A) I encourage you to look online at the prices
      paid for items in that auction.
 (B) Our auctions used to be held at a historic
      hotel called The Faremount Rose.
 (C) Some of our customers are interested in
      antique metal banks from the 1800s.
 (D) All participants in the online auction
      needed credentials to enter the site.

142. (A) although
 (B) since
 (C) nonetheless
 (D) than

GO ON TO THE NEXT PAGE

Questions 143-146 refer to the following memo.

To: All Personnel
From: Harkfield Capital
Subject: Half day
Date: November 10

On Friday, November 19, beginning at 2:00 P.M., the parking garage will be power washed and the lines will be repainted. Before the workers can ------- , the garage needs to be empty.
143.
Therefore, all employees will receive a paid half day off from work. ------- . Those who begin at
144.
9:00 A.M. will finish at 1:00 P.M. No lunch hours will be taken. Employees must ------- the garage
145.
immediately after completing their shifts.

The garage will remain ------- all weekend. Employees who work on the weekend must park on
146.
the street or in a paid lot.

We hope you will enjoy this extra time off.

143. (A) be hired
(B) be paid
(C) rest
(D) start

144. (A) Employees who start work at 8:00
A.M. will leave at noon.
(B) Confidential material should be
disposed of in a secure bin.
(C) Carpooling has become increasingly
popular with employees.
(D) Managers must approve all overtime
requests.

145. (A) vacates
(B) vacate
(C) vacated
(D) be vacated

146. (A) underground
(B) exact
(C) spacious
(D) closed

Directions: In this part you will read a selection of texts, such as magazine and newspaper articles, e-mails, and instant messages. Each text or set of texts is followed by several questions. Select the best answer for each question and mark the letter (A), (B), (C), or (D) on your answer sheet.

Questions 147-148 refer to the following invoice.

Oma Jean's Cakes

Customer Name: Robert Palomino
Customer Phone: (704) 555-0189
Date of Order: October 26
Date of Delivery: October 28
Delivery: Grand Uptown Hotel
Delivery by: Renu Bhatti

Two kg chocolate cake (round)	$75.00
Chocolate icing	free
Strawberry filling	$20.00
Message on cake: *"Congratulations on your retirement, Mary Ellen!"*	free
Special instructions: Decorate cake with yellow icing flowers	$15.00
Delivery Fee	$15.00
Grand Total	**$125.00**

147. According to the invoice, what was purchased?

(A) A hotel stay
(B) Fresh flowers
(C) Chocolate candies
(D) A custom dessert

148. According to the invoice, who most likely is Ms. Bhatti?

(A) A coworker of Mr. Palomino's
(B) A member of the hotel staff
(C) An Oma Jean's Cakes employee
(D) A retiring chef

GO ON TO THE NEXT PAGE

Questions 149-150 refer to the following text-message chain.

Greg Pfaff (1:17 P.M.)
Hi Jessa. I'm running a bit late for our 2:00 P.M. appointment to troubleshoot the problem with your desktop computer. I should arrive around 2:20 P.M.

Jessa Kim (1:18 P.M.)
That's fine. I hope you can fix it. I depend on that desktop for my online craft supply business.

Greg Pfaff (1:19 P.M.)
I know. It may just need a tune-up. My assistant, Kevin Mulford, will be with me too. He may help you out in the future while I work on a maintenance project at a local data center.

Jessa Kim (1:20 P.M.)
That's good to know.

Greg Pfaff (1:21 P.M.)
Good. That's it, then.

Jessa Kim (1:22 P.M.)
All right. See you when you get here.

---

149. Who most likely is Mr. Pfaff?

(A) A studio artist
(B) A seller of craft supplies
(C) A computer technician
(D) A building superintendent

150. At 1:20 P.M., what does Ms. Kim most likely mean when she writes, "That's good to know"?

(A) She is relieved that a problem was solved.
(B) She is glad that she will have help if needed.
(C) She is happy that Mr. Pfaff will arrive soon.
(D) She is satisfied with work done on a maintenance project.

Questions 151-152 refer to the following product review.

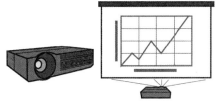

As my company's regional training manager, I am often making presentations to groups of people and rarely in the same place. I needed a portable projector to display what's on my computer screen, and the Veruvatron 800 is perfect because it is slim and light. I did quite a bit of research comparing different brands in terms of image resolution and other specifications. Many were comparable in terms of those specifications, but the Veruvatron 800 is especially easy to bring to all my presentations, and that is ultimately why I chose this one. One flaw is that both the power cord and the VGA cord are surprisingly short. I have needed to use an extension cord pretty much every time I use it, so be prepared to do the same.

– Horace Offerman

151. Why did Mr. Offerman choose one projector over others?

(A) It is durable.
(B) It is easy to carry.
(C) It has the best image quality.
(D) It includes more accessories.

152. What does Mr. Offerman warn readers about?

(A) The life span of a device
(B) The length of some cables
(C) The need for a separate case
(D) The lack of compatibility with certain computers

GO ON TO THE NEXT PAGE

Questions 153-154 refer to the following e-mail.

To:	Demetri Owens
Cc:	Theodore Scott, Halina Kibera
From:	Janice Kovack
Date:	January 10
Subject:	Next interview

Dear Mr. Owens,

It was great to speak to you about the security systems manager position. I am pleased to report that I would like you to move on to the next level of interviews. You will speak with the director of security, Mr. Scott, and his assistant, Ms. Kibera.

I will send another e-mail before the meeting with instructions on how to join the virtual conference call.

Meeting date/time: January 12 at 2:30 P.M. Eastern Standard Time

Please confirm that you can make the conference call.

Sincerely,

J. Kovack
Human Relations Agent

153. What is the purpose of the e-mail?

(A) To advertise a job opening
(B) To change the time of a virtual meeting
(C) To offer a job to a candidate
(D) To schedule an interview

154. Who is Mr. Scott?

(A) An agent in the human relations department
(B) The head of security
(C) An applicant for a job in the security systems department
(D) Ms. Kibera's personal assistant

To:	board@sunnervalleyalliance.org
From:	kathleen.huff@sunnervalleyalliance.org
Date:	Tuesday, August 17
Subject:	Sunner Planning Commission meeting

Dear Board Members,

I am preparing to speak at the upcoming Sunner Planning Commission meeting and will be creating a slideshow to accompany my presentation. I have some great data to reinforce my points, but I think it will be easier for people to understand if the information is presented visually. Is anybody interested in helping me develop the visual component of my presentation? Some pie charts and diagrams would make a big impact in the slideshow.

The goal is to present the advantages and disadvantages of the three proposals for using the Holt property in northeast Sunner Valley. I am hoping that the commission accepts Ken Jansen's offer to buy the property, which is next to his land. He would expand his orchard and this would help maintain the rural nature of northern Sunner Valley.

The speaker sign-up guidelines state that I will need to submit my presentation materials before the agenda gets posted online, but they do not specify when this will happen. I will call today to find out more details.

Kathleen Huff

155. What is the purpose of the e-mail?

(A) To coordinate speakers
(B) To collect more statistics
(C) To get assistance with graphics
(D) To argue against some evidence

156. What does Ms. Huff hope the planning commission will do?

(A) Decline a proposal
(B) Tighten a restriction
(C) Preserve rural land
(D) Restore some waterways

157. What will Ms. Huff confirm?

(A) The boundaries of a property
(B) The deadline for submissions
(C) The allowed length of a presentation
(D) The regulations for new businesses

GO ON TO THE NEXT PAGE

Waypave Hardscapes
The Finest in Residential Driveways, Walls, and Patios

ESTIMATE: #20987
DATE: 09/28
TOTAL AMOUNT: $4,000

PREPARED FOR

Lurene Toyo
23000 S Henry Street
Fairville, GA 30013

JOB DESCRIPTION

Remove grass and old concrete patio behind the house. Lay a cement foundation for the new patio. Install Tropical Sunset tiles per client's approved plan.

MATERIALS	RATE	QUANTITY	AMOUNT
Cement	$50 per bag	5	$250
Tropical Sunset tiles	$3 each	500	$1,500
Delivery of materials			$350
Disposal of debris			$150
Labor			$1,750
TOTAL			**$4,000**

TERMS

$2,000 due upon signing of contract
$2,000 due upon completion of project
Payable by credit card, check, or bank transfer

This estimate serves as your contract. Please sign and return this document to estimates@waypavehardscapes.com.

---

158. For what type of work was the estimate created?

(A) Painting a house
(B) Paving a driveway
(C) Building a stone fence
(D) Creating an outdoor patio

159. What most likely happened before Waypave provided the estimate?

(A) A design proposal was accepted.
(B) An old patio was removed.
(C) A discount was offered.
(D) Dirt and debris were removed from a yard.

160. How much will Ms. Toyo owe when she signs the contract?

(A) $1,500
(B) $1,750
(C) $2,000
(D) $4,000

Questions 161-163 refer to the following e-mail.

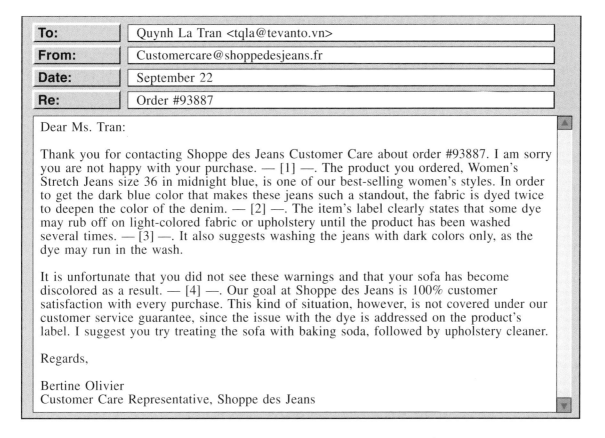

To:	Quynh La Tran <tqla@tevanto.vn>
From:	Customercare@shoppedesjeans.fr
Date:	September 22
Re:	Order #93887

Dear Ms. Tran:

Thank you for contacting Shoppe des Jeans Customer Care about order #93887. I am sorry you are not happy with your purchase. — [1] —. The product you ordered, Women's Stretch Jeans size 36 in midnight blue, is one of our best-selling women's styles. In order to get the dark blue color that makes these jeans such a standout, the fabric is dyed twice to deepen the color of the denim. — [2] —. The item's label clearly states that some dye may rub off on light-colored fabric or upholstery until the product has been washed several times. — [3] —. It also suggests washing the jeans with dark colors only, as the dye may run in the wash.

It is unfortunate that you did not see these warnings and that your sofa has become discolored as a result. — [4] —. Our goal at Shoppe des Jeans is 100% customer satisfaction with every purchase. This kind of situation, however, is not covered under our customer service guarantee, since the issue with the dye is addressed on the product's label. I suggest you try treating the sofa with baking soda, followed by upholstery cleaner.

Regards,

Bertine Olivier
Customer Care Representative, Shoppe des Jeans

161. Why did Ms. Tran contact Shoppe des Jeans Customer Care?

(A) She received jeans that were the wrong color.
(B) Her jeans ruined her light-colored clothing.
(C) She was unhappy with the style of her jeans.
(D) Her jeans stained an item of furniture.

162. How does Ms. Olivier help Ms. Tran?

(A) By sending a new pair of jeans
(B) By offering a full refund
(C) By offering a discount on future orders
(D) By suggesting a way to fix a problem

163. In which of the positions marked [1], [2], [3], and [4] does the following sentence best belong?

"Each pair of jeans comes with a large label displaying the care instructions."

(A) [1]
(B) [2]
(C) [3]
(D) [4]

GO ON TO THE NEXT PAGE

Lado Shopping Center

Rebbly Development is pleased to announce the approval of a new project, the Lado Shopping Center in Springfield. This rapidly expanding city is conveniently located near the capital, and Lado Shopping Center is set to deliver an excellent shopping experience for all. We expect to finish construction next year.

Property Highlights
- 150,000 square feet of retail and office space
- $25 per square foot (ground floor)
- $20 per square foot (upper floors)
- Space available for lease or rent
- Space can be custom-built in consultation with Rebbly Development

Area Attractions
- Located near the aquarium, several parks, and the river
- Two major access roads: Hemley Boulevard and Route 82, with additional connection to Highway 35 to be completed in five years
- 4,000 new homes to be built in Springfield within three years
- Nearby parking structure with ports for electric vehicles to be completed within two years
- Movie theaters, amusement park, and other attractions nearby

164. What is indicated about the new property?

(A) It will contain movie theaters.
(B) It will offer private residences.
(C) Ground-floor units cost more than upper-level units.
(D) Parking is included for free with all spaces.

165. The word "deliver" in paragraph 1, line 3, is closest in meaning to

(A) carry
(B) provide
(C) send
(D) purchase

166. What is indicated about Springfield?

(A) It is owned by Rebbly Development.
(B) Its population is expected to increase.
(C) It does not have river access.
(D) Its economy is based on manufacturing.

167. When will the connection to Highway 35 be completed?

(A) In one year
(B) In two years
(C) In three years
(D) In five years

Jack Elling (10:35 A.M.)
Hi, everyone. Would anyone be able to come into the shop to work tonight? Kelly is having car problems and can't work her shift.

Emily Chin (10:37 A.M.)
I can't, sorry. But aren't Maria and Koji also working? Don't we usually have two people in the evenings?

Jack Elling (10:39 A.M.)
Yes, we usually have two people, and those two are working tonight. But we are having our special promotion, giving away samples of our new ice cream flavors. I need a third person to help with that.

Emily Chin (10:40 A.M.)
I'm attending a birthday party this afternoon, so I can't do it.

Cameron Stein (10:42 A.M.)
I could stay on after my day shift is over.

Emily Chin (10:43 A.M.)
Actually, I could work 6–9 P.M. if you don't want to stay. My party is only a few hours. What do you think?

Cameron Stein (10:44 A.M.)
Well, I could really use the overtime hours.

Emily Chin (10:45 A.M.)
OK.

Jack Elling (10:46 A.M.)
Thanks, Cameron!

168. Why does Mr. Elling start the text-message chain?

(A) To tell Ms. Chin that she missed a work shift
(B) To ask someone to cover a work shift
(C) To extend an invitation to a special event
(D) To ask for a ride to work

169. What is happening at the shop tonight?

(A) Staff will work on new recipes.
(B) Staff will offer free ice cream tastings.
(C) Staff will participate in a training session.
(D) Staff will hold a going-away party for a colleague.

170. Where is Ms. Chin going today?

(A) To Mr. Stein's house
(B) To a car repair shop
(C) To a party
(D) To a movie

171. At 10:44 A.M., what does Mr. Stein most likely mean when he writes, "Well, I could really use the overtime hours"?

(A) He is accepting Ms. Chin's apology.
(B) He is declining Ms. Chin's offer.
(C) He enjoys working at the shop.
(D) He prefers to work in the evening.

GO ON TO THE NEXT PAGE

Kiame Tire Factory Productivity Report

Preparer: Wilma Najjar, Systems Engineer
Date of review: April 10
Reason for review: Quarterly inspection

Summary: I have completed my inspection of all equipment and machinery at the plant. — [1] —. The main components of the production line are running as expected. These components include mixers, rollers, and the textile production system. — [2] —. The rotating drums for assembling the tires that were added last quarter have also been functioning as expected. Finally, the molds for the tire treads are beginning to show some signs of wear. Employees have flagged these molds, and the molds will be removed from the production line.

Recommendations: Purchasing new replacement molds is the top priority. See the report in the section dedicated to tire molds for details. — [3] —. Finally, as the Kiame plant increases its production, adding more mixers will be crucial to making more tires. The company must decide at that point whether to purchase newer mixer models or to upgrade those that we are currently using. — [4] —. However, replacing the older mixers will speed up production, which will likely outweigh any additional cost.

172. Why did Ms. Najjar most likely prepare the report?

(A) To explain why the mixing equipment is not working properly
(B) To document findings of a factory inspection
(C) To explain why productivity has recently decreased
(D) To justify the purchase of new rotating drums

173. What is true about the tire molds?

(A) There is a separate section about them in the report.
(B) They have all been replaced recently.
(C) They are not produced within the factory.
(D) More tires can now be produced with fewer molds.

174. What is indicated about the Kiame Tire Factory?

(A) Most of its equipment is old.
(B) It is less expensive to maintain than anticipated.
(C) It is likely to grow in the future.
(D) It has recently lost several employees.

175. In which of the positions marked [1], [2], [3], and [4] does the following sentence best belong?

"Of course, replacing existing models would be more costly."

(A) [1]
(B) [2]
(C) [3]
(D) [4]

GO ON TO THE NEXT PAGE

Call for Entries: Annual Sustainability Competition

Sponsored by the League of New Zealand Builders

PURPOSE: The League of New Zealand Builders (LNZB) wants to recognize an individual whose contribution to a new construction features design innovations that are environmentally friendly. The winner will be featured at an on-site celebration and show guests and journalists around the finished building, explaining its environmental highlights.

ENTRANTS: Priority consideration will be given to members of the LNZB, but any professional builder who completes a project in New Zealand before 15 December of this year may apply. Go to the LNZB Web site for the submission form.

DUE DATE: All submissions are due by 15 December.

JUDGING PROCESS: The application and vetting process includes several steps. After screening the candidates, judges will choose semifinalists. Then a special panel will choose this year's recipient.

FOR MORE INFORMATION: Visit www.leagueofnewzealandbuilders.org.nz to learn more about the LNZB and past winners.

Rahotu Wins LNZB Prize

(17 March)—The League of New Zealand Builders (LNZB) yesterday announced that Maia Rahotu won this year's Sustainability Competition. Ms. Rahotu, whose work on building designs throughout New Zealand goes back many years, won the award for her design of the Rowan Community Centre. The centre utilized renewable and recycled materials throughout its construction. In April, Ms. Rahotu will be formally presented with the award during the ceremony at the centre; details will be announced soon. "It was a tough decision this year," said LNZB's director, Thomas Young. "All applicants chose materials that minimize environmental impact. But we were able to narrow the candidates to three top choices, each of whom was interviewed by our panel of experts."

Building components in the Rowan project were thoughtfully selected by Ms. Rahotu to minimize environmental impact, Young added. "However, what is exceptional about Ms. Rahotu's design is how well it harvests solar energy." According to experts at LNZB, her solar design generates a high surplus of electricity beyond the building's requirements. This surplus is transmitted to the region's power grid—in effect reducing strain on local energy production.

176. What does the announcement indicate about the award?

(A) Its winner is chosen by Mr. Young.
(B) Its focus is on making cities smaller.
(C) It is given out every year.
(D) It includes a cash prize.

177. According to the announcement, what is required of candidates for the competition?

(A) Sponsorship from an LNZB mentor
(B) New Zealand citizenship
(C) Membership in the LNZB
(D) Completion of a building project

178. According to the article, what is true about Ms. Rahotu?

(A) She has significant design experience.
(B) She served on the LNZB selection panel.
(C) She recently moved to the region.
(D) She specializes in designing apartment buildings.

179. What will Ms. Rahotu do in April?

(A) Join a special LNZB panel
(B) Become the head of the LNZB
(C) Lead a tour of a building
(D) Submit an entry in a competition

180. According to the article, why is Ms. Rahotu's design exceptional?

(A) It uses a high percentage of recycled materials.
(B) It produces a large amount of electricity.
(C) Its roof and walls have curved shapes.
(D) It has a garden that covers most of the roof.

GO ON TO THE NEXT PAGE

LAZON COLOR SWIRL CUTTING BOARD

Model #B875

Always wash the product soon after each use, especially after cutting acidic fruits and vegetables like oranges and tomatoes.

Refrain from using bleach or cleaners with chlorine, which the board can absorb. For tough food stains, soak the board in soapy water for five minutes. Be sure to remove the leather hanging strap before cleaning, since water will make the leather tough and brittle.

To store your product, hang it upright from the leather strap on a wall or shelf. Do not store it in direct sunlight, since this will cause the vibrant colors of the board to fade. Periodically, polish the board with a light coat of olive oil to help the board's colors stay bright.

Like all Lazon products, our cutting boards are handmade. With minimal upkeep, you can keep your product looking like new.

If you have any problems with your board, please e-mail us at support@lazonproducts.com. Our policy is to replace at no cost any defective parts or products within three months of purchase. At Lazon Products, quality is our top priority!

From:	Jonas E. Iversen <jonaseiversen@daylightcommerce.com>
To:	support@lazonproducts.com
Date:	August 2, 4:58 P.M.
Subject:	Model #B875

Hello,

I'm writing in regard to a defect in my Lazon Model #B875 board. I was very careful to follow all the maintenance tips that came with the product, but when I was taking off the leather strap as instructed, I noticed a small tear had formed in the middle. It's not very large now, but it will only get bigger after a couple more months of use. Even though I purchased the product four months ago, I only started using it one month ago. Is the leather strap still covered under your defective parts policy? I'd like to get a new one.

Thank you for your assistance.

Jonas E. Iversen

181. What do the instructions describe?

    (A) How to display a piece of artwork
    (B) How to prepare a type of gourmet food
    (C) How to use a construction tool
    (D) How to take care of a piece of kitchen
        equipment

182. According to the instructions, what can oil
    be used for?

    (A) To make a product taste better
    (B) To make a product look better
    (C) To make a product run faster
    (D) To make a product stronger

183. What was Mr. Iversen most likely about to
    do when he noticed a problem?

    (A) Clean the product
    (B) Store the product
    (C) Display the product
    (D) Assemble the product

184. How long has Mr. Iversen owned the
    product?

    (A) For one month
    (B) For two months
    (C) For three months
    (D) For four months

185. What does Mr. Iversen ask Lazon Products
    to do?

    (A) Give him maintenance tips
    (B) Give him a full refund
    (C) Send a replacement part
    (D) Offer to repair the product

GO ON TO THE NEXT PAGE

TEST 5

https://www.flutteringwings.com.mx

| About Us | Reservations | FAQ | Contact Us |

Fluttering Wings Resort

Located just minutes from the entrance to the Tall Trees Monarch Butterfly Sanctuary, Fluttering Wings Resort is Mexico's finest eco-friendly destination. Open year-round, our facilities include a full-service restaurant, a relaxing swimming pool, and a rooftop deck with an amazing view.

Butterfly season is from mid-November to early March, and millions of monarch butterflies pass the winter at the Tall Trees sanctuary. Visitors can hike up the mountain on foot, but most prefer to participate in our guided horseback tours. Our expert guides, who escort visitors up the mountain, are all local villagers. They continuously scout the sanctuary for the best viewing locations.

At all times of the year, we offer hiking trails, bird-watching, and horseback riding. Electric vehicle tours of the villages and farms outside the sanctuary are also available.

To:	Carmen Sanchez <c.sanchez@flutteringwings.com.mx>
From:	James Norville <jnorville@itiaworld.org>
Date:	June 12
Subject:	International Travel Industry Association Guardian Award

Congratulations, Carmen Sanchez!

Fluttering Wings Resort has been named a recipient of an International Travel Industry Association Guardian Award. The ITIA Guardian Award includes a $5,000 cash award and one year of free support from our advisory team. ITIA experts can advise Fluttering Wings on ways to operate your business more efficiently and to use the Web to promote your services to potential visitors. A member of our advisory team, Rosa Del Vio, would like to present the award to you and visit your resort in July or August. She will be in touch with you before the end of the month.

Sincerely,

James Norville

Executive Director, International Travel Industry Association

```
┌─────────────────────────────────────────────────────┐
│  Fluttering Wings Resort              INVOICE         │
│                                                       │
│  Name: Julio and Lisa Bardom                          │
│  Prepayment received on: February 1                   │
│  Dates of stay: February 25–27                        │
│                                                       │
│  King-size room: two nights at $95/night    $190.00   │
│  Guided butterfly sanctuary tour: $40 x 2    $80.00   │
│  Total                                      $270.00   │
│  ─────────────────────────────────────────────────   │
│  Amount Paid:                               $270.00   │
│  Balance Due:                                 $0.00   │
│                                                       │
│  Note: Regarding your question, don't worry—the       │
│  butterflies don't depart the reserve until early     │
│  March.                                               │
└─────────────────────────────────────────────────────┘
```

186. What can guests do at Fluttering Wings Resort?

(A) Learn to scuba dive
(B) Take a cooking class
(C) Observe birds
(D) Rent scooters

187. According to the e-mail, in what way can ITIA help Fluttering Wings Resort?

(A) By teaching employees how to raise butterflies
(B) By helping the resort improve its online advertising effort
(C) By providing the resort with new laptop computers
(D) By constructing additional guest rooms

188. What resort activity will Ms. Del Vio be unable to do during her visit?

(A) Tour the local villages in an electric vehicle
(B) Take a guided horseback tour
(C) Visit a sanctuary while millions of butterflies are there
(D) Use the resort swimming pool

189. What is the purpose of the note on the receipt?

(A) To reassure the Bardoms about the timing of their trip
(B) To explain why the bill included an extra charge
(C) To thank the Bardoms for visiting a resort
(D) To warn the Bardoms of a possible disappointment

190. How will the Bardoms most likely tour the butterfly sanctuary?

(A) On foot
(B) On bicycles
(C) On horseback
(D) In all-terrain vehicles

GO ON TO THE NEXT PAGE

15th Annual Innovations in Horticulture and Agriculture Conference
At the renovated Blane Hotel and Conference Centre, London, UK
10–12 November
innovationsinhorticulture.org.uk

Featured Speakers:

- Chen Wan, China
- Hope O'Brian, United Kingdom
- Piet Bax, Netherlands
- Emil Savov, Bulgaria

For more information and to register, visit the Innovations in Horticulture and Agriculture Web site. Student discounts available with ID. A limited number of hotel rooms are available at the conference site. There is a complimentary bus service for attendees staying at nearby hotels.

E-Mail Message

To: Piet Bax <pbax@mailcrate.com>
From: Jacob Brewster <jbrewster@sootenfarms.co.uk>
Subject: Lighting Information
Date: 18 December

Dear Mr. Bax:

It was wonderful meeting you in London last month. Thank you for taking the time to talk to me after your speech and for agreeing to the video meeting on 5 January. I'm going to ask my project manager, Ms. Woo-Jin Ko, to join us. Among other things, Ms. Ko has some questions about lighting for my greenhouses. I think she has some questions about the products offered by the Brillante Luxlight company. I understand you helped design some of their products, so perhaps you can offer some advice. I know we'll both have many other questions, so I do appreciate this opportunity. I also hope I will be able to visit sometime in the spring and get an in-person look at your greenhouses.

Sincerely,

Jacob Brewster

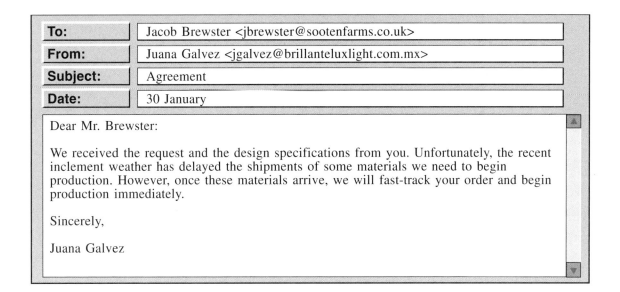

To:	Jacob Brewster <jbrewster@sootenfarms.co.uk>
From:	Juana Galvez <jgalvez@brillanteluxlight.com.mx>
Subject:	Agreement
Date:	30 January

Dear Mr. Brewster:

We received the request and the design specifications from you. Unfortunately, the recent inclement weather has delayed the shipments of some materials we need to begin production. However, once these materials arrive, we will fast-track your order and begin production immediately.

Sincerely,

Juana Galvez

191. What does the advertisement indicate?

(A) The number of student discounts is limited.
(B) The conference will last for fifteen days.
(C) Free busing from hotels is available.
(D) The conference center is being renovated.

192. Where did Mr. Brewster and Mr. Bax most likely meet?

(A) At a conference
(B) On a plane flight
(C) At a charity fund-raiser
(D) At the Brillante Luxlight office

193. In the first e-mail, what does Mr. Brewster say he will do?

(A) Reschedule a video meeting
(B) Hire a new project manager
(C) Change an order he made
(D) Include someone else in a meeting

194. What is the purpose of the second e-mail?

(A) To ask Mr. Brewster to send a shipment
(B) To discuss the status of an order
(C) To explain some specifications
(D) To complain about the quality of a product

195. What is suggested about Mr. Brewster?

(A) He owns farmland in both the United Kingdom and Bulgaria.
(B) He wants to start a new business with Mr. Bax.
(C) He developed a new agricultural product.
(D) He ordered lights for some indoor plants.

GO ON TO THE NEXT PAGE

ORANGE LIGHT GYM
GRAND OPENING WEEK

Orange Light Gym is coming to Singapore! Join us as we open our newest and best gym in April. This will be our first location in Singapore, and we will add two other locations later this year.

- 10 percent off for new Orange Light Gym members who sign up during our Orchard Road grand opening event from 4 April until 8 April
- Singapore bodybuilding legend Ronny Cho appearing on 5 April
- World-famous trainer Lina Sitaman appearing on 6 April

ORANGE LIGHT GYM ▪ 1140 Orchard Road ▪ Singapore

Orange Light Gym Marina South   183 Reviews
2 October

Max Halle

I have been a regular Orange Light Gym member for ten years and generally like their service. I live in Dubai but travel to Singapore for work regularly, so it's great to belong to a gym with locations in both countries! The Marina South gym in Singapore is very clean and well designed, but there are two areas that need improvement. There are not enough machines, especially compared to the much larger Orchard Road location. Also, I have visited the gym about ten times and on nearly half of those occasions, the pool was not available for use. I will still use this gym because of the global membership, but I hope they address the cause of the pool closures.

To:	Sam Adawi
From:	Ani Wayanti
Date:	14 October
Subject:	Stokner Service

Mr. Adawi,

I know we have a one-year contract with Stokner Service, but I am very concerned. The problems that we have had at the Orange Light Gyms in Singapore are due to improper maintenance. Quite simply, I don't think the workers that Stokner employs are trained well enough to do their jobs. Can we meet to discuss this? The sooner we resolve this issue, the better.

Ms. Wayanti

Regional Manager

Orange Light Gym

196. According to the advertisement, what is indicated about Orange Light Gym's Orchard Road location?

(A) It is Orange Light Gym's only location with a pool.
(B) It is the first Orange Light Gym in Singapore.
(C) It is owned by a famous bodybuilder.
(D) It offers classes led by a popular trainer.

197. What does Mr. Halle indicate about the Orange Light Gym Marina South location?

(A) It is not conveniently located.
(B) It is not very clean.
(C) It has more machines than the Orchard Road location.
(D) It is smaller than the Orchard Road location.

198. What is true about Mr. Halle's membership in the Orange Light Gym?

(A) He plans to cancel it.
(B) He received a 10 percent discount.
(C) He never used it to enter the Dubai location.
(D) He started it before locations opened in Singapore.

199. Why did Ms. Wayanti send the e-mail?

(A) To express concern about a hired company's poor work
(B) To ask about becoming a gym member
(C) To discuss an overpayment
(D) To recommend hiring better trainers

200. What is suggested about Stokner Service?

(A) It services Orange Light Gym locations in Dubai.
(B) It fixes the exercise machines at Orange Light Gyms in Singapore.
(C) It is not maintaining the pools at Orange Light Gyms well.
(D) It was recently bought by another company.

Stop! This is the end of the test. If you finish before time is called, you may go back to Parts 5, 6, and 7 and check your work.

토익 정기시험
실전 ❶1000
RC

실전 TEST

06

In the Reading test, you will read a variety of texts and answer several different types of reading comprehension questions. The entire Reading test will last 75 minutes. There are three parts, and directions are given for each part. You are encouraged to answer as many questions as possible within the time allowed.

You must mark your answers on the separate answer sheet. Do not write your answers in your test book.

PART 5

Directions: A word or phrase is missing in each of the sentences below. Four answer choices are given below each sentence. Select the best answer to complete the sentence. Then mark the letter (A), (B), (C), or (D) on your answer sheet.

101. Mobile phone upgrades will be discounted with the ------- of a one-year service plan.

(A) purchase
(B) purchaser
(C) purchased
(D) purchasers

102. Meeting coordinators are ------- to make sure the projection equipment is turned off after each use.

(A) proposed
(B) supported
(C) reminded
(D) suggested

103. For questions ------- to the use of personal time off, please contact Ms. Matz in the human resources department.

(A) relate
(B) related
(C) relation
(D) relates

104. Ammeto software ------- team members to view project-related schedules, resources, and costs.

(A) allowance
(B) allows
(C) allowing
(D) allowable

105. Customer service representatives are ------- to answer your inquiries 24 hours a day.

(A) urgent
(B) invested
(C) available
(D) secure

106. The audience laughed so ------- during the play that some of the actors' lines were drowned out.

(A) loudest
(B) louder
(C) loudness
(D) loudly

107. Customers may request parking validation ------- before or after they dine with us.

(A) either
(B) since
(C) if
(D) as

108. Prestige Apartment Homes offers ------- apartments for an additional cost.

(A) furnishing
(B) furnished
(C) furnishes
(D) furnish

109. Mr. Park must wait for ------- from human resources before posting the job announcement.

(A) admission
(B) approval
(C) favor
(D) opinion

110. Please direct inquiries to the appropriate person listed in our ------- staff directory.

(A) update
(B) updated
(C) updates
(D) updating

111. The Blakewood store had been waiting for the shipment of gift boxes ------- finally arrived on Friday morning.

(A) that
(B) though
(C) over
(D) still

112. Wheller's software tools make market research quick and easy ------- any entrepreneur.

(A) onto
(B) except
(C) upon
(D) for

113. Da-Xia Ting is seeking a patent for the heat-exchange valve she -------.

(A) inventor
(B) inventing
(C) invented
(D) invention

114. The library has newspapers dating from the 1700s and is ------- a prime destination for historians.

(A) toward
(B) where
(C) thus
(D) yet

115. A small water leak often leads to major problems if not fixed -------.

(A) immediately
(B) especially
(C) previously
(D) relatively

116. ------- construction, more than 400 meters of public water pipes will be replaced.

(A) Until
(B) Within
(C) During
(D) Among

117. The electrical work in the lobby today is not expected to interfere with normal business -------.

(A) operator
(B) operates
(C) operations
(D) operational

118. Because the accounting team worked so -------, the report was completed ahead of schedule.

(A) securely
(B) efficiently
(C) respectively
(D) usually

119. The proposal submitted by Ferrisa Associates did not ------- an itemized budget.

(A) contain
(B) fold
(C) count
(D) refuse

120. The employee handbook ------- states that uniforms must be worn by all customer service providers.

(A) clear
(B) clears
(C) clearer
(D) clearly

GO ON TO THE NEXT PAGE

121. Andara Ebele taught ------- to paint by copying the styles of famous portrait and landscape artists.

(A) hers
(B) her own
(C) she
(D) herself

122. Mr. Zasio will need to reschedule his appointment today as his train was unexpectedly -------.

(A) delay
(B) delays
(C) delayed
(D) delaying

123. The bottling machine should be turned off ------- it is being cleaned.

(A) while
(B) so
(C) whereas
(D) also

124. Ms. Ogawa is adamantly ------- to the redevelopment project in its current form.

(A) objectionable
(B) negative
(C) close
(D) opposed

125. ------- the statistical report is drafted, Ms. Arista will edit it.

(A) How
(B) Then
(C) When
(D) Where

126. Having strong partnerships throughout Southeast Asia has been ------- to Srisati Company's success.

(A) critical
(B) criticize
(C) critic
(D) critically

127. Sarah Davidson ------- Chikara Architects' creative vision more enthusiastically than any other associate did.

(A) caught up
(B) gave away
(C) prepared
(D) embraced

128. ------- with more than a year of employment can apply for tuition assistance if they wish to pursue an academic degree.

(A) Those
(B) These
(C) Whoever
(D) Who

129. Factilis Capital is mainly concerned about the enormous ------- of the Ito Wind Farm project.

(A) difference
(B) confusion
(C) scale
(D) spiral

130. All Loreen wristwatches come with ------- black, white, and blue bands.

(A) variable
(B) probable
(C) companionable
(D) interchangeable

PART 6

Directions: Read the texts that follow. A word, phrase, or sentence is missing in parts of each text. Four answer choices for each question are given below the text. Select the best answer to complete the text. Then mark the letter (A), (B), (C), or (D) on your answer sheet.

Questions 131-134 refer to the following article.

A New Season at the Farmers Market

Lee Valley Farmers Market is ------- exciting changes. Jerry Carver, who has been the market's
131.

------- for the last three years, stepped down last week. He was replaced by Paul Frankson, who
132.

oversaw operations at Garden Haven Farm.

The main market area is expanding from ten to fifteen booths to include more than just produce.

------- . There are also plans for a coffee stand and a craft section. "We really appreciate our loyal
133.

customers who have been purchasing produce from us for many years," said Frankson. "We

hope that by offering a ------- range of products, we can encourage more people to shop locally."
134.

Lee Valley Farmers Market is open year-round, seven days a week, from 8:00 A.M. to 6:00 P.M.

TEST 6

131. (A) resulting
    (B) attaching
    (C) competing
    (D) undergoing

132. (A) shipper
    (B) grower
    (C) driver
    (D) manager

133. (A) However, there is a pharmacy next door.
    (B) It will be closed over the winter months.
    (C) Meat, cheese, and honey are among the
        new products.
    (D) Currently, parking is available in the
        garage across the street.

134. (A) widen
    (B) wider
    (C) widest
    (D) widely

GO ON TO THE NEXT PAGE

MARCHETTI TIRES

Don't let tires that are cracked, bulging, or worn slow you down. Cruise into the new year on fresh Marchetti premium tires! Now at all Greenback Discount Warehouse Club locations, members can save $75 on a ------- of four this month.
135.

------- . Sign up for an annual membership before December 31 and take an extra $20 off tire
136.

installation. Some exclusions ------- , and sizes may not be available for all vehicle makes and
137.

models. For ------- details, go to your nearest Greenback Discount Warehouse Club or visit the
138.

Web site at www.gdwc.com/tires.

135. (A) file
(B) packet
(C) set
(D) round

136. (A) Are you tired of sitting in traffic?
(B) Would you like to become a member?
(C) Do you need a trusted mechanic?
(D) Are you interested in a new car?

137. (A) apply
(B) to apply
(C) applying
(D) had applied

138. (A) modern
(B) optional
(C) inflated
(D) further

To: Ezgi Inan
From: Tina Yun
Date: 15 April
Subject: Event Confirmation

Dear Ms. Inan,

It was a pleasure ------- with you today. Thank you for booking your 21 May team-building event
139.

at Bonner Trampoline Park. As I mentioned, Bonner offers a variety of lunch packages. I have put

you down for the basic option. This ------- one slice of pizza, one can of lemonade, and one
140.

small bag of crisps for £8 per person. You may upgrade your package to add a fruit or vegetable

tray for £35. Bonner can also provide a sheet cake for an additional £30. ------- , you may bring
141.

your own cake or another dessert. ------- . Food orders can be changed up to 48 hours prior to
142.

your event.

Sincerely,

Tina Yun
Events Manager, Bonner Trampoline Park

139. (A) speaking
(B) presenting
(C) performing
(D) celebrating

140. (A) includes
(B) including
(C) has included
(D) would have included

141. (A) Similarly
(B) In short
(C) Alternatively
(D) For example

142. (A) Our vegetable tray is a popular item.
(B) Check-in for your party begins at noon.
(C) Each guest will need to sign a waiver
prior to the event.
(D) Please reply to this message if you
would like to upgrade your menu.

Questions 143-146 refer to the following notice.

Thank you for initiating the setup of your Paxton Mobile Banking account. ------ .
                                                                                143.

Once your account is fully activated, you will receive notifications of any account activity,

------ deposits, withdrawals, and fund transfers. You can ------ your notification settings on the
144.   145.

"My Account" page on our mobile app or Web site. For security purposes, you will be prompted

to request a one-time ------ code before changing your settings. If you have any questions,
                       146.

please visit www.paxtonmobilebanking.com/FAQ.

143. (A) To open a new line of credit, call your
        local branch office.
     (B) To complete the process, follow the
        instructions we sent to your e-mail.
     (C) Please respond to this survey so we can
        learn how to serve you better.
     (D) You can order a replacement bank card
        directly from the app.

144. (A) without
     (B) as soon as
     (C) instead of
     (D) such as

145. (A) adjust
     (B) interrupt
     (C) spend
     (D) allow

146. (A) verify
     (B) verifies
     (C) verifiability
     (D) verification

Directions: In this part you will read a selection of texts, such as magazine and newspaper articles, e-mails, and instant messages. Each text or set of texts is followed by several questions. Select the best answer for each question and mark the letter (A), (B), (C), or (D) on your answer sheet.

Questions 147-148 refer to the following article.

Mayor Lizette Set to Deliver State of the City Address

FALCON HEIGHTS (21 April)—Mayor Loretta Lizette will deliver her fifth State of the City address at Falcon Heights City Hall, Room 101, on Wednesday, 30 April, beginning at 7:00 P.M. The event is open to the public, but seating is first come, first served.

Mayor Lizette, who was reelected to her second four-year term last month, will discuss her vision for the future of the city. One issue on her agenda is the controversial application by Panhandle Eatery, a fast-food restaurant, to open a location on historic Hedgerow Boulevard. The speech will be followed by a question-and-answer period. Doors open at 6:30 P.M.

147. What is NOT mentioned about the event?

(A) Its starting time
(B) Its main purpose
(C) Its location
(D) Its duration

148. What is indicated about Mayor Lizette?

(A) She owns a fast-food restaurant.
(B) She recently won an election.
(C) She has a home on Hedgerow Boulevard.
(D) She will present an award to a city employee.

GO ON TO THE NEXT PAGE

YOU'RE INVITED!

**Corozal Digital's
Tenth Anniversary**

Join us to celebrate your hard work and dedication
that got us to this milestone!

Saturday, June 15

6:00 P.M. Appetizers and Music
7:00 P.M. Dinner

Bayshore Hotel
22 Atlantic Avenue

RSVP by June 1 to j.bovel@corozaldigital.com.

149. For whom is the invitation intended?

(A) Corozal Digital's clients
(B) Corozal Digital's employees
(C) Bayshore Hotel staff
(D) Bayshore Hotel patrons

150. What is mentioned about the event?

(A) It will mark a retirement.
(B) No response is required.
(C) Food will be served.
(D) Guests of invitees are welcome.

https://www.firststreetcinema.com/classic_film

| Season Program | **News** | Tickets | Contact |

Classic Film Festival

The new First Street Cinema is celebrating its opening in June by welcoming filmgoers with these free screenings for fans of classic films. The films will start at 7:00 P.M. Seating is limited, and guests are asked to reserve tickets on our Web site, as tickets will not be offered on-site.

The Hillside Farm   Saturday, June 2
   The story features a mysterious farm on a hill and three generations of the family living there.

Just Two Wheels   Saturday, June 9
   A young cyclist spends years preparing for an elite race. This is a heartwarming story of overcoming adversity.

The Missing Papers   Saturday, June 16
   The puzzling theft of a writer's manuscript causes a search for the culprit.

A Rambling Homecoming Saturday, June 23
   The Khan's family reunion celebration is marked by a series of comical incidents and misunderstandings. If you need a good laugh, this is the film for you.

TEST 6

151. What is true about the classic film screenings?

(A) They are offered to the public for a small fee.
(B) They are scheduled throughout one month.
(C) They are shown during the morning.
(D) They are being held outdoors.

152. What film is most likely to be humorous?

(A) *The Hillside Farm*
(B) *Just Two Wheels*
(C) *The Missing Papers*
(D) *A Rambling Homecoming*

Questions 153-156 refer to the following online chat discussion.

Aisa Ito [10:08 A.M.] I'm so glad I found this forum for users of Canomatik products! Has anyone tried the S20 can opener? The electric can opener I've had for years finally broke.

Tanveer Kumar [10:10 A.M.] I bought one several years ago, but I don't think it was worth the money I spent.

Ingrid Vogel [11:15 A.M.] I like mine. I used to struggle opening cans. This one makes it easier to open cans of all sizes.

Laurie Jacobs [2:12 P.M.] The commercial version is expensive, but there is also a consumer version that costs less.

John Burwood [2:14 P.M.] I ordered mine online, and it was defective. I contacted the company's customer service department, and they sent me a new one that works just fine.

Laurie Jacobs [2:16 P.M.] I used to be a cook at a restaurant years ago, and we had a commercial-grade Canomatik can opener back then. I've been using the consumer version at home for nearly a decade. It opens cans safely and easily.

Aisa Ito [5:15 P.M.] Thanks, everyone. I'll give it a try.

---

153. Who responded to Ms. Ito's question?

(A) Customer service agents
(B) Advertising sales representatives
(C) Participants in an online cooking course
(D) Owners of a particular type of appliance

154. What is Mr. Kumar's opinion of the Canomatik product?

(A) He likes its size.
(B) He is dissatisfied with its quality.
(C) He finds it convenient to use.
(D) He is concerned that it might break.

155. Who once worked in the food-service industry?

(A) Ms. Vogel
(B) Ms. Jacobs
(C) Mr. Burwood
(D) Mr. Kumar

156. At 5:15 P.M., what does Ms. Ito most likely mean when she writes, "I'll give it a try"?

(A) She will make a purchase.
(B) She will eat at a restaurant.
(C) She will contact a manufacturer.
(D) She will attempt to open a container.

Questions 157-158 refer to the following text-message chain.

Gerald Anast [8:58 A.M.]
Hi, Laura. You have enough people to work in our showroom this morning, right?

Laura Huu [8:59 A.M.]
I do. Brenda, our part-time helper, is here now.

Gerald Anast [9:01 A.M.]
Good. I'm at the distributor's warehouse on Crosby Street. It turns out they have the exact style of pendant lights we need for our latest client, Alsford Guesthouse.

Laura Huu [9:02 A.M.]
I'm surprised you had to go there. We have such a large variety of styles here.

Gerald Anast [9:04 A.M.]
Well, Alsford's management was very specific about their design preference. I'm just glad we'll be able to get those lights. I should be back by late morning. Have you looked over our purchase orders and inventory spreadsheets?

Laura Huu [9:05 A.M.]
I've only been here about ten minutes.

Gerald Anast [9:06 A.M.]
No problem. When you are caught up, let me know if we're short on any items.

Laura Huu [9:07 A.M.]
Will do.

157. Where most likely do the writers work?

(A) At a guesthouse
(B) At an accounting firm
(C) At a lighting store
(D) At a manufacturing company

158. At 9:05 A.M., what does Ms. Huu most likely mean when she writes, "I've only been here about ten minutes"?

(A) She has not yet reviewed some documents.
(B) She had to make a delivery to a client.
(C) She will not be able to substitute for an absent employee.
(D) She has not had time to unpack some boxes.

GO ON TO THE NEXT PAGE

To:	Nick Foster
From:	Natural Spring Garden Products Customer Support
Subject:	Follow-up
Date:	October 28

Dear Mr. Foster,

Thank you for your recent purchase of a Serene Bird Bath from Natural Spring Garden Products. Its steady, cascading flow of water down several levels will attract native birds to your garden and is sure to provide a cool, calming environment.

I see that your order was placed on October 21 and arrived on October 24. I hope that you have been pleased with the product thus far. Please remember that your purchase is covered by a three-year warranty. If you experience any issues with its operation, feel free to reach out to our customer service team at 1-800-555-0168.

Would you mind taking two minutes to complete a brief survey? Your responses will enable us to learn more about our customers so that we can more effectively market our products and services. To access the survey, please visit our Web site at www.naturalspringgardenproducts.com/review.

Sincerely,

Ken Iwata
Customer Support, Natural Spring Garden Products

---

159. What product did Mr. Foster most likely purchase?

(A) A water purifier
(B) A bird feeder
(C) A book about gardens
(D) An outdoor fountain

160. What is Mr. Foster asked to do?

(A) Write an online review
(B) Provide feedback
(C) Confirm a delivery date
(D) Update his address

161. The word "covered" in paragraph 2, line 3, is closest in meaning to

(A) described
(B) protected
(C) continued
(D) allowed

Questions 162-164 refer to the following article.

Home Style Clothing Line Debuts

MANILA (September 18)—Inspired by the handmade crafts of the Philippines, local designer Maritess Bautista has introduced Home Style, a clothing brand that features fabrics woven by area artisans using traditional practices.

Bautista first learned basic weaving techniques from her mother and aunts in her youth and built on that knowledge as she studied at the Manila School of Fashion Design. — [1] —. She then spent the next ten years working as a junior designer for Trendy Today. — [2] —. Finally, she returned to her hometown of San Jacinto to found Home Style.

Home Style's debut collection includes clothing and hair accessories that utilize the weaving techniques and designs that the area is known for. — [3] —. Ms. Bautista purchases all the textiles she uses from local craftspeople.

Currently, Home Style merchandise is available only in select San Jacinto-area stores. — [4] —.

"I want to keep production local," said Ms. Bautista. "That's good for the artisans, and it's authentic. But I don't want the *products* to remain local. I want to bring our designs to the whole country—maybe even the world."

162. Who introduced Ms. Bautista to weaving?

(A) Her family
(B) Her teachers
(C) Senior designers
(D) Local craftspeople

163. What is indicated about Ms. Bautista?

(A) She was born in Manila.
(B) She buys materials from nearby sources.
(C) She has started many businesses.
(D) She regularly travels around the world.

164. In which of the positions marked [1], [2], [3], and [4] does the following sentence best belong?

"However, Ms. Bautista has broader goals."

(A) [1]
(B) [2]
(C) [3]
(D) [4]

TEST 6

GO ON TO THE NEXT PAGE

Questions 165-167 refer to the following Web page.

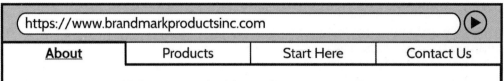

https://www.brandmarkproductsinc.com ▶

| About | Products | Start Here | Contact Us |

Make your mark with your logo on our products!

There is no better way to advertise your organization than with our attractive fashion apparel featuring your logo or company slogan. Provide us with your logo file, and Brandmark Products, Inc., will adorn selected items and deliver your order within four business days. We will produce your order with color printing or embroidery of the highest quality.

Our 25 years in operation have revealed one important fact about developing name recognition. Forget water bottles and key chains—items that are frequently put aside or misplaced. Your message will be more effective and longer lasting with our quality shirts, sweatshirts, jackets, and hats.

To place an order, use the "Start Here" tab or call 1-800-555-0155 to speak with a customer service representative.

---

165. What is indicated about Brandmark Products, Inc.?

(A) It has discontinued making some products.
(B) It offers discounts on large orders.
(C) It specializes in making athletic uniforms.
(D) It helps companies promote themselves.

166. The phrase "put aside" in paragraph 2, line 3, is closest in meaning to

(A) saved up
(B) classified
(C) ignored
(D) closed up

167. According to the Web page, why should someone contact customer service?

(A) To get assistance with an order
(B) To request a sample product
(C) To set up an appointment
(D) To finalize the design of a logo

---

https://www.clarrellestate.com.au/about

| **About** | Events | Photos | The Foundation |

Welcome to the Clarrell Estate—Ballarton's premier centre for the arts! The exquisite grounds of the estate are situated on 60 hectares of hilly terrain featuring lush English gardens and an impressive manor house that was designed by noted architect Owen Barton. Ten years ago, the Clarrell Foundation decided to transform the estate into an arts centre. Initially, the foundation opened the manor house to the public, highlighting the Clarrell family art collection. In the last three years, a large, multiuse complex was built near the property entrance, complete with art studios and a theatre.

The Clarrell Estate's museum and gardens are open to the public free of charge. In addition, the theatre hosts public lectures as well as musical performances, and the studios showcase individual artists' curated works. For a complete schedule, a list of current artists, and information on admission fees for the theatre and studios, please visit the Events page.

Join the Clarrell Foundation to enjoy members-only special events and discounts on performances. Members also have the opportunity to reserve the gardens for private events. To become a member, contact Alicia Ji at aji@clarrellestate.com.au.

---

168. What does the Web page focus on?

(A) An overview of an attraction
(B) A town's cultural festival
(C) A local gardening club
(D) An opportunity to buy art

169. What is indicated about the manor house?

(A) It is available for private parties.
(B) It is part of an old estate.
(C) It hosts concerts by local musicians.
(D) It has recently been renovated.

170. According to the Web page, what has happened over the last three years?

(A) A new building has been constructed.
(B) A school of arts has been founded.
(C) A public park has been cleaned up.
(D) A film about Mr. Barton has been made.

171. According to the Web page, why should a person e-mail Ms. Ji?

(A) To purchase tickets to a performance
(B) To get help in using a Web page
(C) To request an updated event schedule
(D) To inquire about a foundation membership

GO ON TO THE NEXT PAGE

Finance Director

The Palliz Foundation seeks a finance director to be a member of our senior leadership team. This is a supervisory position reporting directly to the foundation president. — [1] —. The finance director manages the seven-member finance department, including the payroll manager and accounting director. The finance director is responsible for the oversight and maintenance of accounting and purchasing systems. — [2] —. The person in this position monitors internal control procedures and ensures compliance with legal obligations. — [3] —. Additional responsibilities include disbursement, investment, and management of all company funds, development of financial policies and practices, budget preparation, and creation of reports for the board of directors.

Preference will be given to current employees. — [4] —. Interested parties should submit a résumé listing their qualifications to the human resources department at humanresources@pallizfoundation.org no later than 4:30 P.M. on Friday, April 23.

172. Who supervises the finance director?

(A) The foundation president
(B) The payroll manager
(C) The accounting director
(D) The board of directors

173. What information about the position is included in the job advertisement?

(A) Salary
(B) Schedule
(C) Qualifications
(D) Duties

174. How can candidates apply for the position?

(A) By visiting a booth at a job fair
(B) By e-mailing a résumé to the personnel office
(C) By uploading a résumé to a Web page
(D) By completing an online application form

175. In which of the positions marked [1], [2], [3], and [4] does the following sentence best belong?

"However, highly qualified external candidates are encouraged to apply."

(A) [1]
(B) [2]
(C) [3]
(D) [4]

GO ON TO THE NEXT PAGE

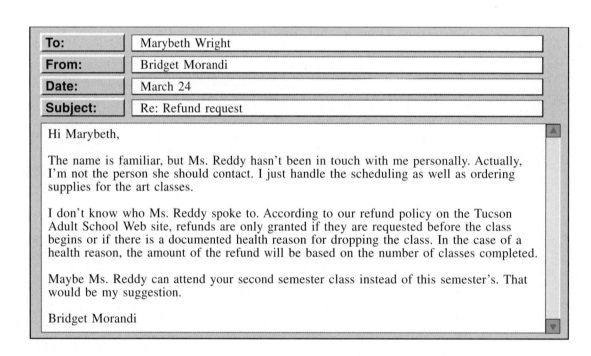

To:	Bridget Morandi
From:	Marybeth Wright
Date:	March 23
Subject:	Refund request

Hi Bridget,

I was wondering if you have heard from Sujata Reddy. She was enrolled in the painting class I teach on Tuesday and Thursday. She was only able to attend for the first week because another commitment came up. She said she asked someone in the Tucson Adult School office if she could drop the class, and she has requested a refund of the course tuition.

She said she hasn't received her refund yet. Did she contact you?

Best,

Marybeth Wright

To:	Marybeth Wright
From:	Bridget Morandi
Date:	March 24
Subject:	Re: Refund request

Hi Marybeth,

The name is familiar, but Ms. Reddy hasn't been in touch with me personally. Actually, I'm not the person she should contact. I just handle the scheduling as well as ordering supplies for the art classes.

I don't know who Ms. Reddy spoke to. According to our refund policy on the Tucson Adult School Web site, refunds are only granted if they are requested before the class begins or if there is a documented health reason for dropping the class. In the case of a health reason, the amount of the refund will be based on the number of classes completed.

Maybe Ms. Reddy can attend your second semester class instead of this semester's. That would be my suggestion.

Bridget Morandi

176. Who most likely is Ms. Wright?

    (A) A scheduling coordinator
    (B) A vice principal
    (C) An art gallery owner
    (D) An adult education teacher

177. Why did Ms. Wright send an e-mail to Ms. Morandi?

    (A) To decline an invitation
    (B) To propose a solution
    (C) To ask for information
    (D) To reschedule a meeting

178. In the first e-mail, the word "drop" in paragraph 1, line 4, is closest in meaning to

    (A) slip
    (B) quit
    (C) lower
    (D) slow

179. Why most likely has Ms. Reddy not yet received a tuition refund?

    (A) The registration office has been closed.
    (B) The refund check is still in the mail.
    (C) She failed to submit her request in writing.
    (D) She already attended part of the class.

180. What does Ms. Morandi suggest that Ms. Reddy may be able to do?

    (A) Use her previously paid tuition to take a future class
    (B) Find the same class at another adult school
    (C) Attend half the class and still receive credit
    (D) Contact the teacher to arrange for private tutoring

GO ON TO THE NEXT PAGE

New Bakery Coming to Town

OREVALE CITY (October 14)—A Cresson's Bakery is opening soon at the corner of Canton Avenue and Ridley Street. The location will be the national chain's first within the city limits. Like all Cresson's Bakery stores, it will operate seven days a week.

The only similar business in the vicinity is the Donut Station on the Kupperman University campus. Cresson's Bakery will offer breakfast sandwiches and fruit juices in addition to its signature coffee and baked goods. The company is following its revised business model to open compact facilities rather than sit-down eateries. This means the Orevale City location will offer takeout and drive-through service only.

The bakery will occupy Canton Avenue's smallest vacant lot. Approval for the project followed a public hearing where area residents voiced mixed opinions.

Gina Holton, who lives on Paxton Road, said she liked the idea of having a new bakery in her neighborhood but worries about traffic congestion on Ridley Street. As evidence, she presented pictures of heavy vehicle traffic there. Wofford Drive resident Steven Lu said he would enjoy having a convenient place to grab a quick snack.

Cresson's Bakery is slated to welcome its first customers in early March.

Dear Editor,

As a lifelong resident of Orevale City, I appreciate your coverage of Cresson's Bakery. Unfortunately, the October 14 article contained some inaccurate information. The photos that I shared during the public hearing captured images of traffic congestion in front of my house. Also, as a member of the city's Historic Preservation Committee, I was primarily concerned about the bakery's architecture. The initial building design for Cresson's Bakery was contemporary. I am pleased to report that the chain has agreed to modify the exterior so that it blends in better with the older structures surrounding it.

Sincerely,
Gina Holton

181. What is indicated about Orevale City?

    (A) It has little open land for development.
    (B) It has two warehouse districts.
    (C) It is home to a university.
    (D) It has a growing population.

182. What is different about new Cresson's Bakery locations?

    (A) They replicate historic architectural features.
    (B) They offer a wider variety of baked goods.
    (C) They do not offer seating for customers.
    (D) They are located outside of city centers.

183. What is indicated about Mr. Lu?

    (A) He is Ms. Holton's next-door neighbor.
    (B) He plans to patronize Cresson's Bakery.
    (C) He recently moved to Orevale City.
    (D) He is a member of a historic preservation group.

184. Where did Ms. Holton take photos of vehicle traffic?

    (A) On Canton Avenue
    (B) On Wofford Drive
    (C) On Ridley Street
    (D) On Paxton Road

185. What does the letter suggest about Ms. Holton?

    (A) She is happy that a building design was changed.
    (B) She is planning to start her own bakery business.
    (C) She did not attend a public hearing.
    (D) She wants to submit an article to the newspaper.

GO ON TO THE NEXT PAGE

Brandy Mortimer
Raxconnect, Inc.
620 Weir Road
Glasgow G91 9HX

11 March

Alyssa Susilo
29 Lefroy Street
Glasgow G3 7BQ

Dear Ms. Susilo,

As you may know, Raxconnect has been expanding its services in the Glasgow area over the past year. Our new fibre-optic cable lines offer faster and more reliable service and eliminate the need for aboveground wiring. In order for the system to work, we need to install Internet connection devices throughout the city. Phase 1 of our construction work involved City Centre. Phase 2 involved West End. Although Phase 2 took longer than expected, we were able to expedite Phase 3 and get back on schedule. Phase 4 is now ready to begin in your area.

Raxconnect would like to place a small Internet connection hub on your property at 29 Lefroy Street. Because of its central location on the street, your front yard would make an optimal connection point. Please call us at 0141 496 0001 by 10 April to let us know whether we may proceed. Thank you.

Sincerely,

Brandy Mortimer

Brandy Mortimer, Utilities Adviser

Raxconnect Expands Service

GLASGOW (14 March)—After unexpected delays in West End, Raxconnect has finally completed the latest phase of its project to install fibre-optic cable throughout the city. Residents and businesses in Southside are now enjoying faster Internet service.

For the next phase of the project, in Finnieston, Raxconnect has identified key locations for connection hubs and is currently reaching out to residents and homeowners so that work can begin as soon as possible.

The moves follow an announcement made earlier this year that Raxconnect had invested £350 million to expand its network. Local officials hope that the project brings new business and spending to their neighbourhoods.

Notice of Temporary Road Closure

Please be aware that construction at 29 Lefroy Street will result in the closure of the entire street. The closure will last from Monday, 31 May, until Tuesday, 8 June. During that period, automobile access will be limited to residents who live on Lefroy Street.

186. What is the main purpose of the letter?

(A) To apologize for poor Internet service
(B) To seek permission from a property owner
(C) To provide an explanation for a delay
(D) To persuade a customer to switch Internet providers

187. What is suggested about Finnieston in the article?

(A) It recently experienced power outages.
(B) It houses Raxconnect's headquarters.
(C) It will require only one connection hub.
(D) It will soon have upgraded Internet service.

188. Which phase of Raxconnect's project took place in Southside?

(A) Phase 1
(B) Phase 2
(C) Phase 3
(D) Phase 4

189. What can be concluded about Ms. Susilo?

(A) She agreed to Ms. Mortimer's request.
(B) She is employed by Raxconnect.
(C) She plans to move to a different Glasgow neighborhood.
(D) She produces video content for the Internet.

190. What does the notice suggest about people who live on Lefroy Street?

(A) They will have access to a shuttle service to their homes.
(B) They will receive free Internet service for one week.
(C) They will be asked to fill out a form when Raxconnect's work is done.
(D) They will be able to use the street during construction.

TEST 6

GO ON TO THE NEXT PAGE

Questions 191-195 refer to the following press release, e-mail, and review.

FOR IMMEDIATE RELEASE

Contact: Kevin Oessenich, kevin.o@albertandannies.com.au

GOOLWA (2 November)—Yesterday, Albert and Annie's, a leading maker of gourmet frozen desserts, unveiled several new treats: Triple Time Chocolate ice cream, a waltz of light and dark chocolate with a chocolate crumb swirl; Toffee Spree, a vanilla and toffee ice cream with sweet biscuit infusions; and a raspberry sorbet, featuring bits of real fruit. The new products are expected to be in Australian stores by mid-November.

The company was founded 25 years ago by Albert and Annie Grundon, president and CEO, respectively. Earlier this year, they announced the opening of a South African division. South African retailers will get access to a number of Albert and Annie's products in mid-December.

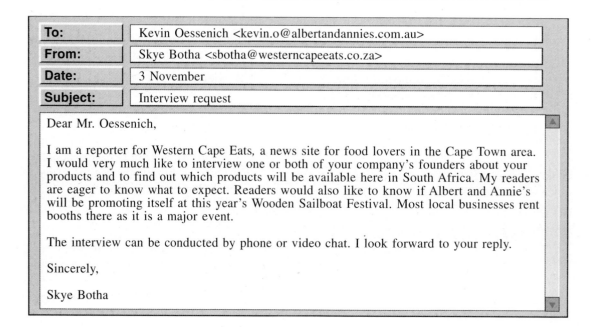

To:	Kevin Oessenich <kevin.o@albertandannies.com.au>
From:	Skye Botha <sbotha@westerncapeeats.co.za>
Date:	3 November
Subject:	Interview request

Dear Mr. Oessenich,

I am a reporter for Western Cape Eats, a news site for food lovers in the Cape Town area. I would very much like to interview one or both of your company's founders about your products and to find out which products will be available here in South Africa. My readers are eager to know what to expect. Readers would also like to know if Albert and Annie's will be promoting itself at this year's Wooden Sailboat Festival. Most local businesses rent booths there as it is a major event.

The interview can be conducted by phone or video chat. I look forward to your reply.

Sincerely,

Skye Botha

https://www.westerncapeeats.co.za/reviews

| About | News | Events | **Reviews** |

Jim Sato, 31 December

Your article informing me about Albert and Annie's, an ice-cream company that just came to South Africa, gave me one more reason to attend the annual Wooden Sailboat Festival. I got to sample some sensational ice creams at Albert and Annie's booth. The booth offered three amazing flavours: Coffee Truffle, Fudge Mint, and Chocolate Pretzel Delight. In your article, Mr. Oessenich stated that these would be the first flavours to be rolled out to grocery outlets in South Africa and that more will become available over time. I can't wait!

191. What is announced in the press release?

(A) The merger of two companies
(B) The retirement of a company's leaders
(C) The expansion of a product line
(D) The relocation of a production plant

192. What does the press release suggest about Albert and Annie's South African division?

(A) It will open in mid-November.
(B) It will not be hiring until mid-December.
(C) It will soon launch its own Web site.
(D) It will not sell ice cream directly to consumers.

193. According to the e-mail, what are Ms. Botha's readers interested in?

(A) Tasting new foods
(B) Renting a festival booth
(C) Opening a business
(D) Writing reviews of food products

194. What is indicated about Ms. Botha?

(A) She plans to attend the Wooden Sailboat Festival.
(B) She grew up in the Cape Town area.
(C) She wants to talk to Mr. and Ms. Grundon.
(D) She applied for a job in Albert and Annie's South African division.

195. What can be concluded about Albert and Annie's booth at the festival?

(A) It was staffed by Mr. Oessenich.
(B) It did not have coffee ice cream when Mr. Sato arrived.
(C) It was one of three booths featuring frozen desserts.
(D) It did not offer samples of the company's newest flavors.

GO ON TO THE NEXT PAGE

Ben's Nonprofit Burst—*Resources for those who work in the nonprofit sector*

Getting Grants

Posted on August 18 by Ben Fineman

Grant writing is the art of completing applications for financial aid offered by government agencies, schools, corporations, or other entities. There is huge competition for grants and no room for mediocrity in grant writing. To improve your grant-writing skills, consider taking an online course taught by Kristina Gilliam of Meadow Park University. Her Writing Great Grants course is divided into four 90-minute interactive sessions. It is designed for people with some basic knowledge of grant writing. These Monday evening classes run from November 15 to December 6. For details and registration, visit www.kristinagilliam.ca/course. Use the promo code NPBURST at checkout to get 15 percent off the $350 tuition. This code expires on September 30. On October 1, only full-price registration will be available until the final registration day, November 1.

---

www.kristinagilliam.ca/feedback

Thank you for participating in my Writing Great Grants course. Please take a moment to tell me about your experience by filling out the form below.

Name: Natalie Ballard

Location: Winnipeg

Comment: Relatively short compared to other writing courses I've taken, Writing Great Grants provided a decent overview. I was impressed to learn that the instructor helped companies get millions of dollars in grants during her career, and I'm glad to now have her as a resource if I ever get hired as a grant writer. Fortunately, I used Ben's Nonprofit Burst's promo code when I registered. Otherwise, I'd have considered the tuition too high. The Web site gave me the impression that Ms. Gilliam would include more specifics about the actual writing process than she did.

www.kristinagilliam.ca/feedback

Thank you for participating in my Writing Great Grants course. Please take a moment to tell me about your experience by filling out the form below.

Name: Paul Voigt

Location: Toronto

Comment: This was a great course overall. The instructor shared a wealth of valuable insights, including her experiences as the founder of Orden International. I never realized that grant-writing firms even existed! I might start one of my own if I ever leave my current grant-writing job. The course focused mainly on researching grant opportunities and analyzing samples of successful grant applications. When several of us asked for specific writing tips during the final session, Ms. Gilliam simply referred us to other resources. The course description on her Web site was a bit misleading in that regard.

196. What is the purpose of the blog post?

(A) To provide grant-writing tips
(B) To recommend a learning experience
(C) To spotlight an employee
(D) To preview changes to a Web site

197. According to Mr. Fineman, when does the registration period end?

(A) On September 30
(B) On October 1
(C) On November 1
(D) On December 6

198. What is indicated about Ms. Ballard?

(A) She registered for the grant-writing course before October 1.
(B) She currently works as a grant writer.
(C) She took a course from Ms. Gilliam on a previous occasion.
(D) She edits Mr. Fineman's blog posts.

199. What is true about Ms. Ballard and Mr. Voigt?

(A) They attended a class together in Winnipeg.
(B) They have been interviewed by Mr. Fineman.
(C) They want to learn how to research grant opportunities.
(D) They noticed the same weakness in the Writing Great Grants course.

200. What does Mr. Voigt indicate about Ms. Gilliam?

(A) She lives in Toronto.
(B) She started a grant-writing firm.
(C) She wrote a grant for Mr. Fineman.
(D) She authored a grant-writing manual.

Stop! This is the end of the test. If you finish before time is called, you may go back to Parts 5, 6, and 7 and check your work.

토익 정기시험
실전 ❶ 1000
RC

실전 TEST

07

PART 5

Directions: A word or phrase is missing in each of the sentences below. Four answer choices are given below each sentence. Select the best answer to complete the sentence. Then mark the letter (A), (B), (C), or (D) on your answer sheet.

101. The Sandville Community Center received ------- of art supplies.

(A) donating
(B) donated
(C) donations
(D) donate

102. The sales associates often ------- potential client accounts at the weekly meeting.

(A) discusses
(B) discuss
(C) discussion
(D) discussing

103. Ravelia Hotels is building a hotel ------- Wingate Mall.

(A) up to
(B) since
(C) next to
(D) throughout

104. Starting this Thursday, all Tenacore employees will be required to wear ------- official uniforms.

(A) their
(B) themselves
(C) they
(D) them

105. Mr. Kwon ------- guided the proposal through the difficult approval process.

(A) skillful
(B) skilled
(C) skill
(D) skillfully

106. The Standbridge Company ------- its staff to work remotely one or two days each week.

(A) understands
(B) participates
(C) encourages
(D) remembers

107. Please arrive ten minutes before your appointment to allow enough ------- to fill out some paperwork.

(A) time
(B) staff
(C) seats
(D) funds

108. ------- you have any questions about the updated contract, please contact Human Resources.

(A) If
(B) Though
(C) Either
(D) Beyond

109. The printed ------- for the upcoming musical are kept in the theater director's office.

(A) advertisements
(B) advertises
(C) advertised
(D) advertise

110. Laboratory chemicals should be stored no ------- than eye level and never on top of a tall cabinet.

(A) upper
(B) further
(C) longer
(D) higher

111. According to Reilly's vehicle fleet manager, ------- company delivery vans will be serviced in August.

(A) much
(B) total
(C) all
(D) highly

112. Because airlines ------- revise baggage-check policies, passengers should check for updates before a flight.

(A) occasion
(B) occasional
(C) occasions
(D) occasionally

113. Contracts for the Queen's Landing project should be placed in an ------- stack on the supervisor's desk.

(A) organize
(B) organizer
(C) organized
(D) organizing

114. Some board members ------- that Mr. Saito's sales forecasts are too optimistic.

(A) need
(B) pause
(C) refuse
(D) suspect

115. Ms. Koffler is confident ------- the new manager will improve the department's productivity.

(A) in
(B) well
(C) that
(D) both

116. The wooden barn on the Eastwood property is so ------- deteriorated that it is unlikely to be salvaged.

(A) formerly
(B) badly
(C) briefly
(D) exactly

117. Roseville Resort is offering discounted accommodations ------- its first month of operation.

(A) during
(B) among
(C) in front of
(D) away from

118. Although the look of the new mobile phone model is ------- the previous one, the call quality is much improved.

(A) similar to
(B) involved in
(C) happy with
(D) occupied by

119. Dr. Simone Beaumont ------- to head of Research and Development at Brodeur Technology last week.

(A) promoted
(B) was promoted
(C) promotes
(D) is promoting

120. Enertek Industries is developing an ------- safe method for refining lithium.

(A) environmentalist
(B) environments
(C) environmental
(D) environmentally

GO ON TO THE NEXT PAGE

TEST 7

121. Before starting the motor, make sure the brake is -------.

(A) engage
(B) engages
(C) engagement
(D) engaged

122. Henderson Technical College offers introductory computer ------- for free to community members.

(A) purchases
(B) lessons
(C) graphics
(D) users

123. No fees will be charged for the time the agency ------- to search for records.

(A) looks
(B) examines
(C) takes
(D) inspects

124. The Durand Concert Hall, ------- was built 80 years ago, has undergone a complete renovation.

(A) where
(B) each
(C) there
(D) which

125. There may be flaws in the computer code that we are not ------- aware of.

(A) yet
(B) soon
(C) far
(D) lately

126. ------- who wishes to make a monetary gift to the Voltra Museum should fill out the form at the back of the brochure.

(A) Anyone
(B) Whichever
(C) Each other
(D) Those

127. Companies that seek a stable workforce should focus on employee ------- as well as recruitment.

(A) agents
(B) coverage
(C) retention
(D) authentication

128. ------- a new user-friendly interface on its Web site, the Kramer-Lee Company reported improved customer satisfaction.

(A) Furthermore
(B) Owing to
(C) Subsequently
(D) At one time

129. Chef Wingert is reluctant to open a second location of Antoine's Pizza ------- interest from many of his customers.

(A) overall
(B) in addition to
(C) despite
(D) on the whole

130. ------- thinking by Ms. Blakely's marketing team helped increase sales of the Mindi motorcycle.

(A) Relative
(B) Potential
(C) Distant
(D) Creative

PART 6

Directions: Read the texts that follow. A word, phrase, or sentence is missing in parts of each text. Four answer choices for each question are given below the text. Select the best answer to complete the text. Then mark the letter (A), (B), (C), or (D) on your answer sheet.

Questions 131-134 refer to the following Web page.

Slipcovers

Glen and Meadows Home Goods now sells a variety of practical covers ------- your chairs and
         131.
sofas. Our slipcovers are available in a wide selection of sizes and colors. We have many

options for your most heavily used ------- . There are many beautiful stain-resistant fabrics to
                                    132.
choose from. ------- . If the use of synthetic materials is a concern, you can select from our
              133.
Naturals Collection. Whatever your interior design plans, you can ------- change the look of any
                                                                    134.
room with Glen and Meadows slipcovers.

131. (A) protect
     (B) to protect
     (C) are protecting
     (D) protected

132. (A) furniture
     (B) systems
     (C) appliances
     (D) routes

133. (A) They do not hold up well with
         frequent use.
     (B) They are no longer available on our
         online store.
     (C) And we are adding more options
         every week.
     (D) We find them fun and easy to wear.

134. (A) quicken
     (B) quickly
     (C) quicker
     (D) quick

GO ON TO THE NEXT PAGE

Questions 135-138 refer to the following e-mail.

To: All Staff <staff@kelseytech.co.uk>
From: Kosei Masutani <kmasutani@kelseytech.co.uk>
Subject: Information
Date: 26 January

Some of you may have felt a bit ------- while sitting at your desk this morning. That's because
                                135.
one of the heating units in our building is broken. Unfortunately, the repair crew cannot come to

fix the problem until Thursday. The open office space on the lower level is the most affected

area, with only some heat. Our interns are ------- there, so they will be assigned temporary office
                                         136.
spaces on other floors. ------- , upon arrival tomorrow morning, interns will need to check in with
                        137.
Ms. Connor to receive their alternative work-space assignments. ------- . In the meantime, be
                                                               138.
assured we will ensure everyone's safety and resolve this quickly.

Kosei Masutani, Facilities Manager

135. (A) uncomfortable
     (B) lonely
     (C) prompt
     (D) overwhelmed

136. (A) a location
     (B) to locate
     (C) locating
     (D) located

137. (A) However
     (B) Likewise
     (C) Consequently
     (D) Otherwise

138. (A) The interns will not arrive here until
         June.
     (B) I apologize for the inconvenience.
     (C) We will soon be renovating the open
         office space.
     (D) Heater maintenance is sometimes
         costly.

Southerby Designs

Southerby Designs is the leading firm in designing retail spaces and product displays in the greater Chennington area. For nearly three decades, Southerby Designs has collaborated with countless stores, ------- beautiful designs for their retail spaces. We have ------- worked with
                                                     139.   **140.**
several museums and event production companies to create captivating, streamlined, and inviting visitor experiences. ------- designing retail displays to completing projects for leading cultural
                                          141.
institutions, Southerby Designs can partner with your organization to develop the perfect design solution to fit your needs. ------- . We are confident that we can develop a solution to help you!
                                                  142.

139. (A) produced
     (B) have produced
     (C) was producing
     (D) producing

140. (A) even
     (B) instead
     (C) therefore
     (D) nevertheless

141. (A) By
     (B) Over
     (C) After
     (D) From

142. (A) We worked with a large portfolio of
         designers and artists at that time.
     (B) Contact us today and let us know what
         design challenges you are facing.
     (C) In fact, we raised our rates for the first
         time last year.
     (D) In contrast, our business has grown
         substantially over the past ten years.

TEST 7

Questions 143-146 refer to the following Web page.

Central Train Service makes it ------ than ever to give the gift of travel. Our gift cards are the
                                        143.
perfect way to give someone special an unforgettable journey. Traveling by train can provide

passengers with a worry-free experience. ------- . Enjoy visiting amazing cities and beautiful
                                               144.
national parks.

Central Train Service gift cards never ------- . They can be redeemed online or at any major train
                                            145.
station. Cards can be purchased in amounts up to $500. There are no additional ------- . The full
                                                                                     146.
value of the gift card can be applied to any ticket purchase.

143. (A) easily
     (B) easier
     (C) easy
     (D) ease

144. (A) The tourists often visit Paris and London.
     (B) There are several ways to change your
         seat selection.
     (C) Travelers are free to relax and enjoy the
         adventure.
     (D) Passengers must travel with personal
         identification.

145. (A) expire
     (B) expiring
     (C) expired
     (D) expiration

146. (A) comments
     (B) instructions
     (C) dates
     (D) fees

PART 7

Directions: In this part you will read a selection of texts, such as magazine and newspaper articles, e-mails, and instant messages. Each text or set of texts is followed by several questions. Select the best answer for each question and mark the letter (A), (B), (C), or (D) on your answer sheet.

Questions 147-148 refer to the following Web page.

https://www.aci.com/childrens-oral-care/availableoptions			
Available Options	Toothbrushes	Mouthwash	Other Products

Artemis Consolidated Industries (ACI) is the country's leading manufacturer of a range of oral hygiene products for children and adults. Among our best sellers is Oraglitz, the nation's most popular children's toothpaste. It has won various industry awards, including the Product Excellence Prize. In addition to being available on this Web site, Oraglitz can also be purchased at supermarkets, pharmacies, and health food stores nationwide.

Some Basic Facts About Oraglitz

Flavor	Designed for Ages	Size
Peach	18 months to 3 years	5 and 6 ounce
Strawberry	3 to 4 years	4, 5, and 6 ounce
Vanilla	4 to 7 years	4 and 5 ounce
Mint	7 years and up	4 and 6 ounce

147. What is NOT stated about Oraglitz?

(A) It is widely available.
(B) It comes in three sizes.
(C) It has seen an increase in sales recently.
(D) It is highly regarded within the industry.

148. What flavor of Oraglitz is best for an eight-year-old child?

(A) Peach
(B) Strawberry
(C) Vanilla
(D) Mint

GO ON TO THE NEXT PAGE

```
*E-mail*
```

To:	Parsons Road Distribution List
From:	Alfredo Moreno
Date:	October 12
Subject:	Parsons Road

Dear Parsons Road Businesses:

Beginning in March, Parsons Road will be widened between Memorial Boulevard and Hallam Road. The project will add a center turn lane, bicycle paths, pedestrian paths, and streetlights. In addition, a side gutter will be added to improve water flow.

The Parsons Road project ties into work completed between Hallam Road and Ingraham Avenue earlier this year. This work will improve access to your businesses and increase pedestrian safety on Parsons Road, which can be quite busy. The roadwork is expected to take three months to complete. Please visit www.yorkcity.gov/parsonsroadproject for more information.

Sincerely,

Alfredo Moreno
Community Relations Manager
Bethany Construction and Engineering

149. What is the purpose of the e-mail?

(A) To inform local companies about upcoming construction
(B) To request feedback on a road-improvement plan
(C) To advise businesses about a new traffic light
(D) To ask for help in distributing information

150. What is indicated about the Parsons Road project?

(A) It was delayed three times.
(B) It requires additional funding.
(C) It is expected to begin on October 12.
(D) It will make walking near the road safer.

Questions 151-152 refer to the following text-message chain.

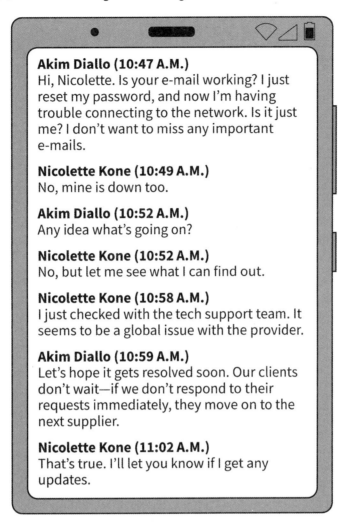

Akim Diallo (10:47 A.M.)
Hi, Nicolette. Is your e-mail working? I just reset my password, and now I'm having trouble connecting to the network. Is it just me? I don't want to miss any important e-mails.

Nicolette Kone (10:49 A.M.)
No, mine is down too.

Akim Diallo (10:52 A.M.)
Any idea what's going on?

Nicolette Kone (10:52 A.M.)
No, but let me see what I can find out.

Nicolette Kone (10:58 A.M.)
I just checked with the tech support team. It seems to be a global issue with the provider.

Akim Diallo (10:59 A.M.)
Let's hope it gets resolved soon. Our clients don't wait—if we don't respond to their requests immediately, they move on to the next supplier.

Nicolette Kone (11:02 A.M.)
That's true. I'll let you know if I get any updates.

151. What is Mr. Diallo unable to do?

(A) Access his e-mail account
(B) Locate his Internet provider
(C) Update his résumé information
(D) Contact the tech support team

152. At 11:02 A.M., what does Ms. Kone most likely mean when she writes, "That's true"?

(A) She feels that the supplier makes unreasonable requests.
(B) She understands that customers can be impatient.
(C) She thinks her company needs a new service provider.
(D) She expects to receive a status update soon.

GO ON TO THE NEXT PAGE

Questions 153-154 refer to the following sign.

Attention!

Some park visitors have been intentionally stacking piles of rocks as an art form or for amusement. Please refrain from doing this on park grounds, as these unofficial rock stacks can disrupt sensitive habitats and affect the area's natural beauty.

New rock piles can also endanger hikers who traditionally rely on stacked rock markers as navigational tools. Park officials are the only ones who should be stacking rocks, and they do so strategically on trails where the path may be unclear. If you see rocks that have been stacked, please leave them alone, and do not create confusion by making your own stack.

---

153. What is the purpose of the sign?

(A) To describe a historic monument
(B) To warn hikers about dangerous trails
(C) To change a behavior of visitors
(D) To ask for help with a building project

154. According to the sign, what do park officials do?

(A) They coordinate group activities.
(B) They create directional markers.
(C) They issue resource permits.
(D) They grant access to a scenic overlook.

Questions 155-157 refer to the following article.

Orinti Explains Web Site Updates

SAN DIEGO (May 2)—Orinti, Inc., one of North America's largest purveyors of tea, recently added a page to its Web site, listing the sources of all the tea leaves that end up in its final products. The page was created in response to recent public scrutiny over whether the company is justified in claiming that its tea is pesticide-free.

"The rumors being circulated do not reflect reality," Orinti CEO Giovanni Shaw said in a public statement issued on Tuesday. "We procure tea leaves only from producers who meet our strict quality standards. We never settle for anything less."

According to Mr. Shaw, the company also utilizes software that tracks the producer, the processing date, and other pertinent data for each batch of tea leaves.

"This level of detail is not displayed on our packaging for the simple reason that we do not have the space for it," said Mr. Shaw. "As we are committed to transparency, this information can be viewed on our Web site."

The popular blog foodnews.org was the first to call into question Orinti's assertion that its tea leaves are grown without the use of pesticides. The issue has since attracted national attention.

155. What does the company's new Web page display?

(A) The origin of its ingredients
(B) The steps in a production process
(C) The results of some product testing
(D) The process for evaluating new vendors

156. Why did Mr. Shaw issue a public statement?

(A) To announce a policy change
(B) To apologize for an oversight
(C) To correct some misinformation
(D) To reveal a new regional partner

157. What does the article suggest about Orinti, Inc.?

(A) It is considering some packaging alternatives.
(B) It is changing its leadership team.
(C) It wants to keep its recipes confidential.
(D) It gets information from an electronic tracking system.

GO ON TO THE NEXT PAGE

Questions 158-160 refer to the following notice.

Learn about Woodworking

Multonia Hardware, Inc., is offering an online video course about basic woodworking. — [1] —. The course is fun and can be completed at your own pace, and, best of all, it's free! It is divided into four prerecorded sections. — [2] —. Section 1 is an introduction to woodworking equipment, tools, and safety. — [3] —. Section 2 describes various types of wood and their appropriate uses. Section 3 introduces the fundamentals of cabinet and furniture repair. — [4] —. The final section describes the preparation of wood surfaces and a variety of popular and beautiful finishing techniques.

The course includes a downloadable instruction guide and an online chat feature that can connect participants with an experienced woodworking artisan. Sign up today at multoniahardware.com/tips/basicwoodworking.

---

158. What section most likely covers how to choose wood for a project?

(A) Section 1
(B) Section 2
(C) Section 3
(D) Section 4

159. According to the notice, how can participants find help while taking the course?

(A) By buying a textbook from Multonia Hardware
(B) By reaching out to other course participants
(C) By visiting a Multonia Hardware location
(D) By contacting an expert through the Web site

160. In which of the positions marked [1], [2], [3], and [4] does the following sentence best belong?

"Participants may take and retake as many of the sections as they wish."

(A) [1]
(B) [2]
(C) [3]
(D) [4]

Questions 161-164 refer to the following e-mail.

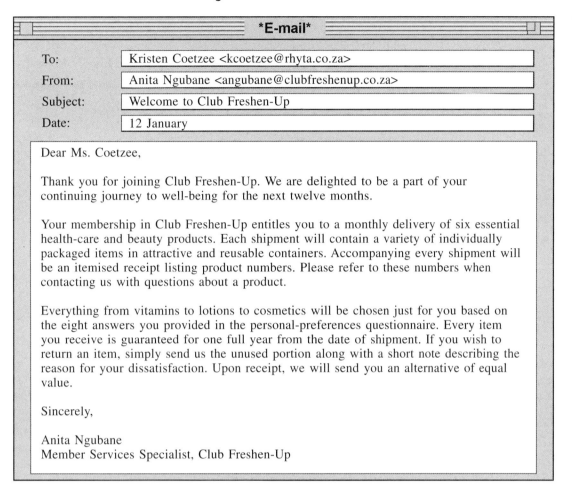

E-mail

To:	Kristen Coetzee <kcoetzee@rhyta.co.za>
From:	Anita Ngubane <angubane@clubfreshenup.co.za>
Subject:	Welcome to Club Freshen-Up
Date:	12 January

Dear Ms. Coetzee,

Thank you for joining Club Freshen-Up. We are delighted to be a part of your continuing journey to well-being for the next twelve months.

Your membership in Club Freshen-Up entitles you to a monthly delivery of six essential health-care and beauty products. Each shipment will contain a variety of individually packaged items in attractive and reusable containers. Accompanying every shipment will be an itemised receipt listing product numbers. Please refer to these numbers when contacting us with questions about a product.

Everything from vitamins to lotions to cosmetics will be chosen just for you based on the eight answers you provided in the personal-preferences questionnaire. Every item you receive is guaranteed for one full year from the date of shipment. If you wish to return an item, simply send us the unused portion along with a short note describing the reason for your dissatisfaction. Upon receipt, we will send you an alternative of equal value.

Sincerely,

Anita Ngubane
Member Services Specialist, Club Freshen-Up

161. What will a Club Freshen-Up subscriber receive every month?

(A) Vegetarian cooking ingredients
(B) Fitness training equipment
(C) Household cleaning supplies
(D) Personal care merchandise

162. What does Club Freshen-Up offer its customers?

(A) Monthly consultations
(B) Free shipping
(C) A product guarantee
(D) A print catalog

163. According to the e-mail, what should accompany every product return?

(A) The original shipping material
(B) A written explanation
(C) A copy of the receipt
(D) The preferences questionnaire

164. What will Club Freshen-Up do when it receives a product return?

(A) Provide the customer with a discount on a future membership fee
(B) Refund the purchase price
(C) Replace the item with another product
(D) Increase the number of products included in a future shipment

GO ON TO THE NEXT PAGE

Questions 165-167 refer to the following letter.

9 September

Soraya Delgado
Carrer de Bergara, 2, 08139
Sant Cugat del Valles
Barcelona, Spain

Dear Ms. Delgado,

I am writing to notify you that the board of directors has selected you to receive the Ondae Award for Leadership for the Mediterranean region. Your contributions to Allegrino Travel Agency helped place our company on the radar this year. Due to your relentless work, your direction of the "Find a New Way" marketing initiative, and your strategic development and placement of advertising, our travel agency is now one of the most recognized brands in Europe.

The award ceremony will be held at the next shareholders' meeting of Allegrino Travel Agency in Copenhagen on 19 November. I would like to ask you to consider being a featured speaker at the meeting in addition to accepting your award. I believe your insights into boosting market share and finding new ways to reframe our services would be incredibly valuable for shareholders and other employees to hear. Of course, all the expenses associated with your travel to Copenhagen would be covered by the company. Please let me know whether you will be available to accept your award and speak about your recent initiatives.

Sincerely,

Noor Darwish

Noor Darwish, CEO
Allegrino Travel Agency

165. What is indicated about Ms. Delgado's work?

(A) It has increased public awareness of her company.
(B) It involves evaluating contributions made by employees.
(C) It includes collecting feedback from consumer surveys.
(D) It was instrumental in launching a new award.

166. What is Ms. Delgado asked to do?

(A) Share her travel arrangements
(B) Present an award to a colleague
(C) Consider becoming a shareholder
(D) Give a speech at a company meeting

167. The word "covered" in paragraph 2, line 7, is closest in meaning to

(A) paid
(B) hidden
(C) insured
(D) guarded

Questions 168-171 refer to the following text-message chain.

Vincent Benedict (9:45 A.M.) Hello. I was given your contact information by my neighbor, Ms. Ryan. You did some work in her home yesterday. I was wondering if you would be able to move a power outlet in my house.

Matt Clayton (9:55 A.M.) We can help with that. Where is the outlet? By the way, I'm adding my business partner, Denise Bosworth, to this message.

Vincent Benedict (9:57 A.M.) It's in my living room, near the floor. I want to move it up. I am going to have a television screen mounted on my wall, and it will look ugly if there are cords hanging down to the outlet.

Matt Clayton (10:00 A.M.) OK. We can do this type of work for you.

Vincent Benedict (10:02 A.M.) How much would something like that cost?

Matt Clayton (10:03 A.M.) That will probably be between one and two hours of labor. We charge $50 per hour.

Denise Bosworth (10:05 A.M.) However, we might find pipes, insulation, or other wiring in the wall once we open it.

Vincent Benedict (10:08 A.M.) I understand. Thank you for the information. Are you available to come out and see what needs to be done?

Matt Clayton (10:12 A.M.) I will have someone from our office get in touch with you by phone to schedule a visit.

168. Why did Mr. Benedict contact Mr. Clayton?

(A) To apply for a job
(B) To request a service
(C) To complain about a repair
(D) To welcome a new neighbor

169. What most likely is Mr. Clayton's job?

(A) Electrician
(B) Inspector
(C) Plumber
(D) Salesperson

170. At 10:08 A.M., what does Mr. Benedict most likely mean when he writes, "I understand"?

(A) He will reschedule a visit.
(B) He will follow up with Ms. Bosworth.
(C) He knows that the final cost may vary from the estimate.
(D) He knows what materials need to be purchased.

171. What should Mr. Benedict expect next?

(A) Delivery of a television
(B) Removal of some wires
(C) A call from Mr. Clayton's office
(D) An invoice for completed work

GO ON TO THE NEXT PAGE

Questions 172-175 refer to the following e-mail.

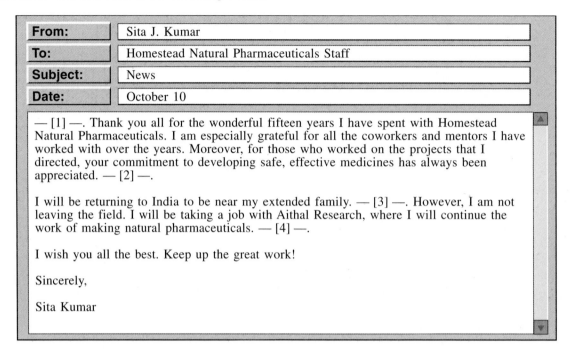

From: Sita J. Kumar

To: Homestead Natural Pharmaceuticals Staff

Subject: News

Date: October 10

— [1] —. Thank you all for the wonderful fifteen years I have spent with Homestead Natural Pharmaceuticals. I am especially grateful for all the coworkers and mentors I have worked with over the years. Moreover, for those who worked on the projects that I directed, your commitment to developing safe, effective medicines has always been appreciated. — [2] —.

I will be returning to India to be near my extended family. — [3] —. However, I am not leaving the field. I will be taking a job with Aithal Research, where I will continue the work of making natural pharmaceuticals. — [4] —.

I wish you all the best. Keep up the great work!

Sincerely,

Sita Kumar

172. What is one purpose of the e-mail?

 (A) To request a job transfer
 (B) To describe some pharmaceutical products
 (C) To ask for help with a new project
 (D) To announce a decision to colleagues

173. What most likely is Ms. Kumar's position at Homestead Natural Pharmaceuticals?

 (A) Accountant
 (B) Project manager
 (C) Chief executive officer
 (D) Administrative assistant

174. What is indicated about Ms. Kumar?

 (A) She is retiring from work.
 (B) She has started her own company.
 (C) She is relocating to be closer to her relatives.
 (D) She completed an internship at Aithal Research.

175. In which of the positions marked [1], [2], [3], and [4] does the following sentence best belong?

"I am proud that, together, we have made positive advances in our industry."

 (A) [1]
 (B) [2]
 (C) [3]
 (D) [4]

GO ON TO THE NEXT PAGE

In the Kitchen
Reviewed by Peter Gottlieb

Qi Chien understands how restaurants work. Her new book, *In the Kitchen: How to Thrive in the Restaurant Business*, expertly advises restaurant managers on handling challenges in the industry, from creating reasonable schedules for chefs to appeasing picky diners. Throughout the book, Chien offers concise, practical suggestions with easy-to-understand concepts. Overall, the book offers a colorful snapshot of the various tasks involved in the day-to-day operations of a restaurant.

Chien's book is unique among other industry guides in that she interviewed restaurant owners, managers, and customers as part of her research. She even spoke to journalists who write restaurant reviews to get a good sense of what they most prize in a dining experience. My only criticism is that the book should have also included the perspective of chefs, especially since their role is crucial to a restaurant's success. This caveat aside, *In the Kitchen* is an insightful and instructive read.

To:	editor@lakecountyherald.com
From:	qichien@rapidonline.com
Date:	August 5
Subject:	*In the Kitchen*

To the Editor:

I was delighted to read Peter Gottlieb's review of my latest book, *In the Kitchen,* in your newspaper. I have appreciated his thoughtful comments about my works over the years, even if they are sometimes negative. In this case, I was especially glad that he liked the chapter about restaurant reviewers, since initially I had been reluctant to interview journalists for the book. It is true that I could have included a greater variety of insights, but unfortunately the people whose views he most wanted to hear were just too busy to speak with me before the publishing deadline. Perhaps this is something I can address in an updated edition of the book.

Qi Chien

176. What is the focus of Ms. Chien's book?

(A) How to properly train chefs
(B) How to develop recipes
(C) How to manage a restaurant
(D) How to write an engaging story

177. What does Mr. Gottlieb indicate about Ms. Chien's writing?

(A) It is informative.
(B) It is outdated.
(C) It is imaginative.
(D) It is well organized.

178. In the review, the word "sense" in paragraph 2, line 3, is closest in meaning to

(A) intelligence
(B) idea
(C) chance
(D) direction

179. What is suggested about Mr. Gottlieb in the e-mail?

(A) He has worked at the same company as Ms. Chien.
(B) He met Ms. Chien at a restaurant industry conference.
(C) He was interviewed by Ms. Chien for one of her books.
(D) He has reviewed other books written by Ms. Chien.

180. What group of people was Ms. Chien unable to speak to before her deadline?

(A) Chefs
(B) Diners
(C) Journalists
(D) Restaurant owners

GO ON TO THE NEXT PAGE

Questions 181-185 refer to the following e-mail and text message.

To:	Harriet Trimble <htrimble@decobusinessdesign.com>
From:	Karl Vinton <karl.vinton@vintapparel.com>
Date:	May 26
Subject:	Layout for Vint Apparel store
Attachment:	 Store layout

Hello, Harriet,

I am delighted you are available for this latest project; we were very pleased with your previous work. Here are some general instructions to start.

On the back wall, hang the Vint Apparel neon sign high enough to be seen over other furniture in the store. The sign has already shipped and should be delivered next Monday.

The rectangular light fixtures will also arrive on Monday. There should be four—two for each of the side walls. The racks and shelving to display clothing are already there. Please place the three circular racks in the center of the store and put the two shelving units along the left side as you enter the store. Finally, place the cashier station to the right as you enter the store.

I have attached a drawing of the layout that includes more detail.

Regards,

Karl Vinton, Owner

Harriet Trimble [8:05 A.M.]
I stopped by the Vint Apparel job site. We will have to put everything in place by June 15 because the grand opening is fast approaching. Mr. Vinton stressed that they need to start stocking merchandise the week of June 20 to be ready for the official event on July 1.

Jackson Ortega [8:06 A.M.]
We can do that.

Harriet Trimble [8:07 A.M.]
Also, there has been a change to the layout drawing. Now we are to install a mannequin display where the two shelving units were and then move the shelving units to the side walls. I will bring an updated copy for you when I come over this afternoon.

181. What does Mr. Vinton suggest in the e-mail?

(A) He has worked with Ms. Trimble before.
(B) A neon sign has already been delivered to Vint Apparel's new location.
(C) He plans to inspect the store on Monday.
(D) Vint Apparel's new location is in a shopping center.

182. According to the e-mail, how many rectangular light fixtures will be delivered?

(A) One
(B) Two
(C) Three
(D) Four

183. Where will the mannequin display be installed?

(A) Against the back wall
(B) In the center of the store
(C) To the left of the entrance
(D) To the right of the cashier station

184. What does Ms. Trimble suggest is the date of the new Vint Apparel location's grand opening?

(A) May 26
(B) June 15
(C) June 20
(D) July 1

185. What will Ms. Trimble do with the updated layout drawing?

(A) She will hang it in her office.
(B) She will review it with Mr. Vinton.
(C) She will take it to Mr. Ortega.
(D) She will mail it to Vint Apparel.

GO ON TO THE NEXT PAGE

Foursquare Housing offers corporate housing with apartment units in the greater Miltonville area. The apartments are fully furnished and include wireless Internet service. Floor plans and photos of apartment interiors can be viewed online.

Center Tower
Located in downtown Miltonville, the ten-story building has shops on the ground level. Center Tower is on the southwest corner of Beeman Square, features a rooftop garden, and is close to public transportation.

Angora Plaza
Located near downtown Miltonville, the building has a self-service laundromat and a large parking garage. It is also close to two subway stations.

Regent Apartments
Located approximately six miles outside of Miltonville, the building features an on-site business center and is within walking distance of public transportation.

Cityview Gardens
Cityview Gardens is a complex of four two-story buildings located in Dayton, about a twenty-minute drive from downtown Miltonville. The property boasts a fitness center and a swimming pool and is adjacent to a community park. A bus line operates a route through the neighborhood.

From:	gsteuber@wardertechnology.com
To:	info@foursquarehousing.com
Date:	July 12
Subject:	Inquiry

Foursquare Housing,

I work in the human resources office of Warder Technology's Miltonville division. We are seeking an apartment that can be used by employees from outside the area who will work at our headquarters temporarily.

We need an apartment for employees who will be in Miltonville for two months or more. The apartment should have amenities like a gym and a pool.

Sincerely,

Gina Steuber

From:	info@foursquarehousing.com
To:	gsteuber@wardertechnology.com
Date:	July 12
Subject:	Information you requested
Attachment:	📎 Pricing_ Leases.pdf

Dear Ms. Steuber,

Thank you for your interest in Foursquare Housing. We have a two-bedroom apartment that will be available on August 15 that should meet your requirements. I have attached a price list for this unit and our other apartments as well. If you agree that this meets your needs, I can send a contract.

I should point out that your corporate headquarters in Beeman Square is next to apartments owned by Foursquare. One apartment here will also become available in August. This would be very convenient if you have short-term visitors.

Sincerely,

Sam Flannery
Leasing Agent

186. What is true about all of the apartments listed on the Web site?

(A) They are in downtown Miltonville.
(B) They are near public transportation.
(C) They have swimming pools.
(D) They are in high-rise buildings.

187. What apartment would best fit the requirements mentioned by Ms. Steuber?

(A) Center Tower
(B) Angora Plaza
(C) Regent Apartments
(D) Cityview Gardens

188. According to Mr. Flannery, what will happen in August?

(A) Two apartments will become available.
(B) Foursquare Housing will purchase a new building.
(C) Warder Technology will reach the end of its lease.
(D) An apartment building will be renovated.

189. What does Mr. Flannery offer to send Ms. Steuber?

(A) A map of Miltonville
(B) A rental contract
(C) Photos of apartments
(D) Resident reviews of properties

190. What does Mr. Flannery suggest about Warder Technology's corporate headquarters?

(A) It is a twenty-minute drive from Miltonville.
(B) It is next to the Center Tower building.
(C) It is on the same road as the Regent Apartments.
(D) It has a large parking garage.

GO ON TO THE NEXT PAGE

To:	Everlast Hospital Nursing Staff
From:	Gretchen Robertson
Date:	February 3
Subject:	Deonardo pilot testing

Thank you for agreeing to work with the team at Cybernetic Robotics as they tested their new robot, Deonardo, in our hospital. As you know, Deonardo was developed to allow you, our nursing staff, more time to focus on patients. This is exciting work.

It has been a month, and Cybernetic Robotics would like to hear about your experiences with Deonardo. Please use the following link to complete an online survey. The team especially wants to know about your experiences with Deonardo during the state reviewers' inspection on January 28. At the end of the survey, you may leave any additional comments you have about the robot.

www.cyberneticrobotics.com/survey/everlast/

Best regards,

Gretchen Robertson
Director, Everlast Hospital

---

https://www.cyberneticrobotics.com/survey/everlast/01282

Deonardo is easy to work with. I like that I don't have to tell Deonardo directly what to do. When I update patient information in our system, Deonardo's tasks are updated as well. I have been better able to concentrate on my patients because I know Deonardo takes care of little things that used to take up so much of my time. Deonardo was particularly helpful during a recent state review because it delivered patients' medications for all the nurses so that we didn't have to, and we were able to focus on patient care. I believe Deonardo helped us receive positive comments from the inspectors.

I do wish Deonardo could respond to voice commands. And occasionally, its wheels squeak as it moves around. But patients like watching it work, and everyone wants to take pictures with it. I wonder if you could get Deonardo to stand still for pictures?

Lan Duy, BSN

To:	Everlast Hospital Nursing Staff
From:	Gretchen Robertson
Date:	February 13
Subject:	Deonardo in-house pilot

Thank you all for your help with Deonardo, our nursing robot. I'm glad that our staff has been able to take part in such groundbreaking work.

Those of you who work directly with Deonardo can expect it to behave a bit differently in the coming week. It will be programmed to perform some new tasks. Previously, it waited at the nurse's station between tasks. Now, it will spend some of this time interacting with patients who may want to pose for pictures with it. When Deonardo is in this socializing mode, the eyes on its LED face will be heart-shaped instead of the round eyes that indicate that it is in work mode.

Finally, the hospital will be purchasing two additional robots in the next few months to work in other areas of the hospital. I appreciate your willingness to work with this new technology. We look forward to learning how robots can further improve employee and patient experiences.

Sincerely,

Gretchen Robertson
Director, Everlast Hospital

191. What is the purpose of the first e-mail?

(A) To describe an upcoming inspection
(B) To invite nurses to give feedback
(C) To announce an employment opportunity
(D) To request suggestions for naming a robot

192. What task did Deonardo perform on January 28?

(A) It analyzed patients' health data.
(B) It made copies of patients' records.
(C) It brought medications to patients.
(D) It played music to entertain patients.

193. In the second e-mail, what does Ms. Robertson indicate about Deonardo?

(A) It has a display that looks like a face.
(B) It works closely with doctors.
(C) It will begin serving patients their meals.
(D) It has a special charging base.

194. What suggestion from Ms. Duy did the robotics company most likely apply?

(A) The robot will now play games with patients.
(B) The robot will get quieter wheels.
(C) The robot will respond to voice commands.
(D) The robot will now be available for photographs with patients.

195. What does the hospital plan to do in the near future?

(A) Replace the robot
(B) Buy more robots
(C) Advertise its robot
(D) Repair the robot

GO ON TO THE NEXT PAGE

Questions 196-200 **Questions 196-200** refer to the following e-mail, advertisement, and online form.

```
╔══════════════════════════════════════════════════════════════════╗
║                              *E-mail*                              ║
╠══════════════════════════════════════════════════════════════════╣
```

To:	management_team@pfi.co.uk
From:	schakravarty@pfi.co.uk
Subject:	R&D Director Search
Date:	24 July
Attachment:	⫐ Files.txt

Dear Management Team Members,

On behalf of the hiring committee, I am pleased to report that the search for a new research and development director is nearing completion.

Given the key selection criteria the suitable candidate must meet—a demonstrated ability to improve product offerings, a keen awareness of consumers' tastes, and in-depth knowledge of nutritional science—we have narrowed the applicant pool to Alex Mooring and Inez Fuentes. While either makes for an excellent choice, I believe that Ms. Fuentes is better suited to the role. Though somewhat less experienced than Mr. Mooring, she has innovative ideas that are in line with our company's needs.

Attached are the résumés and references of the two candidates. The dates, times, and location of their final interviews will be forthcoming in another e-mail when that information is finalized. We look forward to your participation in these meetings as well as your final hiring decision.

Sincerely,

Supriya Chakravarty, Chair, Hiring Committee
Primidian Food Industries

Upcoming Events at Primidian Food Industries

On 7 October at 10 A.M., Ms. Inez Fuentes, director of research and development at Primidian Food Industries (PFI), will facilitate a workshop titled Food Innovation for the Future. Among other things, she will explain why PFI recently reformulated its pasta products and demonstrate how they can be prepared in novel, tasty ways.

Ms. Fuentes is a certified nutritionist with a degree in food science from Mexico City's Academy of Science and Technology. Upon graduation, she accepted a two-year internship at Italy's prestigious Rome Institute of Culinary Arts. Before joining PFI's executive team, she served for five years as lead product development manager at Zesty Meals, based in Montreal, Canada.

Register for this free event at www.pfi.co.uk/events/register, specifying whether you will attend online or in person at our corporate headquarters in Birmingham.

https://www.pfi.co.uk/contact-us			
Who We Are	Our Brands	News and Events	**Contact Us**

Please complete the form below so someone from our team can contact you.

Name: Chaim Auerbach

E-mail: chaim_auerbach@equisend.net.uk

Your Message:

I thoroughly enjoyed the Food Innovation for the Future workshop led by Ms. Fuentes on 28 October. I almost missed it, though. Apparently, when details about the workshop were updated, including that it would be an online-only event, my registration—and, I learned, that of some other participants—was not transferred over. Luckily, a staffer charged with online registration was able to quickly reregister me. PFI may want to analyse its electronic registration system and make improvements where necessary so that this problem does not reoccur.

196. Why did Ms. Chakravarty write the e-mail?

(A) To describe her work experience
(B) To propose a new line of products
(C) To provide information about some job applicants
(D) To offer feedback on a pending research project

197. According to the e-mail, what will Ms. Chakravarty send to committee members in the near future?

(A) An interview schedule
(B) A list of desired leadership skills
(C) An analysis of a consumer survey
(D) A collection of tips for revising résumés

198. What can be concluded about the management team?

(A) It agreed with Ms. Chakravarty's recommendation.
(B) It recently added more members.
(C) It updated the key selection criteria for a job in July.
(D) It contacted Mr. Mooring for references.

199. Based on the advertisement, where most likely does Ms. Fuentes currently live?

(A) In Rome
(B) In Montreal
(C) In Mexico City
(D) In Birmingham

200. What is suggested about the workshop?

(A) It was mainly an in-person event.
(B) It was held later than originally scheduled.
(C) It cost more than was budgeted.
(D) It had more participants than expected.

Stop! This is the end of the test. If you finish before time is called, you may go back to Parts 5, 6, and 7 and check your work.

토익 정기시험
실전 ❶ 1000
RC

실전 TEST
08

READING TEST

In the Reading test, you will read a variety of texts and answer several different types of reading comprehension questions. The entire Reading test will last 75 minutes. There are three parts, and directions are given for each part. You are encouraged to answer as many questions as possible within the time allowed.

You must mark your answers on the separate answer sheet. Do not write your answers in your test book.

PART 5

Directions: A word or phrase is missing in each of the sentences below. Four answer choices are given below each sentence. Select the best answer to complete the sentence. Then mark the letter (A), (B), (C), or (D) on your answer sheet.

101. The building contract was ------- awarded to Zhong Builders of Manchester.

(A) slowly
(B) exactly
(C) greatly
(D) recently

102. A small salad is included with the lunch special ------- Wednesday.

(A) as
(B) every
(C) eventually
(D) those

103. Mapsoar Airways redesigned its seats to make it much ------- to recline them.

(A) easy
(B) easily
(C) easier
(D) ease

104. Employees may visit the company cafeteria on weekday evenings ------- 8:00 P.M.

(A) since
(B) until
(C) along
(D) over

105. Mr. Yang sent one copy of his résumé but was asked to bring ------- to his interview.

(A) another
(B) anyone
(C) itself
(D) all

106. Once payment ------- are submitted, it takes several days for any corporate expenditures to be approved.

(A) offices
(B) debates
(C) delays
(D) requests

107. The Outsourced Kitchen Company's cross-back apron is ------- by chefs around the world.

(A) favor
(B) favorite
(C) favored
(D) favoring

108. Mr. Toskala was able to ------- an agreement with the supplier for lower-cost replacement parts.

(A) arrive
(B) reach
(C) call
(D) touch

109. Lucior Shoes saw a ------- in expenses after adjusting its production processes.

(A) drop
(B) drops
(C) dropped
(D) to drop

110. Ms. Easley was asked to limit ------- to two 10-minute breaks per day.

(A) their
(B) she
(C) herself
(D) they

111. Since the Orchid Ridge Hotel is in a remote area, the Web site includes a map and detailed -------.

(A) renovations
(B) directions
(C) settings
(D) appearances

112. Ms. Dolin ------- requested that order number 42 be hand delivered to avoid breakage.

(A) specific
(B) specify
(C) specifically
(D) specification

113. Gahee's Market is located ------- the northeast corner of Welsh Avenue and Zilla Drive.

(A) among
(B) at
(C) into
(D) to

114. ------- of Hamilton County are looking forward to the restored waterfront promenade.

(A) Residing
(B) Residents
(C) Resides
(D) Residential

115. The Wakeshuka Manufacturing Council is made up of regional factory leaders ------- help set industry standards.

(A) whichever
(B) whose
(C) who
(D) what

116. Inquiries regarding long-term advertising contracts should be ------- to Juan Mendes in the sales department.

(A) arranged
(B) prepared
(C) addressed
(D) obtained

117. Interns at Biocorps ------- participated in the collection and analysis of water samples from the city reservoir.

(A) tremendously
(B) exponentially
(C) severely
(D) eagerly

118. Mr. Melo argued that Vantimore's inventory tracking system is too -------.

(A) complexes
(B) complex
(C) complexity
(D) complexness

119. Years of experience in the industry is the most ------- factor in predicting one's success in a supervisory role.

(A) temporary
(B) valuable
(C) purposeful
(D) respective

120. Iron Nail Hardware sells a wide ------- of kitchen and bathroom fixtures.

(A) vary
(B) various
(C) variously
(D) variety

GO ON TO THE NEXT PAGE

121. The popular Zeni Flex athletic shoes are sold ------- at Sports Now Shops.

    (A) exclusively
    (B) eligibly
    (C) extremely
    (D) explicitly

122. The newest Pala's Pasta House operates as a delivery-only restaurant, ------- its older locations continue to offer dine-in service.

    (A) owing to
    (B) apart from
    (C) whereas
    (D) during

123. ------- three weeks of completing the training sessions, the factory workers' efficiency improved by 24 percent.

    (A) Within
    (B) Experiencing
    (C) Further
    (D) Considering

124. A portfolio of promising uniform designs was submitted to the client for -------.

    (A) evaluation
    (B) description
    (C) inscription
    (D) expectation

125. The sales representatives ------- samples of the company's latest medications to doctors' offices throughout the region.

    (A) to distribute
    (B) is distributing
    (C) will be distributing
    (D) have been distributed

126. Performing regular maintenance on your delivery vehicles will help prevent service disruptions and ------- emergency repairs.

    (A) annoyed
    (B) damaged
    (C) costly
    (D) steady

127. Despite past business failures, Mr. Bharati ------- and now runs a successful shipping operation.

    (A) persevered
    (B) acknowledged
    (C) determined
    (D) criticized

128. Mr. Chen spoke -------, and his material was very well organized.

    (A) distinct
    (B) distinctly
    (C) distinctive
    (D) distinction

129. Ms. Marcus is scheduled to arrive at City Station at 7:13 P.M. ------- her train is on time.

    (A) unless
    (B) in order to
    (C) provided that
    (D) as much as

130. In the report, the researchers described the methodology they used in ------- their conclusions.

    (A) formulating
    (B) formulate
    (C) formulated
    (D) being formulated

PART 6

Directions: Read the texts that follow. A word, phrase, or sentence is missing in parts of each text. Four answer choices for each question are given below the text. Select the best answer to complete the text. Then mark the letter (A), (B), (C), or (D) on your answer sheet.

Questions 131-134 refer to the following information.

Signs Press Plus is the region's oldest and most trusted sign ------- . Our company creates signs
131.

in many sizes and forms—banners, storefront signs, and even vehicle wraps. ------- . We use our
132.

------- experience to design signs that allow our customers' enterprises to stand out from the
133.

competition. We can help you get your business noticed! Call 575-555-0161 to ------- a consultation.
134.

131. (A) is made
(B) making
(C) to make
(D) maker

132. (A) Your order has been given prompt attention.
(B) We have been doing this for over 30 years.
(C) Some companies have delivery trucks.
(D) These clients include signs in their marketing plans.

133. (A) permanent
(B) rewarding
(C) extensive
(D) memorable

134. (A) cancel
(B) set up
(C) provide
(D) turn down

GO ON TO THE NEXT PAGE

Questions 135-138 refer to the following article.

Fill-Your-Cup Day Returns

COLUMBUS (June 16)—Nationwide convenience store chain Abel's Market is announcing the return of a well-known promotion not seen in three years. On June 22, customers

------- their own cups to participating Abel's Markets to receive half-price fountain drinks. The
135.

retailer urges creativity when defining a cup and posted a picture of a flower vase filled with

soda as an example on ------- social media account. ------- . Abel's Market encourages customers
136.   137.

to post pictures of their creative cups to their own social media accounts and to mention the

company in their posts.

Abel's Market has not stated whether Fill-Your-Cup Day will become an annual event as it

------- was.
138.

---

135. (A) brought
     (B) can bring
     (C) would bring
     (D) were bringing

136. (A) its
     (B) our
     (C) your
     (D) them

137. (A) The company has increased its online
         advertising budget.
     (B) Note that Abel's Market no longer
         provides vases.
     (C) Fill-Your-Cup Day was once a highly
         popular event.
     (D) Any container that fits under the store's
         soda machine may be used.

138. (A) smoothly
     (B) kindly
     (C) previously
     (D) constantly

Castak Recruiting: What We Do

Since we started our operations more than ten years ago, we have helped countless job

seekers find employment ------- our online listings of job openings. However, that is not all we
        139.

------- . We also help employers find the most qualified candidates to fill their vacant positions in
140.

the shortest amount of time possible. Most human resources directors who use Castak

Recruiting ------- hire new staff within two weeks of posting their job openings on our Web site.
     141.

Castak Recruiting's service for companies is subscription based and provides numerous

affordable and customizable plans. ------- .
        142.

139. (A) between
(B) versus
(C) over
(D) through

140. (A) offer
(B) assess
(C) suggest
(D) investigate

141. (A) successful
(B) successfully
(C) succeed
(D) success

142. (A) Fees vary based on each company's
usage requirements.
(B) Our database contains many similar
positions.
(C) We recommend that you personalize
your messages.
(D) We are excited to welcome you to the
area.

Questions 143-146 refer to the following information.

Medical and Research Space for Lease

Etoile Centre, in the city of Brussels, is an outstanding place to work. Its ideal location

------- on-site staff unbeatable access to public parks and local amenities. Etoile Centre's campus
143.

is also in close proximity to top medical and academic institutions. Consequently, tenants report

how easy it is to nurture collaborations with leading ------- who live and work in the area.
144.

------- , Etoile Centre's campus itself offers access to large conference rooms, several cafés, and
145.

two cafeterias. While Etoile Centre's North Tower is currently fully occupied, much of the

soon-to-be-opened South Tower is still available. ------- .
146.

---

143. (A) affords
 (B) afforded
 (C) had to afford
 (D) would be affording

144. (A) retailers
 (B) scientists
 (C) designers
 (D) chefs

145. (A) In contrast
 (B) As a result
 (C) On one hand
 (D) In addition

146. (A) However, hiring is down compared with
 last year.
 (B) Some companies are investing instead in
 the local economy.
 (C) Time is running out for these firms to join
 the program.
 (D) Construction is expected to finish in
 early October.

PART 7

Directions: In this part you will read a selection of texts, such as magazine and newspaper articles, e-mails, and instant messages. Each text or set of texts is followed by several questions. Select the best answer for each question and mark the letter (A), (B), (C), or (D) on your answer sheet.

Questions 147-148 refer to the following advertisement.

CALLA DANCE STUDIO IS NOW OPEN!

Come to our beautiful, spacious studio in Hopkins Bay for our grand opening on Saturday, March 5, and Sunday, March 6, from noon to 5:00 P.M.

During the celebration, you can

- mingle and chat with our highly trained instructors;

- enjoy fun, free, easygoing dance classes; and

- receive a 10 percent discount on one of our dance lesson packages.

We believe that everyone can benefit from dancing, so whether you are a beginner or an expert, we have a class for you!

Visit us online at www.calladancestudio.com for class descriptions, instructor profiles, directions to the studio, and more.

---

147. What is NOT listed as something visitors can do during the celebration?

(A) They can meet dance instructors.
(B) They can take a dance class.
(C) They can get a discount.
(D) They can purchase gift cards.

148. What is true about Calla Dance Studio?

(A) It has locations in multiple cities.
(B) It provides certification for dance instructors.
(C) It offers classes for a range of experience levels.
(D) Its grand opening will be held on a single day.

GO ON TO THE NEXT PAGE

Travel with Confidence—the Simple Trip Way!

Does your travel plan include taking one or more flights? Save time and avoid inconvenience with Simple Trip. Recommended by leading companies in the travel industry, the award-winning Simple Trip application allows Web check-in at the airport and keeps you up-to-date regarding local weather conditions and any changes to departure and arrival times. — [1] —.

Download Simple Trip from any app store onto your mobile phone. — [2] —. Simple Trip is completely secure, with multiple layers of encryption to keep your personal information hidden from hackers. Once your documentation has been successfully loaded into the app, Simple Trip provides you with digital passes that can be scanned at security checkpoints, check-in kiosks, and boarding gates. — [3] —.

Bypass the ticket counter and check in to your flight through the app. Stay up-to-date with the latest entry requirements at your destination. — [4] —. Make your journey a breeze with Simple Trip!

149. What is suggested about the Simple Trip application?

(A) An update for the app will be released soon.
(B) It is focused on air travel.
(C) It provides information only for major airports.
(D) Travel experts developed it.

150. What is a benefit of using Simple Trip?

(A) Secure user information
(B) Airline seating upgrades
(C) Discounts on airline fares
(D) Complimentary checked bags

151. In which of the positions marked [1], [2], [3], and [4] does the following sentence best belong?

"It will guide you through the steps to set up and personalize your account."

(A) [1]
(B) [2]
(C) [3]
(D) [4]

Questions 152-153 refer to the following text-message chain.

Manuel Cabrera [9:18 A.M.]
Hello, Sara. Our client Mr. Forsyth is changing his mind about the color scheme for his kitchen. Can you send me the photos from the Maroney project we completed last autumn?

Sara Baird [9:20 A.M.]
Sure. Do you want me to send just the kitchen pictures?

Manuel Cabrera [9:21 A.M.]
Send those of the kitchen and living room, please.

Sara Baird [9:22 A.M.]
They are on their way. I have also included pictures of the Thackers' kitchen from a couple of years ago. We created a similar style for them.

Manuel Cabrera [9:23 A.M.]
Good thinking. Thank you!

152. In what type of business do the writers most likely work?

(A) Interior decorating
(B) Fine dining
(C) Photography
(D) Appliance sales

153. At 9:23 A.M., what does Mr. Cabrera most likely mean when he writes, "Good thinking"?

(A) He expects that the additional pictures Ms. Baird sent will be helpful.
(B) He is certain that the client will like the new color scheme.
(C) He is impressed with the work Ms. Baird did on the Maroney project.
(D) He remembers how much the Thackers liked their kitchen.

GO ON TO THE NEXT PAGE

Questions 154-155 refer to the following notice.

Please Note

The views expressed by the speakers shown in this documentary film are their own and do not necessarily reflect the opinions of the filmmakers. The filmmakers' goal was to present the topic from diverse points of view. The inclusion of the speakers does not constitute an endorsement of their perspectives, nor does it imply the filmmakers' support for any organization that those speakers may represent.

154. What is the purpose of the notice?

(A) To generate enthusiasm for an upcoming film
(B) To express support for a charitable organization
(C) To apologize for some factual errors
(D) To discourage assumptions about the filmmakers

155. What does the notice suggest about the speakers in the film?

(A) They are members of the same organization.
(B) They will participate in follow-up interviews.
(C) They were all paid the same fee by the filmmakers.
(D) They expressed different opinions about a topic.

Centre Touts New Adventure

TORONTO (28 May)—The trustees of Toronto's Earth and Space Centre announced the opening of an exciting new educational film. The two-hour immersive experience called *Out of This World* explains through live footage, interviews, and first-rate animation what the next outer-space missions might involve with respect to both vehicles and people.

Out of This World will be presented on the Envelop system, which has been installed in the theatre and is now undergoing testing and fine-tuning. The system promises to delight the senses, not only through vivid visuals but also through superb, lifelike sound projected to the listeners from all sides.

Single-ticket prices for adults and special rates for youngsters, families, and school groups will be announced soon. The anticipated public debut for the programme is 1 July.

156. What is indicated about *Out of This World*?

(A) It requires a tour guide.
(B) It includes animated video.
(C) It will run for only one month.
(D) It is open only to school groups.

157. The word "projected" in paragraph 2, line 6, is closest in meaning to

(A) planned
(B) proposed
(C) calculated
(D) transmitted

158. What is mentioned about the Envelop system?

(A) It was expensive to build.
(B) It is used to record videos.
(C) It will be operational by July 1.
(D) It is currently being shipped to Toronto.

GO ON TO THE NEXT PAGE

Questions 159-160 refer to the following e-mail.

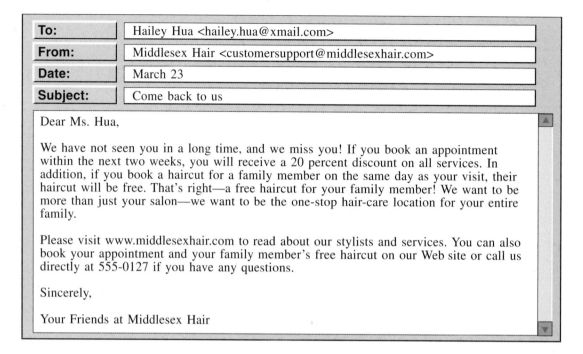

To:	Hailey Hua <hailey.hua@xmail.com>
From:	Middlesex Hair <customersupport@middlesexhair.com>
Date:	March 23
Subject:	Come back to us

Dear Ms. Hua,

We have not seen you in a long time, and we miss you! If you book an appointment within the next two weeks, you will receive a 20 percent discount on all services. In addition, if you book a haircut for a family member on the same day as your visit, their haircut will be free. That's right—a free haircut for your family member! We want to be more than just your salon—we want to be the one-stop hair-care location for your entire family.

Please visit www.middlesexhair.com to read about our stylists and services. You can also book your appointment and your family member's free haircut on our Web site or call us directly at 555-0127 if you have any questions.

Sincerely,

Your Friends at Middlesex Hair

159. How can Ms. Hua receive a 20 percent discount at Middlesex Hair?

(A) By presenting a coupon
(B) By referring new customers
(C) By booking more than one service
(D) By making an appointment within two weeks

160. What does the e-mail indicate that a member of Ms. Hua's family can receive?

(A) A photo posted on the salon's Web site
(B) The same offer as Ms. Hua's
(C) A haircut at no charge
(D) A tour of a new location

Rapido Airline Coming Soon to Encino Pass

ENCINO PASS (March 11)—Encino Pass Airport officials have announced that Rapido Airline will begin offering flights in and out of Encino Pass this summer. Rapido joins Gamma Air and Southern Skylines in serving the regional airport.

As the city of Encino Pass has grown in recent years, Encino Pass Airport has seen increased air traffic, despite being the smallest airport in the state. With flights to Encino Pass regularly booked to capacity, travelers often had to use other regional airports. The Encino Pass Airport and the city council have both been working to attract more airlines to the area to better accommodate the increase in the number of travelers.

"Rapido Airline was our top choice as an expansion airline," said Encino Pass Mayor Chris Donovan. "It is known for offering low fares, maintaining on-time schedules, and surpassing safety inspections. We're pleased that it has decided to join us here in Encino Pass. This addition will expand options and make air travel more convenient for residents and visitors alike."

The city and airport are also in talks to provide shuttle bus service between the airport and surrounding parking facilities, refurbish the rental car booths, and add another terminal to the airport. The negotiations are part of the city's long-term plan to increase tourism in the area.

Rapido Airline's flights between Encino Pass and Summerset begin on July 9, with more routes to be added later in the month.

161. Why are more airlines being sought to service the Encino Pass Airport?

(A) To offer lower-priced flights in the region
(B) To respond to complaints from neighboring airports
(C) To carry cargo on behalf of shipping companies
(D) To improve air travel to and from Encino Pass

162. What is suggested about Rapido Airline?

(A) It has lost business to other airlines.
(B) It offers more flights than other airlines.
(C) It has a reputation for prioritizing safety.
(D) It is used primarily by business travelers.

163. What is NOT mentioned as part of the city's plan to increase tourism in the area?

(A) Providing discounted parking
(B) Offering shuttle bus service
(C) Building a new terminal
(D) Improving car rental booths

TEST 8

Casey Willard (7:43 A.M.)
Can either of you come in to work this morning? We have a huge order to fill, and two of the forklift drivers scheduled for today have called in sick. So, we only have one working. One or two more would be really helpful. The shipping clerks can't get the products out fast enough.

Kazuko Yoneda (7:46 A.M.)
Sorry, I wish I could, but I have other commitments today. Maybe try Claudia Kwon? She is usually very flexible.

Casey Willard (7:47 A.M.)
She has the weekend off and went to Ford Harbor to visit her family. It's too bad because she always appreciates an opportunity to earn overtime pay.

Lucas Suarez (7:51 A.M.)
I'm busy until about 10 A.M., but I could come in after that.

Casey Willard (7:52 A.M.)
Thank you, Lucas. We need all the help we can get! If the order is not on the truck by 6 tonight, it won't go out for delivery until Monday.

Lucas Suarez (7:54 A.M.)
Got it. I'll be there as soon as I can.

164. Why did Ms. Willard text her colleagues?

(A) Some workers are unexpectedly absent.
(B) Shipping clerks are working ahead of schedule.
(C) Two of the company's forklifts are having mechanical difficulties.
(D) Too few forklift drivers were scheduled to work.

165. What does Ms. Yoneda suggest that Ms. Willard do?

(A) Work longer hours
(B) Offer additional pay
(C) Contact another employee
(D) Bring in temporary workers

166. What must happen by 6:00 P.M.?

(A) A truck must be loaded.
(B) An employee must go home.
(C) A payment must be received.
(D) A customer must confirm an order.

167. At 7:54 A.M., what does Mr. Suarez most likely mean when he writes, "Got it"?

(A) He will cancel an order.
(B) He understands a situation.
(C) He knows how to reach Ms. Kwon.
(D) He has received the key to a truck.

GO ON TO THE NEXT PAGE

Yum and Walk Food Tours
Adding a New Destination

COLLEGE STATION (May 15)—On June 2, Yum and Walk Food Tours will add College Station to its statewide list of culinary destinations.

"College Station has been overlooked as a culinary destination for too long," said tour-company owner Ed Lopez. A former chef, Lopez also once worked as a journalist and wrote about cuisine for the *Texas Beacon*.

Yum and Walk Food Tours offers outings in nine other cities in Texas and brings visitors to restaurants, bakeries, and specialty stores to sample both sweet and savory treats. Visitors walk through the city with an experienced guide, who also shares information about each neighborhood's history. Mr. Lopez himself will serve as the tour guide in College Station, his home before working in San Antonio and then returning to the area.

"From the beginning, my goal has been to help people discover great food," said Mr. Lopez.

The local itinerary includes five stops in a three-hour time span—Giuseppina's Trattoria, Yucatan Plate, Kerala Kebabs, Spice Rub Stop, and Delicious Doughnuts. Customers can schedule private tours if they have any specific dietary preferences or requirements.

Local officials are excited about the tour company's move into the area.

"We're thrilled to have Yum and Walk Food Tours add us to their list of destinations," said College Station Mayor Maria Garcia. "Their presence is sure to have a positive impact on our area's dining establishments."

Tickets are $50 each. The ten-week touring season begins on July 2 and lasts until September 3. Tours take place on Sundays from 1 P.M. to 4 P.M.

168. Why most likely did Mr. Lopez start Yum and Walk Food Tours?

(A) To take advantage of his experience leading tours
(B) To share his love of food with people
(C) To provide advertising opportunities for local restaurants
(D) To allow himself to work closer to home

169. What is NOT indicated about the Yum and Walk Food Tour in College Station?

(A) It will last for three hours.
(B) It will be led by Mr. Lopez.
(C) It will be advertised in the *Texas Beacon*.
(D) It will bring visitors to five restaurants.

170. What is indicated about private tours?

(A) They cost extra to attend.
(B) They are not available in all cities.
(C) They must be scheduled at least ten weeks in advance.
(D) They can be arranged for people who avoid certain foods.

171. What is true about Ms. Garcia?

(A) She thinks the tours will be good for local businesses.
(B) She owns the Spice Rub Stop.
(C) She has participated in the food tour.
(D) She is from San Antonio.

To:	All employees
From:	Janice Capaldi
Date:	October 23
Subject:	Guests

Good afternoon, everyone,

We will soon host a group of employees from Seongnam Electronics. — [1] —. They will arrive on November 10 and be with us for a week to observe our research and production methods. We encourage everyone to interact with the visitors while they are here. — [2] —.

The executives in the group are leaders in the field of electronics development and manufacturing. Dr. Sung-Hye Kim leads Research and Development. Her individual contributions have focused on how magnetic fields influence the efficiency of components within electrical devices. She has also been called on by other physicists and professors to write and edit texts that explain electromagnetic phenomena. Dr. Kim's work is influential throughout the international electronics industry. Also, Jin-Woong Lee, chief production officer at Seongnam Electronics, heads the team that designed the manufacturing processes at the plant near Seoul. — [3] —. The award-winning techniques developed by Mr. Lee's team assure both cost-effectiveness and quality.

On the afternoon of November 10, we will hold a reception in the conference room on the third floor to welcome our guests. Specifics will be sent to the entire staff in an e-mail from Stewart Lark, who is serving as the event's coordinator. — [4] —. Please plan on attending. Contact Mr. Lark and me with any questions you may have.

Thank you,

Janice Capaldi, Director of Operations, Dolesley Electronics, Inc.

172. What is suggested about Dr. Kim?

(A) She is a physicist.
(B) She usually works alone.
(C) She lectures at a university.
(D) She launched Seongnam Electronics.

173. What is Mr. Lee responsible for?

(A) Negotiating sales deals
(B) Choosing marketing strategies
(C) Establishing a product assembly process
(D) Managing a human resources department

174. What new information about the reception will Mr. Lark most likely include in his e-mail?

(A) A purpose
(B) The date
(C) A location
(D) The time

175. In which of the positions marked [1], [2], [3], and [4] does the following sentence best belong?

"Please share your work processes with them and answer any of their questions."

(A) [1]
(B) [2]
(C) [3]
(D) [4]

```
╔══════════════════════════════════════════════════════════╗
║                        *E-mail*                          ║
╠══════════════════════════════════════════════════════════╣

     From:      efeehan@rossfieldhotels.ie

     To:        customerservice@parleganispublishing.com

     Date:      15 December

     Sent:      Course books

   ┌──────────────────────────────────────────────────────┐
   │ Dear Customer Service Representative:                 │
   │                                                       │
   │ In October my company ordered 60 paperback copies of  │
   │ the *Food Safety Course Book* for our employees so    │
   │ they could study for their mandatory food safety      │
   │ certification. I just learned from one of our         │
   │ managers that you offer this course book in languages │
   │ other than English. May I send back twenty of the     │
   │ English language versions and get ten Polish and ten  │
   │ Portuguese books instead? Some of our new employees   │
   │ said they would really appreciate being able to read  │
   │ the crucial information in their first language.      │
   │                                                       │
   │ The books I wish to return are still in their         │
   │ original packaging. I can have them boxed and shipped │
   │ quickly, but I will wait for your acknowledgement and │
   │ instructions regarding paperwork.                     │
   │                                                       │
   │ Sincerely,                                            │
   │                                                       │
   │ Ella Feehan                                           │
   │ Food Services Director                                │
   │ Rossfield Hotels Ltd.                                 │
   └──────────────────────────────────────────────────────┘
```

Parleganis Publishing

Returns and Exchanges Policy

We accept products under the following conditions.

- Unmarked, unused materials may be returned or exchanged within 90 days of purchase.

- Items returned or exchanged more than 30 days after purchase are subject to a restocking fee equal to 20% of the cover price.

- Paperback books come in plastic-wrapped bundles of ten. Unopened bundles may be returned for full credit. Individual paperback books will receive partial credit.

- Software products and subscription fees are not refundable.

- No credit will be issued for damaged or out-of-print books.

176. Why did Ms. Feehan write to Parleganis Publishing?

(A) She offered feedback on a publication.
(B) She would like to exchange some training materials.
(C) She received an incorrect shipment.
(D) She needs to return some damaged books.

177. What is indicated about Rossfield Hotels Ltd.?

(A) Some of its workers must earn certificates.
(B) It recently hired a food services manager.
(C) It advertises in several European countries.
(D) Some of its guests come from Poland and Portugal.

178. In the e-mail, the word "original" in paragraph 2, line 1, is closest in meaning to

(A) odd
(B) initial
(C) ancient
(D) creative

179. What will Rossfield Hotels Ltd. most likely pay in December?

(A) A restocking fee
(B) A subscription fee
(C) A past-due invoice
(D) A refund for unused services

180. What is stated about the *Food Safety Course Book*?

(A) It is available in electronic format.
(B) It was published in October.
(C) It will soon be out of print.
(D) It is sold in packs of ten.

GO ON TO THE NEXT PAGE

Questions 181-185 refer to the following online review and menu.

Review: Pizza in Bobbingworth   **Submitted by: Gerard Landis**

There is a new pizza restaurant in town called Maple Pizza House. Not to my surprise, it offers a number of signature pizzas with maple flavoring, including dessert pizzas. While I personally did not like the maple-flavored pizza at all, the rest of my party enjoyed a large maple-ham pizza as a main course. The others in my group also devoured the maple-walnut dessert pizza, which, to me, tasted like an overly sweet, sticky pie.

Fortunately for me, the menu includes some pizzas that do not have maple flavoring. I ordered a traditional cheese pizza. It was served piping hot and was delicious. Because there were tasty menu options that pleased everyone, I rate the Maple Pizza House 4 stars out of 5, and I would recommend visiting.

Maple Pizza House
83 Fox Lane, Bobbingworth, CM2 9B
077 5014 0314
We now accept credit cards.

Signature Maple Pizzas (with red sauce)	Personal	Large
Chicken maple	£4.5	£15
Maple ham	£5	£17
Pineapple	£4	£14
Traditional Pizzas (select red or white sauce)		
Cheese	£4	£13
Vegetable	£4	£13
Meatball	£4	£13
Dessert Pizzas (with brown butter sauce)		
Cinnamon maple		£11
Maple walnut		£11

ALL BEVERAGES: £2

181. What does Mr. Landis think about the restaurant's menu?

    (A) There are too few vegetarian options.
    (B) He preferred the restaurant's previous menu.
    (C) The dessert pizzas are too expensive.
    (D) He does not care for the taste of the signature pizzas.

182. In the review, the word "sweet" in paragraph 1, line 5, is closest in meaning to

    (A) moderate
    (B) pleasing
    (C) sugary
    (D) dear

183. How much was the pizza that Mr. Landis' group ordered for their main course?

    (A) £5
    (B) £11
    (C) £13
    (D) £17

184. Which pizza is available with a white sauce?

    (A) Maple ham
    (B) Pineapple
    (C) Meatball
    (D) Cinnamon maple

185. What is suggested about the restaurant?

    (A) It prepares dessert pizza in only one size.
    (B) It accepts payments in cash only.
    (C) It makes home deliveries.
    (D) It has moved to a larger location.

GO ON TO THE NEXT PAGE

TEST 8

https://www.northamcarparts.co.uk/home

| Home | Catalogue | Contact Form | About Us |

We Have the Parts You Need

Northam Car Parts is a leading seller of rare and hard-to-find car parts. We have a huge selection of car transmissions, body and frame parts, and steering-repair kits, just to name a few. Check out our online catalogue page for a detailed list of parts currently available in our warehouse. We specialise in vintage European cars, but we have plenty of parts for American-made and Japanese-made vehicles. If you do not see what you need in our catalogue, please fill out a contact form—we can help you find the part you need! Please note that our response time is now two to four business days because of a rise in the number of requests we receive.

Parts can be delivered to any address within the United Kingdom, France, Belgium, or Spain.

Northam Car Parts Contact Form

Contact Information	
Name:	Gerald Aldegunde
E-mail:	carmanga55@saffronmail.de
Phone:	+52 (164) 5559183
Address:	Kanalstrasse 60 01067 Dresden, Germany
Date:	6 August

Vehicle Information	
Manufacturer:	Exceller
Model:	Dragonfire
Year:	1988
Transmission:	Manual
Drive:	2WD

Message:

I've been looking for a part for a transmission in a 1988 Exceller Dragonfire I purchased last year. I have been unable to find this part, so a friend who found a new steering wheel through your company recommended that I contact you. I was wondering how much you would charge for locating a vintage British car part like this. Also, I noticed that Germany is not listed on your Web site as a shipping destination. Do you ever ship to areas other than the countries that are currently listed there? Thanks for your help! Working on this car has been a great experience, but I'm eager to get this thing on the road!

To:	Gerald Aldegunde <carmanga55@saffronmail.de>
From:	Bethany Turnhout <bturnhout@northamcarparts.co.uk>
Date:	28 August
Subject:	Shipping notification

Dear Mr. Aldegunde:

Your item will arrive on 30 August, no later than 8:00 P.M., at the following address: Kanalstrasse 60, 01067 Dresden, Germany. It will be arriving via the IHE insured delivery service, so you or a designated representative must be present to accept and sign for the package. IHE will contact you in advance of the driver's arrival. Please make sure that the path from the street to your door is clear of obstructions so the driver can have free access.

Thank you for choosing Northam Car Parts to help find your part!

Bethany Turnhout
Sales Representative, Northam Car Parts

186. According to the Web page, what has changed recently at Northam Car Parts?

(A) The hours of operation
(B) The number of customer inquiries
(C) The amount of warehouse space
(D) The availability of Japanese car parts

187. What is indicated about Mr. Aldegunde on the contact form?

(A) He is eager to finish rebuilding his car.
(B) He needs a new steering wheel.
(C) He has owned his car for many years.
(D) He has a friend who works for Northam Car Parts.

188. What is most likely true about the part that Mr. Aldegunde needs?

(A) It was manufactured in Germany.
(B) It will take four business days to ship.
(C) It is too large to transport internationally.
(D) It is not included in Northam Car Parts' catalog.

189. According to the e-mail, what service does IHE provide?

(A) It sells car insurance.
(B) It repairs vintage cars.
(C) It transports packages.
(D) It cleans streets.

190. What can be concluded about Northam Car Parts?

(A) It was recently purchased by Ms. Turnhout.
(B) It maintains warehouses in several countries.
(C) It ships to countries that are not listed on its Web page.
(D) It does not respond to customer inquiries after 8:00 P.M.

GO ON TO THE NEXT PAGE

Questions 191-195 refer to the following press release, Web page, and text message.

RHC Continues to Impress

FOR IMMEDIATE RELEASE
Contact: Dora Su, +65 0555 1294

SINGAPORE (3 August)—In operation for five years, Rayder Holdings Corporation (RHC) is announcing the completion of its sixth renovation project, Bay Commons. The company, founded by real estate agents Rayna Wong and Derrick Lim, specializes in converting industrial buildings into apartment complexes.

"Turning commercial buildings into residential spaces has its challenges," Ms. Wong said. "However, we are committed to repurposing buildings instead of constructing new ones."

This commitment was recently cited in a speech by Yamina Badawi, Singapore's minister of Housing and Urban Development, who applauded RHC's contribution to the nation's housing supply.

RHC completed its first conversion project four years ago—the Kallang Overlook apartment complex. Since then, RHC has completed five more projects: Asten Estates, Tampines Tower, Lakeside Manor, Yishun Terrace, and now Bay Commons.

"Bay Commons represents a departure from our previous projects," Ms. Wong noted. "This housing complex is designed primarily for students at the nearby Changi Technological Institute."

Units at Bay Commons are now available for rent or purchase, she added.

---

https://www.rayderholdingscorporation.com.sg/current-listings

About Us	**Current Listings**	News	Careers

Rayder Holdings Corporation turns vacant commercial properties into pleasant residential buildings. Below are our current offerings in alphabetical order.

Asten Estates: 14-unit building with pool, fitness centre, and car park

Bay Commons: 60 studio apartments with shared kitchen areas and other common rooms

Kallang Overlook: 40-unit apartment complex situated on the Kallang River

Lakeside Manor: 28-unit building with indoor pool, outdoor tennis and basketball courts, playground, and on-site cafeteria

Tampines Tower: 36-unit apartment complex with pool and fitness room

Yishun Terrace: 55-unit apartment complex with outdoor sports facilities (tennis, basketball, football), indoor swimming pool, catch-and-release fishing pond, and picnic area

For details and other queries, contact info@rayderholdingscorporation.com.sg.

Today 9:53 A.M.

Hello, Mr. Goh. A fellow resident found your wallet on the cafeteria counter and dropped it off here at the RHC leasing office. Please stop by to pick it up. We are open until 6:00 P.M. For after-hours service, call 0904 6802, and someone will assist you.

Alicia Rajani, Office Manager

191. According to the press release, what is true about RHC?

(A) It has an international presence.
(B) It specializes in designing work spaces.
(C) It was founded by two construction engineers.
(D) It has been in business for five years.

192. What does the press release suggest about Ms. Badawi?

(A) She appreciates RHC's approach to expanding housing.
(B) She owns a unit at one of RHC's properties.
(C) She advises students at Changi Technological Institute.
(D) She has hired Mr. Lim to be one of her advisers.

193. How many units does the first housing complex built by RHC have?

(A) 14
(B) 28
(C) 40
(D) 60

194. Why did Ms. Rajani send a text message to Mr. Goh?

(A) To introduce him to a new neighbor
(B) To notify him that his wallet was found
(C) To respond to his request for information
(D) To provide the leasing office's hours of operation

195. Where does Mr. Goh most likely live?

(A) At Asten Estates
(B) At Lakeside Manor
(C) At Tampines Tower
(D) At Yishun Terrace

TEST 8

GO ON TO THE NEXT PAGE

Questions 196-200 refer to the following Web page, text-message chain, and online review.

https://www.camsfurniture.ca/about_us

About Us	Catalogue	Reviews	Contact Us

Cam's Furniture has been a fixture in Ottawa for more than 50 years. With our focus on exceptional customer service, we guarantee that your time in our store will be both pleasant and worthwhile!

Our daily business operations are overseen by George Meara, the eldest son of founder Cam Meara. George is joined by his sister, Elise Meara, and an enthusiastic team of sales associates who will help you choose the best furniture for your needs. Our enormous showroom features a broad selection of high-quality furniture arranged in different types of residential rooms and office spaces. And, along with all the top brands of furniture, we are proud to carry unique and environmentally friendly items sourced from the Green Directions Trade Fair. Our head buyer, Debbie Sarno, attends this event annually to choose fantastic new products for our store.

We offer complimentary delivery and setup for all customers whose home or business is within the boundaries of the city of Ottawa.

Linda Fei (1:57 P.M.)
Toby, I'm at Cam's Furniture. The items you chose for our reception area look great! The salesperson told me the bill is going to be a little more than expected because there will be a charge for delivery and setup. The crew can come out to our office on Friday, so we'll definitely be able to have everything in place before our clients arrive on Monday.

Toby Pesenti (1:59 P.M.)
Great! The slightly higher cost shouldn't be a problem. We have enough in our budget.

Online Reviews

Customer review posted by Linda Fei on 23 July at 5:32 P.M.

The staff at Cam's Furniture is extraordinarily helpful and professional. I was pleased that we could get eco-friendly pieces for our company's reception area. The furniture is beautiful—we've been receiving many compliments. Cam's delivery team spent extra time at our new office space to make sure that the furniture was arranged in exactly the right way. We look forward to shopping at Cam's again!

196. What does the Web page indicate about Cam's Furniture?

(A) It is currently hiring new staff.
(B) It has two store locations.
(C) It is a family business.
(D) It specializes in used furniture.

197. In her text message, what does Ms. Fei mention will happen on Monday?

(A) Some furniture will be delivered.
(B) Some clients will visit.
(C) A bill will be paid in full.
(D) A reception area will be closed for remodeling.

198. What is suggested about Ms. Fei's company?

(A) It raised its prices.
(B) It is located outside Ottawa.
(C) It is an interior design firm.
(D) It recently merged with another organization.

199. What can be concluded about the new furniture purchased by Ms. Fei's company?

(A) It was sourced by Ms. Sarno.
(B) It comes with a money-back guarantee.
(C) It can be used indoors or outdoors.
(D) It was purchased from Ms. Fei.

200. In the online review, what does Ms. Fei indicate about the members of the delivery team?

(A) They used custom-made equipment.
(B) They arranged the new furniture incorrectly.
(C) They offered to haul away the old furniture.
(D) They stayed for longer than expected.

TEST 8

Stop! This is the end of the test. If you finish before time is called, you may go back to Parts 5, 6, and 7 and check your work.

토익 정기시험
실전 ❶ 1000
RC

실전 TEST

09

In the Reading test, you will read a variety of texts and answer several different types of reading comprehension questions. The entire Reading test will last 75 minutes. There are three parts, and directions are given for each part. You are encouraged to answer as many questions as possible within the time allowed.

You must mark your answers on the separate answer sheet. Do not write your answers in your test book.

PART 5

Directions: A word or phrase is missing in each of the sentences below. Four answer choices are given below each sentence. Select the best answer to complete the sentence. Then mark the letter (A), (B), (C), or (D) on your answer sheet.

---

101. Edison Delivery's trucks leave the warehouse promptly ------- 6:00 A.M. each morning.

(A) at
(B) on
(C) for
(D) with

102. A ------- copy of the rental agreement for the apartment has been delivered to the main office.

(A) signature
(B) sign
(C) signs
(D) signed

103. ------- can be made online or by calling customer service between 6:30 A.M. and 5:30 P.M.

(A) Reserve
(B) Reserved
(C) Reservations
(D) Reservable

104. Ms. Shimabukuro rose through the ranks ------- and became the manager in less than two years.

(A) quick
(B) quicken
(C) quickly
(D) quickening

105. The Highland Museum of Robotics will be ------- for renovations until further notice.

(A) bought
(B) closed
(C) stopped
(D) held

106. The Hollytown Arena designates an area where fans can meet their ------- athletes after each game.

(A) favorite
(B) favoritism
(C) favorites
(D) favoring

107. Billboards that advertise legal services are most effective when placed ------- business districts.

(A) from
(B) down
(C) of
(D) in

108. Ms. Ueda was quite ------- with the wholesale prices offered by Rea's International Restaurant Suppliers.

(A) advised
(B) true
(C) pleased
(D) strong

109. *Geology Monthly* is a professional journal with articles written ------- for experts in the field.
    (A) specify
    (B) had specified
    (C) specifics
    (D) specifically

110. ------- the year-end sale at Arthur's Camping Supplies, all winter items are discounted by 25 percent.
    (A) During
    (B) Although
    (C) As long as
    (D) In addition

111. In the ------- future, a hardware store will open on the corner of Oak Boulevard and Primrose Avenue.
    (A) nears
    (B) nearly
    (C) nearness
    (D) near

112. Mr. Careni requested that ------- from the technical support team come immediately to the Harrisburg office.
    (A) who
    (B) someone
    (C) which
    (D) themselves

113. The time-entry system was ------- unavailable this afternoon, but it is functioning normally now.
    (A) directly
    (B) urgently
    (C) precisely
    (D) briefly

114. The upcoming career fair ------- by more than 100 employers and job-recruiting agencies.
    (A) attend
    (B) were attended
    (C) was attending
    (D) will be attended

115. ------- theater at Landon Cinema is decorated with a different theme.
    (A) Even
    (B) Much
    (C) Each
    (D) All

116. Changes to course content have been halted ------- the Salinas Academy transitions to a new online platform.
    (A) while
    (B) though
    (C) regarding
    (D) whether

117. Bricktown Mayor Julian Trent will ------- help plant flowers in Evans Park this weekend.
    (A) personal
    (B) personalize
    (C) personally
    (D) personality

118. Please replace pages 28 to 35 in the employee handbook with the ------- pages.
    (A) careful
    (B) updated
    (C) consistent
    (D) sizable

119. ------- we increased our Internet speed, we can download large documents much faster.
    (A) Since
    (B) Provided
    (C) Yet
    (D) Instead

120. The lead graphic artist decides which photographs submitted by freelancers ------- to the creative director.
    (A) are sending
    (B) sender
    (C) should be sent
    (D) send

GO ON TO THE NEXT PAGE

TEST 9

121. ------- you visit the Star Hotel, the cheerful staff makes you feel welcome.

(A) Whenever
(B) Whichever
(C) Nevertheless
(D) Altogether

122. Ms. Matlou considered a legal career before ------- deciding to go to business school.

(A) strictly
(B) politely
(C) ultimately
(D) slightly

123. Patrons of the festival enjoying picnic lunches on the concert hall's lawn is a ------- dating back almost a century.

(A) traditional
(B) tradition
(C) traditionalist
(D) traditions

124. Many people ------- their online shopping carts when they discover what the shipping charge will be.

(A) eject
(B) abandon
(C) resign
(D) discourage

125. The state's tourism Web site provides information on many of the area's popular -------.

(A) situations
(B) appeals
(C) demands
(D) attractions

126. ------- interested in learning more about Shana Fabian's sculptures should attend her talk at Deana Gallery on May 2.

(A) Enough
(B) Whoever
(C) Each other
(D) Those

127. The merger between the Oznaze and Tellurisq companies was ------- settled following months of tough negotiations.

(A) exactly
(B) instantly
(C) finally
(D) easily

128. Auto parts are shipped ------- two to three days unless the customer requests expedited delivery.

(A) within
(B) here
(C) afterward
(D) perhaps

129. The interior designer selected some very ------- colors for the lobby walls.

(A) massive
(B) intense
(C) direct
(D) sudden

130. Experts recommend that the cooling system be checked by a service technician at regular -------.

(A) expanses
(B) intervals
(C) classifications
(D) detachments

PART 6

Directions: Read the texts that follow. A word, phrase, or sentence is missing in parts of each text. Four answer choices for each question are given below the text. Select the best answer to complete the text. Then mark the letter (A), (B), (C), or (D) on your answer sheet.

Questions 131-134 refer to the following e-mail.

To: Roger Wall <rogerwall@openemail.com>
From: Guillermo Torres <gtorres@supplyflow.com>
Date: May 2
Subject: RE: Missing delivery

Dear Mr. Wall,

This is in response to your ------- e-mail notifying us that you did not receive your April shipment
__131.__
of office supplies. We verified that your annual subscription is up-to-date and that everything is in

order on your side. This error is, therefore, an oversight on ------- part. We have transitioned to
__132.__
new shipping software, and some customer information was not transferred correctly. Rest

assured that this has been fixed and that the error will not ------- again.
__133.__

We sent your box of office supplies today using an overnight shipping service. ------- . Inside the
__134.__
box, you will also find a complimentary token of appreciation for your patience.

If you have further questions or concerns, do not hesitate to contact me directly.

Sincerely,

Guillermo Torres, Customer Assistant, Supply Flow, Inc.

---

131. (A) constant
(B) nearby
(C) early
(D) recent

132. (A) either
(B) its
(C) our
(D) their

133. (A) combine
(B) revise
(C) affect
(D) occur

134. (A) You should receive it tomorrow.
(B) This order will take longer than usual
to process.
(C) The box is very heavy.
(D) Please review the invoice attached to
this e-mail.

GO ON TO THE NEXT PAGE

To: Marketing Department, Tavola Foods Distributors
From: Victor Cotillo
Date: March 4
Subject: Information

Please look at the proposed survey that was just added to our team folder. The first section asks

------- to rate their favorite vegetables. We felt shoppers might prefer a particular vegetable only if
135.

it is fresh and in season. ------- , we also ask what frozen vegetables they buy most frequently
136.

and why. In addition, we ------- a series of questions about food preparation and convenience.
137.

We feel this survey will give us a better picture of what our customers want. Please look over

everything and quickly respond with any thoughts. ------- .
138.

135. (A) farmers
(B) executives
(C) consumers
(D) merchants

136. (A) In effect
(B) Therefore
(C) On occasion
(D) Nevertheless

137. (A) were inserting
(B) have inserted
(C) had been inserting
(D) could have inserted

138. (A) We want to start distributing the
survey next week.
(B) We value the feedback provided
by you, our customers.
(C) Despite higher costs, demand for
our products has risen.
(D) As we all know, fresh vegetables
are good for you.

To: vendors@grovecenterfleamarket.org
From: alanc@spicebest.com
Date: October 22
Subject: Parking issue

Dear Vendors,

Starting next month, the owners of the Grove Center Flea Market will charge a flat daily rate of $10 to use the onsite parking deck. This means customers who drive to our weekly flea market will no longer enjoy free parking. I'm concerned that this might ------- some shoppers from
139.
coming, which will hurt our businesses.

As president of the Grove Center Flea Market, I have asked the owners to consider waiving or reducing the fee. ------- . The nearest other large-scale parking facility is at city hall, three long
140.
blocks from our site. Street parking is available but can be ------- to find.
141.

Please reply to all if you have any thoughts on alternative ------- .
142.

Best,

Alan Coleman

139. (A) remove
(B) carry
(C) discourage
(D) manage

140. (A) Their offices are not open on
Sundays.
(B) I also asked them to expand the
garage.
(C) Nevertheless, we have more vendors
than last year.
(D) Unfortunately, we could not reach a
compromise.

141. (A) difficult
(B) pleasant
(C) expensive
(D) specific

142. (A) solution
(B) solutions
(C) solve
(D) solving

TEST 9

GO ON TO THE NEXT PAGE

QUEENSVILLE (November 3)—Recycling just became easier for many local residents thanks to the opening of the township's second recycling center. "West Queensville residents now have a more ------- location to drop off their materials," Mayor Dustin Larson said at yesterday's
143.
ribbon-cutting ceremony. "No longer must they travel to the east part of the town."

------- . However, Ida Aguirre of the Queensville Clean Coalition criticized the town council's
144.
decision to eliminate curbside pickup of recyclables. "Curbside pickup should be resumed

------- elected officials want to make recycling easier," she said in a telephone interview. Open
145.
6 A.M. to 8 P.M. on weekdays, the new 18 Darren Street facility takes only mixed paper and some

plastics. Aluminum is not currently ------- .
146.

143. (A) widespread
(B) convenient
(C) ordinary
(D) stable

144. (A) The percentage of household waste sent to landfills has decreased recently.
(B) Those who attended the ceremony applauded the new facility.
(C) Employees at both drop-off sites can help unload materials.
(D) The drop-off site in West Queensville opens next year.

145. (A) by
(B) so
(C) if
(D) through

146. (A) accepted
(B) accepting
(C) accepts
(D) accept

PART 7

Directions: In this part you will read a selection of texts, such as magazine and newspaper articles, e-mails, and instant messages. Each text or set of texts is followed by several questions. Select the best answer for each question and mark the letter (A), (B), (C), or (D) on your answer sheet.

Questions 147-148 refer to the following e-mail.

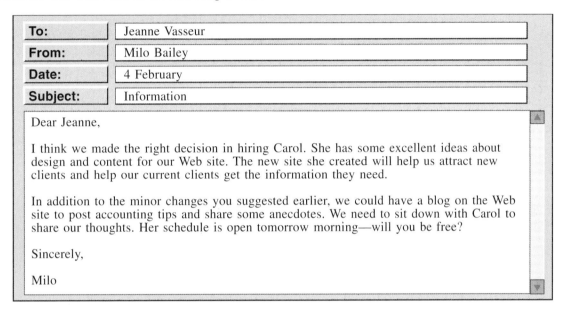

To:	Jeanne Vasseur
From:	Milo Bailey
Date:	4 February
Subject:	Information

Dear Jeanne,

I think we made the right decision in hiring Carol. She has some excellent ideas about design and content for our Web site. The new site she created will help us attract new clients and help our current clients get the information they need.

In addition to the minor changes you suggested earlier, we could have a blog on the Web site to post accounting tips and share some anecdotes. We need to sit down with Carol to share our thoughts. Her schedule is open tomorrow morning—will you be free?

Sincerely,

Milo

147. Why did Mr. Bailey send the e-mail to Ms. Vasseur?

(A) To inquire about a product
(B) To explain a new process to her
(C) To discuss changes to a Web site
(D) To ask her to contact a new client

148. What does Mr. Bailey want to do?

(A) Review a schedule
(B) Hire additional staff
(C) Open a new account
(D) Meet with a new employee

GO ON TO THE NEXT PAGE

Green's Athletic Shoes

18502 Oriole Avenue
Chicago, IL 60800
(312) 555-0132

August 5, 11:27 A.M.

Receipt number: 5926

Lunarwave running shoes Style: Fleetfoot, men's size 10	$119.00
Suresocks cotton running socks men's size large	$4.99
Coolbreeze T-shirt men's size medium Regularly $14.00, now 15% off	$11.90
Subtotal	$135.89
Sales tax (6.25%)	$8.49
Total	**$144.38**

Thank you for shopping at Green's Athletic Shoes!
Please fill out a customer survey at www.greensathletic.com.

All returns must be made within 30 days.
A receipt is required to make a return.

149. What is indicated about the T-shirt?

(A) It was made by Lunarwave.
(B) It is a size large.
(C) It is made of cotton.
(D) It was sold at a discounted price.

150. What must a customer do to return an item?

(A) Complete an online form
(B) Bring the item back within six months
(C) Show an original store receipt
(D) Mail the item to the manufacturer

Questions 151-152 refer to the following text-message chain.

Monica Blanco (10:43 A.M.)
Hi, Carrie. Are you working this Friday? I'm working a half shift, and I was wondering if you could cover it. My brother's birthday party is that day.

Carrie Morgan (11:25 A.M.)
I'm working a half shift too. What time are you scheduled?

Monica Blanco (11:37 A.M.)
8 A.M. to noon.

Carrie Morgan (11:39 A.M.)
I might be able to. I could do a full day, actually. I'm scheduled after you.

Monica Blanco (11:40 A.M.)
OK.

Carrie Morgan (11:41 A.M.)
I'm at work right now. When I see Mr. Cho, I'll ask him if it is OK to do your shift as well as mine.

Monica Blanco (11:50 A.M.)
Thank you! I appreciate it.

---

151. At 11:39 A.M., what does Ms. Morgan mean when she writes, "I might be able to"?

(A) She could help organize a weekend event.
(B) She could work Ms. Blanco's hours on Friday.
(C) She could pick up some food for a party.
(D) She could meet with Ms. Blanco during her break.

152. Who most likely is Mr. Cho?

(A) A temporary worker
(B) A party planner
(C) A supervisor
(D) A friend of Ms. Blanco's

GO ON TO THE NEXT PAGE

TEST 9

MEMO

To: All Avisomark Employees
From: Eugenia Bajorek, Assistant Communications Director
Date: January 30
Re: Our company newsletter

As part of a company-wide effort to reduce waste, we will be discontinuing the print version of our weekly company newsletter, effective March 1. From that date forward, the newsletter will be published in its online format only. In addition, beginning in March, the submission deadline for the Employee News section of the newsletter will be changed from the third Friday of each month to the second Friday of each month. This change will give Markus Quimby the time he needs to process and edit submissions. The submission process remains the same: simply e-mail Markus directly at mquimby@avisomark.com.

153. Why was the memo written?

   (A) To announce a recent decision
   (B) To introduce a new staff member
   (C) To describe a volunteer opportunity
   (D) To invite feedback on a new practice

154. According to the memo, why would employees e-mail Mr. Quimby?

   (A) To update their personal information
   (B) To request a copy of a newsletter
   (C) To express their opinion on the
        newsletter format
   (D) To send in their latest news

Driverless Buses in Swansea?

SWANSEA (12 May)—A consortium of city government officials and local business leaders is considering the purchase of driverless buses for some city routes. Commissioned with exploring options to improve transportation in Swansea and surrounding areas, the group recently sent three members to Malaga, Spain, where driverless buses run an eight-kilometre loop several times a day.

Consortium member Gareth Elias was impressed by what he learned. Despite concerns about safety and traffic regulations, Mr. Elias could see driverless buses becoming a reality before long, but only in specific cases. "I believe they would be particularly useful during festivals and special events," he said. "I can't imagine them being on the roads every day."

Anisha Deepak, an engineer specialising in transportation innovation, served as a technical consultant on the trip. She was struck by the complexity of the buses' artificial intelligence system, which allows them to learn as they collect data on every trip.

"Artificial intelligence makes these buses very safe in real-world situations," she said. "Nevertheless, it's best to have a human operator on board at all times in case of emergencies."

A public community forum is scheduled for 2 June to discuss the benefits and drawbacks of driverless buses. Visit the Swansea Town Council's Web site at www.swanseatowncouncil.gov.uk to learn more.

155. What is the purpose of the article?

(A) To explain how a new technology works
(B) To report on a group's recent activities
(C) To recruit participants for a travel forum
(D) To announce changes to a bus schedule

156. What opinion does Mr. Elias express about driverless buses?

(A) They are not safe under any circumstances.
(B) Traffic regulations must be revised to accommodate them.
(C) They are practical for limited purposes.
(D) They are appropriate for Malaga but not for Swansea.

157. What is indicated about Ms. Deepak?

(A) She was recently elected to the Swansea Town Council.
(B) She collected data for a computer system.
(C) She took notes during an emergency meeting.
(D) She traveled to Malaga as a consultant.

TEST 9

Questions 158-161 refer to the following job posting.

Morves Laboratories of Seoul is seeking an associate research scientist who will work collaboratively with a team of other scientists within the Research and Development Division.

Morves Laboratories has more than 85,000 employees in offices and laboratories in Asia, Europe, and North America who are involved in developing, manufacturing, and selling cutting-edge medicines. The Research and Development Division is responsible for achieving the company's primary goal of creating new and effective medications for worldwide use.

Primary Job Functions:

• Design and conduct laboratory experiments

• Perform rigorous data analysis

• Collaborate to write detailed reports

• Present research findings internally and externally to clients at specific meetings

Position Requirements:

• A master's degree in biology

• At least five years of laboratory experience

• Excellent oral and written communication skills

To apply, submit a résumé and cover letter to www.morveslaboratories.co.kr/careers by November 10.

---

158. What does the job posting indicate about Morves Laboratories?

(A) It offers excellent employee benefits.
(B) Its workforce is primarily based in Europe.
(C) Its main purpose is to develop new medicines.
(D) It partners with another company for product distribution.

159. What is one responsibility of the position?

(A) Analyzing information from experiments
(B) Designing safe packaging materials
(C) Operating manufacturing equipment
(D) Responding to patient inquiries

160. According to the job posting, what should an applicant possess?

(A) Knowledge of medical regulations
(B) Expertise in editing medical journals
(C) A background in teaching biology
(D) Experience working in a laboratory

161. How should someone apply for the position?

(A) By visiting the company's offices
(B) By submitting a résumé online
(C) By calling a recruiting professional
(D) By e-mailing a current employee

```
══════════════════ E-Mail Message ══════════════════

To:        team@rosettipasta.com.au
From:      valentina_rosetti@rosettipasta.com.au
Date:      20 August
Subject:   Update
```

Dear Team,

The past several years have been fast-paced. — [1] —. Five years ago, when I began selling my homemade pasta, I never expected to need a space larger than the kitchen in my own house. How things have changed! This week, the business won a contract to supply a regional food distributor here in Eastern Australia.

This achievement certainly would not have been possible without you. — [2] —. You have all worked hard to keep pace with such tremendous growth, and it was not always easy. To show my appreciation, I have decided that each of you will receive a bonus. — [3] —.

With our solid team and our streamlined production process, I am optimistic that we will see our product placed on even more supermarket shelves soon. — [4] —. The future looks bright.

Sincerely,

Valentina Rosetti
Chief Executive Officer, Rosetti Pasta Company Ltd.

---

162. Why did Ms. Rosetti send the e-mail?

(A) To thank employees
(B) To present a business plan
(C) To announce a postponement
(D) To request assistance with a project

163. What does Ms. Rosetti express confidence about?

(A) The development of a new product line
(B) The potential for more company growth
(C) The success of an advertising campaign
(D) The possibility of replacing old machinery

164. In which of the positions marked [1], [2], [3], and [4] does the following sentence best belong?

"It will appear in your accounts on Friday."

(A) [1]
(B) [2]
(C) [3]
(D) [4]

GO ON TO THE NEXT PAGE

To:	Sid Shepard
From:	Corporate Security
Date:	July 2
Subject:	Your ID badge

Dear Mr. Shepard:

We received your request this morning for assistance in acquiring a new physical identification badge. As your current badge was misplaced, it has been deactivated. To receive a replacement, visit the corporate security office in Paulsen Hall between 7 a.m. and 5:30 p.m. You will be required to show a form of government-issued identification.

In the meantime, you can take advantage of a new corporate initiative. The company app installed on all employees' mobile devices now includes a digital identification card that can be used to gain entry to the corporate parking garage and campus buildings. To access the digital ID card in the app, look for the "ID Card" tab. You can then scan your digital ID to enter all secure areas.

If you have questions or need additional help, please call corporate security at 863-555-0171.

Thank you,

Hopper Technology Corporate Security

165. What is the purpose of the e-mail?

(A) To respond to a request for help
(B) To promote the sale of a new product
(C) To alert authorities to a security problem
(D) To announce a new company policy

166. What is suggested about Mr. Shepard?

(A) He first contacted corporate security two days ago.
(B) He does not use the corporate parking garage.
(C) He does not know where Paulsen Hall is located.
(D) He has the company app installed on his mobile device.

167. The word "gain" in paragraph 2, line 3, is closest in meaning to

(A) win
(B) obtain
(C) collect
(D) increase

Questions 168-171 refer to the following online chat discussion.

Margo Basset [9:16 A.M.] Hi, All. Where are we with the schedule for the weekly New Assets lunch series for our new hires?

Stephan Ruess [9:18 A.M.] We've finalized the session topics. I believe we have confirmed one speaker.

Alban Mithat [9:20 A.M.] That is correct. Salima Abubakar from our north suburban office agreed to take on the first session of the series.

Margo Basset [9:24 A.M.] Fantastic. Is she able to present on June 10 as we planned?

Alban Mithat [9:26 A.M.] She is, and she suggested that a panel discussion might be more engaging for her topic, renewable resources. She will moderate the discussion. I've e-mailed the three employees she suggested as panelists.

Margo Basset [9:27 A.M.] That sounds good. And the other sessions?

Stephan Ruess [9:28 A.M.] So, the topics for the other six sessions will be cryptocurrencies, commodities, investments, start-ups, real estate, and virtual interfaces. I hope to have speakers for those sessions lined up by the end of this week.

Margo Basset [9:31 A.M.] And they'll all be held at the midtown office.

Stephan Ruess [9:32 A.M.] Correct. Four of our seven new hires are permanently assigned to the midtown office. The other new hires will be there on session days for required training.

---

168. What is suggested about the New Assets lunch session on June 10 ?

(A) It will be led by Ms. Abubakar.
(B) It will be introduced by Mr. Mithat.
(C) It will feature Ms. Basset.
(D) It will include information about cryptocurrencies.

169. At 9:27 A.M., what does Ms. Basset mean when she writes, "That sounds good"?

(A) She is eager to attend the New Assets lunch series.
(B) She approves of Ms. Abubakar's idea.
(C) She is pleased with all the session topics.
(D) She looks forward to meeting the recently hired employees.

170. How many sessions still need speakers?

(A) One
(B) Three
(C) Four
(D) Six

171. What is true about the New Assets lunch series?

(A) It is the main component of employee training.
(B) It will be held in the same location every week.
(C) It will consist exclusively of panel discussions.
(D) It will include presenters from outside the company.

GO ON TO THE NEXT PAGE

Questions 172-175 refer to the following article.

Research Findings Presented

GALWAY (1 July)—Eva Urban and her research team at the Ireland Agronomy Association presented their findings to the Galway Department of Transportation on Thursday. During their three-year study, the team was tasked with researching ways to improve the success of tree and shrub plantings along roadways. — [1] —.

"The ground next to newly paved roads is often compacted by heavy machinery associated with construction," Ms. Urban said. "As a result, the soil can't absorb water or nutrients well, which makes it difficult for new growth to establish itself. — [2] —. My team set up different experimental plots alongside highways and tried various combinations of planting, tilling, and amending soils to determine what worked."

The final results of the government-sponsored research project were compiled into a 50-page handbook. Although the handbook was written specifically for the Galway Department of Transportation, its recommendations can be applied by municipal agencies throughout the country. — [3] —.

"Each chapter explores one of the ten best practices identified by the team," said Ms. Urban. "These basic techniques are relevant regardless of where they are implemented. The only site-specific variable is plant selection, as that will depend upon the particular geographic region."

Another point conveyed by the study is that successful plant establishment requires an integrated approach. — [4] —. Improving roadside planting requires a thorough assessment of a site's existing conditions as well as a wide variety of management practices to address the specific issues involved.

172. What is the subject of the research discussed in the article?

(A) Keeping vegetation alive along roadways
(B) Preventing damage to highway surfaces
(C) Advocating for the use of native plants
(D) Improving roadside visibility for drivers

173. Why does Ms. Urban mention heavy machinery?

(A) To explain why plants may grow poorly in some soil
(B) To argue that roads can be built more efficiently
(C) To suggest that road maintenance crews should be careful with young plants
(D) To describe equipment used by her research team

174. In the article, what is indicated about a handbook?

(A) It is only ten pages long.
(B) It will be distributed to the public.
(C) It was the subject of a local dispute.
(D) It is appropriate for use in other parts of the country.

175. In which of the positions marked [1], [2], [3], and [4] does the following sentence best belong?

"In other words, one action is not enough."

(A) [1]
(B) [2]
(C) [3]
(D) [4]

GO ON TO THE NEXT PAGE

Questions 176-180 refer to the following invoice and article.

Dawn Sky Catering
525 Horseshoe Lane
Gardendale, PA 19061

Invoice date: December 6   **Invoice number:** 5688

Customer name	Maureen Shibata		
Company	Gardendale Neighborhood Association (GNA)		
Address	4069 Strother Street, Gardendale, PA 19061		
Phone number	484-555-0152	**E-mail**	mshibata@gardendalena.org
Event date	December 15	**Balance due date**	December 13

Description	Quantity	Price
Platter of assorted raw vegetables with dips	5	$125.00
Grilled chicken skewers (tray)	5	$150.00
Quiche tarts (tray)	5	$175.00
Small chocolate cakes (custom decorated)	50	$250.00
SUBTOTAL		$700.00
Deposit (received November 25)		−$200.00
BALANCE DUE		$500.00

Comments or special instructions:
See November 30 e-mail from Ms. Shibata about cake design. This will be for the GNA's annual reception.

GARDENDALE (December 20)—The Gardendale Neighborhood Association (GNA) honored Mayor Karla Fugate at its annual reception last Saturday. Mayor Fugate had been asked to give a short speech about the city's plans to build a new recreational center, after which she was presented with a special plaque to thank her for her role in the Westside Park project. According to GNA president Manuel Yuen, "Mayor Fugate was instrumental in making last year's fund-raising festival for the park a huge success." The festival raised thousands of dollars more than the GNA expected.

"It was a delightful surprise," said Mayor Fugate. "We set ourselves a difficult mission with the park project, but everybody in the GNA and the community at large came through admirably," the mayor continued.

The GNA reception was held in the Gardendale Botanical Garden, which offered a beautiful setting. The food was provided by Dawn Sky Catering, which included an individual chocolate cake for each guest decorated with the GNA logo.

176. What does the invoice suggest about Ms. Shibata?

(A) She will be the guest of honor at an event.
(B) She charged the GNA for its catering order.
(C) She is the organizer of the GNA's reception.
(D) She will be decorating some cakes herself.

177. When was the GNA required to pay $500 to Dawn Sky Catering?

(A) On November 30
(B) On December 6
(C) On December 13
(D) On December 15

178. According to the article, what happened at the reception?

(A) Mayor Fugate was given an award.
(B) Mayor Fugate was asked to reduce her speech.
(C) Mayor Fugate took questions from the audience.
(D) Mayor Fugate was invited to join the GNA.

179. In the article, the word "instrumental" in paragraph 1, line 12, is closest in meaning to

(A) mechanical
(B) informal
(C) musical
(D) essential

180. How many people most likely attended the GNA reception?

(A) 5
(B) 50
(C) 100
(D) 200

GO ON TO THE NEXT PAGE

Chisaka Gaming Systems
410-1109, Nijo Dencho, Nakagyo-ku Kyoto-shi
Kyoto, Japan

Toby Heisenberger
1226 Lark Street
Albany, New York 12210
USA

May 7

Product Recall:
CGS-P27 High-Speed Gaming Computer

Dear Mr. Heisenberger,

This is to inform you that the CGS-P27 High-Speed Gaming Computer has been recalled. We have received reports of units overheating and becoming unusable. To address this issue, an additional fan needs to be installed in your computer. Please return the gaming system to the store in which it was purchased, using your personal customer identification number, PCI-70734. Your system will then be sent back to the manufacturer and repaired at no expense to you.

We apologize for any inconvenience.

Sincerely,
Kobu Matsui
Kobu Matsui, Vice President
Chisaka Gaming Systems

To:	Virginia Granger <v.granger@chisakagamingsystems.jp>
From:	Jennifer Kinkaid <jkinkaid@albancgm.com>
Date:	June 12
Subject:	Product recall

Dear Ms. Granger,

Our retail stores have been accepting your CGS-P27 High-Speed Gaming Computers for repairs as arranged. As you may know, owners of your gaming system are reluctant to give up their devices for repair once they find that they will be without the system for two to three weeks. Today alone, three customers (PCI-70734, PCI-17503, and PCI-90022) declined to have their systems repaired.

The good news is that users of your gaming system are very loyal. However, to increase compliance with the recall and as a public relations gesture, you could provide us with several devices as part of a loaner program. Let me know how I can assist with this arrangement.

Thank you!

Jennifer Kinkaid
Alban Computers, Games, and More

181. Why did Mr. Matsui send the letter?

(A) To advertise a new product
(B) To alert a customer to a problem
(C) To confirm that a refund had been issued
(D) To offer a customer an upgrade

182. What type of company does Ms. Granger work for?

(A) A computer manufacturer
(B) A retail store
(C) A repair company
(D) A game rental service

183. In the e-mail, the word "program" in paragraph 2, line 3, is closest in meaning to

(A) schedule
(B) plan
(C) broadcast
(D) software

184. What can be concluded about Mr. Heisenberger?

(A) He was not satisfied with his purchase.
(B) He called Ms. Granger to discuss options.
(C) He did not bring his system in for repair.
(D) He requested a two-week turnaround.

185. What does Ms. Kinkaid request in her e-mail?

(A) Free products
(B) System upgrades
(C) Computer monitors
(D) Temporary replacements

TEST 9

GO ON TO THE NEXT PAGE

Questions 186-190 refer to the following e-mail and Web pages.

To:	Marcella Wairimu <m.wairimu@theushindigroup.co.ke>
From:	Henry Bunyasi <h.bunyasi@theushindigroup.co.ke>
Date:	3 February
Subject:	Survey

Dear Ms. Wairimu,

The management team has asked us to find out how satisfied our clients are with our digital marketing services. To that end, we will conduct a survey during the month of April.

Given your expertise in survey design and analysis, I would like you to develop a customer satisfaction survey that includes an evaluation of the digital marketing services we advertise on our Web site. It will be sent to each of our longtime clients here in Kenya. Please have a draft ready by 17 February and distribute it to the members of the management team for their review. You and I will present the draft at the management team's meeting on 23 February at 2:00 P.M.

Regards,

Henry Bunyasi

---

https://www.theushindigroup.co.ke/services_survey

About Us	**Services**	Plans and Pricing	Company News

Satisfaction Survey
1 May

At The Ushindi Group, we strive to provide you with top-quality marketing services. That is why we are asking our longtime clients to complete this short survey about our digital marketing services. With the information you provide, we can identify areas for improvement. Please submit your responses on or before 19 May. Thank you for helping us to serve you better.

Please type one of the following values into the appropriate box for each service.
1 = very dissatisfied, 2 = dissatisfied, 3 = no opinion, 4 = satisfied, 5 = very satisfied

Digital Marketing Services
   A. Advertising on social media
   B. Content creation, including written content, photos, and videos
   C. E-mail marketing to existing and potential customers
   D. Web and mobile app development and design

Client name (optional):

https://www.theushindigroup.co.ke/companynews

| About Us | Services | Plans and Pricing | **Company News** |

Improvements to Our Services

In response to customer feedback, The Ushindi Group will introduce a new e-mail marketing strategy on 15 July.

Our new focus will be on triggered e-mails. Triggered e-mails are sent out automatically based on customer behaviour and have a much higher response rate than traditional marketing e-mails. Triggered e-mails help companies turn casual buyers into loyal customers.

We anticipate that this change will result in a noticeable increase in repeat customers for our clients. The price of our services will remain the same. For more information, you may contact your marketing account manager directly, call The Ushindi Group at 0800 205 555, or send an e-mail to info@theushindigroup.co.ke.

186. What is stated about Ms. Wairimu in the e-mail?

(A) She resolved a complaint from one of her clients.
(B) She responded to an employee questionnaire.
(C) She is a member of the management team.
(D) She is highly skilled in survey development.

187. What will most likely happen on February 23 ?

(A) The Ushindi Group's Web site will be updated.
(B) Mr. Bunyasi will review the advertising budget.
(C) Ms. Wairimu will attend a meeting in the afternoon.
(D) The management team will vote on a policy revision.

188. What can be concluded about the satisfaction survey?

(A) It was sent by mail.
(B) It was not distributed to clients according to the original timetable.
(C) It was revised after the management team's meeting.
(D) It was sent to clients around the world.

189. What news is reported on the second Web page?

(A) Service rates will soon increase.
(B) A marketing manager has been replaced.
(C) Surveys will be conducted on a monthly basis.
(D) An automated customer contact system will launch.

190. What digital marketing service will The Ushindi Group change based on responses to its survey?

(A) Service A
(B) Service B
(C) Service C
(D) Service D

GO ON TO THE NEXT PAGE

Questions 191-195 refer to the following article and Web pages.

Director Rubio Celebrated

MERRINGTON (July 20)—Although Pedro Rubio retired from directing ten years ago, his award-winning films still influence today's cinema.

Rubio's childhood home was near a movie house, where he fell in love with the art form. He saw several movies a week, sometimes watching the same movie multiple times.

His extensive familiarity with a range of genres is apparent in his work. Titles range from the romantic *Send Me Some Roses* to the horror classic *That House*.

Rubio retired from filmmaking at age 65 after almost 40 years of directing, but he has kept busy. Most recently, he has been working as a guest lecturer at the nearby Weberton Film School.

Readers will be pleased to hear that our own Merrington Cinema will be showing Rubio's films throughout August. Whether you are a longtime fan or have never seen a Rubio film, you will surely enjoy this offering at Merrington Cinema.

---

https://www.merringtoncinema.com

Home	Schedule	Reviews	Contact Us

Choose Your Own Double Feature

In August, we will celebrate the acclaimed director Pedro Rubio's birthday by showing many of his movies. And you can purchase tickets to two movies for the price of one! Rubio made the films listed below at the beginning of his directing career. See the Schedule page for the complete list of films and their weekly viewing times.

Put a Roof on It, Comedy, 102 minutes
Construction workers do their best to build a wealthy man's dream home while his brother tries to take over the project.

Through a Diamond Rain, Science Fiction, 124 minutes
Two teams of researchers travel to Neptune and try to send their findings back to Earth.

Weekends and Memories, Drama, 115 minutes
A group of old friends gather at a country house and discover that much has changed since they were last together. This film won the Gold Dreamer Award.

The Strange Drive, Western, 107 minutes
Cowboys on a cattle drive encounter a series of interesting and unusual strangers.

| Home | Schedule | **Reviews** | Contact Us |

I recently read a great article about director Pedro Rubio. It contained a lot of information about his work and life, including some surprising information about what he has been doing since he retired from filmmaking. The article also mentioned that Merrington Cinema would be showing his films. So I went to the cinema's Web site and saw the two-for-one deal. I thought this would be an excellent way to spend a Saturday, so I went! I saw two wonderful movies. One of the films I saw was new to me: it was about scientists on a mission in space. I loved it!

For a movie fan like me, Merrington Cinema's promotion was perfect. I understand there will be a similar promotion for Meredeth Bui's films in October. I'll be sure to take advantage of great offers like this again.

—Talia Pak

191. According to the article, how did Mr. Rubio become interested in the cinema?

(A) His family worked in the movie business.
(B) He participated in a film club at school.
(C) He visited a movie theater frequently in his youth.
(D) He used to be a ticket seller in a movie theater.

192. According to the first Web page, why is Merrington Cinema offering a promotion?

(A) It recently opened and wants to attract customers.
(B) It is celebrating a director's birthday.
(C) It has partnered with a movie studio to show certain movies.
(D) It wants to advertise its new upgraded premises.

193. According to the first Web page, what do the four listed movies have in common?

(A) They are all less than 120 minutes long.
(B) They all focus on friendships.
(C) They are all early films of Mr. Rubio's.
(D) They have all received awards.

194. What did Ms. Pak find surprising about Mr. Rubio?

(A) He is teaching at a local film school.
(B) He directed movies for nearly 40 years.
(C) He worked in many genres.
(D) He has opened his own movie theater.

195. What movie did Ms. Pak see recently for the first time?

(A) *Put a Roof on It*
(B) *Through a Diamond Rain*
(C) *Weekends and Memories*
(D) *The Strange Drive*

TEST 9

GO ON TO THE NEXT PAGE

Questions 196-200 refer to the following policy and e-mails.

Submission Policy

Undeniable is an ad-supported literary journal of short fiction and nonfiction by emerging writers. We waive our $5 fee for first-time submitters.

• Stories must be between 250 and 1,000 words (no poetry, please).

• Do not include illustrations. All illustrations are produced in-house.

• Attach your story in an e-mail to: submissions@undeniable.com. Please include a brief synopsis of your piece, and tell us how you discovered *Undeniable*.

• We pay a $50 honorarium upon acceptance for publication.

• If we accept your story, we will send you a contract and a form to set up an electronic money transfer.

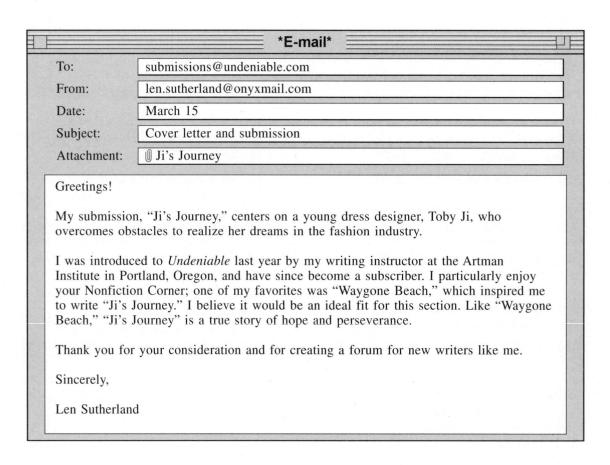

E-mail	
To:	submissions@undeniable.com
From:	len.sutherland@onyxmail.com
Date:	March 15
Subject:	Cover letter and submission
Attachment:	📎 Ji's Journey

Greetings!

My submission, "Ji's Journey," centers on a young dress designer, Toby Ji, who overcomes obstacles to realize her dreams in the fashion industry.

I was introduced to *Undeniable* last year by my writing instructor at the Artman Institute in Portland, Oregon, and have since become a subscriber. I particularly enjoy your Nonfiction Corner; one of my favorites was "Waygone Beach," which inspired me to write "Ji's Journey." I believe it would be an ideal fit for this section. Like "Waygone Beach," "Ji's Journey" is a true story of hope and perseverance.

Thank you for your consideration and for creating a forum for new writers like me.

Sincerely,

Len Sutherland

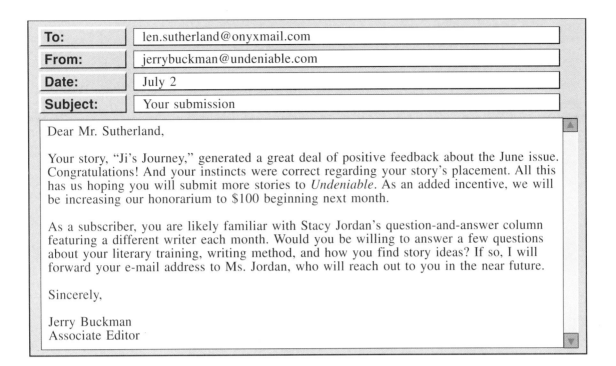

To:	len.sutherland@onyxmail.com
From:	jerrybuckman@undeniable.com
Date:	July 2
Subject:	Your submission

Dear Mr. Sutherland,

Your story, "Ji's Journey," generated a great deal of positive feedback about the June issue. Congratulations! And your instincts were correct regarding your story's placement. All this has us hoping you will submit more stories to *Undeniable*. As an added incentive, we will be increasing our honorarium to $100 beginning next month.

As a subscriber, you are likely familiar with Stacy Jordan's question-and-answer column featuring a different writer each month. Would you be willing to answer a few questions about your literary training, writing method, and how you find story ideas? If so, I will forward your e-mail address to Ms. Jordan, who will reach out to you in the near future.

Sincerely,

Jerry Buckman
Associate Editor

196. What does the policy indicate about *Undeniable* ?

(A) It does not accept poems.
(B) It has no advertisements.
(C) It requires writers to submit drawings.
(D) It publishes the work of famous authors.

197. According to the first e-mail, where did Mr. Sutherland discover *Undeniable* ?

(A) In a public library
(B) In a school bookstore
(C) In a writing class
(D) In a clothing shop

198. What can be concluded about "Waygone Beach"?

(A) It takes place in Portland, Oregon.
(B) It was not accepted for publication.
(C) It is Mr. Sutherland's first story.
(D) It does not exceed 1,000 words.

199. How much did Mr. Sutherland receive for his story in the June issue of *Undeniable* ?

(A) $5
(B) $50
(C) $100
(D) $250

200. What does the second e-mail suggest about Ms. Jordan?

(A) She plans to renew her subscription.
(B) She writes a column for *Undeniable*.
(C) She teaches writing classes.
(D) She has an unusual writing method.

TEST 9

Stop! This is the end of the test. If you finish before time is called, you may go back to Parts 5, 6, and 7 and check your work.

토익 정기시험
실전 ❶ 1000
RC

기출 TEST

10

READING TEST

In the Reading test, you will read a variety of texts and answer several different types of reading comprehension questions. The entire Reading test will last 75 minutes. There are three parts, and directions are given for each part. You are encouraged to answer as many questions as possible within the time allowed.

You must mark your answers on the separate answer sheet. Do not write your answers in your test book.

PART 5

Directions: A word or phrase is missing in each of the sentences below. Four answer choices are given below each sentence. Select the best answer to complete the sentence. Then mark the letter (A), (B), (C), or (D) on your answer sheet.

---

101. Aberdeen Bank offers a range of financial services ------- the needs of its customers.

(A) meet
(B) to meet
(C) is meeting
(D) meetings

102. ------- staff are asked to provide a backup cell phone number and e-mail address.

(A) Every
(B) All
(C) Each
(D) Any

103. Today, Mr. Rahn will present ------- ideas to improve the company's accounting software.

(A) he
(B) him
(C) his
(D) himself

104. The firm's one-hour lunch policy is ------- enforced, so do not return late.

(A) strictly
(B) hungrily
(C) punctually
(D) bravely

105. Ms. Martinova's promotion to chief financial officer is contingent ------- approval by our board of executives.

(A) within
(B) on
(C) around
(D) beside

106. The peninsula's southernmost portion is rarely visited because it is not ------- accessible to travelers.

(A) easy
(B) easily
(C) easier
(D) easiest

107. The Vaknis Group ------- all clients a flat consultation fee, to be paid in advance.

(A) informs
(B) considers
(C) charges
(D) suggests

108. On August 19, employees will not be able to access their e-mail account ------- time sheet.

(A) like
(B) so
(C) or
(D) first

109. Walk-in clients are ------- a reliable source of business for the Auburn Hair Salon.

(A) typically
(B) fairly
(C) sharply
(D) evenly

110. By the end of the year, all packaging used for Schaefer's food products will be ------- recyclable.

(A) critically
(B) initially
(C) freshly
(D) fully

111. Highbrook Hotel staff are trained to provide each guest with an exceptional -------.

(A) experiencing
(B) is experienced
(C) experience
(D) to experience

112. In ------- for their help, volunteers at the library's book sale were given personalized tea mugs.

(A) appreciate
(B) appreciative
(C) appreciation
(D) appreciates

113. Because employees must learn to use the new software, several training sessions will take place ------- the next two weeks.

(A) by
(B) over
(C) against
(D) at

114. Flight attendants asked passengers to take their seats ------- upon boarding the plane.

(A) quicken
(B) quickened
(C) quickly
(D) quickest

115. Last July, Rojas Rieper LLC ------- a grand opening celebration.

(A) hosts
(B) hosted
(C) will host
(D) is hosting

116. Mr. Kim was one ------- three people who received the firm's Competitive Edge award.

(A) by
(B) of
(C) for
(D) to

117. Interviews begin today for the production manager ------- at Zhu Pharmaceuticals.

(A) participation
(B) outline
(C) arrangement
(D) position

118. Tours of the historic courthouse are offered twice a week ------- the summer.

(A) onto
(B) during
(C) about
(D) at

119. ------- the next few months, Abundi Ltd. will open its fourth pharmaceutical laboratory in New Zealand.

(A) Within
(B) Soon
(C) Even
(D) When

120. The ------- at Yohanan Company organizes the delivery of supplies to all conference locations.

(A) coordinating
(B) coordinates
(C) coordinated
(D) coordinator

TEST 10

GO ON TO THE NEXT PAGE

121. The owners of Rowecroft Porcelain ------- to begin production of casual dinnerware sets next month.

   (A) intend
   (B) intending
   (C) intentional
   (D) intentionally

122. Mykos Auto Makers agreed to grant long-term factory employees ------- vacation time.

   (A) exhausted
   (B) every
   (C) extended
   (D) any

123. The customer ------- believed that the coat he had purchased was waterproof.

   (A) mistakenly
   (B) mistaken
   (C) mistook
   (D) mistake

124. All cars built by Roadway Motors come ------- with an alarm reminding drivers to buckle their seat belts.

   (A) equips
   (B) equipped
   (C) equipping
   (D) equipment

125. The components of the CT640 dishwasher are largely the same as ------- of earlier models.

   (A) they
   (B) them
   (C) those
   (D) themselves

126. The Nakato Group has won several industry awards for its innovative marketing -------.

   (A) strategize
   (B) strategic
   (C) strategically
   (D) strategies

127. Krit Pinthong's new mystery novel is the most widely ------- book of the year.

   (A) estimated
   (B) anticipated
   (C) assumed
   (D) predicted

128. The leadership team was quite relieved ------- the Tovyar building project was completed under budget.

   (A) especially
   (B) following
   (C) when
   (D) than

129. -------- two floors of offices, the building offers several retail spaces.

   (A) In addition to
   (B) Fortunately
   (C) In order that
   (D) Especially

130. ------- regarding construction noise and traffic delays should be directed to Mr. Jasdi, the project manager.

   (A) Materials
   (B) Concerns
   (C) Expansions
   (D) Selections

PART 6

Directions: Read the texts that follow. A word, phrase, or sentence is missing in parts of each text. Four answer choices for each question are given below the text. Select the best answer to complete the text. Then mark the letter (A), (B), (C), or (D) on your answer sheet.

Questions 131-134 refer to the following advertisement.

JOIN THE RGBS AUTOMOTIVE TEAM

RGBS Automotive is ------- hiring full-time and part-time workers. Apply today! ------- could
                            131.   **132.**

become part of our manufacturing team! We make high-tech products ------- found in cars and
                                                                        133.

trucks of all kinds.

RGBS Automotive pays well, and we provide ongoing training plus opportunities for promotion.

------- . Go to www.rgbsautomotive.com for more details and to fill out an application.
134.

---

131. (A) now
  (B) likewise
  (C) there
  (D) instead

132. (A) It
  (B) You
  (C) They
  (D) Everyone

133. (A) can be
  (B) that are
  (C) and being
  (D) that had been

134. (A) Ours is a highly competitive industry.
  (B) RGBS Automotive began doing business 45 years ago.
  (C) We also offer a generous number of vacation days.
  (D) RGBS Automotive sells a wide selection of merchandise.

GO ON TO THE NEXT PAGE

Questions 135-138 refer to the following memo.

MEMO

To: Marketing Team
From: Alyssa Jacobs, Project Manager
Date: 27 September
Subject: Meeting wrap-up

Thank you again to all of you for your fine work on the upcoming marketing campaign for the Turbo Omega 2 smartphone. As ------- during yesterday's meeting, our goal is to launch the
135.
television, radio, and social media advertisements on 1 November. The phone itself will be in stores by 1 December. ------- .
136.

------- , Gary Carollo will draft the press release and post it on our shared drive, where all of you
137.
will be able to read it. Please e-mail any ------- for changes to Gary within one week. He will
138.
present his final draft at our next regular meeting. We will also tie up any loose ends at that time.

---

135. (A) taken
     (B) driven
     (C) earned
     (D) decided

136. (A) Remember to turn off your phone at the end of the workday.
     (B) This gives us one month to generate consumer excitement.
     (C) The wholesale price can also be adjusted if necessary.
     (D) These new features will surely increase Turbo Omega 2 sales.

137. (A) Rather
     (B) Soon
     (C) After all
     (D) That is

138. (A) suggesting
     (B) suggested
     (C) suggestions
     (D) suggests

Handmade Silk Blouse by Coreopsis Textiles, Size Medium, £45

Coreopsis Textiles' silk blouses are created from vintage fabrics and other recycled components that we sew together in a patchwork fashion. Because all ------- garments are handcrafted, each is
139.
one of a kind. ------- . Unique variations within each piece are part of the charm of Coreopsis
140.
Textiles' products. The blouse you receive will be similar in style but not identical to the one pictured.

Please note that this garment is ------- . It is recommended that you either hand-wash it or wash it
141.
in cold water on the gentle cycle in a mesh bag. While the item has been prewashed, dryer heat may cause it to shrink. ------- , it is important that it be hung to air dry.
142.

139. (A) its
(B) our
(C) your
(D) their

140. (A) This is a hassle-free return policy.
(B) Always check your receipt.
(C) They cannot be exactly replicated.
(D) Extra shipping charges may apply.

141. (A) popular
(B) delicate
(C) mild
(D) unavailable

142. (A) If not
(B) Likewise
(C) Therefore
(D) On the contrary

GO ON TO THE NEXT PAGE

To: Shu Jiang <sjiang@rowanatech.ca>
From: Maxwell Baschet <mbaschet@mapleroadstorage.ca>
Date: 4 April
Subject: Your contract
Attachment: Jiang contract

Dear Ms. Jiang,

We are pleased you ------- Maple Road Storage for your storage needs. I have attached a copy
                       143.
of your signed contract. ------- .
                         144.

Do you know about our referral program? You will receive one free month of storage if someone

you recommend signs a contract with us. The new tenant will receive a free month

------- . You can find more information about this program and all our special ------- on our Web
145.   **146.**
site at www.mapleroadstorage.ca.

Sincerely,

Maxwell Baschet, Site Manager

---

143. (A) chooses
 (B) will choose
 (C) chosen
 (D) have chosen

144. (A) If your contact information changes, please let us know.
 (B) We hope you will enjoy working here.
 (C) We will reply as soon as possible.
 (D) However, business contracts can be difficult to understand.

145. (A) after all
 (B) again
 (C) as well
 (D) since

146. (A) offers
 (B) schedules
 (C) classes
 (D) amounts

PART 7

Directions: In this part you will read a selection of texts, such as magazine and newspaper articles, e-mails, and instant messages. Each text or set of texts is followed by several questions. Select the best answer for each question and mark the letter (A), (B), (C), or (D) on your answer sheet.

Questions 147-148 refer to the following notice.

Cardinal Street Project—Update

Because of unusually wet and cold weather conditions, the road closure on Cardinal Street between Lee Drive and Petunia Lane will be extended until late spring. Construction will continue; however, final paving on Cardinal Street cannot occur until the weather conditions improve. Workers will begin the pavement work once construction of the bridge on Cardinal Street has been completed. If you have questions or comments, please contact Vy Nguyen in the city planning office at 615-555-0184.

---

147. What is a purpose of the notice?

(A) To report a change in weather patterns
(B) To announce a new detour route
(C) To explain a change in road construction plans
(D) To highlight causes of road deterioration

148. What is indicated about the Cardinal Street project?

(A) It includes building a bridge.
(B) It is being handled by Ms. Nguyen's company.
(C) It does not involve street paving.
(D) It cannot be completed in hot weather.

GO ON TO THE NEXT PAGE

George's Orchard Farm

2232 Alpine Lane

Pick your own! Select from five varieties of juicy peaches in our orchard!
Buckets provided at no cost.

Stop by our market to purchase jams, pies, and sauces made from
farm-fresh fruit.
We sell lunches to enjoy in our picnic area.

Follow the signs ahead for designated parking areas.

Wednesday to Friday, 12 noon to 5:00 P.M.
Saturday and Sunday, 10:00 A.M. to 6:00 P.M.

149. What does George's Orchard Farm offer visitors?

(A) Free buckets for fruit gathering
(B) Customized picnic baskets
(C) Samples of pies and jams
(D) Tours of the farm

150. What is indicated about the market?

(A) It has a new parking area.
(B) It sells products made with peaches.
(C) It is under new management.
(D) It is open every day of the week.

Questions 151-152 refer to the following e-mail.

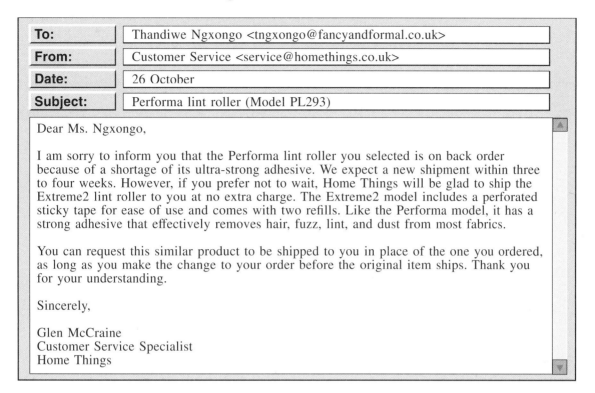

To:	Thandiwe Ngxongo <tngxongo@fancyandformal.co.uk>
From:	Customer Service <service@homethings.co.uk>
Date:	26 October
Subject:	Performa lint roller (Model PL293)

Dear Ms. Ngxongo,

I am sorry to inform you that the Performa lint roller you selected is on back order because of a shortage of its ultra-strong adhesive. We expect a new shipment within three to four weeks. However, if you prefer not to wait, Home Things will be glad to ship the Extreme2 lint roller to you at no extra charge. The Extreme2 model includes a perforated sticky tape for ease of use and comes with two refills. Like the Performa model, it has a strong adhesive that effectively removes hair, fuzz, lint, and dust from most fabrics.

You can request this similar product to be shipped to you in place of the one you ordered, as long as you make the change to your order before the original item ships. Thank you for your understanding.

Sincerely,

Glen McCraine
Customer Service Specialist
Home Things

151. Why did Mr. McCraine write the e-mail?

(A) To highlight a new product
(B) To apologize for a delay
(C) To respond to a question
(D) To provide details about a return

152. What is indicated about the Extreme2 lint roller?

(A) It is less expensive than the Performa model.
(B) It comes with additional tape.
(C) It is more effective than the Performa model.
(D) It has received high user ratings.

GO ON TO THE NEXT PAGE

Questions 153-154 refer to the following text-message chain.

Sen Chai (6:51 P.M.):
We're on a dinner break from the negotiation meeting. Mr. Geraci did not accept our offer.

Mateo Michelacci (6:52 P.M.):
That's frustrating. Do you think if we offered another €10,000 he would sell? You and I have agreed that this is the right facility: it's in a convenient location for customers, the access from the highway is perfect for incoming and outgoing deliveries, and potential tenants have already expressed interest.

Sen Chai (6:53 P.M.):
I can't see that happening. But I'll try again. How high can I go?

Mateo Michelacci (6:54 P.M.):
The bank approved us for another €20,000. Offer Mr. Geraci €10,000 more, plus we will fix any building code violations at our expense. Go up to the full €20,000 only if necessary.

Sen Chai (6:55 P.M.):
I'll do my best.

153. What is suggested about Mr. Geraci?

(A) He owns a building.
(B) He recently renovated a facility.
(C) He will approve a loan.
(D) He will meet with Mr. Michelacci.

154. At 6:53 P.M., what does Ms. Chai most likely mean when she writes, "I can't see that happening"?

(A) She thinks that renters will be difficult to attract.
(B) She believes that an offer will still be rejected.
(C) She doubts that shipping will be easy to organize.
(D) She thinks that clients will have trouble finding a location.

Blossom Sales Systems

Blossom Sales Systems (BSS) makes running your business a breeze with its sleek, intuitive point-of-sale devices. As a small business owner, you have many responsibilities and a reputation to build. BSS has all the tools needed to make transactions safe, seamless, and hassle-free.

Enjoy the convenience of a system that has you covered wherever you conduct your business. Whether you sell in a store, over the phone, or online, BSS simplifies the transaction process while backing you with 24-7 technical expertise. Our innovative devices enable you to accept a variety of payment types—from magnetic-stripe and chip readers for credit cards to digital scanners for checks to popular mobile app payment services—ensuring that no potential sales are missed.

Sign up for BSS today and enjoy a free ten-day trial. Registration takes just fifteen minutes to complete. Once approved, save $50 on the purchase of any BSS device that connects to your phone or tablet. Call 931-555-0148 to schedule a demonstration and see how BSS can make your sales bloom!

---

155. The word "backing" in paragraph 2, line 3, is closest in meaning to

(A) favoring
(B) reversing
(C) supporting
(D) establishing

156. What payment method is NOT mentioned in the advertisement?

(A) Cash
(B) Check
(C) Credit card
(D) Mobile app

157. What is BSS offering as a sales promotion?

(A) A new mobile phone
(B) A fifteen-day free trial
(C) A free device for a tablet
(D) A discount on equipment

```
┌──────────────────────────────────────────────────────────────────────┐
│                              *E-mail*                                  │
├──────────────────────────────────────────────────────────────────────┤
│                                                                        │
│   To:        cbrandt@prebleevents.com                                  │
│                                                                        │
│   From:      chsiao@yanvillefestival.com                               │
│                                                                        │
│   Date:      May 15                                                    │
│                                                                        │
│   Subject:   Festival support                                          │
│                                                                        │
├──────────────────────────────────────────────────────────────────────┤
│  Dear Mr. Brandt,                                                      │
│                                                                        │
│  Thank you for contacting us regarding the Yanville Festival. — [1] —. │
│  We have already contracted with Breemer's Staging to provide lighting │
│  equipment for our main stages.                                        │
│                                                                        │
│  — [2] —. Do you provide catering services? — [3] —. We do not have    │
│  anyone yet to manage the food for our actors and stage crews. Would   │
│  you be interested in this work? Please let me know. — [4] —.          │
│                                                                        │
│  Best regards,                                                         │
│                                                                        │
│  Cecily Hsiao                                                          │
│  Vice-Chair, Yanville Festival                                         │
│                                                                        │
└──────────────────────────────────────────────────────────────────────┘
```

158. What is one reason that Ms. Hsiao wrote the e-mail?

(A) To confirm an order
(B) To request a price
(C) To provide a report
(D) To make an offer

159. What most likely is the focus of the Yanville Festival?

(A) Music
(B) Books
(C) Theater
(D) Fashion

160. In which of the positions marked [1], [2], [3], and [4] does the following sentence best belong?

"However, we have heard good reports about your company, Preble Events, from our partners."

(A) [1]
(B) [2]
(C) [3]
(D) [4]

Questions 161-163 refer to the following advertisement.

Kramer's Emporium
2323 Raleigh Street • Houston, TX 77021

After 25 years in business, our store is closing. Everything must go!

From refrigerators to washing machines, we have hundreds of brand-new appliances for your home or office. Most items have been marked down by 30 percent. Delivery is available within 60 miles of our store for a flat fee of $50.00. We are open daily from 9:00 A.M. to 7:00 P.M.

Don't wait! Merchandise is selling fast!

---

161. What most likely can be purchased at Kramer's Emporium?

(A) Computers
(B) Sofas
(C) Dishwashers
(D) Food

162. Why is Kramer's Emporium selling merchandise at a discount?

(A) It will soon move to a new location.
(B) It wants to promote a specific brand.
(C) It needs to make room for new items.
(D) It will soon go out of business.

163. What is mentioned about delivery?

(A) It is free for purchases of two or more items.
(B) It is available only in a specific area.
(C) It is limited to large items.
(D) It is included in the price of the item.

GO ON TO THE NEXT PAGE

TEST 10

To:	Bruce Holt
From:	Shamonica Walker
Date:	April 9
Subject:	Immediate and confidential

Dear Bruce,

Beginning with the new fiscal year, a change in retirement benefits will be applied for all full-time employees here at Blanen Industries. They will no longer be given their matching retirement funds in the form of cash. Instead, their retirement funds will be provided in the form of company stock to be deposited in their retirement portfolios.

Our current retirement management firm, Proxave Futures, has been informed of this change in retirement benefits. The firm will manage the transition and will continue to provide customer support to Blanen Industries employees. Questions should be directed to Pierre Dehaene at Proxave Futures rather than our human resources department.

Please work with Yua Suzuki, head of human resources, to provide her with the information she should include in her all-staff communication about this important change in employee benefits. Our president notified me that he would like to receive all reports related to this transition. Also, please continue to send me daily financial reports.

Best,

Shamonica Walker, CFO
Blanen Industries

164. What is a purpose of the e-mail?

(A) To inquire about a transaction
(B) To plan a meeting agenda
(C) To provide instructions
(D) To ask for an opinion

165. The word "applied" in paragraph 1, line 1, is closest in meaning to

(A) requested
(B) delayed
(C) discussed
(D) implemented

166. What is suggested about Proxave Futures?

(A) It is giving employees a bonus.
(B) It offers company stock shares to its employees.
(C) It will address any concerns of Blanen Industries employees.
(D) It is merging with Blanen Industries.

167. Who is responsible for notifying all employees about the policy change?

(A) Mr. Holt
(B) Ms. Walker
(C) Mr. Dehaene
(D) Ms. Suzuki

Monica Zia (8:27 A.M.) Hi, Yuji and Sung-ho. I wonder if one of you could help me later today. Dejani Jones was going to help, but she's going to be out of the office today.

Yuji Saito (8:28 A.M.) That's too bad. Did she say why?

Monica Zia (8:28 A.M.) She said she had a slight cold but that she should be able to work from home on the data analyses for her clients.

Sung-ho Suh (8:29 A.M.) So, she won't be coming in at all today?

Monica Zia (8:31 A.M.) No. And Dejani and I were going to go to Willi's Market to buy food and beverages for tomorrow's office picnic. You remember, right? Saturday at noon at City Park. Anyhow, Dejani has a car and was going to drive us to the store and use her credit card to purchase the supplies. I know that both of you drive to work, so I thought one of you could help.

Sung-ho Suh (8:32 A.M.) When were you thinking of going?

Yuji Saito (8:32 A.M.) Sure. I can help, and we can use my credit card.

Monica Zia (8:33 A.M.) Around two.

Yuji Saito (8:34 A.M.) No problem. Just stop by my cubicle, and we can take my car to go to the store.

Sung-ho Suh (8:35 A.M.) That's great, Yuji. I have several meetings this afternoon, so I wouldn't be able to get away.

Monica Zia (8:35 A.M.) Thanks, Yuji. I'll see you this afternoon.

---

168. Why is Ms. Jones going to be out of the office today?

(A) She is feeling ill.
(B) She works from home every Friday.
(C) She is meeting with clients.
(D) She is having car trouble.

169. What had Ms. Jones previously agreed to do?

(A) Drive Ms. Zia to work
(B) Choose a location for a picnic
(C) Move to a new office cubicle
(D) Help with some shopping

170. Who most likely will purchase food and beverages for the picnic?

(A) Ms. Zia
(B) Ms. Jones
(C) Mr. Saito
(D) Mr. Suh

171. At 8:33 A.M., what does Ms. Zia mean when she writes, "Around two"?

(A) She needs at least two people to help her at Willi's Market.
(B) She has reserved two tickets for an event at City Park.
(C) She plans to meet with Mr. Suh in about two hours.
(D) She wants to leave the office this afternoon at about two o'clock.

To:	Dorota Kucharski <dkucharski@internationaltechnologicalsociety.org>
From:	Luciano Moretti <lmoretti@internationaltechnologicalsociety.org>
Date:	8 August
Subject:	Research results

Ms. Kucharski,

The following is a summary of what I have learned in my research about where to hold our next annual technology conference in June of next year.

In Rome, the best option I have found is Hotel al Ponte. The total cost for conference events there would be €31,500. — [1] —. Individual hotel rooms would cost €80 per night for participants. In the event that attendance is high, we could also house participants in the nearby Hotel Milvio at €120 per night. — [2] —.

I also looked into hotels in Genoa and Florence, but I could not find any that would be much cheaper in overall conference costs. — [3] —. More importantly, I am concerned that the greater cost of flights to those smaller cities could discourage some attendees. Rome, on the other hand, has affordable direct flights from most European cities. — [4] —. It will also be more affordable for our colleagues coming from Buenos Aires.

If you would like to pursue the Hotel al Ponte option, I will provide a detailed write-up of the anticipated costs and of the amenities offered by the hotel.

Best,

Luciano Moretti
Secretary, International Technological Society

172. What is the main purpose of the e-mail?

(A) To book travel for a conference
(B) To compare possible venues for a conference
(C) To request a budget increase for organizing a conference
(D) To inquire about the cost of attending a conference

173. What is indicated about the conference?

(A) It is for professionals in the travel industry.
(B) It takes place every year.
(C) It is usually held in Buenos Aires.
(D) It will occur in August.

174. What is true about Hotel Milvio?

(A) It is more expensive than Hotel al Ponte.
(B) It is usually fully booked.
(C) It has locations in Genoa and Florence.
(D) It has more rooms than Hotel al Ponte.

175. In which of the positions marked [1], [2], [3], and [4] does the following sentence best belong?

"The savings to host the conference in one of those cities would be €500 at most."

(A) [1]
(B) [2]
(C) [3]
(D) [4]

GO ON TO THE NEXT PAGE

TEST 10

https://www.centraluniversity.edu/nutrition/newsletter

| **Home** | Customer Service | Subscribe | Account | Log In |

Central University Health Newsletter—Your Guide to Nutrition and Well-Being

Tips on healthful eating are available almost everywhere—from TV shows to online cooking forums. It's often difficult to know whether the advice you encounter is based on scientific evidence. That's why the *Central University Health Newsletter* is indispensable. Each month, it delivers informative, easy-to-understand articles that summarize findings by researchers at the Central University School of Nutrition. For example, last April's issue evaluated nutritional supplements that are sold in supermarkets. The back page features our Ask an Expert column, in which the director of the School of Nutrition answers readers' questions.

A one-year subscription is $20 and includes online access to all previous issues. We also offer a 10 percent discount on your first subscription renewal. What's more, subscribers receive our free weekly "Healthy Living" e-mail update, which includes special reports plus links to videos and podcasts.

To get started, simply go to our Subscribe page and follow the instructions.

---

https://www.centraluniversity.edu/nutrition/newsletter/reviews

Publication: *Central University Health Newsletter*
★★★★★
Reviewed by: Ari Kipp

Date posted: August 4

This is my second year subscribing to the *Central University Health Newsletter*, which I read cover to cover. I'm particularly impressed with the Ask an Expert column, and I always learn something new. This month, for instance, Dr. Stella Booth gives a surprising answer to the question of which pasta is most nutritious. I didn't know that bean-based pasta even existed, much less how much fiber it contains. I tried it and will never go back to regular pasta. My sole complaint is that the newsletter is only twelve pages long!

176. What is the purpose of the Web page?

(A) To explain the reason for a price increase
(B) To increase the size of the audience for a publication
(C) To recruit volunteers for a research project
(D) To sell nutritional supplements

177. In the Web page, the word "delivers" in paragraph 1, line 4, is closest in meaning to

(A) presents
(B) transports
(C) guides
(D) claims

178. What is true about Mr. Kipp?

(A) He is a health-care professional.
(B) He received a 20 percent discount on a subscription.
(C) He gets nutrition tips from a television program.
(D) He gets a weekly e-mail from Central University.

179. What is indicated about the Central University School of Nutrition?

(A) It creates lesson plans for local teachers.
(B) It is headed by Dr. Booth.
(C) It offers online cooking classes.
(D) It has a job opening for a researcher.

180. According to the online review, what is a weakness of the newsletter?

(A) The limited range of topics
(B) The complexity of the articles
(C) The lack of photographs
(D) The overall length

GO ON TO THE NEXT PAGE

TEST 10

Brit-Revision Editing Services Invoice

Freelance Editor: Lisa Yamashita

Invoice Date: 30 September

Address: 178 Upsala Road
LONDON
E16 1DJ

Contact: (020) 7946 0612
lisa.yamashita@bluesun.co.uk
Stashcash ID: Lisa.Yamashita8

Client Name	Project Description	Date Completed	Time
Eddie Kent	University thesis editing	5 September	2 hours
Ben Gallagher	Grant proposal editing	9 September	10 hours
Lydia Quinn of Hyden Interiors	Marketing copy editing	17 September	8.5 hours
Winona Rogers	Journal article editing	22 September	2 hours
Tony Withers	CV and cover letter editing	28 September	2.5 hours

To:	Lisa Yamashita <lisa.yamashita@bluesun.co.uk>
From:	Claudio Aguilar <caguilar@britrevision.co.uk>
Date:	1 October
Subject:	Your recent invoice

Dear Lisa,

Thank you for sending your invoice for services rendered in the month of September. I want to commend you on your superb start as one of our independent freelance editors. Our clients had nothing but positive things to say about your work. As you know, we do not dictate how you structure your workday; instead, Brit-Revision (BRV) guidelines require simply that deadlines be met and that work quality be maintained. You have done both admirably.

Also, we will pay you for an additional 30 minutes of work that you did for Mr. Kent. He reported that you did consulting work for him over the phone on a short oral presentation that he created. As for the work that you did for our long-standing corporate client Lydia Quinn, you will see on your receipt that we have paid you at a higher hourly rate.

I have initiated the transfer of £750 into your Stashcash account. The funds should appear in your account by tomorrow morning.

Sincerely,

Claudio Aguilar
Accounts Payable, Brit-Revision Editing Services

181. What client of BRV's is most likely seeking new employment?

   (A) Mr. Gallagher
   (B) Ms. Quinn
   (C) Ms. Rogers
   (D) Mr. Withers

182. What does the e-mail indicate about Ms. Yamashita?

   (A) She can set her own hours.
   (B) She visits the BRV office every week.
   (C) She must find new clients for BRV.
   (D) She will be eligible for a job promotion soon.

183. According to the e-mail, what did Ms. Yamashita NOT include on the invoice?

   (A) A change of address
   (B) An additional task
   (C) A project end date
   (D) An account number

184. For what project will Ms. Yamashita earn the most per hour?

   (A) The university thesis
   (B) The grant proposal
   (C) The marketing copy
   (D) The journal article

185. When can Ms. Yamashita expect a payment to arrive?

   (A) On September 28
   (B) On September 30
   (C) On October 1
   (D) On October 2

GO ON TO THE NEXT PAGE

TEST 10

Questions 186-190 refer to the following e-mails and instructions.

To:	New Employees
From:	Hemi Amos <hamos@motmanmotors.com>
Date:	June 8
Subject:	Welcome to Motman Motors
Attachment:	📎 Information

Dear New Employees,

Welcome! We are thrilled that all of you are joining Motman Motors.

New-employee orientation for all is on June 10 from 9:00 A.M. to 12:00 noon. Please report to the proper room in the Pimzler Building on our campus as indicated below. I will come around to each room to meet the new employees briefly.

• Marketing and Customer Service: both groups report to room 320.

• Engineering: report to room 215.

• Technology Services: report to room 158.

I can confirm that the employee paperwork has been finalized for most of you, so at this point we just need to ensure that your Motman Motors portal account is set up using the employee identification number recently sent to you and that your bank account information is entered there. Please follow the attached instructions to complete this final step. It should not take any more than fifteen minutes, and I ask that you do this by June 17. Don't hesitate to reach out if you have any questions.

Welcome aboard!

Hemi Amos
Human Resources, Motman Motors

Please follow these steps to create and activate your new Motman Motors portal account. Go to https://motmanmotors.com/portal/activation to begin.

1. Go to the "New User Registration" page and enter your employee ID number.
2. Your name and address will appear. Confirm that this information is correct.
3. A new screen titled "Bank Account" will appear. Fill in your bank account information.
4. Finally, you will be asked to select two security questions and provide the answers.

Once you have created your account, your account will become active, the payroll department will be alerted, and your payment schedule will be set. Please e-mail Mr. Hemi Amos at hamos@motmanmotors.com if you have any difficulties or questions.

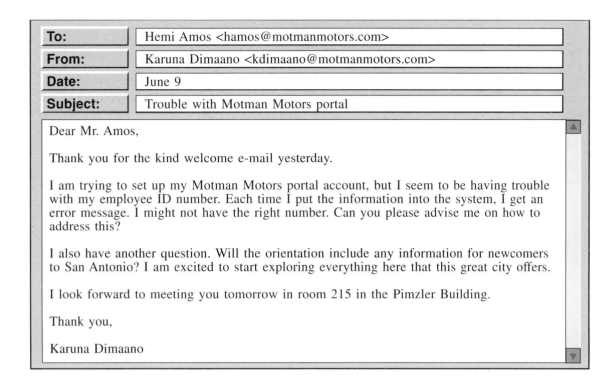

To:	Hemi Amos <hamos@motmanmotors.com>
From:	Karuna Dimaano <kdimaano@motmanmotors.com>
Date:	June 9
Subject:	Trouble with Motman Motors portal

Dear Mr. Amos,

Thank you for the kind welcome e-mail yesterday.

I am trying to set up my Motman Motors portal account, but I seem to be having trouble with my employee ID number. Each time I put the information into the system, I get an error message. I might not have the right number. Can you please advise me on how to address this?

I also have another question. Will the orientation include any information for newcomers to San Antonio? I am excited to start exploring everything here that this great city offers.

I look forward to meeting you tomorrow in room 215 in the Pimzler Building.

Thank you,

Karuna Dimaano

186. According to the first e-mail, what was previously sent to new employees?

(A) An advertisement
(B) An application form
(C) An employee ID number
(D) Directions to an office complex

187. According to the first e-mail, what is the deadline to complete an online task?

(A) June 8
(B) June 10
(C) June 15
(D) June 17

188. What step is Ms. Dimaano having trouble with?

(A) Step 1
(B) Step 2
(C) Step 3
(D) Step 4

189. What department will Ms. Dimaano join?

(A) Marketing
(B) Customer Service
(C) Engineering
(D) Technology Services

190. In the second e-mail, what is suggested about Ms. Dimaano?

(A) She has just graduated from university.
(B) She has met Mr. Amos before.
(C) She is concerned about finding a building.
(D) She has recently moved to San Antonio.

GO ON TO THE NEXT PAGE

To:	Felix Herman <felixh@videogenieproductions.com>
From:	Sapna Mathai <smathai@thehospitalequipmentco.com>
Date:	September 17
Subject:	Notes on rough cut of video
Attachment:	📎 Information

Dear Mr. Herman,

Thank you for sending the rough version of the informational video for our new Fluorolook Imager. I think that the video looks great so far. It clearly demonstrates why the Fluorolook is the best medical imaging device available. I have just a few notes before you proceed to create the final version.

- At 20 seconds: Could you insert a short timeline of the history of The Hospital Equipment Company? I have attached the relevant information to this e-mail.
- At 1 minute: I had a hard time seeing the details of the control panel in this scene. Could you please replace it with a close-up shot?
- At 2 minutes: The sequence in which the medical technician positions the patient and adjusts the machine moves too quickly. Can this be slowed down?

I look forward to seeing the final version on September 23. As always, thank you and your colleagues at Video Genie Productions for the excellent work.

Sincerely,

Ms. Sapna Mathai, Project Manager
The Hospital Equipment Company

The Hospital Equipment Company

Invoice 9984
Billing date: October 25
Installation date: October 26

Bill to:
All-City Hospital
3 Shoreline Road
Clear Lake, Minnesota 55319

Quantity	Item Number	Description	Unit Price	Total
2	62630	Fluorolook Imager	$242,300	$484,600
			Delivery and Installation	$2,350
			Total	**$486,950**

MEMO

To: All The Hospital Equipment Company Employees
From: Marcia Oliver, Vice President of Sales
Date: October 27
Re: Good work!

Congratulations on the successful launch of the Fluorolook Imager! The Hospital Equipment Company has made its first sale—to a hospital in Clear Lake. And MDP Delivery has informed us that the two devices have been delivered.

I would especially like to commend Ms. Mathai. She was instrumental in getting us to this point. The administrator of the hospital that made the purchase, Mr. Fabrice Lamontagne, credited his decision to the informational video. He remarked that the video effectively demonstrated why the Fluorolook Imager was the right device for his medical institution.

191. What is attached to the e-mail?

(A) Details about an invoice
(B) Reviews of Video Genie Productions
(C) A timeline for completing a project
(D) A graphic outlining a company's history

192. Why does Ms. Mathai want to replace the scene at 1 minute?

(A) Some content is not clearly visible.
(B) Some equipment is labeled incorrectly.
(C) The video of the scene moves too quickly.
(D) The medical technician speaks too quietly.

193. What does the invoice indicate about the Fluorolook Imagers?

(A) They were sold at a discount.
(B) The delivery was free of charge.
(C) The purchaser ordered two of them.
(D) They were installed on October 25.

194. Whom does Ms. Oliver specifically praise?

(A) A medical technician
(B) A hospital administrator
(C) A project manager
(D) A video producer

195. Where does Mr. Lamontagne most likely work?

(A) At MDP Delivery
(B) At Video Genie Productions
(C) At The Hospital Equipment Company
(D) At All-City Hospital

GO ON TO THE NEXT PAGE

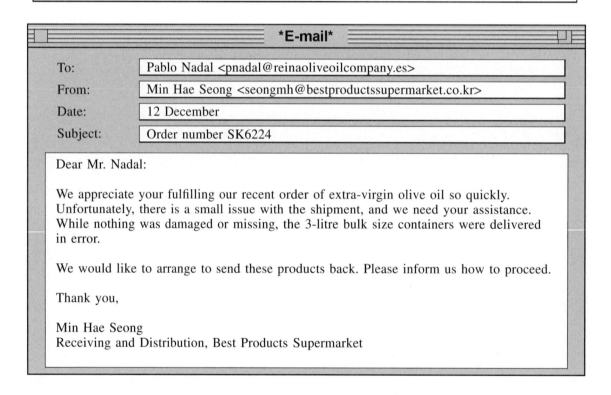

To:	Min Hae Seong <seongmh@bestproductssupermarket.co.kr>
From:	Pablo Nadal <pnadal@reinaoliveoilcompany.es>
Date:	14 December
Subject:	RE: Order number SK6224

Dear Ms. Seong,

I apologise for the error in order number SK6224. We have determined that your order was accidentally combined with another in our electronic database. Unfortunately, we are unable to restock any items that have left our warehouse. Therefore, you may keep the additional olive oil and sell it in your stores. Also, you will receive a refund for the extra charge within the next five to ten business days because of our mistake.

We are currently celebrating peak olive season by offering 10 percent off of your next order. Also, during our Olive Harvest Festival in December, every shipment includes samples of our company's classic olive oil that we encourage you to give to your shoppers with our compliments.

We hope to continue providing Best Products Supermarket with the finest olive oils.

Sincerely yours,

Pablo Nadal
Export Division Manager, Reina Olive Oil Company

196. What is the purpose of the first e-mail?

(A) To place an order
(B) To inquire about delivery costs
(C) To discuss a shipping mistake
(D) To make a payment

197. What item number does Ms. Seong refer to?

(A) EVO160
(B) EVO161
(C) EVO162
(D) EVO163

198. What does the second e-mail suggest about Reina Olive Oil Company?

(A) It is seeking new clients.
(B) It cannot accept returns.
(C) It is owned by Mr. Nadal.
(D) It distributes more than olive oil.

199. What does Mr. Nadal mention he will do for Ms. Seong?

(A) Begin an investigation
(B) Send some company brochures
(C) Arrange for a refund
(D) Send a revised bill

200. Why was item number EVO001 included in the shipment?

(A) To recognize and celebrate a festival
(B) To introduce a company's new product
(C) To replace an item that was out of stock
(D) To resolve an issue with a company's database

Stop! This is the end of the test. If you finish before time is called, you may go back to Parts 5, 6, and 7 and check your work.

ANSWER SHEET

한글
한자
영자

성 명

수험번호

응시일자 : 20   년   월   일

Test 01 (Part 5~7)

101 102 103 104 105 106 107 108 109 110 111 112 113 114 115 116 117 118 119 120
121 122 123 124 125 126 127 128 129 130 131 132 133 134 135 136 137 138 139 140
141 142 143 144 145 146 147 148 149 150 151 152 153 154 155 156 157 158 159 160
161 162 163 164 165 166 167 168 169 170 171 172 173 174 175 176 177 178 179 180
181 182 183 184 185 186 187 188 189 190 191 192 193 194 195 196 197 198 199 200

Test 02 (Part 5~7)

101 102 103 104 105 106 107 108 109 110 111 112 113 114 115 116 117 118 119 120
121 122 123 124 125 126 127 128 129 130 131 132 133 134 135 136 137 138 139 140
141 142 143 144 145 146 147 148 149 150 151 152 153 154 155 156 157 158 159 160
161 162 163 164 165 166 167 168 169 170 171 172 173 174 175 176 177 178 179 180
181 182 183 184 185 186 187 188 189 190 191 192 193 194 195 196 197 198 199 200

ANSWER SHEET

ETS® TOEIC® 토익 정기시험 실전 1000

수험번호

응시일자 : 20 년 월 일

Test 03 (Part 5~7)

성명 한글 한자 영자

Test 04 (Part 5~7)

ANSWER SHEET

ETS® TOEIC® 토익 정기시험 실전 1000

수험번호

응시일자 : 20   년   월   일

성 명	한글
	한자
	영자

Test 05 (Part 5~7)

101 102 103 104 105 106 107 108 109 110 111 112 113 114 115 116 117 118 119 120
121 122 123 124 125 126 127 128 129 130 131 132 133 134 135 136 137 138 139 140
141 142 143 144 145 146 147 148 149 150 151 152 153 154 155 156 157 158 159 160
161 162 163 164 165 166 167 168 169 170 171 172 173 174 175 176 177 178 179 180
181 182 183 184 185 186 187 188 189 190 191 192 193 194 195 196 197 198 199 200

Test 06 (Part 5~7)

101 102 103 104 105 106 107 108 109 110 111 112 113 114 115 116 117 118 119 120
121 122 123 124 125 126 127 128 129 130 131 132 133 134 135 136 137 138 139 140
141 142 143 144 145 146 147 148 149 150 151 152 153 154 155 156 157 158 159 160
161 162 163 164 165 166 167 168 169 170 171 172 173 174 175 176 177 178 179 180
181 182 183 184 185 186 187 188 189 190 191 192 193 194 195 196 197 198 199 200

ANSWER SHEET

ETS® TOEIC® 토익® 정기시험 실전 1000

수험번호						

응시일자 : 20 년 월 일

성명		
	한 글	
	한 자	
	영 자	

Test 07 (Part 5~7)

101	ⓐ ⓑ ⓒ ⓓ	121	ⓐ ⓑ ⓒ ⓓ	141	ⓐ ⓑ ⓒ ⓓ	161	ⓐ ⓑ ⓒ ⓓ	181	ⓐ ⓑ ⓒ ⓓ
102	ⓐ ⓑ ⓒ ⓓ	122	ⓐ ⓑ ⓒ ⓓ	142	ⓐ ⓑ ⓒ ⓓ	162	ⓐ ⓑ ⓒ ⓓ	182	ⓐ ⓑ ⓒ ⓓ
103	ⓐ ⓑ ⓒ ⓓ	123	ⓐ ⓑ ⓒ ⓓ	143	ⓐ ⓑ ⓒ ⓓ	163	ⓐ ⓑ ⓒ ⓓ	183	ⓐ ⓑ ⓒ ⓓ
104	ⓐ ⓑ ⓒ ⓓ	124	ⓐ ⓑ ⓒ ⓓ	144	ⓐ ⓑ ⓒ ⓓ	164	ⓐ ⓑ ⓒ ⓓ	184	ⓐ ⓑ ⓒ ⓓ
105	ⓐ ⓑ ⓒ ⓓ	125	ⓐ ⓑ ⓒ ⓓ	145	ⓐ ⓑ ⓒ ⓓ	165	ⓐ ⓑ ⓒ ⓓ	185	ⓐ ⓑ ⓒ ⓓ
106	ⓐ ⓑ ⓒ ⓓ	126	ⓐ ⓑ ⓒ ⓓ	146	ⓐ ⓑ ⓒ ⓓ	166	ⓐ ⓑ ⓒ ⓓ	186	ⓐ ⓑ ⓒ ⓓ
107	ⓐ ⓑ ⓒ ⓓ	127	ⓐ ⓑ ⓒ ⓓ	147	ⓐ ⓑ ⓒ ⓓ	167	ⓐ ⓑ ⓒ ⓓ	187	ⓐ ⓑ ⓒ ⓓ
108	ⓐ ⓑ ⓒ ⓓ	128	ⓐ ⓑ ⓒ ⓓ	148	ⓐ ⓑ ⓒ ⓓ	168	ⓐ ⓑ ⓒ ⓓ	188	ⓐ ⓑ ⓒ ⓓ
109	ⓐ ⓑ ⓒ ⓓ	129	ⓐ ⓑ ⓒ ⓓ	149	ⓐ ⓑ ⓒ ⓓ	169	ⓐ ⓑ ⓒ ⓓ	189	ⓐ ⓑ ⓒ ⓓ
110	ⓐ ⓑ ⓒ ⓓ	130	ⓐ ⓑ ⓒ ⓓ	150	ⓐ ⓑ ⓒ ⓓ	170	ⓐ ⓑ ⓒ ⓓ	190	ⓐ ⓑ ⓒ ⓓ
111	ⓐ ⓑ ⓒ ⓓ	131	ⓐ ⓑ ⓒ ⓓ	151	ⓐ ⓑ ⓒ ⓓ	171	ⓐ ⓑ ⓒ ⓓ	191	ⓐ ⓑ ⓒ ⓓ
112	ⓐ ⓑ ⓒ ⓓ	132	ⓐ ⓑ ⓒ ⓓ	152	ⓐ ⓑ ⓒ ⓓ	172	ⓐ ⓑ ⓒ ⓓ	192	ⓐ ⓑ ⓒ ⓓ
113	ⓐ ⓑ ⓒ ⓓ	133	ⓐ ⓑ ⓒ ⓓ	153	ⓐ ⓑ ⓒ ⓓ	173	ⓐ ⓑ ⓒ ⓓ	193	ⓐ ⓑ ⓒ ⓓ
114	ⓐ ⓑ ⓒ ⓓ	134	ⓐ ⓑ ⓒ ⓓ	154	ⓐ ⓑ ⓒ ⓓ	174	ⓐ ⓑ ⓒ ⓓ	194	ⓐ ⓑ ⓒ ⓓ
115	ⓐ ⓑ ⓒ ⓓ	135	ⓐ ⓑ ⓒ ⓓ	155	ⓐ ⓑ ⓒ ⓓ	175	ⓐ ⓑ ⓒ ⓓ	195	ⓐ ⓑ ⓒ ⓓ
116	ⓐ ⓑ ⓒ ⓓ	136	ⓐ ⓑ ⓒ ⓓ	156	ⓐ ⓑ ⓒ ⓓ	176	ⓐ ⓑ ⓒ ⓓ	196	ⓐ ⓑ ⓒ ⓓ
117	ⓐ ⓑ ⓒ ⓓ	137	ⓐ ⓑ ⓒ ⓓ	157	ⓐ ⓑ ⓒ ⓓ	177	ⓐ ⓑ ⓒ ⓓ	197	ⓐ ⓑ ⓒ ⓓ
118	ⓐ ⓑ ⓒ ⓓ	138	ⓐ ⓑ ⓒ ⓓ	158	ⓐ ⓑ ⓒ ⓓ	178	ⓐ ⓑ ⓒ ⓓ	198	ⓐ ⓑ ⓒ ⓓ
119	ⓐ ⓑ ⓒ ⓓ	139	ⓐ ⓑ ⓒ ⓓ	159	ⓐ ⓑ ⓒ ⓓ	179	ⓐ ⓑ ⓒ ⓓ	199	ⓐ ⓑ ⓒ ⓓ
120	ⓐ ⓑ ⓒ ⓓ	140	ⓐ ⓑ ⓒ ⓓ	160	ⓐ ⓑ ⓒ ⓓ	180	ⓐ ⓑ ⓒ ⓓ	200	ⓐ ⓑ ⓒ ⓓ

Test 08 (Part 5~7)

101	ⓐ ⓑ ⓒ ⓓ	121	ⓐ ⓑ ⓒ ⓓ	141	ⓐ ⓑ ⓒ ⓓ	161	ⓐ ⓑ ⓒ ⓓ	181	ⓐ ⓑ ⓒ ⓓ
102	ⓐ ⓑ ⓒ ⓓ	122	ⓐ ⓑ ⓒ ⓓ	142	ⓐ ⓑ ⓒ ⓓ	162	ⓐ ⓑ ⓒ ⓓ	182	ⓐ ⓑ ⓒ ⓓ
103	ⓐ ⓑ ⓒ ⓓ	123	ⓐ ⓑ ⓒ ⓓ	143	ⓐ ⓑ ⓒ ⓓ	163	ⓐ ⓑ ⓒ ⓓ	183	ⓐ ⓑ ⓒ ⓓ
104	ⓐ ⓑ ⓒ ⓓ	124	ⓐ ⓑ ⓒ ⓓ	144	ⓐ ⓑ ⓒ ⓓ	164	ⓐ ⓑ ⓒ ⓓ	184	ⓐ ⓑ ⓒ ⓓ
105	ⓐ ⓑ ⓒ ⓓ	125	ⓐ ⓑ ⓒ ⓓ	145	ⓐ ⓑ ⓒ ⓓ	165	ⓐ ⓑ ⓒ ⓓ	185	ⓐ ⓑ ⓒ ⓓ
106	ⓐ ⓑ ⓒ ⓓ	126	ⓐ ⓑ ⓒ ⓓ	146	ⓐ ⓑ ⓒ ⓓ	166	ⓐ ⓑ ⓒ ⓓ	186	ⓐ ⓑ ⓒ ⓓ
107	ⓐ ⓑ ⓒ ⓓ	127	ⓐ ⓑ ⓒ ⓓ	147	ⓐ ⓑ ⓒ ⓓ	167	ⓐ ⓑ ⓒ ⓓ	187	ⓐ ⓑ ⓒ ⓓ
108	ⓐ ⓑ ⓒ ⓓ	128	ⓐ ⓑ ⓒ ⓓ	148	ⓐ ⓑ ⓒ ⓓ	168	ⓐ ⓑ ⓒ ⓓ	188	ⓐ ⓑ ⓒ ⓓ
109	ⓐ ⓑ ⓒ ⓓ	129	ⓐ ⓑ ⓒ ⓓ	149	ⓐ ⓑ ⓒ ⓓ	169	ⓐ ⓑ ⓒ ⓓ	189	ⓐ ⓑ ⓒ ⓓ
110	ⓐ ⓑ ⓒ ⓓ	130	ⓐ ⓑ ⓒ ⓓ	150	ⓐ ⓑ ⓒ ⓓ	170	ⓐ ⓑ ⓒ ⓓ	190	ⓐ ⓑ ⓒ ⓓ
111	ⓐ ⓑ ⓒ ⓓ	131	ⓐ ⓑ ⓒ ⓓ	151	ⓐ ⓑ ⓒ ⓓ	171	ⓐ ⓑ ⓒ ⓓ	191	ⓐ ⓑ ⓒ ⓓ
112	ⓐ ⓑ ⓒ ⓓ	132	ⓐ ⓑ ⓒ ⓓ	152	ⓐ ⓑ ⓒ ⓓ	172	ⓐ ⓑ ⓒ ⓓ	192	ⓐ ⓑ ⓒ ⓓ
113	ⓐ ⓑ ⓒ ⓓ	133	ⓐ ⓑ ⓒ ⓓ	153	ⓐ ⓑ ⓒ ⓓ	173	ⓐ ⓑ ⓒ ⓓ	193	ⓐ ⓑ ⓒ ⓓ
114	ⓐ ⓑ ⓒ ⓓ	134	ⓐ ⓑ ⓒ ⓓ	154	ⓐ ⓑ ⓒ ⓓ	174	ⓐ ⓑ ⓒ ⓓ	194	ⓐ ⓑ ⓒ ⓓ
115	ⓐ ⓑ ⓒ ⓓ	135	ⓐ ⓑ ⓒ ⓓ	155	ⓐ ⓑ ⓒ ⓓ	175	ⓐ ⓑ ⓒ ⓓ	195	ⓐ ⓑ ⓒ ⓓ
116	ⓐ ⓑ ⓒ ⓓ	136	ⓐ ⓑ ⓒ ⓓ	156	ⓐ ⓑ ⓒ ⓓ	176	ⓐ ⓑ ⓒ ⓓ	196	ⓐ ⓑ ⓒ ⓓ
117	ⓐ ⓑ ⓒ ⓓ	137	ⓐ ⓑ ⓒ ⓓ	157	ⓐ ⓑ ⓒ ⓓ	177	ⓐ ⓑ ⓒ ⓓ	197	ⓐ ⓑ ⓒ ⓓ
118	ⓐ ⓑ ⓒ ⓓ	138	ⓐ ⓑ ⓒ ⓓ	158	ⓐ ⓑ ⓒ ⓓ	178	ⓐ ⓑ ⓒ ⓓ	198	ⓐ ⓑ ⓒ ⓓ
119	ⓐ ⓑ ⓒ ⓓ	139	ⓐ ⓑ ⓒ ⓓ	159	ⓐ ⓑ ⓒ ⓓ	179	ⓐ ⓑ ⓒ ⓓ	199	ⓐ ⓑ ⓒ ⓓ
120	ⓐ ⓑ ⓒ ⓓ	140	ⓐ ⓑ ⓒ ⓓ	160	ⓐ ⓑ ⓒ ⓓ	180	ⓐ ⓑ ⓒ ⓓ	200	ⓐ ⓑ ⓒ ⓓ

ANSWER SHEET

ETS® TOEIC® 토익 정기시험 실전 1000

수험번호

응시일자 : 20 ___ 년 ___ 월 ___ 일

성명 | 한글
명 | 한자
| 영자

Test 09 (Part 5~7)

101	102	103	104	105	106	107	108	109	110	111	112	113	114	115	116	117	118	119	120
121	122	123	124	125	126	127	128	129	130	131	132	133	134	135	136	137	138	139	140
141	142	143	144	145	146	147	148	149	150	151	152	153	154	155	156	157	158	159	160
161	162	163	164	165	166	167	168	169	170	171	172	173	174	175	176	177	178	179	180
181	182	183	184	185	186	187	188	189	190	191	192	193	194	195	196	197	198	199	200

Test 10 (Part 5~7)

101	102	103	104	105	106	107	108	109	110	111	112	113	114	115	116	117	118	119	120
121	122	123	124	125	126	127	128	129	130	131	132	133	134	135	136	137	138	139	140
141	142	143	144	145	146	147	148	149	150	151	152	153	154	155	156	157	158	159	160
161	162	163	164	165	166	167	168	169	170	171	172	173	174	175	176	177	178	179	180
181	182	183	184	185	186	187	188	189	190	191	192	193	194	195	196	197	198	199	200

ANSWER SHEET

수험번호

응시일자 : 20   년   월   일

성 명
| 한 글 |
| 한 자 |
| 영 자 |

Test (Part 5~7)

(Answer bubbles for questions 101–200, columns with A B C D options)

101–120, 121–140, 141–160, 161–180, 181–200

Test (Part 5~7)

(Answer bubbles for questions 101–200, columns with A B C D options)

101–120, 121–140, 141–160, 161–180, 181–200

ANSWER SHEET

ETS TOEIC® 토익 정기시험 실전 1000

수험번호

응시일자 : 20 　 년 　 월 　 일

성명 한글

성명 한자

성명 영자

Test (Part 5~7)

| 101 | 102 | 103 | 104 | 105 | 106 | 107 | 108 | 109 | 110 | 111 | 112 | 113 | 114 | 115 | 116 | 117 | 118 | 119 | 120 |

| 121 | 122 | 123 | 124 | 125 | 126 | 127 | 128 | 129 | 130 | 131 | 132 | 133 | 134 | 135 | 136 | 137 | 138 | 139 | 140 |

| 141 | 142 | 143 | 144 | 145 | 146 | 147 | 148 | 149 | 150 | 151 | 152 | 153 | 154 | 155 | 156 | 157 | 158 | 159 | 160 |

| 161 | 162 | 163 | 164 | 165 | 166 | 167 | 168 | 169 | 170 | 171 | 172 | 173 | 174 | 175 | 176 | 177 | 178 | 179 | 180 |

| 181 | 182 | 183 | 184 | 185 | 186 | 187 | 188 | 189 | 190 | 191 | 192 | 193 | 194 | 195 | 196 | 197 | 198 | 199 | 200 |

Test (Part 5~7)

| 101 | 102 | 103 | 104 | 105 | 106 | 107 | 108 | 109 | 110 | 111 | 112 | 113 | 114 | 115 | 116 | 117 | 118 | 119 | 120 |

| 121 | 122 | 123 | 124 | 125 | 126 | 127 | 128 | 129 | 130 | 131 | 132 | 133 | 134 | 135 | 136 | 137 | 138 | 139 | 140 |

| 141 | 142 | 143 | 144 | 145 | 146 | 147 | 148 | 149 | 150 | 151 | 152 | 153 | 154 | 155 | 156 | 157 | 158 | 159 | 160 |

| 161 | 162 | 163 | 164 | 165 | 166 | 167 | 168 | 169 | 170 | 171 | 172 | 173 | 174 | 175 | 176 | 177 | 178 | 179 | 180 |

| 181 | 182 | 183 | 184 | 185 | 186 | 187 | 188 | 189 | 190 | 191 | 192 | 193 | 194 | 195 | 196 | 197 | 198 | 199 | 200 |

ETS® TOEIC®

RC

All New
토익®
정기시험
실전 1

1000

정답 및 해설

101 (C)	102 (B)	103 (A)	104 (B)	105 (D)
106 (D)	107 (A)	108 (B)	109 (C)	110 (D)
111 (C)	112 (B)	113 (D)	114 (D)	115 (A)
116 (B)	117 (B)	118 (A)	119 (C)	120 (D)
121 (B)	122 (C)	123 (D)	124 (B)	125 (D)
126 (A)	127 (B)	128 (B)	129 (C)	130 (B)
131 (B)	132 (C)	133 (C)	134 (A)	135 (D)
136 (A)	137 (C)	138 (D)	139 (A)	140 (A)
141 (D)	142 (D)	143 (B)	144 (D)	145 (A)
146 (C)	147 (A)	148 (B)	149 (B)	150 (C)
151 (C)	152 (B)	153 (D)	154 (C)	155 (C)
156 (C)	157 (B)	158 (C)	159 (B)	160 (C)
161 (A)	162 (A)	163 (B)	164 (D)	165 (D)
166 (C)	167 (A)	168 (B)	169 (A)	170 (C)
171 (C)	172 (B)	173 (C)	174 (D)	175 (A)
176 (C)	177 (C)	178 (B)	179 (D)	180 (C)
181 (A)	182 (B)	183 (B)	184 (D)	185 (D)
186 (C)	187 (A)	188 (C)	189 (B)	190 (A)
191 (B)	192 (B)	193 (D)	194 (A)	195 (D)
196 (C)	197 (A)	198 (D)	199 (B)	200 (C)

PART 5

101 동사 자리 _ 복합문제

해설 Ms. Toba가 주어, her sales staff가 목적어인 문장이므로 빈칸에는 목적어를 취할 수 있는 능동태 동사가 와야 한다. When절의 last meeting에서 일어난 일에 대해 언급하고 있으므로 주절의 동사 또한 과거 시제가 되어야 한다. 따라서 (C) encouraged가 정답이다.

번역 토바 씨는 지난번 회의를 열었을 때 영업 사원들에게 다음 분기에 훨씬 더 좋은 성과를 내도록 격려했다.

어휘 perform 성과를 내다, 성취하다   quarter 분기(3개월)

102 전치사 어휘

해설 '파트너십 제안에 대해 통보받았다'는 의미가 되어야 하므로 '~에 대하여'라는 의미를 지닌 (B) about이 정답이다.

번역 전 직원이 ERI 파이낸스와의 파트너십 제안에 대해 통보받았다.

어휘 inform 통지하다   proposed 제안된   partnership 동업

103 인칭대명사의 격 _ 소유격

해설 빈칸에는 뒤에 온 명사 ideas를 수식하는 소유격 인칭대명사가 들어가야 한다. 따라서 (A) his가 정답이다.

번역 금요일에 나카무라 씨는 바쁜 웨이터들을 지원하기 위한 그의 아이디어에 대해 논의할 것이다.

어휘 support 지원하다

104 동사 어휘

해설 '천연자원과 야생 생물을 관리하기 위해'라는 의미가 되어야 적절하므로 '관리하다'라는 의미의 (B) manage가 정답이다.

번역 산림 위원회는 주(州)의 천연자원과 야생 생물을 관리하기 위해 설립되었다.

어휘 forestry 산림 관리   commission 위원회   natural resource 천연자원

105 부사 자리 _ to부정사 수식

해설 빈칸이 없어도 완전한 문장을 이루고 있으므로, 빈칸에는 앞에 나온 to부정사구 to complete their tasks를 수식하는 부사가 들어가야 한다. 따라서 정답은 '안전하게'라는 뜻의 부사인 (D) safely이다.

번역 확립된 지침을 따름으로써 건설 노동자들은 작업을 안전하게 완수할 수 있을 것이다.

어휘 established 확립된

106 형용사 어휘

해설 주어인 Dr. Kwan을 보충 설명하기에 적절한 형용사를 고르는 문제이다. 많은 자격증을 소지하고(With her numerous credentials) 있다는 내용으로 보아 콴 박사가 대학에서 가르칠 자격이 있다는 의미가 되어야 자연스러우므로, '자격이 있는'이라는 의미의 (D) qualified가 정답이다.

번역 많은 자격증을 소지하고 있는 콴 박사는 매스턴 대학에서 중세 역사를 가르칠 자격이 충분하다.

어휘 numerous 많은   credential 자격증   medieval 중세의   arranged 정리된   available 시간[여유]이 있는

107 명사 자리 _ 동사의 주어

해설 빈칸은 동사 is 앞 주어 자리이며, 빈칸 뒤 전치사구 at the annual technology conference의 수식을 받는 명사가 와야 한다. 따라서 '참석'이라는 뜻의 명사인 (A) Attendance가 정답이다.

번역 연례 기술 회의의 참석은 트리몬트 사의 모든 엔지니어들에게 의무이다.

어휘 mandatory 의무적인

108 부사 어휘

해설 '특별히 출연시키다, 특징으로 삼다'라는 의미의 동사 features를 수식하여 '가끔 시인, 포크 송 가수, 극단이 무대에 선다'는 내용이 되어야 자연스러우므로 '가끔, 때때로'라는 뜻의 빈도 부사 (B) occasionally가 정답이다.

번역 그 카페는 가끔 시인, 포크 송 가수, 극단이 무대에 선다.

어휘 poet 시인   vaguely 애매하게   realistically 현실적으로

109 명사절 _ that절

해설 동사 assure는 'be assured+that절'의 형태로 즉, 수동태 뒤에 목적어 역할을 하는 that절을 취해 '(that절의 내용)을 확인받다, 확신하다'라는 의미를 나타낸다. 뒤에 절이 있으므로 빈칸에는 동사 were assured의 목적어 역할을 하는 명사절을 이끄는 접속사가 필요하고, '~라는 것을 확인받았다'는 의미가 되어야 하므로 정답은 (C) that이다. 참고로 (A) who 또한 목적어절을 이끌 수 있지만 뒤에 불완전한 절이 와야 하므로 답이 되지 않는다.

번역 세미나가 시작되기 전, 참석자들은 예정된 발표자들이 모두 나올 것이라는 확인을 받았다.

어휘 attendee 참석자   presenter 발표자

110 전치사 자리

해설 빈칸은 뒤에 온 명사구 Fun Bone and Chew Right를 목적어로 취하는 전치사 자리이다. 따라서 보기 중 유일한 전치사로 '~와 같은'의 의미로 예시를 나타낼 때 쓰는 (D) such as가 정답이다.

번역 포에버펫은 펀본과 츄라이트와 같은 신제품을 시장에 출시하는 데 있어 선두 주자였다.

111 동명사 _ 전치사의 목적어

해설 빈칸은 전치사 of의 목적어 자리이므로 명사나 동명사가 들어갈 수 있는데, 빈칸 뒤에 the organization of records라는 목적어가 나오므로 목적어를 취할 수 있는 동명사가 들어가야 한다. 따라서 (C) improving이 정답이다.

번역 터너 씨는 인사지원부에서 기록 체계를 개선하는 일을 맡고 있다.

어휘 in charge of ~을 맡고 있는   organization 구성, 체계

112 명사 어휘 _ 복합명사

해설 빈칸은 동사 receive의 목적어 자리로, 등위접속사 or로 명사 e-mail과 대등하게 연결되면서 빈칸 앞의 text와 함께 복합명사를 만들 수 있는 명사가 들어가야 한다. '이메일 또는 문자 알림을 받는다'는 내용이 되어야 자연스러우므로 '알림, 경보'라는 뜻의 (B) alert이 정답이다.

번역 쉬폰 뱅크 고객은 계좌 비밀번호에 변경이 있을 시 항상 이메일 또는 문자 알림을 받는다.

어휘 following ~ 이후에   issue 발행   claim 청구

113 형용사 자리 _ 명사 수식

해설 빈칸은 앞에 부정관사 a, 뒤에 명사 decrease가 있으므로 명사를 수식하는 형용사 자리이다. '수요 감소가 현저한 생산 감소로 이어졌다'는 내용이 적절하므로 '현저한, 주목할 만한'이라는 뜻의 (D) remarkable이 정답이다. remark는 자동사로 쓰일 때 '언급하다', 타동사로 쓰일 때 '알아차리다'라는 뜻으로 분사 형태로 바꾸더라도 명사 decrease를 수식하기에 의미상 적절하지 않다.

번역 소비자 수요 감소로 대형 픽업트럭의 생산이 현저하게 줄었다.

어휘 demand 수요   decrease 감소   production 생산

114 부사 어휘

해설 동사 place를 수식하여 '곧바로 튀김기에 넣어야 한다'는 의미가 되어야 자연스러우므로 '곧바로, 곧장'을 뜻하는 (D) directly가 정답이다.

번역 요리사는 감자에 밀가루와 양념을 입힌 뒤 곧바로 튀김기에 넣어야 한다.

어휘 flour 밀가루   spice 양념   place 놓다   deep fryer 튀김용 냄비   rarely 드물게   doubtfully 미심쩍게

115 인칭대명사의 격 _ 소유격

해설 빈칸에는 뒤에 온 명사 customers를 수식하는 소유격 인칭대명사가 들어가야 한다. 따라서 정답은 (A) their이다.

번역 몇몇 은행들은 고객들이 전화로 쉽게 요금을 낼 수 있게 해 주는 앱을 출시했다.

어휘 release 출시하다   bill 청구서

116 동사 어휘

해설 '인사부는 ~한 지원자들만 고려할 것이다'는 내용이 되어야 적절하므로 '고려하다'라는 의미의 (B) consider가 정답이다. (C) grant는 '(내키지 않지만) 인정하다'라는 의미를 나타내므로 문맥상 어울리지 않는다.

번역 인사부는 해당 직위에 5년 이상 경력이 있는 지원자들만 고려할 것이다.

어휘 personnel department 인사부   applicant 지원자   participate 참가하다

117 부사 자리 _ 동사 수식

해설 빈칸은 be동사와 p.p. 사이에서 동사를 수식하는 부사 자리이다. 따라서 '활발하게'라는 뜻의 (B) actively가 정답이다.

번역 벨포어 일렉트로닉스 유한회사의 직원들은 지역 사회 지원 프로그램에 활발하게 참여하고 있다.

어휘 involve 참여시키다

118 동사 어휘

해설 빈칸 뒤의 명사 the contract를 목적어로 취해 '계약을 갱신하지 않을 것'이라는 내용이 되어야 자연스러우므로 '갱신하다'라는 뜻의 (A) renew가 정답이다.

번역 맥캘터 장비의 경영진들은 주요한 변화 없이는 계약을 갱신하지 않기로 결정했다.

어휘 executive 경영진   major 주요한   consume 소비하다   identify 확인하다   resemble 닮다

119 형용사 자리 _ 명사 수식

해설 빈칸은 앞에 부정관사 a, 뒤에 명사 layer가 있으므로 명사를 수식하는 형용사 자리이다. 따라서 '보호용의'라는 뜻의 (C)

protective가 정답이다.

번역 잠수복은 열을 가두어 잠수부를 따뜻하게 해 주는 고무 보호막으로 만들어진다.

어휘 wet suit 잠수복   layer 막, 층   rubber 고무   trap 가두다

120 명사 어휘

해설 빈칸 뒤에서 빈칸에 들어갈 명사를 수식하는 of 이하의 전치사구에서 '세 지점을 하나로'라고 했으므로, 빈칸에는 '합병'을 의미하는 명사가 들어가야 적절하다. 따라서 (D) merger가 정답이다.

번역 뉴캠프 서비스 관리자들은 세 개의 소규모 지점을 하나의 대형 지점으로 합병하자는 제안에 대해 논의하기 위해 만날 예정이다.

어휘 security 보안   bracket 괄호; (동류의) 그룹

121 형용사 자리 _ 주격 보어

해설 빈칸은 be동사 뒤 주격 보어 자리이므로 형용사나 명사가 들어갈 수 있다. '고객의 기록은 기밀이다'는 내용이 되어야 하므로 '기밀의'라는 뜻의 형용사 (B) confidential이 정답이다. 주어인 records와 명사 confidentiality(기밀성)는 동격이 아니므로 (D)는 오답이다.

번역 야르젠 테크놀로지에서 고객의 기록은 기밀 사항이며 소수의 펀드 매니저들만이 접근할 수 있다.

어휘 confide 털어놓다   confidentially 은밀히

122 명사 어휘

해설 빈칸은 동사 discuss의 목적어 자리이므로 논할 대상이 되기에 적절한 명사를 골라야 한다. 의학 학회의 패널이 온라인 의료 서비스에 관해 논할 주제로 보기 중 가장 적절한 명사는 '동향'을 의미하는 (C) trends이다.

번역 NHJ 의학 학회의 주요 패널들은 온라인 의료 서비스의 최근 동향에 대해 논할 예정이다.

어휘 panel 패널, 토론자단   variety 품종, 종류   rehearsal 리허설

123 능동태 vs. 수동태

해설 빈칸 뒤에 목적어가 없고, '모든 식당은 점검받는다'는 내용이 되어야 하므로 수동태 (D) are inspected가 정답이다.

번역 밀빌의 모든 식당은 시 보건부에 의해 일 년에 수차례 점검을 받는다.

어휘 inspect 점검[검사]하다

124 형용사 어휘

해설 빈칸 뒤의 명사 base를 수식하여 전치사구 of customers와 함께 '충성 고객층'이라는 의미를 만들어야 자연스러우므로 '충성스러운'이라는 뜻의 형용사 (B) loyal이 정답이다.

번역 스위트 선라이트 베이커리는 맛있는 쿠키와 케이크로 충성도 높은 고객층을 꾸준하게 쌓아 왔다.

어휘 steadily 꾸준히   base 기반   brief 간단한   strict 엄격한

125 명사 자리 _ 동사의 주어

해설 빈칸은 동사 are expected 앞 주어 자리이며, 빈칸 뒤 전치사구 in medical technology companies의 수식을 받는 명사가 와야 한다. 따라서 '투자'라는 뜻의 명사인 (D) investments가 정답이다.

번역 금융 분석가들에 따르면, 의료 기술 기업에 대한 투자 가치가 증가할 것으로 예상된다.

126 형용사 어휘

해설 문맥상 '항구는 모든 크기의 배가 접근 가능하다'는 내용이 되어야 자연스러우므로 '접근 가능한'이라는 의미의 형용사 (A) accessible이 정답이다.

번역 그 도시의 항구는 모든 크기의 컨테이너선과 어선이 접근 가능하다.

어휘 harbor 항구   fishing vessel 어선   reasonable 합리적인

127 부사 자리 _ 동사 수식

해설 빈칸이 have와 p.p. 사이에 있으므로 동사를 수식하는 부사 자리이다. 따라서 정답은 '그 결과'라는 의미의 부사 (B) consequently이다. (C) beneath도 부사로 쓰일 수 있으나 위치를 나타내는 '밑에, 아래쪽에'라는 뜻이므로 답이 되지 않는다.

번역 마야스 댄스웨어는 광고 시장을 확대했고, 그 결과 매출이 증가했다.

어휘 expand 확장하다

128 접속사 자리 _ 부사절 접속사

해설 빈칸 뒤에 주어와 동사를 갖춘 완전한 절이 왔으므로 부사절 접속사가 들어가야 한다. 따라서 '~할 때까지'를 뜻하는 부사절 접속사 (B) until이 정답이다.

번역 돕슨 아이스크림은 고객 설문 조사 결과가 분석될 때까지 어떤 새로운 맛도 선보이지 않을 예정이다.

어휘 flavor 맛   analyze 분석하다

129 능동태 vs. 수동태

해설 빈칸 뒤에 목적어가 없고, '체육관은 기구가 갖추어져 있다'는 내용이 되어야 하므로 수동태 (C) has been equipped가 정답이다.

번역 새로 단장한 회사 체육관에는 프리 웨이트와 운동 기구들이 갖춰져 있다.

어휘 free weight (덤벨, 바벨 등의) 프리 웨이트   equip 장비를 갖추다

130 전치사 자리

해설 빈칸은 뒤에 있는 동명사구를 콤마 뒤 절에 연결하는 자리이다. 문맥상 '자가용을 운전하는 대신 버스를 이용해야 한다'는 내용이 되어야 자연스러우므로 '~ 대신에'라는 뜻의 전치사 (B) Instead of가 정답이다. 참고로 driving their cars를 분사구문으로 볼 경우 빈칸에 부사절 접속사인 (C) Whenever와 (D) Although도 들어갈 수 있지만 문맥상 어울리지 않는다.

번역 도심으로 이동하는 근로자들은 자가용을 운전하는 대신 버스 노선을 이용해야 한다.

PART 6

131-134 기사

> **지역 이발소, 주 대회에서 우승하다**
>
> **미란다 워렌 작성**
>
> 말렌다 카운티 (1월 12일)—그랜드 가 3949번지에 **131위치한** 팻 앤 케니스 이발소가 이발사 및 미용사 연합에 의해 주 최고의 이발소로 지정되었다. 선정 기준에는 평판, 가격 적정성, 전문성, 인가 여부가 포함된다. **132팻 앤 케니스 이발소는 네 가지 부문에서 모두 뛰어났다.**
>
> 창립자이자 소유주인 케네스 웨버와 패트릭 밀러는 어린 시절부터 가장 친한 친구였다. **133그들은** 34년 전에 가게를 열었다. 이발소는 고풍스러운 매력을 유지하고 **134있지만** 이발사들은 전통적인 스타일뿐 아니라 최신 스타일에도 통달했다. 머리를 자르거나 새로운 스타일을 찾는 남녀 노소 모두 팻 앤 케니스 이발소를 이용해 봐야 할 것이다.

> 어휘 barbershop 이발소 competition 대회 name 지명하다, 지정하다 barber 이발사 coalition 연합 criteria 기준(criterion의 복수형) reputation 평판 affordability 가격 적정성 accreditation 인가, 승인 founder 창립자 retain 유지하다 charm 매력 traditional 전통적인 people of all ages 남녀노소, 모든 연령대의 사람들

131 과거분사

해설 문장에 동사 has been named가 있으므로, 빈칸부터 Grand Street까지는 주어인 Pat and Kenny's Barbershop을 수식하는 수식어구임을 알 수 있다. 따라서 빈칸에는 명사를 수식할 수 있는 분사가 들어가야 하므로 과거분사인 (B) located가 정답이다.

132 문맥에 맞는 문장 고르기

해설 빈칸 앞에서 팻 앤 케니스 이발소가 주 최고의 이발소로 지정되었다며 선정 기준 네 가지를 열거했다. 따라서 이발소가 앞 문장에서 언급된 네 가지 선정 기준을 모두 충족시켰다는 내용이 와야 자연스러우므로 팻 앤 케니스 이발소가 네 가지 부문에서 모두 뛰어났다고 언급한 (C)가 정답이다.

번역 (A) 결과는 이달 말에 발표될 것이다.
　　(B) 우리는 우리 지역 사회에 우수한 서비스를 제공하는 것을 자랑스럽게 생각한다.
　　(C) 팻 앤 케니스 이발소는 네 가지 부문에서 모두 뛰어났다.
　　(D) 예약을 잡으려면 미리 전화하세요.

어휘 excel 뛰어나다 in advance 미리

133 인칭대명사

해설 빈칸은 동사 opened의 주어 자리로 이 주어가 34년 전에 가게를 열었다고 했는데, 앞 문장에서 창립자가 케네스 웨버와 패트릭 밀러라

고 언급했다. 따라서 빈칸에는 케네스 웨버와 패트릭 밀러를 지칭하는 3인칭 복수 대명사가 들어가야 하므로 (C) They가 정답이다.

134 접속사 자리 _ 부사절 접속사

해설 빈칸은 빈칸 뒤의 완전한 절을 콤마 뒤의 절에 연결하는 자리이므로 접속사가 들어가야 한다. 따라서 '~이지만'라는 뜻의 부사절 접속사 (A) While이 정답이다. '그렇지만'이라는 의미의 등위접속사 (D) Yet은 뒤의 절을 앞의 절에 연결하므로 답이 될 수 없다.

135-138 설명서

> **가스고 프로판가스 탱크 교환**
>
> 귀하께서는 가스레인지, 그릴, 히터, 벽난로 또는 기타 장치를 위한 연료를 구하는 데 안전하고 **135경제적인** 방법을 선택하셨습니다. **136아래** 지시 사항을 따르기만 하면 됩니다.
>
> 탱크에 프로판가스가 떨어지면 저희 가게로 가져오셔서 가게 밖에 명확하게 표시된 녹색 선반 중 하나에 놓아두십시오. **137그것을 안으로 가지고 들어오지 마십시오.** 그러고 나서 가게 안에 있는 출납원에게 새 프로판가스 탱크값을 계산하십시오. 그런 다음, 출납원이나 다른 직원이 실외 교환 구역으로 귀하와 동행할 것입니다. 직원이 댁으로 가져갈 연료가 가득 찬 탱크를 드리고, 운반할 탱크가 여러 개일 경우 도움을 드릴 것입니다. 탱크에 붙어 있는 설명서에 따라 귀하의 장치에 탱크를 연결하십시오.
>
> **138교체가** 필요할 때 꼭 다시 방문해 주십시오.

> 어휘 propane 프로판가스 exchange 교환, 대체 obtain 구하다 stove 가스레인지 fireplace 벽난로 device 장치 directions 지시 run out of ~이 떨어지다 accompany 동행하다 instructions 설명(서)

135 형용사 자리 _ 명사 수식

해설 빈칸은 부정관사 a와 명사 way 사이에서 명사를 수식하는 형용사 자리이다. 또한 등위접속사 and 앞의 형용사 safe와 동등한 품사로 연결되어야 하므로 '경제적인'이라는 뜻의 형용사 (D) economical이 정답이다.

어휘 economize 절약하다, 아끼다

136 부사 어휘

해설 빈칸이 있는 문장에서 지시 사항을 따르라고 언급하고 있고, 그 문장 아래 단락에서 빈 탱크를 가져와 녹색 선반에 두라는 등 지시 사항을 구체적으로 설명하고 있으므로 '아래 지시 사항을 따르라'는 문장이 되어야 적절하다. 따라서 '아래에, 밑에'라는 뜻의 부사 (A) below가 정답이다.

137 문맥에 맞는 문장 고르기

해설 빈칸 앞에서 탱크를 가져와 가게 밖에 명확하게 표시된 녹색 선반에 놓아두라(leave it on one of the clearly marked green shelves outside the store)고 강조했고, 빈칸 뒤에서 그러고 나서

가게 안에 있는 출납원에게 계산하라(pay the cashier inside the store)고 했다. 따라서 빈칸에는 탱크를 가게 밖에 두고 들어오라는 당부의 내용이 들어가야 자연스러우므로, 탱크(it)를 가게 안으로 가지고 들어오지 말라고 언급한 (C)가 정답이다.

번역 (A) 곧 다시 오십시오.
(B) 가게 안이 더 따뜻합니다.
(C) 그것을 안으로 가지고 들어오지 마십시오.
(D) 탱크는 미리 채워져 있습니다.

138 명사 어휘

해설 업체에서 빈 탱크를 가스를 채운 새 탱크로 교환해 가는 방법에 대해 안내하는 글이다. 따라서 가스 탱크 교환이 필요할 때 자사를 다시 이용해 달라는 내용으로 마무리되어야 자연스러우므로, '교체'라는 뜻의 명사 (D) replacement가 정답이다.

139-142 이메일

수신: 테크니칸 엔터프라이즈 고객
발신: 테크니칸 엔터프라이즈 고객 서비스
날짜: 9월 10일
제목: 고객 서비스 제공

소중한 고객님께:

저희는 귀하께서 테크니칸 엔터프라이즈를 쉽고 즐겁게 **139경험하시기**를 바랍니다. 이를 위해 고객 친화적인 특징을 강화해 새롭게 구성된 웹사이트를 발표하게 되어 기쁩니다. 당사의 새로운 웹사이트는 연중무휴 24시간 내내 귀하의 질문에 답변을 제공합니다. 저희 홈페이지에서 시스템 설정에 대한 정보를 얻으실 수 있고, 인터넷 문제 페이지**140나** TV 및 스트리밍 문제 페이지를 방문하여 문제를 해결하실 수도 있습니다. **141또한**, 계정 관리, 접속, 요금 청구 및 결제에 대한 상세한 정보를 확인하실 수 있습니다. **142온라인에서 필요한 항목을 찾을 수 없는 경우, 지원 번호로 전화 주십시오.** www.technicarnenterprises.com에서 가능한 한 빨리 새로운 웹사이트를 살펴보십시오. 늘 그렇듯이 귀하께 서비스를 제공할 수 있게 해 주셔서 감사합니다.

테크니칸 엔터프라이즈 고객 서비스팀

어휘 to that end 그러기 위해서 enhanced 향상된 customer-friendly 고객 친화적인 feature 특징, 특성 troubleshoot 문제를 해결하다 detailed 상세한 concerning ~에 관한 account 계정 billing 청구서 발부 explore 살피다 at one's earliest convenience 가급적 빨리

139 명사 자리 _ 동사의 목적어

해설 빈칸은 동사 want의 목적어 자리이며 소유격 뒤에는 명사가 와야 하므로 (A) experience가 정답이다. 동명사 (C) experiencing은 experience가 타동사로 뒤에 목적어를 취해야 하므로 오답이다.

140 상관접속사

해설 빈칸 뒤의 or가 문제 해결의 단서로, 문맥상 '인터넷 문제 페이지나 TV 및 스트리밍 문제 페이지 둘 중 하나'라는 의미가 되어야 한다. 따라서 or와 상관접속사를 이루는 (A) either가 정답이다.

141 접속부사

해설 앞 문장에서 홈페이지에서 시스템 설정에 대한 정보를 얻거나 문제를 해결할 수 있다고 했고, 뒤 문장에서 계정 관리, 접속, 요금 청구 및 결제에 대한 정보를 확인할 수 있다며 홈페이지를 통해 할 수 있는 일을 추가로 언급하고 있다. 따라서 '게다가, 또한'을 의미하는 접속부사 (D) Moreover가 정답이다.

142 문맥에 맞는 문장 고르기

해설 빈칸 앞에서 시스템 설정 관련 정보, 문제 해결 방법, 계정 관리, 접속, 요금 청구 및 결제에 관한 정보 등 회사의 홈페이지를 통해 확인할 수 있는 정보에 대해 나열하고 있다. 따라서 앞서 언급된 정보 이외에 찾을 수 없는 항목이 있을 경우 대처 방법을 알려 주는 내용이 이어지는 것이 자연스러우므로 (D)가 정답이다.

번역 (A) 저희는 또한 귀하의 지불 기한이 5일 경과했다는 것을 알려 드려야 합니다.
(B) 저희는 모든 관련 부대용품을 당사 소매점에서 구입하실 것을 권해 드립니다.
(C) 오류 메시지가 뜰 경우, 인터넷 연결을 끊고 다시 시도하십시오.
(D) 온라인에서 필요한 항목을 찾을 수 없는 경우, 지원 번호로 전화 주십시오.

어휘 past due 만기가 지난 related 관련된 accessories 부대용품 disconnect 연결을 끊다

143-146 공지

환경을 생각하는 가너 시티 교통

5월 1일부로, 모든 가너 시티 교통의 버스와 지하철 노선에서 종이 승차권과 통행권의 판매 및 사용이 **143중단됩니다.** 해당 변경 사항은 주간 및 월간 통행권**144뿐만 아니라** 1회용 승차권에도 적용됩니다. 종이를 없애는 것은 환경에 유익하고 쓰레기가 줄게 됩니다.

탑승객은 무료 가너 시티 교통 앱을 다운로드할 수 있습니다. 이 앱으로 계정에 돈을 입금하고, 승차권을 구입하고, **145경로를 짜고,** 도착 및 출발 시간을 확인할 수 있습니다.

그렇지 않으면, 승객들은 어느 역에서나 충전식 교통카드를 구입할 수도 있습니다. **146오래 사용 가능한 이 카드는 재활용 재료로 만들어집니다.** 가너 시티 교통 웹사이트 www.garnercitytransport.org에서 카드에 금액을 충전할 수 있습니다.

어휘 transit pass 통행권, 교통패스 apply to ~에 적용되다 eliminate 제거하다 benefit 유익하다 litter 쓰레기 track 추적하다 alternatively 그 대신에, 그렇지 않으면 rechargeable 재충전되는 value (금전적) 가치, 가격

143 형용사 어휘

해설 빈칸 뒤 문장에서 종이를 없애는 것은 환경에 유익하고 쓰레기가 줄어든다고 언급한 것으로 보아 '종이 승차권과 통행권의 판매 및 사용이 중단된다'는 내용이 되어야 적절하다. 따라서 '중단[단종]된'을 뜻하는 (B) discontinued가 정답이다.

어휘 enlarged 확대된 accessible 접근[이용] 가능한 refreshed 상쾌한

144 상관접속사

해설 빈칸 앞의 전치사구 to single-ride tickets와 뒤의 전치사구 to weekly and monthly passes를 연결해 '주간 및 월간 통행권뿐만 아니라 1회용 승차권에도 변화가 적용된다'는 내용이 되어야 하므로 '~뿐만 아니라 …도'라는 뜻의 상관접속사 (D) as well as가 정답이다.

145 명사 어휘

해설 빈칸 앞 문장에서 가너 시티 교통 앱을 소개하고 있고, 빈칸이 있는 문장에서는 앱으로 할 수 있는 일에 대해 언급하고 있으므로 동사 plan과 함께 '경로를 짜다'라는 내용이 되어야 적절하다. 따라서 '경로'를 뜻하는 명사 (A) routes가 정답이다.

146 문맥에 맞는 문장 고르기

해설 빈칸 앞 문장은 충전식 교통카드를 처음 언급했고, 빈칸 뒤 문장은 웹사이트에서 카드에 금액을 충전할 수 있다며 카드 사용법과 관련해 안내하고 있다. 따라서 빈칸에도 충전식 교통카드에 대해 소개하는 내용이 들어가야 글의 흐름이 일관적이므로, 카드가 만들어진 소재에 관해 설명하고 있는 (C)가 정답이다.

번역 (A) 사람들은 종종 비행 중에 식사를 구입하기 위해 신용카드를 사용합니다.
(B) 많은 사람들이 저렴하다는 이유로 대중교통을 선호합니다.
(C) 오래 사용 가능한 이 카드는 재활용 재료로 만들어집니다.
(D) 지난달에 약간의 가격 인상이 있었습니다.

어휘 durable 오래가는, 내구성 있는 material 재료

PART 7

147-148 광고

하비스 문구점 재고 정리 세일

표시된 가격은 매장 내 구매에만 해당됩니다.

500 핀스톤 가 / 셰필드 / S12HN

시즌 품목	
사전 인쇄된 시즌 카드 10장들이 상자 (25% 할인)	£ 8.99
148맞춤 제작 가능한 시즌 카드 또는 초대장 5장들이 상자 (50% 할인)	£ 11.99

147모든 학용품 10% 할인	
펜 24개들이 상자	£ 1.79
탁상용 램프	£ 19.99
무선 마우스	£ 17.99
배낭	£ 29.99

www.harbisstationery.uk에서 하비스 문구를 방문하세요.

어휘 stationery 문구류 clearance sale 재고 정리 판매 indicated 표시된 seasonal 시즌[계절]에 따른 preprinted 사전 인쇄된 customizable 맞춤 제작할 수 있는 supplies 용품

147 Not / True

번역 하비스 문구점에 대해 명시된 것은?
(A) 학생을 위한 물품을 제공한다.
(B) 여러 곳에 매장이 있다.
(C) 기념일을 기념하고 있다.
(D) 온라인 주문 시 무료 배송을 제공한다.

해설 광고의 두 번째 항목에서 모든 학용품을 10% 할인(All school supplies 10% off)한다고 했으므로 학생들을 위한 품목을 판매하고 있음을 알 수 있다. 따라서 (A)가 정답이다.

어휘 materials 용구, 도구 multiple 다수의 anniversary 기념일

Paraphrasing	지문의 school supplies → 정답의 materials for students

148 세부 사항

번역 가장 큰 비율로 할인되는 제품은?
(A) 카드 10장들이 상자
(B) 초대장 5장들이 상자
(C) 무선 마우스
(D) 탁상용 램프

해설 시즌 품목에서는 사전 인쇄된 시즌 카드 10장들이 상자(Box of ten preprinted seasonal cards)가 25% 할인(25% off), 맞춤 제작 가능한 시즌 카드 또는 초대장 5장들이 상자(Box of five customizable seasonal cards or invitations)가 50% 할인(50% off)된다고 했고, 모든 학용품(All school supplies)은 10% 할인(10% off)된다고 했다. 따라서 보기의 항목 중 50% 할인되는 초대장 5장들이 상자가 가장 많이 할인되므로 (B)가 정답이다.

149-150 이메일

수신: 웬빈 펑 〈wpeng@chenconstruction.com〉
발신: 토시 자동차 그룹 〈cs@toshiautogroup.com〉
날짜: 2월 26일
제목: 임대 차량

펑 씨께:

아시다시피 150토시 자동차 그룹은 첸 건설 직원들의 임대 차량에 필요한 모든 서비스를 처리하고 있습니다. 당사의 기록에 따르면, 귀하께서는 작년 3월 1일에 임대 차량을 인수하셨습니다. 149귀하의 차량은 현재 필수 연간 서비스 및 정비 점검을 받을 시기입니다. 예약을 하려면 (215) 555-0109로 전화하시거나 온라인으로 www.toshiautogroup.com/serviceappointments를 방문해 주십시오.

토시 자동차 그룹
고객 서비스

어휘 lease 임대[임차]하다 take possession of ~을 입수하다 due ~하기로 되어 있는 maintenance 유지 book an appointment 예약하다, 약속을 잡다

149 주제 / 목적

번역 이메일의 목적은?
(A) 차량 임대에 대해 문의하려고
(B) 고객에게 필수 차량 정비에 대해 알리려고
(C) 신차 출시를 발표하려고
(D) 연장된 보증 서비스에 중고차를 등록하려고

해설 세 번째 문장에서 귀하의 차량은 현재 필수 연간 서비스 및 정비 점검을 받을 시기(Your car is now due for its required annual service and maintenance check)라고 알려 주고 있으므로 (B)가 정답이다.

어휘 inquire 문의하다 extended 연장된 warranty 보증(서)

150 추론 / 암시

번역 첸 건설에 대해 암시된 것은?
(A) 회사 차량의 정비를 수행한다.
(B) 3월 1일부터 새로운 프로젝트를 시작한다.
(C) 일부 직원들에게 임대 차량을 제공한다.
(D) 곧 토시 자동차 그룹을 위한 건설 프로젝트를 시작한다.

해설 첫 문장에서 토시 자동차 그룹은 첸 건설사 직원들의 임대 차량에 필요한 모든 서비스를 처리하고 있다(Toshi Auto Group handles all the service needs for cars leased by employees of Chen Construction)고 한 것으로 보아, 첸 건설이 직원들에게 임대 차량을 지원하고 있음을 알 수 있다. 따라서 정답은 (C)이다.

어휘 perform 수행하다 servicing (차량) 정비

151-153 기사

런던 (2월 2일)—151**목요일에 틸포드 출판사는 새로운 출판 독립 브랜드인 틸포드 이그절트의 출시를 발표했다.** 이 새로운 라인은 건강한 생활 방식을 권장하는 책과 희망을 주는 메시지를 담은 회고록, 생일과 결혼식 같은 특별한 행사를 위한 지침을 제공하는 서적을 선보일 것이다. 틸포드 이그절트는 주력 제품을 보완하는 달력과 연하장도 발행할 예정이다.

회고록을 쓰기로 이미 계약한 사람들로는 수상 경력이 있는 여배우 알렉시아 레오즈, 런던에 기반을 두고 있는 지휘자이자 작곡가 배승현, 유명 요리사 레인 라이가 있다. 152**라이 씨의 삶과 경력에 대한 이야기가 첫 번째로 출간될 것이다.** 이 책은 12월에 공개 예정이다.

프레데릭 비셋 틸포드 부사장은 회사가 다양한 관점에서 업적과 인생 사건을 기념하는 책에 대한 필요성을 인식했다고 말했다. 153**"우리는 다양한 문화적 배경을 가진 작가들을 원했고, 출발이 좋다고 생각합니다."**라고 그는 말했다. 그는 틸포드 이그절트의 작가들이 항상 유명했던 것은 아니라며, 이 책들이 그들의 성취뿐 아니라 초창기, 일상생활, 첫 직업, 결혼과 가족에 대해 살펴볼 것이라고 언급했다.

틸포드 출판사는 맨체스터에 본사를 두고 있다. 뉴욕, 토론토, 시드니에 사무실이 있지만, 출판물은 전 세계적으로 판매되고 있다.

어휘 launch 출시; 출시[출간]하다 imprint 출판사 내 독립 브랜드 feature 특징으로 하다 memoir 회고 uplifting 희망을 주는 volume 서적, 책 occasion (특별한) 행사, 경우 greeting card 연하장 complement 보완하다 conductor 지휘자 composer 작곡가 release 발표, 공개 accomplishment 업적, 성취 perspective 관점, 시각 be off to a good[great] start 출발이 좋다 publication 출판(물)

151 주제 / 목적

번역 기사의 주요 목적은?
(A) 새로운 조리기구 제품 라인 홍보
(B) 오케스트라 콘서트 광고
(C) 새로운 서적 시리즈 발표
(D) 지역 행사 일정표 제공

해설 첫 문장에서 목요일에 틸포드 출판사는 새로운 출판 독립 브랜드인 틸포드 이그절트 출시를 발표했다(On Thursday, Tilford Press announced the launch of its new imprint, Tillford Exalt)며 새로운 출간물 시리즈가 발표된 일에 대해 전하고 있으므로 (C)가 정답이다.

어휘 cookware 조리기구

Paraphrasing	지문의 the launch of its new imprint → 정답의 a new series of books

152 세부 사항

번역 12월에 계획된 것은?
(A) 시상식
(B) 인생 이야기 출판
(C) 새 앨범 발매
(D) 유명인사의 식당 개점

해설 두 번째 단락의 두 번째 문장에서 라이 씨의 삶과 경력에 대한 이야기가 첫 번째로 출간될 것(Ms. Lai's story of her life ~ first to be launched)이라고 했고, 이 책은 12월에 공개 예정(It is set for release in December)이라고 했으므로 정답은 (B)이다.

153 세부 사항

번역 프레데릭 비셋이 틸포드 이그절트에 대해 강조하는 것은?
(A) 기록적인 매출
(B) 맨체스터에 둔 기반
(C) 소설과 시에 맞춘 초점
(D) 다양한 저자

해설 세 번째 단락의 두 번째 문장에서 프레데릭 비셋이 우리는 다양한 문화적 배경을 가진 작가들을 원했고 출발이 좋다고 생각한다(We wanted authors from a wide variety of cultural backgrounds, and we think we're off to a great start)고 말했다고 했으므로 정답은 (D)이다.

어휘 emphasize 강조하다 fiction 소설 poetry 시 a broad range of 다양한, 폭넓은

Paraphrasing	지문의 authors from a wide variety of cultural backgrounds → 정답의 Its broad range of authors

154-155 문자 메시지

그레그 스카겐 (오전 8시 58분) 안녕하세요, 브렌다. 저는 창고에 있어요. 수습 직원들이 모두 도착했는데, **154B 하역장의 파워 도어가 제대로 작동하지 않는 걸 발견했어요.**

브렌다 사다우스카스 (오전 8시 59분) 또요?

그레그 스카겐 (오전 8시 59분) 도어를 열려고 버튼을 누르면, 도어가 끝까지 올라가지만 그러다가 약 30초 후에 다시 닫힌 상태로 내려와요.

브렌다 사다우스카스 (오전 9시) 제가 정비 기술자들과 함께 내려갈게요. **155수습 직원들을 제 구역으로 데려오는 게 어떨까요? 배송 라벨 만드는 방법을 가르쳐 준 다음 오늘 아침 배송물을 포장하고 라벨을 붙이게 할 수 있어요.**

그레그 스카겐 (오전 9시 2분) 네, 그러면 되겠네요.

브렌다 사다우스카스 (오전 9시 3분) 감사합니다. 그럼 오후에 하역장 작업을 보여줄 수 있을 거예요.

어휘 warehouse 창고 trainee 수습 (직원) loading dock 하역장 act up 제 기능을 못하다 label 라벨[상표]; 라벨[상표]을 붙이다 operation 작업

154 세부 사항

번역 스카겐 씨가 언급하는 문제는?
(A) 신입 사원 몇 명이 결근했다.
(B) 일부 상자에 라벨이 잘못 붙어 있다.
(C) 물품 배송이 지연되고 있다.
(D) 출입문이 오작동하고 있다.

해설 8시 58분에 스카겐 씨가 B 하역장의 파워 도어가 작동하지 않는 것을 발견했다(I noticed the power door ~ is acting up)고 언급했으므로 (D)가 정답이다.

어휘 absent 결근한 incorrectly 틀리게 malfunction 오작동하다

Paraphrasing	지문의 is acting up → 정답의 is malfunctioning

155 의도 파악

번역 오전 9시 2분에 스카겐 씨가 "네, 그러면 되겠네요"라고 쓴 의도는?
(A) 전기 기술자가 작업 현장에 도착했다.
(B) 일부 장비가 순조롭게 작동 중이다.
(C) 수습 직원들이 배송물 작업을 도울 수 있다.
(D) 사다우스카스 씨는 그녀의 직업에 매우 적합하다.

해설 9시에 사다우스카스 씨가 수습 직원들을 자신의 구역으로 데려오는 게 어떨지(Why don't you bring your trainees to my area?)를 제안하면서 배송 라벨 만드는 방법을 가르쳐 준 다음 오늘 아침 배송물을 포장하고 라벨을 붙이게 할 수 있다(You can teach them

~ this morning's shipments)고 하자, 9시 2분에 스카겐 씨가 그러면 되겠다(Yes, that works)고 대답했다. 따라서 스카겐 씨는 사다우스카스 씨의 제안을 받아들여 수습 직원들이 배송물 작업을 돕게 하겠다는 의도로 한 말임을 알 수 있으므로 정답은 (C)이다.

어휘 electrician 전기 기술자 smoothly 순조롭게 suited 적합한

156-157 양식

서비스 요청 양식
모든 영역을 작성해 기술 서비스부(412호)로 전달하세요.

요청자 이름: <u>엘레노라 데코우</u>
요청자 사무실: <u>718호</u>
요청자 전화: <u>내선 5709</u>

서비스 장소: <u>500호</u>
서비스 유형 (택1):
☐ 청소   156☒ **수리**   ☐ 설치/설정   ☐ 기타

요청 사항
<u>156텔레비전 오디오에 문제가 있습니다. 온라인 동영상을 재생했을 때, 영상은 괜찮았지만 아무 소리도 들리지 않았습니다. 모든 설정을 확인했으며, 다른 텔레비전에서는 같은 동영상을 문제없이 들을 수 있었습니다. 157다음 주 월요일에 500호실에서 고객을 위한 제품 시연회를 진행할 예정이므로 이번 주 금요일까지 이 문제가 해결될 수 있으면 정말 감사하겠습니다.</u>

어휘 field 영역 requester 요청자 repair 수리; 수리하다 installation 설치 description 설명, 서술 demonstration 시연

156 주제 / 목적

번역 양식은 왜 제출되었는가?
(A) 영상이 선명하게 보이지 않는다.
(B) 프로젝터가 설치되어야 한다.
(C) 오디오가 제대로 작동하지 않는다.
(D) 마이크가 수리되어야 한다.

해설 양식 중반부의 서비스 유형에서 수리(Repair)를 선택했고, 요청 사항의 첫 문장에서 텔레비전 오디오에 문제가 있다(There is a problem with the television audio)고 했다. 따라서 오디오가 제대로 작동하지 않아 수리를 요청하기 위해 양식을 제출했음을 알 수 있으므로 (C)가 정답이다.

어휘 function 작동하다 properly 제대로, 적절히

Paraphrasing	지문의 There is a problem → 정답의 is not functioning properly

157 세부 사항

번역 데코우 씨가 다음 주에 하려고 계획하는 것은?
(A) 고객 위치 방문
(B) 제품 배송
(C) 온라인 동영상 제작
(D) 프레젠테이션

해설 요청 사항의 네 번째 문장에서 다음 주 월요일에 500호실에서 고객을 위한 제품 시연회를 진행할 예정(I'm supposed to deliver a product demonstration ~ in room 500 next Monday)이라고 했으므로 (D)가 정답이다.

> Paraphrasing 지문의 deliver a product demonstration
> → 정답의 Give a presentation

158-161 문자 메시지

> **엘라 글랫 (오전 11시 34분)**
> 안녕하세요. 오늘 바쁜 날인 건 알지만, 재무팀에서 마케팅 회의에 참석할 수 있는 사람이 있는지 알고 싶어서요.
>
> **스테프 골드버그 (오전 11시 35분)**
> 안녕하세요, 엘라. 그러고 싶지만 회의가 2시에 시작하잖아요. **158저는 2시 30분에 다른 회의에 참석해야 해요.**
>
> **엘라 글랫 (오전 11시 36분)**
> 아, 그렇군요. **158골드버그 씨가 경영진 회의에 가는 걸 깜빡했어요.**
>
> **다니엘 세이달 (오전 11시 36분)**
> 저도 2시 30분 회의에 참석하기로 되어 있어요. 우리 중 한 명이 마케팅 회의에 반드시 참석해야 하나요?
>
> **엘라 글랫 (오전 11시 37분)**
> 글쎄요, **159적어도 15분 정도는 재무팀 사람이 거기에 있으면 도움이 될 것 같아요.**
>
> **빌 아이버먼 (오전 11시 38분)**
> **159분기별 보고서가 방금 들어와서 다니엘, 스테프, 그리고 저는 오늘 안으로 검토를 해야 해요.**
>
> **엘라 글랫 (오전 11시 39분)**
> 여러분 모두 할 일이 많네요.
>
> **다니엘 세이달 (오전 11시 41분)**
> 맞아요! **161그래도 저는 2시부터 2시 15분까지는 있을 수 있어요.** 그게 제가 할 수 있는 전부예요.
>
> **엘라 글랫 (오전 11시 43분)**
> 좋아요. **160그냥 여러분 중 한 명이 다음 광고 캠페인을 위한 예산에 대해 간단히 몇 가지 요점을 설명해 주면 되거든요.**

어휘 executive 경영진 essential 필수적인 quarterly 분기별의 commit to ~에 헌신하다 clarify 명확하게 말하다 budget 예산

158 세부 사항

번역 경영진 회의는 몇 시에 시작할 것인가?
(A) 오후 2시
(B) 오후 2시 15분
(C) 오후 2시 30분
(D) 오후 3시

해설 11시 35분에 골드버그 씨가 2시 30분에 다른 회의에 참석해야 한다 (I need to be at a different meeting at 2:30)고 하자, 11시 36분에 글랫 씨가 골드버그 씨가 경영진 회의에 가는 걸 깜빡했다

(I forgot you were going to the executive board meeting)고 했다. 따라서 골드버그 씨가 2시 30분에 경영진 회의에 참석한다는 것을 알 수 있으므로 (C)가 정답이다.

159 추론 / 암시

번역 아이버먼 씨는 어느 분야에서 근무할 것 같은가?
(A) 마케팅
(B) 재무
(C) 광고
(D) 경영진

해설 11시 37분에 글랫 씨가 적어도 15분 정도는 재무팀 사람이 거기에 있으면 도움이 될 것 같다(it would be helpful ~ at least for 15 minutes or so)고 하자 11시 38분에 아이버먼 씨가 분기별 보고서가 방금 들어와서 다니엘, 스테프, 그리고 저는 오늘 안으로 검토를 해야 한다(The quarterly reports just came in ~ review them by the end of the day)며 마케팅 회의 참석 요청에 응할 수 없음을 알리고 있다. 따라서 아이버먼 씨는 다니엘, 스테프와 함께 재무팀에 속한 사람임을 알 수 있으므로 (B)가 정답이다.

160 세부 사항

번역 글랫 씨는 왜 동료가 회의에 참석하기를 원하는가?
(A) 이전 회의의 요약을 위해
(B) 홍보 캠페인의 설명을 위해
(C) 예산에 대한 정보 제공을 위해
(D) 최근에 승인된 문서의 검토를 위해

해설 11시 43분에 글랫 씨가 여러분 중 한 명이 다음 광고 캠페인을 위한 예산에 대해 간단히 몇 가지 요점을 설명해 주면 된다(We just need one of you to clarify ~ next advertising campaign)고 했으므로 정답은 (C)이다.

어휘 summarize 요약하다 previous 이전의 promotional 홍보[판촉]의

> Paraphrasing 지문의 clarify a few quick points
> → 정답의 provide information

161 의도 파악

번역 오전 11시 43분에 글랫 씨가 "좋아요"라고 쓴 의도는?
(A) 세이달 씨의 제안을 받아들인다.
(B) 아이버먼 씨가 오후 3시 회의에 참석하는 것에 동의한다.
(C) 제안된 예산안에 만족한다.
(D) 프로젝트가 완료된 것을 기뻐한다.

해설 11시 41분에 세이달 씨가 2시부터 2시 15분까지는 있을 수 있다 (I could come from 2:00 to 2:15)며 그게 자신이 할 수 있는 전부(That's all I can commit to)라고 하자 11시 43분에 글랫 씨가 좋다(Sounds great)고 대답했으므로 글랫 씨는 세이달 씨의 참석 제안을 수락하려는 의도로 한 말임을 알 수 있다. 따라서 정답은 (A) 이다.

어휘 accept 받아들이다 complete 완료하다, 끝마치다

162-165 이메일

수신: amal.abboud@bunzifoundation.org
발신: maria_mcfarland@myemail.com
날짜: 8월 22일 목요일
제목: 프로젝트 진행자 자리
첨부: 📎 résumé_m.mcfarland.pdf

아부드 씨께,

162저의 친구 조시아 윌킨스가 귀하께서 귀사의 프로젝트 진행자를 구하고 있다고 말해 주었습니다. 저는 경영학 학위를 가지고 있고 제가 귀하의 요구에 딱 맞는 적임자라고 생각하여 이력서를 첨부해 드립니다. 보시다시피, 저는 여러 클라우드 기반의 프로젝트 관리 프로그램을 사용한 경험이 있습니다. 또한, 저는 저의 조직력을 이용해 다수의 활동을 동시에 진행할 수 있으며, 프로젝트의 각 단계에 참여하는 팀원들에게 기대 사항을 명확하게 163전달할 수 있습니다.

지난 5년간 근무해 온 국제 엔지니어링 회사에서 프로젝트 진행자로서의 현재 역할 또한 팀, 일정 및 예산을 관리하는 데 충분한 경험을 제공해 주었습니다. **164제가 하고 있는 일이 즐겁기는 하지만, 저에게 강력한 임무로부터 동기부여가 필요하다는 것이 분명해졌습니다.** 지속 가능한 주택 단지를 개발하고자 하는 귀사의 목표야말로 제가 강력하게 지지하고 기쁘게 일할 수 있는 것입니다.

165저는 업무 및 자원봉사 활동을 통해 아시아와 중동의 여러 국가에서 수개월을 보냈습니다. 이는 제가 지리적으로 그리고 문화적으로 다양한 팀을 이끄는 일에 익숙하다는 점에서 특히 관련성이 있는 것 같아 말씀 드립니다.

읽어 주셔서 감사드리며, 빠른 시일 내에 말씀 나눌 수 있기를 기대합니다.

마리아 맥팔랜드

어휘 coordinator 진행자, 코디네이터 degree 학위 business administration 경영학 attach 첨부하다 organizational 조직하는 enable 할 수 있게 하다 coordinate 조정하다, 조직화하다 simultaneously 동시에 convey 전달하다 phase 단계 afford 제공하다 ample 충분한 sustainable 지속 가능한 housing project 주택 단지 particularly 특히 relevant 관련 있는, 적절한 geographically 지리적으로 diverse 다양한

162 Not / True

번역 맥팔랜드 씨가 윌킨스 씨에 대해 언급한 것은?
(A) 그가 일자리에 대해 알려 주었다.
(B) 그는 전문가 추천서가 필요할 것이다.
(C) 그는 좋은 사업 파트너가 될 것이다.
(D) 그는 직책에서 사직하는 것을 고려하고 있다.

해설 첫 문장에서 맥팔랜드 씨가 저의 친구 조시아 윌킨스가 귀하께서 귀사의 프로젝트 진행자를 구하고 있다고 말해 주었다(My friend Josiah Wilkins told me ~ a project coordinator for your company)고 했으므로 (A)가 정답이다.

어휘 reference 추천서 resign 사직하다

163 동의어

번역 첫 번째 단락 5행의 "convey"와 의미가 가장 가까운 단어는?
(A) 수송하다
(B) 전하다
(C) 추천하다
(D) 조정하다

해설 의미상 팀원들에게 기대 사항을 '전달하다'라는 뜻으로 쓰인 것이므로 정답은 (B) communicate이다.

164 세부 사항

번역 맥팔랜드 씨는 왜 현재의 직책을 떠나고 싶어하는가?
(A) 자신의 노력에 대해 더 높은 연봉을 받고 싶어 한다.
(B) 경험이 더 많은 팀과 일하고 싶어 한다.
(C) 더 많은 승진 기회를 원한다.
(D) 자신을 좀 더 고취시켜 줄 역할을 원한다.

해설 두 번째 단락의 두 번째 문장에서 맥팔랜드 씨는 자신이 하고 있는 일이 즐겁기는 하지만 강력한 임무로부터 동기부여가 필요하다는 것이 분명해졌다(While I enjoy the kind of work ~ need motivation from a strong mission)고 했으므로 (D)가 정답이다.

어휘 advancement 승진, 발전 inspire 고무하다, 고취시키다

Paraphrasing	지문의 need motivation → 정답의 inspires her more

165 세부 사항

번역 맥팔랜드 씨는 왜 그녀의 여행을 언급하는가?
(A) 특정 국가에 배치를 요청하려고
(B) 그녀가 어떻게 전략적 산업 인맥을 쌓게 되었는지 논하려고
(C) 그녀가 어떻게 특정 국제 문제를 인지하게 되었는지 설명하려고
(D) 다른 배경을 가진 사람들과의 경험을 강조하려고

해설 세 번째 단락의 첫 문장에서 맥팔랜드 씨는 업무 및 자원봉사 활동을 통해 아시아와 중동의 여러 국가에서 수개월을 보냈다(Through my work ~ throughout Asia and the Middle East)며, 이는 자신이 지리적으로 그리고 문화적으로 다양한 팀을 이끄는 일에 익숙하다는 점에서 특히 관련성이 있는 것 같아 말씀드린다(This seems particularly ~ culturally diverse teams)고 했다. 따라서 맥팔랜드 씨는 다양한 배경의 사람들과 일한 경험을 부각시키고자 해외에서 지낸 일을 언급한 것이므로 (D)가 정답이다.

어휘 placement 배치 particular 특정한 acquire 얻다 strategic 전략적인 emphasize 강조하다

Paraphrasing	지문의 geographically and culturally diverse teams → 정답의 people of different backgrounds

https://trexdale.com/aboutus

회사 소개

트렉스데일 서플라이는 모든 종류의 과학 연구소를 위한 가구의 설계, 생산 및 설치를 전문으로 합니다. **166우리는 다양한 종류의 완전 조립 캐비닛, 워크스테이션, 벤치 등을 제공하며, 이 모든 것은 텍사스주 댈러스에 있는 당사의 생산 시설에서 전적으로 제작됩니다.** 당사의 연구소용 가구는 어떤 연구 용도의 요구 사항이라도 맞출 수 있도록 매우 다양한 크기와 구성으로 이용 가능합니다.

우리 회사는 제품뿐만 아니라 디자인 컨설팅 서비스 또한 제공합니다. 창업 연구소의 경우, 컨설팅 전문가 팀이 있어서 시설의 구체적인 요구 사항을 평가하여 공간을 배치하고 가장 적합한 가구를 선택하는 데 도움을 줍니다. **167예를 들어, 최근에 당사는 대형 바이오 연료 생산업체의 선택을 받아 이용 가능한 공간을 극대화하도록 연구소 배치를 변경하는 데 전문적인 도움을 제공했습니다.** 이 프로젝트의 결과로, 이 고객사는 연구소의 에너지 사용량을 줄임으로써 상당한 비용 절감을 실현했습니다.

연구소 시설의 건축 혹은 개조에 관하여 자세히 알고 싶으시다면 **168이 웹사이트의 '연구소 계획' 섹션을 방문하십시오. 거기서 관심 양식을 작성하여 귀하의 향후 프로젝트에 대해 당사 컨설턴트에게 문의하실 수 있습니다.**

어휘 specialize in ~을 전문으로 하다 laboratory 연구소, 실험실 a range of 다양한 assembled 조립된 workstation 근무[작업] 장소 exclusively 전적으로 configuration 배치, 구성 application 특정의 용도[목적] start-up 창업 단계의 specialist 전문가 evaluate 평가하다 specific 구체적인 suitable 적합한 biofuel 바이오 연료 expert 전문적인 layout 배치 maximize 극대화하다 realize 실현하다 substantial 상당한 reduce 줄이다 usage 사용량

166 세부 사항

번역 트렉스데일 서플라이가 제작하는 것은?
(A) 의료용품
(B) 농기구
(C) 캐비닛 및 가구
(D) 유리 실험실 장비

해설 두 번째 문장에서 우리는 다양한 종류의 완전 조립 캐비닛, 워크스테이션, 벤치 등을 제공하며 이 모든 것은 텍사스주 댈러스에 있는 당사의 생산 시설에서 전적으로 제작된다(We provide a range of ~ production facility in Dallas, Texas)고 했으므로 (C)가 정답이다.

167 세부 사항

번역 트렉스데일 서플라이가 최근 프로젝트에서 한 일은?
(A) 고객의 연구소 구조를 재구성했다.
(B) 바이오 연료를 사용할 수 있도록 차량을 개조했다.
(C) 생산 시설에 인력을 확충했다.
(D) 고객이 무역 박람회를 조직하는 일을 도왔다.

해설 두 번째 단락의 세 번째 문장에서 최근에 당사는 대형 바이오 연료 생산업체의 선택을 받아 이용 가능 공간을 극대화하도록 연구소 배치를 변경하는 데 전문적인 도움을 제공했다(Recently, for example, ~ maximize available space)고 했으므로 (A)가 정답이다.

어휘 reorganize 재조직[재편성]하다 convert 개조하다 expand 확대하다 staffing 직원 채용 trade show 무역 박람회

> Paraphrasing 지문의 changing the layout
> → 정답의 reorganized

168 세부 사항

번역 트렉스데일 서플라이에 연락할 수 있는 방법으로 언급된 것은?
(A) 이메일
(B) 전화
(C) 인스턴트 메시지
(D) 온라인 양식

해설 세 번째 단락의 첫 문장에서 이 웹사이트의 '연구소 계획' 섹션을 방문하라(Please visit the "Lab Planning" section of this Web site)고 했고, 거기서 관심 양식을 작성하여 귀하의 향후 프로젝트에 대해 당사 컨설턴트에게 문의할 수 있다(There, you can fill out an interest form ~ about your next project)고 했으므로 (D)가 정답이다.

어휘 instant 즉각적인

제품 시연자 모집!

외향적이고 열정적이신가요? 모든 유형의 사람들과 이야기하는 것을 즐기시나요? 여러분의 성격과 소통 능력을 일하는 데 활용해 보세요! **171BBD 스태핑은 고객의 상품을 쇼핑객들에게 홍보하는 매장 내 제품 시연자를 모집하고 있습니다.** 세계적으로 유명한 많은 브랜드들이 제품에 긍정적인 인상을 창출하기 위해 우리 제품 시연자들에게 의지하고 있습니다. **171우리 팀의 일원으로서 여러분은 식료품점과 기타 소매점에서 다양한 소형 주방용품 및 도구를 시연하게 될 것입니다.**

일부 제품의 경우에는 간단한 조리법을 준비하는 것이 요구됩니다. 또한 쇼핑객들의 질문에도 답변해야 합니다. 따라서 고객의 제품을 잘 파악해 소비자들에게 핵심 정보를 제공할 수 있어야 합니다. **169많은 시연에 식품을 다루는 일이 필요하므로 지원자는 전문 식품 취급 자격증을 가지고 있어야 합니다.**

170지원하시려면, 여러분이 왜 성공적인 제품 시연자가 될지 보여 주는 1분 이내의 동영상을 www.bbdstaffing.com/applications**에 업로드해 주세요.**

어휘 demonstrator (제품) 시연자 outgoing 외향적인 enthusiastic 열정적인 promote 홍보하다 merchandise 상품 demonstrate 시연하다 kitchen appliance 주방용품 grocery store 식료품점 venue 장소 familiar with ~을 잘 아는 consumer 소비자 candidate 지원자 food handler 음식을 다루는 사람 certificate 자격증

169 추론 / 암시

번역 어떤 업무 경력이 이 직책의 지원자에게 가장 적합하겠는가?

(A) 요리사
(B) 출납원
(C) 인테리어 디자이너
(D) 행사 기획자

해설 두 번째 단락의 네 번째 문장에서 많은 시연에 식품을 다루는 일이 필요하므로 지원자는 전문 식품 취급 자격증을 가지고 있어야 한다(Because many of the demonstrations ~ a Professional Food Handler certificate)고 했으므로 요리 경험이 지원자에게 가장 필요한 경력임을 알 수 있다. 따라서 (A)가 정답이다.

170 세부 사항

번역 광고에 따르면, 지원하는 데 관심 있는 사람들은 다음에 무엇을 해야 하는가?

(A) 설문 조사 응답
(B) 면접 준비
(C) 녹화물 제출
(D) 추천서 제출

해설 세 번째 단락에서 지원하려면 여러분이 왜 성공적인 제품 시연자가 될지 웹사이트에 1분 이내의 동영상을 업로드하라(To apply, upload a video ~ at www.bbdstaffing.com/applications)고 했으므로 (C)가 정답이다.

어휘 arrange for (일정·계획 등을) 준비하다 reference 추천서

> **Paraphrasing** 지문의 upload a video
> → 정답의 Submit a recording

171 문장 삽입

번역 [1], [2], [3], [4]로 표시된 곳 중에서 다음 문장이 들어가기에 가장 적합한 위치는?

"세계적으로 유명한 많은 브랜드들이 제품에 긍정적인 인상을 창출하기 위해 우리 제품 시연자들에게 의지하고 있습니다."

(A) [1]
(B) [2]
(C) [3]
(D) [4]

해설 제시된 문장에서 '많은 세계적인 브랜드들이 우리의 제품 시연자들에게 의지한다'며 제품 시연자(product demonstrators)를 언급했다. 따라서 BBD 스태핑은 매장 내 제품 시연자를 모집한다(BBD Staffing is seeking to hire in-store product demonstrators ~)는 문장과 팀의 일원으로서 다양한 소형 주방용품 및 도구를 시연하게 될 것이다(As a member for our team, you will demonstrate ~)라며 제품 시연자 업무를 소개하는 문장 사이, 즉 [3]에 들어가는 것이 글의 흐름상 자연스러우므로 (C)가 정답이다.

어휘 generate 만들어 내다 impression 인상

172-175 기사

> ### [172]고먼, 최신 스마트폰 모델 공개
>
> 런던 (4월 20일)—[172]고먼 모바일이 연례 테크노브릿 컨퍼런스에서 열렬한 환영을 받으며 최신 스마트폰을 공개했다. 512기가바이트 저장 용량, 7인치 스크린 디스플레이, 선택 사항인 스타일러스 펜이 포함된 프로폰 4는 6월 11일 매장에 출시될 예정이다. 전작인 프로폰 3과 달리 더 커진 스크린, 초광폭 카메라 렌즈, 8K 해상도 촬영 기능이 특징이다.
>
> 이러한 업그레이드에는 비용이 따른다. [175]시작 가격인 999파운드는 이전 모델보다 100파운드 더 비싸다. [173]스타일러스 펜, 보호 케이스, 무선 헤드폰과 같은 추가 부속품은 각각 39파운드, 59파운드, 79파운드의 추가 비용이 든다.
>
> 고먼 제품 관리자 이언 힐은 가격 인상이 고객들을 단념시킬 것이라고 생각하지 않는다.
>
> "프로폰 4는 화질과 매끈한 디자인 측면에서 판도를 바꾸는 제품입니다."라고 힐은 말했다. "전 모델의 가장 큰 단점으로 빈약한 카메라 기능을 꼽은 직접적인 고객 피드백을 바탕으로 개선이 이루어졌습니다. 고객들이 이야기를 했고, 우리는 경청하고 거기에 맞춰 조정했습니다."
>
> [174]프로폰 4가 이전 모델과 유사한 한 가지는 충전기이다. 경쟁 무선 통신사의 동향에 맞서 고먼은 대신 편의성에 초점을 맞추고 있다.
>
> "우리는 고객들이 이미 구입한 다른 고먼 기기의 구성품을 재사용할 수 있게 하기를 원합니다."라고 힐은 말했다. "이미 사용 중인 케이블이 넘쳐나는데 더할 이유가 있나요?"

어휘 unveil 발표하다 eager 열렬한 reception 환영, 반응 storage 저장 (용량) stylus pen (패드용) 스타일러스 펜 hit the selves (가게 등에) 나오다 predecessor 이전 것[모델] resolution 해상도 add-on 추가물 respectively 각각 dissuade 단념시키다 game changer 상황 전개를 완전히 바꿀 수 있는 것 in terms of ~ 면에서 sleek 매끈한, 날렵한 cite (이유·예를) 들다 functionality 기능(성) drawback 결점 prior 이전의 adapt 조정하다 accordingly 그에 맞춰 similarity 유사성 charger 충전기 element 요소 overload 지나치게 많음, 과부하 in circulation 현재 쓰이고 있는

172 주제 / 목적

번역 기사의 목적은?

(A) 기술 전시회 홍보
(B) 제품 소개
(C) 스마트폰 사용자 인터뷰
(D) 기기 리콜 발표

해설 고먼, 최신 스마트폰 모델 공개(Gorman Unveils Newest Smartphone Model)라는 기사 제목하에 첫 문장에서 고먼 모바일이 연례 테크노브릿 컨퍼런스에서 열렬한 환영을 받으며 최신 스마트폰을 공개했다(Gorman Mobile unveiled ~ at the annual Technobrit Conference)고 전한 뒤 512기가바이트 저장 용량, 7인치 스크린 디스플레이, 선택 사항인 스타일러스 펜이 포함된 프로폰 4가 6월 11일 매장에 출시될 예정(The Pro Phone 4 ~ will hit the shelves on 11 June)이라면서 새로 출시되는 스마트폰에 대한 소개를 이어가고 있으므로 (B)가 정답이다.

173 세부 사항

번역 고먼 프로폰 4 무선 헤드폰은 얼마인가?
(A) 39파운드
(B) 59파운드
(C) 79파운드
(D) 100파운드

해설 두 번째 단락의 두 번째 문장에서 스타일러스 펜, 보호 케이스, 무선 헤드폰과 같은 추가 부속품은 각각 39파운드, 59파운드, 79파운드의 추가 비용이 든다(Add-ons, such as ~ £79, respectively)고 했으므로 스타일러스 펜은 39파운드, 보호 케이스는 59파운드, 무선 헤드폰은 79파운드임을 알 수 있다. 따라서 (C)가 정답이다.

174 세부 사항

번역 프로폰 4가 이전 모델과 공통적인 것은?
(A) 화면 크기
(B) 카메라 해상도
(C) 가격
(D) 충전기

해설 다섯 번째 단락의 첫 문장에서 프로폰 4가 이전 모델과 유사한 한 가지는 충전기(One similarity ~ is the charger)라고 했으므로 (D)가 정답이다.

어휘 in common with ~와 공통적으로

175 문장 삽입

번역 [1], [2], [3], [4]로 표시된 곳 중에서 다음 문장이 들어가기에 가장 적합한 위치는?
"이러한 업그레이드에는 비용이 따른다."
(A) [1]
(B) [2]
(C) [3]
(D) [4]

해설 제시된 문장은 '이러한 업그레이드에는 비용이 따른다'며 가격이 인상되었음을 암시하고 있다. [1] 뒤에서 시작 가격인 999파운드는 이전 모델보다 100파운드 더 비싸다(The £999 starting price is £100 more than that of the previous model)며 가격 인상에 대한 내용을 언급하고 있으므로, (A)가 정답이다.

176-180 작업 주문서 + 이메일

작업 주문: 7549	
요청자:	시, 지나
입력일:	4월 9일 수요일
마감일:	4월 10일 목요일
유형:	기술 최종 사용자 요청
요약:	음성 메일 보안 설정
지정 정비사:	아놀드, 샘
컴퓨터 워크스테이션 ID:	HYS31

내용:

176새 전화 시스템의 음성 메일에서 새로운 보안 단계를 없앨 수 있을까요? 179저는 정말 비밀번호를 사용하고 싶지 않고, 매달 비밀번호를 변경하고 싶지도 않습니다. 저의 일은 기밀 사항이 아니어서 높은 수준의 보안이 필요하지 않습니다. 다른 누군가가 제 메시지에 접근하더라도 큰 피해를 끼치지 않을 것입니다.

어휘 requester 요청자 end-user (정보기술) 최종 사용자 assigned 배정된 degree 정도 security 보안 confidential 기밀의 gain access 접근하다 do harm 해를 끼치다

수신: 지나 시
발신: 샘 아놀드
날짜: 4월 10일 목요일
제목: 기술 지원 요청 7549

안녕하세요, 시 씨.

178이 메일은 새로운 전화 시스템과 관련된 당신의 작업 주문서 7549에 관한 내용입니다. 이 일로 당신을 도울 수 있어서 기쁩니다. 음성 메일 설정에 높은 수준의 보안이 필요하다고 생각하지 않는다는 점은 이해합니다만, 179새로운 시스템에서는 음성 메일을 검색하기 위해 암호가 있어야 합니다. 그러나 회사 정책에 따라 기밀 자료로 작업하지 않는 직원에 대한 설정을 제가 변경할 수 있습니다. 177,179정기적으로 비밀번호를 재설정할 필요가 없도록 보안 설정을 업데이트해 드릴 수 있습니다.

저는 당신이 낮은 수준의 보안에 수반되는 위험을 이해하고 있는지 확인하고 싶습니다. 당신의 음성 메일 계정에 접근할 수 있는 사람은 누구든지 단순히 메시지를 듣는 것 이상의 일을 할 수 있습니다. 메시지를 삭제하거나 인사말을 변경하거나 당신이 음성 메일에 접근할 수 없도록 비밀번호를 변경할 수 있습니다 (적어도 여기 IT 부서의 누군가가 비밀번호 변경을 무효화할 수 있을 때까지요). 180여전히 그 정도의 위험을 감수할 수 있는지 저에게 알려 주시면, 비밀번호가 만료되지 않도록 설정을 변경해 드리겠습니다.

샘 아놀드
기술 지원 직원

어휘 in reference to ~에 관하여 related 관련된 retrieve (정보를) 검색하다 material 자료 involved 수반된 delete 삭제하다 greeting 인사말 override 무효화하다 expire 만료되다 associate (직장) 동료

176 추론 / 암시

번역 시 씨의 요청에서 회사에 대해 암시된 것은?
(A) 일부 직원들에게 휴대전화를 제공한다.
(B) 직원들이 기밀 유지를 중시한다.
(C) 최근에 전화 시스템을 바꿨다.
(D) 직원들에게 기술 교육을 제공한다.

해설 작업 주문서의 내용란 첫 문장에서 시 씨가 새 전화 시스템의 음성 메일에서 새로운 보안 단계를 없앨 수 있을지(Is it possible to remove ~ in the new phone system?)를 묻고 있는 것으로 보아 회사가 최근에 전화 시스템을 교체했다는 것을 알 수 있다. 따라서 정답은 (C)이다.

어휘 value 소중하게 생각하다 confidentiality 기밀성

177 동의어

번역 이메일에서 첫 번째 단락 6행의 "regular"와 의미가 가장 가까운 단어는?
(A) 주기적인
(B) 질서 있는
(C) 관례적인
(D) 합법적인

해설 의미상 '정기적인'이라는 뜻으로 쓰인 것이므로 정답은 (A) periodic이다.

178 세부 사항

번역 아놀드 씨는 시 씨의 요청에 대한 세부 사항을 어디에서 알게 되었는가?
(A) 주간 관리자 회의
(B) 작업 주문서
(C) 전화 통화
(D) 개인 음성 메일

해설 이메일의 첫 문장에서 아놀드 씨가 시 씨에게 이 메일은 새로운 전화 시스템과 관련된 당신의 작업 주문서 7549에 관한 내용(This is in reference to your work order 7549 related to the new phone system)이라고 했으므로 시 씨의 작업 주문서를 통해 시 씨의 요청 내용에 대해 알게 되었음을 알 수 있다. 따라서 (B)가 정답이다.

179 연계

번역 아놀드 씨는 어떻게 시 씨의 요청을 들어주려고 하는가?
(A) 시 씨가 요청한 모든 것에 동의함으로써
(B) 시 씨의 전화기에 비밀번호를 재설정함으로써
(C) 다른 기술자에게 문제를 맡김으로써
(D) 시 씨의 요청 중 일부만 이행하겠다고 제안함으로써

해설 작업 주문서의 내용란 두 번째 문장에서 시 씨는 정말 비밀번호를 사용하고 싶지 않고 매달 비밀번호를 변경하고 싶지도 않다(I really don't want ~ change it every month)고 했는데, 이메일의 첫 단락 세 번째 문장에서 아놀드 씨는 새로운 시스템에서는 음성 메일을 검색하기 위해 암호가 있어야 한다(the new system does require ~ your voice mail)고 한 반면, 다섯 번째 문장에서는 정기적으로 비밀번호를 재설정할 필요가 없도록 보안 설정을 업데이트할 수 있다(I can update ~ on a regular basis)고 했다. 따라서 아놀드 씨는 시 씨가 요청한 두 가지 사항 중 한 가지만 들어줄 수 있다고 한 것이므로 (D)가 정답이다.

어휘 satisfy 충족시키다 refer (문제 등을) 위탁하다 fulfill 이행하다

180 세부 사항

번역 아놀드 씨는 시 씨에게 무엇을 하라고 요청하는가?
(A) 음성 메일 시스템에 필요한 변경을 할 것
(B) 새로운 음성 메일 시스템에 대한 교육에 참석할 것
(C) 그가 그녀의 음성 메일 시스템을 변경해 주기를 원하는지 확인해 줄 것
(D) 음성 메일 시스템의 문제에 대해 명확한 설명을 제공할 것

해설 이메일의 두 번째 단락 마지막 문장에서 아놀드 씨가 시 씨에게 그 정도의 위험을 감수할 수 있는지 알려 주면 비밀번호가 만료되지 않도록 설정을 변경하겠다(If you still feel comfortable ~ your password never expires)고 했으므로 정답은 (C)이다.

Paraphrasing 지문의 let me know → 정답의 confirm

181-185 이메일 + 후기

수신: 린다 한슈
발신: 클리프 머슨
제목: 조명 문제
날짜: 9월 4일 오전 10시 12분

안녕하세요, 한슈 씨:

〈타이탄 어드벤처〉의 최신 챕터에서 조명에 대해 논의했던 문제를 확인하고 싶습니다. ¹⁸³과거 버전의 게임에서는 녹색과 파란색 영역의 반사 이미지와 조명을 정확하게 맞추는 것이 특히 어려웠고, 계속해서 발생하는 문제였습니다. 새로운 출시작인 〈해왕성의 항해〉는 주로 수중 탐험으로, 이 문제를 처리하는 것이 매우 중요합니다. ¹⁸³당신이 이 일을 책임지겠다고 했는데, 문제의 해결책을 찾았다는 소식을 듣게 되기를 바랍니다. 팀에서는 사전 예행을 위해 10월 10일까지 게임 조명의 최종 렌더링을 실행해 보기를 기대하고 있었습니다. 그때까지 조명의 최종 버전이 준비될까요?

¹⁸¹게임의 다른 모든 측면은 일정대로 진행되고 있습니다. 가능한 빠른 시일 내에 조명에 대한 업데이트를 보내 주세요.

클리프 머슨
¹⁸¹리머코 게임즈 프로젝트 매니저

어휘 reflection 반사된 상 arise 생기다 release 출시(작) Neptune 해왕성 voyage 항해 primarily 주로 underwater 수중의 address (문제 등을) 다루다, 처리하다 crucial 중대한 take charge of ~을 책임지다 rendering 렌더링(그래픽 이미지 합성 기술) preliminary 예비의 run-through 예행연습, 리허설 aspect 측면 on schedule 예정대로

〈타이탄 어드벤처〉의 후기: 〈해왕성의 항해〉

4월 1일, 레오 웨버 작성

〈타이탄 어드벤처〉의 이번 신작은 새로운 플레이어들과 이 시리즈에 친숙한 오래된 마니아들 모두에게 놀라움과 즐거움을 줄 것이다. ¹⁸²비록 오픈 월드 형식이 최근 몇 년간 널리 퍼져 있기는 하지만, 〈해왕성의 항해〉는 이 형식에 새로움을 불어넣는다. ¹⁸⁴지침서를 삭제함으로써 이 게임은 사용자에게 새로운 영역과 장치를 발견할 수 있는 기회를 제공한다. 〈해왕성의 항해〉에서 당신은 수중 동굴에서 해왕성을 구출하는 임무를 맡은 돌고래 테티스로 깨어난다. 그런 다음 사용자는 게임의 세계에서 오르고, 달리고, 타고, 항해하고, 날아다니며, 그 과정에서 새로운 마을과 폐허, 그리고 다른 생물체들을 마주친다. 이 생물체들 중 일부는 오랜 팬들에게는 익숙하겠지만 참신함 또한 많다. ¹⁸³이 최신 버전은 또한 〈타이탄 어드벤처〉의 전작에서 종종 문제가 되었던 녹색과 파란색 이미지 렌더링을 바로잡았다.

¹⁸⁵〈해왕성의 항해〉는 5월 5일 리머코 클러치와 FS5에서 출시된다. 영어, 한국어, 일본어, 프랑스어, 스페인어로 이용 가능하다.

181 추론 / 암시

번역 이메일에서 머슨 씨에 대해 암시된 것은?
(A) 게임 개발팀을 총괄한다.
(B) 〈타이탄 어드벤처〉가 너무 비싸다고 확신한다.
(C) 리머코 게임즈의 신입 사원이다.
(D) 10월 10일에 출장을 떠날 예정이다.

해설 이메일의 두 번째 단락 첫 문장에서 게임의 다른 모든 측면은 일정대로 진행되고 있다(All other aspects of the game are on schedule)고 한 것으로 보아 머슨 씨가 게임 개발 업무를 조율하고 있음을 알 수 있다. 또한 이메일 마지막 줄에 머슨 씨의 직함이 리머코 게임즈 프로젝트 매니저(Project Manager, Rimerko Games)인 것으로 보아 머슨 씨가 관리자임을 알 수 있으므로 정답은 (A)이다.

어휘 coordinate 조직화하다 convinced 확신하는 overpriced 너무 비싼

182 Not / True

번역 후기에서 〈해왕성의 항해〉에 대해 명시된 것은?
(A) 〈타이탄 어드벤처〉의 주요 경쟁작이다.
(B) 오픈 월드 형식이 특징이다.
(C) 시리즈의 첫 번째 비디오 게임이다.
(D) 리머코의 가장 도전적인 게임이다.

해설 후기의 두 번째 문장에서 비록 오픈 월드 형식이 최근 몇 년간 널리 퍼져 있기는 하지만 〈해왕성의 항해〉는 이 형식에 새로움을 불어넣는다(Though open-world formats ~ brings something new to the format)고 했으므로, 〈해왕성의 항해〉가 오픈 월드 형식 기반이라는 것을 알 수 있다. 따라서 (B)가 정답이다.

어휘 competitor 경쟁자 challenging 도전적인

183 연계

번역 한슈 씨에 대해 결론지을 수 있는 것은?
(A) 〈해왕성의 항해〉의 대본을 썼다.
(B) 머슨 씨의 우려를 성공적으로 해결했다.
(C) 게임 디자인 상을 받았다.
(D) 프로젝트 매니저이다.

해설 이메일의 첫 단락 두 번째 문장에서 머슨 씨가 한슈 씨에게 과거 버전의 게임에서는 녹색과 파란색 영역의 반사 이미지와 조명을 제대로 맞추는 것이 특히 어려웠고 계속해서 발생하는 문제였다(In past versions of the game ~ a problem that kept arising)고 한 다음, 네 번째 문장에서 당신이 이 일을 책임지겠다고 했는데 문제의 해결책을 찾았다는 소식을 듣게 되기를 바란다(You said you would ~ found a solution to the problem)고 했는데, 후기의 첫 단락 마지막 문장에서 이 최신 버전은 또한 〈타이탄 어드벤처〉의 전작에서 종종 문제가 되었던 녹색과 파란색 이미지 렌더링을

바로잡았다(This newest version also corrects ~ in earlier installments of Titan Adventure)고 했다. 따라서 한슈 씨가 머슨 씨가 걱정했던 렌더링 문제를 제대로 해결했다는 것을 알 수 있으므로 (B)가 정답이다.

Paraphrasing 지문의 found a solution to the problem
→ 정답의 successfully addressed ~ concern

184 세부 사항

번역 웨버 씨는 〈해왕성의 항해〉에 대해 무엇이 흥미롭다고 생각하는가?
(A) 플레이어들이 해왕성 역할을 하게 한다.
(B) 플레이어들에게 어디로 가야 하는지 보여주기 위해 조명을 이용한다.
(C) 완전히 새롭게 구성된 캐릭터들을 소개한다.
(D) 플레이어들이 안내 없이 새로운 기능을 탐색할 수 있게 한다.

해설 후기의 세 번째 문장에서 지침서를 삭제함으로써 이 게임은 사용자에게 새로운 영역과 장치를 발견할 수 있는 기회를 제공한다(By stripping down instructional guides ~ discover new areas and devices)고 했다. 따라서 정답은 (D)이다.

어휘 navigate 길을 찾다 explore 탐험하다 feature 기능 guidance 안내

Paraphrasing 지문의 stripping down instructional guides → 정답의 without guidance

185 세부 사항

번역 〈해왕성의 항해〉는 언제 이용할 수 있는가?
(A) 9월 4일
(B) 10월 10일
(C) 4월 1일
(D) 5월 5일

해설 후기의 두 번째 단락 첫 문장에서 〈해왕성의 항해〉는 5월 5일 리머코 클러치와 FS5에서 출시된다(Neptune's Voyage launches May 5 on Rimerko Clutch and FS5)고 했으므로 정답은 (D)이다.

186-190 일정표 + 이메일 + 구인 광고

원더 리지 라디오 방송 일정, 월요일-금요일			
오전 6시 - 정오	정오 - 오후 4시	오후 4시 - 오후 7시	오후 7시 - 오후 10시
190 〈커피 브레이크〉 지역 뉴스 및 지역 사회 구성원과의 인터뷰	〈애프터눈 재즈〉 전통 재즈부터 퓨전 재즈에 이르는 음악	188 〈포크 프렌지〉 전 세계의 민속 음악	186 〈조시스 조인트〉 우리 방송국 음악 감독이 직접 선정한 현대 음악
진행자: 펠리스 피니	진행자: 말라치 므지	진행자: 페니 아리자	진행자: 조시 존스

어휘 traditional 전통의 folk 민속 음악; 민속의 frenzy 광란 select 선정하다 host 진행자

수신: feedback@wonderridgeradio.org
발신: pfabre@sendmail.net
제목: 나의 새 라디오 방송국!
날짜: 10월 22일

원더 리지 라디오 관계자분들께:

지난주에 운전을 하다가 188스포츠 토크를 듣는 게 지겨워서 다이얼을 돌렸습니다. 갑자기 제 차는 여러 해 동안 듣지 못했던 노래 한 곡으로 가득 찼습니다. 그 곡은 제 할머니께서 태어나신 프랑스의 전통 음악이었습니다. 할머니는 제가 어렸을 때 그 노래를 연주하시곤 했습니다. 187그 곡을 여기 원더 리지 라디오에서 듣게 되리라고는 전혀 예상하지 못했습니다. 이 경험과 귀사의 모든 훌륭한 프로그램에 감사드립니다.

귀사의 새로운 팬,
피에르 파브르

어휘 folks 사람들 be filled with ~로 가득 차다

원더 리지 라디오 채용 공고: 프로그래밍 보조

11월 2일 게시

직무 내용
프로그래밍 보조는 프로그래밍 책임자에게 보고하며 다양한 조사 및 소통 역할을 수행하여 라디오 방송을 지원합니다. 이 역할은 신입 파트타임 직책입니다.

업무
- 190인터뷰 대상자에 대한 배경 조사 실시
- 190방송 인터뷰에 잠재적인 주제와 게스트를 제안할 수 있도록 뉴스 및 뉴스메이커에 대한 최신 정보 유지
- 189방송국의 웹사이트 및 프로그램 진행자 약력 페이지 업데이트
- 189일정 관리 소프트웨어를 사용하여 방송 일정 업데이트
- 189특히 이메일과 소셜 미디어를 통한 청취자와의 소통

지원하시려면 이메일 hiring@wonderridgeradio.org로 이력서와 자기소개서를 보내 주세요.

어휘 description 기술, 설명 perform 수행하다 function 기능, 역할 entry-level 신입의, 초급의 conduct (특정 활동을) 하다 background 배경 up-to-date 최신의 news maker 뉴스거리가 되는 사람 potential 잠재적인 biography 전기 cover letter 자기소개서

186 세부 사항

번역 일정표에 따르면, 존스 씨는 누구인가?
(A) 라디오 방송국의 광고 관리자
(B) 지역 사회 뉴스 프로그램의 진행자
(C) 원더 리지 라디오의 음악 감독
(D) 스포츠 라디오 프로그램의 진행자

해설 일정표의 네 번째 프로그램인 〈조시스 조인트〉(JOSIE'S JOINT)의 진행자가 조시 존스(Host: Josie Jones)이고, 프로그램 설명에 우

리 방송국의 음악 감독이 직접 선정한 현대 음악(Modern sounds selected by our station's own music director)이라고 했으므로 존스 씨가 원더 리지 라디오의 음악 감독임을 알 수 있다. 따라서 (C)가 정답이다.

187 주제 / 목적

번역 이메일의 목적은?
(A) 라디오 방송국에 대한 칭찬
(B) 취업 기회에 대한 문의
(C) 더 많은 스포츠 토크쇼 프로그램 요청
(D) 노래 제목 문의

해설 이메일의 다섯 번째 문장에서 파브르 씨는 앞서 언급한 곡을 여기 원더 리지 라디오에서 듣게 되리라고는 전혀 예상하지 못했다(I never expected to hear it ~ in Wonder Ridge)며 이 경험과 귀사의 모든 훌륭한 프로그램에 감사드린다(Thanks for this experience and for all your great programs)며 라디오 방송국에 찬사를 보내고 있다. 따라서 (A)가 정답이다.

어휘 express praise 칭찬하다 inquire 문의하다

188 연계

번역 파브르 씨는 언제 원더 리지 라디오를 처음 들었을 것 같은가?
(A) 오전 6시에서 정오 사이
(B) 정오에서 오후 4시 사이
(C) 오후 4시에서 오후 7시 사이
(D) 오후 7시에서 오후 10시 사이

해설 이메일의 첫 문장에서 파브르 씨는 스포츠 토크를 듣는 게 지겨워서 다이얼을 돌렸는데(I got tired ~ turned the dial) 갑자기 제 차는 여러 해 동안 듣지 못했던 노래 한 곡으로 가득 찼으며(Suddenly, my car was filled with ~ in many years) 그 곡은 할머니께서 태어나신 프랑스의 전통 음악이었다(It was traditional music ~ my grandmother was born)고 했는데, 일정표의 세 번째 프로그램인 〈포크 프렌지〉(FOLK FRENZY)에서 전 세계의 민속 음악(folk music from around the world)를 들을 수 있다고 소개하고 있다. 따라서 파브르 씨는 오후 4시에서 오후 7시 사이에 하는 〈포크 프렌지〉를 통해 처음으로 원더 리지 라디오를 들었다는 것을 알 수 있으므로 (C)가 정답이다.

189 추론 / 암시

번역 구인 광고에서 지원자들이 반드시 갖추어야 한다고 암시하는 것은?
(A) 여행에 대한 자발성
(B) 컴퓨터에 익숙함
(C) 커뮤니케이션 학위
(D) 라디오 업계에서의 폭넓은 경험

해설 구인 광고 업무의 세 번째 항목에서 방송국의 웹사이트 및 프로그램 진행자 약력 페이지 업데이트(Updating the station's Web site ~ biography pages), 네 번째 항목에서 일정 관리 소프트웨어를 사용하여 방송 일정 업데이트(Using scheduling software ~ broadcast schedule), 다섯 번째 항목에서 특히 이메일과 소셜 미디어를 통한 청취자와의 소통(Communicating with listeners ~ social media)을 언급하고 있는 것으로 보아 지원자는 컴퓨터 작업에 익숙해야 한다는 것을 알 수 있다. 따라서 (B)가 정답이다.

어휘 willingness 기꺼이 하는 마음 familiarity 익숙함 degree 학위 extensive 폭넓은

190 연계

번역 어떤 라디오 프로그램이 프로그래밍 보조로부터 가장 많은 지원을 받을 것 같은가?
(A) 〈커피 브레이크〉
(B) 〈애프터눈 재즈〉
(C) 〈포크 프렌지〉
(D) 〈조시스 조인트〉

해설 일정표의 첫 프로그램인 〈커피 브레이크〉(COFFEE BREAK)는 지역 뉴스 및 지역 사회 구성원과의 인터뷰(Local news and interview with community members)를 다룬다고 나와 있고, 프로그래밍 보조 구인 광고에서 업무 중 첫 항목이 인터뷰 대상자에 대한 배경 조사 실시(Conducting background research on interviewees), 두 번째 항목이 방송 인터뷰에 가능한 주제와 게스트를 제안할 수 있도록 뉴스 및 뉴스메이커에 대한 최신 정보 유지(Keeping up-to-date on news ~ guests for on-air interviews)라고 나와 있다. 프로그래밍 보조의 다섯 가지 업무 중 두 가지가 〈커피 브레이크〉를 지원하는 업무이므로 (A)가 정답이다.

191-195 안내문 + 이메일 + 안내판

기록물 요청을 위한 안내

아빌렌 시에서 관리하는 공식 기록물과 문서에 관심을 가져 주셔서 감사합니다. 공공 정보 요청을 제출하시려면 다음 단계를 따라 주십시오.

1. 기록물 센터 웹포털에서 계정을 만듭니다. 191**현재 모든 요청은 포털을 통해 이루어져야 합니다.**

2. 드롭다운 메뉴를 이용하여 정보를 찾고 있는 부서를 찾아서 요청을 제출합니다. 참조 번호가 포함된 확인 이메일을 받습니다.

3. 부서 직원이 요청받은 기록물을 찾아보고 준비되면 연락드립니다. 기록물을 배송받을 수도 있고, 직접 가지러 올 수도 있습니다. 직접 가지러 오기를 원하는 경우 부서 직원과 약속을 잡아야 합니다.

4. 194**요청과 관련된 수수료가 있는 경우, 제공되는 서비스와 해당 특정 서비스에 대한 요금이 상세히 나온 항목별 명세서를 받습니다.**

어휘 instruction 설명, 안내 maintain 유지하다, 보존하다 file 제출하다 drop-down menu 버튼을 클릭하면 아래로 하위 항목이 펼쳐지는 방식의 메뉴 locate (위치를) 찾아내다 confirmation 확인 reference 참조, 조회 in person 직접 associated with ~와 관련된 itemized 항목별로 구분한 statement 명세서 detail 상술하다 charge 요금 specific 특정한

수신: 박주희 〈jhpark@coa.net〉
발신: 키스 브란덴버그 〈kbrandenberg@mailcurrent.com〉
날짜: 5월 3일
제목: RE: 참조 번호 W2486

박 씨께,

제 서류가 입수 가능한지 확인해 주셔서 감사합니다. 가능한 한 빨리 직접 가지러 가고 싶습니다. 이번 주에 약속을 잡을 수 있을까요?

수수료에 관해 질문이 하나 있습니다. 보아하니, 제 서류에 대해 300달러가 청구되어 있습니다. 수수료가 이렇게 높은 이유를 이해할 수 없고, 194**귀하의 이메일에는 어떠한 설명도 없었습니다.** 저는 과거 RJ 환경 엔지니어링에서 일할 당시 기록물을 여러 번 요청한 적이 있는데 이렇게 높은 수수료를 지불한 적은 없습니다. 192,195**이번 경우에 저는 도시의 지하 배관 지도 두 개를 요청했을 뿐이며, 이는 시의 하수 관리 자문에 응하는 우리 회사의 현재 작업에 정보를 제공해 줄 것입니다.**

수수료에 대해 명확히 설명해 주시고, 이번 주에 서류를 가지러 갈 수 있는지 알려 주시기 바랍니다. 감사합니다.

키스 브란덴버그

어휘 apparently 보아[듣자]하니 underground 지하의 pipeline 배관 inform 정보를 제공하다 advise 자문에 응하다, 조언하다 wastewater 하수 clarify 명확하게 하다

아빌렌 시 행정 건물
193**방문객들은 이 시설에 들어가기 전에 서명해야 합니다.**
이름과 방문할 호실을 일지에 기입하세요.

1층 안내:
IT 서비스 – 100호
공원 및 레크리에이션 – 101호
교통 – 102호
195**하수 – 103호**

어휘 administrative 행정의 facility 시설 logbook 일지 directory 건물 안내판

191 Not / True

번역 안내문에서 기록물 요청에 대해 명시하는 것은?
(A) 특정일에만 할 수 있다.
(B) 온라인으로만 할 수 있다.
(C) 허가받은 직원만 제출할 수 있다.
(D) 수수료를 수납한 후에만 제출할 수 있다.

해설 안내문의 첫 번째 단계 두 번째 문장에서 현재 모든 요청은 포털을 통해 이루어져야 한다(Currently, all requests must be made through the portal)고 했으므로 (B)가 정답이다.

어휘 certain 특정한 authorized 허가를 받은 personnel 직원

Paraphrasing 지문의 through the portal → 정답의 online

192 세부 사항

번역 이메일에 따르면, 브란덴버그 씨는 공공 정보를 어떻게 사용할 계획인가?
(A) 웹포털에 정보를 추가할 것
(B) 그의 회사에서 시에 조언하는 일을 도울 것
(C) 회계 오류를 확인할 것
(D) 기관이 조직된 방법을 알아낼 것

해설 이메일의 두 번째 단락 다섯 번째 문장에서 브란덴버그 씨는 이번 경우에 자신은 도시의 지하 배관 지도 두 개를 요청했을 뿐이며, 이는 시의 하수 관리 자문에 응하는 당사의 현재 작업에 정보를 제공해 줄 것(In this case, I am only requesting ~ on wastewater management)이라고 했다. 따라서 (B)가 정답이다.

어휘 identify 확인하다 structure 조직하다

193 세부 사항

번역 안내판에서 방문객들이 건물에 들어가기 전에 해야 하는 것으로 명시하는 것은?
(A) 보안 검색을 거친다.
(B) 주차증을 받는다.
(C) 신분증을 제시한다.
(D) 일지에 서명한다.

해설 안내판의 첫 문장에서 방문객들은 이 시설에 들어가기 전에 서명해야 한다(Visitors must sign in prior to entering this facility)면서 이름과 방문할 호실을 일지에 기입하라(Please enter your name ~ in the logbook)고 했으므로 (D)가 정답이다.

어휘 screening 검색, 심사 permit 허가증 identification 신분증

194 연계

번역 브란덴버그 씨가 받기를 기대한 것은?
(A) 수수료 항목별 명세서
(B) 회사에서 보낸 편지
(C) 시 공무원의 전화
(D) 웹포털의 비밀번호

해설 안내문의 마지막 단계에는 요청과 관련된 수수료가 있는 경우 제공되는 서비스와 해당 특정 서비스에 대한 요금이 상세히 나온 항목별 명세서를 받는다(If there are any fees ~ those specific services)고 나와 있는데, 이메일의 두 번째 단락 세 번째 문장에서 귀하의 이메일에는 (수수료에 대한) 어떠한 설명도 없었다(there was no explanation included in your e-mail)고 했다. 따라서 브란덴버그 씨는 수수료에 대한 항목별 명세서를 제공받기를 예상하고 있었다는 것을 알 수 있으므로 (A)가 정답이다.

195 연계

번역 브란덴버그 씨는 몇 호실을 방문할 것 같은가?
(A) 100호
(B) 101호
(C) 102호
(D) 103호

해설 이메일의 두 번째 단락 다섯 번째 문장에서 브란덴버그 씨는 이번 경우에 저는 도시의 지하 배관 지도 두 개를 요청했을 뿐이며, 이는 시의 하수 관리 자문에 응하는 우리 회사의 현재 작업에 정보를 제공해 줄 것(In this case, I am only requesting ~ on wastewater management)이라고 했고, 아빌렌 시 행정 건물 안내판에 하수는 103호(Wastewater – Room 103)라고 나와 있다. 따라서 정답은 (D)이다.

196-200 논평 + 이메일 + 이메일

196유명 배우, 첫 번째 책

런던 (2월 25일)—**196,200사이먼 에클룬드의 팬들은 배우로서 잘 알려진 그의 경력에서 쓴 첫 번째 책인 자서전 〈극장 조명이 어두워지면〉에 기뻐할 것이다.** 이 책은 **197그의 모국인 스웨덴에서** 영화에서의 첫 역할을 시작으로 프랑스와 이탈리아에서의 활동을 거쳐 영국에서의 최근 연극 작품으로 마무리되는, 그의 경력에 대한 훌륭한 통찰력을 제공한다.

책에서 에클룬드 씨는 스톡홀름에서 초기에 자신의 능력을 개발하는 데 도움을 준 멘토인 찰스 군나르손에 대해 언급하는 데 상당량의 지면을 할애한다. 그는 또한 특히 코미디에서 드라마 연기로, 다른 유형의 역할로 전환하는 데 있어 어려움을 설명한다. 그는 이곳 런던에서 무대 연기를 처음 시도한 일에 관한 몇 가지 재미난 일화를 수록한다. 그는 그 시도들이 처참했다고 서술하지만, 〈인생과 게임〉에서 그의 최근 공연을 본 사람은 누구든지 그 반대라고 말할 것이다.

에클룬드 씨는 오랫동안 무대와 스크린에서 마음을 사로잡아 온 배우이자, 지금은 대단히 매력적인 작가이다.

- 우마 조시

어휘 autobiography 자서전 dim 어두워지다 storied (이야기로) 잘 알려진, 유명한 insight 통찰력 native 태어난 곳의 dedicate 바치다, 헌정하다 fair 상당한 transition 전환하다 anecdote 일화 disastrous 처참한, 형편없는 captivating 마음을 사로잡는 thoroughly 완전히 engaging 매력적인

수신: 이디스 호킹
발신: 우마 조시
198날짜: 3월 2일
제목: RE: 기회

이디스 씨께,

197에클룬드 씨와의 인터뷰 주선에 응해 주셔서 감사합니다. 저는 이것이 제 최근 글의 훌륭한 후속편이 될 것이라고 생각합니다.

유익한 우연의 일치로, **197,198저는 다음 달에 언론인 총회에서 연설을 하기 위해 그의 고국을 방문할 예정입니다.** 저는 특별 연사로서 저널리즘에 있어 다양성의 이점에 대해 논의할 것입니다. 저의 연설 직전이나 직후에 에클룬드 씨와 할 일을 계획할 수 있을 거라고 생각합니다.

우마 조시
예술과 문화 편집자
톱 뉴스 U.K.

어휘 arrange 주선하다 follow-up 후속편 coincidence 우연의 일치 address 연설하다 diversity 다양성

수신: 우마 조시 〈ujoshi@topnews.co.uk〉
발신: 마리아 카잘라 〈mcazalla@zephyrmail.se〉
날짜: 3월 20일
제목: RE: 정보

조시 씨께,

199다음 달에 있을 에클룬드 씨와의 인터뷰에 대해 우리 모두 매우 기대

하고 있습니다. **200그는 당신이 〈톱 뉴스 U.K.〉에 기고하는 보도 기사, 인터뷰, 그리고 물론 〈극장 조명이 어두워지면〉에 대한 최근 기사까지 모든 글을 좋아합니다.**

199저는 단지 당신과 몇 가지 세부 사항을 마무리 짓고 싶습니다. 당신을 위해 호텔에서 에클룬드 씨의 집까지 가는 교통편을 마련해 두었습니다. 에클룬드 씨가 점심 식사에 당신의 일행 모두가 함께하기를 원하기 때문에 일행이 몇 명이 될지 알려 주세요.

마리아 카잘라

어휘   finalize 마무리 짓다

196 Not / True

번역   논평에서 에클룬드 씨에 대해 언급하는 것은?
(A) 감독으로서 자신의 일을 즐긴다.
(B) 많은 젊은이들의 멘토였다.
(C) 유명한 배우이다.
(D) 많은 책을 썼다.

해설   논평 제목이 유명 배우, 첫 번째 책(Famous Actor, First Book)이고, 첫 문장에서 사이먼 에클룬드의 팬들은 배우로서 잘 알려진 그의 경력에서 쓴 첫 번째 책인 자서전 〈극장 조명이 어두워지면〉에 기뻐할 것(Fans of Simon Eklund will be delighted ~ his storied career as an actor)이라고 했으므로 에클룬드 씨가 유명한 배우라는 것을 알 수 있다. 따라서 (C)가 정답이다.

Paraphrasing   지문의 famous → 정답의 well-known

197 연계

번역   조시 씨는 어디에서 에클룬드 씨를 만날 것 같은가?
(A) 스웨덴
(B) 프랑스
(C) 이탈리아
(D) 영국

해설   논평의 두 번째 문장에서 에클룬드 씨의 모국이 스웨덴(his native Sweden)이라고 나와 있고, 첫 번째 이메일의 첫 문장에서 조시 씨가 에클룬드 씨와의 인터뷰 주선에 응해 주셔서 감사하다(Thank you for agreeing ~ with Mr. Eklund for me)면서 두 번째 단락 첫 문장에서 다음 달에 언론인 총회에서 연설을 하기 위해 그의 고국을 방문할 예정(I will be visiting his home country ~)이라고 했다. 따라서 조시 씨와 에클룬드 씨는 에클룬드 씨의 모국인 스웨덴에서 만날 예정임을 알 수 있으므로 (A)가 정답이다.

198 세부 사항

번역   첫 번째 이메일에 따르면, 조시 씨가 4월에 여행하는 이유는?
(A) 휴가를 가기 위해
(B) 새 직장을 위한 면접을 보기 위해
(C) 국제 영화제에 참석하기 위해
(D) 총회에서 연설하기 위해

해설   조시 씨가 첫 번째 이메일을 작성한 날짜가 3월 2일(Date: 2 March)이고, 두 번째 단락의 첫 문장에서 다음 달에 언론인 총회에서 연설을 하기 위해 그의 고국을 방문할 예정(I will be visiting ~ to address a journalists' convention)이라고 했다. 따라서 조시 씨는 언론인 총회에서 연설을 하기 위해 4월에 여행을 하는 것이므로 정답은 (D)이다.

Paraphrasing   지문의 address a journalists' convention
→ 정답의 speak at a conference

199 주제 / 목적

번역   두 번째 이메일의 목적은?
(A) 호텔 객실 예약
(B) 만남 준비 확인
(C) 영화를 위한 아이디어 논의
(D) 교통편 요청

해설   두 번째 이메일의 첫 문장에서 다음 달에 있을 에클룬드 씨와의 인터뷰에 대해 우리 모두 매우 기대하고 있다(We are all very excited ~ with Mr. Eklund)고 했고, 두 번째 단락의 첫 문장에서 당신과 몇 가지 세부 사항을 마무리 짓고 싶다(I just wanted to finalize a few details with you)고 했다. 따라서 만남을 위한 준비 사항을 확인하기 위해 이메일을 쓴 것이므로 (B)가 정답이다.

200 연계

번역   에클룬드 씨에 대해 결론지을 수 있는 것은?
(A) 영국의 뉴스 사이트에 글을 쓰고 싶어 한다.
(B) 방금 새로운 조수를 고용했다.
(C) 그의 책에 대한 조시 씨의 논평에 만족했다.
(D) 특별한 요리를 자주 한다.

해설   논평의 첫 문장에서 조시 씨는 사이먼 에클룬드의 팬들은 배우로서 잘 알려진 그의 경력에서 쓴 첫 번째 책인 자서전 〈극장 조명이 어두워지면〉에 기뻐할 것(Fans of Simon Eklund will be delighted ~ his storied career as an actor)이라고 했고, 카잘라 씨가 조시 씨에게 쓴 두 번째 이메일의 두 번째 문장에서 에클룬드 씨가 당신이 〈톱 뉴스 U.K.〉에 기고하는 보도 기사, 인터뷰, 그리고 물론 〈극장 조명이 어두워지면〉에 대한 최근 기사까지 모든 글을 좋아한다(He enjoys all your writing ~ The Theatre Lights Dimmed!)고 했다. 따라서 에클룬드 씨가 그의 책에 대해 조시 씨가 쓴 논평에 만족했다는 것을 알 수 있으므로 (C)가 정답이다.

어휘   frequently 자주

실전 TEST 2

101 (C)	**102** (D)	**103** (A)	**104** (B)	**105** (D)
106 (C)	**107** (A)	**108** (D)	**109** (B)	**110** (C)
111 (C)	**112** (A)	**113** (B)	**114** (A)	**115** (A)
116 (A)	**117** (B)	**118** (B)	**119** (B)	**120** (A)
121 (A)	**122** (C)	**123** (D)	**124** (B)	**125** (C)
126 (C)	**127** (D)	**128** (A)	**129** (D)	**130** (C)
131 (D)	**132** (B)	**133** (C)	**134** (A)	**135** (C)
136 (D)	**137** (A)	**138** (C)	**139** (D)	**140** (B)
141 (C)	**142** (A)	**143** (D)	**144** (B)	**145** (B)
146 (C)	**147** (B)	**148** (D)	**149** (A)	**150** (B)
151 (B)	**152** (B)	**153** (D)	**154** (C)	**155** (D)
156 (B)	**157** (A)	**158** (C)	**159** (C)	**160** (A)
161 (B)	**162** (D)	**163** (A)	**164** (D)	**165** (C)
166 (D)	**167** (D)	**168** (B)	**169** (C)	**170** (D)
171 (C)	**172** (B)	**173** (A)	**174** (C)	**175** (A)
176 (D)	**177** (C)	**178** (B)	**179** (A)	**180** (B)
181 (B)	**182** (C)	**183** (D)	**184** (D)	**185** (A)
186 (A)	**187** (D)	**188** (C)	**189** (D)	**190** (B)
191 (D)	**192** (B)	**193** (B)	**194** (A)	**195** (C)
196 (B)	**197** (A)	**198** (D)	**199** (C)	**200** (B)

PART 5

101 동사 자리 _ 시제

해설 three staff members가 주어인 문장에 동사가 보이지 않으므로 빈칸은 동사 자리이다. 문장의 맨 앞에 과거를 나타내는 시간 부사구 Last week가 있어 '지난주에' 일어난 일에 대해 언급하고 있으므로 동사는 과거 시제가 되어야 한다. 따라서 (C)가 정답이다.

번역 지난주에 직원 세 명이 지역 도서관의 도서 판매 행사에서 자원봉사를 했다.

102 전치사 어휘

해설 문맥상 '20%만큼 하락한다'는 의미가 되어야 적절하므로 수치와 함께 쓰여 차액을 나타내어 '~만큼'을 뜻하는 (D) by가 정답이다. 참고로 도달하는 수치를 나타낼 때는 '~까지'라는 의미로 전치사 'to'를 쓴다.

번역 4월에는 물가가 20%만큼 하락할 것으로 예상된다.

103 재귀대명사

해설 전치사 by의 목적어 역할을 하며, '스스로 많은 업무를 처리한다'는 내용이 되어야 자연스러우므로 전치사 by와 함께 쓰여 '혼자서, 스스로'라는 의미의 관용 표현을 이루는 (A) themselves가 정답이다.

번역 프로젝트 관리 소프트웨어는 직원들이 많은 업무를 스스로 처리할 수 있게 한다.

어휘 allow 허용하다 handle 처리하다 task 업무

104 동사 어휘

해설 '배송 시간을 절감했다'는 의미가 되어야 적절하므로 '줄이다'는 의미의 (B) reduced가 정답이다.

번역 현지 제조사들은 외부 운송사를 고용하여 배송 시간을 절감했다.

어휘 external 외부의 attempt 시도하다 weaken 약화시키다

105 형용사 자리 _ 명사 수식

해설 빈칸은 뒤에 오는 명사 fee를 수식하는 형용사 자리이다. 문맥상 '추가적인 요금'이라는 의미가 되어야 자연스러우므로, '추가적인'이라는 뜻의 형용사 (D) additional이 정답이다. fee(요금)는 add의 주체가 아닌 대상이므로 능동 의미의 현재분사 (B) adding은 답이 될 수 없다.

번역 그램웰사는 지난달 작업에 대해 추가 요금을 청구할 수도 있다.

어휘 corporation 회사 charge 부과하다 fee 수수료

106 인칭대명사의 격 _ 소유격

해설 빈칸에는 뒤에 온 명사구 current project를 수식하는 말이 들어가야 한다. 따라서 명사 앞에 쓰여 한정사 역할을 할 수 있는 소유격 인칭대명사인 (C) her가 정답이다.

번역 강 씨는 재무부로 옮기기 전에 현재의 프로젝트를 완료하고 싶어 한다.

어휘 prefer 선호하다 transfer 옮기다

107 형용사 자리 _ 명사 수식

해설 빈칸은 There 구문의 주어 역할을 하는 명사 criteria 앞에서 명사를 수식하는 형용사 자리이다. 따라서 정답은 '구체적인'을 뜻하는 형용사 (A) specific이다.

번역 비밀번호를 성공적으로 변경하려면 충족해야 하는 특정 기준이 있다.

어휘 criteria (criterion의 복수형) 기준 meet 충족시키다 specify 명시하다

108 명사 자리 _ 복합명사

해설 전치사 to의 목적어 역할을 하는 명사 자리로, 빈칸 뒤의 명사 designer와 함께 '수석 디자이너'라는 의미의 복합명사를 만들 수 있는 (D) lead가 정답이다.

번역 의상 디자이너가 영화를 준비하는 일에 도움이 되도록 옷감 샘플을 수석 디자이너에게 보낼 수 있다.

어휘 costume 의상 fabric 직물 lead 선두; 이끌다

109 과거분사

해설 빈칸은 be동사 뒤에 적절한 보어를 골라 동사의 형태를 완성시켜야 하는 자리이다. 주어가 it(the product presentation)이고 빈칸 뒤에 목적어가 없으며, '발표가 촬영될 수 있다'는 수동의 의미가 되어야 자연스러우므로 수동태를 이루는 과거분사 (B) filmed가 정답이다.

번역 제품 발표회 리허설이 완전히 끝나서 다음 주 아무 때나 촬영이 가능하다.

110 동사 어휘

해설 명사 effort를 수식하는 to부정사에 들어갈 적절한 동사 어휘를 고르는 문제이다. '새로운' 로고에 대해 설명하는 문장이므로 문맥상 '브랜드의 정체성을 새롭게 하기 위한 노력'이라는 내용이 되어야 자연스럽다. 따라서 '새롭게 하다'라는 뜻의 (C) refresh가 정답이다.

번역 새 로고는 브랜드의 정체성을 새롭게 하고 더 젊은 소비자들에게 어필하기 위한 포괄적인 노력의 일환이다.

어휘 comprehensive 포괄적인 identity 정체(성) consumer 소비자

111 부사 자리 _ 동사 수식

해설 The latest sport utility vehicle이 주어, can carry가 동사, eight people이 목적어인 완전한 문장이다. 빈칸에는 동사 can carry를 수식할 부사가 들어가야 하므로 (C) comfortably가 정답이다.

번역 본던 자동차의 최신 SUV는 8명을 편안하게 태울 수 있다.

어휘 latest 최신의 sport utility vehicle SUV(스포츠 유틸리티 차량)

112 전치사 자리

해설 동명사 deciding과 함께 쓰여 '결정하기 전에'라는 의미를 나타내는 전치사인 (A) Before가 정답이다. 'before + -ing(~하기 전에)'와 'after + -ing(~한 후에)'는 빈출 표현이니 암기해 두자.

번역 음식 제공업체를 교체하기로 결정하기 전에 경영진은 전 직원을 대상으로 설문 조사를 실시했다.

113 형용사 자리 _ 주격 보어

해설 빈칸은 be동사 뒤 주격 보어 자리이므로 형용사나 분사, 또는 명사가 들어갈 수 있다. '전근 가는 것에 대해 망설였다'는 내용이 되어야 하므로 (B) hesitant가 정답이다. 자동사 hesitate는 수동태로 쓰지 않으므로 (D) hesitated는 오답, 주어인 Mr. Cho와 명사 hesitation은 동격이 아니므로 (C)도 오답이다.

번역 조 씨는 휴스턴 지사로 옮기는 것에 대해 망설였지만 지금은 그곳에서 자신 있게 그리고 생산적으로 근무하고 있다.

어휘 transfer 옮기다 confidently 자신 있게 productively 생산적으로

114 접속사 자리 _ 부사절 접속사

해설 빈칸 뒤에 주어와 동사를 갖춘 완전한 절이 왔으므로 부사절 접속사가 들어가야 한다. 따라서 '~므로, ~ 때문에'라는 의미의 접속사 (A) as가 정답이다.

번역 무급 휴가는 관리자가 승인할 수 없으므로 인사과에 연락해야 한다.

어휘 personnel office 인사과 leave 휴가 supervisor 관리자

115 to부정사 vs. 동명사

해설 문장의 동사 voted는 to부정사를 목적어로 취하는 동사인데, 빈칸 앞에 to가 있으므로 빈칸에는 동사원형이 들어가야 한다. 따라서 (A) proceed가 정답이다.

번역 어제 이사회는 아틀라스버그 파이낸셜 인수에 대한 논의를 진행하기로 결정했다.

어휘 board 이사회 vote 투표하다 acquire 인수하다 proceed with ~을 진행하다

116 형용사 어휘

해설 빈칸 뒤에 '개인의 이익을 추구하기보다'라는 내용이 온 것으로 보아, 빈칸에는 뒤의 내용과 상반되는 '공동의 목표'라는 의미가 되어야 적절하므로 '공동의'라는 뜻의 (A) common이 정답이다.

번역 로블스사는 직원들이 개인의 이익을 추구하기보다는 공동의 목표를 향해 일하도록 권장한다.

어휘 encourage 권장하다 pursue 추구하다 individual 개인의 plain 분명한

117 명사 자리 _ 동사의 주어

해설 빈칸은 복수동사 are의 주어 자리이므로 복수명사가 들어가야 한다. 따라서 (B) images가 정답이다.

번역 안내 책자에 있는 이미지는 리조트에 머무는 손님들이 기대하는 것에 대해 정확하게 묘사한 것이다.

어휘 accurate 정확한 representation 묘사[표현]

118 동사 어휘

해설 문맥상 적절한 동사이면서 빈칸 뒤에 목적어가 없으므로 자동사가 들어가야 한다. '절차에 대해 문의해야 한다'는 내용이 되어야 자연스러우므로 전치사 about과 함께 '~에 관해 문의하다'는 의미를 만드는 (B) inquire가 정답이다.

번역 새로운 관리직에 관심 있는 현직 직원들은 내부 채용 절차에 대해 문의해야 한다.

어휘 managerial 관리[경영]의 internal 내부의 process 절차

119 부사 어휘

해설 등위접속사 and 뒤에 주어(Colleagues in the accounting department)가 생략된 완전한 절이 왔으므로 빈칸은 부사 자리

이다. 문맥상 '문제가 종결되었다고 간주하므로 더 이상 조언을 제공할 수 없다'는 내용이 되어야 자연스러우므로 인과 관계를 나타내는 '그 결과, 따라서'라는 뜻의 (B) consequently가 정답이다. 빈칸에 명사가 올 수는 있지만, (D) anyone이 아니라 none을 써서, 'none of them can provide ∼'로 써야 '아무도 추가 의견을 낼 수 없다'라는 뜻이 통한다.

번역 회계 부서의 직원들은 그 문제가 종결되었다고 간주하므로 더 이상의 의견을 제공할 수 없다.

어휘 matter 문제   input 의견

120 동사 어휘

해설 higher profits를 목적어로 받아 '더 많은 이익을 내다'라는 문맥이 되어야 자연스러우므로 '내다, 산출하다'는 의미의 (A) yield가 정답이다.

번역 최고 경영자는 컨설턴트의 조언이 궁극적으로 회사에 더 많은 이익을 가져다줄 것으로 기대한다.

어휘 ultimately 궁극적으로   invent 발명하다   resolve 해결하다

121 명사 어휘

해설 문맥상 전문가들이 계약서를 검토하고 있다는 내용의 절을 수식하는 수식구에 들어갈 명사를 고르는 문제로, '재무적인 관점에서 계약서를 검토 중'이라는 의미가 되어야 적절하므로 '관점'을 뜻하는 (A) perspective가 정답이다.

번역 전문가 팀이 재무적인 관점에서 계약서를 검토하는 중이므로 아직 고객과 내용을 공유하지 말아 주십시오.

어휘 expert 전문가   proportion 비율

122 부사 어휘

해설 빈칸 뒤 형용사 open을 수식하기에 적절한 부사를 고르는 문제이다. 문맥상 '소음 방지를 위해 운영되지 않는다'는 의미가 적절하므로 부정 부사인 (C) never가 정답이다.

번역 공연자들의 주의를 산만하게 하는 소음을 방지하기 위해 공연 중에는 로비의 기념품점이 운영되지 않는다.

어휘 prevent 방지하다   distract 산만하게 하다

123 부사 자리 _ 동사 수식

해설 Zuper Brite lightbulbs가 주어이고 reduce가 동사이며, 빈칸은 동사 reduce를 수식하는 부사 자리이다. '에너지 소비를 크게 줄인다'는 내용이 되어야 자연스러우므로 '대단히, 크게'라는 뜻의 (D) greatly가 정답이다. (A) great는 동사 뒤에서 부사로 쓸 때 '아주 잘'을 뜻하므로 문맥상 어울리지 않는다.

번역 주퍼 브라이트 전구는 표준 백열 전구에 비해 에너지 소비를 크게 줄인다.

어휘 lightbulb 전구   consumption 소비   compare 비교하다   incandescent 백열성의

124 명사 어휘

해설 빈칸 뒤 문장에서 프로젝트에 리모델링된 터미널과 개선된 교통 시스템이 포함된다고 했으므로, '공항 현대화 프로젝트'라는 의미가 되어야 적절하다. 따라서 '현대화'를 뜻하는 (B) modernization이 정답이다.

번역 제안된 공항 현대화 프로젝트에는 리모델링된 터미널 두 곳과 개선된 교통 시스템이 포함될 것이다.

어휘 proposed 제안된   transportation 교통   encouragement 격려

125 명사 자리 _ 주격 보어

해설 be동사 뒤에 정관사 the가 있으므로 빈칸은 명사 자리이다. 따라서 '부서'라는 뜻의 명사 (C) division이 정답이다.

번역 마켓 리서치는 고객의 요구를 더 잘 이해하는 것과 관련된 회사 부서이다.

어휘 concerned with ∼와 관련된

126 접속사 자리 _ 부사절 접속사

해설 문장 중의 so가 문제 해결의 단서로, 'so + 형용사/부사'와 함께 쓰여 '너무 ∼해서 …하다'라는 결과의 의미를 이루는 (C) that이 정답이다.

번역 타나카 씨는 분기별 실적 보고서를 보고 몹시 기뻐서 주간 보고를 취소했다.

어휘 quarterly 분기별의

127 접속사 자리 _ 부사절 접속사

해설 빈칸 뒤에 주어와 동사를 갖춘 완전한 절이 왔으므로 부사절 접속사가 들어가야 한다. 또한 문맥상 '서비스의 질적 향상이 있는 경우에만'이라는 내용이 되어야 적절하므로 '∼한 경우에만'이라는 의미의 접속사 (D) only if가 정답이다.

번역 퀸사이콤의 가격 인상은 우리가 받는 인터넷 서비스의 질적 향상이 있는 경우에만 타당하다.

어휘 justifiable 타당한   improvement 향상

128 명사 어휘

해설 빈칸 뒤에 전치사 with와 함께 타사의 휴대전화 모델이 언급된 것으로 보아 '비바시코의 최신 스마트폰과 유스타스 테크의 모델을 비교한 것'이라는 내용이 되어야 자연스러우므로 전치사 with와 어울려 '비교'를 뜻하는 (A) comparison이 정답이다.

번역 이 이메일에 첨부된 차트는 비바시코의 최신 스마트폰과 유스타스 테크의 모델을 비교한 것이다.

어휘 present 보여 주다   latest 최신의   pronouncement 선언   guideline 지침   publicity 홍보

129 명사 자리 _ 주격 보어

해설 가주어 It의 주격 보어 역할로 소유격 뒤에는 명사가 와야 하므로, 빈칸은 명사 자리이다. 따라서 '의무'라는 의미의 명사인 (D) obligation이 정답이다.

번역 행사에 앞서 일찌감치 주방장에게 계획된 메뉴를 알리는 것은 음식 공급 책임자의 의무이다.

어휘 catering 음식 공급 inform 알리다 intended 계획된 in advance 미리 obligation 의무

130 부사 어휘

해설 형용사구 well suited를 수식하여 적절한 문맥을 완성하는 부사를 고르는 문제이다. '경력을 고려해 볼 때 정 씨가 특히 적합하다'는 의미가 되어야 자연스러우므로 '특히'라는 강조의 의미를 지닌 (C) particularly가 정답이다.

번역 건강 관리 분야에서 그녀의 경력을 고려해 볼 때, 정 씨는 회사의 건강 프로그램을 관리하는 데 특히 적합하다.

어휘 given ~을 고려해 볼 때 suited 적합한 formerly 이전에 expectantly 기대하여 avoidably 피할 수 있게

PART 6

131-134 제품 설명

> **샌버그 인더스트리즈: 빅 앵글 텔레비전 월 마운트**
>
> 빅 앵글 텔레비전 월 마운트는 화면을 대각선으로 측정했을 때 40인치에서 75인치 크기의 TV를 설치하기에 완벽합니다. 마운트는 벽에 쉽게 131**연결되므로** 테이블 위를 비워 공간을 절약해 줍니다. 132**플렉시블** 마운트에는 다양한 방향으로 구부러지는 25인치 거치대가 딸려 있어 실내 어디에서나 TV 시청을 즐길 수 있습니다. 또한, 수직 및 수평 기울임 기능이 있어 원하는 위치에 TV를 133**정확하게** 배치할 수 있습니다. 134**샌버그 인더스트리즈의 모든 제품과 마찬가지로 이 제품 또한 5년 보증이 제공됩니다.**

> 어휘 mount 설치; 설치하다 measure 측정하다 diagonally 대각선으로 tabletop 테이블 위 bend 구부러지다 direction 방향 vertical 수직의 horizontal 수평의 tilt 기울어짐 capability 성능, 능력

131 접속부사

해설 빈칸 앞에 완전한 절이 왔고 뒤에는 분사구문이 왔으므로, 빈칸에는 분사구를 절에 자연스럽게 연결할 접속부사가 들어가면 된다. '마운트는 벽에 쉽게 연결되므로 테이블 위를 비워 공간을 아껴 준다'는 의미가 되어야 하므로 '그렇게 함으로써'를 뜻하는 부사 (D) thereby가 정답이다.

132 형용사 어휘

해설 마운트에 다양한 방향으로 구부러지는 25인치 거치대가 딸려 있어 실내 어디에서나 TV 시청을 즐길 수 있다고 했으므로 이러한 마운트를 수식하는 형용사로는 '유연한'이라는 뜻의 (B) flexible이 들어가야 한다. 따라서 정답은 (B)이다.

어휘 mysterious 신비한 flexible 유연한 skillful 능숙한 limited 제한된

133 부사 자리 _ 동사 수식

해설 빈칸이 없어도 완전한 절이 있고 동사구 can be placed를 수식하는 자리이므로 '정확하게'를 뜻하는 부사 (C) exactly가 정답이다.

134 문맥에 맞는 문장 고르기

해설 빈칸 앞에서 플렉시블 마운트에 다양한 방향으로 구부러지는 거치대가 딸려 있고, 수직 및 수평 기울임 기능이 있다며 제품에 대해 설명하고 있으므로 빈칸에도 제품에 대한 정보를 알려 주는 내용이 연결되어야 자연스럽다. 따라서 해당 제품에 5년 보증이 제공된다는 추가 정보를 언급하고 있는 (A)가 정답이다.

번역 (A) 샌버그 인더스트리즈의 모든 제품과 마찬가지로 이 제품 또한 5년 보증이 제공됩니다.
(B) 샌버그 제품에 대한 귀하의 문의는 영업일 기준 2일 이내에 처리될 것입니다.
(C) 샌버그 인더스트리즈에서 수년간 근무해 주셔서 감사합니다.
(D) 고화질 TV는 향상된 시청 경험을 제공합니다.

어휘 guarantee 품질 보증 inquiry 문의 address 처리하다 grateful 감사하는 high-definition 고화질의 viewing 시청

135-138 이메일

> 수신: minjunlee@alto.com
> 발신: contest@asianaturemag.org
> 날짜: 9월 7일
> 제목: 제10회 연례 대회
>
> 〈아시아 네이처〉 잡지는 귀하의 135**제출**에 감사드립니다. 제10회 연례 아마추어 사진 대회에 참여해 주셔서 감사합니다. 저희가 받은 각 사진은 전문가 패널에 의해 심사됩니다. 136**이 전문가들은 각자의 분야에서 최고에 속합니다.** 이들의 작품은 전 세계 갤러리에 전시되었습니다.
>
> 〈아시아 네이처〉 잡지는 귀하와 같이 환경을 아끼고 자연의 아름다움을 137**소중히 여기는** 사람들에게 의존하고 있습니다. 오늘 저희 웹사이트를 방문하셔서 기부해 주시기 바랍니다. 귀하와 같은 138**관대한** 독자가 없다면 저희는 일을 계속할 수 없을 것입니다.

> 어휘 participation 참여 judge 심사하다 panel 패널(조언 등을 제공하는 전문가 집단) expert 전문가 depend on ~에 의존하다 contribution 기부금, 기여

135 명사 어휘

해설 빈칸 뒤 문장에서 제10회 연례 아마추어 사진 대회에 참여해 주셔서 감사하다고 한 것으로 보아 빈칸이 있는 문장은 사진을 제출해 주어 감사하다는 내용이 되어야 적절하다. 따라서 '제출'을 뜻하는 (C) submission이 정답이다.

136 문맥에 맞는 문장 고르기

해설 빈칸 앞에는 사진이 전문가 패널(our panel of experts)에 의해 심사된다고 했고, 빈칸 뒤에는 이들의 작품(their works)이 전 세계 갤러리에 전시되었다고 전문가 패널에 대해 소개하고 있다. 따라서 빈칸에도 전문가 패널에 대한 내용이 들어가야 앞뒤 연결이 자연스러우므로 전문가 패널을 이 전문가들(These professionals)로 받아 추가적인 설명을 하고 있는 (D)가 정답이다.

번역 (A) 자연을 촬영하는 것은 배우기 어려운 기술입니다.
　　(B) 우리 잡지의 모든 독자들은 야생 동물이 소중하다는 것을 알고 있습니다.
　　(C) 〈아시아 네이처〉 잡지는 14년 동안 발행되었습니다.
　　(D) 이 전문가들은 각자의 분야에서 최고에 속합니다.

어휘 wildlife 야생 동물　precious 소중한　professional 전문가　field 분야

137 동사 자리 _ 복합문제

해설 빈칸은 등위접속사 and 뒤에 주격 관계대명사 who가 생략된 동사 자리이다. 관계사절의 동사는 선행사에 수를 일치시키는데, 선행사가 people like you이므로 복수동사가 들어가야 한다. 또한 앞 절의 동사 care가 현재 시제이고 일반적인 사실을 설명하는 내용이므로 빈칸에도 현재 시제 동사가 와야 한다. 따라서 정답은 (A) value이다.

138 형용사 어휘

해설 앞 문장에서 오늘 저희 웹사이트를 방문하셔서 기부해 주시기 바란다고 했으므로, 빈칸이 있는 문장에서 말하는 독자는 '기부해 주는 독자'를 의미하는 것임을 알 수 있다. 따라서 '관대한, 후한'이라는 뜻의 (C) generous가 정답이다.

139-142 기사

개점을 앞둔 새 이탈리아 식품점

캘거리 (3월 28일)—이번주 토요일에는 캘거리의 최신 이탈리아 전문 식품점의 개점을 축하한다. 살레르노즈 이탈리안 푸드는 수입품 ¹³⁹**뿐 아니라** 자체 브랜드의 신선한 파스타와 소스도 판매할 예정이다. 매장은 매콜 가와 아른헴 가의 모퉁이에 위치한다. ¹⁴⁰**이 지역은 이미 여러 빵집, 식당, 커피숍이 모여 있다.** 캘거리의 이 작은 지역은 고급 음식을 맛보기 위해 가는 매우 인기 있는 장소가 되고 있다. 가게의 주인인 레오 사리는 ¹⁴¹**이전에** 밀라노즈의 주방장이었다. 그는 토요일을 손꼽아 기다리고 있으며 처음으로 ¹⁴²**소매업계에** 진출하게 되어 흥분된다고 말했다.

어휘 mark 기념[축하]하다　specialty (식당의) 전문 음식　imported 수입된　goods 제품　gourmet food 고급 식료품　thrilled 아주 흥분한

139 상관접속사

해설 Salerno's Italian Food가 주어, will sell이 동사, its own brand of fresh pastas and sauces와 imported goods가 목적어인 문장이다. 따라서 빈칸에는 목적어인 두 명사구를 이어주며, '수입품뿐 아니라 자체 브랜드의 신선한 파스타와 소스도 판매한다'는 의미를 만드는 '~뿐만 아니라 …도'라는 뜻의 상관접속사 (D) as well as가 정답이다.

140 문맥에 맞는 문장 고르기

해설 빈칸 앞에는 매장의 위치(located on the corner of ~)에 대해 안내하고 있고, 빈칸 뒤에는 이 지역(This small part of Calgary)이 매우 인기 있는 장소가 되고 있다고 설명하고 있다. 따라서 빈칸에도 매장이 위치한 지역에 대한 내용이 들어가야 앞뒤 연결이 자연스러우므로 이 지역(This area)은 이미 여러 음식점이 모여 있다고 언급하고 있는 (B)가 정답이다.

번역 (A) 토요일 날씨는 아름다울 것으로 예상된다.
　　(B) 이 지역은 이미 여러 빵집, 식당, 커피숍이 모여 있다.
　　(C) 신선한 파스타와 소스는 대량 생산된 것들보다 우수하다.
　　(D) 우리는 곧 살레르노즈가 제공하는 제품에 대한 소비자들의 생각을 알게 될 것이다.

어휘 bistro 작은 식당　superior (~보다 더) 우수한　mass-produced 대량 생산의　consumer 소비자

141 부사 어휘

해설 빈칸에 적절한 부사를 선택하는 문제이다. 빈칸 앞에서 새로 문을 여는 가게에 대해 계속 현재 시제로 소개하다가 빈칸이 있는 문장에서만 과거 시제(was)를 사용했고, '가게의 주인인 레오 사리는 이전에 밀라노의 주방장이었다'는 내용이 되어야 적절하므로 '이전에'라는 뜻의 (C) previously가 정답이다.

142 명사 어휘

해설 빈칸이 있는 문장의 주어인 He는 앞 문장의 레오 사리이고, 레오 사리는 가게의 주인(the store's owner)이라고 했으므로 그가 진출하는 업계는 '소매업계'임을 알 수 있다. 따라서 '소매'를 뜻하는 (A) retail이 정답이다.

143-146 구인 광고

숙련 기술자 모집

칼리파 테크 인더스트리즈에서는 당사의 주요 생산 공장에서 문제를 ¹⁴³**분석하고**, 기기를 설치 및 작동하며, 기계의 고장을 해결할 수 있는 숙련된 기술자를 구하고 있습니다. ¹⁴⁴**우리 공장은 산업 설비에 사용되는 부품을 생산합니다.** 우리가 만드는 장비의 예로는 다양한 산업용 펌

프와 팬이 있습니다.

칼리파 테크 인더스트리즈는 마감 시한이 촉박한 빠른 작업 환경을 특징으로 합니다. 우리는 압박감 ¹⁴⁵**속에서** 함께 일할 수 있는 팀원이 필요합니다. 우리는 ¹⁴⁶**높은** 급여와 우수한 복지를 제공합니다. humanresources@caliphartechindustries.com으로 연락 주십시오.

> 어휘 machinist 기계 제작[수리] 기술자 seek 구하다 set up 설치하다 operate 작동하다 troubleshoot 문제를 해결하다 plant 공장 manufacture 제조하다 fan 팬, 환풍기 various 다양한 feature 특징을 이루다 fast-paced 진행 속도가 빠른 pressure 압박 benefits 복리 후생

143 to부정사의 형용사적 용법

해설 Caliphar Tech Industries가 주어, is seeking이 동사, experienced machinists가 목적어인 완전한 문장에서, 명사 machinists를 뒤에서 수식하면서 목적어 problems를 취할 수 있는 준동사가 빈칸에 와야 한다. 준동사인 (C) analyzing, (D) to analyze 중에서, 콤마 뒤에 오는 set up and operate, troubleshoot과 병렬 구조를 이루어야 하므로 (D) to analyze가 정답이다. 명사 뒤에서 to부정사가 명사를 수식하면 '~할'이라는 의미로, '문제를 분석할 기술자를 구한다'라는 뜻이 되므로 구인 광고에 적합하다.

144 문맥에 맞는 문장 고르기

해설 빈칸 뒤에서 우리가 만드는 장비의 예로는 다양한 산업용 펌프와 팬이 있다며 업체에서 생산하는 장비의 구체적인 예시를 들고 있으므로 빈칸에는 업체에서 생산하는 제품의 종류에 대한 내용이 들어가야 연결이 자연스럽다. 따라서 공장에서 산업 설비용 부품을 생산한다고 언급한 (B)가 정답이다.

번역 (A) 귀하의 프로젝트에 대한 시방서를 우리의 생산 책임자에게 보내십시오.
(B) 우리 공장은 산업 설비에 사용되는 부품을 생산합니다.
(C) 우리의 혁신적인 제조 공장의 견학을 즐기시기 바랍니다.
(D) 칼리파 테크 인더스트리즈에 채용된 것을 축하드립니다.

어휘 specification 시방서, 사양 component 부품 industrial 산업용의 innovative 혁신적인

145 전치사 어휘

해설 뒤의 pressure를 목적어로 연결해 '압박감 속에서'라는 의미를 만드는 (B) under가 정답이다.

146 형용사 자리 _ 명사 수식

해설 빈칸은 뒤에 온 명사 salaries를 수식하는 형용사 자리이고, '높은 급여'라는 의미가 되어야 자연스러우므로 '(가격 등이) 남에게 뒤지지 않는, 경쟁력 있는'이라는 의미의 형용사인 (C) competitive가 정답이다.

PART 7

147-148 광고

> ¹⁴⁷**엉클 피트의 마리오네트 극장 공연**
> **〈무스 레이크〉**
> 3월 27일-5월 7일
>
> ¹⁴⁸**엉클 피트의 마리오네트 극장이 설립된 이래로, 유명한 발레인 〈무스 레이크〉를 각색한 작품은 우리의 가장 사랑받는 공연 중 하나입니다.** 100개의 수공예 마리오네트가 여러분을 〈무스 레이크〉의 짜릿한 모험의 세계로 데려다줄 것입니다.
>
> 능숙한 퍼페티어들이 줄을 잡아당겨 인형들을 움직이는 동안 여러분은 마리아와 무스 왕자를 응원하게 될 것입니다. 도마뱀 왕과 그의 부하들 때문에 언짢아질지도 모릅니다. 여러분은 날아다니는 잠자리떼에 매료될 것입니다!
>
> 엉클 피트의 〈무스 레이크〉 버전은 30년 이상 모든 연령대의 관객들을 즐겁게 해 주었습니다. 쇼는 매년 매진되므로 오늘 바로 표를 구입하세요.
>
> 입장권은 펜튼 페리 가 521번지에 있는 매표소에서 구입하실 수 있습니다.

> 어휘 marionette 꼭두각시 인형 present (연극·방송 등을) 공연하다 founding 설립 adaptation 각색 (작품) handcrafted 수공예품인 thrilling 신나는 adventure 모험 puppeteer 인형을 조종하는 사람 string 줄 puppet 꼭두각시 cheer 응원하다 lizard 도마뱀 minion 하인 enthralled 매혹된 drifting 떠다니는 dragonfly 잠자리 delight 아주 즐겁게 하다

147 주제 / 목적

번역 광고되고 있는 것은?
(A) 호수 유람선
(B) 인형극
(C) 현악 4중주단
(D) 놀이공원

해설 광고의 제목이 엉클 피트의 마리오네트(꼭두각시 인형) 극장 공연 (Uncle Pete's Marionette Theater Presents) 〈무스 레이크〉 (Moose Lake)이므로 인형극을 광고하고 있음을 알 수 있다. 따라서 (B)가 정답이다.

148 세부 사항

번역 엉클 피트 버전의 〈무스 레이크〉는 무엇을 바탕으로 한 것인가?
(A) 고전 아동 도서
(B) 인기 영화
(C) 비디오 게임
(D) 무용 공연

해설 첫 단락의 첫 문장에서 엉클 피트의 마리오네트 극장이 설립된 이래로 유명한 발레인 〈무스 레이크〉를 각색한 작품은 우리의 가장 사랑받는 공연 중 하나(Ever since the founding ~ most beloved shows)라고 했으므로 정답은 (D)이다.

Paraphrasing 지문의 ballet → 정답의 dance performance

149-150 쿠폰

클린 하우스 청소 용역 서비스
149 1972년 이래 코퍼 카운티의 신뢰할 수 있고 효율적인 청소 해결사

150 신규 고객 판촉 행사
*코퍼 카운티 주민 전용

집안 청소 첫 해 이용 시 15% 할인!
*카펫 청소 서비스 미포함

자세한 내용을 확인하시거나 첫 서비스를 예약하시려면
오늘 916-555-0137로 전화하십시오.

이 행사는 12월 31일까지 유효합니다.

어휘 janitorial service 청소 용역 서비스 trustworthy 신뢰할
수 있는 promotion 판촉 (행사) resident 주민 valid 유효한

149 Not / True

번역 클린 하우스 청소 서비스에 대해 명시된 것은?
(A) 1972년에 설립되었다.
(B) 사무실 청소를 전문으로 한다.
(C) 카펫 청소에 할인을 제공한다.
(D) 온라인 소통 방식을 선호한다.

해설 두 번째 줄에서 1972년 이래로 코퍼 카운티의 신뢰할 수 있고 효율
적인 청소 해결사(Copper County's ～ since 1972)라고 클린 하
우스 청소 서비스에 대해 소개하고 있으므로 업체가 1972년부터 운
영되어 왔음을 알 수 있다. 따라서 (A)가 정답이다.

어휘 found 설립하다 specialize in ～을 전문으로 하다

150 세부 사항

번역 코퍼 카운티에서 쿠폰을 사용할 수 있는 사람은?
(A) 모든 대형 소매점
(B) 신규 고객
(C) 재방문 고객
(D) 모든 거주자

해설 세 번째 줄에서 신규 고객 판촉 행사(NEW CUSTOMER
PROMOTION)이며 코퍼 카운티 주민 전용(Copper County
residents ONLY)이라고 나와 있으므로 쿠폰을 사용할 수 있는 사
람은 코퍼 카운티 주민 중 신규 고객임을 알 수 있다. 따라서 (B)가
정답이다.

151-152 편지

피에르 기탄
벤트 트리 로 26
샬롯, NC 28804

4월 15일

기탄 씨께,

151 이 편지는 6개월마다 받으시는 치과 진료 방문 시기가 되었음을 알
려 드리기 위한 것입니다. 저희 웹사이트를 방문하셔서 예약 신청서를
작성해 주십시오. 또는, 원하신다면 (704) 555-0138로 전화하셔서 저
희 접수원과 통화하십시오.

152 본원에서 이제는 더 멋진 미소를 위한 치아 미백과 투명 교정기를 제
공하게 되었음을 알려 드리게 되어 기쁩니다. 이 서비스 중 하나 또는 둘
다에 관심이 있으시면 저희에게 알려 주십시오.

곧 연락 주시기를 기대합니다.

사라 하마디
레드 스트리트 치과 사무장

어휘 inform 알리다 due ～하기로 예정된 semiannual
반년마다의 fill out 작성하다 form 양식 appointment 예약
reach 연락하다 invisible 보이지 않는 brace 치아 교정기

151 주제 / 목적

번역 기탄 씨는 왜 편지를 받았는가?
(A) 최근에 새 치과를 구했다.
(B) 정기 검진을 받을 시기이다.
(C) 레드 스트리트 치과에서 그의 피드백을 요청하고 있다.
(D) 지난번 방문에 불만이 있다.

해설 첫 문장에서 기탄 씨에게 이 편지는 6개월마다 받으시는 치과 진
료 방문 시기가 되었음을 알려 드리기 위한 것(This letter is to
inform ～ dental care visit)이라고 했으므로 (B)가 정답이다.

어휘 routine checkup 정기 검진 dissatisfied 불만스러워하는

Paraphrasing 지문의 semiannual ～ care
→ 정답의 routine checkup

152 Not / True

번역 치아 미백 서비스에 대해 편지에 언급된 것은?
(A) 투명 교정기와 비용이 거의 같다.
(B) 최근에서야 레드 스트리트 치과에서 이용할 수 있게 되었다.
(C) 원하는 결과를 얻으려면 최대 6개월이 걸린다.
(D) 치과 보험이 적용되지 않는다.

해설 두 번째 단락의 첫 문장에서 본원에서 이제는 더 멋진 미소를 위
한 치아 미백과 투명 교정기를 제공하게 되었음을 알려 드리게 되
어 기쁘다(We are happy to announce that we now offer ～
improve your smile)고 했으므로 치아 미백 서비스는 최근에 추가
된 것임을 알 수 있다. 따라서 (B)가 정답이다.

어휘 obtain 얻다 desired 바라는 cover (보험으로) 보장하다
insurance plan 보험

153-154 문자 메시지

텔레시아 토마스 (오전 8시 12분) 로라, 153 이미 사무실에 있나요, 아니면 들어오는 중인가요? 부탁이 하나 있어요.
로라 펜 (오전 8시 14분) 저 여기 있어요.
텔레시아 토마스 (오전 8시 16분) 오늘 아침에 잭의 송별 조찬이 있잖아요. 주스, 커피, 과일 그리고 빵은 준비가 되었는데, 동료들에게 그의 행운을 기원하는 카드를 돌려 사인받는 일을 못 했어요. 대신해 주실 수 있을까요? 제 책상 위에 카드들이 있어요.
로라 펜 (오전 8시 18분) 154 실은 제가 이메일을 보내 직원들에게 당신의 사무실로 가서 카드에 서명해 달라고 부탁하려고요. 구석에 있는 원탁에 그것들을 준비해 놓겠습니다. 지금 바로 해 드릴게요.

어휘 favor 부탁 farewell 송별 pass around ~을 돌리다 colleague 동료 arrange 준비하다 straightaway 바로

153 의도 파악

번역 오전 8시 14분에 펜 씨가 "저 여기 있어요"라고 쓴 의도는?
(A) 주의를 기울이고 있다.
(B) 토마스 씨와 같은 방에 있다.
(C) 토마스 씨가 도착하기를 기다리고 있다.
(D) 이미 사무실에 있다.

해설 8시 12분에 토마스 씨가 사무실에 있는지 아니면 들어오는 중인지(are you in the office ~ on your way in?)를 묻자 8시 14분에 펜 씨가 저 여기 있다(I'm here)고 대답했으므로, 펜 씨가 자신이 이미 사무실에 와 있음을 알리려는 의도로 한 말임을 알 수 있다. 따라서 (D)가 정답이다.

154 추론 / 암시

번역 펜 씨가 다음에 할 것 같은 일은?
(A) 발표
(B) 회의 연기
(C) 탁자에 카드 놓기
(D) 직원실에 좌석 배치

해설 8시 18분에 펜 씨가 제가 이메일을 보내 직원들에게 당신의 사무실로 가서 카드에 서명해 달라고 부탁하겠다(I can send out ~ sign the cards)고 했고, 구석에 있는 원탁에 그것들을 준비해 놓겠다(I'll arrange them ~ in the corner)며 지금 바로 해 주겠다(I'll do that straightaway)고 했으므로 펜 씨는 직원들이 서명할 수 있도록 원탁에 카드를 준비해 놓을 것임을 알 수 있다. 따라서 (C)가 정답이다.

어휘 postpone 연기하다

Paraphrasing 지문의 **arrange** → 정답의 **Put**

155-157 메뉴

역사
역사적인 H. G. 월시 빌딩과 노스 리버뷰 레스토랑에 오신 것을 환영합니다! 1897년 H. G. 월시에 의해 건축된 이 건물은 1942년까지 아스토리아의 우체국으로 155 **사용되었다**. 이후 이 건물은 잡화점, 부티크, 가족이 운영하는 신선한 해산물을 제공하는 레스토랑이 되었다. 지난 세기 동안, 건물의 2층은 생일과 결혼식 같은 사적인 파티를 위해 사용되어 왔다. 1970년대 후반에 철거 가능성에 직면했던 이 건물은 1981년에 현 소유주인 헨리 토마슨과 후아나 토마슨에 의해 매입되었다. 이후 투자와 대대적인 보수공사로 H. G. 월시 빌딩이 보존되었고, 1996년에 국가 역사 유산 등록 명부에 등재되었다. 156 컬럼비아강을 바라보는 멋진 전망과 다양한 계절 메뉴로 H. G. 월시 빌딩은 오리건 주의 태평양 해안을 찾는 방문객들에게 최고의 목적지가 되었다.

가을 메뉴	
157 **해산물 차우더 | 컵: 5달러, 볼: 8달러** 크림을 베이스로 하며 조개, 새우, 홍합이 들어간 요리	**청경채 | 12달러** 마늘 생강 굴 소스로 팬에 볶아 쌀국수 위에 올린 요리
피시 앤 칩스 | 대구: 12달러, 넙치: 15달러 버터밀크 반죽을 입혀 튀긴 세 조각	**셰프 샐러드 | 11달러** 구운 아몬드, 블루 치즈 드레싱, 아보카도를 섞은 각종 야채
구운 연어 | 20달러 레몬 마늘 소스와 샐러드를 곁들인 요리	

어휘 subsequently 그 뒤에 general store 잡화점 family-run 가족 경영의 face 직면하다 potential 가능성이 있는 demolition 철거 subsequent 그 다음의 investment 투자 extensive 광범위한, 다양한 status 지위 National Register of Historic Places 국가 역사 유산 등록 명부 stunning 멋진 clam 조개 mussel 홍합 bok choy 청경채 pan-seared 팬에 볶은 cod 대구 halibut 큰 넙치 breaded 빵가루를 묻힌 batter 반죽 greens 녹색 채소 toss (음식 재료를) 섞다

155 동의어

번역 첫 번째 단락 2행의 "served"와 의미가 가장 가까운 단어는?
(A) 제공했다
(B) 배송했다
(C) 제시했다
(D) 기능했다

해설 의미상 건물이 우체국으로 '사용되었다'는 뜻으로 쓰인 것이므로 정답은 (D) functioned이다.

156 추론 / 암시

번역 H. G. 월시 빌딩에 대해 암시된 것은?
(A) 1층짜리 건물이다.
(B) 물가에 위치해 있다.
(C) 우체국 옆에 있다.
(D) 거의 변하지 않았다.

해설 두 번째 단락의 마지막 문장에서 컬럼비아강을 바라보는 멋진 전망과 다양한 계절 메뉴로 H. G. 웰시 빌딩은 오리건 주의 태평양 해안을 찾는 방문객들에게 최고의 목적지가 되었다(With its stunning views ~ Oregon's Pacific coast)고 했으므로 (B)가 정답이다.

157 세부 사항

번역 10달러 미만으로 살 수 있는 것은?
(A) 해산물 차우더
(B) 피시 앤 칩스
(C) 청경채
(D) 셰프 샐러드

해설 메뉴에 따르면 해산물 차우더가 컵은 5달러, 볼은 8달러(Seafood chowder | Cup: $5, Bowl: $8)로 10달러 미만으로 살 수 있는 유일한 요리이므로 (A)가 정답이다.

158-160 회사 소식지 기사

본사 팀, 매장 일 돕는다

한넨은 1962년 이래로 남서부에서 가장 큰 백화점 체인 중 하나를 운영해 왔다. 2월 7일에 시작한 인스토어 프로젝트는 한넨 백화점 기업 운영 팀의 새로운 사업 계획이다. **158 다양한 직위에 있는 직원들의 권고에 따라, 이 사업 계획은 본사가 개별 매장에서의 일상적인 운영을 더 잘 이해할 수 있도록 개발되었다.**

159 인스토어 프로젝트는 본사 직원들을 매장에 배치하고, 매장 직원들과 짝을 이뤄 일상적인 근무를 하도록 한다. 이를 통해 양쪽의 한넨 직원들이 서로의 업무에 대해 질문을 하고 배울 수 있다. 지금까지 이 사업 계획은 매장 직원들 사이에서 기업 차원에서 이루어진 결정에 대한 이해도를 높이고, 본사 직원들 사이에서 기업의 계획이 어떻게 실행되는지에 대한 이해도를 높였다.

160 한넨은 향후 두 달 이내에 매장 방문을 완료하고 매년 방문을 반복 실시할 계획이다.

어휘 headquarters 본사 operate 운영하다 launch 시작하다 initiative (특정 목적 달성을 위한) 계획 corporate 기업의 individual 개별의 place 배치하다 pair 짝을 짓다 shift 교대 근무 (시간) so far 지금까지 implement 시행하다 conduct 실시[수행]하다

158 세부 사항

번역 회사가 프로젝트를 시작한 이유는?
(A) 대기업들 사이에서 현재 유행 중이다.
(B) 모회사가 요구했다.
(C) 일부 직원들이 제안했다.
(D) 일부 고객들이 요청했다.

해설 첫 단락의 세 번째 문장에서 다양한 직위에 있는 직원들의 권고에 따라 이 사업 계획이 개발되었다(Following recommendations from employees ~ individual store level)고 했으므로 정답은 (C)이다.

어휘 parent company 모회사

Paraphrasing 지문의 recommendations from employees → 정답의 suggested by some employees

159 세부 사항

번역 프로젝트에 포함된 것은?
(A) 매장 직원들의 다른 백화점 체인점 방문
(B) 현장 교육을 받기 위한 인턴 고용
(C) 본사 직원들의 매장 일시 근무
(D) 직원 팀의 매장 재설계 작업

해설 두 번째 단락 첫 문장에서 인스토어 프로젝트는 본사 직원들을 매장에 배치하고 매장 직원들과 짝을 이뤄 일상적인 근무를 하도록 한다(The In-Store Project ~ work typical shifts)고 했으므로 (C)가 정답이다.

어휘 on-the-job training 현장 교육

160 Not / True

번역 기사에서 프로젝트의 미래에 대해 명시한 것은?
(A) 회사는 매년 프로젝트를 다시 할 계획이다.
(B) 회사는 소유하고 있는 다른 매장으로 프로젝트를 확대할 계획이다.
(C) 성공하지 못하여 중단되고 있다.
(D) 너무 많은 비용이 들어 완료되지 않을 것이다.

해설 마지막 문장에서 한넨은 매년 방문을 반복 실시할 계획(Hannen plans to ~ conduct repeat visits annually)이라고 했으므로, 본사 직원들의 매장 방문 프로젝트를 매년 반복할 것임을 알 수 있다. 따라서 (A)가 정답이다.

어휘 expand 확대하다 discontinue 중단하다

Paraphrasing 지문의 annually → 정답의 each year

161-164 온라인 기사

칼링가 해변

(12월 4일)—**161 문화 관광을 촉진하기 위해 이 지역에 더 많은 자원이 할당되어야 한다고 칼링가 해변 관광부 (KBTD) 관계자들이 어제 열린 기획 회의에서 결론지었다.** 관광부는 또한 이 지역의 다채로운 역사와 문화를 강조하는 "칼링가 해변과 만나요"라는 제목의 신규 마케팅 캠페인의 초안도 구성했다. "앞으로 전통적인 해변 활동을 광고하는 것보다는 새로운 친환경 관광 활동에 더 집중해야 한다는 데 모두가 동의했습니다."라고 관광 책임자인 아놀드 바트는 말했다.

162 회의 동안, 바트 씨는 이 지역 대학 학생들이 제작한 온라인 설문지의 결과를 분석하는 발표를 했다. 응답자에는 지역 주민과 관광객 모두가 포함되었다. 한 가지 중요한 결과에서 전체 응답자의 80% 이상이 친환경 관광을 촉진하는 데 더 중점을 두어야 한다는 데 동의했다. 또 다른 결과에서 75% 이상이 더 다양한 현지 조달 유기농 식품을 선택할 수 있기를 원한다고 밝혔다. **163 "저로서는 관광객들의 응답이 뜻밖이었습니다. 하지만 전체적인 그림을 보면 해변 인근의 땅에 많은 가족 농장이 있기 때문에 일리가 있습니다." 163 라고 바트 씨는 말했다.**

이 설문 조사로 파악된 사항들은 164 **KLP 유기농 농장**을 운영하는 캐시 리에게 반가운 소식이다. 164 **농장 부지에 위치한 식료품점은 신선하고 계절에 따라 다른 유기농 재배 농산물로 일년 내내 채워져 있다.** 향후 관광객 방문이 증가하면 리 씨는 준비된 음식과 음료를 제공할 계획이다.

어휘 resource 자원 allocate 할당하다 official 공무원[관리] conclude 결론 짓다 draft 초안을 작성하다 title 제목을 붙이다 traditional 전통적인 eco-friendly 친환경적인 respondent 응답자 resident 주민 emphasis 강조 finding 결과 indicate 명시하다 sourced 공급된 response 응답 insight 통찰력 operate 운영하다 grocery store 식료품점 property 토지 stock (상품을 갖추고) 있다 seasonal 계절적인 produce 농산물 beverage 음료

161 주제 / 목적

번역 기사의 주요 목적은?
(A) 최근 인사 이동에 대한 발표
(B) 제안된 마케팅 계획에 대한 개요 설명
(C) 지역 관광의 감소에 대한 설명
(D) 설문 조사에 대한 참여 권장

해설 첫 문장에서 문화 관광을 촉진하기 위해 이 지역에 더 많은 자원이 할당되어야 한다고 칼링가 해변 관광부 (KBTD) 관계자들이 어제 열린 기획 회의에서 결론지었다(More resources ~ meeting held yesterday)고 했고, 관광부는 또한 이 지역의 다채로운 역사와 문화를 강조하는 "칼링가 해변과 만나요"라는 제목의 신규 마케팅 캠페인의 초안도 구성했다(The department ~ rich history and culture)며 칼링가 해변 관광부의 회의에 따른 관광 마케팅 계획에 대해 서술하고 있으므로 (B)가 정답이다.

어휘 personnel 인사, 직원들 outline 개요를 서술하다 decrease 감소 encourage 권장하다 participation 참여

162 추론 / 암시

번역 칼링가 해변에 대해 암시된 것은?
(A) 관광 시즌이 짧다.
(B) 비싸지 않은 숙박 시설을 제공한다.
(C) 주로 페리로 접근한다.
(D) 대학과 가깝다.

해설 두 번째 단락의 첫 문장에서 회의 동안 바트 씨는 이 지역 대학 학생들이 제작한 온라인 설문지의 결과를 분석하는 발표를 했다(During the meeting ~ region's university)고 한 것으로 보아 칼링가 해변 지역에 대학교가 있음을 알 수 있다. 따라서 (D)가 정답이다.

어휘 inexpensive 비싸지 않은 accommodation 숙박 시설 access 접근하다 ferry 연락선[페리]

163 Not / True

번역 기사에 따르면, 바트 씨에 대해 사실인 것은?
(A) 한 조사 결과에 놀랐다.
(B) 설문지의 구성을 변경했다.
(C) 지역의 농경지 손실에 대해 우려하고 있다.
(D) 공개 회의의 참석률을 높이고 싶어 한다.

해설 두 번째 단락의 다섯 번째 문장에서 저로서는 관광객들의 응답이 뜻밖이었다고 바트 씨가 말했다("For me ~ said Mr. Bhatt)고 했으므로 (A)가 정답이다.

어휘 questionnaire 설문지 concerned 우려하는 lose 잃다 attendance 참석률

Paraphrasing 지문의 response was unexpected
→ 정답의 surprised by a survey result

164 Not / True

번역 KLP 유기농 농장에 대해 언급된 것은?
(A) 호텔 투숙객들에게 무료 투어를 제공한다.
(B) 자체 소식지를 발행한다.
(C) 최근에 식당을 열었다.
(D) 현장에서 과일과 채소를 판다.

해설 세 번째 단락의 첫 문장에서 KLP 유기농 농장(the KLP Organic Farm)을 언급하며, 이 농장 부지에 위치한 식료품점은 신선하고 계절에 따라 다른 유기농 재배 농산물로 일년 내내 채워져 있다(Its grocery store ~ organically grown produce)고 했으므로 (D)가 정답이다.

어휘 on-site 현장에서

Paraphrasing 지문의 produce → 정답의 fruits and vegetables

165-167 광고

트렉스 오토

차량 주행이 원활하도록 유지하는 일에는 올바른 작업이 요구됩니다. 트렉스 오토의 전문가 손에 차량을 맡기시고 필요 없는 것은 빼고 항상 정확히 필요한 것만 받으십시오. 저희 정비소는 165 (B) **1963년 토니 레커가 첫 번째 차량 정비소를 연 이후 줄곧** 165 (A) **리즈에 본사를 두고 있습니다.** 165 (D) **3대에 걸쳐** 165 (C) **저희 가족이 운영하는 업체는 공정한 가격과 정직한 서비스를 위한 헌신으로 서부 요크셔 지역에 서비스를 제공해 온 것을 자랑스럽게 생각하고 있습니다.**

트렉스 오토는 다양한 오일 교환 패키지를 제공합니다. 각 패키지에는 무료 타이어 공기압 점검, 타이어 교대, 166 (C) **오일 주입**, 표준 오일 필터, 5리터 오일 교환, 브레이크 검사가 포함되어 있습니다. 167 **아래 나열된 오일 옵션 중에서 선택하십시오. 귀하의 자동차에 가장 적합한 종류를 모르실 경우 저희 서비스 기술자에게 문의하십시오.**

합성유 혼합	고급유	완전 합성유
166 (A) 25파운드	166 (A) 40파운드	166 (A) 50파운드
166 (D) 125,000 마일 미만 또는 10년 미만인 차량에 권장	166 (D) 125,000 마일 이상 또는 10년 이상인 차량에 적합	166 (D) 125,000마일 이상이고 제조업체 권장 특별 정비 요구 사항이 있는 차량에 적합

어휘 smoothly 순조롭게 demand 요구하다 based in ~에 본사를 둔 garage 차고, 차량 정비소 generation 세대

family-run 가족 운영의 commitment 전념 a variety of
다양한 complimentary 무료의 rotation 교대 fluid 유체
fill-up (자동차의) 기름 탱크 가득 채우기 inspection 검사
synthetic 합성 물질 blend 혼합 maintenance 정비

165 Not / True

번역　트렉스 오토에 대해 명시된 것은?
　　(A) 런던에 본사가 있다.
　　(B) 1983년에 창업했다.
　　(C) 훌륭한 고객 서비스에 주력하고 있다.
　　(D) 5대째 가족 운영 업체이다.

해설　첫 단락의 마지막 문장에서 저희 가족이 운영하는 업체는 공정한
　　가격과 정직한 서비스를 위한 헌신으로 서부 요크셔 지역에 서비
　　스를 제공해 온 것을 자랑스럽게 생각하고 있다(our family-run
　　business ~ commitment to honest service)고 했으므로
　　(C)가 정답이다. 리즈에 본사를 두고 있다고 했으므로 (A)는 오답,
　　1963년에 첫 정비소를 열었다고 했으므로 (B)도 오답, 3대에 걸쳐
　　가족이 운영한다고 했으므로 (D)도 오답이다.

166 Not / True

번역　오일 교환 패키지에 대해 명시된 것은?
　　(A) 모두 같은 가격이다.
　　(B) 무료 브레이크 패드 교체가 각각 포함되어 있다.
　　(C) 패키지 중 한 개만 오일 주입을 제공한다.
　　(D) 차량이 주행된 마일 수를 기준으로 한다.

해설　광고 하단의 각 오일 교환 패키지를 보면 합성유 혼합(Synthetic
　　Blend)은 125,000마일 미만 또는 10년 미만 차량에 권장
　　(Recommended ~ ten years old), 고급유(High Mileage)
　　는 125,000 마일 이상 또는 10년 이상 차량에 적합(Best ~ ten
　　years old), 완전 합성유(Full Synthetic)는 125,000 마일 이상
　　이고 특별 정비가 요구되는 차량에 적합(Ideal ~ maintenance
　　needs)이라고 차량의 주행 거리를 기준으로 패키지가 분류되어 있
　　으므로 (D)가 정답이다. 패키지의 가격이 25, 40, 50파운드로 모두
　　다르므로 (A)는 오답, 각 패키지에 무료 오일 주입이 포함되어 있다
　　고 나와 있으므로 (C)도 오답, 무료 브레이크 패드를 교체해 준다는
　　언급은 없으므로 (B)도 오답이다.

어휘　cost (값이) ~이다 replacement 교체 base ~에 근거를 두다

167 문장 삽입

번역　[1], [2], [3], [4]로 표시된 곳 중에서 다음 문장이 들어가기에 가장
　　적합한 위치는?

　　"귀하의 자동차에 가장 적합한 종류를 모르실 경우 저희 서비스 기술
　　자에게 문의하십시오."
　　(A) [1]
　　(B) [2]
　　(C) [3]
　　(D) [4]

해설　제시된 문장은 '자동차에 적합한 종류를 모를 경우 문의하라'며 적
　　절한 서비스를 선택해야 하는 상황에 대해 조언하고 있다. 따라서 아
　　래 나열된 오일 옵션 중 선택하라(Choose from the oil options

listed below)는 문장 뒤에 들어가는 것이 글의 흐름상 자연스러우
므로 (D)가 정답이다.

168-171 기사

> ### 셰이드사이드 플라자의 새로운 매장
>
> 버치 시티 (11월 12일)—버치 시티에서 평생을 살아온 타마라 반다가
> 운영하는 보석 업체인 디자인 글로리가 셰이드사이드 플라자 쇼핑 지역
> 에 오프라인 매장을 열었다. **168 반다 씨는 11월 9일 문을 연 이 매장이
> 어떤 공간에서든 중앙 장식이 될 수 있는 아름다운 원석 크리스탈과 그
> 녀의 모든 수제 보석 제품 라인을 특징으로 한다고 말했다.**
>
> **169 반다 씨는 예산을 넘지 않는 가격대의 수제 디자인을 제공함으로
> 써 자신의 보석 브랜드를 다른 브랜드로부터 차별화한다고 강조한다.**
> 그녀는 간접비를 통제하기 위해 다양한 지역 금속 공급업체로부터 창
> 의적으로 재료를 조달한다고 말한다. 화요일부터 토요일, 오전 11시부
> 터 오후 5시까지 문을 여는 매장을 관리하기에는 많은 시간이 들겠지만,
> **171 반다 씨는 그럼에도 지역 예술 축제에서 부스를 운영할 계획이라고
> 말했다.** 그녀는 또한 다음 달에 시립 미술관의 공예품 전시회에도 참가
> 할 것이라고 언급했다. 그녀는 보석 세공 기술을 배웠던 센트럴 예술 대
> 학에서 열리는 연례 아트 쇼의 기획 위원회에서도 계속 일할 예정이다.
>
> 반다 씨는 친구인 **170 브랜드 마차도가 현재 디자인 글로리가 위치한 셰
> 이드사이드 플라자의 맞은편에 있는 자신의 소매 서점 운영에 대해 긍
> 정적인 경험을 이야기했을 때 오프라인 매장을 연다는 아이디어를 떠올
> 렸다.** 그는 이 쇼핑 구역이 인근의 많은 유동 인구로부터 혜택을 입고
> 있다고 말했다.

어휘　brick-and-mortar store 오프라인 매장 feature (~의)
특징을 이루다 centerpiece 중앙부 장식 emphasize 강조하다
set ~ apart from ~을 돋보이게 만들다 keep ~ in check ~을
통제[억제]하다 overhead cost 간접비용 source 공급자를 찾다
material 재료 creatively 창의적으로 occupy 차지하다 retail
소매 on the opposite side of ~ 맞은편의 heavy 많은[심한]
foot traffic 유동 인구 규모

168 Not / True

번역　디자인 글로리에 대해 명시된 것은?
　　(A) 개점 날짜가 늦어졌다.
　　(B) 장식용 돌을 판매한다.
　　(C) 매주 공예 시연회를 한다.
　　(D) 토요일에는 문을 닫는다.

해설　첫 단락의 두 번째 문장에서 반다 씨는 11월 9일 문을 연 이 매장(디
　　자인 글로리)이 어떤 공간에서든 중앙 장식이 될 수 있는 아름다운
　　원석 크리스탈과 그녀의 모든 수제 보석 제품 라인을 특징으로 한다
　　고 말했다(Ms. Banda said ~ centerpiece of any room)고 했
　　으므로 디자인 글로리는 장식용 석조 및 보석을 판매하는 가게임을
　　알 수 있다. 따라서 (B)가 정답이다.

어휘　delay 미루다 decorative 장식용의 craft 공예
demonstration 시연

> Paraphrasing　지문의 can become the centerpiece
> 　　　　　　　→ 정답의 decorative

169 세부 사항

번역 반다 씨는 자신의 보석에 대해 무엇이 특별하다고 말하는가?
(A) 지역 학생들이 디자인했다.
(B) 고풍스럽다.
(C) 저렴하다.
(D) 가볍다.

해설 두 번째 단락의 첫 문장에서 반다 씨는 예산을 넘지 않는 가격대의 수제 디자인을 제공함으로써 자신의 보석 브랜드를 다른 브랜드로부터 차별화한다고 강조한다(Ms. Banda emphasizes ~ won't break a budget)고 했으므로 (C)가 정답이다.

Paraphrasing   지문의 price points that won't break a budget → 정답의 affordable

170 세부 사항

번역 마차도 씨는 누구인가?
(A) 부동산 개발업자
(B) 금속 공급업자
(C) 사진작가
(D) 서점 주인

해설 세 번째 단락의 첫 문장에서 브랜드 마차도가 현재 디자인 글로리가 위치한 셰이드사이드 플라자의 맞은편에 있는 자신의 소매 서점 운영에 대해 긍정적인 경험을 이야기했다(Brad Machado ~ Design Glory is now)고 했으므로 마차도 씨는 서점 주인임을 알 수 있다. 따라서 (D)가 정답이다.

Paraphrasing   지문의 operating his retail bookshop → 정답의 bookseller

171 문장 삽입

번역 [1], [2], [3], [4]로 표시된 곳 중에서 다음 문장이 들어가기에 가장 적합한 위치는?

"그녀는 또한 다음 달에 시립 미술관의 공예품 전시회에도 참가할 것이라고 언급했다."
(A) [1]
(B) [2]
(C) [3]
(D) [4]

해설 제시된 문장의 She noted as well ~ craft fair가 문제 해결의 단서이다. 반다 씨가 공예품 전시회에도 참가할 것이라고 언급했다면서 as well(또한)을 사용했으므로 주어진 문장 앞에서는 반다 씨의 다른 활동 언급에 대한 내용이 와야 한다. 따라서 반다 씨가 예술 축제에서 부스를 운영할 계획이라고 말했다(Ms. Banda said ~ arts festivals)는 문장 뒤에 들어가는 것이 글의 흐름상 자연스러우므로 (C)가 정답이다.

어휘 note 언급하다 craft 공예(품) fair 박람회[전시회]

172-175 문자 메시지

산드라 카일 (오전 8시 19분)
좋은 아침입니다. 172지금 가는 길인데 로즈웨이 대로에 차선 폐쇄가 있어서 늦을 것 같아요. 교통이 정체되어 버스가 거의 움직이지 않고 있어요.

루카스 보딘 (오전 8시 20분)
끔찍하네요!

산드라 카일 (오전 8시 21분)
아침 8시 30분 회의에서 제가 필기를 하기로 되어 있어요. 제가 도착할 때까지 두 분 중 한 분이 대신해 주실 수 있을까요?

캐롤리나 마타 (오전 8시 23분)
잠깐만요, 174못 들으셨어요? 173,174회의는 목요일로 변경되었어요.

산드라 카일 (오전 8시 24분)
정말요? 174다행이네요.

캐롤리나 마타 (오전 8시 26분)
173장 씨가 포츠빌에서 새 창고 건물의 최종 설계에 대해 고객과 회의 중이에요. 그는 내일 돼야 돌아와요.

산드라 카일 (오전 8시 27분)
네, 저도 그가 포츠빌로 간다고 들었어요.

루카스 보딘 (오전 8시 30분)
고객이 막판 변경을 몇 가지 요청해서 장 씨의 출장이 예상보다 오래 걸리고 있어요. 175이미 할당받은 예산을 초과했기 때문에 변경 사항이 크지 않으면 좋겠어요.

캐롤리나 마타 (오전 8시 33분)
목요일 회의에서 최신 정보를 받을 예정이에요. 좋은 소식이면 좋겠네요.

어휘 lane 차선 closure 폐쇄 backed up 차가 정체된 barely 거의 ~않는 terrible 끔찍한 be supposed to ~하기로 되어 있다 fill in for ~을 대신하다 relief 안도 warehouse 창고 minor 작은 allocated 할당된

172 세부 사항

번역 카일 씨는 왜 직장에 늦을 것으로 예상하는가?
(A) 날씨가 좋지 않아 버스가 느리다.
(B) 버스가 교통 체증으로 움직이지 못하고 있다.
(C) 버스를 놓쳤다.
(D) 버스가 그녀가 타는 정류장에 늦게 도착했다.

해설 8시 19분에 카일 씨가 지금 가는 길인데 로즈웨이 대로에 차선 폐쇄가 있어서 늦을 것 같다(I'm on my way ~ Roseway Boulevard)며 교통이 정체되어 버스가 거의 움직이지 않고 있다(It's all backed up ~ barely moving)고 했으므로 (B)가 정답이다.

어휘 stuck 움직일 수 없는 miss 놓치다

Paraphrasing   지문의 backed up → 정답의 stuck in traffic

173 세부 사항

번역 회의는 왜 연기되었는가?

(A) 동료가 사무실에 없다.

(B) 고객이 준비할 시간을 더 필요로 한다.

(C) 보딘 씨가 일정이 맞지 않다.

(D) 마타 씨가 업데이트를 준비해야 한다.

해설 8시 23분에 마타 씨가 회의는 목요일로 변경되었다(The meeting was moved to Thursday)고 했고, 다시 8시 26분에 장 씨가 포츠빌에서 새 창고 건물의 최종 설계에 대해 고객과 회의 중(Mr. Chang is ~ warehouse building)이라면서 그는 내일 돼야 돌아올 것(He won't be back until tomorrow)이라고 이유를 언급했으므로 (A)가 정답이다.

어휘 scheduling conflict 일정 겹침

Paraphrasing 지문의 won't be back
→ 정답의 out of the office

174 의도 파악

번역 오전 8시 24분에 카일 씨가 "정말요?"라고 쓴 의도는?

(A) 특정 디자인에 실망했다.

(B) 결정에 동의하지 않는다.

(C) 마타 씨의 말에 놀랐다.

(D) 이미 그 소식을 들었다.

해설 8시 23분에 마타 씨가 못 들었는지(haven't you heard?) 물으며 회의가 목요일로 변경되었다(The meeting ~ Thursday)고 소식을 전하자 8시 24분에 카일 씨가 정말요?(Really?)라고 되물으며 다행(What a relief)이라고 안도하는 것으로 보아, 카일 씨는 회의 일정 변경 소식을 접하고 놀라서 한 말임을 알 수 있다. 따라서 (C)가 정답이다.

175 Not / True

번역 프로젝트에 대해 명시된 것은?

(A) 계획보다 비용이 더 들고 있다.

(B) 기술적인 어려움이 있다.

(C) 관리가 허술하다.

(D) 제시간에 완수할 수 없다.

해설 8시 30분에 보딘 씨가 이미 할당받은 예산을 초과했다(we're already over the allocated budget)고 언급했으므로 프로젝트 경비가 원래 계획했던 금액을 넘어섰음을 알 수 있다. 따라서 (A)가 정답이다.

Paraphrasing 지문의 over the allocated budget
→ 정답의 more expensive than planned

176-180 구인 광고 + 이메일

톰슨 앤 그로브스

톰슨 앤 그로브스 법률 사무소는 우리의 저명한 환경 소송 팀에 합류할 전담 보조를 찾고 있습니다.

이 보조는 다음과 같은 다양한 법률 서비스 관련 일을 할 것입니다.

• 재판을 위해 준비 중인 사건과 관련된 증거 조사

• 정보 제시를 위한 증거물, 차트 및 도표 준비

• 의뢰인과의 연락 및 지속적인 파일 업데이트

176 이 직책에 가장 적합한 후보

• 자발적이고 책임감이 있으며 동시에 많은 프로젝트를 처리할 수 있는 자

• 뛰어난 소통 능력, 조직력 및 컴퓨터 실력을 갖춘 자

177 지원하려면 이력서를 이메일 julia.powell@thompsonand-groves.com으로 인사부 줄리아 파월에게 5월 25일까지 보내십시오. **180 면접은** 6월 초에 진행될 예정이며 채용은 7월 초에 이루어질 것입니다.

어휘 dedicated 전념하는 established 저명한 environmental 환경의 litigation 소송 legal 법률과 관련된 investigate 조사하다 evidence 증거 related to ~와 관련된 court 법정 exhibit 증거물 diagram 도표 self-directed 자발적인 juggle 잘 처리하다 at once 동시에[한꺼번에] organization 구성, 조직 apply 지원하다

수신: julia.powell@thompsonandgroves.com

발신: jonas_ivanov@sidmail.com

날짜: 7월 12일

제목: 답장: 법무보조직

파월 씨께,

저에게 법무보조직을 제안한다는 당신의 편지를 읽고 기뻤습니다. 하지만 **178 고심 끝에 지금은 윌슨 법률 사무소를 떠나기에 좋은 시기가 아니라고 결정했습니다.** 퇴사 가능성에 직면하고 나서야 이곳 프로젝트 업무에 제가 얼마나 깊이 투입되어 있는지를 깨달았습니다. **179 세간의 이목을 끄는 수많은 환경 소송에서 승소한 저명한 법률 사무소에서 근무한다는 생각에 흥분됐지만** 지금은 제가 변화를 이룰 때가 아닙니다.

180 당신과 당신의 동료들을 만나 뵙게 되어 즐거웠고 앞으로도 인연이 닿기를 바랍니다.

요나스 이바노프

어휘 consideration 고려 realize 깨닫다 be invested in 투입되다 face 직면하다 thrilled 아주 흥분한 illustrious 저명한 high-profile 세간의 이목을 끄는 cross paths 마주치다

176 Not / True

번역 구인 광고에 포함된 것은?

(A) 톰슨 앤 그로브스 법률 사무소의 간략한 역사

(B) 회사 사무실로 오는 길 안내

(C) 직무의 급여 및 복지 혜택에 대한 설명

(D) 이상적인 지원자에 대한 설명

해설 구인 광고의 세 번째 단락에서 이 직책에 가장 적합한 후보(The best candidate for this position)에 대해 자발적이고 책임감이 있으며 동시에 많은 프로젝트를 처리할 수 있는 자(is self-directed ~ at once; and)와 뛰어난 소통 능력, 조직력 및 컴퓨터 실력을 갖춘 자(has strong ~ computer skills)라고 명시하고 있으므로 정답은 (D)이다.

> Paraphrasing 지문의 The best candidate
> → 정답의 the ideal applicant

177 추론 / 암시

번역 파월 씨의 업무 책임 중 하나일 것 같은 것은?
(A) 증거물 및 차트 준비
(B) 컴퓨터 파일 업데이트
(C) 신입 사원 채용
(D) 환경 문제에 관한 집필

해설 구인 광고의 네 번째 단락 첫 문장에서 지원하려면 이력서를 인사부 줄리아 파월에게 5월 25일까지 보내라(To apply ~ by May 25)고 한 것으로 보아 파월 씨는 인사부 소속이며 신입 사원 채용 업무를 담당하고 있음을 짐작할 수 있다. 따라서 (C)가 정답이다.

178 Not / True

번역 이바노프 씨가 그의 이메일에 명시한 것은?
(A) 진로 목표를 바꾸었다.
(B) 현재 직장에 남기로 결정했다.
(C) 은퇴하기로 결심했다.
(D) 다른 직장에 지원할 것이다.

해설 이메일의 두 번째 문장에서 이바노프 씨가 고심 끝에 지금은 윌슨 법률 사무소를 떠나기에 좋은 시기가 아니라고 결정했다(after much consideration ~ leave Wilson Law)고 언급했으므로 현 직장인 윌슨 법률 사무소에 남기로 결정했음을 알 수 있다. 따라서 (B)가 정답이다.

어휘 career 경력, 진로 present 현재의 retire 은퇴하다

> Paraphrasing 지문의 not the best time to leave
> → 정답의 stay

179 Not / True

번역 이메일에서 톰슨 앤 그로브스 법률 사무소에 대해 언급한 것은?
(A) 성공한 소송들로 유명하다.
(B) 더 큰 공간으로 이전할 것이다.
(C) 더 이상 환경 문제를 전문으로 하지 않는다.
(D) 국제 회의를 주최할 예정이다.

해설 이메일의 네 번째 문장에서 이바노프 씨가 톰슨 앤 그로브스 법률 사무소에 대해 세간의 이목을 끄는 수많은 환경 소송에서 승소한 저명한 법률 사무소에서 근무한다는 생각에 흥분됐다(I was thrilled ~ high-profile environmental cases)고 했으므로 (A)가 정답이다.

어휘 specialize in ~을 전문으로 하다

> Paraphrasing 지문의 illustrious → 정답의 well-known

180 연계

번역 이바노프 씨에 대해 암시된 것은?
(A) 5월에 승진했다.
(B) 6월에 파월 씨를 만났다.
(C) 파월 씨와 공통으로 아는 친구가 있다.
(D) 이제 막 자격증 프로그램을 수료했다.

해설 구인 광고의 마지막 문장에서 면접은 6월 초에 진행될 예정 (Interviews will be conducted at the beginning of June)이라고 했고, 이메일의 마지막 문장에서 이바노프 씨가 파월 씨에게 당신과 당신의 동료들을 만나 뵙게 되어 즐거웠다(It was a pleasure meeting you and your colleagues)고 했으므로 이바노프 씨와 파월은 6월 면접에서 만났음을 알 수 있다. 따라서 (B)가 정답이다.

어휘 mutual 공통의 certification 증명서 교부

181-185 회람 + 공지

> **회람**
>
> 수신: 킬데어 레크리에이션 센터 직원
> 발신: 매들린 번
> 날짜: 4월 11일
> 제목: 일일 이용권
>
> ¹⁸²4월 직원 회의에서 논의된 바와 같이 ^{181,185}일일 이용권 가격을 5유로에서 9유로로 인상하는 것을 고려 중입니다. 정확한 인상가는 5월 회의에서 결정될 것입니다. ^{181,183}이번 변경으로 내년도에 5천 유로를 추가로 벌어들일 것으로 예상되며, 실외 육상 트랙을 교체하는 비용으로 사용할 것입니다. 요금 변경으로 인한 수익 증가로 공사에 필요한 7천 유로 확보에 근접하게 될 것입니다.
>
> 저는 야외 육상 시즌이 짧다는 것을 인식하고 있으며, ¹⁸²회의에서 일부 직원들이 돈을 다른 용도에 사용하는 것을 고려하고 싶어 했다는 것도 알고 있습니다. 리셉션 구역 보수, 댄스 스튜디오를 위한 새로운 바닥, 센터 전체 더 많은 평면 TV를 위한 자금 사용 가능성이 제기되었습니다. 그러나 ¹⁸³이사회는 우리 회원들에 의해 가장 빈번히 요청되는 개선 사항에 초점을 맞추는 것이 더 현명하다고 생각했습니다. 직원들이 제안한 업그레이드는 천 유로에서 2천 유로 범위에 속하며, 향후 연도에 이를 검토할 수 있기를 바랍니다.
>
> 어휘 pass 통행권 revenue 수익 improvement 개조 (공사) realize 깨닫다 raise (문제 등을) 제기하다 board of directors 이사회 fall into (특정 영역에) 속하다[들다]

> **공지**
> 킬데어 레크리에이션 센터 방문객
>
> ¹⁸⁵6월 1일부터 비회원용 일일 이용권료는 8유로입니다. 이 ¹⁸⁴소소한 인상으로 방문객들에게 훨씬 더 좋은 야외 육상 트랙을 제공할 수 있게 될 것입니다. 월회비와 연회비는 변동이 없습니다. 회원 관련 문제를 상담하시려면 정규 영업시간 동안 등록 사무실을 방문해 주십시오.
>
> 어휘 effective 시행되는 modest 별로 크지 않은 registration 등록 related 관련된

181 주제 / 목적

번역 회람의 목적은?
(A) 회원 수의 증가에 대한 공지
(B) 특정 자금이 어떻게 사용될지에 대한 설명
(C) 행사 관련 수행 업무 설명
(D) 프로젝트를 위한 기부 요청

해설 회람의 첫 문장에서 일일 이용권 가격을 5유로에서 9유로로 인상하는 것을 고려 중(we are considering ~ €5 to €9)이라고 했고, 세 번째 문장에서 이번 변경으로 내년도에 5천 유로를 추가로 벌어들일 것으로 예상되며 실외 육상 트랙을 교체하는 비용으로 사용할 것(This change is ~ outdoor running track)이라고 했다. 즉, 이용권 가격 인상으로 인해 증대된 수익금의 활용 방안에 대해 논의하고 있으므로 (B)가 정답이다.

어휘 describe 설명하다 task 업무 solicit 요청하다 donation 기부

182 세부 사항

번역 4월 회의에서 직원들이 한 것은?
(A) 레크리에이션 센터 회원들을 위한 설문 조사 설계
(B) 가격 인상 반대
(C) 레크리에이션 센터에 대한 업그레이드 제안
(D) 리셉션 구역의 이전 고려

해설 회람의 첫 문장에서 4월 직원 회의(April's staff meeting)에 대해 언급했고, 두 번째 단락의 첫 문장에서 회의에서 일부 직원들이 돈을 다른 용도에 사용하는 것을 고려하고 싶어 했다는 것도 알고 있다(I know that ~ use for the money)며 리셉션 구역 보수, 댄스 스튜디오를 위한 새로운 바닥, 센터 전체 더 많은 평면 TV를 위한 자금 사용 가능성이 제기되었다(The possibilities ~ were raised)고 했다. 따라서 4월 회의에서 직원들은 센터에 개선이 필요한 곳들에 대해 제안했음을 알 수 있으므로 (C)가 정답이다.

어휘 object to ~에 반대하다

183 세부 사항

번역 회람에 따르면, 레크리에이션 센터 회원들이 가장 빈번히 요청하는 것은?
(A) 리셉션 구역 보수
(B) 댄스 스튜디오의 새로운 바닥
(C) 평면 TV 추가
(D) 야외 육상 트랙 개선

해설 회람의 첫 단락 세 번째 문장에서 이번 변경으로 내년도에 5천 유로를 추가로 벌어들일 것으로 예상되며 실외 육상 트랙을 교체하는 비용으로 사용할 것(This change is ~ outdoor running track)이라고 했고, 두 번째 단락 세 번째 문장에서 이사회는 우리 회원들에 의해 가장 빈번히 요청되는 개선 사항에 초점을 맞추는 것이 더 현명하다고 생각했다(the board of directors ~ requested by our members)고 했다. 추가 수익금을 육상 트랙 교체에 사용하겠다는 결정을 발표하며 그 이유로 회원들이 가장 빈번히 요청하는 개선 사항에 맞춘 것이라고 했으므로 정답은 (D)이다.

184 동의어

번역 공지에서 첫 번째 단락 2행의 "modest"와 의미가 가장 가까운 단어는?
(A) 수줍은
(B) 현대적인
(C) 창의적인
(D) 소규모의

해설 의미상 크지 않은 즉, '소소한' 인상이라는 뜻으로 쓰인 것이므로 정답은 (D) small이다.

185 연계

번역 비회원용 일일 이용권의 새로운 요금에 대해 사실인 것은?
(A) 원래 고려되었던 것보다 낮다.
(B) 5월 1일부터 시행될 것이다.
(C) 온라인으로 결제할 수 있다.
(D) 6월 회의에서 승인되었다.

해설 회람의 첫 문장에서 일일 이용권 가격을 5유로에서 9유로로 인상하는 것을 고려 중(we are considering ~ €5 to €9)이라고 했는데, 공지의 첫 문장에서 6월 1일부터 비회원용 일일 이용료는 8유로(Effective 1 June ~ will be €8)라고 했다. 따라서 일일 이용권 요금이 원래 고려되었던 가격보다 1유로 낮다는 것을 알 수 있으므로 (A)가 정답이다.

186-190 이메일 + 구인 공고 + 이메일

수신: jsantos@coloniamenor.com
발신: markash@amtrcorp.com
날짜: 9월 4일
186 제목: 일자리 정보

안녕하세요, 후안.

멕시코시티에서 열린 기술 작가 회의에서 다시 만나게 되어 반가웠습니다. 당신의 사촌인 카를로스 크루즈가 이곳 댈러스에서 제품 디자인 일자리를 구하고 싶어 한다고 말씀하셨는데요. **186,187 제가 근무하는 AMTR사에서 곧 주니어 산업 디자이너에 대한 채용 공고를 내려고 하는데 그분이 관심 있으실 것 같아요.** 지금까지는 회사에서 기존 직원들에게만 채용 공고를 냈지만, 다음 주에는 회사 웹사이트에 게시될 예정입니다. 급여도 좋고 내부에는 적임자가 없을 수도 있어요. 그분께 이 기회에 대해 알려 주세요.

하이데 마르카스

어휘 post a job 채용 공고를 내다 industrial 산업의 appear 나오다, 나타나다 qualified 자격이 있는 candidate 지원자 in-house (조직) 내부에

AMTR사   홈   소개   **일자리**   연락처   블로그

현재 기회

주니어 산업 디자이너: 정규직, 텍사스 주 댈러스에 있는 AMTR사에서 제조되는 전 제품 개발 및 개선

직무 예시:

- 187개인용 컴퓨터, 태블릿, 복사기 및 인쇄기를 포함한 소비자 및 사무용 제품 디자인
- 엔지니어링, 마케팅 및 제조 부서의 동료 그리고 디자인 팀과 협력하여 신제품 개발
- 재활용된 재료와 재활용 및 재사용 가능한 재료의 사용 촉진을 통한 지속력 향상

자격:

- 디자인 원리, 이론 및 개념에 대한 이해
- 고객 피드백을 분석하고 적용하는 능력
- 입증된 분석 및 문제 해결 기술
- 스케치, 스토리보드, 모델 및 시제품 제작 경험
- 190산업 디자인 학사 또는 석사 학위

어휘 range 범위 manufacture 제조하다 duty 의무 consumer 소비자 office supply 사무용품 collaborate 협력하다 sustainability 지속 가능성 reusable 재사용 가능한 material 재료 qualification 자격 principle 원리 theory 이론 apply 적용하다 proven 입증된 analytical 분석적인 prototype 시제품 bachelor 학사 master 석사 degree 학위

수신: 카를로스 크루즈 〈ccruz@bmail.com〉
발신: 파멜라 왕 〈wangp@amtrcorp.com〉
날짜: 11월 11일
제목: 취업 지원

크루즈 씨께,

AMTR사의 주니어 산업 디자이너 자리에 지원서를 제출해 주셔서 감사합니다. 190우리 채용 위원회는 귀하의 지원서를 검토했고 해당 직책에 대한 자격을 갖추었다고 판단했습니다. 189첫 면접 일정을 잡기 위해 곧 연락 드리겠습니다. 188,189면접은 12월 첫 2주간 댈러스 본사 현장에서 열릴 것입니다. 그 사이 이메일로 직장 추천서를 요청받게 될 것입니다. 요청받는 즉시 응답해 주십시오.

파멜라 왕
인사 담당자
AMTR사

어휘 application 지원서 determine 결정하다 initial 처음의 on-site 현장에서 headquarters 본사 reference 추천서

---

186 주제 / 목적

번역 첫 번째 이메일의 목적은?
(A) 새로운 채용 공고에 대한 정보 공유
(B) 회사의 신규 직원 채용 여부에 대한 문의
(C) 동료의 다가오는 총회 참석 여부 확인
(D) 새로 취업한 일에 대한 축하

해설 첫 이메일의 제목이 일자리 정보(Subject: Job tip)이고, 세 번째 문장에서 제가 근무하는 AMTR사에서 곧 주니어 산업 디자이너에 대한 채용 공고를 내려고 하는데 그분(수신인의 사촌)이 관심있으실 것 같다(the company I work for ~ might interest him)고 일자리 정보에 대해 알려 주고 있으므로 (A)가 정답이다.

> Paraphrasing   지문의 tip → 정답의 information

187 연계

번역 마르카스 씨가 근무하는 회사가 생산하는 것은?
(A) 웹사이트 제작 가이드
(B) 여객기 운행 매뉴얼
(C) 교통 체계 지도
(D) 사무기기

해설 첫 이메일의 세 번째 문장에서 마르카스 씨가 제가 근무하는 AMTR사(the company I work for, AMTR Corporation)라고 했고, AMTR사 구인 공고의 직무 예시 첫 항목에서 개인용 컴퓨터, 태블릿, 복사기 및 인쇄기를 포함한 소비자 및 사무용 제품을 디자인한다(Design consumer ~ copiers, and printers)고 나온 것으로 보아 마르카스 씨가 일하는 AMTR사는 사무용 기기를 만드는 회사임을 알 수 있다. 따라서 (D)가 정답이다.

어휘 guide 안내(서) manual 설명서 passenger 승객

> Paraphrasing   지문의 personal computers, tablets, copiers, and printers
> → 정답의 Office equipment

188 Not / True

번역 두 번째 이메일에 설명된 것은?
(A) 지원서 제출 절차
(B) 지원자가 면접에서 예상할 수 있는 것
(C) 채용 절차의 다음 단계
(D) 디자이너에 대한 AMTR사의 기대

해설 두 번째 이메일의 네 번째 문장에서 면접은 12월 첫 2주간 댈러스 본사 현장에서 열릴 것(Interviews will be held ~ December)이라고 했고, 그 사이 이메일로 직장 추천서를 요청받게 될 것(In the meantime ~ via e-mail)이라고 다음 단계의 채용 절차에 대해 설명하고 있으므로 (C)가 정답이다.

어휘 procedure 절차 applicant 지원자 process 과정 expectation 기대

189 세부 사항

번역 AMTR사는 12월 첫 2주 동안 무엇을 할 예정인가?
(A) 댈러스로 본사 이전
(B) 지원서 검토 시작
(C) 직장 추천서 발송
(D) 1차 면접 수행

해설 두 번째 이메일의 세 번째 문장에서 AMTR사의 왕 씨가 첫 면접 일정을 잡기 위해 곧 연락하겠다(We will contact you ~ initial interview)고 했고, 면접이 12월 첫 2주간 댈러스 본사 현장에서 열릴 것(Interviews will be held ~ December)이라고 했으므로 (D)가 정답이다.

> **Paraphrasing**   지문의 an initial interview
> → 정답의 the first round of interviews

190 연계

번역 크루즈 씨에 대해 사실일 것 같은 것은?
(A) 11월에 일을 시작할 것이다.
(B) 산업 디자인 학위가 있다.
(C) 댈러스로 이사했다.
(D) 최근에 새 직장을 구하기 위한 면접을 보았다.

해설 구인 공고의 자격 마지막 항목에 산업 디자인 학사 또는 석사 학위(Bachelor's or master's degree in industrial design)가 명시되어 있고, 두 번째 이메일의 두 번째 문장에서 크루즈 씨에게 우리 채용 위원회는 귀하의 지원서를 검토했고 해당 직책에 대한 자격을 갖추었다고 판단했다(Our hiring committee has reviewed ~ meet the qualifications for the position)고 했다. 크루즈 씨가 구인 공고의 직책에 대한 자격을 갖추었다고 했으므로 산업 디자인 학위의 소지자임을 알 수 있고 따라서 (B)가 정답이다.

어휘 relocate 이사하다

191-195 목록 + 편지 + 일정표

싱글 타운 루핑
색상 옵션

오래가고 아름다운 지붕을 위한 고품질의 저렴한 지붕널을
다양한 색상 중에서 선택하세요.

색상	제품 번호
194 론우드 블루	**(302번)**
차콜 블리스	(702번)
폭스우드 그레이	(704번)
미션 그레이	(707번)
시더우드	(203번)
히코리 넛	(209번)
브릭 레드	(505번)

어휘 shingle 지붕널, 널빤지 지붕 affordable 저렴한 long-lasting 오래가는

조앤 웨슬리
195대퍼딜 로 8021번지
헌든, 버지니아 22090

웨슬리 씨께,

191이 편지는 8월 4일 버지니아 주 헌든에 위치한 귀하의 지붕을 교체하기로 한 계약을 확인하기 위한 것입니다. 논의된 대로 우리는 히코리 넛 색상 판넬로 당사의 독점 프라임 테크놀로지 시스템을 사용할 것입니다. **192프라임 테크놀로지 시스템은 귀하의 주택에 비가 새지 않도록 보장하며**, 작업 및 자재에 대해 10년간 보증합니다.

우리 작업팀은 오전 8시 30분에 도착할 예정입니다. 귀하의 착수금과 서명된 계약서를 받았습니다. 나머지 요금은 작업이 완료되는 대로 지불하시면 됩니다. 문의 사항이 있으시면 연락 주십시오.

마틴 세이지, 고객 서비스 담당자
싱글 타운 루핑

어휘 exclusive 독점적인 guarantee 보장하다 warranty 품질 보증서 labor 노동 material 자재 crew 작업팀 deposit 보증금 remainder 나머지 charge 요금 due (돈을) 지불해야 하는 completion 완료

193싱글 타운 루핑: 8월 1-7일자 설치 일정

설치 작업팀에 대한 참고 사항: 작업 장소와 필요한 자재를 반드시 확인하세요.

일요일	월요일	화요일	195수요일	목요일	금요일	토요일
1	2 해리스 주택 (702번)	1933 랜스포드 아파트 E-3 (505번)	4 195웨슬리 주택 (209번)	5 194켄델 우드 모텔 (302번)	6 호프웰 가든 (704번)	7 호프웰 가든 (704번)

어휘 installation 설치

191 주제 / 목적

번역 편지의 목적은?
(A) 새 지붕에 대한 비용 견적 문의
(B) 작업 착수금 요청
(C) 시공사에 프로젝트 의뢰
(D) 사업 계약 마무리

해설 편지의 첫 문장에서 이 편지는 8월 4일 버지니아 주 헌든에 위치한 귀하의 지붕을 교체하기로 한 계약을 확인하기 위한 것(This is to confirm ~ on August 4)이라고 했으므로 정답은 (D)이다.

어휘 estimate 견적 contractor 도급업자, 시공사 finalize 마무리 짓다

> **Paraphrasing**   지문의 agreement → 정답의 arrangement

192 Not / True

번역 세이지 씨가 프라임 테크놀로지 시스템에 대해 명시한 것은?
  (A) 10년 보증을 받으려면 별도의 수수료가 필요하다.
  (B) 집 안으로 물이 새는 것을 방지한다.
  (C) 특정 유형의 지붕널에만 이용 가능하다.
  (D) 설치하는 데 많은 작업팀원이 필요하다.

해설 편지의 세 번째 문장에서 세이지 씨가 프라임 테크놀로지 시스템은 귀하의 주택에 비가 새지 않도록 보장한다(The Prime Technology ~ keep your house dry)고 했으므로 (B)가 정답이다.

어휘 separate 별도의 prevent 방지하다 leak 새다

> **Paraphrasing** 지문의 keep your house dry
> → 정답의 prevents water from leaking into a house

193 세부 사항

번역 8월 3일에 지붕널 설치가 예정된 곳은?
  (A) 해리스 주택
  (B) 랜스포드 아파트
  (C) 켄델우드 모텔
  (D) 호프웰 가든

해설 일정표가 싱글 타운 루핑의 8월 1-7일자 설치 일정(Shingle Town Roofing: Installation Schedule for August 1-7)을 나타내고 있고, 3일에는 랜스포드 아파트 E-3(Landsford Apartments E-3)이라고 나와 있으므로 (B)가 정답이다.

194 연계

번역 작업팀은 켄델우드 모텔에 어떤 색상의 지붕널을 설치할 예정인가?
  (A) 론우드 블루
  (B) 차콜 블리스
  (C) 미션 그레이
  (D) 브릭 레드

해설 일정표에 따르면 켄델우드 모텔에는 302번(Kendelwood Motel (#302))을 설치한다고 나와 있고, 목록에서 제품 번호 302번은 론우드 블루(Lawnwood Blue (#302))라고 나와 있으므로 (A)가 정답이다.

195 연계

번역 싱글 타운 루핑은 언제 대퍼딜 로 8021번지에서 작업할 예정인가?
  (A) 월요일
  (B) 화요일
  (C) 수요일
  (D) 목요일

해설 편지의 상단에 웨슬리 씨의 주소가 대퍼딜 로 8021번지(8021 Daffodil Lane)라고 나와 있고, 일정표에 따르면 웨슬리 주택(Westley residence)은 수요일(Wednesday)에 작업하는 것으로 나와 있으므로 (C)가 정답이다.

196-200 웹페이지 + 고객 후기 + 회사 답변

---

https://carinasolutions.com/home

홈	서비스	연락처	후기

카리나 솔루션즈
호텔 관리를 위한 최고의 소프트웨어 옵션

저희는 귀하께서 호텔의 모든 측면을 관리하실 수 있도록 도움을 드릴 것입니다. 예약 시스템, 직원 관리, 광고 및 온라인 입지 개선 등 어떤 도움이 필요하시든 저희 소프트웨어를 이용하세요!

다음은 저희 소프트웨어로 할 수 있는 업무 중 일부입니다.
  • 온라인 예약 및 결제 관리
  • 직원 근무 시간 및 휴무 기록
  • 일류 예약 웹사이트에서 호텔 홍보
  • 건물 유지 관리

196,197오늘 바로 연락하셔서 3개월 동안 소프트웨어 체험판 버전을 완전 무료로 사용해 보세요. **196**프리미어 소프트웨어 버전의 가격 및 기능에 대한 자세한 내용은 당사 웹사이트의 서비스 페이지에서 확인하실 수 있습니다.

어휘 aspect 측면 reservation 예약 presence 존재(감) task 업무 track 추적하다 property 건물 maintenance 유지 trial 체험, 시험 feature 특징

---

https://carinasolutions.com/reviews

홈	서비스	연락처	후기

197카리나 솔루션즈 호텔 관리 소프트웨어의 체험판이 내일 만료되므로 프리미어 버전을 구입할지 아니면 더 좋은 버전을 찾을지 결정해야 합니다.

저는 주요 우려 사항이 두 가지 있습니다.
1. **198**예약 모듈에서 재방문 손님에 대한 정보를 파일에 보관할 수 없습니다. 이로 인해 직원들이 재방문 손님의 정보를 수동으로 재입력해야 하므로 시간이 낭비됩니다.

2. **200**이 소프트웨어는 데스크톱 컴퓨터에서 접속할 때만 완전한 기능을 제공하는데, 저는 휴대폰으로 거의 모든 일을 하기 때문에 이 점이 아쉽습니다. 어떤 장치를 사용하든 인터페이스는 동일해야 합니다.

—**197**제출자: 수잔 얀

어휘 expire 만료되다 concern 걱정 force ~하게 만들다 reenter 재입력하다 manually 수동으로 waste 낭비하다 functionality 기능(성) device 장치

---

https://carinasolutions.com/reviews_response

홈	서비스	연락처	후기

얀 씨께,

좋은 소식이 있습니다! 귀하께서 체험판 이용을 시작하신 이후 저희는 카리나 솔루션즈의 일부 기능을 개선했습니다. 이제 재방문 고객을 등록하

는 데 사용하실 수 있는 자동 재예약 기능이 있어 수동 데이터 입력을 줄일 수 있습니다.

또한 **200 체험판과 프리미어 버전의 차이점 중 하나는 인터페이스가 모든 장치에서 동일하다는 점입니다.**

카리나 솔루션즈 호텔 관리 소프트웨어는 단순한 예약 도구 이상이라는 점을 기억해 주세요. **199 프리미어 버전의 모든 기능을 익히시면 귀하의 호텔을 만족한 고객들로 채우는 데 도움이 될 겁니다. 저희의 교육용 영상을 보시려면 carinasolutions.com을 방문하세요.**

마커스 펠드만
카리나 솔루션즈 담당자

> 어휘 subscription 구독, (서비스의) 사용   register 등록하다
> manual 수동의   entry 입력   tool 도구   fill 채우다
> instructional 교육용의

196 Not / True

번역 웹페이지에 따르면, 카리나 솔루션즈 소프트웨어의 제조사에 대해 사실인 것은?
(A) 운송 산업을 위한 제품을 만든다.
(B) 두 가지 버전의 소프트웨어를 만든다.
(C) 여행자들은 할인된 호텔 가격을 찾기 위해 이 회사의 제품을 사용한다.
(D) 제품이 아직 판매되지 않았다.

해설 웹페이지의 마지막 단락에서 오늘 바로 연락하셔서 3개월 동안 소프트웨어 체험판 버전을 완전 무료로 사용해 보라(Contact us ~ for three months)고 했고, 프리미어 소프트웨어 버전의 가격 및 기능에 대한 자세한 내용은 당사 웹사이트의 서비스 페이지에서 확인할 수 있다(More information ~ our Web site)고 했으므로 카리나 솔루션즈 소프트웨어는 두 가지 버전이 있음을 알 수 있다. 따라서 (B)가 정답이다.

197 연계

번역 얀 씨에 대해 암시된 것은?
(A) 거의 3개월 동안 카리나 솔루션즈를 사용해 왔다.
(B) 다른 고객으로부터 카리나 솔루션즈를 소개받았다.
(C) 다음 여행 동안 호텔에 숙박할 계획이다.
(D) 소프트웨어 회사에서 일한다.

어휘 refer 소개하다

해설 웹페이지의 마지막 단락 첫 문장에 오늘 바로 연락하셔서 3개월 동안 소프트웨어 체험판 버전을 완전 무료로 사용해 보라(Contact us ~ for three months)고 나와 있고, 고객 후기의 하단에 후기를 제출한 사람이 수잔 얀(Submitted by Susan Yan)이고 첫 문장에서 카리나 솔루션즈 호텔 관리 소프트웨어의 체험판이 내일 만료된다(My trial version ~ expires tomorrow)고 했다. 따라서 얀 씨는 지난 3개월 동안 카리나 솔루션즈 체험판 버전을 사용했음을 알 수 있으므로 (A)가 정답이다.

198 세부 사항

번역 호텔 투숙객 정보에 대한 얀 씨의 걱정은?
(A) 쉽게 다운로드할 수 없다.
(B) 시스템이 안전한 비밀번호로 고객 정보를 보호하지 않는다.
(C) 철자가 틀린 이름이나 주소에 대해 수정 사항을 입력할 수 없다.
(D) 손님이 예약할 때마다 재입력해야 한다.

해설 고객 후기의 두 번째 단락 1번 항목에서 얀 씨가 예약 모듈에서 재방문 손님에 대한 정보를 파일에 보관할 수 없다(The reservations ~ repeat guests on file)며 이로 인해 직원들이 재방문 손님의 정보를 수동으로 재입력해야 하므로 시간이 낭비된다(This forces staff ~ which wastes time)고 했다. 따라서 정답은 (D)이다.

어휘 secure 안전한   correction 수정   misspelled 철자가 틀린

199 추론 / 암시

번역 펠드만 씨가 회사의 영상에 대해 암시하는 것은?
(A) 방문할 만한 흥미로운 장소들에 대한 정보가 들어 있다.
(B) 손님들이 호텔 객실에서 시청할 수 있다.
(C) 회사의 소프트웨어가 사용될 수 있는 많은 방법에 대해 설명한다.
(D) 회사에서 아주 최근에 제작했다.

해설 회사 답변의 마지막 단락 두 번째 문장에서 펠드만 씨가 프리미어 버전의 모든 기능을 익히시면 귀하의 호텔을 만족한 고객들로 채우는 데 도움이 될 것(Learning about all ~ happy customers)이라며 교육용 영상을 보려면 carinasolutions.com을 방문하라(Make sure to ~ instructional videos)고 했다. 따라서 영상에는 소프트웨어의 모든 기능에 대한 설명이 나와 있음을 알 수 있으므로 (C)가 정답이다.

어휘 contain 들어 있다   describe 설명하다

200 연계

번역 카리나 솔루션즈 소프트웨어의 프리미어 버전에 대해 암시된 것은?
(A) 3개월마다 업데이트해야 한다.
(B) 얀 씨의 두 번째 우려 사항을 해결한다.
(C) 선택 기능은 유료로 추가할 수 있다.
(D) 얀 씨는 할인 쿠폰을 받기 위해 펠드만 씨에게 연락할 수 있다.

해설 고객 후기의 2번 항목에서 얀 씨가 이 소프트웨어는 데스크톱 컴퓨터에서 접속할 때만 완전한 기능을 제공하는데 저는 휴대폰으로 거의 모든 일을 하기 때문에 이 점이 아쉽다(The software offers ~ my mobile phone)며 어떤 장치를 사용하든 인터페이스는 동일해야 한다(The interface should ~ device you use)고 했는데, 회사 답변의 두 번째 단락에서 체험판과 프리미어 버전의 차이점 중 하나는 인터페이스가 모든 장치에서 동일하다는 점(you should know ~ across all devices)이라고 했으므로 프리미어 버전에서는 얀 씨의 우려 사항이 해소될 수 있음을 알 수 있다. 따라서 정답은 (B)이다.

어휘 address 해결하다   optional 선택적인

101 (A)	**102** (A)	**103** (B)	**104** (B)	**105** (A)
106 (D)	**107** (C)	**108** (C)	**109** (A)	**110** (D)
111 (A)	**112** (C)	**113** (A)	**114** (B)	**115** (C)
116 (D)	**117** (C)	**118** (A)	**119** (B)	**120** (C)
121 (D)	**122** (D)	**123** (A)	**124** (C)	**125** (B)
126 (B)	**127** (D)	**128** (C)	**129** (D)	**130** (D)
131 (A)	**132** (C)	**133** (A)	**134** (D)	**135** (B)
136 (D)	**137** (B)	**138** (C)	**139** (B)	**140** (B)
141 (C)	**142** (A)	**143** (A)	**144** (A)	**145** (D)
146 (C)	**147** (B)	**148** (D)	**149** (B)	**150** (A)
151 (B)	**152** (A)	**153** (A)	**154** (C)	**155** (D)
156 (A)	**157** (C)	**158** (C)	**159** (C)	**160** (B)
161 (D)	**162** (D)	**163** (C)	**164** (D)	**165** (C)
166 (A)	**167** (C)	**168** (B)	**169** (D)	**170** (A)
171 (A)	**172** (A)	**173** (A)	**174** (D)	**175** (C)
176 (A)	**177** (C)	**178** (B)	**179** (D)	**180** (B)
181 (B)	**182** (C)	**183** (D)	**184** (C)	**185** (A)
186 (C)	**187** (D)	**188** (D)	**189** (B)	**190** (A)
191 (B)	**192** (D)	**193** (D)	**194** (C)	**195** (A)
196 (D)	**197** (B)	**198** (C)	**199** (A)	**200** (C)

PART 5

101 명사 자리 _ 동사의 목적어

해설 빈칸은 동사 need의 목적어 역할을 하며 부정관사 a와 형용사 broad의 수식을 받는 명사 자리이므로, 정답은 (A) knowledge 이다.

번역 비디오 게임 디자이너들은 컴퓨터 프로그래밍에 대한 폭넓은 지식을 필요로 한다.

어휘 broad 폭넓은

102 인칭대명사의 격 _ 목적격

해설 빈칸은 전치사 for의 목적어 자리이고, 단수 사물명사인 the item 을 받는 대명사가 필요하므로 정답은 (A) it이다.

번역 운송 중에 분실된 물품에 관해서는 저희가 책임지겠습니다.

어휘 concerning ~에 관한   in transit 운송 중에

103 to부정사의 부사적 용법

해설 빈칸 앞에 완전한 절이 있고 빈칸 뒤에 명사구가 왔으므로, 빈칸에 는 앞에 나온 완전한 절을 수식하면서 뒤에 온 명사구를 목적어로 취할 수 있는 to부정사가 와야 한다. 따라서 정답은 (B) to promote 이다.

번역 스프링리 에너지 마케팅 팀은 당사의 최신 제품을 홍보하기 위해 열심히 일하고 있다.

104 명사 어휘

해설 구인 광고에 열거되어 있고, 면접을 위해 고려되어야 하는 것이므로 문맥상 빈칸에는 '자격'이 들어가야 자연스럽다. 따라서 '자격'을 뜻 하는 (B) qualifications가 정답이다.

번역 구인 광고에는 면접을 위해 고려되어야 할 여러 자격 요건이 열거되 어 있다.

어휘 list 열거하다   specialist 전문가   engagement 업무 assortment 구색

105 형용사 자리 _ 주격 보어

해설 2형식 동사 become 뒤에는 주격 보어가 와야 하므로, '시행되는, 발효되는'을 뜻하는 형용사인 (A) effective가 정답이다. 명사도 보 어 역할을 할 수 있으나, 주어인 it(the contract)과 effect(효과)는 동격이 아니므로 (B) effect는 답이 될 수 없다.

번역 계약서가 날인되고 수령되면 즉시 효력이 발생할 것이다.

어휘 immediately 즉시   effectively 효과적으로

106 동사 어휘

해설 the financial challenge를 목적어로 받아 '재정난을 예방할 수 있 었을 것 같지 않다'라는 문맥이 되어야 자연스러우므로 '막다, 예 방하다'는 의미의 (D) prevented가 정답이다. (B) banned와 (C) forbidden은 금(지)하다는 뜻이므로 문맥에 어울리지 않는다.

번역 정책 변화로 건설사가 직면한 재정난을 예방할 수 있었을 것 같지는 않다.

어휘 challenge 어려움[난제]   face 직면하다   ban 금지하다   forbid 금지하다

107 현재분사

해설 '바산 포토가 ~라는 것을 인정하고 있다'는 내용으로 빈칸 뒤의 that절이 동사의 목적어 역할이 되어야 문맥에 맞다. 따라서 be 동사 is 뒤에서 능동태 진행형 문장을 만들 수 있는 현재분사 (C) acknowledging이 정답이다.

번역 바산 포토는 3분기가 시작되기 전에는 자사의 최신 프린터가 공급되 지 않을 것이라고 인정하고 있다.

어휘 acknowledge 인정하다   latest 최신의

108 부사 어휘

해설 동사구 turn on을 수식하여 적절한 문맥을 완성하는 부사를 고 르는 문제이다. '사무실에 들어오면 전등 및 장치들이 자동으로 켜 진다'는 내용이 되어야 자연스러우므로 '자동으로'라는 뜻의 (C) automatically가 정답이다.

번역 새로 설치한 시스템 덕분에 사무실에 들어오면 모든 전등 및 기타 장 치들이 자동으로 켜진다.

어휘 install 설치하다   device 장치   heavily (정도가) 심하게 furiously 분노하여

109 전치사 자리

해설 빈칸은 쉼표 뒤 완전한 절에 명사구 the high demand (for apartments)를 연결하는 자리이므로 전치사가 들어가야 한다. 따라서 '~에도 불구하고'라는 의미의 전치사 (A) Despite가 정답이다.

번역 아파트에 대한 높은 수요에도 불구하고, 본 연구는 단독 주택이 5년 안에 가장 인기 있는 주거지가 될 것임을 보여준다.

어휘 demand 수요 single detached home 단독 주택 dwelling 주거지 apparently 분명히

110 형용사 어휘

해설 문맥상 '절차가 완료되어'라는 내용이 되어야 적절하므로 '완료된'을 뜻하는 (D) complete가 정답이다.

번역 연간 경비 산정 절차가 완료되었으므로 내년을 위한 직원 채용 계획을 시작할 수 있다.

어휘 process 절차 estimate 추산하다 expense 경비 staffing 직원 채용 careless 부주의한 full 가득한 entire 전체의

111 명사 자리 _ 동사의 주어

해설 빈칸은 주어 자리이며 동사 had called(전화했다)의 주체가 되어야 하므로 사람명사가 주어로 와야 한다. 따라서 정답은 '전시자, 전시 업체'를 뜻하는 (A) exhibitor이다.

번역 6월 26일 현재, 오직 한 전시 업체만이 무역 박람회에 자리를 요청하기 위해 전화했다.

어휘 as of ~ 현재로 request 요청하다; 요청

112 전치사 어휘

해설 문맥상 '정해진 예산 내에서'라는 의미가 되어야 적절하므로 '~ 이내에, ~ 안에서'를 뜻하는 (C) within이 정답이다.

번역 정해진 예산 내에서 비용을 유지하기 위해 소유주는 건축될 차고의 크기를 줄이기로 결정했다.

어휘 established 확정된 garage 차고

113 전치사 자리

해설 빈칸은 완전한 절에 명사구 the cold and rainy weather를 연결하는 자리이므로 전치사가 들어가야 한다. 따라서 '~에도 불구하고'라는 의미의 전치사 (A) in spite of가 정답이다.

번역 춥고 비 오는 날씨에도 불구하고 야외 판매 행사는 대성공이었다.

어휘 provided that (만약) ~라면

114 명사 어휘

해설 빈칸에 들어갈 명사는 책과 관련된 것이면서 저자의 통찰력 있는 분석을 언급하지 않고는 완전하지 않다고 했으므로 '책의 요약(본)'이라는 의미가 되어야 문맥상 적절하다. 따라서 '요약'을 뜻하는 (B) summary가 정답이다.

번역 비즈니스 블로그 세계에 대한 통찰력 있는 분석을 언급하지 않고는 핸슨 씨의 책에 대한 어떠한 요약도 완전하지 않을 것이다.

어휘 insightful 통찰력 있는 analysis 분석 composition 구성 organization 조직

115 명사 자리 _ 동사의 목적어

해설 빈칸은 동사 will send의 목적어 역할을 하는 명사 자리이며, 문맥상 '소중한 고객들에게 분명한 메시지를 전달할 것이다'는 의미가 되어야 하므로 (C) message가 정답이다.

번역 구매자들이 불평했던 제품군을 업데이트하면 우리의 소중한 고객들에게 분명한 메시지가 전달될 것이다.

어휘 complain 불평하다 obvious 분명한 valued 소중한

116 부사 어휘

해설 문맥상 '의심할 여지없이 중요한 부분이 될 것이다'는 의미가 되어야 적절하므로 '의심할 여지없이, 틀림없이'라는 뜻의 강조 부사 (D) undoubtedly가 정답이다.

번역 인터넷은 의심할 여지없이 가까운 미래에 경제의 중요한 부분이 될 것이다.

어휘 crucial 중요한 foreseeable future 가까운 미래 concisely 간결하게

117 명사 자리 _ 동사의 목적어

해설 동사 required의 목적어 역할로 형용사 little의 수식을 받는 명사가 와야 하므로 (A) deliberation이 정답이다.

번역 경영진은 양 씨를 승진시키기로 결정하기 전에 고심할 필요가 거의 없었다.

118 형용사 어휘

해설 명사 policy를 수식하기에 적절한 형용사를 고르는 문제이다. 빈칸 뒤에서 정책을 수식하는 말로 '직원들에게 추가 휴가를 주는 정책'이라고 했으므로 해당 내용과 일관성을 이루려면 '관대한 정책'이 되어야 한다. 따라서 '관대한, 후한'이라는 뜻의 (A) generous가 정답이다.

번역 인사부는 직원들에게 추가 휴가를 주는 좀 더 관대한 정책을 채택하고 있다.

어휘 adopt 채택하다 generous 관대한 collaborative 공동의 severe 극심한 regional 지역의

119 인칭대명사의 격 _ 소유격

해설 빈칸에는 뒤에 온 명사 handling을 수식하는 말이 들어가야 한다. 따라서 명사 앞에 쓰여 한정사 역할을 할 수 있는 소유격 인칭대명사인 (B) their가 정답이다.

번역 그리브스 씨는 우리의 공급업체들에게 운송 상황에 대한 그들의 처리에 대해 말할 예정이다.

어휘 supplier 공급업체 handling 처리 transportation 운송 situation 상황

120 동사 어휘

해설 앞에서 이것은 단지 예비 명단일 뿐이라고 한 것으로 보아 '막판 추가 가능성을 예상해야 한다'는 내용이 되어야 적절하다. 따라서 '예상하다'는 뜻의 (C) expect가 정답이다.

번역 이것은 단지 예비 입사 지원자 명단일 뿐이므로 면접관들은 막판 추가 가능성에 대해 예상하고 있어야 한다.

어휘 preliminary 예비의 candidate 지원자 addition 추가 figure ~라고 판단하다, 계산하다

121 형용사 자리 _ 주격 보어

해설 주어 Market conditions를 수식하는 형용사 자리이다. 보기 중 형용사는 (B) favorite과 (D) favorable인데, 문맥상 '시장 상황이 유리했다'는 의미가 되어야 적절하므로 정답은 (D) favorable이다.

번역 작년에 시장 상황은 우리가 몇몇 새로운 인수를 할 수 있을 만큼 충분히 유리했다.

어휘 condition 상황 acquisition 인수 favorite 선호하는 favorable 좋은, 유리한

122 전치사 어휘

해설 문맥상 '정확성을 가지고, 정확하게'라는 의미가 되어야 하므로 어떤 일을 할 때의 태도나 방식을 나타낼 때 쓰는 전치사 (D) with가 정답이다. 참고로 'with ease 쉽게, with care 주의 깊게, with enthusiasm 열정적으로' 등의 표현이 흔히 쓰인다.

번역 웹 광고는 매우 구체적이고 아주 정확하게 시장을 공략할 수 있다는 점에서 훌륭하다.

어휘 specific 구체적인 target 겨냥하다 accuracy 정확도

123 명사 자리 _ 동사의 목적어

해설 빈칸은 동사 obtain의 목적어로 직원들이 취득하는 대상이 와야 한다. 또한 certifier는 가산명사이므로 한정사 없이 단독으로는 단수형으로 쓸 수 없다. 따라서 '증명(서)'을 뜻하는 (A) certification이 정답이다.

번역 도서관장은 직원들이 도서관의 교육 프로그램을 더 잘 지원할 수 있도록 교육 기술학 자격증을 취득할 것을 요청한다.

어휘 obtain 얻다 instructional 교육용의 educational 교육의 certifier 증명자

124 전치사 어휘

해설 빈칸 뒤로 명사구가 왔으므로 빈칸은 전치사 자리이다. 문맥상 기존 제품과 신제품을 비교하는 문장이므로 '~와 달리'라는 비교의 의미를 지닌 (C) Unlike가 정답이다.

번역 기술적 전문 지식을 가진 사람들을 위해 설계된 기존 제품과 달리, 이 새로운 프로그램은 더 많은 이용자들의 관심을 끌 것이다.

어휘 existing 기존의 expertise 전문 지식 appeal 관심[흥미]을 끌다 audience 청중[독자]

125 병렬 구조

해설 주어가 Some functions(일부 기능들), 동사가 are인 문장에서 보어 자리에 주어와 동격으로 to부정사가 온 구조이다. 등위접속사 and로 문장이 연결되므로 병렬 구조를 이루어야 하며, to부정사가 대등하게 연결될 때는 to를 생략하고 to identify … and (to) prioritize로 쓰므로 (B) prioritize가 정답이다.

번역 웹 팀의 일부 기능은 애플리케이션의 문제를 파악하고 그 다음 수정의 우선순위를 정하는 것이다.

어휘 function 기능 identify 발견하다 fix 수정[수리]

126 동사 어휘

해설 a great opportunity를 목적어로 취해 '이 파트너십은 좋은 기회를 의미한다'는 문맥이 되어야 자연스러우므로 '나타내다, 의미하다'는 의미의 (B) represents가 정답이다.

번역 이 파트너십은 우리 스톨런트 테크가 사용할 수 있는 소프트웨어 목록을 확장할 좋은 기회를 의미한다.

어휘 broaden 넓히다 inventory 물품 목록, 재고 correspond 일치하다 intend 의도하다

127 부사 자리 _ 동사 수식

해설 빈칸이 have와 p.p. 사이에 있으므로 동사를 수식하는 부사 자리이다. 따라서 정답은 (D) partially이다.

번역 관련 계약이 일부만 완료되어 광고 캠페인 시작을 미뤄야 할 필요가 있다.

어휘 delay 미루다 relevant 관련된 partially 부분적으로

128 접속사 자리 _ 부사절 접속사

해설 빈칸 뒤에 주어와 동사를 갖춘 완전한 절이 왔으므로 부사절 접속사가 들어가야 한다. 문맥상 '직원들 대부분이 휴가이기 때문에'가 되어야 자연스러우므로 '~ 때문에'라는 의미의 접속사 (C) Because가 정답이다.

번역 다음 주에 회계부서 직원들 대부분이 휴가이기 때문에 사무실에 남아 있는 직원들은 매우 바쁠 것이다.

129 전치사 자리

해설 빈칸은 뒤에 있는 동명사구를 콤마 뒤 절에 연결하는 자리이므로 전치사가 와야 한다. 따라서 '~하기보다, ~ 대신'이라는 뜻의 전치사 (D) Rather than이 정답이다.

번역 아이디어를 공유하고 결정을 내리기 위해 팀장은 여러 건의 이메일을 보내기보다는 이 문제를 논의하기 위해 한 시간짜리 회의를 소집했다.

어휘 multiple 다수의 reach 도달하다

130 동사 어휘

해설 승무원직 지원자가 침착한 통솔력을 '보여주어야 한다'는 문맥이 적절하므로 '보여 주다, 나타내다'라는 뜻을 지닌 (D) project가 정답이다.

번역 조이어스 항공의 승무원직 지원자들은 항상 침착한 통솔력을 보여주어야 한다.

어휘 applicant 지원자 flight attendant 승무원 calm 침착한 authority 권위, 지휘권 estimate 추산하다 appear 나타나다 involve 포함하다

PART 6

131-134 공지

> **다르웨이 시립 공원 프로젝트 업데이트**
>
> 다르웨이 시립 공원 관리부는 공사 작업이 진행 중인 동안 모든 방문객 산책로를 ¹³¹**개방하기** 위해 노력하고 있습니다. 현재, 작업팀이 공원의 우드모어 자전거 도로를 따라 방향 표지판 주위의 식물을 다듬고 있기 때문에 자전거를 타는 사람들은 이 지역에서 조심해서 주행해야 합니다. 비수기에는 공원을 이용하는 사람들이 더 적기 때문에 가능할 ¹³²**때마다** 보수 공사를 진행하도록 예정되어 있다는 점을 알고 계시기 바랍니다. 주변 자연 환경의 구체적인 특징을 강조하는 새로운 안내 표지판 또한 산책로 구간을 따라 설치될 것입니다. ¹³³**이것들은 방문객들이 공원을 더 즐길 수 있도록 하기 위한 것입니다.** 이번 프로젝트 단계는 다음 달에 완료될 예정이며, 진행되는 동안 공원 이용객에 ¹³⁴**방해가** 되는 일은 거의 없을 것으로 예상합니다. 시의 공원 관리 부처는 공사 프로젝트 동안 산책로 폐쇄 및 우회로 발생을 피하기 위해 모든 노력을 기울이고 있습니다.

> 어휘 strive 노력하다 trail 산책로 underway 진행 중인 crew 작업반 trim 다듬다 vegetation 초목[식물] directional 방향의 off-peak 비수기의 informational 정보를 제공하는 specific 구체적인 feature 특징 surrounding 주위의 phase 단계 progress 진행하다 closure 폐쇄 detour 우회

131 형용사 어휘

해설 빈칸은 to keep의 목적어인 all visitor trails를 수식하는 보어 자리이므로, 방문객 산책로를 수식하기에 적절한 형용사를 골라야 한다. '작업이 진행 중인 동안 산책로를 개방하려고 노력하고 있다'는 내용이 되어야 자연스러우므로 (A) open이 정답이다.

어휘 noticeable 뚜렷한 practical 현실적인 genuine 진짜의

132 복합관계부사

해설 that절에서 빈칸 뒤에 형용사만 남아 있는 것으로 보아 부사절 접속사 절의 주어와 be동사가 생략되고 보어 자리의 형용사만 남아 있는 것을 알 수 있다. 부사절 접속사 역할을 하는 복합관계부사 whenever가 들어가면 '가능할 때마다'라는 의미가 되어 자연스러우므로 (C) whenever가 정답이다.

133 문맥에 맞는 문장 고르기

해설 빈칸 앞에서 주변 자연 환경의 특징을 강조하는 새로운 안내 표지판(New informational signs)이 설치될 것이라고 했으므로, 이를 They로 받아 표지판의 설치 목적에 대해 설명하는 내용이 들어가야 연결이 자연스럽다. 따라서 방문객들의 더욱 즐거운 공원 이용을 목적으로 한다고 언급하고 있는 (A)가 정답이다.

번역 (A) 이것들은 방문객들이 공원을 더 즐길 수 있도록 하기 위한 것입니다.
　　 (B) 이것들은 이러한 업데이트된 규정을 알리기 위해 고안되었습니다.
　　 (C) 방문객들은 특히 공원 카페 및 기타 편의 시설의 이용을 즐깁니다.
　　 (D) 새로운 나무를 심는 것은 적절한 계획과 부지 선정이 요구됩니다.

어휘 regulation 규정 amenity 편의 시설 plant 심다 proper 적절한 site 부지

134 명사 어휘

해설 뒤 문장에서 공사 동안 산책로 폐쇄 및 우회로 발생을 피하기 위해 모든 노력을 기울이고 있다고 했다. 따라서 공사가 진행되는 동안 공원 이용객들에게 '방해가 되는 일은 거의 없을 것'으로 예상한다는 내용이 되어야 뒤 문장과의 연결이 자연스러우므로 정답은 '방해, 중단'을 뜻하는 (D) disruption이다.

어휘 supplement 보충 reduction 감소 implementation 시행

135-138 이메일

> 발신: 맥거킨, 에드워드
> 수신: 모든 여름철 투숙객
> 날짜: 5월 15일 수요일, 오전 8시 2분
> 제목: 지역 해변을 즐기는 것
>
> 귀하께서 미라클 해변의 그랜드 호텔에 방문하시기를 고대하고 있습니다! 시 의회에서 최근 해수욕객들이 지역 해변 ¹³⁵**이용**에 대해 비용을 지불할 것을 요구하는 법령을 통과시켰습니다. 우리는 무료 해변 출입이 우리의 투숙객들에게 얼마나 중요했는지 알고 있습니다. ¹³⁶**따라서** 무료로 이용 가능한 해변 통행권을 준비했습니다. 체크인하실 때 통행권을 요청하시고 체크아웃하실 때 반납하시기만 하면 됩니다.
>
> 시 소속 해안 순찰대 직원들이 ¹³⁷**정기적으로** 해변을 따라 순찰하며 저희가 제공하는 것과 같은 통행권을 확인할 것입니다. ¹³⁸**지역 해변 통행권을 지참하지 않은 사람에게는 과태료가 부과될 것입니다.** 반드시 통행권을 확보하셔서 벌금 발생 가능성을 피하시기 바랍니다.

> 어휘 town council 시 의회 ordinance 법령 entry 입장 arrange for 준비하다 pass 통행권 free of charge 무료로 municipal 시의 beach-patrol 해안 순찰대 penalty 벌금

135 명사 자리 _ 전치사의 목적어

해설 빈칸은 전치사 for의 목적어 자리이므로 명사나 동명사가 들어갈 수 있다. 빈칸 뒤에 목적어가 없고 전치사구 to the local beaches가 나오므로 명사인 (B) access가 정답이다.

136 접속부사

해설 앞 문장에서 해변 이용 시 비용을 지불해야 한다는 새로운 법령에 대해 알리면서 무료 해변 출입이 투숙객에게 중요한 것(how important free beach entry has been)을 알고 있다고 했고, 뒤 문장에는 무료로 이용 가능한 해변 통행권을 준비했다(arranged for beach passes to be available for you – free of charge)고 했다. 두 문장이 무료 해변 출입이 중요하므로 무료 통행권을 준비했다는 인과 관계를 나타내고 있으므로 '그러므로, 따라서'를 뜻하는 (D) Therefore가 정답이 된다.

137 부사 자리 _ 동사 수식

해설 빈칸이 없어도 완전한 절이 있고, 빈칸은 동사 will be walking을 수식하는 부사 자리이다. 따라서 부사인 (B) regularly가 정답이다.

138 문맥에 맞는 문장 고르기

해설 빈칸 앞에는 해안 순찰대 직원들이 통행권을 확인할 것(check for passes)이라고 했고, 빈칸 뒤에는 통행권을 꼭 확보해 벌금 발생 가능성을 피하라(get your pass and avoid the possible penalty)고 했다. 따라서 빈칸에는 통행권과 관련해 벌금이 부과되는 상황에 대한 내용이 들어가야 연결이 자연스럽다. 따라서 해변 통행권이 없는 사람에게는 과태료가 부과된다고 언급하고 있는 (C)가 정답이다.

번역 (A) 해변을 떠나실 때 모든 개인 소지품을 챙기십시오.
(B) 안타깝게도, 해변 이용료 지불은 전국적으로 증가하고 있는 현상입니다.
(C) 지역 해변 통행권을 지참하지 않은 사람에게는 과태료가 부과될 것입니다.
(D) 요청하시는 손님께는 비치 타월도 제공해 드립니다.

어휘 belongings 소지품   phenomenon 현상   nationwide 전국적으로   fine 벌금   impose 부과하다   secure 확보하다

139-142 이메일

발신: 박은미
수신: 신한국 금융그룹 전 직원 (NKFG)
제목: 근무 공간 개선
날짜: 3월 12일

직원들에게 편안한 환경을 제공하기 위한 노력의 일환으로, 개별 근무 공간을 ¹³⁹**향상시키는 것**을 목표로 유지 보수 작업이 이번 주에 시작될 예정입니다. 작업은 단계적으로 진행될 것입니다. 먼저, 내일 각 사무실과 칸막이 공간에 새 카펫이 설치될 예정입니다. 이 프로젝트가 원활히 ¹⁴⁰**진행될** 수 있도록 오늘 퇴근하기 전에 각자의 근무 구역에 있는 모든 개인 물품을 바닥으로부터 치워 주십시오. ¹⁴¹**다음으로**, 이번 주 후반에 개방형 철제 책꽂이가 미닫이 문이 달린 최신식 고강도 플라스틱 책꽂이로 교체될 것입니다. 이번 작업으로 회사 전체 근무 공간의 외관이 개선될 것으로 확신합니다. ¹⁴²**이번 주에 이러한 조치로 인해 발생할 수 있는 불편함에 대해 유감스럽게 생각합니다.** 여러분의 이해와 협조에 미리 감사드립니다.

어휘 commitment 전념, 약속   maintenance 유지 보수   enhance 향상시키다   proceed 진행하다   in stages 단계적으로

cubicle 칸막이 공간   smoothly 순조롭게   state-of-the-art 최신의   high-density 고밀도의   initiative 계획   appearance 외관   cooperation 협조

139 동사 어휘

해설 전치사 of의 목적어 역할을 하는 동명사 자리에 들어갈 동사 어휘를 고르는 문제이다. 빈칸 앞에서 직원들에게 편안한 환경을 제공하기 위한 노력의 일환으로 유지 보수 작업을 시작한다고 했으므로, 문맥상 '개별 근무 공간을 개선하는 것'을 목표로 한다는 내용이 되어야 자연스럽다. 따라서 '개선하다, 향상시키다'는 뜻의 (B) enhancing이 정답이다.

어휘 combine 결합하다   reassign 다시 할당하다

140 동사 자리 _ 복합문제

해설 빈칸은 that절의 주어 this project의 동사 자리이므로 동사인 (B) runs나 (C) ran이 답이 될 수 있다. 앞 문장에서 언급한 내일 있을 새 카펫 설치를 this project로 받아 이 프로젝트의 원활한 진행을 위해 오늘 퇴근 전 할 일에 대해 당부하는 내용의 문장이므로 과거 시제는 답이 될 수 없고 현재 시제인 (B) runs가 정답이다.

141 접속부사

해설 앞 내용에서 먼저(First), 내일 새 카펫이 설치될 것이라고 했고, 빈칸 뒤에는 이번 주 후반에 철제 책꽂이가 플라스틱 책꽂이로 교체될 것이라고 했다. 두 문장이 앞으로 있을 작업 일정에 대해 안내하는 내용이므로, 첫 번째(First) 작업의 다음 순서를 의미하는 말이 들어가야 자연스럽다. 따라서 '다음으로'라는 뜻의 (C) Next가 정답이다.

142 문맥에 맞는 문장 고르기

해설 빈칸 뒤에서 여러분의 이해와 협조에 미리 감사드린다고 한 것으로 보아, 빈칸에는 양해를 구하는 내용의 문장이 들어가야 자연스럽게 연결될 수 있다. 따라서 이러한 조치로 발생할 수 있는 불편함에 대해 유감이라고 언급하고 있는 (A)가 정답이다.

번역 (A) 이번 주에 이러한 조치로 인해 발생할 수 있는 불편함에 대해 유감스럽게 생각합니다.
(B) 우리는 오랜 고객들에게 제공하는 금융 서비스를 자랑스럽게 여깁니다.
(C) 철제 책꽂이는 불과 5년 전에 설치되었습니다.
(D) 지역 자선 단체에서 도서는 언제나 환영받습니다.

어휘 regret 유감스럽게 생각하다   inconvenience 불편   measure 조치   charity 자선 단체

143-146 기사

새롭게 단장한 클레어몬트 시네마

사라 랭글리 작성

브리스톨 (9월 12일)—6개월이 지난 뒤 마침내 클레어몬트 시네마가 재

개관했다. 소유주들이 계획에 대해 **143모호했기** 때문에 영화 관람객들은 어젯밤 극장 문이 열렸을 때 무엇을 기대해야 할지 알지 못했다. 가장 큰 변화는 이제 복합 상영관 내에 하나가 아닌 세 개의 상영관이 있다는 점이다. **144여기에는 장점과 단점이 있다.** 한편으로, 영화 관람객들은 이제 클레어몬트 시네마가 오랫동안 자랑스럽게 제공해 온 독립 영화들을 더 많이 접할 수 있게 되었다. 반면, 이 영화들은 아주 작은 스크린에서 상영되고 있다. **145사실** 나는 집에서 TV를 보고 있는 것처럼 느꼈다. 그럼에도, 복합 상영관은 새로운 매점과 마찬가지로 환상적이다. 그러니 모든 영화 애호가들이 새로운 클레어몬트 시네마가 제공하는 것을 **146스스로** 발견해 보기를 권한다.

> 어휘 filmgoer 영화 관람객 complex 복합 건물 independent film 독립 영화 offering 제공된 것 refreshments 다과 stand 가판대

143 형용사 어휘

해설 빈칸 뒤에서 영화 관람객들이 어젯밤 극장 문이 열렸을 때 무엇을 기대해야 할지 몰랐다고 했으므로 계획에 대해 '불분명했다' 또는 '모호했다'는 의미가 되어야 자연스럽다. 따라서 '모호한, 애매한'이라는 뜻의 (A) vague가 정답이다.

어휘 flexible 유연한 joyful 아주 기뻐하는 encouraging 고무적인

144 문맥에 맞는 문장 고르기

해설 빈칸 앞에는 상영관이 세 개로 늘었다는 변화를 언급했고, 빈칸 뒤에서는 독립 영화를 더 많이 접할 수 있게 되었다는 장점과 너무 작은 스크린에서 상영된다는 단점을 차례로 언급하고 있다. 따라서 빈칸에는 상영관의 수가 증가했다는 변화를 This로 받아 여기에는 장단점이 공존한다고 언급하고 있는 문장이 들어가야 연결이 자연스럽다. 따라서 (A)가 정답이다.

번역 (A) 여기에는 장점과 단점이 있다.
(B) 많은 영화 관람객들이 재개관식에 왔다.
(C) 큰 변화는 종종 어렵지만 필요하다.
(D) 소유주들은 상당한 수익을 누리게 될 것 같다.

어휘 advantage 장점 disadvantage 단점 significant 상당한

145 접속부사

해설 빈칸 앞 문장에서 영화가 아주 작은 스크린에서 상영되고 있다고 했고, 뒤 문장에서 집에서 TV를 보고 있는 것처럼 느꼈다고 했다. 앞 문장에서 언급한 작은 스크린(very small screens)에 대해 강조하려고 뒤 문장에 자신의 느낌(felt like I was at home watching television)을 덧붙인 것이므로, 방금 한 말에 대해 실상을 강조하거나 자세한 내용을 덧붙일 때 사용하는 '사실은'이라는 뜻의 (D) In fact가 정답이다.

146 재귀대명사

해설 전치사 for의 목적어 자리에 들어갈 대명사를 고르는 문제이다. all film lovers를 대신하면서 모든 영화 애호가들이 '스스로 발견해 보기를 권한다'는 의미가 되어야 하므로, 전치사 for와 함께 쓰여 '스스

로'라는 의미의 관용 표현을 이루는 (C) themselves가 정답이다.

PART 7

147-148 공지

> 이웃 여러분,
>
> **147길고 추운 겨울이 이제 막 지나갔으니** 새로 조성된 문 타운십 커뮤니티 가든을 개선하는 데 여러분의 도움을 청하고 싶습니다. 주민 위원회가 마을 수영장이 있던 땅을 취득했고, 아름다운 우리 마을의 녹지를 와서 즐길 수 있는 가족을 위한 공간을 이 땅에 만들고자 합니다. **148이번 달 남은 주말 동안 자원봉사자들의 도움을 받아 가족들이 직접 선택한 꽃, 관목, 나무를 배치하고 심을 수 있도록 지원할 예정입니다.** 우리의 아름다운 마을 정원을 꾸미는 데 여러분의 참여를 바랍니다!
>
> 문 타운십 녹지 위원회

> 어휘 neighbor 이웃 established 설립된 township 군구(county 아래의 행정 구역 단위), 그 주민 committee 위원회 acquire 얻다 on hand (도움을) 구할 수 있는 remainder 나머지 arrange 배열하다 plant 심다 shrub 관목

147 추론 / 암시

번역 공지는 어느 계절에 작성되었을 것 같은가?
(A) 겨울
(B) 봄
(C) 여름
(D) 가을

해설 첫 문장에서 이제 길고 추운 겨울이 막 지나갔다(Now that the long, cold winter is just behind us)고 했으므로 공지가 봄에 작성되었음을 짐작할 수 있다. 따라서 (B)가 정답이다.

148 세부 사항

번역 가족들이 하도록 장려되는 일은?
(A) 마을 수영장 사용
(B) 꽃 구입
(C) 타운십 위원회 위원 선출 투표
(D) 정원에 식물 심는 일 돕기

해설 세 번째 문장에서 이번 달 남은 주말 동안 자원봉사자들의 도움을 받아 가족들이 직접 선택한 꽃, 관목, 나무를 배치하고 심을 수 있도록 지원할 예정(We will have volunteers ~ of their choice)이라며 우리의 아름다운 마을 정원을 꾸미는 데 여러분의 참여를 바란다(We hope ~ community garden!)고 했으므로 (D)가 정답이다.

어휘 vote 투표하다

> Paraphrasing 지문의 planting the flowers, shrubs, and trees → 정답의 plant a garden

149-150 상품권

150스파클링 크릭 커피하우스 & 그릴

상품권

받는 분: 나타샤 터커

금액: 75달러

보내신 분: 후아 시에

메시지: 149제 기사를 도와주셔서 감사합니다.
편집을 멋지게 해 주셨어요!

150승인자: 제니 레녹스

어휘 gift certificate 상품권 present 주다 authorize 인가하다

---

149 세부 사항

번역 터커 씨가 상품권을 받은 이유는?

(A) 레스토랑에서 수고한 일에 대한 감사 표시

(B) 제공된 도움에 대한 감사 표시

(C) 보상금 승인

(D) 대출금 상환

해설 상품권의 메시지에서 시에 씨가 터커 씨에게 제 기사를 도와주셔서 감사하다(Thank you for your help with my article)고 했으므로 터커 씨는 시에 씨를 도운 일에 대한 보답으로 상품권을 받았음을 알 수 있다. 따라서 정답은 (B)이다.

어휘 acknowledge (공식적으로) 감사를 표하다, 인정하다 gratitude 감사 reward 보상(금) repay 갚다 loan 대출(금)

Paraphrasing 지문의 Thank you
→ 정답의 express gratitude

---

150 추론 / 암시

번역 레녹스 씨는 누구일 것 같은가?

(A) 식당 직원

(B) 터커 씨의 친구

(C) 편집자

(D) 시에 씨의 조수

해설 상품권의 상단에 상품권을 발행한 곳이 스파클링 크릭 커피하우스 & 그릴(Sparkling Creek Coffeehouse & Grill)이라고 표기되어 있고, 하단에 제니 레녹스가 승인했다(Authorized by: Jenny Lenox)고 나와 있는 것으로 보아 레녹스 씨는 해당 식당 소속 직원임을 알 수 있다. 따라서 (A)가 정답이다.

151-152 확인 목록

151환영 이메일

☐ 우리 팀에 새로 온 직원들에 대한 따뜻한 환영 인사

☐ 교육 세션 날짜 포함

☐ 일일 교육 일정 포함(첨부 파일 참조)

☐ 멘토 전화번호 제공

☐ 지참할 서류 목록 작성

151신입 직원 교육

☐ 시작 날짜 공지

☐ 152신입 사원을 환영하고 회사 관리자들을 만나볼 수 있는 사교 모임에 대한 정보 포함

☐ 기술 팀에 문의하여 이메일 계정 생성

☐ 새 ID 배지와 열쇠 준비

☐ 복지 후생 준비(건강 보험 및 퇴직금)

☐ 신입 사원이 도착 시 개별 만남

어휘 onboarding 신입 직원 교육 gathering 모임 hire 신입 사원 benefits package 복리 후생 insurance 보험 retirement 은퇴

---

151 주제 / 목적

번역 확인 목록의 목적은?

(A) 새 이메일 시스템 공지

(B) 신입 사원을 위한 준비

(C) 퇴사자 지원

(D) 강사들에게 일정 통보

해설 주요 항목 두 가지가 환영 이메일(Welcome E-mail)과 신입 직원 교육(Onboarding)인 것으로 보아 신입 사원을 맞이하기 위한 준비 사항 목록임을 알 수 있다. 따라서 (B)가 정답이다.

어휘 notify 통지하다

---

152 세부 사항

번역 사교 모임의 한 가지 목표는?

(A) 관리자와의 만남

(B) 복지에 대해 배우기

(C) 신분 확인 서류 수령

(D) 교육 실습 시작

해설 신입 직원 교육의 두 번째 항목인 신입 사원을 환영하고 회사 관리자들을 만나볼 수 있는 사교 모임에 대한 정보 포함(Include information ~ meet company leaders)에 따르면 사교 모임의 목표는 신입 사원 환영과 회사 관리자들과의 만남이므로 (A)가 정답이다.

어휘 benefit 복지, 혜택 identification 신분 확인

Paraphrasing 지문의 company leaders
→ 정답의 managers

153-154 문자 메시지

루시 오말리 (오후 1시 36분)
제가 지금 사무실인데 밀러 파일을 도무지 찾을 수가 없어요.

스탠리 햄스테드 (오후 1시 37분)
153향후 사업 계획 파일 캐비닛은 확인해 보셨나요?

루시 오말리 (오후 1시 39분)
운이 없네요. 153다른 생각나는 곳이 있을까요?

스탠리 햄스테드 (오후 1시 40분)

찰스 와다의 사무실에 있는 게 분명해요. 그의 책상을 확인해 보시고 알려 주세요.

루시 오말리 (오후 1시 47분)

찾았어요! 어떻게 가져다 드리면 될까요?

스탠리 햄스테드 (오후 1시 48분)

가져다 달라고 부탁드리면 무리일까요? **154**서명이 있는 원본 서류가 필요하거든요. 가능한 한 빨리 와 주세요.

루시 오말리 (오후 1시 50분)

154문제없어요. 택시를 타고 갈게요.

어휘 bet ~이 분명하다[틀림없다]

153 의도 파악

번역 오후 1시 39분에 오말리 씨가 "운이 없네요"라고 쓴 의도는?
(A) 향후 사업 계획을 지지하지 않는다.
(B) 동료의 사무실이 어디에 있는지 모른다.
(C) 물건을 찾을 수 없었다.
(D) 와다 씨로부터 추가 설명이 필요하다.

해설 1시 37분에 햄스테드 씨가 향후 사업 계획 파일 캐비닛을 확인해 봤는지(Did you check ~ file cabinet?) 묻자 1시 39분에 오말리 씨가 운이 없다(No luck)며 다른 생각나는 곳이 있는지(Any other ideas?)를 묻고 있으므로 파일 캐비닛에 찾고 있는 물건이 없었다는 의도로 한 말임을 알 수 있다. 따라서 (C)가 정답이다.

어휘 support 지원하다 unsure 확신하지 못하는 instruction 설명

154 추론 / 암시

번역 오말리 씨는 다음에 무엇을 할 것 같은가?
(A) 일부 문서를 이메일로 보낸다.
(B) 택배사에 전화한다.
(C) 직접 서류를 전달한다.
(D) 와다 씨에게 연락한다.

해설 1시 48분에 햄스테드 씨가 서명이 있는 원본 서류가 필요하다(We need ~ with signatures)며 가능한 한 빨리 와 달라(Please get here as soon as you can)고 하자 1시 50분에 오말리 씨가 문제없다(Not a problem)며 택시를 타고 가겠다(I'll take a taxi)고 한 것으로 보아 오말리 씨가 햄스테드 씨에게 직접 원본 서류를 가져다 줄 것임을 알 수 있다. 따라서 (C)가 정답이다.

어휘 courier 택배 회사

155-157 공지

155페틀러 항공 활주로 지연 비상 계획

기내 출발 지연은 저희가 최대한 피하고자 하는 상황입니다. 날씨, 가시성, 공항 상황, 혹은 기타 상황으로 인해 드물게 불가피한 지상 지연이 발생할 수 있습니다. 이러한 경우, **156**지연이 60분 이상 지속되면 무료 간식 및 음료를 제공합니다. 지연이 2시간(국내선) 또는 3시간(국제선)

이상 지속될 경우 항공기가 탑승구로 복귀하고 승객들이 비행기에서 내릴 수 있습니다. 승객들은 매 30분마다 탑승구에서 지연 **157**상황에 대한 통지를 듣게 되실 겁니다. 이러한 통지에는 지연 사유 및 식사 또는 호텔 이용권과 같은 추가적인 편의 시설 이용 가능 여부가 포함됩니다.

어휘 tarmac 활주로 delay 지연 contingency plan 비상 계획 onboard 탑승한 rare 드문 occasion 경우 visibility 가시성 circumstance 상황 unavoidable 불가피한 complimentary 무료의 domestic 국내의 passenger 승객 notification 통지 status 상황 amenity 편의 시설 voucher 이용[할인]권

155 주제 / 목적

번역 공지의 목적은?
(A) 항공편 지연에 대한 사과
(B) 기내 음료 옵션 안내
(C) 비행 안전 절차 설명
(D) 항공사 정책 설명

해설 공지의 제목이 페틀러 항공 활주로 지연 비상 계획(Fetler Airlines Tarmac Delay Contingency Plan)으로 활주로가 지연될 경우 항공사의 대책에 대해 설명하는 안내문이므로 (D)가 정답이다.

어휘 in-flight 기내의 describe 설명하다 procedure 절차

156 세부 사항

번역 승객들은 어떤 상황에서 무료 다과를 제공받는가?
(A) 항공편이 한 시간 이상 지연될 경우
(B) 가시거리 불량으로 인해 항공편이 취소된 경우
(C) 비행 시간이 2시간 이상일 경우
(D) 비행기가 일시적으로 탑승구로 돌아올 경우

해설 세 번째 문장에서 지연이 60분 이상 지속되면 무료 간식 및 음료를 제공한다(if the delay lasts ~ complimentary snacks and beverages)고 했으므로 (A)가 정답이다.

어휘 temporarily 일시적으로

Paraphrasing 지문의 60 minutes → 정답의 one hour

157 동의어

번역 첫 번째 단락 7행의 "status"와 의미가 가장 가까운 단어는?
(A) 순위
(B) 지각
(C) 상태
(D) 감독관

해설 의미상 지연 '상황'에 대한 통지라는 뜻으로 쓰인 것이므로 정답은 (C) condition이다.

158-160 기사

마리골드 시티 (5월 11일)—마리골드 시 의회는 마리골드 외곽에 새로운 스포츠 경기장을 건설하기 위한 계획 158안을 받았다. 159경기장은 스포츠 행사와 콘서트를 모두 주최하게 될 것이며 이전의 마리골드 가구 공장 부지에 건축될 것이다. 이 건물은 마리골드 가구가 5여 년 전 다른 장소로 생산지를 이전한 이후 계속 비어 있었다.

160경기장의 설계자들은 이제 건축 계획을 도시 기획 위원회로 보내 인가를 받아야 한다. 건설은 계획 및 수정 사항이 통과되는 대로 시작할 수 있다. 공사는 내년 초에 시작되어 약 2년이 걸릴 것으로 예상된다.

> 어휘 council 위원회 draft 초안 arena 경기장 site 부지 former 예전의 planning commission 계획 위원회 acceptance 승인 revision 수정 accept 수락하다 approximately 거의

158 동의어

번역 첫 번째 단락 2행의 "draft"와 의미가 가장 가까운 단어는?
(A) 바람
(B) 비용
(C) 버전
(D) 변경

해설 의미상 '계획안'에서 '안'이라는 뜻으로 쓰인 것이므로 정답은 (C) version이다.

159 세부 사항

번역 새 건축물은 무엇을 대체할 것인가?
(A) 공터
(B) 시립 공원
(C) 사용하지 않는 건물
(D) 쇼핑몰

해설 첫 단락의 두 번째 문장에서 경기장은 스포츠 행사와 콘서트를 모두 주최하게 될 것이며 이전의 마리골드 가구 공장 부지에 건축될 것 (The arena ~ Marigold Furniture Factory)이라고 했고, 이 건물은 마리골드 가구가 5여 년 전 다른 장소로 생산지를 이전한 이후 계속 비어 있었다(The building has remained empty ~ five years ago)고 했으므로 (C)가 정답이다.

어휘 lot 부지[땅]

> Paraphrasing 지문의 empty → 정답의 unused

160 세부 사항

번역 기사에 따르면, 절차상 다음 단계는?
(A) 새 건축물의 공사가 시작될 것이다.
(B) 승인을 받기 위한 계획이 제출될 것이다.
(C) 건설 회사가 투자자를 찾을 것이다.
(D) 주민들이 계획에 대해 투표할 것이다.

해설 두 번째 단락의 첫 문장에서 경기장의 설계자들은 이제 건축 계획을 도시 기획 위원회로 보내 인가를 받아야 한다(The arena's designers ~ for acceptance)고 했으므로 (B)가 정답이다.

어휘 structure 건축물 present 제출[제시]하다 approval 승인 seek 찾다 investor 투자자 resident 주민 vote 투표하다

> Paraphrasing 지문의 acceptance → 정답의 approval

161-163 광고

> **더 좋아진 영국 최다 판매 페인트**
>
> **더 다양해진 재스민 리프 페인트**
>
> 161재스민 리프 페인트는 지난 5년 연속 가정용 페인트 판매 1위를 차지했습니다. 하지만 베스트 셀러가 되는 것만으로는 충분하지 않습니다. 그래서 161저희는 여러분의 집을 더욱 아름답게 만들어 줄 방법들을 더 가져왔습니다!
>
> 특수 혼합된 블렌덱스 포뮬러 실내 페인트와 프라이머는 얼룩 방지, 우수한 커버력, 냄새가 적은 포뮬러, 쉬운 청소 그리고 평생 보증으로 높이 평가됩니다. 162게다가 저희는 이제 5가지 크기의 캔으로 페인트를 제공하고 있습니다. 그리고 163여러분은 이제 완전 무광, 무광, 새틴, 반광택, 고광택의 5가지 아름다운 마감 칠을 경험하실 수 있습니다. 이 모든 것은 여러분을 위한 더 편리한 옵션을 의미합니다.
>
> 만약 여러분의 집 내부에 좋은 재질의 오래가는 아름다운 벽과 천장을 원하신다면 가까운 고급 페인트 가게에서 재스민 리프 페인트를 찾으세요.

> 어휘 in a row 연속으로 blend 혼합하다 formula 포뮬러, 혼합물 primer 밑칠 페인트 prize 높이 평가하다 stain 얼룩 resistance 저항 odour (불쾌한) 냄새 ease 쉬움 guarantee 품질 보증 finish (페인트 광택제 등의) 마감 칠 (상태) flat 완전 무광 eggshell 무광의 satin (새틴같이) 광택이 고운 gloss 유광의 ceiling 천장 quality 고급의

161 세부 사항

번역 광고는 누구를 주요 대상으로 하는가?
(A) 조경사
(B) 페인트 가게 소유주
(C) 미술을 배우는 학생
(D) 주택 소유자

해설 첫 단락의 첫 문장에서 재스민 리프 페인트는 지난 5년 연속 가정용 페인트 판매 1위를 차지했다(Jasmine Leaf Paint ~ in a row)고 했고, 세 번째 문장에서 여러분의 집을 더욱 아름답게 만들어 줄 방법들을 더 가져왔다(That's why ~ home more beautiful!)고 한 것으로 보아 광고는 주택 소유자를 대상으로 한 것임을 알 수 있다. 따라서 (D)가 정답이다.

162 세부 사항

번역 재스민 리프 페인트에 대해 새로운 점은?
(A) 얼룩을 방지한다.
(B) 평생 보증을 제공한다.
(C) 더 두껍다.
(D) 더 다양한 크기로 이용할 수 있다.

163 문장 삽입

번역 [1], [2], [3], [4]로 표시된 곳 중에서 다음 문장이 들어가기에 가장 적합한 위치는?

"이 모든 것은 여러분을 위한 더 편리한 옵션을 의미합니다."

(A) [1]
(B) [2]
(C) [3]
(D) [4]

해설 제시된 문장에서 이 모든 것(This all)은 여러분을 위한 더 편리한 옵션을 의미한다고 했으므로, 주어진 문장 앞에 '이 모든 것' 즉, 선택할 수 있는 다수의 옵션 사항이 나열되어 있어야 한다. 따라서 완전 무광, 무광, 새틴, 반광택, 고광택의 5가지 페인트(flat, eggshell, satin, semigloss, and high gloss)가 언급되어 있는 문장 뒤인 (C)가 정답이다.

164-167 보도 자료

긴급 보도

연락처: 릴리 콴, lkwan@itamitheater.com

시애틀 (4월 10일)—예술 감독 루카스 프리랜드가 사임했다는 최근 발표 이후, 이타미 극장 이사회는 수 리를 임시 예술 감독으로 임명했다. **164,165(B)리 씨는 이타미에서 10년 동안 일했으며,** 신작 연극 개발 담당 이사를 맡고 있다.

리 씨는 이타미의 예술적 방향에 있어서 중심이 되어 왔다. 그녀는 다음 시즌을 위한 연극 선별을 계속해서 주도할 것이다. "이사회가 저를 믿고 이타미 극장의 전체 팀이 확립해 온 작업을 진행하도록 해 주셔서 영광입니다. 내년에 신명 나는 시즌을 만들기 위해 무대 담당자부터 의상 디자이너에 이르기까지 우리의 모든 헌신적인 스태프들과 함께 일하게 되어 흥분됩니다."라고 리 씨는 말했다. **165(C)극장을 위해 신작 연극 개발을 감독하는 일 외에도,** **167리 씨는 연출가이기도 하다.** 그녀는 연극 〈여름과 가을 그리고 사랑과 눈 속의 다른 모험들〉을 연출했다. 이번 시즌 말에, 그녀는 수상 경력이 있는 극작가 메이 누네스가 쓴 〈숲속 생명체〉를 연출할 예정이다.

"리 씨가 이타미의 임시 예술 감독을 맡도록 한 선택은 현명했습니다. 그녀의 깊은 연극 지식은 프리랜드 씨가 떠나고 상임 예술 감독을 찾는 동안 이타미 극장이 예술적인 노력을 지속하는 데 도움이 될 것입니다."라고 존 스토야노브스키 전무 이사는 말했다. **166이사회는 시간을 들여 상임 예술 감독을 물색하는 데 전념하고 있다. 이사회는 전국에서 지원자를 모집하고 있으며 채용 절차는 6개월에서 9개월이 소요될 것으로 예상된다.**

어휘 step down 사퇴하다 appoint 임명하다 interim 임시의 play 연극 pivotal 중심이 되는 board 이사회 carry forward 진행하다 dedicated 헌신적인 stagehand 무대 담당자

164 추론 / 암시

번역 이타미 극장에 대해 암시된 것은?
(A) 새로운 극작가들에 중점을 두고 있다.
(B) 새로운 의상 디자이너를 찾고 있다.
(C) 두 번째 무대를 짓고 있다.
(D) 10년 이상 운영해 왔다.

해설 첫 단락의 두 번째 문장에서 리 씨가 이타미에서 10년 동안 일했다(Ms. Li has been at Itami for ten years)고 했으므로 이타미 극장이 운영되어 온 지 10년이 넘었음을 알 수 있다. 따라서 (D)가 정답이다.

165 Not / True

번역 리 씨에 대해 명시된 것은?
(A) 많은 희곡을 썼다.
(B) 이타미 극장에 새로 합류했다.
(C) 현재 직장에서 각기 다른 역할을 수행한다.
(D) 새로운 배우들을 고용하고 있다.

해설 두 번째 단락의 다섯 번째 문장에서 극장을 위해 신작 연극 개발을 감독하는 일 외에도 리 씨는 연출가이기도 하다(In addition to overseeing ~ is a director)고 했으므로 정답은 (C)이다. 리 씨는 이타미에서 10년 동안 일했다고 나와 있으므로 (B)는 오답, 희곡을 썼다는 것과 새로운 배우 고용에 대한 언급은 없으므로 (A)와 (D)는 답이 될 수 없다.

166 Not / True

번역 상임 예술 감독의 채용 과정에 대해 명시된 것은?
(A) 9개월 내에 완료될 것이다.
(B) 면접은 6개월 뒤에 실시된다.
(C) 현지 구직자만 고려될 것이다.
(D) 합격자들은 감독 경험이 있을 것이다.

해설 세 번째 단락의 세 번째 문장에서 이사회는 시간을 들여 상임 예술 감독을 물색하는 데 전념하고 있다(The board of directors ~ artistic director)고 했고, 전국에서 지원자를 모집하고 있으며 채용 절차는 6개월에서 9개월이 소요될 것으로 예상된다(The board is pursuing ~ nine months)고 했으므로 예술 감독의 채용은 9개월 뒤에는 마무리될 것임을 알 수 있다. 따라서 (A)가 정답이다.

Paraphrasing	지문의 take six to nine months → 정답의 be completed within nine months

167 문장 삽입

번역 [1], [2], [3], [4]로 표시된 곳 중에서 다음 문장이 들어가기에 가장 적합한 위치는?

"그녀는 연극 〈여름과 가을 그리고 사랑과 눈 속의 다른 모험들〉을 연출했다."
(A) [1]
(B) [2]
(C) [3]
(D) [4]

해설 제시된 문장은 '그녀가 〈여름과 가을 그리고 사랑과 눈 속의 다른 모험들〉 연극을 연출했다'며 그녀가 실제로 연출한 연극의 이름을 알려 주고 있다. 따라서 리 씨는 연출가이기도 하다(Ms. Li is a director)며 '그녀(She)'의 이름을 명시한 후, 연출 일을 한다는 점에 대해서도 언급한 문장 뒤에 들어가는 것이 글의 흐름상 자연스러우므로 (C)가 정답이다.

168-171 회의록

> **회의록―8월 10일**
>
> 참석자: 미구엘 루나, 제니퍼 린, 아말 테일러, 블라디미르 이크람, 네베나 이바노바
>
> 제품 관리자인 아말 테일러가 회의를 시작했다. 그녀는 우리의 신제품 허브차가 9월 25일부터 지역 매장 진열대와 식당에서 판매될 것이라고 보고했다. ¹⁶⁸첫 출시에는 페퍼민트, 레몬 생강, 히비스커스 세 가지 맛이 포함된다. 내년에는 더 많은 종류가 추가될 것으로 예상된다.
>
> 다음으로, ¹⁶⁹미구엘 루나는 차를 담는 상자의 시제품을 공유하고 이를 생산하는 데 사용되는 재료의 지속 가능성에 대해 논의했다. 다채로운 색감의 디자인이 회의 참석자들로부터 긍정적인 피드백을 받았다.
>
> 그 다음으로, 제니퍼 린은 제품 출시를 위한 마케팅 예산에 대한 간략한 개요를 제공했다. 지금은 현재 광고 캠페인 한 가지로 한정되어 있다. ¹⁷⁰마케팅 예산에 대한 더 자세한 내용은 린 씨에게 직접 문의할 것.
>
> 마지막으로, 블라디미르 이크람은 광고 옵션에 대한 논의를 주도했다. 라디오 광고는 과거에 성공적이었고 TV 광고보다 더 저렴하다. 디지털 광고 또한 고려되었다. ¹⁷¹최종 결정은 〈사우스타운 타임즈〉에 지면 광고를 시작하자는 것이었다.
>
> 다음 회의는 8월 17일에 있을 예정이다.
>
> 어휘 meeting minutes 회의록 attendance 참석 initial 처음의 launch 출시 flavor 맛, 향미 ginger 생강 variety 품종[종류] prototype 시제품 sustainability 지속 가능성 material 재료 attendee 참석자 brief 간단한 overview 개요 detailed 상세한 directly 바로

168 세부 사항

번역 회사가 향후에 하려고 계획하는 것은?
(A) 찻집을 몇 군데 개점하는 일
(B) 제품군을 확장하는 일
(C) 차 이외의 음료를 개발하는 일
(D) 기존 차 종류를 교체하는 일

해설 첫 단락의 세 번째 문장에서 첫 출시에는 페퍼민트, 레몬 생강, 히비스커스 세 가지 맛이 포함된다(The initial launch ~ hibiscus flower)고 했고 내년에는 더 많은 종류가 추가될 것으로 예상된다(More varieties ~ next year)고 했으므로 회사는 판매 제품인 차의 종류를 확장하려고 계획하고 있음을 알 수 있다. 따라서 (B)가 정답이다.

어휘 expand 확장하다 other than ~ 외에

> Paraphrasing 지문의 more varieties ~ to be added
> → 정답의 Expand its product line

169 추론 / 암시

번역 루나 씨는 누구일 것 같은가?
(A) 운송 직원
(B) 공장 관리자
(C) 가게 주인
(D) 포장 디자이너

해설 두 번째 단락에서 미구엘 루나는 차를 담는 상자의 시제품을 공유하고 이를 생산하는 데 사용되는 재료의 지속 가능성에 대해 논의했다(Miguel Luna ~ to produce them)고 했고, 다채로운 색감의 디자인이 회의 참석자들로부터 긍정적인 피드백을 받았다(The colorful designs ~ meeting attendees)고 했으므로 루나 씨는 포장 디자이너임을 알 수 있다. 따라서 정답은 (D)이다.

170 세부 사항

번역 마케팅 예산에 대한 정보를 제공할 수 있는 사람은 누구인가?
(A) 린 씨
(B) 테일러 씨
(C) 이크람 씨
(D) 이바노바 씨

해설 세 번째 단락의 마지막 문장에서 마케팅 예산에 대한 더 자세한 내용은 린 씨에게 직접 문의하라(For more detailed ~ contact Ms. Lin directly)고 했으므로 정답은 (A)이다.

171 세부 사항

번역 제품이 처음 광고될 곳은?
(A) 신문
(B) 온라인 잡지
(C) 라디오
(D) 소셜 미디어

해설 네 번째 단락의 네 번째 문장에서 최종 결정은 〈사우스타운 타임즈〉에 지면 광고를 시작하자는 것(The final decision ~ in the Southtown Times)이라고 했으므로 정답은 (A)이다.

172-175 문자 메시지

> **조안 마토스 (오전 11시 45분)**
> 투엣 그리고 짐, 우리가 안에서 세일을 할 때 보통 입구에 광고하기 위해서는 ¹⁷²큰 게시판을 어디서 찾을 수 있는지 아세요?

투옛 응우옌 (오전 11시 58분)

최근에는 못 봤어요. 왜요?

조안 마토스 (오전 11시 59분)

173카페 바깥 뜰에 있는 텐트 아래에서 오늘 오후에 있을 파티를 준비 중인데, 사람들이 도착하면 볼 수 있게 좌석 정보를 게시하려고요.

투옛 응우옌 (오후 12시 1분)

짐한테 있을 수 있어요. 그가 평소 그런 세일을 위한 물품들을 준비하거 든요. 그런데 짐이 퇴근한 것 같아요.

짐 토마스 (오후 12시 2분)

아녜요. 저 퇴근 안 했어요! **174지금 배달을 하러 나왔지만 곧 돌아갈 거 예요.** 게시판은 우리 건물 배달 출입구 안쪽 벽감에서 찾을 수 있어요. **175다음에 필요할 때 제가 찾을 수 있게 다 쓰고 나면 제자리에 가져다 두세요.**

조안 마토스 (오후 12시 4분)

그럴게요. 감사합니다!

어휘   signboard 간판, 게시판   post 게시하다   entrance 입구
set up 설치하다   courtyard 뜰   alcove 벽감(벽을 우묵하게
들어가게 해서 만든 공간)

172 주제 / 목적

번역   마토스 씨는 왜 문자 메시지를 시작했는가?
　　(A) 물건을 찾는 데 도움이 필요해서
　　(B) 토마스 씨가 몇 시에 도착하는지 궁금해서
　　(C) 오늘 텐트를 친 이유를 알고 싶어서
　　(D) 장식물 설치에 도움을 원해서

해설   11시 45분에 마토스 씨가 큰 게시판을 어디서 찾을 수 있는지 아는 지(do you know where I can find that big signboard?)를 묻고 있으므로 물건을 찾는 데 도움을 구하려고 메시지를 보냈음을 알 수 있다. 따라서 (A)가 정답이다.

어휘   locate 찾다   decoration 장식품

173 세부 사항

번역   오늘 오후에 일어날 일은?
　　(A) 야외 행사가 있을 것이다.
　　(B) 세일이 있을 것이다.
　　(C) 응우옌 씨가 게시판을 주문할 것이다.
　　(D) 토마스 씨가 추가 텐트를 배송할 것이다.

해설   11시 59분에 마토스 씨가 카페 바깥 뜰에 있는 텐트 아래에서 오늘 오후에 있을 파티를 준비 중(I'm setting up ~ out in the café courtyard)이라고 했으므로 (A)가 정답이다.

Paraphrasing   지문의 party under the tent out in the café
　　　　　　　 courtyard → 정답의 outdoor event

---

174 추론 / 암시

번역   토마스 씨가 문자 메시지를 보내고 있을 것 같은 장소는?
　　(A) 텐트
　　(B) 건물 입구
　　(C) 그의 집
　　(D) 배달 장소

해설   12시 2분에 토마스 씨가 지금 배달을 하러 나왔지만 곧 돌아갈 것 (I'm out making a delivery right now, but I'll be back soon) 이라고 했으므로 토마스 씨는 현재 배송지에서 문자를 보내고 있음 을 짐작할 수 있다. 따라서 정답은 (D)이다.

175 의도 파악

번역   오후 12시 4분에 마토스 씨가 "그럴게요"라고 쓴 의도는?
　　(A) 아마 일이 곧 끝날 것이다.
　　(B) 토마스 씨와 입구에서 만날 것이다.
　　(C) 물건을 원래 위치에 가져다 놓을 것이다.
　　(D) 응우옌 씨의 설명을 이해한다.

해설   12시 2분에 토마스 씨가 다음에 필요할 때 자신이 찾을 수 있게 다 쓰고 나면 제자리에 가져다 두라(Just put it back ~ I need it)고 하자 12시 4분에 마토스 씨가 그러겠다(No problem)고 대답한 것 이므로, 마토스 씨는 토마스 씨의 요청대로 물건을 쓰고 나면 제자 리에 가져다 놓겠다는 의도로 한 말임을 알 수 있다. 따라서 정답은 (C)이다.

176-180 일정표 + 후기

중앙 미술관
다가오는 특별 전시

176월드와이드 패션

11월 1일 – 28일

세계 여러 지역에서 시대에 따라 의복과 장신구가 어떻게 변화했는지 알 아보세요. **176의복 샘플과 역사적인 소품, 스케치를 감상해 보세요.**

180제프리 램: 동식물 연구가

12월 1일 – 29일

과학자 제프리 램은 6개 대륙의 야생 동물을 연구하고 사진을 찍는 데 그의 삶을 쏟았습니다. **180이 연구원이 40년 경력 동안 찍은 개인 컬렉 션에서 동물과 풍경 사진을 살펴보세요.**

예술 속 인간

1월 1일 – 29일

과거와 현재를 막론한 수십 명의 예술가들의 그림과 조각 컬렉션은 예 술들이 인간이라는 주제를 묘사하는 수많은 방법을 보여줍니다. 유명 예술가와 비교적 알려지지 않은 예술가들의 작품이 모두 포함됩니다.

일상의 예술

1772월 1일 – 26일

일상 속 예술을 보여주는 이 전시회에는 다양한 수제품이 전시되어 있습 니다. **177수제 퀼트에서 가구까지 가정용품들을 완전히 새로운 방식으 로 보세요.**

중앙 미술관 후기

후기 작성자: 메리 월시

별: ★★★★★

미술뿐 아니라 역사에도 관심있는 사람들에게 중앙 미술관을 추천합니다. 저는 최근 이 미술관에 두 번 다녀왔습니다. **178,180저의 첫 번째 방문은 학교의 사진 동아리와 함께 간 것이었습니다. 178,180우리는 사진을 전시한 특별 전시회만 보았지만 저는 떠나면서 미술관의 나머지 부분도 보고 싶어졌습니다. 178며칠 뒤 다시 방문해서 미술관 전체를 둘러볼 기회를 가졌습니다.** 각각의 전시는 서로 달랐지만 흥미로운 작품들로 가득했습니다. **179직접 체험해 보려면 선물 가게 근처의 체험실에도 꼭 들러 보세요.** 첫 방문했을 때 그 방은 재미난 배경과 함께 카메라들이 있었습니다. 방문객들은 본인들의 사진을 찍었고, 저는 적은 비용으로 달에서 깃발을 들고 있는 것처럼 사진을 찍어 인화를 했습니다. **179특별 전시회처럼 체험실 활동은 매달 바뀌기 때문에 항상 새롭고 흥미로운 할 거리를 발견하게 될 겁니다.**

176 추론 / 암시

번역 일정표에 따르면, 방문객이 첫 번째 특별 전시에서 볼 수 있을 것 같은 것은?
(A) 신발
(B) 가구
(C) 라디오
(D) 그림

해설 일정표의 첫 번째 전시회의 이름이 월드와이드 패션(Worldwide Fashion)이고, 의복 샘플과 역사적인 소품, 스케치를 감상해 보라(See clothing samples ~ sketches)고 했으므로 패션 용품에 속하는 (A)가 정답이다.

177 Not / True

번역 2월에 열리는 특별 전시회에 대해 명시된 것은?
(A) 현지 예술가들이 그린 그림으로 주로 구성된다.
(B) 웹사이트에 나열된 다른 전시회보다 먼저 종료된다.
(C) 방문객들은 집에 갖고 있는 것과 비슷한 물건들을 볼 수 있다.
(D) 인기있던 이전 전시 이후 미술관으로 다시 돌아왔다.

해설 일정표의 마지막 전시회가 2월 1일에서 26일까지(February 1-26) 열린다고 나와 있고, 수제 퀼트에서 가구까지 가정용품들을 완전히 새로운 방식으로 보라(From handmade ~ whole new way)고 했으므로 정답은 (C)이다.

어휘 appearance 출현

178 세부 사항

번역 월시 씨는 왜 미술관에 두 번 갔는가?
(A) 사진을 더 많이 찍고 싶어서
(B) 미술관을 더 구경하고 싶어서
(C) 미술관에 실수로 물건을 두고 와서
(D) 표를 할인 받아서

해설 후기의 세 번째 문장에서 저의 첫 번째 방문은 학교의 사진 동아리와 함께 간 것이었다(My first trip ~ photography club)고 했고, 우리는 사진을 전시한 특별 전시회만 보았지만 자신은 미술관의 나머지 부분도 보고 싶어졌다(We only saw ~ rest of the museum)며 며칠 뒤 다시 방문해서 미술관 전체를 둘러볼 기회를 가졌다(I returned ~ the entire museum)고 했다. 따라서 월시 씨는 미술관을 더 둘러보고 싶어서 두 번 방문한 것이므로 (B)가 정답이다.

어휘 accidentally 실수로

179 세부 사항

번역 월시 씨는 독자들에게 무엇을 권하는가?
(A) 미술관 가이드 투어를 해 볼 것
(B) 상세 정보 확인을 위해 미술관에 전화할 것
(C) 미술관 선물 가게에서 물건을 구입할 것
(D) 미술관에서 하는 활동에 참가할 것

해설 후기의 일곱 번째 문장에서 직접 체험해 보려면 선물 가게 근처의 체험실에도 꼭 들러 보라(Be sure to stop at ~ hands-on experience)고 했고, 마지막 문장에서 특별 전시회처럼 체험실 활동은 매달 바뀌기 때문에 항상 새롭고 흥미로운 할거리를 발견하게 될 것(Like the special exhibits ~ interesting to do)이라고 덧붙이며 체험실에서 하는 활동에 참여해 볼 것을 권하고 있으므로 (D)가 정답이다.

180 연계

번역 월시 씨는 미술관 첫 방문 때 어느 전시회를 방문했는가?
(A) 월드와이드 패션
(B) 제프리 램: 동식물 연구가
(C) 예술 속 인간
(D) 일상의 예술

해설 후기의 세 번째 문장에서 월시 씨가 저의 첫 번째 방문은 학교의 사진 동아리와 함께 간 것이었다(My first trip ~ photography club)고 했고, 우리는 사진을 전시한 특별 전시회만 보았다(We only saw ~ featuring photography)고 했는데, 일정표의 두 번째 전시회인 제프리 램: 동식물 연구가(Jeffrey Lamb: Naturalist)의 설명에 이 연구원이 40년 경력 동안 찍은 동물과 풍경 사진을 살펴보라(See photos ~ forty-year career)고 나와 있다. 따라서 월시 씨는 첫 방문 때 사진 전시회인 '제프리 램: 동식물 연구가'를 관람했음을 알 수 있으므로 (B)가 정답이다.

181-185 제품 정보 + 양식

주택 공사 물자 – 자재 개요

조리대	캐비닛	바닥재
세라믹 타일	골든 오크	원목
스테인리스	다크 레드우드	비닐
185대리석 - 고급	블랙 월넛	돌
185화강암 - 고급	합성 합판	콘크리트

181스타일 및 색상 전 종류는 제품 카탈로그를 참조하십시오. 가격은 판매 직원에게 문의하십시오. 주문 배송은 보통 영업일 기준 7-10일이 걸립니다.

참고: 184블랙 월넛 캐비닛과 원목 바닥재는 소규모 지역 제조업체가 제작하는 지역 제품입니다. 주문을 처리하는 데 최소 3주를 감안해 주십시오.

어휘 improvement 개조 (공사) material 자재 overview 개요 countertop 조리대, 작업대 marble 대리석 granite 화강암 synthetic 합성 laminate 합판 flooring 바닥재 range 범위 fabricate 제작하다 fulfill 이행하다

모던 스타일
당신의 리모델링 전문가

고객 접수 양식

고객 성명: 테레사 델만	전화번호: 555-0130
완료 희망일: 4월 21일	
프로젝트 설명: 상업용 □ 주거용 □	

184고객은 새 조리대, 캐비닛, 바닥재와 가전제품(냉장고, 식기세척기, 가스레인지, 오븐)을 포함하여 3주 이내에 리모델링이 완료되기를 원합니다.

고객 선호 사항:
• 조리대: 검정 화강암
• 182,183캐비닛: 고객이 샘플을 갖고 있으며 4월 3일 주문 마감일까지 저에게 알려 줄 것입니다.
• 183바닥재: 고객이 4월 3일까지 알려 줄 것입니다.

참고:
185재료 구매 시 10% 할인 쿠폰 적용. 고급 소재에는 해당 없음.
프로젝트 계약서와 보증금은 4월 1일에 수령함.

어휘 expert 전문가 intake form 접수 양식 desired 희망하는 description 설명 commercial 상업용 residential 주거용의 appliance 가전제품 apply 적용하다 valid 유효한 deposit 보증금

181 세부 사항

번역 제품 정보에 따르면, 고객들은 어디에서 전 제품 목록을 볼 수 있는가?
(A) 웹사이트
(B) 제품 카탈로그
(C) 가게
(D) 신문 광고

해설 표 아래 첫 문장에서 스타일 및 색상 전 종류는 제품 카탈로그를 참조하라(See the product catalog ~ styles and colors)고 했으므로 (B)가 정답이다.

182 추론 / 암시

번역 누가 양식을 작성했을 것 같은가?
(A) 가전제품 수리 기사
(B) 레스토랑 요리사
(C) 디자인 매장 직원
(D) 요리 강사

해설 양식의 고객 선호 사항(Client preferences) 두 번째 항목에서 캐비닛은 고객이 샘플을 갖고 있으며 4월 3일 주문 마감일까지 저에게 알려 줄 것(Cabinets: Client ~ for ordering)이라고 한 것으로 보아 디자인 담당 직원이 작성했음 직하다. 따라서 정답은 (C)이다.

183 세부 사항

번역 양식에 따르면, 고객은 무엇을 제공해야 하는가?
(A) 계약서 서명
(B) 작업 시작 승인
(C) 자가주택자 보험 증서
(D) 두 가지 재료에 대한 결정

해설 양식의 고객 선호 사항(Client preferences) 두 번째 항목에서 캐비닛은 고객이 샘플을 갖고 있으며 4월 3일 주문 마감일까지 저에게 알려 줄 것(Cabinets: Client ~ for ordering)이라고 했고, 바닥재도 고객이 4월 3일까지 알려 줄 것(Flooring: Client ~ by April 3)이라고 했다. 따라서 고객은 4월 3일까지 캐비닛과 바닥재에 대해 결정한 사항을 업체에 알려 주어야 하므로 (D)가 정답이다.

어휘 signature 서명 proof 증거 insurance 보험

184 연계

번역 프로젝트를 위한 캐비닛을 만드는 데 사용될 것 같지 않은 재료는?
(A) 골든 오크
(B) 다크 레드우드
(C) 블랙 월넛
(D) 합성 합판

해설 제품 정보의 참고(Notes)에 블랙 월넛 캐비닛과 원목 바닥재는 소규모 지역 제조업체가 제작하는 지역 제품(Black walnut cabinets and hardwood flooring ~ regional manufacturers)이고 주문을 처리하는 데 최소 3주를 감안해 달라(Please allow a minimum ~ to fulfill orders)고 했고, 양식의 프로젝트 설명(Project description)에 고객은 새 조리대, 캐비닛, 바닥재와 가전제품을 포함하여 3주 이내에 리모델링이 완료되기를 원한다(Client wants a complete remodel ~ flooring, and appliances)고 했다. 고객이 3주 이내에 리모델링 완료를 원하고 있으므로 최소 3주가 소요되는 블랙 월넛은 캐비닛 제작에 사용되지 않을 것임을 알 수 있다. 따라서 (C)가 정답이다.

185 연계

번역 대리석과 화강암에 대해 명시된 것은?
(A) 할인 제공 대상이 아니다.
(B) 더 이상 생산되지 않는다.
(C) 한정된 색상으로만 생산된다.
(D) 고객들에게 매우 인기 있다.

해설 제품 정보의 표에 대리석과 화강암은 고급 자재(Marble – premium, Granite – premium)라고 나와 있고, 양식의 참고(Notes)에 따르면 재료 구매 시 10% 할인 쿠폰이 적용(Ten percent off ~ materials purchase)되지만 고급 소재에는 해당되지 않는다(Not valid on premium materials)고 나와 있다. 따라서 고급 소재인 대리석과 화강암은 할인 쿠폰 적용 대상이 아니므로 (A)가 정답이다.

어휘 be eligible for ~의 대상이다

186-190 기사 + 웹페이지 + 후기

알렉산드리아의 레스토랑 쇼케이스

(6월 5일)—알렉산드리아의 레스토랑 쇼케이스가 돌아왔다! **190 7월 8일부터 7월 25일까지** 알렉산드리아 지역의 참가 레스토랑들이 할인된 가격으로 세트 메뉴를 제공한다. 과거와 마찬가지로, **189 레스토랑들은 2코스 점심 메뉴를 15달러에, 2코스 저녁 메뉴를 20달러에, 3코스 저녁 메뉴를 30달러에 제공할 수 있다.** **186 손님들과 레스토랑 주인들은 모두 이 쇼케이스를 사랑한다.** 음식 애호가들은 더 저렴한 비용으로 새로운 옵션을 맛보고, **186 레스토랑들은 이때가 일년 중 식당 지역이 가장 활기찬 시기라고 말한다.**

187 알렉산드리아는 15년 전에 첫 레스토랑 쇼케이스를 열었다. 월마르 해변 마을의 비슷한 쇼케이스를 모델로 삼은 것이었다. 원래 레스토랑 8곳만이 참여했었다. **187 그 이후로 더 많은 레스토랑이 추가되고 매년 행사 일수도 늘어나면서 쇼케이스는 성장했다.** 올해는 알렉산드리아에 있는 전체 레스토랑의 약 70%인 40곳이 참여할 예정이다. 테이블을 예약하려는 사람들은 서둘러야 한다. 일부 레스토랑은 예약이 필요하고 가장 인기 있는 장소들은 예약이 빨리 찬다. 참가 레스토랑 목록을 확인하고 예약을 하려면 www.alexandriarestaurants.com/showcase를 방문하면 된다.

어휘 participating 참가하는 enthusiast 애호가 dining 식사 model 본보기로 삼다, 모방하다 extend 연장하다 reservation 예약

---

https://www.alexandriarestaurants.com/showcase/reservations

188 검색 결과 표시: 센터 시티 지역

클레어즈
프랑스 음식
점심 식사와 3코스 저녁 식사 제공
화요일-일요일 영업
(703) 555-0102로 전화 예약

프레시 피시 그릴
해산물
점심 식사와 3코스 저녁 식사 제공

월요일-일요일 영업
(703) 555-0195로 전화 예약

진이네 집
한국 음식
2코스 저녁 식사 제공
수요일-토요일 영업
(703) 555-0198로 전화 예약

189 로베르토즈 피제리아
이탈리아 음식
189 점심 식사만 제공
화요일-일요일 영업
예약 필요 없음

어휘 neighborhood 지역

---

https://www.foodreviews.com/alexandria/freshfishgrill

노리 사토

190 프레시 피시 그릴을 적극 추천합니다. 거기에서 처음 먹어봤는데 음식도 훌륭할 뿐 아니라 직원들도 친절하고 능률적이었습니다. 고객 몇 분이 지역을 방문 중이셨는데 **190 다행히 레스토랑 쇼케이스 마지막 날에 예약을 할 수 있었습니다.** 우리 모두에게 아주 즐거운 경험이었습니다. 기꺼이 고객들을 그곳에 다시 모시고 갈 생각입니다.

어휘 efficient 능률적인

186 Not / True

번역 기사에서 알렉산드리아의 레스토랑 쇼케이스에 대해 언급한 것은?
(A) 알렉산드리아의 모든 레스토랑이 참여한다.
(B) 레스토랑들은 일주일에 7일 문을 연다.
(C) 레스토랑이 1년 중 가장 바쁜 때이다.
(D) 레스토랑들은 저녁에만 문을 연다.

해설 기사의 첫 단락 네 번째 문장에서 손님들과 레스토랑 주인들은 모두 이 쇼케이스를 사랑한다(Both customers ~ the showcase)고 했고, 마지막 문장에서 레스토랑들은 이때가 일년 중 식당 지역이 가장 활기찬 시기라고 말한다(restaurants report ~ at their fullest)고 했으므로 정답은 (C)이다.

> **Paraphrasing** 지문의 at their fullest
> → 정답의 the busiest time

187 추론 / 암시

번역 알렉산드리아의 첫 번째 레스토랑 쇼케이스에 대해 암시된 것은?
(A) 8년 전에 열렸다.
(B) 40개의 레스토랑이 참여했다.
(C) 월마르에서 비슷한 쇼케이스가 시작되기 전에 열렸다.
(D) 올해의 레스토랑 쇼케이스보다 기간이 짧았다.

해설 기사의 두 번째 단락 첫 문장에서 알렉산드리아는 15년 전에 첫 레스토랑 쇼케이스를 열었다(Alexandria had ~ 15 years ago)고

했고, 네 번째 문장에서 그 이후로 더 많은 레스토랑이 추가되고 매년 행사 일수도 늘어나면서 쇼케이스가 성장했다(Since then ~ the number of days each year)고 했으므로 첫 레스토랑 쇼케이스의 기간은 현재보다 더 짧음을 알 수 있다. 따라서 (D)가 정답이다.

어휘 duration 기간

> Paraphrasing 지문의 the number of days
> → 정답의 duration

188 Not / True

번역 웹페이지에 있는 모든 레스토랑에 대해 사실인 것은?
(A) 월요일에 문을 연다.
(B) 같은 종류의 음식을 제공한다.
(C) 예약이 필요하다.
(D) 같은 지역에 있다.

해설 웹페이지 상단의 검색 결과 표시에 센터 시티 근처(Showing search results for: Center City Neighborhood)라고 나와 있는 것으로 보아 웹페이지에 나열되어 있는 레스토랑은 모두 같은 지역에 있는 곳임을 알 수 있다. 따라서 (D)가 정답이다.

189 연계

번역 알렉산드리아의 레스토랑 쇼케이스 동안 로베르토즈 피제리아에서의 식사 비용은 얼마인가?
(A) 8달러
(B) 15달러
(C) 20달러
(D) 30달러

해설 기사의 첫 단락 세 번째 문장에서 레스토랑들은 2코스 점심 메뉴를 15달러에, 2코스 저녁 메뉴를 20달러에, 3코스 저녁 메뉴를 30달러에 제공할 수 있다(restaurants can offer ~ menu for $30)고 했고, 웹페이지의 하단에 로베르토즈 피제리아(Roberto's Pizzeria)는 점심 식사만 제공(Serving lunch only)한다고 나와 있으므로, 쇼케이스 기간 동안 점심 식사만 제공하는 로베르토즈 피제리아에서는 15달러에 식사를 할 수 있음을 알 수 있다. 따라서 (B)가 정답이다.

190 연계

번역 사토 씨에 대해 암시된 것은?
(A) 7월 25일에 프레시 피시 그릴에 갔다.
(B) 가족과 함께 프레시 피시 그릴에 갔다.
(C) 프레시 피시 그릴에서 여러 번 식사를 했다.
(D) 프레시 피시 그릴의 주인을 안다.

해설 기사의 두 번째 문장에서 7월 8일부터 7월 25일까지 알렉산드리아 지역의 참가 레스토랑들이 할인된 가격으로 세트 메뉴를 제공한다(From July 8 ~ discounted prices)고 했고, 후기의 첫 문장에서 사토 씨가 프레시 피시 그릴을 적극 추천한다(I highly recommend Fresh Fish Grill)며 세 번째 문장에서 다행히 레스토랑 쇼케이스 마지막 날에 예약을 할 수 있었다(was lucky enough ~ restaurant showcase)고 했다. 따라서 사토 씨는 행

사 마지막 날인 7월 25일에 프레시 피시 그릴을 방문했다는 것을 알 수 있으므로 (A)가 정답이다.

어휘 dine 식사하다

191-195 구인 광고 + 이메일 + 이메일

학생 활동 진행 담당자
롤러비 대학교
메이너드, MA 01754

업무:
- 학생회, 예술, 연극, 문화 단체, 봉사 단체, 체육 동아리 등의 캠퍼스 과외 활동 참여 촉진
- 롤러비 대학교 학생 활동 웹사이트 업데이트 및 모든 소셜 미디어 관리
- ¹⁹¹보스턴 도시 지역의 지역 스포츠 및 문화 행사에 학생 견학 편성
- 전화 응답, 이메일 응답, 미예약 방문자 응대를 통한 문의 사항 처리

¹⁹³지원하시려면 이메일에 자기소개서를 작성하고 ¹⁹⁵이력서를 첨부하여 인사 담당자에게 jobs@rollervy.edu로 보내십시오. ¹⁹³다음 사항에 답변해 주십시오.

- ¹⁹³어떤 관련 직무 경험이 있는가?
- 자신이 적임자라고 생각하는 이유는 무엇인가?
- 자신의 직업상 강점은 무엇인가?
- 어느 부분에서 개선할 수 있는가?

어휘 coordinator 진행자 promote 촉진하다 involvement 참여 extracurricular 과외의 organization 단체 athletic 운동의 coordinate 조직[편성]하다 outing 견학, 야유회 address 처리하다 inquiry 문의 walk-in 예약이 안 된 relevant 관련 있는 fit 맞는 것[사람]

수신: 일자리 〈jobs@rollervy.edu〉
발신: 사만다 브래드버리 〈sambradbury25@rapidonet.com〉
날짜: 9월 10일
제목: 학생 활동 진행 담당자
첨부: ⏸이력서

관계자께,

¹⁹³⁽ᴬ⁾롤러비 대학교에서는 활동을 조율하고, 학생들의 참여를 촉진하며, 전문적인 고객 서비스를 제공할 사람을 찾고 있습니다. 저는 파바톤 대학교에서 캠퍼스 레크리에이션 관리자로 재직하는 동안 ¹⁹³이 세 가지를 모두 담당했습니다.

¹⁹²파바톤 대학에서 저는 학생 활동 참여도를 37% 늘렸습니다. 또한 달리기 동아리를 창설했고 캠퍼스 외부 견학을 기획했습니다. 저는 대학 지도 강사와 학교 공부에 도움이 필요한 지역 고등학생들을 짝지어 주는 프로젝트를 포함한 자원봉사 활동에 큰 중점을 두었습니다.

전반적으로, ¹⁹³⁽ᴮ⁾,⁽ᶜ⁾저는 제가 이 자리에 훌륭한 적임자라고 믿습니다. 저는 시간을 엄수하고, 꼼꼼하며, 학생들과 학교간 연결을 증진시키는 데 열성적입니다. 면접 가능성에 대해 답변을 듣게 되기를 기대합니다.

사만다 브래드버리

수신: 사만다 브래드버리 〈sambradbury25@rapidonet.com〉
195발신: 리사 쿠퍼 〈jobs@rollervy.edu〉
날짜: 10월 2일
제목: 면접

사만다 씨께,

195학생 활동 진행 담당자직을 위한 면접을 보실 수 있는지 확인하고 자 글을 씁니다. 당신의 예비 면접은 온라인상으로 진행될 예정입니다. 194다음 단계에 선발되실 경우 2차 면접은 롤러비 대학 본교에서 대면 으로 진행될 것입니다. 아직 관심이 있으시면 10월 8일 또는 10월 9일 오전 9시에 시간이 되는지에 대해 회신해 주십시오.

리사 쿠퍼

191 세부 사항

번역 구인 광고에 따르면, 학생 활동 진행 담당자의 업무 중 한 가지는?
(A) 학생들의 어려운 과제를 돕는 일
(B) 지역 행사에 대해 학생들에게 알리는 일
(C) 학생들의 발표 수행 교육
(D) 웹사이트 개발에 대한 워크숍 진행

해설 구인 광고의 업무 세 번째 항목에서 보스턴 도시 지역의 지역 스 포츠 및 문화 행사에 학생 견학을 편성(Coordinates student ~ metropolitan area)한다고 했으므로 (B)가 정답이다.

어휘 assignment 과제 inform 알리다

192 세부 사항

번역 첫번째 이메일에 따르면, 브래드버리 씨가 학생 참여를 촉진시킨 한 가지 방법은?
(A) 지역 레크리에이션 센터에서 자원봉사를 했다.
(B) 여러 문화 탐방에 참여했다.
(C) 고등학생을 지도 교사로 채용했다.
(D) 스포츠 동아리를 시작했다.

해설 첫 번째 이메일의 두 번째 단락 첫 번째 문장에서 자신이 학생 활 동 참여도를 37% 늘렸다(I increased participation ~ by 37 percent)며, 달리기 동아리도 창설했다(I also created a running club)고 했으므로 정답은 (D)이다.

Paraphrasing 지문의 created a running club
→ 정답의 started a sports group

193 연계

번역 브래드버리 씨가 자기소개서에서 누락한 정보는?
(A) 관련 직무 경험
(B) 직책에 대한 관심
(C) 직업상 강점
(D) 개선해야 할 분야

해설 구인 광고의 두 번째 단락에서 지원하려면 이메일에 자기소개서 를 작성(To apply ~ in an e-mail)하고 다음 사항에 답변하라 (Please address the following)며 어떤 관련 직무 경험이 있는지 (What relevant ~ you have?), 자신이 적임자라고 생각하는 이유 는 무엇인지(Why do ~ the position?), 자신의 직업상 강점은 무 엇인지(What are ~ strengths?), 어느 부분에서 개선할 수 있는 지(In which ~ you improve?)에 대한 질문을 제시했고, 첫 이메 일에서 브래드버리 씨는 롤러비 대학교에서 활동을 조율하고, 학생 들의 참여를 촉진하며 전문적인 고객 서비스를 제공할 사람을 찾고 있는데(Rollervy University ~ customer service) 자신은 이 세 가지를 모두 담당했다(I did all three)며 직무 경험, 자신이 이 자 리에 훌륭한 적임자라고 믿는다(I believe ~ available position) 며 직책에 대한 관심, 시간을 엄수하고, 꼼꼼하며, 학생들과 학교 간 연결을 증진시키는 데 열성적(I am punctual ~ academic institution)이라며 강점에 대해 언급했다. 구인 광고에 제시된 질문 중 개선해야 할 부분에 대한 답변은 없으므로 정답은 (D)이다.

194 Not / True

번역 두 번째 이메일에서 채용 과정에 대해 명시한 것은?
(A) 모든 지원자는 온라인으로 양식을 작성해야 한다.
(B) 지원자들은 두 장의 추천서를 제출해야 한다.
(C) 일부 지원자들은 대면 면접을 볼 것이다.
(D) 4년제 학위를 소지한 지원자가 선호된다.

해설 두 번째 이메일의 세 번째 문장에서 다음 단계에 선발될 경우 2차 면접은 롤러비 대학 본교에서 대면으로 진행될 것(If selected ~ main campus)이라고 했으므로 지원자 중 1차 면접 통과자만 대면 면접을 보는 것이므로 (C)가 정답이다.

어휘 applicant 지원자 fill in 작성하다 reference letter 추천서 degree 학위

195 연계

번역 쿠퍼 씨는 누구일 것 같은가?
(A) 인사 담당자
(B) 사무 보조원
(C) 대학 입학 상담원
(D) 학생 활동 진행 담당자

해설 구인 광고의 두 번째 단락 첫 문장에서 이력서를 첨부하여 인사 담 당자에게 jobs@rollervy.edu로 보내라(To apply, write your cover letter ~ at jobs@rollervy.edu)고 했고, 두 번째 이메일 의 발신인이 리사 쿠퍼 〈jobs@rollervy.edu〉로 첫 문장에서 학생 활동 진행 담당자직을 위한 면접을 볼 수 있는지 확인하고자 글을 쓴다(I am writing to check Student Activities Coordinator position)며 인사 관련 업무에 대해 언급하고 있으므로 쿠퍼 씨는 구인 광고에 언급된 인사 담당자임을 알 수 있다. 따라서 (A)가 정답 이다.

196-200 이메일 + 회의 안건 + 정책

수신: 셀레스테 오브라이언
197발신: 모니카 청
날짜: 10월 15일
196제목: 휴대폰 환급 정책

오브라이언 씨께,

197회계부 차장으로서 저는 휴대 전화 비용 관련 정책에 대해 글을 쓰고자 합니다. 많은 퍼드 데이터 서비스 직원이 업무 통화를 위해 개인 휴대 전화를 사용합니다. 환급을 받기 위해서는 매달 양식을 제출해야 합니다. 그리고 나면 퍼드는 전화 비용의 30%까지 지급합니다. 우리 부서는 각 직원의 산정액을 확인하고 매달 변동되는 지급일을 정합니다.

196일부 기업들은 정액 요금제로 전환하여 자격이 되는 모든 직원이 매달 고정 금액(예: 20달러)을 받습니다. 월별 처리에 직원 시간이 소요되지 않으며, 수당은 각 급여에 자동으로 포함됩니다.

196,198인사부 부서장으로서 이러한 정책의 채택을 고려해 주시길 바랍니다.

모니카 청

어휘 reimbursement 환급 expense 비용 reimburse 환급하다 calculation 계산, 산출 vary 달라지다 flat-rate 정액 요금 whereby (그에 따라) ~하는 qualify 자격을 얻다 fixed 고정된 processing 처리 allowance 수당 paycheck 급여 adopt 채택하다

퍼드 데이터 서비스
회의 안건

장소: 온라인
200날짜: 10월 24일
시간: 오후 3시
198진행자: 셀레스테 오브라이언, 인사 담당 부사장
198참석자: 인사 담당자, 재무 담당자, 부서장

목표:
1. 현재 휴대 전화 환급 프로그램의 문제 고려
2. 장단점과 함께 다른 옵션 검토
3. **198적합할 시, 새로운 환급제 채택**

옵션:
1. 직원들의 업무용 휴대 전화 사용의 최대 30%에 대한 환급을 지속한다.
2. **200자격이 있는 직원들에게 매월 고정 금액을 지급하고, 비용이 높은 직원은 추가 보상 신청서를 제출할 수 있다.**
3. **200자격이 있는 직원들에게 업무용 휴대 전화를 제공한다.**

어휘 agenda 안건 host 진행자 attendee 참석자 objective 목표 advantage 장점 disadvantage 단점 appropriate 적절한 compensation 보상 qualified 자격이 있는

퍼드 데이터 서비스 직원 정책

휴대 전화 환급 정책
10월 30일 개정

원격 근무 및/또는 업무상 출장을 가는 직원은 휴대 전화의 업무용 사용에 대해 환급을 받게 됩니다. 세 가지 옵션이 가능합니다:

- **200자격이 있는 직원은** 실제 비용에 상관없이 월 20달러의 휴대 전화 수당을 받게 됩니다. 프로그램에 등록하려면 직원은 상사의 서명이 포함된 휴대 전화 수당 양식을 제출해야 합니다. 20달러 수당은 매월 급여에 적용될 것입니다.

- **200요금이 높은 직원은** 실제 비용을 제출하여 추가 환급을 받을 수 있습니다.

- **199,200관리자 및 임원은** 업무용으로만 사용할 수 있는 회사 휴대 전화를 선택할 수 있습니다.

어휘 remotely 원격으로 purpose 목적 regardless of ~에 상관없이 enroll in ~에 등록하다 supervisor 상관 signature 서명 apply 적용하다 charge 요금 executive 임원 opt for 선택하다

---

196 주제 / 목적

번역 이메일의 목적은?
(A) 직원 행동 패턴 설명
(B) 특정 기술에 대한 업데이트 제안
(C) 납품업체 교체에 대한 고려
(D) 환급 정책에 대한 개정 요청

해설 이메일의 제목이 휴대폰 환급 정책(Subject ~ policy)이고, 두 번째 단락의 첫 문장에서 일부 기업들은 정액 요금제로 전환하여 자격이 되는 모든 직원이 매달 고정 금액을 받는다(Some companies ~ each month)고 타사 정책을 소개하며 마지막 단락에서 인사부 부서장으로서 이러한 정책의 채택을 고려해 주길 바란다(I hope ~ a policy like this)고 했다. 따라서 이메일은 환급 정책의 개정을 요청하기 위한 것이므로 (D)가 정답이다.

어휘 describe 설명하다 behavior 행동 vendor 판매업체 revision 개정

197 세부 사항

번역 이메일에 따르면, 청 씨는 누구인가?
(A) 텔레마케터
(B) 회계 팀 직원
(C) 인사 담당자
(D) 전자 기술자

해설 이메일의 발신인이 모니카 청(From: Monica Cheung)이고 첫 문장에서 자신이 회계부 차장(As the Assistant Director of Accounting, I)이라고 언급했으므로 (B)가 정답이다.

Paraphrasing 지문의 Assistant Director of Accounting → 정답의 A member of the accounting team

TEST 3 **57**

198 연계

번역 오브라이언 씨가 청 씨의 이메일을 받은 뒤 한 일은?
(A) 청 씨를 회의에 초대했다.
(B) 청 씨의 제안을 거절했지만 대안을 제시했다.
(C) 문제를 해결하기 위해 다른 회사 관리자들과 협력했다.
(D) 다른 부서로 이동했다.

해설 이메일의 마지막 문장에서 오브라이언 씨는 인사부 부서장으로서 이러한 정책의 채택을 고려해 주길 바란다(I hope ~ a policy like this)는 요청을 받았고, 회의 안건에 따르면 진행자는 셀레스테 오브라이언 인사 담당 부사장(Host: Celeste ~ Human Resources), 참석자는 인사 담당자, 재무 담당자, 부서장(Attendees ~ Department Heads)이며 회의 목표의 3번에 적합할 시 새로운 환급제 채택(Select a new ~ if appropriate)이라고 나와 있다. 따라서 오브라이언 씨는 이메일에서 요청받은 대로 정책 전환 문제를 놓고 회사 관리자들과 논의했으므로 (C)가 정답이다.

어휘 reject 거절하다 alternative 대안 address 해결하다 transfer 이동하다

Paraphrasing	지문의 Human Resources Managers ~ Department Heads → 정답의 company leaders

199 세부 사항

번역 정책에 따르면, 회사 휴대 전화를 받을 자격이 되는 사람은 누구인가?
(A) 퍼드 데이터 서비스 관리자 및 임원
(B) 재택근무를 하는 모든 퍼드 데이터 서비스 직원
(C) 업무상 출장을 가는 직원
(D) 월별 양식을 제출하는 직원

해설 정책의 마지막 문장에서 관리자 및 임원은 업무용으로만 사용할 수 있는 회사 휴대 전화를 선택할 수 있다(Managers and ~ business use only)고 했으므로 정답은 (A)이다.

어휘 work from home 재택근무하다

200 연계

번역 10월 24일 회의 결과를 가장 잘 설명한 것은?
(A) 참석자들은 원래의 절차를 계속 따르기로 합의했다.
(B) 참석자들은 결정을 내리기 전에 더 많은 정보를 수집하기로 결정했다.
(C) 참석자들은 논의된 옵션 중 일부를 채택하기로 결정했다.
(D) 참석자들은 휴대폰 사용에 대해 설문 조사를 완료했다.

해설 회의 안건에 따르면 회의 날짜가 10월 24일(Date: October 24)이고, 옵션 2에 자격이 있는 직원들에게 매월 고정 금액을 지급하고 비용이 높은 직원은 추가 보상 신청서를 제출할 수 있다(Provide a flat ~ additional compensation), 옵션 3에 자격이 있는 직원들에게 업무용 휴대 전화를 제공한다(Provide qualified ~ business use)는 내용이 나와 있고, 정책의 첫 항목에 자격이 있는 직원은 실제 비용에 상관없이 월 20달러의 휴대 전화 수당을 받게 된다(Employees who ~ actual expenses), 두 번째 항목에 요금이 높은 직원은 실제 비용을 제출하여 추가 환급을 받을 수 있다(Employees with ~ reimbursement), 세 번째 항목에 관리자 및 임원은 업무용으로 사용할 수 있는 회사 휴대 전화를 선택할 수 있다(Managers and ~ use only)고 나와 있다. 회의 안건에 나온 옵션 2, 옵션 3의 내용이 정책에 언급되어 있고 옵션 1에 대한 내용은 빠져 있는 것으로 보아 논의된 옵션 중 일부가 채택되었다고 볼 수 있으므로 (C)가 정답이다.

실전 TEST 4

101 (B)	**102** (A)	**103** (B)	**104** (D)	**105** (A)
106 (D)	**107** (C)	**108** (A)	**109** (D)	**110** (D)
111 (A)	**112** (C)	**113** (D)	**114** (A)	**115** (A)
116 (B)	**117** (D)	**118** (C)	**119** (A)	**120** (C)
121 (B)	**122** (C)	**123** (A)	**124** (D)	**125** (B)
126 (A)	**127** (D)	**128** (C)	**129** (B)	**130** (C)
131 (A)	**132** (A)	**133** (D)	**134** (D)	**135** (D)
136 (B)	**137** (A)	**138** (D)	**139** (A)	**140** (A)
141 (C)	**142** (D)	**143** (B)	**144** (C)	**145** (A)
146 (D)	**147** (B)	**148** (D)	**149** (D)	**150** (C)
151 (D)	**152** (B)	**153** (B)	**154** (C)	**155** (A)
156 (D)	**157** (C)	**158** (B)	**159** (C)	**160** (A)
161 (C)	**162** (D)	**163** (A)	**164** (B)	**165** (A)
166 (C)	**167** (B)	**168** (A)	**169** (B)	**170** (B)
171 (A)	**172** (C)	**173** (B)	**174** (D)	**175** (B)
176 (C)	**177** (A)	**178** (B)	**179** (D)	**180** (C)
181 (B)	**182** (D)	**183** (C)	**184** (A)	**185** (B)
186 (B)	**187** (A)	**188** (D)	**189** (C)	**190** (D)
191 (D)	**192** (D)	**193** (C)	**194** (C)	**195** (B)
196 (A)	**197** (D)	**198** (B)	**199** (C)	**200** (D)

PART 5

101 명사 자리 _ 동사의 목적어

해설 빈칸은 동사 report의 목적어 역할을 하며 형용사 significant의 수식을 받는 명사 자리이므로 정답은 명사인 (B) improvements 이다.

번역 소프트웨어 업데이트 후 속도와 신뢰도가 크게 향상되었다고 우리 고객들은 말합니다.

어휘 report 알리다, 전하다 significant 상당한 reliability 신뢰도

102 전치사 어휘

해설 빈칸 뒤의 명사구 the project plan을 목적어로 취해 '프로젝트 계획에 명시된'이라는 내용이 되어야 하므로 '~에'를 뜻하는 (A) in이 정답이다.

번역 맥닐 언리미티드의 시장 프로필은 프로젝트 계획에 명시된 기한 전에 완료되었다.

103 인칭대명사의 격 _ 소유격

해설 빈칸은 as long as가 이끄는 절의 주어 자리이므로 명사 requests 를 수식할 수 있는 한정사가 와야 한다. 따라서 소유격 인칭대명사인 (B) their가 정답이다.

번역 직원은 사전에 그들의 요청이 승인된다면 한 번에 최대 2주까지 휴가를 낼 수 있다.

어휘 at a time 한 번에 approve 승인하다 in advance 미리, 사전에

104 형용사 어휘

해설 빈칸 뒤의 명사 contact를 수식하여 '주요 연락처'라는 의미가 되어야 적합하므로 '주요한'을 뜻하는 (D) primary가 정답이다.

번역 서비스 담당자는 각 고객의 주요 연락처가 되는 역할을 담당한다.

어휘 representative 대리인 abundant 풍부한

105 명사 자리 _ 동사의 주어

해설 빈칸 앞에 정관사 The가 있으므로 빈칸은 명사 자리이다. 문맥상 '모금 행사의 취소'라는 내용이 되어야 하므로 '취소'라는 뜻의 추상 명사 (A) cancellation이 정답이다.

번역 모금 행사가 취소된 것은 악천후 때문이므로 행사는 다음 주말로 일정이 변경될 예정이다.

어휘 fund-raiser 모금 행사

106 부사 어휘

해설 목적격 보어로 쓰인 원형부정사 master를 수식하여 '더 효과적으로 통달하도록'이라는 의미가 되어야 하므로 '효과적으로'라는 뜻의 (D) effectively가 정답이다.

번역 AVB 에듀케이션의 온라인 과정은 사용자들이 다른 학습 방법보다 더 효과적으로 많은 컴퓨터 기술에 통달할 수 있도록 도와줍니다.

어휘 method 방법 nearly 거의 lightly 가볍게 previously 전에

107 명사 자리 _ 동사의 주어

해설 동사 attracted의 주어가 되는 명사 자리이다. 문맥상 '유명 인사들이 있다는 점'이라는 내용이 되어야 하므로 '있음, 존재'라는 뜻의 추상명사 (C) presence가 정답이다.

번역 사사키 박물관에 여러 유명 인사가 있다는 점은 사진을 원하는 지역 주민들의 마음을 끌었다.

108 동사 어휘

해설 부사 enthusiastically의 수식을 받아 문맥상 '보조금 신청을 적극 승인했다'는 내용이 되어야 자연스러우므로 '승인하다'는 뜻의 (A) approved가 정답이다.

번역 위원회가 극단의 보조금 신청을 적극 승인한 것은 지역 사회의 참여를 장려하고 있기 때문이다.

어휘 enthusiastically 열성적으로 grant 보조금 application 신청 participation 참여 practice 실행하다

109 부사 자리 _ 동사 수식

해설 '(일이 어떻게) 진행되다'는 뜻일 때 자동사 go는 'go+부사/전치사구'의 형태로 쓰인다. '계획대로 진행되고 있다'는 의미의 이미 완전한 문장에 빈칸이 있으므로 부사가 들어가면 된다. 따라서 '정확하게'라는 뜻의 부사 (D) precisely가 정답이다.

번역 이브라힘 씨는 경영진에게 연례 주주 총회 준비가 계획대로 정확히 진행되고 있다고 말했다.

어휘 preparation 준비   shareholder 주주

110 전치사 어휘

해설 문맥상 '소포의 무게'라는 의미가 되어야 적절하므로 '~의'를 뜻하는 (D) of가 정답이다.

번역 에어릭스코의 배송비는 목적지와 소포의 무게에 따라 달라진다.

어휘 vary 달라지다   based upon ~에 근거하여   destination 목적지   weight 무게

111 형용사 자리 _ 명사 수식

해설 빈칸 앞에는 부정관사 a, 뒤에는 명사 server가 있으므로 명사를 수식하는 형용사 (A) secure가 정답이다.

번역 우리 고객의 건강 기록은 승인된 사용자만 열람할 수 있는 보안 서버에 저장됩니다.

어휘 store 저장하다   accessible 접근[이용] 가능한   authorized 승인된

112 명사 어휘

해설 '충족시키다'는 뜻의 동사 meet는 '요건, 요구'를 뜻하는 명사가 목적어로 와야 자연스럽다. 빈칸 앞의 installation과 함께 복합명사를 이루어 '설치 요건을 충족시킨다'는 내용이 되어야 하므로 '요건'을 의미하는 (C) requirements가 정답이다.

번역 난방 회사와 계약을 맺기 전에 그 회사의 제안이 우리의 설치 요건을 충족하는지 확인해야 한다.

어휘 installation 설치

113 현재분사

해설 문장에 본동사 is가 있으므로 빈칸부터 headquarters까지는 The area를 수식하는 수식어구임을 알 수 있다. 문맥상 '새로운 본사를 둘러싼 지역'이 되어야 하므로 '둘러싸는'을 의미하는 현재분사 (D) surrounding이 정답이다. 이때 현재분사는 앞에 놓인 명사 area를 수식하며, 뒤에 놓인 the new Furniture Vine headquarters를 목적어로 취한다. 참고로 among은 복수명사 앞에서 '여러 개 사이에'를 뜻하는데 headquarters는 그 자체로 본사를 의미하므로 의미가 맞지 않다.

번역 퍼니처 바인의 새로운 본사를 둘러싸고 있는 구역은 울창한 숲으로 덮여 있다.

어휘 headquarters 본사   dense 빽빽한   foreseeable 예측할 수 있는

114 형용사 어휘

해설 명사 future를 수식하여 '번영하는 미래'라는 의미가 되어야 적절하므로 '번영하는'이라는 뜻의 (A) prosperous가 정답이다.

번역 회사의 최고 분석가들은 밸류웨스트사의 인수가 주주들에게 번영하는 미래를 가져다줄 것으로 기대한다.

어휘 acquisition 인수   shareholder 주주   voluntary 자발적인   sizable 상당한 크기의   calculating 계산적인

115 전치사 자리

해설 빈칸은 완전한 절에 명사구 any concerns를 연결하는 자리로 전치사가 들어가야 하므로 부사인 (B) afterward와 접속사인 (D) as soon as는 답이 될 수 없다. 문맥상 '우려 사항과 관련하여'라는 내용이 되어야 하므로 '~에 관하여'를 뜻하는 전치사 (A) regarding이 정답이다.

번역 합의서 초안을 검토하는 대로 수석 변호사가 우려 사항과 관련하여 관 씨의 팀에 통지할 것이다.

어휘 draft 초안   notify 통지하다   afterward 후에

116 동사 어휘

해설 career-building workshops를 목적어로 받아 '워크숍을 제공한다'는 문맥이 되어야 자연스러우므로 '제공하다'는 의미의 (B) providing이 정답이다.

번역 2년간의 공백 후, 그리어 연구소는 다시 한번 의료 종사자들을 위한 경력 개발 워크숍을 제공한다.

117 형용사 자리 _ 명사 수식

해설 빈칸 앞에는 소유격, 뒤에는 명사 prices가 있으므로 명사를 수식하는 형용사가 와야 한다. 가격을 수식하여 '경쟁력 있는 가격'이라는 뜻이 적합하므로 (D) competitive가 정답이다.

번역 시더 레이크 호텔은 성장하는 시장에서 점유율을 높이기 위한 시도로 경쟁력 있는 가격을 조정했다.

어휘 adjust 조정하다   in an attempt to부정사 ~하려는 시도로   share 점유율

118 명사 어휘

해설 빈칸 앞 형용사 local과 빈칸 뒤 과거분사 enforced의 수식을 받고 있으므로 '시행되는 지역 규제'라는 의미가 적합하다. 따라서 정답은 '규정'을 뜻하는 (C) regulations이다.

번역 빅 미드웨스트 카페의 운영 시간은 카페가 위치한 시에서 시행되는 지역 규정에 따른다.

어휘 be subject to ~의 대상이다   enforce (법률 등을) 시행하다   fragment 조각   equality 평등

119 동사의 시제

해설 The legal department가 주어, 빈칸이 동사 자리인 절 끝에 과거를 나타내는 시간 부사구 last week가 나왔으므로 동사는 과거 시제가 되어야 한다. 따라서 (A) completed가 정답이다.

번역 법무부는 지난주에 개정안의 수정을 완료했고 쾰러 씨는 검토를 위해 이 수정안을 기업 그룹에 보냈다.

어휘 revision 수정 amendment (법 등의) 개정[수정]안

120 명사 어휘

해설 동사 asked의 목적어 자리로 요청 대상이 되는 사람명사가 와야
한다. 따라서 '참가자'를 뜻하는 (C) participants가 정답이다.

번역 아리아타 씨는 어제 있었던 생산성과 기술 워크숍의 모든 참가자들에
게 설문지를 제출해 달라고 요청했다.

어휘 productivity 생산성 questionnaire 설문지 objective 목적

121 부사 자리 _ 형용사 수식

해설 빈칸은 2형식 동사 taste와 보어 역할을 하는 형용사 different 사
이에서 형용사를 수식하는 부사 자리이다. 따라서 정답은 '구별 가능
하게'라는 뜻의 (B) distinguishably이다.

번역 소비자들은 써니사이드 초콜릿이 다른 모든 초콜릿과 구별될 정도로
다른 맛이 난다는 점을 알았다.

어휘 consumer 소비자 distinguish 구별하다

122 동사 어휘

해설 동사 plans의 목적어 역할을 하는 to부정사에 들어갈 동사 어휘를
고르는 문제이다. the number of bicycle lanes를 목적어로 받아
'자전거 도로의 수를 늘릴 계획'이라는 내용이 되어야 자연스러우므
로 '확대하다'는 뜻의 (C) expand가 정답이다.

번역 자전거 타기가 어느 때보다 더 인기를 끌고 있어 시 의회는 도시 거리
에 자전거 도로의 수를 늘릴 계획이다.

어휘 lane 도로, 차선 generate 발생시키다 invent 발명하다
organize 조직하다

123 동사 자리 _ 복합문제

해설 that절의 주어는 equipment ~ suppliers이며, equipment 뒤
에 온 ordered는 목적어가 없으므로 동사가 아니라 앞에 온 명사
equipment를 수식하는 분사임을 파악해야 한다. 따라서 빈칸에는
빈칸 뒤의 safety standards를 목적어로 취하는 능동태 동사가 와
야 하므로 정답은 '충족시키다'를 뜻하는 (A) meets이다.

번역 클러스턴 인더스트리의 지침은 모든 공급업체로부터 주문한 장비가
안전 기준을 충족시키는지 확인하는 데 도움이 된다.

어휘 guideline 지침 supplier 공급업체

124 부사 어휘

해설 콤마 뒤에 오는 절에서 특별 임무가 있을 때는 메이 씨가 대신한다며
예외가 되는 경우에 대해 언급하고 있으므로 빈칸이 있는 절은 '다
이유 씨가 보통 고객 문의를 담당한다'는 내용이 되어야 한다. 따라
서 '보통, 평소'라는 의미의 (D) usually가 정답이다.

번역 다이유 씨는 보통 고객 문의를 담당하지만 관리자로부터 특별 임무를
받을 때는 메이 씨가 대신한다.

어휘 inquiry 문의 take over 인계받다 assignment 임무, 과제

125 동사 자리 _ 복합문제

해설 조동사인 can 뒤에는 동사원형이 와야 한다. 또한 타동사인
pursue(추구하다)의 뒤에 목적어가 보이지 않으므로 수동태가 와
야 한다. 따라서 (B) be pursued가 정답이다.

번역 아크시카 메디컬은 비용과 이익에 대한 면밀한 분석 없이는 성장의
기회를 추구할 수 없다.

126 상관접속사

해설 not only가 문제 해결의 단서로, 문맥상 '매출뿐 아니라 혁신에 있어
서도'라는 의미가 되어야 한다. 따라서 not only와 상관접속사를 이
루어 'A뿐 아니라 B도'라는 의미를 나타내는 (A) but also가 정답
이다.

번역 메이슨 테크놀로지는 매출뿐 아니라 수상 경력이 있는 혁신에 있어서
도 경쟁사를 앞지르고 있다.

어휘 revenue 수익 award-winning 수상을 한

127 상관접속사

해설 and가 문제 해결의 단서로, 문맥상 '이론적 측면과 실질적 측면 둘
다'라는 의미가 되어야 한다. 따라서 and와 상관접속사를 이루어 'A
와 B 둘 다'라는 뜻을 나타내는 (D) both가 정답이다.

번역 우리의 발표는 기계 학습의 이론적 측면과 실질적 측면 모두에 대한
개요를 제공할 것이다.

어휘 overview 개요 theoretical 이론적인 practical 실질적인
aspect 측면

128 부사 어휘

해설 접속사 as와 비교급 more를 통해 '더 ~함에 따라'라는 의미를 잡
을 수 있고, 동사 '증가하다(increase)'를 수식하는 부사 자리이므로
'점점 늘어난다'라는 의미가 적합하다. 따라서 '점차적으로'를 뜻하
는 (C) progressively가 정답이다.

번역 스트림라인 자동차 공장 신임 조립 라인 관리자의 책임은 경험이 더
쌓일수록 점차 늘어난다.

어휘 assembly-line 조립 라인의 supervisor 관리자 gain 얻다
diligently 부지런히 cooperatively 협동하여

129 동사의 시제

해설 주절에 과거 시제(opened)가 왔고, 빈칸 앞에 '처음에(initially)'
를 뜻하는 과거 시간 부사가 있으므로 빈칸에는 opened와 일치
하는 과거 시제, 또는 opened보다 먼저 일어난 일이므로 과거완
료 시제가 올 수 있다. 따라서 정답은 동사의 과거형으로 쓰인 (B)
complicated이다.

번역 비록 예기치 못한 요인들이 처음에 풍력 발전소의 건설을 복잡하게
만들었지만 발전소는 예정대로 문을 열었다.

어휘 unforeseen 예기치 못한 factor 요인 initially 처음에 wind
farm 풍력 발전소 complicate 복잡하게 만들다

130 복합관계사

해설 빈칸 뒤에 완전한 절이 왔으므로 접속사가 필요하고, 문맥상 '하루토는 기회를 볼 때마다'라는 의미가 되어야 하므로 부사절 접속사로 쓰인 복합관계부사 (C) Whenever가 정답이다.

번역 하루토는 전문적으로 발전할 수 있는 기회를 볼 때마다 반드시 그것을 활용한다.

어휘 take advantage of ~을 활용하다 owing to ~ 때문에 whereas ~인 반면에

PART 6

131-134 웹페이지

에버그린 산악 관광 철도

에버그린 산악 관광 철도가 1년간의 보수 공사 끝에 재개장했다. 100여 년 전에 처음 건설된 이 철도는 국내에서 가장 오래된 철도 중 하나이다. 최근 폐쇄는 노후한 선로와 열차를 대대적으로 업그레이드하기 위해 필수적이었다. **131또한** 유서 깊은 역사에도 보수 공사가 이루어졌다.

이 철도의 관광객은 기차를 **132타고** 에버그린 숲을 통과하여 월든산 꼭대기까지 가는 여행을 즐긴다. 여기서 기차는 방문객들이 새로운 방문객 센터를 둘러보거나 아니면 **133간단히** 이 지역에서 가장 높은 산에서 바라보는 경관을 즐길 수 있도록 한 시간 동안 정차한다. 돌아오는 길에는 역까지 다른 경로를 통해 온다. **134전체 여행은 약 두 시간 반 정도 소요된다.** 이 멋진 여정을 위한 탑승권은 온라인에서 구매 가능하다.

어휘 scenic 경치가 좋은 yearlong 1년간의 century 세기 closure 폐쇄 extensive 광범위한 aging 노후한 track 선로 sightseer 관광객 hour-long 1시간의 journey 여정

---

131 접속부사

해설 앞 문장에서 최근 폐쇄는 노후한 선로와 열차를 대대적으로 업그레이드하기 위해 필수적이었다고 했고, 뒤 문장에서 역사에도 보수 공사가 이루어졌다며 철도 및 열차뿐 아니라 역사 또한 보수되었음을 언급하고 있다. 따라서 '게다가, 또한'을 뜻하는 (A) Additionally가 정답이다.

132 동사의 수 일치

해설 빈칸은 부사절 접속사 as절의 동사 자리이며, 주어가 they이므로 복수동사가 와야 한다. 따라서 (A) ride가 정답이다.

133 부사 자리 _ 동사 수식

해설 빈칸은 등위접속사 or로 연결된 to부정사구에서 to가 생략된 동사 enjoy를 수식하는 자리이다. 따라서 부사인 (D) simply가 정답이다.

134 문맥에 맞는 문장 고르기

해설 빈칸 앞에서 철도의 관광객은 숲을 지나 산꼭대기까지 기차를 타고 가며 한 시간 동안 정차하고 다른 경로로 되돌아온다고 했다. 앞 내용에서 철도 여행의 경로에 대해 안내하고 있으므로, 이 여행에 걸리는 소요 시간에 대해 안내하는 내용이 연결되어야 자연스럽다. 따라서 전체 여행은 두 시간 반 정도 소요된다고 언급하고 있는 (D)가 정답이다.

번역 (A) 보수 공사는 예상보다 더 오래 걸렸다.
(B) 월든산은 에버그린 산맥에서 가장 높다.
(C) 근처의 다른 산에는 관광 명소가 없다.
(D) 전체 여행은 약 두 시간 반 정도 소요된다.

어휘 nearby 근처의 tourist attraction 관광 명소 approximately 대략

135-138 이메일

수신: 마커스 위트 〈mwitt@bmail.com〉
발신: 줄리 멘델 〈contracts@nevycorp.com〉
날짜: 6월 1일
제목: 네비와의 계약
첨부: 갱신 양식

위트 씨께:

네비사에서 인사 말씀드립니다. 별일 없이 잘 지내고 계시기를 바랍니다.

최근 통화에서 말씀드렸듯이, 우리는 현재 **135협력사들**에 대해 검토하고 있습니다. 여기에는 귀하의 대행사도 포함됩니다. 힘들었던 한 해 **136에도 불구하고**, 귀하의 대행사가 보여준 전문성과 긍정적인 결과에 깊은 인상을 받았습니다. **137따라서 우리는 귀하와의 계약을 2년 더 연장하기를 원합니다.** 첨부된 서류에 서명한 뒤 가급적 빨리 저희 측에 보내주십시오.

우리는 귀하와 귀하의 팀과의 관계를 강화하기를 **138기대합니다.** 문의나 우려 사항이 있으시면 알려 주십시오.

줄리 멘델
협력 관계 관리자

어휘 renewal 갱신 greetings 인사(말) conduct 수행[실시]하다 impressed 인상 깊게 생각하는 at your earliest convenience 가급적 빨리 strengthen 강화하다

---

135 명사 어휘

해설 빈칸에는 현재 검토 중인 대상이 들어가야 하는데, 뒤 문장에서 검토 대상에 귀하의 대행사(your agency)도 포함된다고 했다. 따라서 대행사를 나타낼 수 있는 단어로 '협력사'를 뜻하는 (D) partnerships가 정답이다.

136 전치사 자리

해설 빈칸은 쉼표 뒤 완전한 절에 명사구 the difficult year를 연결하는 자리이므로 전치사가 들어가야 한다. 문맥상 '힘들었던 한 해에도 불

구하고'라는 내용이 되어야 자연스러우므로 '~에도 불구하고'를 뜻하는 전치사 (B) Despite가 정답이다.

137 문맥에 맞는 문장 고르기

해설 빈칸 앞에서 기존 협력사들을 검토 중인데 힘든 시기에도 불구하고 귀하의 대행사가 보여준 전문성과 성과가 인상적이었다고 했다. 따라서 빈칸에는 대행사에 대한 이러한 긍정적인 검토 결과에 따라 계약을 연장하기로 했다는 내용이 연결되어야 자연스러우므로 정답은 (A)이다.

번역 (A) 따라서 우리는 귀하와의 계약을 2년 더 연장하기를 원합니다.
　　 (B) 유감스럽게도, 우리는 귀하께 제때 연락할 수 없었습니다.
　　 (C) 가급적 빨리 귀하의 연락 정보를 확인해 주십시오.
　　 (D) 우리는 지난번에 대화했을 때 귀하께서 제기하신 우려를 확실히 이해합니다.

138 동사의 시제

해설 앞 문단에서 계약 연장을 제안하며 서류에 서명한 뒤 보내줄 것을 요청한 것으로 보아, 귀사와의 관계를 강화하기를 '기대한다'며 현재 시제로 현재의 입장을 나타내는 것이 자연스럽다. 따라서 정답은 (D) look이다.

139-142 광고

부엘로 피트니스에서 대폭 할인 받으세요!

부엘로 피트니스는 모든 카버 주민들의 신체적, 정신적 건강을 증진시키고자 노력하고 있습니다. 본 체육관은 지역 소유이므로 **139우리는** 여러분의 신체 건강을 극대화하는 데 필요한 관심과 지도를 제공할 것입니다. 또 한 해가 저물어 가고 **140있으므로** 건강한 신체를 가꾸는 게 어떨까요? **141여러분의 시작을 돕기 위해 두 가지 특별 할인을 제공하고 있습니다.** 하지만 서두르셔야 합니다! 이 기간 한정 할인은 12월 31일까지만 유효합니다.

부엘로 번들은 3개월 동안 단돈 100달러에 15개의 클래스로 구성되어 있습니다. 부엘로 언리미티드 패키지는 첫 달에는 단돈 10달러, 그 이후에는 매달 100달러이며, 6개월간 **142의무 계약**이 요구됩니다.

어휘 physical 신체의　own 소유하다　attention 관심
guidance 지도　maximize 극대화하다　get in shape 좋은 몸 상태[몸매]를 유지하다　valid 유효한　consist of ~로 구성되다
thereafter 그 후에

139 인칭대명사의 격 _ 주격

해설 해당 글은 부엘로 피트니스의 광고문으로 빈칸 앞 문장에서 부엘로 피트니스를 we로 지칭하고 있다. 빈칸은 will give의 주어 자리로 부엘로 피트니스가 제공하는 서비스에 대해 언급하고 있으므로 부엘로 피트니스를 지칭하는 인칭대명사 주격인 (A) we가 정답이다.

140 접속사 자리 _ 부사절 접속사

해설 빈칸 뒤에 주어와 동사를 갖춘 완전한 절이 왔으므로 접속사가 들어가야 한다. 따라서 부사절 접속사 역할을 할 수 있는 (A) As가 정답이다. 나머지는 모두 전치사이므로 오답이다.

141 문맥에 맞는 문장 고르기

해설 빈칸 앞에는 운동을 시작할 것을 제안하고 있고, 빈칸 뒤에는 할인 혜택의 기간이 한정되어 있음을 강조하고 있다. 따라서 빈칸에는 운동을 시작하기 위한 동기 부여가 될 수 있도록 할인 혜택을 제공한다는 내용이 들어가면 연결이 자연스러우므로 정답은 (C)이다.

번역 (A) 질문이 있으시면 전화 주십시오.
　　 (B) 고객들의 이러한 긍정적인 후기를 확인하십시오.
　　 (C) 여러분의 시작을 돕기 위해 두 가지 특별 할인을 제공하고 있습니다.
　　 (D) 운동은 건강한 식습관과 병행되어야 합니다.

어휘 combine 결합하다

142 명사 어휘

해설 빈칸 앞 문장에서 부엘로 언리미티드 패키지의 할인 혜택에 대해 설명하고 있고, 빈칸이 있는 문장에서는 이 패키지에 수반되는 요구 사항을 언급하고 있으므로 '이 패키지는 6개월간의 의무 계약을 요구한다'는 내용이 되어야 자연스럽다. 따라서 '약속, 계약'이라는 뜻의 (D) commitment가 정답이다.

어휘 lease 임대차 계약

143-146 이메일

수신: jliu@lle.com
발신: customersupport@gerdenbank.com
제목: 서비스 요금
날짜: 5월 27일 오전 10시 34분

리우 씨께,

당사의 내부 컴퓨터 처리 시스템 오류**143로 인해** 5월 23일에 귀하의 예금 계좌에서 서비스 요금이 잘못 출금되었습니다. 이 오류는 수정되었으며 5월 25일에 귀하의 계좌에 환불이 지급되었습니다. 이 예치금은 귀하의 다음 명세서에 "요금 조정" 항목으로 **144확인하실 수 있을 것입니다.**

이로 인해 **145혼동**이 발생했다면 사과드립니다. 이 문제와 관련하여 우려 사항이 있을 경우 연락 주십시오. **146언제나처럼 저든 은행을 선택해 주셔서 감사합니다.**

제니퍼 에이어스
고객 지원
저든 은행

어휘 internal 내부의　processing 처리　incorrectly 잘못
deduct 공제하다　savings account 예금　deposit 예치금
statement 명세서　description 기재 사항　adjustment
수정[조정]

143 전치사 어휘

해설 빈칸은 쉼표 뒤 완전한 절에 명사구 an error를 연결하는 자리로 전치사가 들어가야 하므로 부사구인 (A) In fact는 답이 될 수 없다. 문맥상 '시스템 오류 때문에 요금이 잘못 인출되었다'는 내용이 되어야 하므로 '~ 때문에'를 뜻하는 전치사구 (B) Because of가 정답이다.

144 동사의 시제

해설 빈칸의 앞 문장에서 오류가 수정되었으며 환불이 지급되었다고 했고, 빈칸이 있는 문장에는 미래의 시점을 나타내는 다음 명세서 (next statement)라는 표현이 있으므로 앞 문장에서 언급된 환불 완료된 '해당 예치금을 다음 명세서에서 확인하게 될 것'이라는 내용이 되어야 한다. 따라서 미래 시제인 (C) will find가 정답이다.

145 명사 어휘

해설 앞 내용에서 시스템 오류로 인해 요금이 잘못 인출되었으며 해당 오류에 대한 수정 조치가 완료되었음을 알리고 있다. 따라서 빈칸이 있는 문장은 앞에서 언급된 문제로 인해 '혼동이 발생했다면 사과한다'는 내용이 되어야 하므로 '혼동'을 뜻하는 (A) confusion이 정답이다.

146 문맥에 맞는 문장 고르기

해설 빈칸 앞에서 문제가 발생되었던 점에 대해 알리고 이에 대해 사과하며 문의 사항이 있다면 연락하라는 당부와 함께 글을 마무리하고 있다. 따라서 이 글의 마지막 문장으로는 자사의 서비스를 이용해 주어 감사하다는 인사말이 와야 자연스러우므로 저든 은행을 선택해 주셔서 감사하다고 언급한 (D)가 정답이다.

번역 (A) 최근 우리 고객 기반에 신규 고객 280명을 추가했습니다.
(B) 당좌 예금 계좌를 개설하실 것인지 알려 주십시오.
(C) 저든 은행은 고객들을 위한 중요한 메시지가 있습니다.
(D) 언제나처럼 저든 은행을 선택해 주셔서 감사합니다.

어휘 base 기반 checking account 당좌 예금

PART 7

147-148 회람

회람

수신: 전 직원
발신: 아마야 소디
제목: 온라인 포털
날짜: 8월 22일

147현재 온라인 포털이 운영되고 있습니다. 포털을 이용하기 위해서 환자들은 먼저 이곳 직원으로부터 활성화 번호를 받아야 합니다. 그러면 환자들은 등록하여 자신의 기록에 접근하고 실험실 결과를 받고 진료 예약을 할 수 있을 것입니다.

148우리는 또한 포털 내에 결제 옵션을 선보일 계획이었습니다. 그러나 웹 개발자들이 아직 청구 시스템 문제를 처리하는 중입니다. 결과적으

로, 해당 부분의 시스템은 나중에 시행될 것입니다.

우리 모두가 포털로 작업하는 방법을 익히는 데는 시간이 좀 걸릴 것입니다. 문의 사항이 있을 경우 내선 244번으로 마리에게 연락하십시오.

어휘 obtain 얻다 activation 활성화 register 등록하다 deal with 처리하다 billing 청구서 발부 implement 시행하다

147 추론 / 암시

번역 소디 씨는 어디에서 근무할 것 같은가?
(A) 호텔
(B) 진료소
(C) 신용 카드사
(D) 취업 알선 업체

해설 첫 문장에서 소디 씨가 현재 온라인 포털이 운영되고 있다(The online portal ~ and running)며 포털을 이용하기 위해서 환자들은 먼저 이곳 직원으로부터 활성화 번호를 받아야 한다(To use it ~ member here)고 한 것으로 보아 소디 씨가 근무하고 있는 이곳은 병원임을 알 수 있다. 따라서 정답은 (B)이다.

148 세부 사항

번역 무엇이 지연되었는가?
(A) 소프트웨어 업데이트
(B) 신입 사원 채용
(C) 마리에게 정보 전달
(D) 온라인 결제 시스템

해설 두 번째 단락의 첫 문장에서 포털 내에 결제 옵션을 선보일 계획이었다(We had also ~ the portal)고 했고, 그러나 웹 개발자들이 아직 청구 시스템 문제를 처리하는 중(However, the Web ~ billing system)이라며 해당 부분의 시스템은 나중에 시행될 것(As a result ~ a later time)이라고 했다. 따라서 정답은 (D)이다.

Paraphrasing 지문의 a payment option within the portal
→ 정답의 An online payment system

149-150 양식

두브로브니크에 있는
미르자나 스프링스 호텔에 오신 것을 환영합니다.

149무료 웹 이용을 위한 네트워크 비밀번호는 "Mirjanawifi"입니다. 호텔 전 구역에서 제공됩니다.

호텔 관련 요청 사항은 안내 데스크로 문의해 주십시오. 150지역 명소와 관광에 관한 정보를 원하시면 레크리에이션 사무실의 노박 씨를 찾으십시오.

즐거운 숙박 되시기를 바랍니다!

객실 번호: 1296	**체크인:** 5월 23일
투숙객: 데본 톨가	**체크아웃:** 5월 25일
점원: 말리나 베이빅	**도착 시간:** 오후 8시 23분

어휘 complimentary 무료의   related 관련된   attraction 명소   excursion 여행

149 Not / True

번역 미르자나 스프링스 호텔의 인터넷 이용에 관해 명시된 것은?
(A) 비밀번호가 필요하지 않다.
(B) 저녁에는 그다지 신뢰할 수 없다.
(C) 1296호실에서는 이용할 수 없다.
(D) 투숙객들은 비용을 지불할 필요가 없다.

해설 첫 문장에서 무료 웹 이용을 위한 네트워크 비밀번호는 "Mirjanawifi"이다(The network ~ "Mirjanawifi")라고 했고, 호텔 전 구역에서 제공된다(It is offered throughout the hotel)고 했으므로 정답은 (D)이다.

어휘 reliable 신뢰할 수 있는

> Paraphrasing   지문의 complimentary
> → 정답의 do not have to pay

150 추론 / 암시

번역 노박 씨에 대해 암시된 것은?
(A) 안내 데스크에서 근무한다.
(B) 5월 25일에 체크아웃할 것이다.
(C) 관광 여행 계획을 돕는다.
(D) 베이빅 씨의 상관이다.

해설 두 번째 단락의 두 번째 문장에서 지역 명소와 관광에 관한 정보를 원하면 레크리에이션 사무실의 노박 씨를 찾으라(For information ~ our recreation office)고 했으므로 노박 씨는 투숙객들이 관광 계획을 짜는 일을 돕고 있음을 알 수 있다. 따라서 정답은 (C)이다.

151-152 광고

> ### 151미니퓨어: 휴대용 공기 청정기
>
> 공기 청정기 선두주자인 마운틴 클리어 에어가 최초의 휴대용 공기 청정기인 미니퓨어를 선보입니다. 선도적인 환경 운동가들과 엔지니어들에 의해 개발된 미니퓨어는 음이온을 사용해 공기를 정화합니다! 게다가 작고 편리해서 어디든 가지고 갈 수 있습니다.
>
> - 친환경적이고 효과적입니다.
> - 152(A)손가방이나 서류 가방에 쏙 들어갑니다.
> - 오염 물질 및 알레르기 유발 물질을 줄여 줍니다.
> - 152(D)일반 전화 충전기로 빠르게 충전됩니다.
> - 151,152(B)가정, 사무실 또는 어디서나 사용할 수 있습니다.
>
> 자세한 내용은 Minipureairclean.com에서 확인하세요.
>
> 어휘 portable 휴대용의   air purifier 공기 청정기   device 장치   environmentalist 환경 운동가   negative ion 음이온   fit 맞다   briefcase 서류 가방   pollutant 오염 물질   allergen 알레르기 유발 물질   charge 충전되다   charger 충전기

151 추론 / 암시

번역 광고는 누구를 대상으로 하겠는가?
(A) 의료 기술자
(B) 호텔 운영자
(C) 환경 전문가
(D) 일반 소비자

해설 광고 제목에 미니퓨어: 휴대용 공기 청정기(Mini-pure: Portable Air Purifier)라고 명시되어 있고, 두 번째 단락의 마지막 항목에 가정, 사무실 또는 어디서나 사용할 수 있다(For use at home, in the office, or anywhere)고 했으므로 일상용품을 구입하는 소비자를 대상으로 하는 광고임을 알 수 있다. 따라서 정답은 (D)이다.

152 Not / True

번역 공기 청정기에 대해 명시되지 않은 것은?
(A) 크기
(B) 용도
(C) 가격
(D) 동력원

해설 두 번째 단락의 두 번째 항목에 손가방이나 서류 가방에 쏙 들어간다(Fits easily into a purpose or briefcase)고 (A) 크기를 언급했고, 네 번째 항목에 일반 전화 충전기로 빠르게 충전된다(Charges quickly with any standard phone charger)고 (D) 동력원을 언급했고, 마지막 항목에 가정, 사무실 또는 어디서나 사용할 수 있다(For use at home, in the office, or anywhere)고 (B) 용도를 언급했다. 가격은 언급되지 않았으므로 정답은 (C)이다.

153-154 문자 메시지

> **짐 시만스키 (오전 9시 42분)**
> 베브, 미리 알려 드릴 게 있어요. 이스트베리 학생 아파트에 수도 밸브가 고장났어요. 그쪽에 물이 2시간 동안 차단될 거예요.
>
> **베브 무노즈 (오전 9시 43분)**
> 문제없습니다. 이 일을 끝낸 뒤 칼튼 아파트에서 손을 씻으면 됩니다.
>
> **짐 시만스키 (오전 9시 44분)**
> 좋습니다. 오늘 아침에도 지난번과 똑같이 할 예정이에요. 153각 아파트에 들어가서 벽면 에어컨의 필터를 진공청소기로 청소할 겁니다. 먼지가 너무 많아 보이는 필터는 모두 교체해야 합니다. 또한 환기구에 있는 잔여물도 제거해야 합니다.
>
> **베브 무노즈 (오전 9시 46분)**
> 알겠습니다. 154모든 아파트가 비어 있을까요?
>
> **짐 시만스키 (오전 9시 47분)**
> 학생들은 학교 방학 중이에요. 그렇지만 혹시 모르니까 노크를 하는 게 좋을 것 같네요.
>
> **베브 무노즈 (오전 9시 48분)**
> 알겠습니다. 근처에 주차해 있어서 A 빌딩은 제가 작업할 수 있습니다. 당신이 B 빌딩을 맡으시면 되겠네요. 그렇게 하면 일을 더 빨리 진행하고 오후에 점심시간을 가질 수 있을 겁니다.

153 세부 사항

번역 시만스키 씨와 무노즈 씨는 오늘 아침에 무엇을 할 예정인가?
(A) 주차장에서 쓰레기 치우기
(B) 일부 에어컨 서비스
(C) 고장 난 수도관 수리
(D) 주방용품 설치

해설 9시 44분에 시만스키 씨가 각 아파트에 들어가서 벽면 에어컨의 필터를 진공청소기로 청소할 것(We'll enter ~ air conditioner)이라면서 먼지가 너무 많아 보이는 필터는 모두 교체해야 한다(Any filter ~ be replaced)고 했으므로 두 사람은 에어컨 필터 서비스를 할 것임을 알 수 있다. 따라서 (B)가 정답이다.

어휘 litter 쓰레기 kitchen appliance 주방용품

154 의도 파악

번역 오전 9시 47분에 시만스키 씨가 "학생들은 학교 방학 중이에요"라고 쓴 의도는?
(A) 주차할 자리를 쉽게 찾을 수 있을 것이다.
(B) A 빌딩에 학생이 살지 않는다.
(C) 아파트는 비어 있을 것이다.
(D) 학생들은 종종 스스로 수리를 한다.

해설 9시 46분에 무노즈 씨가 모든 아파트가 비어 있을지(Will all the apartments be unoccupied?)를 묻자 9시 47분에 시만스키 씨가 학생들은 학교 방학 중(The students are on school holiday)이라고 대답한 것으로 보아, 방학 중이라 아파트에 남아 있는 학생이 없을 것이라는 의도로 한 말임을 알 수 있다. 따라서 (C)가 정답이다.

어휘 vacant 비어 있는

Paraphrasing 지문의 unoccupied → 정답의 vacant

155-157 이메일

155 추론 / 암시

번역 리 씨는 누구일 것 같은가?
(A) 잠재 고객
(B) 영업 사원
(C) 인테리어 디자이너
(D) 창고 직원

해설 이메일의 수신자는 라리사 M. 리 씨(To: Larisa M. Lee), 발신자는 미니치 가구(From: Minnich Furniture), 제목은 가구 세일 금요일 종료(Subject: Furniture Sale Ends Friday)이고 첫 줄의 미니치 가구 시즌 세일(Minnich Furniture Seasonal Sale!)부터 시작해 가구 세일에 대해 홍보하는 내용이 이어지고 있는 것으로 보아 리 씨는 미니치 가구의 잠재 고객임을 알 수 있으므로 (A)가 정답이다.

156 세부 사항

번역 미니치 가구에서 구매할 수 있는 방법은?
(A) 지역 내 여러 소매점 중 하나에서 구입
(B) 중앙 창고 방문
(C) 콜센터에 전화
(D) 온라인 주문

해설 두 번째 단락의 두 번째 문장에서 웹사이트 주소를 제공하며 온라인으로 쇼핑하라(Shop online at www.minnichfurniture.com)고 했으므로 (D)가 정답이다.

Paraphrasing 지문의 Shop online
→ 정답의 placing an online order

157 Not / True

번역 이메일에 명시된 것은?
(A) 할인은 30일 후에 종료된다.
(B) 할인 품목의 반품은 허용되지 않는다.
(C) 고객들은 할인가로 두 개의 제품만 살 수 있다.
(D) 재고가 1,000개만 남아 있다.

해설 두 번째 단락의 첫 항목에 특정 품목에 대해 한정된 수량으로 이용 가능하다(Limited quantities ~ available)고 했고, 고객당 할인 품목 2개로 제한한다(Limit 2 sale items per customer)고 했으므로 (C)가 정답이다.

어휘 in stock 재고로

158-161 편지

요한 크루거
졸라니 출판사
워링 가 291
프리토리아 0002 남아프리카 공화국

6월 16일

나드자 압디, 사무실 관리자
켄다 가 64
나이로비 00606 케냐

압디 씨께,

161(D)⟨모던 스타일 매거진⟩의 무료 체험판을 요청해 주셔서 감사합니다. 무료 잡지를 동봉해 드립니다. 귀사와 같은 사업체들은 저희 잡지 서비스로부터 큰 혜택을 받고 있습니다. **158환자들이 보통 검진이나 스케일링을 받기 전에 최대 20분까지 기다린다는 것을 알고 계십니까? 읽을 잡지가 있으면 대기 시간이 빨리 159지나가는 데 도움이 됩니다.**

정식 구독을 주문할 준비가 되셨습니까? **161(B)동봉된 카드를 반송하시고 신문 가판대의 판매가에서 20%를 할인 받으세요.** 보너스로 저희는 추가 비용 없이 저희의 연간 리뷰 잡지 한 부를 보내 드리겠습니다.

요한 크루거, 졸라니 출판사

160추신: 저희는 ⟨스포츠 투데이⟩, ⟨홈 리페어 저널⟩, ⟨월간 저예산 여행⟩ 등 인기 있는 간행물을 포함해 전 세계의 다양한 독자들을 위한 잡지를 발행하고 있습니다. 161(A)사업체로서 저희 카탈로그에 있는 모든 간행물의 무료 체험판을 요청하실 수 있습니다. 오늘 바로 웹사이트를 방문하세요!

어휘 trial 시험 issue (간행물의) 호 enclosed 동봉된 complimentary 무료의 checkup 검진 subscription 구독 charge 요금 budget 저가의, 저렴한

158 추론 / 암시

번역 압디 씨는 어떤 종류의 사업체를 운영할 것 같은가?
(A) 미용실
(B) 치과
(C) 커피숍
(D) 법률 사무소

해설 첫 단락의 네 번째 문장에서 환자들이 보통 검진이나 스케일링을 받기 전에 최대 20분까지 기다린다는 것을 알고 있는지(Did you know ~ or cleaning?) 물으며, 읽을 잡지가 있으면 대기 시간이 빨리 지나가는 데 도움이 된다(Having magazines ~ time pass quickly)고 압디 씨를 설득하고 있는 것으로 보아 압디 씨는 치과를 운영하고 있다고 짐작할 수 있다. 따라서 (B)가 정답이다.

159 동의어

번역 첫 번째 단락 4행의 "pass"와 의미가 가장 가까운 단어는?
(A) 가로지르다
(B) 일어나다
(C) 시간이 흐르다
(D) 간과하다

해설 의미상 시간이 '지나간다'는 뜻으로 쓰인 것이므로 정답은 (C) elapse이다.

160 추론 / 암시

번역 졸라니 출판사에 대해 암시된 것은?
(A) 취급 제품이 다양한 관심사를 가진 사람들에게 어필한다.
(B) 주로 학술지를 발행한다.
(C) 고객층이 남아프리카 공화국으로 한정되어 있다.
(D) 주로 디지털 구독을 판매한다.

해설 마지막 단락의 추신(P.S.)에서 저희는 ⟨스포츠 투데이⟩, ⟨홈 리페어 저널⟩, ⟨월간 저예산 여행⟩ 등 인기 있는 간행물을 포함해 전 세계의 다양한 독자들을 위한 잡지를 발행하고 있다(We publish ~ *Budget Traveler Monthly*)고 했으므로 다양한 관심사를 가진 독자들에게 어필할 수 있음을 짐작할 수 있으므로 (A)가 정답이다.

161 Not / True

번역 편지에서 압디 씨에게 제공되지 않은 것은?
(A) 다른 잡지의 무료 체험판
(B) 할인된 구독 요금
(C) 신규 구독자 소개에 대한 보너스
(D) 무료 ⟨모던 스타일 매거진⟩ 잡지

해설 첫 문장에서 ⟨모던 스타일 매거진⟩의 무료 체험판을 요청해 주셔서 감사하다(Thank you ~ *Modern Style Magazine*)며 무료 잡지를 동봉한다(Enclosed ~ issue)고 했으므로 (D), 두 번째 단락의 두 번째 문장에서 동봉된 카드를 반송하고 신문 가판대의 판매가에서 20%를 할인 받으라(Return the ~ newsstand price)고 했으므로 (B), 마지막 단락의 두 번째 문장에서 사업체로서 카탈로그에 있는 모든 간행물의 무료 체험판을 요청할 수 있다(As a business ~ our catalogue)고 했으므로 (A)가 압디 씨에게 제공되고, 신규 구독자 소개에 대한 보너스는 언급된 바 없으므로 (C)가 정답이다.

어휘 rate 요금 refer 소개하다

> **Paraphrasing** 지문의 complimentary → 보기 (A), (D)의 free

162-165 보도 자료

긴급 보도

164연락처: 로베르토 바르보자
351 922 555 965

리스본 (6월 18일)—**162올해 국제 사탕 회의는 포르투갈 리스본의 비브 풍선껌 공장 근처에 있는 빌 드 마이트로스 컨벤션 센터에서 열릴 예정이다. 165전 세계 수천 명의 사탕 업계 전문가들이 9월 8일부터 10일까지 이 행사에 참석할 것으로 예상된다.** 비브 풍선껌이 올해의 행사를 주최할 예정이라서 이 수치에는 이제 많은 껌 생산업체가 포함될 것 같다.

162비브 풍선껌의 최고 경영자인 아만다 비브는 츄잉껌 산업을 매우 진지하게 생각한다. 이 회사의 4대 최고 경영자인 **162그녀는 "우리 가족은 이 행사를 후원하게 되어 기쁘고 국제 사탕 회의를 주최하는 최초의 츄잉껌 회사가 되어 무척 흥분됩니다."라고 자랑스럽게 말한다.** 비브 씨는 또한 사탕 회의가 올해 포르투갈에서 열린다는 점에 특히 기뻐하고 있다. "비브 풍선껌은 리스본 근처의 작은 가게에서 시작했습니다. 당사

의 주 공장은 이 지역에 위치해 있지만 현재 우리는 7개국에 껌을 판매하고 있습니다. 우리는 이 행사가 국제 풍선껌 시장뿐 아니라 우리 지역 사회에도 관심과 수익을 가져다주기를 바랍니다."

163,164국제 사탕 회의와 비브 풍선껌 공장 견학에 관한 더 많은 정보는 351 922 555 965로 로베르토 바르보자에게 연락하거나 www. BibbBubblegum.com으로 방문하면 된다.

어휘 immediate 즉각적인 release 발표 generation 세대 proudly 자랑스럽게 thrilled 아주 신이 난 attention 관심 revenue 수익

162 주제 / 목적

번역 보도 자료의 주요 목적은?
(A) 사탕 산업의 역사 설명
(B) 껌 회사의 확장 발표
(C) 새로운 사업체의 최고 경영자 소개
(D) 회의 및 회의 후원사 홍보

해설 첫 단락의 첫 문장에서 올해 국제 사탕 회의는 포르투갈 리스본의 비브 풍선껌 공장 근처에 있는 빌 드 마이트로스 컨벤션 센터에서 열릴 예정(This year's ~ Bubblegum factory)이라고 했고, 두 번째 단락의 첫 문장에서 비브 풍선껌의 최고 경영자인 아만다 비브는 츄잉껌 산업을 매우 진지하게 생각한다(Amanda Bibb ~ very seriously)며 이 행사를 후원하게 되어 기쁘고 국제 사탕 회의를 주최하는 최초의 츄잉껌 회사가 되어 무척 흥분된다고 자랑스럽게 말한다(she proudly ~ Candy Conference!")고 했다. 따라서 보도 자료는 국제 사탕 회의와 그 후원사에 대해 알리기 위한 것이므로 (D)가 정답이다.

어휘 expansion 확장

163 Not / True

번역 비브 풍선껌 회사에 대해 명시된 것은?
(A) 방문객들의 시설 견학을 허용한다.
(B) 리스본에 본사가 있다.
(C) 포르투갈의 새로운 사탕 업체이다.
(D) 다른 껌 회사들보다 더 많은 맛을 제공한다.

해설 마지막 문장에서 국제 사탕 회의와 비브 풍선껌 공장 견학에 관한 더 많은 정보는 351 922 555 965로 로베르토 바르보자에게 연락하거나 www.BibbBubblegum.com으로 방문하면 된다(For more ~ www.BibbBubblegum.com)고 한 것으로 보아 버브 풍선껌 공장에서는 견학을 허용하고 있으므로 (A)가 정답이다.

어휘 facility 시설 headquarters 본사 flavor 맛

164 추론 / 암시

번역 바르보자 씨는 누구일 것 같은가?
(A) 가게 주인
(B) 회사 직원
(C) 신문 기자
(D) 여행사 직원

해설 상단의 연락처에 로베르토 바르보자(Contact: Roberto Barboza)라고 적혀 있고, 마지막 문장에서 국제 사탕 회의와 비브

풍선껌 공장 견학에 관한 더 많은 정보는 351 922 555 965로 로베르토 바르보자에게 연락하거나 www.BibbBubblegum.com으로 방문하면 된다(For more ~ www.BibbBubblegum.com)고 한 것으로 보아 바르보자 씨는 비브 풍선껌에서 근무하고 있음을 짐작할 수 있다. 따라서 (B)가 정답이다.

165 문장 삽입

번역 [1], [2], [3], [4]로 표시된 곳 중에서 다음 문장이 들어가기에 가장 적합한 위치는?

"비브 풍선껌이 올해의 행사를 주최할 예정이라서 이 수치에는 이제 많은 껌 생산업체가 포함될 것 같다."
(A) [1]
(B) [2]
(C) [3]
(D) [4]

해설 제시된 문장의 this year's event와 That number가 문제 해결의 단서로, 주어진 문장 앞에 행사와 관련된 내용과 That number가 가리키는 수치가 있어야 한다. 따라서 수천(Thousands) 명의 사탕 업계 전문가가 이 행사(the event)에 참석할 것으로 예상된다고 언급한 문장 뒤인 (A)가 정답이다.

166-168 공지

> ### 업그레이드된 임팔라 카드가 우편으로 왔습니다!
>
> **166임팔라 신용 조합**에서는 고객님의 안전과 편의가 무엇보다 중요합니다. 이것이 우리가 모든 회원 신용 카드와 체크 카드에 비접촉식 기술을 도입하는 이유입니다. 이 신개발로 고객님은 더 이상 계산대의 카드 리더기에 카드를 읽히거나 삽입할 필요가 없어질 것입니다. 사실, **167실제 지갑에서 카드를 꺼낼 필요조차 없을 것이며** 단지 카드가 읽힐 수 있도록 계산대 근처에 들고만 있으면 됩니다!
>
> 몇 가지 중요한 주의하실 점들이 있습니다. 먼저, 고객님의 현재 카드는 10월 31일자로 정지될 예정입니다. 그때까지는 계속 사용하실 수 있습니다.
>
> 두 번째로 업그레이드된 카드는 현재 카드가 만료되기 전에 도착할 수 있습니다. 새 카드를 활성화하는 즉시 이전 카드는 자동으로 정지되어 더 이상 사용할 수 없습니다. 부착된 스티커의 설명에 따라 새 카드를 수동으로 활성화하셔야 합니다.
>
> 세 번째로 비접촉식 기술 카드에는 새 카드 번호와 유효 기간, 보안 번호가 있을 것입니다. **168활성화할 때 PIN(개인 식별 번호)을 선택하라는 요청을 받게 됩니다.** 현재 카드의 PIN은 자동으로 이전되지 않습니다. 모든 즐겨 찾는 온라인 소매업체와 앱 구독에 저장된 카드를 업데이트하여 계속 이용할 수 있도록 하십시오.
>
> 고객님께서 새로운 카드에 만족하시기를 바랍니다. 비접촉식 기술 임팔라 카드에 관한 문의 사항이 있을 경우 1-610-555-0168로 고객 서비스 센터에 언제든 연락하십시오.

어휘 paramount 가장 중요한 contactless 비접촉식의 debit card 체크 카드 swipe (신용 카드를 인식기에) 읽다 insert 삽입하다 checkout 계산대 deactivate 정지시키다 expire 만료되다 activate 활성화시키다 valid 유효한 manually 수동으로 instruction 설명 expiration date 만기일[유효 기간]

prompt 촉발하다   identification 신원 확인   transfer 옮기다
preferred 선호하는   subscription 구독, 이용

166 주제 / 목적

번역 공지의 목적은?
(A) 고객 피드백을 요청하는 것
(B) 고객에게 신용 카드 사기에 대해 경고하는 것
(C) 고객에게 새로운 결제 방법을 알리는 것
(D) 청구 정책의 변경 사항을 공지하는 것

해설 첫 단락의 첫 문장에서 임팔라 신용 조합에서는 고객의 안전과 편의가 중요하다(At Impala Credit Union ~ are paramount)며 이것이 모든 회원 신용 카드와 체크 카드에 비접촉식 기술을 도입하는 이유(That is why ~ debit cards)라고 했고, 이 신개발로 고객은 더 이상 계산대의 카드 리더기에 카드를 읽히거나 삽입할 필요가 없어질 것(With this new ~ at checkout)이라며 새로 도입하는 결제 방법에 대해 알리고 있으므로 (C)가 정답이다.

어휘 alert (위험 등을) 알리다   fraud 사기   billing 청구서 발부

167 Not / True

번역 새 임팔라 카드에 관해 명시된 것은?
(A) 10월 31일부터 사용 가능하다.
(B) 사용을 위해 지갑에서 꺼낼 필요가 없다.
(C) 앱 이용에 사용할 수 없다.
(D) 이전 카드와 동일한 신원 확인 정보가 포함된다.

해설 첫 단락의 네 번째 문장에서 실제 지갑에서 카드를 꺼낼 필요조차 없을 것(you will not ~ physical wallet)이라고 했으므로 (B)가 정답이다.

168 세부 사항

번역 고객은 새 카드를 활성화할 때 무엇을 해야 하는가?
(A) PIN 선택
(B) 현재 카드 취소
(C) 보안 번호 입력
(D) 미지급금 이체

해설 네 번째 단락 두 번째 문장에서 활성화할 때 PIN(개인 식별 번호)을 선택하라는 요청을 받게 된다(When activating ~ PIN(personal identification number))고 했으므로 (A)가 정답이다.

어휘 outstanding 미지불된   balance 잔액

Paraphrasing   지문의 choose → 정답의 Select

169-172 온라인 채팅

프리다 정 (오전 9시 16분)
169제가 수요일부터 다음 주 월요일까지 사무실에 없을 예정입니다. 지역 입법부에 자금 지원 신청서를 제출해야 합니다. 170두 분께서 금요일에 도시 개발 위원회에게 171새 리버워크에 관한 발표를 잘 하실 수 있을까요?

캐시 알스위드 (오전 9시 18분)
저희끼리 처리할 수 있을 것 같습니다. 그렇죠, 오스틴?

오스틴 에버렛 (오전 9시 20분)
물론이죠. 정 씨, 얼마나 시간을 내실 수 있을지 모르겠습니다만 170원하시면 목요일에 발표에 대한 개요를 보내 드리겠습니다.

프리다 정 (오전 9시 22분)
그러실 필요는 없을 것 같습니다. 171신사업으로 인해 이 지역에 유입될 것으로 예상하는 수익뿐 아니라 우리 연구 그룹이 지적한 긍정적인 환경적 영향도 반드시 강조해 주세요.

오스틴 에버렛 (오전 9시 23분)
알겠습니다. 꼭 그렇게 하겠습니다.

캐시 알스위드 (오전 9시 25분)
172금요일 대신 월요일에 주간 진행 보고서를 제출해도 괜찮을까요? 그러면 발표를 준비할 시간을 좀 더 가질 수 있을 거라서요.

프리다 정 (오전 9시 26분)
네, 좋은 생각입니다.

캐시 알스위드 (오전 9시 26분)
좋습니다. 감사합니다!

프리다 정 (오전 9시 27분)
제가 없는 동안 이메일에 자주 응답 못 할 수도 있지만 긴급한 일이 생기면 언제든 전화나 문자로 연락 주세요.

어휘 legislature office 입법부   urban 도시의   committee 위원회   definitely 분명히   overview 개요   revenue 수익   environmental 환경의   impact 영향   progress 진행   frequently 자주   urgent 긴급한

169 세부 사항

번역 정 씨는 왜 사무실에 없을 예정인가?
(A) 다른 일자리를 위해 면접을 볼 것이다.
(B) 다른 업무가 있다.
(C) 개인적인 이유로 휴가를 낼 것이다.
(D) 병원 진료 예약이 있다.

해설 9시 16분에 정 씨가 수요일부터 다음 주 월요일까지 사무실에 없을 예정(I have to ~ next Monday)이라고 했고, 지역 입법부에 자금 지원 신청서를 제출해야 한다(I need to present ~ legislature office)고 했으므로 정답은 (B)이다.

어휘 obligation 의무   take time off 휴가를 내다

170 의도 파악

번역 오전 9시 22분에 정 씨가 "그러실 필요는 없을 것 같습니다"라고 쓴 의도는?
(A) 에버렛 씨에게 실망했다.
(B) 에버렛 씨와 알스위드 씨의 능력을 확신한다.
(C) 이메일 읽는 것을 즐기지 않는다.
(D) 회의가 취소되어야 한다고 생각한다.

해설 9시 16분에 정 씨가 에버렛 씨와 알스위드 씨에게 두 분이 금요일에 도시 개발 위원회에게 새 리버워크에 관한 발표를 잘 할 수 있을지(Would you both ~ on Friday?)를 물었고, 9시 20분에 에버렛 씨가 정 씨에게 원하면 목요일에 발표에 대한 개요를 보내 주겠다(we could send ~ if you'd like)고 한 데 대해 9시 22분에 정 씨가 그럴 필요 없을 것 같다(I don't ~ necessary)고 했다. 따라서 정 씨는 두 사람이 발표 준비를 잘 할 것으로 믿고 있다는 의도로 한 말이므로 (B)가 정답이다.

어휘 frustrated 불만스러워하는

171 Not / True

번역 리버워크에 대해 명시된 것은?
(A) 이 지역에 추가적인 사업을 유치할 것 같다.
(B) 도시 중심부에 위치해 있다.
(C) 알스위드 씨는 그 혜택에 대해 회의적이다.
(D) 공사가 빠르게 진척되고 있다.

해설 9시 16분에 정 씨가 새 리버워크(the new Riverwalk)를 언급했고, 9시 22분에 정 씨가 신사업으로 인해 이 지역에 유입될 것으로 예상하는 수익뿐 아니라 우리 연구 그룹이 지적한 긍정적인 환경적 영향도 반드시 강조해 달라(Please be sure to ~ research group noted)고 했다. 따라서 새로운 사업으로 이 지역에 새로운 수익이 창출될 것이라고 했으므로 (A)가 정답이다.

어휘 skeptical 회의적인 progress 진전을 보이다

> Paraphrasing 지문의 new → 정답의 extra

172 추론 / 암시

번역 알스위드 씨의 보고서에 대해 암시된 것은?
(A) 늦게 제출된 적이 없다.
(B) 입법부에 제출될 것이다.
(C) 매주 금요일에 제출된다.
(D) 에버렛 씨가 월요일에 검토해야 한다.

해설 9시 25분에 알스위드 씨가 금요일 대신 월요일에 주간 진행 보고서를 제출해도 괜찮을지(Would it be ~ instead of Friday?)를 요청하고 있는 것으로 보아 알스위드 씨는 평소 금요일에 주간 진행 보고서를 제출하고 있음을 짐작할 수 있다. 따라서 정답은 (C)이다.

173-175 편지

웨스트마우스 파이낸셜 서비스
폴 가 1311
엑서터 EX8 9YJ, 영국

7월 14일

타탈 씨께,

귀하의 웨스트마우스 파이낸셜 퇴직 투자 계좌와 관련하여 곧 있을 몇 가지 변경 사항에 대해 알려 드리고자 이 편지를 씁니다. 첫째로, **175이미 알고 계시겠지만 귀하의 주요 금융 서비스 고문인 펠릭스 리어던 씨가**

다음 달에 은퇴할 예정입니다. 따라서 제가 귀하의 계좌 관리를 인수하게 될 것입니다. **173저는 15년 이상 개인 금융 분야에서 일한 경력이 있고 웨스트마우스 파이낸셜에서 그중 3년을 근무해 오면서** 25명 이상의 고객이 노련한 재무 계획을 통해 은퇴 목표를 달성할 수 있도록 도왔습니다. 귀하께서 이 여정을 지속할 수 있도록 돕게 되어 기쁩니다.

둘째로, 귀하의 현재 포트폴리오에 대해 귀하와 만나거나 대화를 나눌 시간을 마련하고 싶습니다. 직접 만나거나 간단한 전화나 영상 통화로 이야기할 수도 있습니다만, 귀하의 은퇴가 임박한 만큼 향후 10년간의 투자 전략 계획을 협의하는 것이 좋을 것 같습니다. 이러한 맥락에서 **174저는 특히 귀하께서 일부 자금을 채권이나 연금 같은 좀 더 안정적인 자산으로 옮기는 것에 관심이 있으신지 알고 싶습니다.** 저는 보통 은퇴에 가까워질수록 더 안전한 이런 옵션으로 옮기실 것을 추천합니다. 대화를 나눌 시간을 잡을 수 있도록 언제든 전화하시거나 이메일을 보내십시오. 감사드리고 더 많은 이야기를 할 수 있기를 기대합니다.

리타 히다얏, 계좌 관리 담당자

어휘 upcoming 다가오는 primary 주된 advisor 고문 savvy 잘 아는, 능통한 journey 여정 touch base 대화[협의]하다 strategy 전략 specifically 특별히 shift 옮기다 stable 안정된 asset 자산 bond 채권 annuity 연금

173 Not / True

번역 히다얏 씨에 대해 명시된 것은?
(A) 개인 금융 분야는 그녀의 두 번째 직업이다.
(B) 3년 동안 현재의 역할을 해왔다.
(C) 리어던 씨의 멘토였다.
(D) 15년 전에 은퇴했다.

해설 첫 단락의 세 번째 문장에서 히다얏 씨가 저는 15년 이상 개인 금융 분야에서 일한 경력이 있고 웨스트마우스 파이낸셜에서 그중 3년을 근무해 왔다(I have over fifteen ~ three of those years)고 했으므로 (B)가 정답이다.

174 추론 / 암시

번역 타탈 씨의 금융 포트폴리오에 대해 암시된 것은?
(A) 가치가 대단히 크지는 않다.
(B) 리어던 씨가 잘 관리하지 못했다.
(C) 타탈 씨는 더 나은 성과를 낼 것으로 기대했다.
(D) 몇 가지 위험 자산이 포함되어 있다.

해설 두 번째 단락의 세 번째 문장에서 히다얏 씨가 타탈 씨에게 저는 특히 귀하께서 일부 자금을 채권이나 연금 같은 좀 더 안정적인 자산으로 옮기는 것에 관심이 있으신지 알고 싶다(I specifically wanted ~ bonds and annuities)고 했다. 따라서 타탈 씨의 금융 포트폴리오에는 위험 자산이 일부 포함되어 있다는 것을 알 수 있으므로 (D)가 정답이다.

어휘 value (경제적인) 가치 risky 위험한 asset 자산

175 문장 삽입

번역 [1], [2], [3], [4]로 표시된 곳 중에서 다음 문장이 들어가기에 가장 적합한 위치는?

"따라서 제가 귀하의 계좌 관리를 인수하게 될 것입니다."

(A) [1]
(B) [2]
(C) [3]
(D) [4]

해설 제시된 문장의 접속부사 Therefore가 문제 해결의 단서이다. 제가 귀하의 계좌 관리 업무를 대신하게 될 것이라며 앞에 Therefore를 사용했으므로, 그 앞에는 주어진 문장에 대한 원인이 와야 한다. 따라서 귀하의 금융 고문인 리어던 씨가 다음 달에 은퇴할 예정 (your primary financial services advisor, Felix Reardon, is retiring next month)이라며 계좌 관리 담당자가 바뀌게 된 원인을 설명하는 내용 뒤인 (B)가 정답이다.

176-180 기사 + 설문 조사

176극단을 위한 새 보금자리

오클랜드 (7월 11일)—178다비 가의 남쪽 끝에는 이전에 태평양 무역 은행의 본점이 있던 위풍당당한 빅토리아 양식의 건물이 우뚝 솟아 있다. 176이 건물은 이제 코나타 극단의 보금자리이다. 화요일 개관식 이후 참석자들에게 새로운 극장에 대한 견학 기회가 주어졌다.

177,179데뷔 쇼는 인기있는 관광지에 대한 여미선의 코미디극인 〈릴렉스〉이다. 공연은 7월 16일 토요일에 시작해 이달 말까지 진행될 예정이다.

코나타 극단의 예술 감독인 노아 라킨스에 따르면, 모든 공연 직후에는 "토크백"이 뒤따를 예정이다. 토크백은 감독과 출연진이 연극에 대한 각자의 생각을 공유할 수 있게 해 주고, 관객들은 그들에게 질문을 할 수도 있다. "우리는 오클랜드와 우리 주변의 더 큰 지역 사회에 있는 예술 공동체의 일부가 되기를 원합니다."라고 라킨스 씨는 말했다.

이 건물에는 약 325명을 수용할 수 있는 주 무대 극장과 위층의 작은 스튜디오 극장이 있다. 회사는 또한 어린이와 성인을 위한 연기 수업도 제공할 예정이다. 자세한 정보를 원하거나 티켓을 구매하려면 회사의 웹페이지인 www.cornatatheatre.nz를 방문하면 된다.

어휘 dominate (어떤 장소에서) 가장 두드러지다 imposing 당당한 formerly 이전에 attendee 참석자 site 장소 talk-back (시청자 등의) 반응 cast member 출연진 audience 관중 house 수용하다 approximately 대략

179〈릴렉스〉를 관람해 주셔서 감사합니다. 잠시 시간을 내어 귀하의 경험에 대해 말씀해 주십시오.

이름 및 이메일 주소: 줄리아 크루즈 〈jcruz@northwing.nz〉

1. 귀하께서 관람하신 공연에 대해 어떻게 평가하십니까?
   매우 좋음 _X_ 좋음 ___ 보통 ___ 별로 ___

2. 극장에서의 전반적인 경험에 대해 어떻게 평가하십니까?
   매우 좋음 ___ 좋음 _X_ 보통 ___ 별로 ___

3. 저희에 대해 어떻게 알게 되셨습니까? (해당 사항에 모두 표기하십시오.)
   지면 광고 _X_ 소셜 미디어 _X_ TV ___ 이메일 ___

의견: 연극의 줄거리는 매혹적이었고 연기는 훌륭했다. 180이번 시즌 극장의 정기 이용 회원이 되어 즐겁다. 모든 쇼가 이렇게 좋다면 매우 행복할 것이다. 구내 매점에는 문제가 있는 것 같았다. 음식과 음료를 위한 줄이 길었고 그다지 빠르게 줄지도 않았다.

어휘 rate 평가하다 fair 괜찮은 overall 전체적인 apply 해당되다 fascinating 매력적인 brilliant 훌륭한 delighted 즐거운 concession stand 매점

176 주제 / 목적

번역 기사의 목적은?

(A) 연극의 토대가 되는 역사 조사
(B) 아마추어 배우들의 참여 유도
(C) 예술 공연장의 개관 발표
(D) 관광객을 위한 서비스 홍보

해설 기사의 제목이 극단을 위한 새 보금자리(New Home for Theatre Group)이고, 첫 단락의 두 번째 문장에서 건물이 이제 코나타 극단의 보금자리(That building is ~ Theatre Company)라고 했고, 화요일 개관식(a grand-opening ceremony on Tuesday)이 언급되었으므로 기사는 새롭게 개관하는 극장에 대한 소식을 전하려고 작성되었음을 알 수 있다. 따라서 정답은 (C)이다.

어휘 examine 조사하다 participation 참여 venue 장소

> **Paraphrasing** 지문의 Theatre → 정답의 arts venue

177 세부 사항

번역 여 씨는 누구인가?

(A) 극작가
(B) 은행원
(C) 부서장
(D) 관광부 책임자

해설 기사의 두 번째 단락 첫 문장에서 데뷔 쇼는 인기있는 관광지에 대한 여미선의 코미디극인 〈릴렉스〉(The debut show ~ popular tourist site)라고 했으므로 여 씨는 극작가임을 알 수 있다. 따라서 (A)가 정답이다.

178 Not / True

번역 기사에서 다비 가의 건물에 대해 언급된 것은?

(A) 다세대 아파트가 있다.
(B) 한때 은행이었다.
(C) 그 거리에서 가장 오래된 건물이다.
(D) 지역 사회 일자리 프로그램을 제공한다.

해설 기사의 첫 문장에서 다비 가의 남쪽 끝에는 이전에 태평양 무역 은행의 본점이 있던 위풍당당한 빅토리아 양식의 건물이 우뚝 솟아 있다 (The south end ~ Pacific Trade Bank)고 했으므로 (B)가 정답이다.

179 연계

번역 크루즈 씨에 대해 암시된 것은?
(A) 이메일로 극장에 대해 들었다.
(B) 제공된 음식과 음료를 즐겼다.
(C) 연기가 매우 좋다고 생각하지 않았다.
(D) 새로운 극장에서 공연된 첫 연극을 보았다.

해설 기사의 두 번째 단락 첫 문장에서 데뷔 쇼는 인기있는 관광지에 대한 여미선의 코미디극인 〈릴렉스〉(The debut show ~ popular tourist site)라고 했고, 크루즈 씨가 작성한 설문 조사의 첫 문장에는 〈릴렉스〉를 관람해 주셔서 감사하다(Thank you for attending *Relax*)며 잠시 시간을 내어 귀하의 경험에 대해 말씀해 달라(Please take ~ your experience)고 했다. 따라서 크루즈 씨는 극장의 첫 공연인 〈릴렉스〉를 보았다는 것을 알 수 있으므로 (D)가 정답이다.

180 Not / True

번역 크루즈 씨가 설문 조사에서 명시한 것은?
(A) 최근에 오클랜드로 이사했다.
(B) 근처 식당에서 일한다.
(C) 시즌 정기 이용자이다.
(D) 쇼핑 후에 극장에 들렀다.

해설 설문 조사의 마지막 단락 두 번째 문장에서 크루즈 씨가 이번 시즌 극장의 정기 이용 회원이 되어 즐겁다(I'm delighted ~ this season)고 했으므로 정답은 (C)이다.

어휘 subscriber 정기 이용자 stop at ~에 들르다

181-185 설명서 + 양식

181블렌도라 커피
18116번 품목: 크리미 바닐라 블렌딜리셔스

181단계	
1811. 에스프레소를 붓는다.	다크 로스트나 182(C)디카페인을 사용하세요. 182(A)스몰 사이즈 음료일 경우 1샷, 미디엄 사이즈일 경우 2샷, 라지 사이즈일 경우 3샷을 넣으세요.
2. 우유를 붓는다.	기본 음료에는 일반 우유를 사용하세요. 고객이 라이트 음료를 요청할 때는 무지방 우유를 사용하세요.
3. 향미료를 넣는다.	183바닐라 파우더를 사용하세요. 스몰 사이즈 음료일 경우 2스쿱, 183미디엄 사이즈일 경우 3스쿱, 라지 사이즈일 경우 4스쿱을 넣으세요.
182(B) 4. 얼음을 넣는다.	얼음 스쿱에 있는 스몰, 미디엄, 라지 사이즈 음료용 표시를 사용하세요.
5. 섞는다.	믹서기에 있는 오렌지 버튼을 누르세요. 크리미한 식감이어야 합니다.
6. 마무리 후 제공한다.	플라스틱 컵에 음료를 따르세요. 184기본 음료에는 생크림을 위에 얹고 반구형 뚜껑을 사용하세요. 182,184라이트 음료에는 생크림을 올리지 말고 납작한 뚜껑을 사용하세요.
7. 뒷정리를 한다.	믹서기 뚜껑과 금속 믹서기 컵을 세척하세요. 카운터를 닦으세요.

어휘 roast 구이 whole milk (지방을 빼지 않은) 전유 flavor 향미료 marking 표시 blend 섞다 texture 질감 domed 반구형의 lid 뚜껑 texture 질감 top 얹다 domed 반구형의 flat 평평한 wipe 닦다

블렌도라 커피 바리스타 교육

교육생: 매트 몰리넬리
강사: 쿠니코 오사와
날짜: 6월 17일

음료: 크리미 바닐라 블렌딜리셔스 (라이트) 사이즈:
□ 스몰 ☑ 183미디엄 □ 라지

완성된 음료의 품질을 평가하시오.
□ 완벽함 □ 매우 좋음 ☑ 좋음 □ 무난함 □ 마음에 들지 않음

교육생이 한 실수는?
184몰리넬리 씨는 미디엄 사이즈 음료를 위해 정확하게 용량을 측정했으며 무지방 우유를 사용했다. 하지만 다른 모든 것은 라이트 음료가 아닌 기본 음료 조리법을 따랐다.

의견: 185몰리넬리 씨는 손을 능숙하게 사용했고, 얼굴에 항상 미소를 띠었다. 조리법을 암기하고 나면 훌륭한 바리스타가 될 것이다.

어휘 rate 평가하다 beverage 음료 measure 측정하다 adept 능숙한

181 세부 사항

번역 설명서는 누구를 위한 것인가?
(A) 식당의 설거지 담당
(B) 커피숍의 신입 직원
(C) 주문하는 고객
(D) 식당용 장비 제조업체

해설 설명서 상단에 블렌도라 커피(Blendora Coffee)라는 상호명이 있고, 16번 품목인 크리미 바닐라 블렌딜리셔스(Item 16: Creamy Vanilla Blendelicious)에 대해 단계(Steps)별로 에스프레소를 붓는다(1. Pour espresso) 등의 설명이 기술되어 있는 것으로 보아 커피숍 직원을 대상으로 커피 제조법을 설명하는 글임을 알 수 있다. 따라서 정답은 (B)이다.

182 Not / True

번역 설명서에 따르면, 크리미 바닐라 블렌딜리셔스에 대해 사실인 것은?
(A) 두 가지 사이즈로만 제공된다.
(B) 뜨겁게 제공된다.
(C) 디카페인으로는 제공되지 않는다.
(D) 때때로 납작한 뚜껑과 함께 제공된다.

해설 설명서의 여섯 번째 단계에서 라이트 음료에는 생크림을 올리지 말고 납작한 뚜껑을 사용하라(For light drinks ~ use a flat lid)고 했으므로 (D)가 정답이다. 1단계에서 디카페인을 사용하라(Use ~ decaf)고 했으므로 (C), 스몰 사이즈 음료일 경우 1샷, 미디엄 사이즈일 경우 2샷, 라지 사이즈일 경우 3샷을 넣으라(For small drinks ~ add 3 shots)고 했으므로 (A), 4단계에서 얼음을 넣는다(Add ice)고 했으므로 (B)는 답이 될 수 없다.

183 연계

번역 몰리넬리 씨는 바닐라 파우더를 몇 스쿱 사용했는가?
(A) 1
(B) 2
(C) 3
(D) 4

해설 양식에서 몰리넬리 씨가 만든 음료는 미디엄 사이즈(Medium)라고 했는데, 설명서의 세 번째 단계에서 바닐라 파우더를 사용하라(Use vanilla powder)며 미디엄 사이즈일 경우 3스쿱(For medium drinks, add 3 scoops)이라고 했으므로 정답은 (C)이다.

184 연계

번역 몰리넬리 씨는 무엇을 잘못했는가?
(A) 음료수에 생크림을 올렸다.
(B) 잘못된 종류의 우유를 사용했다.
(C) 에스프레소를 한 샷만 사용했다.
(D) 비누를 사용하지 않고 믹서기를 세척했다.

해설 양식의 교육생이 한 실수(What errors ~ make?) 항목에 몰리넬리 씨는 미디엄 사이즈 음료를 위해 정확하게 용량을 측정했으며 무지방 우유를 사용했지만 다른 모든 것은 라이트 음료가 아닌 기본 음료 조리법을 따랐다(Mr. Molinelli measured ~ not the light one)고 했다. 설명서의 6단계에서 기본 음료에는 생크림을 위에 얹고 라이트 음료에는 생크림을 올리지 않는다(For regular drinks, ~ whipped cream)고 했는데, 몰리넬리 씨는 기본 음료에 요구되는 생크림을 라이트 음료에 얹는 실수를 했다는 것을 알 수 있으므로 정답은 (A)이다.

Paraphrasing 지문의 top with whipped cream
→ 정답의 put whipped cream on ~

185 추론 / 암시

번역 양식에서 오사와 씨가 몰리넬리 씨에 대해 암시한 것은?
(A) 음료 만드는 것을 도와달라고 요청했다.
(B) 친절한 모습을 보였다.
(C) 전에 믹서기를 사용한 적이 없다.
(D) 기억력이 뛰어나다.

해설 양식의 마지막 단락 첫 문장에서 몰리넬리 씨는 손을 능숙하게 사용했고 얼굴에 항상 미소를 띠었다(Mr. Molinelli was ~ on his face)고 했으므로 몰리넬리 씨의 태도가 친절했다는 것을 알 수 있다. 따라서 정답은 (B)이다.

어휘 appearance 모습

Paraphrasing 지문의 kept a smile on his face
→ 정답의 presented a friendly appearance

186-190 온라인 프로필 + 이메일 + 이메일

다이얼드인: 직업 연결 웹사이트	
쿠엔틴 라인스 다이얼드인 코드 번호: 04404782	원하는 직책: 상업 대출 책임자

경력:
186상업 대출부 대리
186,190바베이도스 제1은행
3년 3개월(현직)

대출 담당자
190바베이도스 제1은행
3년 8개월

창구 직원
190바베이도스 제1은행
1년 2개월

어휘 commercial lending 상업 대출 loan 대출 teller (은행의) 창구 직원

수신: 쿠엔틴 라인스 〈qrines@islandlink.bb〉
발신: 로젤라 휴이 〈rozella.huy@ventana.com〉
날짜: 11월 14일
제목: 일자리 제의

라인스 씨께:

이곳 벤타나 은행의 모든 직원을 대표하여, 지난주 당신을 만나게 되어 얼마나 즐거웠는지 말씀드리고 싶습니다. 당신의 배경과 향후 계획에 대해 논의하는 데 많은 시간을 할애해 주셔서 감사합니다. 188당신에게 상업 대출 책임자직을 제안하게 되어 기쁩니다. 이 직책의 근무지는 케이맨 제도의 조지 타운 지사입니다. 187이 자리를 수락하시면 면접 과정에서 설명된 급여와 복지 수당 및 천 달러의 이사 환급금을 받게 됩니다.

11월 29일까지 이 제안을 수락할지 여부와 원하시는 근무 시작일을 알려 주세요. 저희는 12월 중순까지 이 자리를 충원하기를 바랍니다.

합격을 축하드립니다. 우리 팀에 오시기를 기대하고 있습니다.

로젤라 휴이
벤타나 은행장

어휘 on behalf of ~을 대표하여 accept 수락하다 benefits 복지 후생 describe 서술하다 process 과정 relocation 이전 reimbursement 환급 preferred 선호하는 fill 채우다

수신: 토마스 멜빌 〈tmelville@homenetwork.bb〉
발신: 쿠엔틴 라인스 〈qrines@islandlink.bb〉
날짜: 11월 14일
제목: 새로운 일자리

멜빌 씨께,

월요일에 논의했던 일자리 제의를 방금 벤타나 은행으로부터 받았습니다. 저의 급여 요구를 맞춰 주고 이주비 지급도 제안하고 있습니다.

대학을 졸업하자마자 창구 직원으로 저를 고용하신 이후 이것은 저의 목표였습니다. 하지만 **188제가 꿈꾸던 일자리를 제안받고 나니 의구심이 듭니다. 새로운 장소가 너무 먼 것 같습니다.** 부모님과 형제자매들을 거의 볼 수 없을 것 같습니다.

189이 문제에 있어 당신의 도움을 얻고 싶습니다. 며칠 내에 만나서 점심이나 커피 괜찮을까요? 아시다시피, 저는 항상 당신의 조언을 소중히 여겨 왔고 190당신이 은퇴한 이후 우리가 점심시간에 나누던 대화가 그리웠습니다.

쿠엔틴

어휘 relocate 이전하다 doubt 의심 rarely 드물게 sibling 형제자매 value 소중히 여기다 input 조언

186 세부 사항

번역 온라인 프로필에 따르면, 라인스 씨의 현재 직업은?
(A) 책임자
(B) 대리
(C) 대출 담당자
(D) 창구 직원

해설 온라인 프로필의 경력(Experience)란에 라인스 씨는 바베이도스 제1은행(First Bank of Barbados)의 상업 대출부 대리(Assistant Manager, Commercial Lending)로 3년 3개월째 현직(Three years, three months(present position))으로 근무 중이라고 나와 있으므로 (B)가 정답이다.

187 Not / True

번역 첫 번째 이메일에서 라인스 씨에 대해 명시된 것은?
(A) 이사 비용 지원비로 천 달러를 제안받았다.
(B) 바베이도스 제1은행에서 휴이 씨와 함께 근무했다.
(C) 케이맨 제도로 짧은 여행을 떠날 계획이다.
(D) 최근에 벤타나 은행에 계좌를 개설했다.

해설 첫 이메일의 첫 단락 마지막 문장에서 라인스 씨에게 이 자리를 수락하면 면접 과정에서 설명된 급여와 복지 수당 및 천 달러의 이사 환급금을 받게 된다(Should you accept ~ USD $1,000)고 설명하고 있으므로 정답은 (A)이다.

> Paraphrasing 지문의 a relocation reimbursement
> → 정답의 pay for moving

188 연계

번역 라인스 씨가 일자리에 대해 걱정하는 것은?
(A) 광고된 것보다 급여가 적다.
(B) 케이맨 제도로 이사할 것을 요구한다.
(C) 준비가 되기 전에 시작해야 한다.
(D) 원래 생각했던 것 보다 더 까다로워 보인다.

해설 첫 이메일의 첫 단락 세 번째 문장에서 라인스 씨에게 당신에게 상업 대출 책임자직을 제안하게 되어 기쁘다(We are pleased ~ lending)며 이 직책의 근무지는 케이맨 제도의 조지 타운 지사(The position ~ Cayman Islands)라고 했고, 두 번째 이메일의 두 번째 단락 두 번째 문장에서 라인스 씨는 꿈꾸던 일자리를 제안받고 나니 의구심이 든다(now that I ~ having doubts)며 새로운 장소가 너무 먼 것 같다(The new location ~ far away)고 했다. 따라서 라인스 씨는 새로운 일자리를 위해 케이맨 제도로 이사해야 한다는 점에 대해 걱정하고 있으므로 정답은 (B)이다.

어휘 demanding 힘든, 어려운

189 세부 사항

번역 두 번째 이메일에 따르면, 라인스 씨는 왜 멜빌 씨를 만나고 싶어 하는가?
(A) 일자리를 제안하려고
(B) 대출을 신청하려고
(C) 조언을 구하려고
(D) 그의 도움에 감사하려고

해설 두 번째 이메일의 마지막 단락 첫 문장에서 라인스 씨는 이 문제에 있어 당신의 도움을 얻고 싶다(I would welcome ~ this matter)고 했고, 며칠 내에 만나서 점심이나 커피가 괜찮을지(Could we get ~ or coffee?) 물으며 항상 당신의 조언을 소중히 여겨 왔다(I have always valued your input)고 했다. 따라서 라인스 씨는 멜빌 씨와 만나 그의 조언을 듣고 싶어 하는 것이므로 (C)가 정답이다.

> Paraphrasing 지문의 input → 정답의 advice

190 연계

번역 멜빌 씨에 대해 암시된 것은?
(A) 조지 타운에 산다.
(B) 다이얼드인 웹사이트를 통해 라인스 씨에게 연락했다.
(C) 휴이 씨의 친구이다.
(D) 한때 바베이도스 제1은행에서 근무했다.

해설 온라인 프로필의 경력(Experience)란에 따르면 라인스 씨는 바베이도스 제1은행(First Bank of Barbados)에서만 근무했고, 두 번째 이메일의 마지막 문장에서 라인스 씨가 멜빌 씨에게 당신이 은퇴한 이후 우리가 점심시간에 나누던 대화가 그리웠다(I have missed ~ you retired)고 했다. 따라서 멜빌 씨는 은퇴하기 전 라인스 씨와 바베이도스 제1은행에서 함께 근무했다는 것을 알 수 있으므로 (D)가 정답이다.

191-195 공정도 + 편지 + 제품 목록

마얀 조이 코코아 공정
우리의 유기농 경작지에서 여러분의 부엌 식탁까지!

191 1. 우리는 고대의 전통을 따라 씨를 심고 재배합니다.	192 2. 우리는 씨를 자연적으로 말리고 씻고 준비합니다.	3. 우리는 코코아 원두를 굽고 193손으로 껍질을 제거합니다.	4. 우리는 벗긴 원두를 갈아서 100% 순수 코코아 가루를 생산해냅니다.	5. 여러분은 풍부하고 환상적이며 맛있는 슈퍼 푸드인 멕시코산 코코아를 즐깁니다.

어휘 process 공정　cultivate 재배하다　seed 씨　ancient 고대의　tradition 전통　toast 굽다　shell 껍질　grind 갈다　shelled 껍질을 벗긴　sensational 환상적인

마얀 조이 코코아
아브툴룸 플라자 갈레리아스
칸쿤, 퀸타나 루 97655
멕시코

3월 24일

제임스 그리지오
랜스포드 로 39
밸리 폴스, 캔자스 66088
미국

마얀 조이 코코아 관계자분께:

192저는 최근 멕시코에 있을 때 귀사의 훌륭한 코코아 한 블록을 구매했습니다. 제가 먹어본 것 중 최고였습니다! 귀사의 제품에 대해 조사를 좀 해 봤는데 귀사의 공정에 매우 감명받았습니다. 193특히 귀사의 직원들이 손으로 세심하게 원두의 껍질을 제거한다는 점이 인상 깊었습니다.

집에서 직접 초콜릿을 만들기 위해 조금 더 구매를 하고 싶습니다. 정보와 가격을 보내주세요. 1951파운드짜리 순수 무가당 유카탄 코코아를 사고 싶습니다. 제가 직접 사탕에 설탕을 넣을 거라서 유가당 코코아를 찾고 있지 않습니다.

감사합니다.

제임스 그리지오

어휘 block 사각형 덩어리　impressed 감명받은　appreciate 진가를 인정하다　unsweetened 무가당　sweeten 설탕을 넣다

마얀 조이 코코아 제품 목록

하우스 블렌드	194(B), 195아티잔 블록	194블록 기프트	194(A)마운틴 백
김이 모락모락 나고 거품이 올라간 뜨거운 음료용	음료, 요리, 제빵, 과자에 적합	수공예 나무 선물 상자에 아름답게 장식됨	194(A)과테말라 삽화로 디자인된 봉지에 담긴 무가당 코코아
코코아, 백설탕, 황설탕, 시나몬, 앤쵸, 올스파이스, 아니스, 카옌	195100% 순수 코코아 블록 형태의	블록 형태의 100% 순수 코코아	블록 형태의 100% 순수 코코아
1/2 파운드 봉지 25달러	1951파운드 40달러	1942파운드 98달러	1파운드 65달러
품목: D-23	품목: C-100	품목: C-200	품목: M-42
풍부하고 달콤쌉싸름한 혼합 파우더	194(B), 195유카탄산 순수 코코아	194(B)유카탄산 순수 코코아	과테말라의 고원의 산에서 재배됨

어휘 bittersweet 달콤쌉싸름한　steamy 김이 자욱한　frothy 거품이 떠 있는　ancho 앤쵸(고추)　allspice 올스파이스(향신료)　anise 아니스(향신료)　cayenne 카옌(붉은 고추)　confection 과자　highland 고랭지

---

191 세부 사항

번역　공정도에 따르면, 씨는 재배된 직후 어떻게 되는가?
(A) 음료로 만들어진다.
(B) 가루로 갈린다.
(C) 구워진다.
(D) 건조된다.

해설　공정도에 따르면 1단계에서 고대의 전통을 따라 씨를 심고 재배하고 (We plant ~ ancient traditions) 2단계에서 씨를 자연적으로 말리고 씻고 준비한다(We dry ~ seeds naturally)고 했으므로 정답은 (D)이다.

192 Not / True

번역　그리지오 씨가 편지에 명시한 것은?
(A) 퀸타나 루의 칸쿤에 산다.
(B) 천연 코코아를 재배한다.
(C) 초콜릿 가게를 가지고 있다.
(D) 멕시코에서 코코아를 샀다.

해설　편지의 첫 문장에서 저는 최근 멕시코에 있을 때 귀사의 훌륭한 코코아 한 블록을 구매했다(When I was ~ your fine cocoa)고 했으므로 (D)가 정답이다.

Paraphrasing　지문의 purchased → 정답의 bought

193 연계

번역　그리지오 씨는 마얀 조이 코코아의 제조 공정 중 어느 단계를 칭찬하는가?
(A) 1단계
(B) 2단계
(C) 3단계
(D) 4단계

해설　편지의 첫 단락 마지막 문장에서 그리지오 씨는 특히 귀사의 직원들이 손으로 세심하게 원두의 껍질을 제거한다는 점이 인상 깊었다 (I especially appreciate ~ beans by hand)고 했는데, 공정도에 따르면 껍질을 손으로 제거(remove the shells by hand)하는 것은 3단계이므로 정답은 (C)이다.

194 Not / True

번역 마얀 조이 블록 기프트에 대해 사실인 것은?
(A) 장식된 용기에 들어 있는 유일한 제품이다.
(B) 유일한 유카탄산 제품이다.
(C) 마얀 조이의 다른 제품들보다 크다.
(D) 다른 마얀 조이 제품들보다 더 많은 설탕이 첨가되었다.

해설 제품 목록에 따르면 블록 기프트(Block Gift)는 2파운드(2 pounds)로 제품들 중에서 가장 큰 용량이므로 (C)가 정답이다. 마운틴 백(Mountain Bag)도 과테말라 삽화로 디자인된 봉지에 담겨 있다(in bag designed with artwork from Guatemala)고 했으므로 (A), 아티잔 블록(Artisan Block)도 유카탄산(from the Yucatan)이므로 (B), 더 많은 설탕이 첨가되었는지에 대한 언급은 없으므로 (D)는 답이 될 수 없다.

195 연계

번역 그리지오 씨는 어떤 제품을 구매할 것 같은가?
(A) 하우스 블렌드
(B) 아티잔 블록
(C) 블록 기프트
(D) 마운틴 백

해설 편지의 두 번째 단락 세 번째 문장에서 그리지오 씨는 1파운드짜리 순수 무가당 유카탄 코코아를 사고 싶다(I would prefer ~ Yucatan cocoa)고 했고, 제품 목록에 따르면 아티잔 블록(Artisan Block)이 1파운드로 유카탄산(Pure cocoa from the Yucatan)이며, 100% 순수 코코아(100% pure cocoa)이다. 따라서 정답은 (B)이다.

196-200 보고서 + 쿠폰 + 영수증

고객 설문 조사 피드백 보고서

제작 대상: 플로어시사
수행자: 귀네스 굽타
메달리온 마케팅 컨설턴트

	매우 불만족	다소 불만족	보통	다소 만족	196매우 만족
전반적인 고객 경험	□	□	■	□	□
고객 서비스	□	■	□	□	□
제품 옵션	□	□	■	□	□
제품 가치	□	□	□	■	□
196웹사이트 구성	□	□	□	□	■

의견: 메달리온의 조사 결과가 위에 집계되어 있습니다. 923명이 응답했습니다. 플로어시사가 사업을 성장시키기 위해 서비스를 개선할 수 있는 분야가 몇 가지 있습니다. 첫째, 고객은 적절한 고객 서비스를 받는 데 문제가 있었습니다. 이는 특히 주문을 변경할 때 느린 이메일 응답 시간 때문이었습니다. 197메달리온은 웹용 채팅창에 투자하고 이것을 사용하도록 고객 담당 직원들을 교육할 것을 권합니다. 고객들은 웹사이트 이용을 즐겼으며, 채팅 기능은 고객들이 즉각적인 서비스를 받을 수 있도록 해 줄 것입니다.

제품 옵션과 관련하여 한 가지 일반적인 의견이 눈에 띄었습니다. 199고객들은 다양한 단섬유 단모 카펫을 높이 평가했습니다. 그들은 사람들이 자주 걸어다니는 곳에 대한 해당 카펫의 높은 내구성을 높이 샀습니다. 199그러나 거실과 같은 라운지 구역을 위한 두꺼운 섀그 러그에도 관심을 보였습니다.

어휘 generate 만들어 내다 somewhat 다소 neutral 중립적인 overall 전반적인 organization 구성[조직] compile 편집하다 adequate 적절한 be due to ~ 때문이다 feature 기능 immediate 즉각적인 general 일반적인 stand out 눈에 띄다 low-pile carpet 털이 짧은 카펫 fiber 섬유 durability 내구성 frequently 자주 shag rug 털갈개

플로어시 할인 쿠폰

200고객 설문 조사에 응답해 주셔서 감사합니다!
지원에 대한 보답으로 5월 1일부터 31일까지 다음 온라인 구매 시 20%를 할인 받으세요!

200계산 시 REWARD20 코드를 입력하세요.

198참고: Floorsy.com은 모든 주문에 대해 무료 배송 및 취급을 제공합니다.

어휘 reward 보상 enter 입력하다 checkout 계산대 handling 취급

주문해 주셔서 감사합니다.

린제이 씨께,
전화 주문을 해 주셔서 감사합니다. 귀하의 주문 #104850에 해당하는 다음 품목들이 배송되었습니다.

헨데시아 단모 러그 루비 레드 색상 (6x9)	x 1	180달러
199베레니아 섀그 러그 블루 색상 (6x9)	x 1	250달러
소계		430달러
200할인		86달러 (코드: REWARD20)
총		344달러
전액 지불됨		

성장하는 기업으로서 우리는 모든 후기와 의견을 진지하게 생각합니다. www.floorsy.com/comments를 방문해 후기를 제출하시고 향후 구매 시 10% 할인을 받으십시오. 구매 시 도움이 필요하시면 customerservice@floorsy.com으로 이메일을 보내 주십시오.

196 추론 / 암시

번역 보고서에서 암시된 것은?
(A) 고객들은 웹사이트가 탐색하기 쉽다고 생각한다.
(B) 고객들은 상품이 너무 비싸다고 생각한다.
(C) 고객 서비스 담당자가 높은 점수를 받았다.
(D) 고객들은 이메일로 소통하는 일이 거의 없다.

해설 보고서의 표에 따르면, 고객들이 웹사이트 구성(Web site organization)에 매우 만족했다(Very Satisfied)고 나와 있으므로 고객들은 웹사이트가 검색하기 편하게 짜여 있다고 생각하고 있음을 알 수 있다. 따라서 정답은 (A)이다.

어휘 navigate (인터넷·웹사이트를) 돌아다니다

197 세부 사항

번역 굽타 씨가 보고서에 한 가지 권고는?
(A) 더 많은 인테리어 디자이너를 고용할 것
(B) 러그의 가격을 낮출 것
(C) 반품 정책을 변경할 것
(D) 고객 지원에 더 많은 돈을 지출할 것

해설 보고서의 의견(Comments)란 다섯 번째 문장에서 굽타 씨는 메달리온을 웹용 채팅창에 투자하고 이것을 사용하도록 고객 담당 직원들을 교육할 것을 권한다(Medallion recommends ~ to use it)고 했으므로 (D)가 정답이다.

> Paraphrasing 지문의 investing
> → 정답의 spend more money

198 Not / True

번역 쿠폰에 따르면, 플로어시에 대해 사실인 것은?
(A) 할인을 거의 하지 않는다.
(B) 추가 비용 없이 물품을 배송한다.
(C) 상품권을 제공하지 않는다.
(D) 웹사이트 구성이 형편없다.

해설 쿠폰의 하단에 있는 참고(Note)에서 Floorsy.com은 모든 주문에 대해 무료 배송 및 취급을 제공한다(Floorsy.com offers ~ all orders)고 했으므로 (B)가 정답이다.

어휘 rarely 드물게   organize 구성[조직]하다

> Paraphrasing 지문의 free → 정답의 at no extra cost

199 연계

번역 플로어시에 대해 결론지을 수 있는 것은?
(A) 웹사이트를 완전히 재구성했다.
(B) 굽타 씨에게 관리직을 제안했다.
(C) 판매 제품군에 섀그 러그를 추가했다.
(D) 고객 담당 직원을 추가로 채용했다.

해설 보고서의 의견(Comments) 중 두 번째 단락 두 번째 문장에서 고객들은 다양한 단섬유 단모 카펫을 높이 평가했다(Customers appreciated ~ short fibers)고 했고 마지막 문장에서 그러나 거실과 같은 라운지 구역을 위한 두꺼운 섀그 러그에도 관심을 보였다(However, they were ~ living rooms)고 했다. 그런데 플로어시에서 물건을 구입한 린제이 씨의 영수증에 따르면 결제 품목에 베레니아 섀그 러그 블루 색상(Verenia Shag Rug in Blue)이 있는 것으로 보아 플로어시에서 고객의 관심을 수렴하여 취급 제품에 섀그 러그 제품을 추가했다고 결론 내릴 수 있으므로 (C)가 정답이다.

200 연계

번역 린제이 씨에 대해 사실일 것 같은 것은?
(A) 굽타 씨에게 자신의 주문에 대해 언급했다.
(B) 러그에 다소 만족하지 못했다.
(C) 주문을 변경하기 위해 이메일을 보냈다.
(D) 고객 설문 조사에 응답했다.

해설 쿠폰의 첫 문장에서 고객 설문 조사에 응답해 주셔서 감사하다(Thank you ~ customer survey!)며 보답으로 다음 온라인 구매 시 20%를 할인 받으라(As a reward ~ online purchase)고 했고 계산 시 REWARD20 코드를 입력하라(Enter the ~ checkout)고 했다. 영수증에 따르면 린제이 씨는 REWARD20 코드로 86달러를 할인(Discount $86.00 (Code: REWARD20)) 받았으므로 린제이 씨가 설문 조사에 응했다는 것을 알 수 있다. 따라서 정답은 (D)이다.

TEST 4

실전 TEST 5

101 (A)	102 (A)	103 (C)	104 (C)	105 (A)
106 (A)	107 (B)	108 (A)	109 (A)	110 (A)
111 (C)	112 (D)	113 (C)	114 (D)	115 (A)
116 (C)	117 (C)	118 (D)	119 (B)	120 (D)
121 (C)	122 (B)	123 (A)	124 (D)	125 (B)
126 (C)	127 (D)	128 (B)	129 (B)	130 (D)
131 (B)	132 (A)	133 (D)	134 (D)	135 (A)
136 (D)	137 (C)	138 (B)	139 (C)	140 (B)
141 (A)	142 (D)	143 (D)	144 (A)	145 (B)
146 (D)	147 (D)	148 (B)	149 (C)	150 (B)
151 (B)	152 (D)	153 (D)	154 (B)	155 (C)
156 (C)	157 (D)	158 (D)	159 (A)	160 (C)
161 (D)	162 (B)	163 (B)	164 (B)	165 (B)
166 (B)	167 (D)	168 (B)	169 (B)	170 (C)
171 (B)	172 (B)	173 (A)	174 (C)	175 (D)
176 (C)	177 (D)	178 (A)	179 (C)	180 (B)
181 (D)	182 (C)	183 (A)	184 (D)	185 (C)
186 (D)	187 (B)	188 (C)	189 (A)	190 (C)
191 (C)	192 (A)	193 (D)	194 (B)	195 (D)
196 (B)	197 (D)	198 (D)	199 (A)	200 (C)

PART 5

101 동사 어휘

해설 enough money를 목적어로 받아 '충분한 돈을 모았다'는 문맥이 되어야 자연스러우므로 '(자금 등을) 모으다'는 의미의 (A) raised가 정답이다.

번역 퍼링 타운십은 내년에 새 도서관을 짓기에 충분한 돈을 모았다.

어휘 township (미국의) 군구   convince 확신시키다   observe 준수하다, 관찰하다   tackle (힘든 문제와) 씨름하다

102 인칭대명사의 격 _ 소유격

해설 빈칸에는 뒤에 온 명사구 ground floor café를 수식하는 인칭대명사가 들어가야 한다. 따라서 명사 앞에 쓰여 한정사 역할을 할 수 있는 소유격 인칭대명사 (A) Our가 정답이다.

번역 우리 1층 카페는 건물 거주자들에게 인기가 있다.

103 형용사 어휘

해설 빈칸 뒤의 전치사 with와 어울려 쓸 수 있어야 하며, 문맥상 '절차에 더 익숙해지도록'이라는 내용이 되어야 자연스럽다. 따라서 전치사 with와 함께 쓰여 '~에 익숙한'을 뜻하는 (C) familiar가 정답이다.

번역 추가 교육은 여러분이 RNV 연구소의 절차에 더 익숙해지도록 도울 것입니다.

어휘 procedure 절차   primary 주된   brief 간단한

104 전치사 어휘

해설 빈칸에는 명사구 a quarterly basis와 함께 쓰여 '분기별로'라는 의미를 나타내는 전치사가 들어가야 한다. 따라서 정답은 (C) on이다. 참고로 'on a regular basis 정기적으로, on a first-come-first-served basis 선착순으로' 등의 표현도 익혀 두자.

번역 직원 성과 심사는 분기별로 실시된다.

어휘 conduct 수행[실시]하다   quarterly 분기별의   basis 기준

105 명사 자리 _ 동사의 목적어

해설 빈칸은 동사 record의 목적어 자리이므로 명사가 들어가야 한다. 따라서 (A) attendance와 (B) attendant 중 하나를 선택해야 하는데, 빈칸 앞에 관사나 소유격이 없으므로 가산명사인 attendant는 들어갈 수 없고 문맥상으로도 '참석자 수를 기록한다'는 의미가 되어야 하므로 '참석자 수'를 뜻하는 불가산명사인 (A) attendance가 정답이다.

번역 콘서트 행사장에서는 마케팅 캠페인의 성공을 평가하기 위해 정기적으로 참석자 수를 기록한다.

어휘 venue 장소   routinely 일상적으로   evaluate 평가하다

106 접속사 어휘

해설 문맥상 적절한 부사절 접속사를 고르는 문제이다. '작업을 시작하기 전에 서명해야 한다'는 내용이 되어야 자연스러우므로 '~ 전에'라는 시간의 의미를 나타내는 (A) before가 정답이다.

번역 새 계약서는 작업을 시작하기 전에 서명되고 반송되어야 한다.

107 동사 자리

해설 The park's maps가 주어이고 빈칸이 동사인 문장이다. 따라서 문장에서 본동사 역할을 할 수 있는 (B) explain이 정답이다.

번역 공원의 지도는 각 등산로의 난이도를 설명해 준다.

어휘 hiking trail 등산로

108 형용사 어휘

해설 복합명사 customer service를 수식하여 '신속한 고객 서비스'라는 의미가 되어야 적합하므로 '신속한'을 뜻하는 (A) rapid가 정답이다.

번역 브랠리스 델리는 신선한 재료와 신속한 고객 서비스를 자랑한다.

어휘 pride 자랑하다   ingredient 재료   occasional 가끔의

109 전치사 어휘

해설 문맥상 '팀 회의가 화상 회의로 열릴 것이다'라는 의미가 적절하므로 '~로'라는 수단의 의미를 지닌 전치사 (A) by가 정답이다.

번역 다음 기술 합동 팀 회의는 내일 오후 3시에 화상 회의로 열릴 것이다.

어휘 coordination 합동   teleconference 화상 회의

110 형용사 자리 _ 명사 수식

해설 빈칸 앞에는 부정관사, 뒤에는 명사 grasp가 있으므로 명사를 수식하는 형용사 (A) firm이 정답이다. (B) firmest도 형용사이지만 최상급 앞에 있어야 하는 소유격이나 the가 없으므로 빈칸에 들어갈 수 없다.

번역 와이스 조경은 우수한 고객 서비스로 인해 고객 기반을 확고하게 잡고 있다.

어휘 landscaping 조경   grasp (확실한) 지배   firm 확고한

111 복합관계사

해설 빈칸 뒤에 주어와 동사가 있는 절이 왔으므로 접속사가 필요하고, 문맥상 '우리가 할 수 있을 때마다'라는 의미가 되어야 자연스러우므로 부사절 접속사로 쓰인 복합관계부사 (C) whenever가 정답이다.

번역 예상치 못한 지출에 대비해 수중에 돈을 확실히 확보하기 위해 우리는 가능할 때마다 예금 계좌에 자금을 추가한다.

어휘 savings account 보통 예금 계좌   on hand 구할 수 있는   expense 경비

112 능동태 vs. 수동태

해설 동사 자리인 빈칸 뒤에 타동사 offer의 목적어가 아닌 전치사 at이 이끄는 전치사구가 왔으므로 정답은 수동태인 (D) is being offered이다.

번역 럴스터 전기차의 작년 출시 모델이 대폭 할인가에 제공되고 있다.

어휘 significant 상당히 큰

113 형용사 어휘

해설 명사 method를 수식하는 형용사로 '선호하는 수단'이라는 의미가 되어야 적절하므로 '선호하는'이라는 뜻의 (C) preferred가 정답이다.

번역 시간이 중요하지 않을 경우 화물 열차는 초만 운송이 선호하는 자재 운송 수단이다.

어휘 freight 화물   method 방법   material 자재   factor 요소   valuable 귀중한   plain 소박한

114 명사 자리 _ 동사의 목적어

해설 동사 has collected의 목적어 역할로 관사 the 뒤에 명사가 와야 하므로 빈칸은 명사 자리이다. 따라서 '서신'을 뜻하는 명사 (D) correspondence가 정답이다.

번역 고객 불만에 대응하기 위해 영업부는 발송되는 모든 서신을 모아두었다.

115 명사절 _ 의문사절

해설 빈칸에는 동사 determine의 목적어 역할을 하는 명사절을 이끄는 접속사가 필요한데, 빈칸 뒤에 주어가 빠진 불완전한 문장이 있고 문맥상 '누가 그것들을 소유하고 있는지'라는 내용이 되어야 자연스러우므로 명사절 접속사 (A) who가 정답이다.

번역 축제 관계자들은 행사 후 남겨진 물건들을 누가 주인인지 확인할 수 있을 때까지 보관했다.

어휘 official 관리   store 보관하다   determine 알아내다   own 소유하다

116 동사 어휘

해설 빈칸 뒤에 온 to부정사를 목적어로 취할 수 있는 동사가 필요하다. 또한 문맥상 '퍼레이드를 다시 열기로 결정했다'는 의미가 적절하므로 정답은 '결정하다'는 뜻의 (C) decided이다.

번역 작년에 교통 문제가 있었음에도 불구하고 관계자들은 다시 도심에서 퍼레이드를 열기로 결정했다.

어휘 official 관리   advance 증진되다

117 명사 자리 _ 전치사의 목적어

해설 전치사 for의 목적어 역할로 소유격 뒤에 명사가 와야 하므로 빈칸은 명사 자리이다. 따라서 '도착'이라는 뜻의 명사인 (C) arrival이 정답이다.

번역 다나카 씨의 본사 방문 일정이 마무리되는 대로 우리는 그녀의 도착에 대비할 것이다.

어휘 arrangement 준비   finalize 마무리 짓다   headquarters 본사

118 부사 어휘

해설 감정을 나타내는 분사 excited를 수식하는 자리에서, 그러한 감정을 느끼는 것이 '이해할 만하다, 당연하다'라고 표현하는 것이 가장 적절하므로 '당연히'를 뜻하는 (D) understandably가 정답이다.

번역 새 쇼핑센터가 제공하게 될 이익을 고려해 볼 때, 지역 사회 구성원들이 새 쇼핑센터 제안에 열광하는 것은 당연했다.

어휘 given ~을 고려할 때   responsibly 책임감 있게   mistakenly 실수로

119 형용사 자리 _ 명사 수식

해설 동사 gained의 목적어로 온 명사 savings를 수식하는 자리이므로 '상당한'이라는 뜻의 형용사 (B) substantial이 정답이다.

번역 울트라 스타 건설은 다른 공급업체로부터 자재를 구입함으로써 상당한 비용 절감을 실현했다.

어휘 savings 절약된 금액   material 자재   supplier 공급업체

120 명사 어휘

해설 동사가 '고용하다(hire)'이고, 빈칸 뒤에 '자신의 분야에 폭넓은 경험을 가진'이라는 수식 내용으로 보아 '컨설턴트를 고용한다'가 가장 적합하다. 따라서 정답은 (D) consultants이다.

번역 엔비라 병원의 연구 프로젝트 관리자들은 종종 자신의 분야에 폭넓은 경험을 가진 외부 컨설턴트를 고용한다.

어휘 external 외부의 extensive 광범위한 field 분야 contender 경쟁자

121 부사 어휘

해설 빈칸 뒤의 finished를 수식하여 보고서를 '거의 끝냈다'는 의미가 되어야 적절하므로 '거의'라는 뜻의 (C) almost가 정답이다.

번역 콴 씨는 최종 고객 후기를 받을 때까지 보고서를 거의 마무리했다고 보고했다.

어휘 pending (어떤 일이) 있을 때까지

122 명사 어휘

해설 주어 자리인 빈칸은 보어로 온 that절과 동격을 이루어야 하므로 '신제품이 인기를 얻고 있다'를 대변할 수 있는 명사가 와야 한다. 문맥상 보고서를 근거로 파악한 판매 동향에 대해 설명하는 내용이므로 '추세, 동향'이라는 뜻의 (B) trend가 정답이다.

번역 지난 3개월간의 판매 보고서에 따르면 우리의 최신 제품들이 인기를 얻고 있는 추세인 것 같다.

123 형용사 자리 _ 명사 수식

해설 동사 are hiring의 목적어로 온 명사 contractors를 수식하는 자리이므로 '자격을 갖춘'이라는 뜻의 형용사 (A) qualified가 정답이다.

번역 뉴포트 힐스 부동산 개발업체는 최첨단 정수 시스템을 구축하기 위해 자격을 갖춘 도급업체들을 고용하고 있다.

어휘 property 부동산 contractor 도급업체 state-of-the-art 최첨단의 filtration 여과

124 명사 어휘

해설 빈칸 뒤의 '전치사 to + 잡지명'과 어울려 '~잡지의 기고가'라는 의미를 만드는 '기고가'라는 뜻의 (D) Contributors가 정답이다.

번역 〈알파인 클라이머〉 잡지의 기고가에는 유럽 최고의 사진작가 두 명인 칼 사엔스와 홀리 버깃츠가 포함되어 있다.

어휘 novelist 소설가 passenger 승객 contributor 기고가

125 명사 자리 _ 전치사의 목적어

해설 전치사 on의 목적어 역할로 정관사 the 뒤에 명사가 와야 하므로 빈칸은 명사 자리이다. 따라서 '자금 조달'이라는 뜻의 명사인 (B) financing이 정답이다.

번역 LN 은행과 이스트 웨이 은행의 합병 자금 조달에 관한 내용이 회의록에 포함될 것이다.

어휘 note 주석, 관련 내용 merger 합병 meeting minutes 회의록

126 부사 자리 _ 동사 수식

해설 목적어까지 나온 완전한 절 뒤에 동사 complete를 수식할 부사가 들어가야 하므로 (C) promptly가 정답이다.

번역 아흐마드 씨는 오늘 그녀의 월 예산 보고서에 포함시킬 수 있도록 우리 업무를 지체 없이 완료해 달라고 요청했다.

어휘 assignment 업무 promptly 지체 없이

127 전치사 자리

해설 빈칸은 뒤에 온 명사 labeling을 목적어로 취하는 전치사 자리이다. 따라서 보기 중 유일한 전치사인 (D) such as가 정답이다.

번역 신임 운영 관리자는 임원들이 상표 부착과 같은 사소한 업무에 대해서도 비용 견적을 원하는 것에 놀랐다.

어휘 operation 운영 cost estimate 비용 견적 minor 사소한 task 업무 labeling 상표 부착

128 동사 어휘

해설 '보고서(report)'를 목적어로 받을 수 있는 동사가 와야 하므로 '추가 조사 후, 보고서를 수정했다'는 내용을 이루는 '수정하다'는 뜻의 (B) revised가 정답이다.

번역 추가 조사 후, 헤인즈 씨는 이 지역의 철새 서식률에 대한 보고서를 수정했다.

어휘 prevalence 널리 퍼짐 migratory birds 철새 estimate 추산하다 inflict (괴로움 등을) 가하다

129 전치사 자리

해설 빈칸은 완전한 절에 명사구 a few recent negative reviews를 연결하는 자리이므로 전치사가 들어가야 한다. 문맥상 '부정적 평가에도 불구하고 잘 팔린다'는 내용이 되어야 하므로 '~에도 불구하고'를 뜻하는 전치사 (B) despite가 정답이다.

번역 출판사에 따르면, 클라크 리의 책은 최근의 몇몇 부정적인 평가에도 불구하고 잘 팔리고 있다.

130 부사 자리 _ to부정사 수식

해설 빈칸이 없어도 완전한 문장을 이루고 있으므로 빈칸에는 앞에 나온 to부정사를 수식하는 부사가 와야 한다. 따라서 정답은 '객관적으로'라는 뜻의 부사인 (D) objectively이다.

번역 카노 보험의 인사부 직원들은 모든 지원서를 객관적으로 분석할 수 있어야 한다.

어휘 insurance 보험 personnel 인사부 application 지원(서)

PART 6

131-134 기사

131 동사 자리 _ 시제

해설 Medicatenet이 주어, 빈칸이 동사인 문장으로 빈칸 뒤에 yesterday라는 과거를 나타내는 표현이 있으므로 과거 시제 동사인 (B) announced가 정답이다.

132 명사 어휘

해설 빈칸의 앞 문장에서 2억 달러의 벤처 자금(venture capital)을 조달했다고 했으므로 빈칸이 있는 문장의 'those …'는 앞 문장에서 언급된 자금을 받아 '이 자금을 사용할 계획'이라는 내용이 되어야 적절하다. 따라서 '자금'을 뜻하는 (A) funds가 정답이다.

133 전치사 어휘

해설 빈칸 뒤에 기간을 나타내는 명사구인 the next twelve months가 왔으므로 기간 전치사인 (D) over가 정답이다.

134 문맥에 맞는 문장 고르기

해설 빈칸 앞에서 이번 투자로 인력을 3배로 늘릴 수 있게 될 것이라고 했으므로, 앞 문장에서 언급된 인력 증가를 this increase로 받아 이러한 증가를 수용할 수 있도록 새 시설로 확장하기 위해 임대 계약을 체결했다는 내용이 뒤따르는 것이 가장 자연스럽다. 따라서 (D)가 정답이다.

번역 (A) 메디카테넷은 5년간의 연구 결과를 대대적으로 발표했다.
　　 (B) 대부분의 치료법은 시행착오 과정을 통해 개발된다.
　　 (C) 메디카테넷은 여러 일류 생명 공학 기업 중 하나이다.
　　 (D) 이러한 증가를 수용할 수 있도록 회사는 노워크에 있는 새 시설로 확장하기 위한 임대 계약을 체결했다.

어휘 fanfare 과시, 광고 trial-and-error 시행착오 process 과정 accommodate 수용하다 lease 임대차 계약 expand 확장하다 facility 시설

135-138 이메일

135 명사 어휘

해설 빈칸 앞에서 체크인 시간 전후에 도착할 경우 전화해 달라고 요청하고 있으므로 '사전 연락없이 도착할 경우 객실이 다른 손님에게 배정될 수 있다'는 내용이 되어야 적절하다. 따라서 '통지, 통보'를 뜻하는 (A) notice가 정답이다.

136 관계대명사 _ 주격

해설 빈칸 이하는 선행사 the breakfast buffet를 수식하는 관계절로, 빈칸 뒤에 동사가 나오므로 주격 관계대명사인 (D) which가 정답이다.

137 형용사 어휘

해설 빈칸은 '전경'이라는 뜻의 명사 view를 수식하기에 가장 자연스러운 형용사를 골라야 한다. 따라서 정답은 '환상적인, 장관을 이루는'이라는 뜻의 (C) spectacular이다.

138 문맥에 맞는 문장 고르기

해설 빈칸 앞에서 지역 명소에 대한 정보가 필요하면 서비스 데스크로 오라고 했고, 빈칸 뒤에는 만 일대에는 할 것이 많다고 했다. 따라서 빈칸에는 서비스 데스크에서 도움을 줄 수 있는 부문으로 방문할 만한 장소에 대한 정보 제공 외에 즐길 수 있는 활동에 대한 내용이 들어가면 자연스럽다. 따라서 여러 활동을 위한 계획을 짜는 데 도움을 줄 수 있다고 언급하고 있는 (B)가 정답이다.

번역 (A) 투숙객은 1층 선물 가게에서 한 가지 품목에 대해 할인을 받았습니다.
(B) 스쿠버 다이빙, 보트 타기, 또는 기타 활동들을 즐길 수 있는 계획을 도와드릴 수 있습니다.
(C) 모든 객실에는 인기 영화를 볼 수 있는 케이블 텔레비전이 연결되어 있습니다.
(D) 투숙객은 때때로 추가 요금 없이 호텔에 일찍 체크인할 수 있습니다.

어휘 charge 요금

139-142 편지

> 1월 17일
> 켄지 데이비스
> 26 페어트리 레인
> 볼티모어, MD 21205
>
> 데이비스 씨께,
>
> 이번 달 초 볼티모어에서 열린 연례 모형 기차 쇼에서 당신과 이야기할 수 있어서 즐거웠습니다. 당신이 전시했던 고품질의 골동품 기차에 **139감명받았습니다.**
>
> 골동품 기차 세트 몇 개를 판매하고 싶을 수도 있다고 말씀하셨는데요. 페어마운트 골동품 경매가 이상적인 **140판매 장소**가 될 것입니다. 1년에 두 차례 우리는 전 세계의 모형 기차 수집가들로부터 입찰을 유치하는 골동품 장난감의 온라인 경매를 개최합니다. 우리의 가장 최근 경매는 11월에 있었습니다. **141이 경매에 나온 물건에 지불된 가격을 온라인으로 확인하시기를 권합니다.** 우리 측 경매의 물건들이 다른 사이트에서 팔린 비슷한 물건들**142보다** 더 높은 가격에 팔렸다는 것을 발견하시게 되리라 믿습니다.
>
> 우리의 다음 경매는 5월 21일부터 22일까지 열릴 예정입니다. 참여하실 의향이 있는지 알려 주십시오.
>
> 저스틴 가르시아, 페어마운트 골동품 경매
>
> ---
> 어휘 auction 경매 ideal 이상적인 bid 입찰 collector 수집가

139 능동태 vs. 수동태

해설 빈칸 뒤에 목적어가 없고, 고품질의 골동품 기차에 주어인 I가 '감명받았다'는 내용이 되어야 하므로 (C) was impressed가 정답이다.

140 명사 어휘

해설 빈칸 앞 문장에서 골동품 기차 세트를 팔고 싶다고 말했다고 한 것으로 보아 빈칸이 있는 문장에는 페어마운트 골동품 경매가 골동품 기차 세트를 팔 수 있는 이상적인 장소가 될 것이라는 내용이 되어야 자연스럽다. 따라서 물건을 팔 수 있는 장소, 즉 '판매 장소'라는 뜻의 (B) marketplace가 정답이다.

141 문맥에 맞는 문장 고르기

해설 빈칸 앞에서 가장 최근 경매가 11월에 있었다고 했고, 빈칸 뒤에서 우리 측 경매의 물건들이 다른 사이트의 유사 물건보다 더 높은 가격에 팔렸다는 것을 알게 될 것이라고 했다. 따라서 빈칸에는 앞 문장

에서 언급된 최근 경매를 that auction으로 받아 이 경매에서의 경매가를 확인해 보라는 내용이 들어가야 뒤이어 유리한 경매 가격에 대해 언급한 문장이 자연스럽게 연결되므로 정답은 (A)이다.

번역 (A) 이 경매에 나온 물건에 지불된 가격을 온라인으로 확인하시기를 권합니다.
(B) 우리의 경매는 페어마운트 로즈라고 불리는 역사적인 호텔에서 열리곤 했습니다.
(C) 우리 고객들 중 일부는 1800년대의 골동품 금속 저금통에 관심이 있습니다.
(D) 온라인 경매의 모든 참가자들은 사이트에 들어가기 위한 자격 인증이 필요했습니다.

어휘 participant 참가자 credential 자격 인증

142 비교급

해설 빈칸 앞에 비교급인 higher prices가 있고, 빈칸 뒤에는 비교 대상이 언급되어 '다른 사이트에서 비슷한 물건들이 팔린 것보다'라는 내용이 되어야 하므로 '~보다'라는 의미의 (D) than이 정답이다.

143-146 메모

> 수신: 전 직원
> 발신: 하크필드 캐피탈
> 제목: 반나절
> 날짜: 11월 10일
>
> 11월 19일 금요일 오후 2시부터 주차장을 전기 세척하고 선을 다시 칠할 예정입니다. 작업자들이 일을 **143시작하기** 전에 주차장이 비워져야 합니다. 따라서 모든 직원들은 유급 반나절 휴가를 받게 될 것입니다. **144오전 8시에 근무를 시작하는 직원들은 정오에 퇴근할 것입니다.** 오전 9시에 시작하는 사람들은 오후 1시에 끝날 것입니다. 점심시간은 없을 예정입니다. 직원들은 근무를 마친 뒤 즉시 주차장을 **145비워야 합니다.**
>
> 주차장은 주말 내내 **146폐쇄될** 예정입니다. 주말에 근무하는 직원들은 길가나 유료 주차장에 주차해야 합니다.
>
> 이번 추가 휴가가 즐거우시기를 바랍니다.
>
> ---
> 어휘 personnel 직원들 parking garage 주차장
> immediately 즉시 shift 근무 시간 lot (특정 용도용) 부지

143 동사 어휘

해설 앞 문장에서 주차장 청소와 선을 다시 칠하는 작업 일정을 공지했으므로 빈칸이 있는 문장은 '작업자들이 작업을 시작하기 전에 주차장이 비워져야 한다'는 내용이 되어야 적절하다. 따라서 '시작하다'는 뜻의 (D) start가 정답이다.

144 문맥에 맞는 문장 고르기

해설 빈칸 앞에서 작업을 위해 주차장을 비워야 하는 이유로 직원들이 반나절 휴가를 받게 될 것이라는 일정에 대해 언급했고, 빈칸 뒤에서 오전 9시에 시작하는 직원은 오후 1시에 근무 종료라고 했다. 따라서 빈칸에도 반나절 휴가를 받아 일찍 퇴근하게 되는 직원들의 일

정에 대해 안내하는 내용이 들어가야 문맥이 일관성을 갖게 되므로 오전 8시에 근무를 시작하는 직원들은 정오에 퇴근한다고 언급한 (A)가 정답이다.

번역 (A) 오전 8시에 근무를 시작하는 직원들은 정오에 퇴근할 것입니다.
(B) 기밀 자료는 안전한 통에 폐기되어야 합니다.
(C) 카풀은 직원들 사이에서 점점 인기를 얻고 있습니다.
(D) 관리자들은 모든 초과 근무 신청을 승인해야 합니다.

어휘 confidential 기밀의 material 자료 be disposed of 처리되다 secure 안전한 bin 통 increasingly 점점 더

145 능동태 vs. 수동태

해설 조동사인 must 뒤에는 동사원형이 와야 한다. 또한 주어 Employees는 vacate(비우다, 떠나다)의 주체이고, 빈칸 뒤에 the garage라는 목적어가 있으므로 능동태 동사가 와야 한다. 따라서 (B) vacate가 정답이다.

146 형용사 어휘

해설 빈칸 뒤 문장에서 주말에 근무하는 직원들은 다른 곳에 주차해야 한다고 안내한 것으로 보아 '주차장이 주말 동안 폐쇄된다'는 내용이 되어야 적절하다. 따라서 '문을 닫는, 폐쇄된'을 뜻하는 (D) closed가 정답이다.

어휘 underground 지하의 spacious 널찍한

PART 7

147-148 청구서

148오마 진스 케이크

고객명: 로버트 팔로미노
고객 전화: (704) 555-0189
주문 날짜: 10월 26일
배달 날짜: 10월 28일
배달: 그랜드 업타운 호텔
148배달원: 레누 바티

1472kg 초콜릿 케이크 (원형)	75달러
초콜릿 아이싱	무료
딸기 속 재료	20달러
케이크 위 메시지: "메리 엘렌, 당신의 은퇴를 축하합니다!"	무료
147특별 요청: 케이크를 노란 아이싱 꽃으로 장식해 주세요.	15달러
배송비	15달러
총계	**125달러**

어휘 icing (과자 등의) 당의 filling (파이 등 음식의) 속
instruction 지시 사항 decorate 장식하다

147 세부 사항

번역 청구서에 따르면, 무엇이 구매되었는가?
(A) 호텔 숙박
(B) 싱싱한 꽃
(C) 초콜릿 사탕
(D) 주문 제작 디저트

해설 주문품이 2kg 원형 초콜릿 케이크(Two kg chocolate cake (round))라고 나와 있고, 특별 요청으로 노란 아이싱 꽃 장식 (Decorate cake with yellow icing flowers)이 기입되어 있으므로 (D)가 정답이다.

어휘 custom 주문 제작한

> **Paraphrasing** 지문의 cake → 정답의 dessert

148 추론 / 암시

번역 청구서에 따르면, 바티 씨는 누구일 것 같은가?
(A) 팔로미노 씨의 동료
(B) 호텔 직원 중 한 명
(C) 오마 진스 케이크의 직원
(D) 은퇴하는 요리사

해설 청구서를 발행한 가게의 이름이 오마 진스 케이크(Oma Jean's Cakes)이고, 물건을 배달한 사람이 레누 바티(Delivery by: Renu Bhatti)라고 나와 있다. 따라서 바티 씨는 오마 진스 케이크에서 일하는 사람임을 알 수 있으므로 정답은 (C)이다.

149-150 문자 메시지

그레그 파프 (오후 1시 17분)
안녕하세요, 제사. 149당신의 데스크톱 컴퓨터 문제를 해결하기 위한 오후 2시 약속에 조금 늦어지고 있습니다. 2시 20분쯤 도착할 것 같아요.

제사 킴 (오후 1시 18분)
괜찮습니다. 컴퓨터를 고칠 수 있기를 바랍니다. 저의 온라인 공예품 공급 사업을 그 컴퓨터에 의존하고 있거든요.

그레그 파프 (오후 1시 19분)
알고 있습니다. 단순히 조정이 필요한 걸 수도 있습니다. 150제 조수인 케빈 멀포드도 저와 함께 할 것입니다. 제가 지역 데이터 센터에서 정비 프로젝트를 진행하는 동안 그가 앞으로 여러분을 도와줄 수 있을 겁니다.

제사 킴 (오후 1시 20분)
잘됐네요.

그레그 파프 (오후 1시 21분)
좋습니다. 그럼 됐습니다.

제사 킴 (오후 1시 22분)
알겠습니다. 여기 오시면 뵙겠습니다.

어휘 troubleshoot 문제를 해결하다 depend on ~에 의존하다 craft 공예품 tune-up 조율[조정] maintenance 유지

149 추론 / 암시

번역 파프 씨는 누구일 것 같은가?
(A) 스튜디오 아티스트
(B) 공예품 판매업자
(C) 컴퓨터 기술자
(D) 건물 관리자

해설 1시 17분에 파프 씨가 당신의 데스크톱 컴퓨터 문제를 해결하기 위한 오후 2시 약속에 조금 늦어지고 있다(I'm running ~ troubleshoot the problem with your desktop computer)고 한 것으로 보아 파프 씨는 컴퓨터를 수리하는 기술자임을 알 수 있다. 따라서 정답은 (C)이다.

어휘 superintendent 관리자

150 의도 파악

번역 오후 1시 20분에 킴 씨가 "잘됐네요"라고 쓴 의도는?
(A) 문제가 해결되어 안심했다.
(B) 필요시 도움을 받을 수 있게 되어 기쁘다.
(C) 파프 씨가 곧 도착한다는 것에 기쁘다.
(D) 정비 프로젝트에 대한 작업에 만족한다.

해설 1시 19분에 파프 씨가 조수인 케빈 멀포드도 저와 함께 할 것(My assistant ~ with me, too)이라며 지역 데이터 센터에서 정비 프로젝트를 진행하는 동안 그가 앞으로 여러분을 도와줄 수 있을 것(He may help you out ~ local data center)이라고 하자, 1시 20분에 킴 씨가 잘됐다(That's good to know)고 했다. 따라서 킴 씨는 파프 씨가 없는 동안에도 그의 조수인 멀포드 씨의 도움을 받을 수 있다는 것을 알게 되어 안심이라는 의도로 한 말임을 알 수 있다. 따라서 정답은 (B)이다.

어휘 relieved 안심하는

151-152 제품 후기

우리 회사의 지역 교육 관리자로서, 저는 종종 그룹에게 프레젠테이션을 하고 있고 같은 장소에서는 거의 하지 않습니다. **151컴퓨터 화면에 뜨는 내용을 보여 줄 휴대용 프로젝터가 필요했는데, 베루바트론 800은 얇고 가벼워서 안성맞춤입니다.** 저는 이미지 해상도 및 기타 사양에 있어 여러 브랜드를 꽤 많이 비교 조사했습니다. 사양에 있어서는 많은 제품들이 비슷했지만 베루바트론 800은 특히 모든 프레젠테이션에 쉽게 가지고 다닐 수 있고 그래서 결국 이 제품을 택하게 되었습니다. **152한 가지 결점은 전원 코드와 VGA 코드가 놀라울 정도로 짧다는 점입니다.** 제품 사용 시 거의 매번 연장 코드를 사용해야 했으므로 저와 똑같은 대비를 하시기 바랍니다.

- 호레이스 오퍼맨

어휘 regional 지역의 rarely 드물게 portable 휴대용의 in terms of ~에 관하여 resolution 해상도 specification 사양 comparable 비슷한 ultimately 결국 flaw 결점 extension cord 연장 코드

151 세부 사항

번역 오퍼맨 씨는 왜 다른 것들과 비교해 하나의 프로젝터를 선택했는가?
(A) 내구성이 좋다.
(B) 휴대가 쉽다.
(C) 화질이 가장 좋다.
(D) 더 많은 부속품이 포함되어 있다.

해설 두 번째 문장에서 오퍼맨 씨가 컴퓨터 화면에 뜨는 내용을 보여 줄 휴대용 프로젝터가 필요했는데 베루바트론 800은 얇고 가벼워서 안성맞춤이다(I needed a portable projector ~ slim and light)라고 했으므로, 휴대하기가 편리하여 베루바트론 800을 선택했음을 알 수 있다. 따라서 정답은 (B)이다.

어휘 durable 내구성이 있는 accessories 부속품

> **Paraphrasing** 지문의 slim and light
> → 정답의 easy to carry

152 세부 사항

번역 오퍼맨 씨는 독자들에게 무엇을 충고하는가?
(A) 장치의 수명
(B) 일부 케이블의 길이
(C) 별도 케이스의 필요성
(D) 특정 컴퓨터와의 호환성 부족

해설 다섯 번째 문장에서 한 가지 결점은 전원 코드와 VGA 코드가 놀라울 정도로 짧다는 점(One flaw is ~ surprisingly short)이라면서, 제품 사용 시 거의 매번 연장 코드를 사용해야 했으므로 이와 똑같은 대비를 하기 바란다(I have needed ~ do the same)고 충고하고 있으므로 (B)가 정답이다.

어휘 life span 수명 device 장치 length 길이 separate 별도의 lack 부족 compatibility 호환성

153-154 이메일

수신: 디미트리 오웬스
참조: 시어도어 스콧, 할리나 키베라
발신: 제니스 코백
날짜: 1월 10일
153제목: 다음 면접

오웬스 씨께,

보안 시스템 관리자 직책과 관련해 이야기할 수 있어서 좋았습니다. 다음 단계 면접을 보실 수 있게 되었다고 말씀드리게 되어 기쁩니다. **154보안 담당 이사인 스콧 씨와 부장 키베라 씨와 대화하시게 될 겁니다.**

미팅 전에 가상 전화 회의에 참여하는 방법에 대한 지침을 포함한 이메일을 추가로 보내겠습니다.

153미팅 날짜/시간: 1월 12일 오후 2시 30분 동부 표준시

153전화 회의를 할 수 있는지 확인해 주십시오.

J. 코백
인사부 직원

어휘 cc 참조 security 보안 instruction 지침 virtual 가상의 conference call 전화 회의

153 주제 / 목적

번역 이메일의 목적은?
(A) 일자리 광고
(B) 가상 회의의 시간 변경
(C) 지원자에게 일자리 제의
(D) 면접 일정 잡기

해설 이메일의 제목이 다음 면접(Subject: Next interview)이고, 세 번째 단락에서 미팅 날짜와 시간을 1월 12일 오후 2시 30분 동부 표준시(Meeting date/time ~ Standard Time)라고 알려 주며 전화 회의를 할 수 있는지 확인해 달라(Please confirm ~ the conference call)고 했으므로 구직자와 2차 면접 일정을 잡으려고 글을 쓴 것임을 알 수 있다. 따라서 (D)가 정답이다.

어휘 job opening 일자리 candidate 지원자

154 세부 사항

번역 스콧 씨는 누구인가?
(A) 인사부 직원
(B) 보안 책임자
(C) 보안 시스템 부서의 입사 지원자
(D) 키베라 씨의 개인 비서

해설 첫 단락의 세 번째 문장에서 보안 담당 이사인 스콧 씨와 부장 키베라 씨와 대화하게 될 것(You will speak with the director of security, Mr. Scott ~ Kibera)이라고 한 것으로 보아 스콧 씨는 보안 책임자임을 알 수 있다. 따라서 정답은 (B)이다.

Paraphrasing 지문의 director → 정답의 head

155-157 이메일

수신: board@sunnervalleyalliance.org
발신: kathleen.huff@sunnervalleyalliance.org
날짜: 8월 17일 화요일
제목: 서너 기획 위원회 회의

이사회 여러분께,

저는 다가오는 서너 기획 위원회 회의에서 발표 준비를 하고 있으며, 발표에 수반될 슬라이드쇼를 제작할 예정입니다. 저의 요점을 보강할 수 있는 훌륭한 자료를 갖고 있지만 그 정보가 시각적으로 제시된다면 사람들이 더 쉽게 이해할 것이라고 생각합니다. ¹⁵⁵저의 발표에 들어갈 시각적 요소의 개발을 돕는 데 관심있으신 분이 계실까요? 원형 도표와 도해는 슬라이드쇼에 큰 영향을 미칠 것입니다.

서너 밸리 북동쪽에 있는 홀트 부동산을 활용하는 세 가지 제안의 장단점을 제시하는 것이 목표입니다. ¹⁵⁶저는 위원회가 자신의 땅 옆에 있는 그 부동산을 매입하겠다는 켄 얀센의 제안을 받아들이기를 바랍니다. 그가 자신의 과수원을 확장할 수도 있고 이것이 서너 밸리 북부의 전원풍 자연을 유지하는 데 도움이 될 것입니다.

¹⁵⁷발표자 등록 안내에는 의제가 온라인에 게시되기 전에 발표 자료를 제출해야 한다고 나와 있지만 이때가 언제인지 명시되어 있지 않습니다. 오늘 전화로 자세한 내용을 알아보겠습니다.

캐슬린 허프

어휘 commission 위원회 board 이사회 upcoming 다가오는 accompany 수반하다 reinforce 보강하다 component 요소 diagram 도표 impact 영향 disadvantage 단점 property 부동산, 부지 accept 받아들이다 expand 확장하다 orchard 과수원 rural 시골의 material 자료 agenda 의제 specify 명시하다

155 주제 / 목적

번역 이메일의 목적은?
(A) 발표자 편성
(B) 추가 통계 수집
(C) 도표에 대한 지원 요청
(D) 일부 증거에 대한 반론

해설 첫 단락의 세 번째 문장에서 저의 발표에 들어갈 시각적 요소의 개발을 돕는 데 관심있으신 분이 있을지(Is anybody interested ~ my presentation?)를 물으며 원형 도표와 도해는 슬라이드쇼에 큰 영향을 미칠 것(Some pie charts ~ the slideshow)이라고 했으므로 발표에 들어갈 시각 자료를 만드는 데 도움을 요청하기 위해 이메일을 썼다는 것을 알 수 있다. 따라서 정답은 (C)이다.

어휘 coordinate 편성하다 statistics 통계 argue 주장하다 evidence 증거

Paraphrasing 지문의 pie charts and diagrams → 정답의 graphics

156 세부 사항

번역 허프 씨는 기획 위원회가 무엇을 하기를 바라는가?
(A) 제안 거절
(B) 규제 강화
(C) 전원 지대 보존
(D) 일부 수로 복구

해설 두 번째 단락의 두 번째 문장에서 허프 씨는 위원회가 자신의 땅 옆에 있는 그 부동산을 매입하겠다는 켄 얀센의 제안을 받아들이기를 바란다(I am hoping ~ his land)면서, 그가 자신의 과수원을 확장할 수도 있고 이것이 서너 밸리 북부의 전원풍 자연을 유지하는 데 도움이 될 것(He would expand ~ Sunner Valley)이라고 했다. 따라서 허프 씨는 위원회가 전원 지역을 보존하는 방향으로 결정을 내리기를 바라고 있음을 알 수 있으므로 (C)가 정답이다.

어휘 decline 거절하다 tighten 강화하다 restriction 규제 preserve 보존하다 restore 복구하다

Paraphrasing 지문의 maintain the rural nature → 정답의 Preserve rural land

157 세부 사항

번역 허프 씨는 무엇을 확인할 것인가?
(A) 부동산의 경계
(B) 제출 기한
(C) 발표 허용 시간
(D) 신규 사업에 대한 규정

해설 마지막 단락에서 허프 씨가 발표자 등록 안내에는 의제가 온라인에 게시되기 전에 발표 자료를 제출해야 한다고 나와 있지만 이때가 언제인지 명시되어 있지 않다(The speaker sign-up ~ this will happen)면서 오늘 전화로 자세한 내용을 알아보겠다(I will call ~ more details)고 했으므로 발표 자료 제출 기한을 확인할 것임을 알 수 있다. 따라서 정답은 (B)이다.

어휘 boundary 경계 submission 제출 regulation 규정

158-160 견적서

웨이페이브 하드스케이프스
주택지 진입로, 벽 및 테라스 분야 최고

견적: #20987
날짜: 9월 28일
총액: 4,000달러

준비 대상
루렌 토요
S 헨리 가 23000
페어빌, GA 30013

158작업 설명
집 뒤쪽의 잔디 및 오래된 콘크리트 테라스 제거. 새 테라스를 위한 시멘트 기초 깔기. 158,159의뢰인이 승인한 계획에 따라 트로피칼 선셋 타일 설치.

자재	요율	수량	금액
시멘트	포대당 50달러	5	250달러
트로피칼 선셋 타일	개당 3달러	500	1,500달러
자재 배송			350달러
작업 잔해 처리			150달러
인건비			1,750달러
총			**4,000달러**

조건
160계약서 서명 시 2,000달러 지불
프로젝트 완료 시 2,000달러 지불
신용 카드, 수표 또는 계좌 이체로 지불 가능

이 견적서는 귀하의 계약서로 활용됩니다. 이 문서에 서명하고 estimates@waypavehardscapes.com으로 반송해 주세요.

어휘 residential 주택지의 estimate 견적서 description 설명 lay 깔다 foundation 기초 per ~에 따라 material 자재 rate 가격 disposal 처리 debris 잔해, 쓰레기 labor 노동 terms 조건 due (돈을) 지불해야 하는 payable 지불 가능한 transfer 이체

158 세부 사항

번역 견적서는 어떤 종류의 작업에 대해 작성되었는가?
(A) 주택 페인트칠
(B) 진입로 포장
(C) 돌담 쌓기
(D) 야외 테라스 조성

해설 견적서의 작업 설명(JOB DESCRIPTION)란에 집 뒤쪽의 잔디 및 오래된 콘크리트 테라스 제거(Remove grass ~ the house), 새 테라스를 위한 시멘트 기초 깔기(Lay a cement ~ new patio), 의뢰인이 승인한 계획에 따라 트로피칼 선셋 타일 설치(Install Tropical ~ approved plan)라고 기재되어 있으므로 집 뒤쪽의 야외 테라스 조성을 위해 작성된 견적서임을 알 수 있다. 따라서 정답은 (D)이다.

어휘 fence 울타리

159 추론 / 암시

번역 웨이페이브가 견적서를 제공하기 전에 무슨 일이 일어났을 것 같은가?
(A) 디자인 제안이 받아들여졌다.
(B) 오래된 테라스가 제거되었다.
(C) 할인이 제공되었다.
(D) 마당에서 흙과 잔해가 제거되었다.

해설 견적서의 작업 설명(JOB DESCRIPTION)란 세 번째 문장에 의뢰인이 승인한 계획에 따라 트로피칼 선셋 타일 설치(Install Tropical ~ approved plan)라고 기재되어 있는 것으로 보아 의뢰인에게 디자인 제안을 이미 승인받았다는 것을 알 수 있으므로 (A)가 정답이다.

> **Paraphrasing** 지문의 approved plan → 정답의 A design proposal was accepted.

160 세부 사항

번역 토요 씨는 계약서에 서명할 때 얼마를 지불해야 하는가?
(A) 1,500달러
(B) 1,750달러
(C) 2,000달러
(D) 4,000달러

해설 견적서의 하단에 있는 조건(TERMS) 첫 항목에 계약서 서명 시 2,000달러를 지불해야 한다($2,000 due upon signing of contract)고 나와 있으므로 (C)가 정답이다.

161-163 이메일

수신: 카인 라 트랜 〈tqla@tevanto.vn〉
발신: Customercare@shoppedesjeans.fr
날짜: 9월 22일
제목: 주문 번호 93887

트랜 씨께:

161샵 데 진 고객 관리 센터로 주문 번호 93887에 대해 문의 주셔서 감

사합니다. 구매가 만족스럽지 않으시다니 유감입니다. 고객님께서 주문하신 제품인 여성 스트레치 청바지 36 사이즈 미드나잇 블루 색상은 저희의 가장 잘 팔리는 여성복 스타일 중 하나입니다. 이 청바지를 돋보이게 만드는 다크 블루 색상을 내기 위해 원단은 데님 색상이 짙어지도록 두 번 염색됩니다. 각각의 청바지는 주의 사항을 표시한 큰 라벨이 붙어 있습니다. **163제품의 라벨에는 제품이 여러 번 세탁될 때까지 일부 염료가 밝은 색상의 섬유나 가구 커버에 이염될 수 있다고 분명하게 명시되어 있습니다.** 또한 세탁 시 염료가 빠져나올 수 있으므로 청바지를 어두운 색상의 세탁물과 함께 세탁할 것을 권장합니다.

161이러한 경고를 확인하지 못하셨고 그 결과 고객님의 소파가 변색되었다니 유감입니다. 샵 데 진의 목표는 모든 구매에 대한 100% 고객 만족입니다. 그러나 이러한 상황은 제품 라벨에 염료 문제가 기재되어 있기 때문에 저희 고객 서비스 보증에 해당되지 않습니다. **162베이킹 소다로 소파를 처리한 뒤 가구 커버 세정제를 사용하실 것을 권합니다.**

베르틴 올리비에
고객 관리 담당자, 샵 데 진

어휘 standout 눈에 띄는 것 dye 염색하다; 염료 deepen 짙게 하다 state 명시하다 rub off on ~에 물들다 upholstery (소파 등의) 커버 run (옷에서 염색된) 물이 빠지다 discolored 변색된 situation 상황 cover 포함시키다 guarantee 보증 treat 처리하다

---

161 세부 사항

번역 트랜 씨는 왜 샵 데 진 고객 관리 센터에 연락했는가?
(A) 잘못된 색상의 청바지를 받았다.
(B) 청바지 때문에 밝은 색상의 옷이 망가졌다.
(C) 청바지 스타일이 불만족스러웠다.
(D) 청바지 때문에 가구 제품이 얼룩졌다.

해설 첫 문장에서 트랜 씨에게 샵 데 진 고객 관리 센터로 문의 주셔서 감사하다(Thank you for ~ #93887)고 했고, 구매가 만족스럽지 않으시다니 유감(I am sorry ~ your purchase)이라며 고객님께서 주문하신 제품은 여성 스트레치 청바지 36 사이즈 미드나잇 블루 색상(The product ~ midnight blue)이라고 했으며, 두 번째 단락의 첫 문장에서 경고를 확인하지 못하여 고객님의 소파가 변색되었다니 유감이다(It is unfortunate ~ discolored as a result)라고 했다. 따라서 트랜 씨는 최근 구매한 청바지로 인해 소파가 변색된 문제와 관련하여 고객 센터에 연락한 것이므로 (D)가 정답이다.

어휘 ruin 망치다 stain 얼룩지게 하다

Paraphrasing 지문의 your sofa has become discolored
→ 정답의 stained an item of furniture

162 세부 사항

번역 올리비에 씨는 트랜 씨를 어떻게 돕는가?
(A) 새 청바지 발송
(B) 전액 환불 제공
(C) 향후 주문에 대한 할인 제공
(D) 문제 해결 방법 제안

해설 두 번째 단락의 마지막 문장에서 올리비에 씨가 트랜 씨에게 베이킹 소다로 소파를 처리한 뒤 가구 커버 세정제를 사용하실 것을 권한다(I suggest you ~ upholstery cleaner)며 이염 문제를 해결할 방법을 권하고 있으므로 (D)가 정답이다.

163 문장 삽입

번역 [1], [2], [3], [4]로 표시된 곳 중에서 다음 문장이 들어가기에 가장 적합한 위치는?

"각각의 청바지는 주의 사항을 표시한 큰 라벨이 붙어 있습니다."

(A) [1]
(B) [2]
(C) [3]
(D) [4]

해설 제시된 문장은 '각 청바지는 주의 사항을 표시한 큰 라벨이 붙어 있다'며 각 제품의 라벨마다 주의 사항이 표기되어 있다는 점을 강조하고 있다. 따라서 라벨(The item's label)에 대해 언급하며, 제품의 일부 염료가 이염될 수 있다는 주의 사항이 라벨에 분명히 명시되어 있음을 고객에게 상기시키는 내용의 문장 앞에 들어가는 것이 글의 흐름상 자연스러우므로 정답은 (B)이다.

164-167 안내 책자

라도 쇼핑센터

레블리 개발은 스프링필드의 라도 쇼핑센터 신규 프로젝트의 승인을 발표하게 되어 기쁩니다. 빠르게 확장하고 있는 이 도시는 수도권에 편리하게 위치해 있으며 라도 쇼핑센터는 모두에게 훌륭한 쇼핑 경험을 **165제공해** 줄 것입니다. 공사는 내년에 끝날 것으로 예상됩니다.

건물의 주요 특성	지역 특징
• 150,000 제곱피트의 소매 및 사무실 공간	• 수족관, 다수의 공원, 강과 인접해 있음
• **164제곱피트당 25달러 (1층)**	• 2개의 주요 연결 도로: 헴리 대로와 82번 도로, **16735번 고속도로와 추가 연결로 5년 뒤 완공 예정**
• **164제곱피트당 20달러 (2층 이상)**	
• 공간 임대차 가능	• **166스프링필드에 3년 이내 4,000 가구 신축**
• 레블리 개발과 협의를 통한 공간 주문 제작 가능	• 2년 이내 전기차 충전소를 갖춘 인근 주차 건물 완공 예정
	• 근처의 영화관, 놀이공원, 기타 명소들

어휘 approval 승인 rapidly 빠르게 expand 확대되다 conveniently 편리하게 capital 수도 lease 임대차 custom-built 주문 제작한 consultation 협의 structure 건축물 port 포트(접속 단자) attraction 명소[명물], 매력을 끄는 요소

164 Not / True

번역 새로운 건물에 대해 명시된 것은?
(A) 영화관이 입주할 것이다.
(B) 개인 주거지를 제공할 것이다.
(C) 1층은 상위층보다 더 비싸다.
(D) 모든 공간에 주차가 무료로 포함된다.

해설   건물의 주요 특성(Property Highlights)의 두 번째 항목에 1층은 제곱피트당 25달러($25 per square foot (ground floor))이고 세 번째 항목에 2층 이상은 제곱피트당 20달러($20 per square foot (upper floors))라며 1층이 상위층보다 더 비싸다는 것이 명시되어 있으므로 정답은 (C)이다.

어휘   contain ~이 들어 있다

165 동의어

번역   첫 번째 단락 3행의 "deliver"와 의미가 가장 가까운 단어는?
    (A) 나르다
    (B) 제공하다
    (C) 보내다
    (D) 구입하다

해설   의미상 쇼핑센터가 모두에게 훌륭한 쇼핑 경험을 '제공해 준다'는 뜻으로 쓰인 것이므로 정답은 (B) provide이다.

166 추론 / 암시

번역   스프링필드에 대해 암시된 것은?
    (A) 레블리 개발의 소유이다.
    (B) 인구가 증가할 것으로 예상된다.
    (C) 강에 접근할 수 없다.
    (D) 경제가 제조업에 기반을 두고 있다.

해설   지역 특징(Area Attractions)의 세 번째 항목에서 스프링필드에 3년 이내 4,000 가구가 신축된다(4,000 new homes to be built in Springfield within three years)고 나와 있는 것으로 보아 이 지역의 가구 수가 증가할 것임을 알 수 있으므로 (B)가 정답이다.

167 세부 사항

번역   35번 고속 도로 연결로는 언제 완공되는가?
    (A) 1년 뒤
    (B) 2년 뒤
    (C) 3년 뒤
    (D) 5년 뒤

해설   지역 특징(Area Attractions)의 두 번째 항목에서 35번 고속도로에 추가 연결로가 5년 뒤 완공 예정(with additional connection to Highway 35 to be completed in five years)이라고 나와 있으므로 (D)가 정답이다.

168-171 문자 메시지

잭 엘링 (오전 10시 35분) 안녕하세요, 여러분. **168오늘 밤 가게에 일하러 올 수 있는 사람이 있을까요? 켈리가 차에 문제가 있어서 근무를 할 수가 없대요.**
에밀리 친 (오전 10시 37분) 죄송하지만 전 안돼요. 그런데 마리아와 코지도 근무하지 않나요? 저녁에는 보통 두 명이 있지 않나요?

잭 엘링 (오전 10시 39분)
네, 보통 두 명이 있고 169그 둘은 오늘 밤에 근무할 거예요. 하지만 새로운 맛의 아이스크림을 나눠 주는 특별 판촉 행사를 진행할 예정이라서요. 이 일을 도와줄 한 명이 더 필요해요.

에밀리 친 (오전 10시 40분)
170저는 오늘 오후에 생일 파티에 참석할 계획이라서 안 되겠네요.

카메론 스타인 (오전 10시 42분)
171제 낮 근무가 끝나고 나서 계속 있을 수 있습니다.

에밀리 친 (오전 10시 43분)
171사실, 계속 남아 있고 싶지 않으시면 오후 6시에서 9시까지 제가 일할 수 있어요. 파티가 몇 시간 내로 끝날 거예요. 171어떻게 생각하세요?

카메론 스타인 (오전 10시 44분)
음, 초과 근무 시간을 꼭 썼으면 좋겠어요.

에밀리 친 (오전 10시 45분)
알겠습니다.

잭 엘링 (오전 10시 46분)
고마워요, 카메론!

어휘   shift 근무 시간   promotion 판촉 활동   flavor 맛

168 주제 / 목적

번역   엘링 씨가 문자 메시지를 시작한 이유는?
    (A) 친 씨에게 근무 시간에 결근했다고 말하려고
    (B) 근무 시간을 대체해 줄 사람을 요청하려고
    (C) 특별 행사에 초대하려고
    (D) 직장까지 태워달라고 부탁하려고

해설   10시 35분에 엘링 씨가 오늘 밤 가게에 일하러 올 수 있는 사람이 있을지(Would anyone ~ work tonight?) 물으며, 켈리가 차에 문제가 있어서 근무를 할 수가 없다(Kelly is ~ can't work her shift)고 했으므로 켈리 대신 근무해 줄 사람을 요청하려고 문자 메시지를 보냈음을 알 수 있다. 따라서 정답은 (B)이다.

어휘   extend (초대장을) 보내다   ride (차량 등을) 타고 가기

169 세부 사항

번역   오늘 밤 가게에서 무슨 일이 있을 것인가?
    (A) 직원들이 새로운 조리법을 연구할 것이다.
    (B) 직원들이 무료 아이스크림 시식을 제공할 것이다.
    (C) 직원들이 교육에 참여할 것이다.
    (D) 직원들이 동료의 환송 파티를 열 것이다.

해설   10시 39분에 엘링 씨가 오늘 밤에 둘이 근무할 것(those two are working tonight)이지만 새로운 맛의 아이스크림을 나눠 주는 특별 판촉 행사를 진행할 예정(But we are ~ ice cream flavors)이라고 했으므로 오늘 밤 가게에서는 아이스크림 시식 행사가 있음을 알 수 있다. 따라서 정답은 (B)이다.

어휘   tasting 시식   participate in ~에 참여하다   going-away 이별의

170 세부 사항

번역 친 씨는 오늘 어디에 가는가?
(A) 스타인 씨의 집
(B) 자동차 정비소
(C) 파티
(D) 영화관

해설 10시 40분에 친 씨가 오늘 오후에 생일 파티에 참석할 계획(I'm attending a birthday party this afternoon)이라고 했으므로 (C)가 정답이다.

171 의도 파악

번역 오전 10시 44분에 스타인 씨가 "음, 초과 근무 시간을 꼭 썼으면 좋겠어요"라고 쓴 의도는?
(A) 친 씨의 사과를 받아주고 있다.
(B) 친 씨의 제안을 거절하고 있다.
(C) 가게에서 일하는 것을 좋아한다.
(D) 저녁에 일하는 것을 선호한다.

해설 10시 42분에 스타인 씨가 낮 근무가 끝나고 나서 계속 있을 수 있다(I could stay ~ shift is over)고 초과 근무를 하려 하자, 10시 43분에 친 씨가 자신이 오후 6시에서 9시까지 일할 수 있다(Actually, I could ~ want to stay)며 어떻게 생각하는지(What do you think?) 물었다. 이에 대해 10시 44분에 스타인 씨가 본인이 초과 근무하려는 의지를 다시 한번 강조하며 초과 근무 시간을 꼭 썼으면 좋겠다(Well, I could ~ overtime hours)고 했으므로 친 씨의 제안을 사양하려는 의도를 파악할 수 있다. 따라서 정답은 (B)이다.

어휘 accept 받아들이다 apology 사과 decline 거절하다

172-175 보고서 요약

172키아메 타이어 공장 생산성 보고서

작성자: 윌마 나자르, 시스템 엔지니어
보고서 날짜: 4월 10일
172**보고서 사유:** 분기 검사

요약: 172공장의 모든 장비 및 기기를 검사를 완료했습니다. 생산 라인의 주요 요소들은 예상대로 가동되고 있습니다. 이러한 요소에는 믹서, 롤러 및 직물 생산 시스템이 포함됩니다. 지난 분기에 추가된 타이어 조립용 회전통도 예상대로 기능하고 있습니다. 마지막으로, 타이어 접지면용 금형이 마모의 징후를 보이기 시작했습니다. 직원들은 이 금형들에 표시를 했으며 해당 금형들은 생산 라인에서 제거될 것입니다.

권고 사항: 새로운 교체 금형을 구입하는 것이 최우선 사항입니다. 173자세한 내용은 보고서의 타이어 금형을 다루는 항목을 참조하십시오. 마지막으로, 174키아메 공장의 생산량이 증가함에 따라 추가 믹서를 들이는 것이 더 많은 타이어를 만드는 데 결정적일 것입니다. 그런 점에서 회

사는 새로운 믹서 모델을 구입할지 아니면 현재 사용 중인 것을 업그레이드할지를 결정해야 합니다. 물론, 기존 모델의 교체가 비용이 더 많이 들 것입니다. 175그러나 구형 믹서를 교체하면 생산 속도가 빨라져 추가 비용을 상쇄하고도 남을 것 같습니다.

어휘 productivity 생산성 preparer 준비자 review 보고서 quarterly 분기별의 inspection 검사 summary 요약 plant 공장 component 요소, 부품 rotating drum 회전통 assemble 조립하다 function 기능하다 mold 틀, 금형 tread (타이어의) 접지면 wear 마모 flag 표시를 하다 priority 우선 사항 dedicated 전념하는, 전용의 crucial 중대한 outweigh ~보다 더 크다

172 주제 / 목적

번역 나자르 씨는 왜 보고서를 준비했을 것 같은가?
(A) 혼합 장비가 제대로 작동하지 않는 이유를 설명하려고
(B) 공장 검사의 결과를 기록하려고
(C) 최근에 생산성이 저하된 이유를 설명하려고
(D) 새로운 회전통 구입의 타당성을 주장하려고

해설 보고서의 제목이 키아메 타이어 공장 생산성 보고서(Kiame Tire Factory Productivity Report)이고 보고서 사유가 분기별 검사(Reason for review: Quarterly inspection)이며 요약(Summary)란에서 공장의 모든 장비 및 기기에 대한 검사를 완료했다(I have completed ~ at the plant)고 공장에 대한 검사 내용을 보고하고 있으므로 (B)가 정답이다.

어휘 properly 제대로 document 기록하다 findings 결과 decrease 줄다 justify 옳다고 주장하다

173 Not / True

번역 타이어 금형에 대해 사실인 것은?
(A) 보고서에 이들에 대한 부분이 따로 있다.
(B) 최근에 모두 교체되었다.
(C) 공장 내에서 생산되지 않는다.
(D) 이제 더 적은 금형으로 더 많은 타이어가 생산될 수 있다.

해설 권고 사항(Recommendations)란의 두 번째 문장에서 자세한 내용은 보고서의 타이어 금형을 다루는 항목을 참조하라(See the report ~ for details)고 했으므로 보고서에 타이어 금형에 대해서만 별도로 할애된 부분이 있음을 알 수 있다. 따라서 (A)가 정답이다.

어휘 separate 별개의

174 추론 / 암시

번역 키아메 타이어 공장에 대해 암시된 것은?
(A) 대부분의 장비가 오래되었다.
(B) 예상보다 유지비가 덜 든다.
(C) 앞으로 성장할 것 같다.
(D) 최근에 직원 몇 명을 잃었다.

해설 권고 사항(Recommendations)란의 세 번째 문장에서 키아메 공장의 생산량이 증가함에 따라 추가 믹서를 들이는 것이 더 많은 타이어를 만드는 데 결정적일 것(as the Kiame ~ making more tires)이라는 내용으로 보아, 타이어 생산량이 늘어나면서 공장이 성장할 것임을 알 수 있다. 따라서 정답은 (C)이다.

어휘 maintain 유지하다 anticipate 예상하다

175 문장 삽입

번역 [1], [2], [3], [4]로 표시된 곳 중에서 다음 문장이 들어가기에 가장 적합한 위치는?

"물론, 기존 모델의 교체가 비용이 더 많이 들 것입니다."
(A) [1]
(B) [2]
(C) [3]
(D) [4]

해설 제시된 문장은 '모델 교체가 비용이 더 많이 들 것'이라며 비용 부담이라는 모델 교체 방안의 단점을 언급하고 있다. 따라서 구형 믹서를 교체(replacing)하면 생산 속도를 높여 비용 부담이라는 단점이 상쇄될 것(outweigh any additional cost)이라는 문장 앞에 들어가는 것이 글의 흐름상 자연스러우므로 (D)가 정답이다.

176-180 공지 + 기사

¹⁷⁶참가 요청: 연례 지속 가능성 대회

뉴질랜드 건설 연맹 후원

¹⁷⁶목적: 뉴질랜드 건설 연맹(LNZB)은 친환경적인 설계 혁신을 이룬 신규 건축물에 기여한 개인에 표창하기를 원합니다. ¹⁷⁹수상자는 현장 기념행사에 참가하여 손님과 기자들에게 완성된 건물을 보여 주며 환경적인 주요 특성을 설명하게 될 예정입니다.

참가자: LNZB 회원들이 우선적으로 고려될 것이나 ¹⁷⁷올해 12월 15일 이전에 뉴질랜드에서 프로젝트를 완료한 전문 건축업자는 누구나 지원할 수 있습니다. 제출 양식이 필요하시면 LNZB 웹사이트를 방문하십시오.

마감일: 모든 제출은 12월 15일까지입니다.

심사 절차: 심사 절차는 몇 가지 단계를 포함합니다. 후보자들을 심사한 뒤 심사 위원들은 준결승 진출자를 선정할 것입니다. 그런 다음 특별 패널이 올해의 수상자를 선정할 것입니다.

자세한 정보: LNZB와 과거 수상자에 대해 더 자세히 알아보시려면 www.leagueofnewzealandbuilders.org.nz를 방문하십시오.

어휘 entry 출품[참가] sustainability 지속 가능성 competition 대회 recognize 인정하다 individual 개인 contribution 기여 feature 특징으로 하다, 특별히 포함하다 innovation 혁신 environmentally friendly 친환경적인 on-site 현장의 entrant 출품자[참가자] priority 우선 submission 제출 due ~할 예정인 judging 심사 process 과정 vetting 조사, 검토 screening 검사[심사] semifinalist 준결승자 panel 패널(견해를 제공하는 전문가 집단) recipient 수령자

라호투, LNZB상 수상

(3월 17일)—뉴질랜드 건설 연맹(LNZB)은 어제 마이아 라호투가 올해의 지속 가능성 대회에서 우승했다고 발표했다. ¹⁷⁸뉴질랜드 전역에 걸친 건축 설계 작업을 수년 전부터 해온 라호투 씨는 로완 커뮤니티 센터의 설계로 이 상을 수상했다. 이 센터는 건설되는 내내 재생 및 재활용 자재를 활용했다. ¹⁷⁹4월에 센터에서 열리는 기념행사에서 라호투 씨는 공식적으로 상을 받을 것이다. 자세한 내용은 곧 발표될 예정이다. "올해 결정은 힘들었습니다. 모든 지원자들이 환경적 영향을 최소화하는 자재를 선택했습니다. 그러나 우리는 후보자 선택을 최종 3명으로 좁혔고 각 후보들은 전문가 패널과 인터뷰를 했습니다."라고 LNZB의 이사인 토마스 영은 말했다.

로완 프로젝트의 건물 구성 요소는 환경적 영향을 최소화하기 위해 라호투 씨에 의해 신중하게 선별되었다고 영 씨는 덧붙였다. "하지만 ¹⁸⁰라호투 씨의 설계가 뛰어난 점은 태양광 에너지를 얼마나 잘 모아들이는가 하는 점입니다." LNZB의 전문가들에 따르면, 그녀의 태양광 설계는 건물의 요구 사항을 훨씬 넘어서는 추가 전력을 발생시킨다고 한다. 이 잉여분은 지역의 전력망으로 전송되어 지역 에너지 생산에 대한 부담을 실질적으로 줄일 수 있다.

어휘 utilize 활용하다 renewable 재생 가능한 material 자재 formally 공식적으로 be presented with ~을 받다 minimize 최소화하다 impact 영향 narrow 좁히다 component 부품, 요소 exceptional 출중한 harvest 수확하다 solar 태양의 generate 발생시키다 surplus 잉여 transmit 전송하다 power grid 전력망 in effect 사실상[실제로는] strain 부담

176 추론 / 암시

번역 공지에서 상에 대해 암시된 것은?
(A) 영 씨가 우승자를 선정한다.
(B) 도시를 더 작게 만드는 데 주안점을 둔다.
(C) 매년 수여된다.
(D) 상금이 포함된다.

해설 공지의 제목이 연례 지속 가능성 대회 참가 요청(Call for ~ Competition)이고, 이 대회의 목적은 뉴질랜드 건설 연맹(LNZB)이 친환경적인 설계 혁신을 이룬 신규 건축물에 기여한 개인에 표창하는 것(PURPOSE: The ~ environmentally friendly)이라고 했으므로 해마다 열리는 대회에서 상이 수여되고 있음을 알 수 있다. 따라서 정답은 (C)이다.

Paraphrasing 지문의 Annual → 정답의 every year

177 세부 사항

번역 공지에 따르면 대회 지원자에게 요구되는 것은?
(A) LNZB 멘토의 보증
(B) 뉴질랜드 시민권
(C) LNZB 회원권
(D) 건설 프로젝트 완료

해설 공지의 두 번째 단락 첫 문장에서 올해 12월 15일 이전에 뉴질랜드에서 프로젝트를 완료한 전문 건축업자는 누구나 지원할 수 있다(any professional builder ~ may apply)고 했으므로 (D)가 정답이다.

어휘 sponsorship 후원, 보증

178 Not / True

번역 기사에 따르면, 라호투 씨에 대해 사실인 것은?
(A) 상당한 설계 경력을 가지고 있다.
(B) LNZB 선정 위원이었다.
(C) 최근에 이 지역으로 이사했다.
(D) 아파트 설계를 전문으로 한다.

해설 기사의 첫 단락 두 번째 문장에서 뉴질랜드 전역에 걸친 건축 설계 작업을 수년 전부터 해온 라호투 씨(Ms. Rahotu ~ many years)라고 했으므로 (A)가 정답이다.

어휘 significant 상당한 specialize in ~을 전문으로 하다

179 연계

번역 라호투 씨는 4월에 무엇을 할 예정인가?
(A) LNZB 특별 패널에 합류
(B) LNZB 수장으로 취임
(C) 건물 견학 주도
(D) 대회에 출품작 제출

해설 공지의 첫 단락 두 번째 문장에서 수상자는 현장 기념행사에 참가해 손님과 기자들에게 완성된 건물을 보여 주며 환경적인 주요 특성을 설명하게 될 예정(The winner will ~ environmental highlights)이라고 했고, 기사의 첫 단락 네 번째 문장에서 4월에 센터에서 열리는 기념행사에서 라호투 씨는 공식적으로 상을 받을 것(In April ~ at the centre)이라고 했다. 따라서 수상자인 라호투 씨는 4월에 있을 기념행사에서 건물 견학을 이끌 것임을 알 수 있으므로 (C)가 정답이다.

> Paraphrasing 지문의 show ~ around the ~ building
> → 정답의 Lead a tour of a building

180 세부 사항

번역 기사에 따르면, 라호투 씨의 설계가 뛰어난 이유는?
(A) 재활용된 자재를 높은 비율로 사용한다.
(B) 많은 양의 전력을 생산한다.
(C) 지붕과 벽이 휘어진 모양을 하고 있다.
(D) 지붕의 대부분을 덮는 정원이 있다.

해설 기사의 두 번째 단락 두 번째 문장에서 라호투 씨의 설계가 뛰어난 점은 태양광 에너지를 얼마나 잘 모아들이는가 하는 점(what is exceptional ~ solar energy)이라고 했고, LNZB의 전문가들에 따르면 그녀의 태양광 설계는 건물의 요구 사항을 훨씬 넘어서는 추가 전력을 발생시킨다고 한다(According to ~ building's requirements)고 했으므로 정답은 (B)이다.

181-185 설명서 + 이메일

┌─────────────────────────────
181라존 컬러 스월 도마

모델 #B875
└─────────────────────────────

특히 오렌지와 토마토와 같은 181산성 과일과 채소를 자른 후에는 항상 제품을 사용 즉시 세척하세요.

도마가 흡수할 수 있는 181염소가 함유된 표백제나 세정제의 사용을 삼가 주세요. 잘 지워지지 않는 음식 얼룩이 있을 경우 도마를 비눗물에 5분 동안 담그세요. 물로 인해 가죽이 뻣뻣해지고 끊어지기 쉬우므로 183세척 전에 가죽 걸고리를 반드시 제거하세요.

제품을 보관할 때는 벽이나 선반에 똑바로 세워 가죽 고리로 걸어 두세요. 도마의 선명한 색이 바래므로 직사광선에 보관하지 마세요. 주기적으로, 182도마의 밝은 색이 유지되도록 돕기 위해 가볍게 올리브 오일을 덧발라 닦아 주세요.

모든 라존 제품과 마찬가지로 저희 도마는 수작업으로 제작되었습니다. 최소한의 관리로 제품을 새것처럼 유지할 수 있습니다.

도마에 문제가 있을 경우 support@lazonproducts.com으로 이메일을 보내세요. 구매 후 3개월 내로 결함이 있는 부품이나 제품은 무상으로 교체해 드리는 것이 당사의 방침입니다. 라존 프로덕츠에서는 품질이 최우선 사항입니다!

어휘 swirl 소용돌이 acidic 산성의 refrain 삼가다 bleach 표백제 chlorine 염소 absorb 흡수하다 stain 얼룩 soak 담그다 soapy 비누를 함유한 leather 가죽 brittle 잘 부러지는 store 보관하다 upright 똑바로 vibrant 선명한 fade 바래다 periodically 주기적으로 polish 닦다 upkeep 유지 defective 결함이 있는 priority 우선 사항

발신: 조나스 E. 이베르센 〈jonaseiversen@daylightcommerce. com〉
수신: support@lazonproducts.com
날짜: 8월 2일 오후 4시 58분
제목: 모델 #B875

안녕하세요.

저의 라존 모델 #B875 도마의 결함과 관련하여 글을 씁니다. 제품에 딸려온 모든 유지 관리 정보를 따르려고 매우 주의를 기울였지만, 183지침대로 가죽 끈을 탈착하고 있을 때 가운데 있는 작은 구멍을 발견했습니다. 지금은 그렇게 크지 않지만 몇 개월 더 사용하고 나면 더 커질 것입니다. 비록 1844개월 전에 제품을 구매했지만 고작 한 달 전에 사용하기 시작했습니다. 185가죽 끈이 불량 부품 방침에 아직 적용이 될까요? 새 제품을 받고 싶습니다.

도움 주셔서 감사합니다.

조나스 E. 이베르센

어휘 defect 결함 maintenance 유지 instruct 지시하다 tear 구멍

181 주제 / 목적

번역 설명서에 설명된 내용은?
(A) 예술 작품 전시법
(B) 고급 음식 준비법
(C) 건설 도구 사용법
(D) 주방용품 관리법

TEST 5

해설 설명서의 제목이 라존 컬러 스월 도마(LAZON COLOR SWIRL CUTTING BOARD)이고, 첫 문장에서 산성 과일과 채소를 자른 후에는 항상 제품을 사용 즉시 세척하라(Always wash ~ fruits and vegetables)고 했고, 두 번째 문단에서도 염소가 함유된 표백제나 세정제의 사용을 삼가라(Refrain from ~ with chlorine)고 한 것으로 보아 도마 관리법에 대한 설명문이므로 (D)가 정답이다.

어휘 gourmet 고급, 미식가 tool 도구

182 세부 사항

번역 설명서에 따르면, 오일은 무슨 용도로 사용되는가?
(A) 제품의 맛을 더 좋게 하려고
(B) 제품을 더 좋게 보이게 하려고
(C) 제품을 더 빠르게 작동시키려고
(D) 제품을 더 강하게 만들려고

해설 설명서의 세 번째 단락 마지막 문장에서 도마의 밝은 색이 유지되도록 돕기 위해 가볍게 올리브 오일을 덧발라 닦으라(polish the board ~ colors stay bright)고 했으므로 (B)가 정답이다.

> Paraphrasing 지문의 help the board's colors stay bright
> → 정답의 make a product look better

183 연계

번역 이베르센 씨는 문제를 발견했을 때 무엇을 하려 했을 것 같은가?
(A) 제품 세척
(B) 제품 보관
(C) 제품 진열
(D) 제품 조립

해설 이메일의 두 번째 문장에서 이베르센 씨가 지침대로 가죽 끈을 탈착하고 있을 때 가운데 있는 작은 구멍을 발견했다(when I was ~ in the middle)고 했는데, 설명서의 두 번째 단락 세 번째 문장에서 세척 전에 가죽 걸고리를 반드시 제거하라(Be sure to remove ~ before cleaning)고 했다. 따라서 이베르센 씨는 구멍을 발견했을 때 세척을 위해 가죽 끈을 제거하고 있었음을 알 수 있으므로 (A)가 정답이다.

184 세부 사항

번역 이베르센 씨는 얼마나 오래 제품을 소유했는가?
(A) 1달
(B) 2달
(C) 3달
(D) 4달

해설 이메일의 네 번째 문장에서 이베르센 씨가 4개월 전에 제품을 구매했다(I purchased the product four months ago)고 했으므로 정답은 (D)이다.

185 세부 사항

번역 이베르센 씨는 라존 프로덕츠에 무엇을 요청하는가?
(A) 유지 관리 정보 제공
(B) 전액 환불
(C) 교체 부품 발송
(D) 제품 수리 제안

해설 이메일의 다섯 번째 문장에서 가죽 끈이 불량 부품 방침에 아직 적용이 될지(Is the leather strap ~ parts policy?)를 물으며 새 제품을 받고 싶다(I'd like to get a new one)고 했다. 불량 부품에 대한 교체품을 보내 달라고 요청하고 있으므로 (C)가 정답이다.

186-190 웹페이지 + 이메일 + 청구서

---

http://www.flutteringwings.com.mx

| 소개 | 예약 | 자주 묻는 질문 | 연락처 |

플러터링 윙즈 리조트

거목 왕나비 보호 구역 입구에서 단 몇 분 거리에 위치한 플러터링 윙즈 리조트는 멕시코 최고의 친환경 여행지입니다. 연중무휴로 운영되는 우리 시설은 풀서비스 레스토랑, 편안한 수영장, 멋진 경치를 볼 수 있는 옥상 테라스를 포함합니다.

188나비의 활동 계절은 11월 중순부터 3월 초까지이고, 수백만 왕나비들이 거목 보호 구역에서 겨울을 납니다. **190**방문객은 도보로 산에 등반할 수 있지만 대부분은 가이드가 인솔하는 승마 투어에 참여하는 것을 선호합니다. 방문객을 산 위로 안내하는 우리의 전문 안내원들은 모두 지역 마을 주민들입니다. 그들은 지속해서 보호 구역을 돌아다니며 최고의 관람 장소를 찾습니다.

1861년 내내 우리는 등반 코스, 조류 관찰, 그리고 승마를 제공합니다. 보호 구역 밖의 마을과 농장의 전기차 관광 또한 가능합니다.

어휘 monarch butterfly 왕나비 sanctuary 보호 구역 eco-friendly 친환경적인 destination 목적지 year-round 1년 내내 facility 시설 deck 테라스, 갑판 hike 등반하다 on foot 도보로 participate in ~에 참여하다 horseback 말을 타고 하는 escort 수행하다 villager 마을 사람 scout (무엇을 찾아) 돌아다니다 trail 루트[코스]

수신: 카르멘 산체스 〈c.sanchez@flutteringwings.com.mx〉
발신: 제임스 노빌 〈jnorville@itiaworld.org〉
날짜: 6월 12일
제목: 국제 여행 산업 협회 가디언상

축하합니다, 카르멘 산체스!

플러터링 윙즈 리조트가 국제 여행 산업 협회 가디언상 수상자로 임명되었습니다. ITIA 가디언상에는 5,000달러의 상금과 자문 팀의 1년 무료 지원이 포함됩니다. **187**ITIA 전문가들은 플러터링 윙즈에 보다 효율적으로 사업을 운영하는 방법과 잠재적 방문객들에게 서비스를 홍보하기

위한 웹 사용법에 대해 조언할 수 있습니다. **188우리 자문 팀의 일원인 로사 델 비오가 귀하께 상을 수여하고 7월이나 8월에 귀하의 리조트를 방문하기를 원합니다.** 이번 달 말이 되기 전에 그녀가 연락을 드릴 것입니다.

제임스 노빌

국제 여행 산업 협회 전무 이사

어휘 association 협회 guardian 수호자 name 임명하다 recipient 수령인 advisory 자문의 operate 운영하다 efficiently 효율적으로 potential 잠재적인 present 수여하다 in touch with ~와 연락하여

플러터링 윙즈 리조트	청구서
이름: 줄리오 바돔, 리사 바돔	
선급금 수령일: 2월 1일	
189숙박일: 2월 25-27일	
킹사이즈 객실: 95달러 x 2박	190달러
190나비 보호 구역 안내 투어: 40달러 x 2인	80달러
총	270달러
지불 금액:	270달러
미납 금액:	0달러

189참고: 귀하의 질문에 대해, 걱정 마세요. 나비들은 3월 초까지 보호 구역을 떠나지 않습니다.

어휘 balance due 미납 금액 depart 떠나다 reserve 보호 구역

186 세부 사항

번역 플러터링 윙즈 리조트에서 손님들이 할 수 있는 것은?
(A) 스쿠버 다이빙 배우기
(B) 요리 수업 듣기
(C) 조류 관찰하기
(D) 스쿠터 대여하기

해설 웹페이지의 세 번째 단락 첫 문장에서 1년 내내 우리는 등반 코스, 조류 관찰, 그리고 승마를 제공한다(At all times of the year ~ and horseback riding)고 했으므로 (C)가 정답이다.

어휘 observe 관찰하다

> Paraphrasing 지문의 bird-watching
> → 정답의 Observe birds

187 세부 사항

번역 이메일에 따르면, ITIA는 어떤 방법으로 플러터링 윙즈 리조트를 도울 수 있는가?
(A) 직원들에게 나비 사육법을 가르쳐줌으로써
(B) 리조트가 온라인 광고 활동을 개선하도록 도움으로써
(C) 리조트에 새로운 노트북 컴퓨터를 제공함으로써
(D) 추가 객실을 건설함으로써

해설 이메일의 세 번째 문장에서 ITIA 전문가들은 플러터링 윙즈에 잠재적 방문객들에게 서비스를 홍보하기 위한 웹 사용법에 대해 조언할 수 있다(ITIA experts ~ use the Web to promote your services to potential visitors)고 했으므로 (B)가 정답이다.

> Paraphrasing 지문의 use the Web to promote your services to potential visitors
> → 정답의 improve its online advertising effort

188 연계

번역 델 비오 씨는 방문 중에 어떤 리조트 활동을 할 수 없을 것인가?
(A) 전기차로 지역 마을 관광하기
(B) 가이드가 인솔하는 승마 투어
(C) 수백만 나비가 있는 기간에 보호 구역 방문
(D) 리조트 수영장 이용

해설 웹페이지의 두 번째 단락 첫 문장에서 나비의 활동 계절은 11월 중순부터 3월 초까지이고 수백만 왕나비들이 거목 보호 구역에서 겨울을 난다(Butterfly season ~ Tall Trees sanctuary)고 했고, 이메일의 네 번째 문장에서 우리 자문 팀의 일원인 로사 델 비오가 7월이나 8월에 귀하의 리조트를 방문하기를 원한다(A member of ~ July or August)고 했다. 따라서 보호 구역에서 나비를 볼 수 있는 기간은 겨울인 반면, 델 비오 씨는 여름에 리조트를 방문할 계획이므로 정답은 (C)이다.

189 세부 사항

번역 영수증에 적힌 참고 사항의 목적은?
(A) 바돔 부부에게 여행 시기에 대해 안심시키기
(B) 청구서에 추가 요금이 포함된 이유 설명하기
(C) 리조트 방문에 대해 바돔 부부에게 감사하기
(D) 바돔 부부에게 실망할 가능성에 대해 경고하기

해설 청구서 상단에 바돔 부부의 숙박일이 2월 25-27일(Dates of stay: February 25-27)로 나와 있고, 하단의 참고(Note)에 걱정 말라(Note ~ don't worry)며 나비들은 3월 초까지 보호 구역을 떠나지 않는다(the butterflies ~ until early March)고 한 것으로 보아, 바돔 부부가 여행을 하는 시기에는 보호 구역에서 나비를 볼 수 있다고 안심시키기 위한 것임을 알 수 있다. 따라서 (A)가 정답이다.

어휘 reassure 안심시키다

190 연계

번역 바돔 부부는 어떻게 나비 보호 구역을 관광할 것 같은가?
(A) 도보로
(B) 자전거로
(C) 승마로
(D) 전지형 차량으로

해설 웹페이지의 두 번째 단락 두 번째 문장에서 방문객은 도보로 산에 등반할 수 있지만 대부분은 가이드가 인솔하는 승마 투어에 참여하는 것을 선호한다(Visitors can ~ guided horseback tours)고 했고, 청구서의 결제 내역에 나비 보호 구역 안내 투어(Guided butterfly sanctuary tour)가 있는 것으로 보아 바돔 부부는 리조트에서 안내하는 말을 타고 하는 투어를 할 예정임을 알 수 있다. 따라서 정답은 (C)이다.

어휘 all-terrain 전지형(어떤 지형에도 적응하는)

191-195 광고 + 이메일 + 이메일

---

¹⁹²제15회 연례 원예 농업 혁신 컨퍼런스
¹⁹²영국 런던의 새 단장을 마친 블레인 호텔 앤 컨퍼런스 센터
¹⁹²11월 10-12일
Innovationsinhorticulture.org.uk

¹⁹²주요 연사:

- 첸 완, 중국
- 호프 오브라이언, 영국
- ¹⁹²피에트 백스, 네덜란드
- 에밀 사보프, 불가리아

자세한 정보와 등록을 원하시면 원예 농업 혁신 웹사이트를 방문하세요. 신분증 제시로 학생 할인이 가능합니다. 컨퍼런스 장소에서 한정된 수의 호텔 객실이 이용 가능합니다. ¹⁹¹인근 호텔에 투숙하는 참가자들을 위한 무료 버스 서비스가 있습니다.

어휘 innovation 혁신 horticulture 원예 agriculture 농업 featured 특색으로 한 register 등록하다 complimentary 무료의 attendee 참석자

수신: 피에트 백스 〈pbax@mailcrate.com〉
발신: 제이콥 브루스터 〈jbrewster@sootenfarms.co.uk〉
제목: 조명 정보
¹⁹²날짜: 12월 18일

백스 씨께:

¹⁹²지난달 런던에서 당신을 만나서 기뻤습니다. 연설이 끝난 후 저와 이야기할 시간을 내 주시고 ¹⁹³1월 5일 화상 회의를 하기로 동의해 주셔서 감사합니다. 프로젝트 매니저인 고우진 씨에게 함께하자고 요청하려 합니다. ¹⁹⁵무엇보다도 고 씨는 저의 온실을 위한 조명에 대해 몇 가지 질문이 있습니다. 그녀는 브릴란테 럭스라이트사에서 제공하는 제품에 대해 질문이 있는 것 같습니다. 당신이 그들의 제품 일부를 디자인하는 것을 도왔다고 알고 있어서 아마 조언을 좀 해 주실 수 있을 것 같습니다. 우리 둘 다 궁금한 점이 많을 것을 알고 있어서 이런 기회를 주신데 대해 감사합니다. 또한 봄 중으로 당신의 온실을 방문해 직접 볼 수 있기를 바랍니다.

제이콥 브루스터

어휘 among other things 무엇보다도 lighting 조명 greenhouse 온실 in-person 직접

수신: 제이콥 브루스터 〈jbrewster@sootenfarms.co.uk〉
¹⁹⁵발신: 후아나 갈베즈 〈jgalvez@brillanteluxlight.com.mx〉
제목: 계약
날짜: 1월 30일

브루스터 씨께:

¹⁹⁵귀하로부터 요청서와 설계 사양을 받았습니다. 안타깝게도 ¹⁹⁴최근 악천후로 인해 생산을 시작하는 데 필요한 일부 자재의 배송이 지연되고 있습니다. 그러나 이 자재들이 도착하는 즉시 귀하의 주문을 빠르게 이행하고 곧바로 생산을 시작할 것입니다.

후아나 갈베즈

어휘 specification 사양 inclement 궂은 fast-track 빨리 달성하게 하다

---

191 Not / True

번역 광고에서 명시된 것은?
(A) 학생 할인 횟수가 제한되어 있다.
(B) 컨퍼런스가 15일간 지속될 것이다.
(C) 호텔에서 무료 버스를 이용할 수 있다.
(D) 컨퍼런스 센터가 보수 중이다.

해설 광고의 마지막 문장에 인근 호텔에 투숙하는 참가자들을 위한 무료 버스 서비스가 있다(There is a complimentary ~ nearby hotels)고 했으므로 (C)가 정답이다.

Paraphrasing 지문의 complimentary → 정답의 Free

---

192 연계

번역 브루스터 씨와 백스 씨는 어디서 만났을 것 같은가?
(A) 컨퍼런스
(B) 비행기 기내
(C) 자선 모금 행사
(D) 브릴란테 럭스라이트 사무실

해설 광고의 상단에 제15회 연례 원예 농업 혁신 컨퍼런스(15th Annual ~ Conference)가 영국 런던(London, UK)에서 11월 10-12일(10-12 November)에 열린다고 했고, 주요 연사(Featured Speakers) 목록에 네덜란드의 피에트 백스(Piet Bax, Netherlands)가 있다. 첫 번째 이메일이 작성된 날짜는 12월 18일(Date: 18 December)로 첫 문장에서 브루스터 씨가 백스 씨에게 지난달 런던에서 당신을 만나서 기뻤다(It was wonderful ~ London last month)며 연설이 끝난 후 저와 이야기할 시간을 내 주셔서 감사하다(Thank you for ~ after your speech)고 했다. 따라서 두 사람은 지난달인 11월에 백스 씨가 연설을 한 런던의 컨퍼런스에서 만났음을 알 수 있으므로 (A)가 정답이다.

어휘 charity 자선 fund-raiser 모금 행사

193 세부 사항

번역 첫 번째 이메일에서 브루스터 씨는 무엇을 하겠다고 말하는가?

(A) 화상 회의 일정 변경
(B) 새로운 프로젝트 매니저 채용
(C) 그가 한 주문의 변경
(D) 회의에 다른 사람 포함시키기

해설 첫 이메일의 두 번째 문장에서 브루스터 씨는 1월 5일 화상 회의를 하기로 동의해 주셔서 감사하다(Thank you ~ for agreeing to the video meeting on 5 January)며 프로젝트 매니저인 고우진 씨에게 함께하자고 요청하려 한다(I'm going to ~ to join us)고 했으므로 정답은 (D)이다.

194 주제 / 목적

번역 두 번째 이메일의 목적은?

(A) 브루스터 씨에게 배송 요청
(B) 주문 상태 상의
(C) 일부 사양 설명
(D) 제품 품질에 대한 불평

해설 두 번째 이메일의 두 번째 문장에서 최근 악천후로 인해 생산을 시작하는 데 필요한 일부 자재의 배송이 지연되고 있다(the recent ~ begin production)며, 이 자재들이 도착하는 즉시 귀하의 주문을 빠르게 이행하고 곧바로 생산을 시작할 것(once these materials ~ immediately)이라며 주문의 진행 현황에 대해 알려 주고 있으므로 (B)가 정답이다.

어휘 status 상태

195 연계

번역 브루스터 씨에 대해 암시된 것은?

(A) 영국과 불가리아에 농지를 소유하고 있다.
(B) 백스 씨와 새로운 사업을 시작하길 원한다.
(C) 새로운 농산물을 개발했다.
(D) 실내 식물을 위한 조명을 주문했다.

해설 첫 이메일의 네 번째 문장에서 브루스터 씨는 무엇보다도 고 씨는 저의 온실을 위한 조명에 대해 몇 가지 질문이 있다(Among other things ~ my greenhouses)고 했고, 그녀는 브릴란테 럭스라이트사에서 제공하는 제품에 대해 질문이 있는 것 같다(I think she has ~ Luxlight company)고 했다. 그런데 두 번째 이메일의 발신자인 갈베즈 씨의 이메일 주소(발신: 후아나 갈베즈 〈jgalvez@ brillanteluxlight.com.mx〉)가 브릴란테 럭스라이트사이고, 갈베즈 씨가 브루스터 씨에게 첫 문장에서 귀하로부터 요청서와 설계 사양을 받았다(We received ~ from you)고 한 것으로 보아 브루스터 씨는 브릴란테 럭스라이트사에서 자신의 온실을 위한 조명을 주문했음을 알 수 있다. 따라서 (D)가 정답이다.

Paraphrasing 지문의 greenhouses
→ 정답의 some indoor plants

196-200 광고 + 후기 + 이메일

오렌지 라이트 체육관
그랜드 오프닝 위크

196오렌지 라이트 체육관이 싱가포르에 옵니다! 4월에 최신이자 최고의 체육관을 개관할 때 함께해 주세요. **196,198이곳은 싱가포르에서 우리의 첫 지점이 될 것이고 올해 중으로 두 곳의 다른 지점을 추가할 예정입니다.**

- 4월 4일부터 4월 8일까지 오차드 가 그랜드 오프닝 행사 기간 동안 가입하는 오렌지 라이트 체육관 신규 회원은 10% 할인됩니다.
- 4월 5일에 싱가포르 보디빌딩 전설인 로니 초가 옵니다.
- 4월 6일에 세계적으로 유명한 트레이너인 리나 시타만이 옵니다.

오렌지 라이트 체육관 • **196오차드 가** 1140 • 싱가포르

어휘 sign up 가입하다 legend 전설

오렌지 라이트 체육관 마리나 사우스   183개의 후기
10월 2일

맥스 할리
★★★

198저는 10년간 오렌지 라이트 체육관의 정규 회원이었고 대체적으로 그들의 서비스가 마음에 듭니다. 저는 두바이에 살지만 업무차 싱가포르에 정기적으로 가기 때문에 두 나라에 지점이 있는 체육관에 소속되어 있다는 것은 정말 좋습니다! **197,200싱가포르에 있는 마리나 사우스 체육관은 매우 깨끗하고 설계가 훌륭하지만 두 가지 부분에 개선이 필요합니다. 기계가 충분하지 않습니다. 특히 훨씬 더 큰 오차드 가 지점에 비해서요.** 또한 **200약 열 번 정도 체육관을 방문했는데, 이 중 거의 절반의 경우에 수영장을 사용할 수 없었습니다.** 글로벌 회원권 때문에 이 체육관을 계속 이용할 예정인데 수영장 폐쇄의 원인을 해결해 주기를 희망합니다.

어휘 generally 일반적으로 regularly 정기적으로 belong to ~에 속하다 occasion 경우 address 해결하다

수신: 샘 아다위
발신: 아니 와얀티
날짜: 10월 14일
제목: 스토크너 서비스

아다위 씨께,

저희가 **199,200스토크너 서비스와 1년 계약을 맺고 있는 것으로 알고 있지만 매우 걱정됩니다. 싱가포르에 있는 오렌지 라이트 체육관에서 발생한 문제는 잘못된 유지 관리 때문입니다.** 간단히 말해서 저는 스토크너가 고용한 직원들이 그들의 업무를 수행할 만큼 잘 교육받지 못했다고 생각합니다. 만나서 이 점에 대해 논의할 수 있을까요? 더 빨리 이 문제를 해결할수록 더 좋습니다.

와얀티

지역 관리자

오렌지 라이트 체육관

196 Not / True

번역 광고에 따르면, 오렌지 라이트 체육관의 오차드 가 지점에 대해 명시
된 것은?
(A) 오렌지 라이트 체육관에서 유일하게 수영장이 있는 지점이다.
(B) 싱가포르의 첫 오렌지 라이트 체육관이다.
(C) 유명한 보디빌더가 소유하고 있다.
(D) 인기 있는 트레이너가 이끄는 수업을 제공한다.

해설 광고의 첫 문장에서 오렌지 라이트 체육관이 싱가포르에 온다
(Orange Light Gym is coming to Singapore!)면서 이곳은 싱가
포르에서 우리의 첫 지점이 될 것(This will be our first location
in Singapore)이라고 했고, 광고 하단에 이 지점의 주소가 오차드
가(Orchard Road)이므로 오차드 가 지점은 싱가포르에 생기는 오
렌지 라이트 체육관의 첫 지점이라는 것을 알 수 있다. 따라서 (B)가
정답이다.

197 Not / True

번역 할리 씨가 오렌지 라이트 체육관 마리나 사우스 지점에 대해 명시한
것은?
(A) 위치가 편리하지 않다.
(B) 그다지 깨끗하지 않다.
(C) 오차드 가 지점보다 기계가 더 많다.
(D) 오차드 가 지점보다 작다.

해설 후기의 세 번째 문장에서 할리 씨는 마리나 사우스 체육관은 매우
깨끗하고 설계가 훌륭하지만 두 가지 부분에 개선이 필요하다(The
Marina South gym ~ need improvement)며, 특히 훨씬 더 큰
오차드 가 지점에 비해 기계가 충분하지 않다(There are not ~
Orchard Road location)고 했으므로 (D)가 정답이다.

198 연계

번역 할리 씨의 오렌지 라이트 체육관 회원권에 대해 사실인 것은?
(A) 취소할 계획이다.
(B) 10% 할인을 받았다.
(C) 두바이 지점에 출입하려고 사용한 적이 없다.
(D) 싱가포르 지점이 개점하기 전에 시작했다.

해설 오렌지 라이트 체육관 광고의 세 번째 문장에서 이곳은 싱가포르
에서 우리의 첫 지점이 될 것이고 올해 중으로 두 곳의 다른 지점을
추가할 예정(This will be ~ later this year)이라고 했고, 후기의
첫 문장에서 할리 씨는 저는 10년간 오렌지 라이트 체육관의 정규
회원이었다(I have been ~ for ten years)라고 했다. 따라서 올해
싱가포르 지점이 문을 열기 전부터 할리 씨는 오렌지 라이트 체육관
회원이었으므로 (D)가 정답이다.

199 주제 / 목적

번역 와얀티 씨는 왜 이메일을 보냈는가?
(A) 고용된 회사의 서툰 업무에 대해 우려를 표하려고
(B) 체육관 회원 가입에 대해 문의하려고
(C) 초과 지불에 대해 논의하려고
(D) 더 좋은 트레이너 고용을 추천하려고

해설 이메일의 첫 문장에서 와얀티 씨는 스토크너 서비스와 1년 계약을
맺고 있는 것으로 알고 있지만 매우 걱정된다(I know we ~ very
concerned)며, 싱가포르에 있는 오렌지 라이트 체육관에서 발생
한 문제는 잘못된 유지 관리 때문(The problems ~ improper
maintenance)이라고 했다. 따라서 와얀티 씨는 고용 업체인 스토
크너 서비스가 유지 관리 업무를 제대로 못하고 있는 점이 걱정스
럽다는 점을 알리기 위해 이메일을 보낸 것이므로 (A)가 정답이다.

> Paraphrasing   지문의 improper maintenance
> → 정답의 poor work

200 연계

번역 스토크너 서비스에 대해 암시된 것은?
(A) 두바이의 오렌지 라이트 체육관 지점에 서비스를 제공한다.
(B) 싱가포르의 오렌지 라이트 체육관에 있는 운동 기계를 수리한다.
(C) 오렌지 라이트 체육관의 수영장을 제대로 관리하지 않고 있다.
(D) 최근에 다른 회사에 의해 인수되었다.

해설 이메일의 첫 문장에서 스토크너 서비스와의 계약 관계를 걱정하
며 싱가포르에 있는 오렌지 라이트 체육관에서 발생한 문제는 잘
못된 유지 관리 때문(I know we have a one-year contract ~
improper maintenance)이라고 했는데, 후기의 세 번째 문장에
서 싱가포르에 있는 마리나 사우스 체육관(The Marina South
gym in Singapore)을 언급하면서 약 열 번 정도 체육관을 방문했
는데 이 중 거의 절반의 경우에 수영장을 사용할 수 없었다(I have
visited ~ not available for use)고 했다. 따라서 스토크너 서비
스가 오렌지 라이트 체육관의 수영장 관리를 맡고 있으며, 관리 업
무가 제대로 이루어지지 않고 있음을 알 수 있으므로 (C)가 정답
이다.

어휘 maintain 유지하다

101 (A)	**102** (C)	**103** (B)	**104** (B)	**105** (C)
106 (D)	**107** (A)	**108** (B)	**109** (B)	**110** (B)
111 (A)	**112** (D)	**113** (C)	**114** (C)	**115** (A)
116 (C)	**117** (C)	**118** (B)	**119** (A)	**120** (D)
121 (D)	**122** (C)	**123** (A)	**124** (D)	**125** (C)
126 (A)	**127** (D)	**128** (A)	**129** (C)	**130** (D)
131 (D)	**132** (D)	**133** (C)	**134** (B)	**135** (C)
136 (B)	**137** (A)	**138** (D)	**139** (A)	**140** (A)
141 (C)	**142** (D)	**143** (B)	**144** (D)	**145** (A)
146 (D)	**147** (B)	**148** (B)	**149** (B)	**150** (C)
151 (B)	**152** (D)	**153** (D)	**154** (B)	**155** (B)
156 (A)	**157** (C)	**158** (A)	**159** (D)	**160** (B)
161 (B)	**162** (A)	**163** (B)	**164** (C)	**165** (D)
166 (C)	**167** (A)	**168** (B)	**169** (B)	**170** (D)
171 (D)	**172** (A)	**173** (D)	**174** (B)	**175** (D)
176 (D)	**177** (C)	**178** (B)	**179** (D)	**180** (A)
181 (C)	**182** (C)	**183** (B)	**184** (D)	**185** (A)
186 (A)	**187** (D)	**188** (C)	**189** (A)	**190** (D)
191 (C)	**192** (D)	**193** (A)	**194** (C)	**195** (D)
196 (B)	**197** (C)	**198** (A)	**199** (D)	**200** (B)

PART 5

101 명사 자리 _ 전치사의 목적어

해설 빈칸은 전치사 with의 목적어 역할을 하며 빈칸 앞에 정관사 the가 있으므로 명사 자리이다. 문맥상 '1년 요금제 구매 시 할인된다'는 내용이 되어야 하므로 '구매'를 뜻하는 명사인 (A) purchase가 정답이다. '구매자'를 뜻하는 사람 명사 (B) purchaser와 (D) purchasers는 문맥상 어울리지 않으므로 답이 되지 않는다.

번역 휴대전화 업그레이드는 1년 서비스 요금제 구매 시 할인된다.

102 동사 어휘

해설 앞에 나온 be동사 are와 뒤에 있는 to부정사(to make)와 함께 쓰여 '영사기가 꺼져 있는지 확인하도록 주의받다'는 의미가 되어야 한다. 따라서 '주의[당부]받는, 상기되는'이라는 의미의 (C) reminded가 정답이다. 'be reminded + to부정사'로 암기해 두자.

번역 회의 진행자는 매번 사용 후 영사기가 꺼져 있는지 확인하라는 주의를 받는다.

어휘 coordinator 진행자, 조직자   projection 영사, 투영

103 형용사 자리 _ 명사 수식

해설 빈칸은 앞에 있는 명사 questions를 뒤에서 수식하는 자리이므로 명사 수식 역할을 할 수 있는 형용사가 들어가야 한다. 따라서 전치사 to와 함께 '~와 관련 있는'이라는 뜻을 나타내는 형용사 (B)

related가 정답이다.

번역 개인 휴가 사용과 관련된 질문은 인사부의 마츠 씨에게 문의하십시오.

어휘 time off 휴가   human resources department 인사부

104 동사 자리

해설 Ammeto software가 주어인 문장에 동사가 보이지 않으므로 빈칸은 동사 자리이다. 따라서 '가능하게 하다'라는 뜻의 동사인 (B) allows가 정답이다. 동사 allow는 'allow + 목적어 + to부정사'의 5형식 구조로 쓰여 '목적어가 ~하게 해 주다'라는 의미를 나타내는 것도 함께 알아 두자.

번역 아메토 소프트웨어는 팀원들이 프로젝트와 관련된 일정, 자원 및 비용을 볼 수 있게 해 준다.

어휘 resource 자원   allowance 허용(량); 수당   allowable 허용되는

105 형용사 어휘

해설 문맥상 '고객 서비스 직원이 답변하는 것이 가능하다'는 내용이 되어야 자연스러우므로 '이용 가능한, (일에) 응할 수 있는'이라는 뜻의 형용사 (C) available이 정답이다.

번역 고객 서비스 직원은 24시간 내내 문의에 답변할 수 있다.

어휘 representative 직원, 대표   inquiry 문의   urgent 긴급한   secure 안전한, 확실한

106 부사 자리 _ 동사 수식

해설 The audience가 주어이고 laughed가 동사이며, 빈칸은 부사 so의 수식을 받으면서 자동사 laughed를 수식하는 부사 자리이다. 따라서 '크게'라는 뜻의 부사인 (D) loudly가 정답이다.

번역 연극이 진행되는 동안 관객들이 너무 크게 웃어서 일부 배우들의 대사가 들리지 않았다.

어휘 play 연극   line 대사   drown out (소음이) ~을 들리지 않게 하다

107 상관접속사

해설 빈칸 뒤에 나오는 or가 문제 해결의 단서로, 문맥상 '식사하기 전이나 후에'라는 의미가 되어야 한다. 따라서 or와 상관접속사를 이루어 'A든지 B든지'라는 뜻을 나타내는 (A) either가 정답이다.

번역 고객은 식사를 하기 전이나 후에 주차 확인을 요청할 수 있다.

어휘 validation 확인   dine 식사하다

108 형용사 자리 _ 명사 수식

해설 빈칸은 뒤에 온 명사 apartments를 수식하는 형용사 자리로, '가구가 비치된 아파트'라는 의미가 되어야 자연스러우므로 '가구가 비치된'이라는 의미의 형용사 (B) furnished가 정답이다. 참고로, (A) furnishing은 '가구, 비품'을 뜻하는 명사로 apartments와 복합명사를 이루기엔 어색하므로 답이 되지 않는다.

프레스티지 아파트먼트 홈스는 가구가 비치된 아파트를 추가 비용으로 제공한다.

109 명사 어휘

해설 채용 공고를 내기 전에 인사부로부터 나오기를 기다려야 하는 것이므로 문맥상 빈칸에는 '승인'이라는 말이 들어가야 자연스럽다. 따라서 '승인'을 뜻하는 명사 (B) approval이 정답이다.

번역 박 씨는 채용 공고를 게시하기 전에 인사부의 승인을 기다려야 한다.

어휘 post 게시하다 job announcement 채용공고 admission 입장 favor 호의, 지지

110 형용사 자리 _ 명사 수식 _ 과거분사

해설 빈칸은 소유격 our와 복합명사 staff directory 사이에서 명사를 수식하는 형용사 자리이다. '업데이트된 직원 명부'라는 의미가 되어야 자연스러우므로 '업데이트된'이라는 의미의 과거분사형 형용사인 (B) updated가 정답이다.

번역 문의 사항은 업데이트된 직원 명부에 기재된 적절한 담당자에게 보내 주십시오.

어휘 direct 보내다 appropriate 적절한 staff directory 직원 명부

111 관계대명사 _ 주격

해설 빈칸 이하는 선행사 gift boxes를 수식하는 관계사절로, 빈칸 뒤에 동사 arrived가 나오므로 주격 관계대명사인 (A) that이 정답이다.

번역 블레이크우드 상점은 금요일 아침에 마침내 도착한 선물 상자의 배송을 기다리고 있었다.

어휘 shipment 배송, 수송

112 전치사 어휘

해설 문맥상 '모든 기업가를 위해 시장 조사를 빠르고 쉽게 해 준다'는 의미가 되어야 적절하므로 '(~을 돕기) 위해'라는 의미를 지닌 전치사 (D) for가 정답이다.

번역 휠러의 소프트웨어 도구는 모든 기업가에게 시장 조사를 빠르고 쉽게 해 준다.

어휘 tool 도구 entrepreneur 기업가

113 동사 자리

해설 빈칸은 앞에 있는 she와 더불어 선행사 the heat-exchange valve를 수식하는 관계사절로, 주어 she 앞에 목적격 관계대명사가 생략되어 있다. 관계사절에 주어인 she만 있고 동사가 보이지 않으므로 빈칸에는 동사가 들어가야 한다. 따라서 동사인 (C) invented가 정답이다.

번역 다시아 팅은 그녀가 발명한 열 교환 밸브에 대한 특허를 취득하려고 한다.

어휘 patent 특허권 invent 발명하다

114 부사 자리 _ 접속부사

해설 등위접속사 and 뒤에 주어가 생략된 완전한 절이 왔으므로 빈칸은 부사 자리이다. 문맥상 '과거부터 발행된 신문을 가지고 있어서 주요한 목적지이다'는 내용이 되어야 적절하므로 '그러므로, 따라서'라는 뜻으로 인과 관계를 나타내는 접속부사 (C) thus가 정답이다. 참고로, 접속부사도 일반 부사처럼 명사구를 꾸밀 수 있으므로, thus도 명사구 a prime destination 앞에 놓여 명사구를 수식하고 있다.

번역 그 도서관은 1700년대부터 발행된 신문들을 가지고 있어서 지역 역사가들의 주요한 목적지이다.

어휘 date from ~부터 시작되다 prime 주요한 historian 역사가

115 부사 어휘

해설 과거분사 fixed를 수식하여 '즉시 수리되지 않으면 큰 문제로 이어진다'는 의미가 되어야 하므로 '즉시'라는 뜻의 (A) immediately가 정답이다.

번역 소량의 누수는 즉시 수리되지 않으면 종종 큰 문제로 이어진다.

어휘 water leak 누수 lead to ~로 이어지다 especially 특히 previously 이전에 relatively 비교적

116 전치사 어휘

해설 문맥상 빈칸 뒤 명사 construction과 함께 '공사 기간 동안'이라는 내용이 되어야 자연스러우므로 '~ 동안'이라는 의미의 (C) During이 정답이다. 참고로, (B) Within은 '~ 이내에'라는 뜻으로 기간을 나타낼 때 뒤에 시간 표현이 온다.

번역 공사 기간 동안 400미터 이상의 공공 수도관이 교체될 예정이다.

어휘 water pipe 수도관 replace 교체하다

117 명사 자리 _ 복합명사

해설 전치사 with의 목적어 역할로 형용사 normal의 수식을 받으며 빈칸 앞의 명사 business와 함께 복합명사를 이루는 명사 자리이다. 문맥상 '정상적인 업무 운영'이라는 의미가 적절하므로 '운영'이라는 뜻의 (C) operations가 정답이다.

번역 오늘 로비의 전기 공사는 정상적인 업무 운영에 방해가 되지 않을 것으로 예상된다.

어휘 electrical 전기의 interfere with ~을 방해하다 normal 정상적인

118 부사 어휘

해설 동사 worked를 수식하여 적절한 문맥을 완성하는 부사를 골라야 한다. 뒤에 일정보다 일찍 끝났다는 내용이 이어지는 것으로 보아 '매우 효율적으로 일했다'는 내용이 되어야 자연스럽다. 따라서 '효율적으로'라는 뜻의 (B) efficiently가 정답이다.

번역 회계팀이 매우 효율적으로 일했기 때문에 보고서는 일정보다 일찍 완료되었다.

어휘 accounting 회계 (업무) ahead of ~보다 일찍[앞서] securely 안전하게 respectively 각각

119 동사 어휘

해설 '제안서에 항목별 예산이 포함되어 있지 않다'는 내용이 되어야 적절하므로 '~이 들어 있다, 포함하다'라는 의미의 (A) contain이 정답이다.

번역 페리사 어소시에이츠가 제출한 제안서에는 항목별 예산이 포함되어 있지 않았다.

어휘 itemized 항목별로 구분한 fold 접다 refuse 거절하다

120 부사 자리 _ 동사 수식

해설 빈칸은 주어 The employee handbook과 동사 states 사이에서 동사를 수식하는 부사 자리이다. 따라서 '명확히, 분명히'라는 뜻의 (D) clearly가 정답이다.

번역 직원 안내서에는 모든 고객 서비스 제공자는 유니폼을 입어야 한다고 명확하게 명시되어 있다.

어휘 handbook 안내서 state 서술하다, 명시하다

121 재귀대명사

해설 빈칸은 동사 taught의 목적어 자리이고, 문맥상 '안다라는 스스로에게 그림을 가르쳤다'는 의미가 되어야 적절하다. 즉, 동사의 대상이 되는 목적어가 주어인 Andara와 일치하므로 재귀대명사인 (D) herself가 정답이다.

번역 안다라 에벨레는 유명한 초상화와 풍경화 화가들의 스타일을 모방하면서 스스로 그림을 배웠다.

어휘 portrait 초상화 landscape 풍경화

122 과거분사

해설 빈칸은 부사절에서 be동사 was와 함께 동사구를 이루는 자리이다. 주어가 his train이고 빈칸 뒤에 목적어가 없으며, '기차가 연착되었다'는 수동의 의미가 되어야 자연스러우므로 수동태를 이루는 과거분사 (C) delayed가 정답이다.

번역 자시오 씨는 기차가 갑작스럽게 연착되어 오늘 약속을 다시 잡아야 할 것이다.

어휘 unexpectedly 갑작스럽게

123 접속사 자리 _ 부사절 접속사

해설 빈칸 뒤에 주어와 동사를 갖춘 완전한 절이 왔으므로 부사절 접속사가 들어가야 한다. 문맥상 '기계가 세척되고 있는 동안'이라는 의미가 되어야 자연스러우므로 '~하는 동안'이라는 의미의 접속사 (A) while이 정답이다.

번역 병입 기계는 세척되는 동안 전원을 꺼 놓아야 한다.

어휘 bottling 병에 채워 넣기 whereas ~에 반해서

124 형용사 어휘

해설 문맥상 '오가와 씨는 재개발 사업에 반대한다'는 의미가 되어야 하므로, 전치사 to와 함께 쓰여 '~에 반대하는'이라는 뜻을 나타내는 (D) opposed가 정답이다. opposed to로 암기해 두자.

번역 오가와 씨는 현재 방식의 재개발 사업에 단호하게 반대한다.

어휘 adamantly 단호하게 form 방식, 형태 objectionable 불쾌한 negative 부정적인

125 접속사 자리 _ 부사절 접속사

해설 빈칸 뒤에 주어와 동사를 갖춘 완전한 절이 왔으므로 부사절 접속사가 들어가야 한다. 문맥상 '보고서 초안이 작성되었을 때'라는 의미가 되어야 자연스러우므로 '~할 때, ~하면'이라는 뜻의 접속사 (C) When이 정답이다. 또한, 문맥상 미래의 상황이라도 시간의 부사절에서는 현재 시제가 미래 시제를 대신한다는 점을 유의한다.

번역 통계 보고서 초안이 작성되면 아리스타 씨가 편집할 것이다.

어휘 statistical 통계의 draft 초안[원고]을 작성하다

126 형용사 자리 _ 주격 보어

해설 빈칸은 be동사 has been 뒤 주격 보어 자리이다. 주어인 Having strong partnerships를 보충 설명해 '파트너십 확보는 대단히 중요했다'는 의미가 되어야 하므로 '대단히 중요한'을 뜻하는 형용사 (A) critical이 정답이다. (C) critic도 '평론가'라는 뜻의 명사로 보어 역할을 할 수 있으나, 주어인 Having strong partnerships와 동격 관계가 아니므로 답이 될 수 없다.

번역 동남아시아 전역에 걸친 강력한 파트너십 확보는 스리사티 컴퍼니의 성공에 대단히 중요했다.

어휘 criticize 비평하다, 비판하다

127 동사 어휘

해설 문맥상 '사라 데이비슨은 치카라 아키텍츠의 비전을 열성적으로 받아들였다'는 의미가 되어야 자연스러우므로 '받아들이다, 수용하다'라는 뜻의 동사 (D) embraced가 정답이다.

번역 사라 데이비슨은 치카라 아키텍츠의 창의적인 비전을 다른 동료들보다 더 열성적으로 받아들였다.

어휘 architect 건축가 enthusiastically 열성적으로 associate 동료 catch up 따라잡다 give away 저버리다

128 지시대명사

해설 빈칸은 동사 can apply의 주어 자리로, 문맥상 뒤에 나온 전치사구와 함께 '재직 기간이 1년 이상인 사람들'이라는 의미가 되어야 하므로 '사람들'이라는 뜻으로 쓰일 수 있는 대명사 (A) Those가 정답이다.

번역 재직 기간이 1년 이상인 사람들은 학위 취득을 희망하는 경우 등록금 지원을 신청할 수 있다.

어휘 tuition 등록금 pursue 추구하다 academic degree 학위

129 명사 어휘

해설 크기를 나타내는 형용사 enormous의 수식을 받아 '프로젝트의 막대한 규모'라는 의미가 되어야 적절하므로 '규모'라는 뜻의 명사 (C) scale이 정답이다.

번역 팩틸리스 캐피탈은 주로 이토 풍력 발전 프로젝트의 막대한 규모에 대해 우려하고 있다.

어휘 mainly 주로   enormous 막대한   wind farm 풍력 발전   confusion 혼란   spiral 나선(형)

130 형용사 어휘

해설 빈칸 뒤의 명사 bands를 수식하기에 적절한 형용사를 고르는 문제이다. 문맥상 '바꿔 낄 수 있는 검정색, 흰색, 파란색 밴드'라는 의미가 되어야 자연스러우므로 '교체할 수 있는'이라는 뜻의 (D) interchangeable이 정답이다.

번역 모든 로린 손목시계는 교체 가능한 검정색, 흰색, 파란색 밴드와 함께 제공된다.

어휘 wristwatch 손목시계   variable 변하기 쉬운   probable 있음직한   companionable 다정한

PART 6

131-134 기사

파머스 마켓의 새로운 시즌

리 밸리 파머스 마켓은 흥미진진한 변화를 **131겪는 중이다**. 지난 3년간 마켓의 **132관리자**였던 제리 카버는 지난주에 사임했다. 그는 가든 헤이븐 농장의 운영을 감독했던 폴 프랭크슨으로 대체되었다.

주요 마켓 구역은 농산물뿐 아니라 더 많은 제품을 포함할 수 있도록 10개 부스에서 15개 부스로 확대된다. **133새로운 제품 중에는 고기와 치즈, 꿀이 있다.** 커피 스탠드와 공예 코너에 대한 계획도 있다. "수년간 저희에게서 농산물을 구매해온 단골 고객들에게 정말 감사드립니다."라고 프랭크슨은 말했다. "저희는 **134 더 다양한** 제품을 제공함으로써 더 많은 사람들이 지역에서 쇼핑하도록 장려할 수 있기를 바랍니다."

리 밸리 파머스 마켓은 연중무휴로 오전 8시부터 오후 6시까지 문을 연다.

어휘 step down 사임하다   replace 대체[교체]하다   oversee 감독하다   expand 확대되다   produce 농산물   craft 공예   loyal customer 단골 고객   a range of 다양한   year-round 일년 내내

131 동사 어휘

해설 빈칸 뒤의 목적어 exciting changes와 어울리는 동사를 골라야 한다. '흥미진진한 변화를 겪는 중이다'는 의미가 되어야 자연스러우므로 '(변화 등을) 겪다'라는 의미의 (D) undergoing이 정답이다. (A) resulting과 (C) competing은 자동사로 목적어를 취할 수 없으므로 답이 될 수 없다.

어휘 attach 붙이다, 첨부하다   compete 경쟁하다

132 명사 어휘

해설 빈칸 뒤 문장에서 가든 헤이븐 농장의 운영을 감독했던 폴 프랭크슨이 제리 카버의 후임이 되었다고 했으므로, 제리 카버가 마켓을 감독했던 관리자였다는 내용이 되어야 자연스럽다. 따라서 '관리자'라는 의미의 (D) manager가 정답이다.

133 문맥에 맞는 문장 고르기

해설 빈칸 앞에서 농산물뿐 아니라 더 많은 제품을 포함하도록 마켓 구역이 확대된다고 했고, 빈칸 뒤에서 also(또한)를 써서 커피 스탠드와 공예 코너에 대한 계획도 있다고 했다. 따라서 빈칸에도 커피나 공예품과 마찬가지로 확대되는 구역에 새롭게 추가될 제품에 대한 내용이 들어가야 자연스러우므로 새로운 제품 중에는 고기와 치즈, 꿀이 있다고 열거하고 있는 (C)가 정답이다.

번역 (A) 하지만, 옆에 약국이 있다.
(B) 겨울 동안 문을 닫을 것이다.
(C) 새로운 제품 중에는 고기와 치즈, 꿀이 있다.
(D) 현재, 길 건너편 주차장에 주차가 가능하다.

어휘 pharmacy 약국   garage 주차장, 차고

134 형용사 자리 _ 명사 수식 _ 비교급

해설 빈칸 앞에는 부정관사 a, 뒤에는 명사 range가 있으므로 명사를 수식하는 형용사가 와야 한다. 따라서 형용사의 비교급인 (B) wider가 정답이다. (C) widest도 형용사이지만 최상급 앞에 붙어야 하는 소유격이나 the가 없으므로 빈칸에 올 수 없다. 참고로, a (wide) range of는 '(매우) 다양한'이라는 의미의 관용 표현이다.

135-138 광고

마르케티 타이어

갈라졌거나 불룩하거나 마모된 타이어 때문에 속도를 늦추지 마세요. 새로운 마르케티 프리미엄 타이어로 새해를 맞이하세요! 지금 모든 그린백 할인 창고 클럽 지점에서 회원들은 이번 달에 4개 **135세트**에 75달러를 절약할 수 있습니다.

136회원이 되기를 원하십니까? 12월 31일 이전에 연간 회원권에 가입하고 타이어 설치비에서 20달러를 추가 할인받으세요. 일부 제외 사항이 **137적용되며** 일부 차량 제조사 및 모델의 경우 사이즈가 제공되지 않을 수 있습니다. **138추가적인** 세부 사항은 가까운 그린백 할인 창고 클럽을 방문하거나 웹사이트 www.gdwc.com/tires를 방문하세요.

어휘 cracked 갈라진   bulging 불룩한   worn 마모된   cruise 순항하다   warehouse 창고   installation 설치   exclusion 제외   vehicle 차량   make 제조사, ~제[산]

135 명사 어휘

해설 빈칸 앞 문장에서 새로운 타이어로 새해를 맞이하며 타이어 구매를 권하고 있으므로, 회원들이 할인받을 수 있는 것은 타이어 '4개짜리 한 세트'가 되어야 적절하다. 따라서 (C) set가 정답이다. '꾸러미, 묶음, 갑[곽]'의 의미를 지닌 (B) packet은 일반적으로 서류의 뭉치, 안내서나 씨앗 등을 넣은 작은 봉투 등을 지칭하므로 타이어와 어울

리지 않는다.

어휘 file (세로)줄, 열 round 하나의 경로[과정], 한 차례

136 문맥에 맞는 문장 고르기

해설 빈칸 뒤에서 12월 31일 이전에 회원권에 가입하고 타이어 설치비에서 20달러를 추가 할인받으라며 회원이 되면 받을 수 있는 혜택을 안내하고 있다. 따라서 빈칸에는 회원이 되기를 권하는 내용의 문장이 들어가야 자연스러우므로 회원이 되는 것에 관심이 있는지를 묻고 있는 (B)가 정답이다.

번역 (A) 교통 체증에 지치셨나요?
(B) 회원이 되기를 원하십니까?
(C) 믿을 수 있는 정비사가 필요하십니까?
(D) 새 차에 관심이 있으십니까?

어휘 be tired of ~에 지치다, 진절머리가 나다 trusted 신뢰받는
mechanic 정비사

137 동사 자리 _ 시제

해설 주어 Some exclusions 뒤에 동사가 필요하므로 빈칸은 동사 자리이다. 등위접속사 and로 연결된 절에서 일부 차량의 경우 사이즈가 제공되지 않을 수도 있다며 현재 시제로 판매 제품에 대한 일반적인 사실을 설명하고 있으므로 빈칸에도 '제외 사항이 적용된다'며 현재 시제로 설명하는 내용이 되어야 자연스럽다. 따라서 (A) apply가 정답이다.

어휘 apply 적용되[하]다

138 형용사 어휘

해설 빈칸 앞에서 회원권 가입과 관련된 혜택 및 혜택이 적용될 수 없는 예외 사항에 대해 설명하고 있으므로, 앞서 설명한 내용 외에 '추가적인 세부 사항을 확인하려면 매장이나 웹사이트를 방문하라'는 내용이 되어야 자연스럽다. 따라서 '추가적인'을 의미하는 (D) further가 정답이다.

어휘 optional 선택적인, 임의의 inflated (공기를 넣어) 부푼, 팽창한

139-142 이메일

수신: 에즈기 이난
발신: 티나 윤
날짜: 4월 15일
제목: 행사 확인

이난 씨께,

오늘 고객님과 139 이야기할 수 있어서 즐거웠습니다. 5월 21일 본너 트램펄린 공원에서 열리는 팀워크 행사를 예약해 주셔서 감사합니다. 말씀드렸듯이 본너는 다양한 점심 식사 패키지를 제공합니다. 고객님은 기본 옵션으로 신청해 드렸습니다. 여기에는 1인당 8파운드에 피자 한 조각,

레모네이드 한 캔, 그리고 작은 포테이토칩 한 봉지가 140 포함됩니다. 과일이나 채소 트레이를 추가하기 위해 패키지를 35파운드로 업그레이드하실 수 있습니다. 저희 본너는 또한 추가 금액 30파운드에 시트 케이크를 제공해 드릴 수 있습니다. 141그렇지 않으면, 직접 케이크나 다른 디저트를 가져오셔도 됩니다. 142메뉴를 업그레이드하기를 원하시면 이 메시지에 회신해 주세요. 음식 주문은 행사 48시간 전까지 변경하실 수 있습니다.

티나 윤
본너 트램펄린 공원 행사 기획자

어휘 confirmation 확인 pleasure 즐거움 team-building 팀워크, 팀빌딩 a variety of 다양한 put ~ down for ~을 …의 신청자[예약자]로 이름을 적어 두다 crisp 포테이토칩 tray 쟁반 up to ~까지

139 동사 어휘

해설 빈칸 뒤 문장에서 공원에서 열리는 행사를 예약해 주어 감사하다면서, 말씀드렸듯이 다양한 패키지를 제공한다고 하는 것으로 보아 이메일을 작성하기 전에 수신자인 이난 씨와 행사 예약 건에 대해 논의했다는 것을 알 수 있다. 따라서 '이야기하다'를 뜻하는 (A) speaking이 정답이다.

140 동사 자리 _ 시제

해설 주어가 This인 문장에 동사가 보이지 않으므로 빈칸은 동사 자리이다. 앞 문장에서 고객님은 기본 옵션으로 신청해 드렸다면서, 빈칸이 있는 문장에서는 기본 옵션에 포함되는 항목들에 대해 안내하고 있다. 따라서 빈칸이 있는 문장은 사실을 설명하는 내용으로 현재 시제가 되어야 하므로 (A) includes가 정답이다. 현재완료 시제인 (C) has included는 이미 일어난 일이 현재에 영향을 주고 있어야 하므로 오답이고, (D) would have included는 가정법 과거완료의 주절에 쓰이는 시제이므로 답이 될 수 없다.

141 접속부사

해설 앞 문장에서 추가 금액 30파운드에 케이크를 제공해 준다고 했고, 뒤 문장에서는 직접 케이크나 다른 디저트를 가져와도 된다고 했다. 뒤 문장이 앞 문장에서 설명한 사항을 선택하지 않을 경우 가능한 대안에 대한 내용이므로 '그렇지 않으면, 그 대신에'를 뜻하는 (C) Alternatively가 정답이다.

어휘 similarly 비슷하게 in short 간단히 말해, 요컨대

142 문맥에 맞는 문장 고르기

해설 빈칸 앞에서 과일이나 채소 트레이 추가, 시트 케이크 추가 등의 메뉴 변경 옵션에 대해 설명하고 있으므로, 메뉴 변경을 원할 경우에 대한 안내가 이어져야 자연스럽다. 따라서 메뉴 업그레이드를 원할 경우 메시지에 회신을 달라고 언급하고 있는 (D)가 정답이다.

번역 (A) 저희 채소 트레이는 인기 품목입니다.
(B) 일행을 위한 체크인은 정오에 시작됩니다.
(C) 각 손님은 행사 전에 면책서에 서명해야 할 겁니다.
(D) 메뉴를 업그레이드하기를 원하시면 이 메시지에 회신해 주세요.

어휘 party 단체, 일행 waiver 면책, 포기 증서[서류]

143-146 공지

> 팩스턴 모바일 뱅킹 계정 설정을 시작해 주셔서 감사합니다. **143절차를 완료하시려면 이메일로 보내 드린 지침을 따르십시오.**
>
> 계정이 완전히 활성화되면, 예금, 인출 및 자금 이체**144와 같은** 계정 활동에 대한 알림을 받으시게 됩니다. 알림 설정은 당사 모바일 앱 또는 웹사이트의 "내 계정" 페이지에서 **145조정하실** 수 있습니다. 설정을 변경하기 전에 보안 목적으로 일회성 **146인증** 번호를 요청하라는 알림 창이 표시됩니다. 질문이 있으면 www.paxtonmobilebanking.com/FAQ를 방문해 주십시오.

> 어휘 initiate 시작하다 setup 설정 account 계정, 계좌 activate 활성화시키다 notification 알림 deposit 예금 withdrawal 인출 transfer 이체 purpose 목적 prompt (컴퓨터에서) 알림 창[지시 메시지]으로 안내하다

143 문맥에 맞는 문장 고르기

해설 빈칸 앞 문장에서 모바일 뱅킹 계정 설정을 시작해 주셔서 감사하다고 했고, 빈칸 뒤로는 계정 설정이 완료된 뒤 일어날 일에 대해 설명하고 있다. 따라서 빈칸에는 계정 설정 절차와 관련된 안내가 들어가야 자연스럽게 연결되므로 절차를 완료하려면 이메일의 지침을 따르라고 언급하고 있는 (B)가 정답이다.

번역 (A) 새로운 신용 대출을 신청하시려면 해당 지역 지점에 전화하세요.
(B) 절차를 완료하시려면 이메일로 보내 드린 지침을 따르십시오.
(C) 저희가 더 나은 서비스 제공 방법을 알 수 있도록 이 설문 조사에 응답해 주십시오.
(D) 앱에서 직접 은행 카드 재발급을 신청하실 수 있습니다.

어휘 line of credit 신용 대출 (한도) process 절차 instruction 지침 replacement 교체

144 전치사 어휘

해설 빈칸은 쉼표 앞 완전한 절에 명사구 deposits, withdrawals, and fund transfers를 연결하는 자리이므로 전치사가 들어가야 한다. 문맥상 '예금, 인출 및 자금 이체와 같은 계정 활동'이라는 의미가 되어야 하므로 '~와 같은, 예를 들어'라는 뜻의 (D) such as가 정답이다. such as는 이전 내용에 추가 정보나 예시를 제공할 때 사용되는 전치사이다.

145 동사 어휘

해설 알림 설정(your notification settings)을 목적어로 취했을 때 자연스러운 동사를 골라야 한다. 또한 빈칸 뒤 문장에서 '설정을 변경하기 전에'라고 했으므로, 빈칸에는 설정 변경과 관련된 동사가 들어가 "내 계정" 페이지에서 알림 설정을 조정할 수 있다'는 내용이 되어야

적절하므로 '조정하다'는 뜻의 (A) adjust가 정답이다.

어휘 interrupt 방해하다

146 명사 자리 _ 복합명사

해설 to부정사 to request의 목적어 역할을 하며 부정관사 a와 형용사 one-time의 수식을 받는 명사 자리이다. 문맥상 빈칸 뒤의 명사 code와 함께 쓰여 '인증 번호'라는 의미의 복합명사를 만들 수 있는 '인증, 확인'이라는 뜻의 (D) verification이 정답이다.

어휘 verify 입증[검증]하다, 확인하다 verifiability 검증 가능성

PART 7

147-148 기사

> **리제트 시장, 시정 연설 준비**
>
> 팰컨 하이츠 (4월 21일) – **147(A), 147(C)**로레타 리제트 시장은 4월 30일 수요일 오후 7시부터 팰컨 하이츠 시청 101호에서 다섯 번째 시정 연설을 할 예정이다. 이 행사는 일반인에게 공개되지만 좌석은 선착순이다.
>
> **147(B), 148(B)**지난달 두 번째 4년 임기에 재선된 리제트 시장은 도시의 미래에 대한 자신의 비전을 논의할 것이다. 그녀의 의제 중 하나는 패스트푸드점인 팬헨들 이터리가 역사적인 헤지로우 대로에 지점을 열기 위해 한 신청으로 논란이 많은 문제이다. 연설 후 질의응답 시간이 뒤따를 예정이다. 오후 6시 30분부터 입장 가능하다.

> 어휘 mayor 시장 set 준비가 된 deliver (연설 등을) 하다 address 연설 first come, first served 선착순 reelect 재선하다 term 임기 agenda 의제 controversial 논란이 많은 application 신청 eatery 식당 historic 역사적으로 중요한 boulevard 대로

147 Not / True

번역 행사에 대해 언급되지 않은 것은?
(A) 시작 시간
(B) 주요 목적
(C) 위치
(D) 기간

해설 첫 문장에서 로레타 리제트 시장은 4월 30일 수요일 오후 7시부터 팰컨 하이츠 시청 101호에서 다섯 번째 시정 연설을 할 예정(Mayor Loretta Lizette will deliver ~ at Falcon Heights City Hall, Room 101, on Wednesday, 30 April, beginning at 7:00 P.M.)이라고 했으므로 (A)와 (C)가 언급되어 있고, 두 번째 단락의 첫 문장에서 지난달 두 번째 4년 임기에 재선된 리제트 시장은 도시의 미래에 대한 자신의 비전을 논의할 것(Mayor Lizette ~ discuss her vision for the future of the city)이라고 연설의 목적을 언급하고 있으므로 (B) 또한 기사에 나온 내용이다. 행사 기간에 대한 언급은 없으므로 (D)가 정답이다.

어휘 purpose 목적 duration 기간

148 Not / True

번역 리제트 시장에 대해 명시된 것은?
(A) 패스트푸드점을 소유하고 있다.
(B) 최근에 선거에서 이겼다.
(C) 헤지로우 대로에 집이 있다.
(D) 시 직원에게 상을 수여할 것이다.

해설 두 번째 단락의 첫 문장에서 지난달 두 번째 4년 임기에 재선된 리제트 시장(Mayor Lizette, who was reelected to her second four-year team last month)이라고 했으므로 (B)가 정답이다.

어휘 present 수여하다

> **Paraphrasing** 지문의 was reelected ~ last month
> → 정답의 recently won an election

149-150 초대장

초대합니다!

149 코로잘 디지털의 10주년

**149 우리를 이 이정표로 이끈 당신의 노고와 헌신을
기념하기 위해 함께해 주세요!**

6월 15일 토요일

150 오후 6시 애피타이저와 음악
오후 7시 저녁 만찬

베이쇼어 호텔
애틀랜틱 가 22

6월 1일까지 j.bovel@corozaldigital.com으로
회신 주시기 바랍니다.

어휘 anniversary 기념일 dedication 헌신 milestone 이정표, 중요한 사건 RSVP 회신 주세요(프랑스어 répondez s'il vous plaît의 약자)

149 추론 / 암시

번역 초대는 누구를 대상으로 하는가?
(A) 코로잘 디지털 고객
(B) 코로잘 디지털 직원
(C) 베이쇼어 호텔 직원
(D) 베이쇼어 호텔 고객

해설 초대장의 두 번째 줄에서 코로잘 디지털의 10주년(Corozal Digital's Tenth Anniversary)을 위한 행사임을 밝혔고, 뒤이어 우리를 이 이정표로 이끈 당신의 노고와 헌신을 기념하기 위해 함께해 달라(Join us to celebrate your hard work and dedication that got us to this milestone!)고 한 것으로 보아 코로잘 디지털에서 근무하고 있는 직원들을 행사에 초대하고 있음을 알 수 있다. 따라서 (B)가 정답이다.

어휘 patron 고객

150 Not / True

번역 행사에 대해 언급된 것은?
(A) 은퇴를 기념할 것이다.
(B) 응답할 필요 없다.
(C) 음식이 제공된다.
(D) 초청객의 손님이 환영받는다.

해설 초대장의 다섯 번째 단락에 오후 6시 애피타이저와 음악(6:00 P.M. Appetizers and Music), 오후 7시에 저녁 만찬(7:00 P.M. Dinner)이 제공된다는 안내가 있으므로 정답은 (C)이다.

어휘 mark 기념[축하]하다 retirement 은퇴 invitee 초청객

> **Paraphrasing** 지문의 Appetizers/Dinner → 정답의 Food

151-152 웹페이지

---

https://www.firststreetcinema.com/classic_film

시즌 프로그램	**소식**	입장권	연락처

고전 영화제

새로운 퍼스트 스트리트 시네마는 고전 영화 팬을 위한 다음 영화의 무료 상영으로 영화 관람객들을 환영하며 6월 개관을 기념하고 있습니다. 영화는 저녁 7시에 시작합니다. 좌석 수는 한정되어 있으며, 현장에서는 입장권을 발행하지 않으니 관람하실 분들은 웹사이트에서 입장권을 예약하시기 바랍니다.

151〈언덕 위 농장〉　　　　　6월 2일 토요일

언덕 위에 있는 기묘한 농장과 그곳에 살고 있는 3대 가족을 다룬 이야기.

151〈단 두 개의 바퀴〉　　　　6월 9일 토요일

한 젊은 사이클 선수가 엘리트 경주를 준비하는 데 수년을 보낸다. 역경을 극복하는 가슴 따뜻해지는 이야기.

151〈사라진 서류〉　　　　　6월 16일 토요일

어느 한 작가의 원고가 영문 모를 도난을 당해 범인을 찾기 위한 수사로 이어진다.

151,152〈뒤죽박죽 귀향〉　　　6월 23일 토요일

152 칸의 가족 모임 행사는 일련의 코믹한 사건과 오해로 점철된다. 큰 웃음을 원한다면 당신을 위한 영화.

어휘 filmgoer 영화 관람객 screening 상영 reserve 예약하다 on-site 현장에서 feature 특징으로 다루다[삼다] mysterious 기묘한 generation 세대 cyclist 자전거 타는 사람, 사이클리스트 heartwarming 마음이 따뜻해지는 overcome 극복하다 adversity 역경 puzzling 영문 모를, 당혹스러운 theft 절도 culprit 범인 rambling 뒤죽박죽의, 정처 없이 돌아다니는 homecoming 귀향 reunion 모임, 재회[재결합] mark 특징짓다 incident 사건 laugh 웃음

151 Not / True

번역 고전 영화 상영에 대해 사실인 것은?
(A) 적은 관람료로 대중들에게 제공된다.
(B) 한 달 내내 하는 것으로 예정되어 있다.
(C) 아침 시간에 상영된다.
(D) 야외에서 열린다.

해설 두 번째 단락에 상영되는 고전 영화 목록이 〈언덕 위 농장〉(*The Hillside Farm*) 6월 2일 토요일(Saturday, June 2), 〈단 두 개의 바퀴〉(*Just Two Wheels*) 6월 9일 토요일(Saturday, June 9), 〈사라진 서류〉(*The Missing Papers*) 6월 16일 토요일(Saturday, June 16), 〈뒤죽박죽 귀향〉(*A Rambling Homecoming*) 6월 23일 토요일(Saturday, June 23)로 각 영화마다 일주일 간격으로 6월 초부터 6월 말까지 계속 상영되는 일정이므로 (B)가 정답이다.

152 추론 / 암시

번역 유머러스할 것 같은 영화는?
(A) 〈언덕 위 농장〉
(B) 〈단 두 개의 바퀴〉
(C) 〈사라진 서류〉
(D) 〈뒤죽박죽 귀향〉

해설 마지막 영화 항목 설명에 칸의 가족 모임 행사는 일련의 코믹한 사건과 오해로 점철된다(The Khan's family reunion celebration ~ and misunderstandings)고 했고, 큰 웃음을 원한다면 당신을 위한 영화(If you need a good laugh, this is the film for you)라고 했으므로 〈뒤죽박죽 귀향〉은 코믹 영화임을 알 수 있다. 따라서 (D)가 정답이다.

> **Paraphrasing** 지문의 comical → 질문의 humorous

153-156 온라인 채팅

> 아이사 이토 [오전 10시 8분] **153**카노마틱 제품 사용자를 위한 커뮤니티를 알게 되어 매우 기쁩니다! **153,156**S20 캔 오프너를 사용해 보신 분 계시나요? **156**몇 년 동안 가지고 있던 전기 캔 오프너가 마침내 고장 났습니다.
>
> 탄비어 쿠마르 [오전 10시 10분] **153**몇 년 전에 하나 샀는데, **154**제가 쓴 돈만큼의 가치는 없었던 것 같아요.
>
> 잉그리드 보겔 [오전 11시 15분] **153,156**저는 제 것이 마음에 들어요. 통조림을 따는 데 애를 먹곤 했거든요. 이것 덕분에 모든 크기의 캔을 더 쉽게 딸 수 있습니다.
>
> 로리 제이콥스 [오후 2시 12분] 업소용은 비싸지만 가격이 저렴한 소비자용도 있습니다.
>
> 존 버우드 [오후 2시 14분] 저는 온라인으로 주문했는데 결함이 있었어요. 회사의 고객 서비스 부서에 연락했더니 작동 잘되는 새 제품으로 보내 주셨습니다.
>
> 로리 제이콥스 [오후 2시 16분] **155**저는 몇 년 전에 식당에서 요리사로 일했는데, 그 당시 업소용 등급의 카노마틱 캔 오프너가 있었습니다. **156**집에서는 10년 가까이 소비자용을 사용하고 있어요. 안전하고 쉽게 통조림을 땁니다.

> 아이사 이토 [오후 5시 15분] 감사합니다, 여러분. 저도 한번 써 봐야겠습니다.

> **어휘** forum 온라인 커뮤니티 electric 전기의 worth ~의 가치가 있는 struggle 애쓰다 commercial 업소[상업]의 consumer 소비자 defective 결함이 있는 work 작동하다 grade 등급 decade 10년 give it a try 한번 해 보다

153 추론 / 암시

번역 이토 씨의 질문에 응답한 사람은?
(A) 고객 서비스 담당자
(B) 광고 판매 사원
(C) 온라인 요리 강좌 참가자
(D) 특정 유형의 가전제품 소유자

해설 10시 8분에 이토 씨가 카노마틱 제품 사용자를 위한 커뮤니티를 알게 되어 기쁘다(I'm so glad I found this forum for users of Canomatik products!)고 한 뒤 S20 캔 오프너를 사용해 보신 분이 있는지(Has anyone tried the S20 can opener?) 물었으므로 온라인 커뮤니티의 대화 참여자들은 카노마틱 제품 소비자임을 알 수 있다. 또한 10시 10분에 쿠마르 씨가 몇 년 전에 하나 샀다(I bought one several years ago)고 했고, 11시 15분에 보겔 씨가 저는 제 것이 마음에 든다(I like mine)고 대답했다. 따라서 이토 씨의 질문에 응답한 사람은 S20 캔 오프너의 소유자이자 사용자임을 알 수 있으므로 정답은 (D)이다.

어휘 particular 특정한 appliance 가전제품

> **Paraphrasing** 지문의 the S20 can opener
> → 정답의 a particular type of appliance

154 세부 사항

번역 카노마틱 제품에 대한 쿠마르 씨의 의견은?
(A) 크기를 맘에 들어 한다.
(B) 품질에 불만족한다.
(C) 사용하기 편리하다고 생각한다.
(D) 고장 날까 봐 걱정한다.

해설 10시 10분에 쿠마르 씨가 제가 쓴 돈만큼의 가치는 없었던 것 같다(I don't think it was worth the money I spent)고 했으므로 (B)가 정답이다.

어휘 dissatisfied 불만스러워하는 concerned 걱정하는

> **Paraphrasing** 지문의 don't think it was worth the money
> → 정답의 dissatisfied

155 세부 사항

번역 한때 식품 서비스 산업에서 일했던 사람은?
(A) 보겔 씨
(B) 제이콥스 씨
(C) 버우드 씨
(D) 쿠마르 씨

해설 2시 16분에 제이콥스 씨가 몇 년 전에 식당에서 요리사로 일했다(I used to be a cook at a restaurant years ago)고 했으므로 정답은 (B)이다.

156 의도 파악

번역 오후 5시 15분에 이토 씨가 "저도 한번 써 봐야겠습니다"라고 쓴 의도는?
(A) 구매를 할 것이다.
(B) 식당에서 먹을 것이다.
(C) 제조사에 연락할 것이다.
(D) 용기를 열려고 시도할 것이다.

해설 10시 8분에 이토 씨가 S20 캔 오프너를 사용해 보신 분이 있는지(Has anyone tried the S20 can opener?) 물으며 몇 년 동안 가지고 있던 전기 캔 오프너가 마침내 고장 났다(The electric can opener I've had for years finally broke)고 하자, 11시 15분에 보겔 씨가 저는 제 것이 마음에 든다(I like mine)고 대답했고, 2시 16분에 제이콥스 씨가 집에서 10년 가까이 소비자용을 사용하고 있다(I've been using the consumer version at home for nearly a decade)며 안전하고 쉽게 통조림을 딴다(It opens cans safely and easily)고 했다. 따라서 이토 씨는 사람들로부터 나온 캔 오프너에 대한 긍정적인 후기를 감안하여 새로운 캔 오프너를 구입해서 사용해 보겠다는 의도로 한 말임을 알 수 있으므로 (A)가 정답이다.

어휘 make a purchase 구매하다 manufacturer 제조사 attempt 시도하다 container 용기

157-158 문자 메시지

제럴드 아나스트 [오전 8시 58분]
안녕, 로라. ¹⁵⁷오늘 아침에 우리 쇼룸에서 일할 사람이 충분히 있죠?

로라 후 [오전 8시 59분]
네, 파트타임 도우미인 브렌다가 지금 여기 있어요.

제럴드 아나스트 [오전 9시 1분]
좋아요. ¹⁵⁷저는 크로스비 가에 있는 유통업체의 창고에 있어요. 최근 고객인 알스포드 게스트하우스에 필요한 바로 그 펜던트 조명 스타일이 이쪽에 있더라고요.

로라 후 [오전 9시 2분]
거기까지 가야 했다니 놀랍네요. ¹⁵⁷우리도 여기에 굉장히 다양한 스타일을 갖고 있잖아요.

제럴드 아나스트 [오전 9시 4분]
음, 알스포드의 경영진은 자신들의 디자인 선호도에 대해 매우 구체적이었어요. 우리가 그 조명들을 입수할 수 있게 되어 기쁠 따름이에요. 오전 늦게까지는 돌아갈 거예요. ¹⁵⁸구매 주문서와 재고 스프레드시트는 살펴보셨나요?

로라 후 [오전 9시 5분]
여기 온 지 10분 정도밖에 안 됐어요.

제럴드 아나스트 [오전 9시 6분]
괜찮아요. 일이 좀 잡히면 부족한 품목이 있는지 알려 주세요.

로라 후 [오전 9시 7분]
그럴게요.

어휘 distributor 유통업체 warehouse 창고 turn out ~인 것으로 드러나다 pendant light 펜던트(매달려 있는) 조명 latest 최근의 specific 구체적인 preference 선호도 look over 살펴보다, 검토하다 inventory 재고(품) catch up 밀린 일[업무]을 따라잡다 short on ~이 부족한

157 추론 / 암시

번역 메시지를 작성한 사람들이 근무할 것 같은 곳은?
(A) 게스트하우스
(B) 회계 법인
(C) 조명 매장
(D) 제조 회사

해설 8시 58분에 아나스트 씨가 오늘 아침에 우리 쇼룸에서 일할 사람이 충분히 있는지(You have enough people ~ morning, right?) 물었고, 9시 1분에 크로스비 가에 있는 유통업체의 창고에 있다(I'm at the distributor's warehouse on Crosby Street)면서 알스포드 게스트하우스에 필요한 바로 그 펜던트 조명 스타일이 이쪽에 있다(It turns out they have the exact style of pendant lights we need for our latest client, Alsford Guesthouse)고 하자, 9시 2분에 후 씨가 우리도 여기에 굉장히 다양한 스타일을 갖고 있다(We have such a large variety of styles here)고 했다. 따라서 두 사람이 일하는 곳은 쇼룸을 갖추고 있고 다양한 조명을 취급하는 곳임을 알 수 있으므로 (C)가 정답이다.

158 의도 파악

번역 오전 9시 5분에 후 씨가 "여기 온 지 10분 정도밖에 안 됐어요"라고 쓴 의도는?
(A) 아직 일부 문서를 검토하지 않았다.
(B) 고객에게 배달을 해야 했다.
(C) 부재중인 직원을 대신할 수 없을 것이다.
(D) 몇 개의 상자를 풀 시간이 없었다.

해설 9시 4분에 아나스트 씨가 구매 주문서와 재고 스프레드시트는 살펴보았는지(Have you looked over our purchase orders and inventory spreadsheets?) 묻자 9시 5분에 후 씨가 여기 온 지 10분 정도밖에 안 됐다(I've only been here about ten minutes)고 대답했다. 따라서 후 씨는 아직 구매 주문서와 재고 스프레드시트를 확인할 시간이 없었다는 의도로 한 말임을 알 수 있으므로 (A)가 정답이다.

어휘 substitute for ~을 대신하다 absent 부재한

> Paraphrasing 지문의 looked over our purchase orders and inventory spreadsheets
> → 정답의 reviewed some documents

159-161 이메일

수신: 닉 포스터
발신: 내추럴 스프링 가든 제품 고객 지원
제목: 후속 조치
날짜: 10월 28일

포스터 씨께,

159최근에 내추럴 스프링 가든 제품에서 세린 버드 배스를 구입해 주셔서 감사합니다. 여러 층으로 꾸준히 계속해서 흘러내리는 물의 흐름은 귀하의 정원에 토종 새들을 끌어들이고 시원하고 차분한 환경을 제공할 것입니다.

귀하의 주문은 10월 21일에 이루어졌고 10월 24일에 도착한 것으로 알고 있습니다. 지금까지 제품에 만족하셨기를 바랍니다. 구입하신 제품은 3년 보증으로 **161보장된다**는 것을 기억하세요. 작동상 문제를 경험하게 되실 경우 고객 서비스팀인 1-800-555-0168로 연락 주시기 바랍니다.

1602분 정도 시간을 내서서 간단한 설문 조사를 작성해 주시겠습니까? 귀하의 답변은 저희가 고객들에 대해 더 많이 알게 되어 제품과 서비스를 더 효과적으로 마케팅하는 데 도움이 될 것입니다. 설문 조사에 응하시려면 www.naturalspringgardenproducts.com/review로 저희 웹사이트를 방문해 주세요.

켄 이와타
내추럴 스프링 가든 제품 고객 지원

어휘 follow-up 후속 조치[처리] serene 고요한 steady 꾸준한 cascading 계속적인, 폭포처럼 흐르는 flow 흐름 level 층 native 토종의 calming 차분한 thus far 지금까지 cover (보험 등으로) 보장하다 warranty 품질 보증 reach out 연락하다 brief 간단한 enable 가능하게 하다 effectively 효과적으로

---

159 추론 / 암시

번역 포스터 씨가 구매했을 것 같은 제품은?
(A) 정수기
(B) 새 먹이통
(C) 정원 관련 책
(D) 야외 분수대

해설 첫 문장에서 포스터 씨에게 최근에 내추럴 스프링 가든 제품에서 세린 버드 배스를 구입해 주어 감사하다(Thank you for your recent purchase ~ Spring Garden Products)며, 여러 층으로 꾸준히 계속해서 흘러내리는 물의 흐름은 귀하의 정원에 토종 새들을 끌어들이고 시원하고 차분한 환경을 제공할 것(Its steady, cascading flow of water ~ provide a cool, calming environment)이라고 제품에 대해 설명하고 있는 것으로 보아 포스터 씨가 구입한 것은 정원에 놓을 분수대임을 알 수 있다. 따라서 정답은 (D)이다.

어휘 purifier 정화 장치 feeder 먹이통

---

160 세부 사항

번역 포스터 씨가 요청받는 것은?
(A) 온라인 후기 작성
(B) 의견 제공
(C) 배송 날짜 확인
(D) 주소 업데이트

해설 세 번째 단락의 첫 문장에서 포스터 씨에게 간단한 설문 조사를 작성해 줄 수 있는지(Would you ~ complete a brief survey?) 묻고 있고, 귀하의 답변은 저희가 고객들에 대해 더 많이 알게 되어 제품과 서비스를 더 효과적으로 마케팅하는 데 도움이 될 것(Your responses will enable ~ effectively market our products

and services)이라고 했다. 본문의 survey는 고객들을 더 잘 알고 제품과 서비스를 더 효과적으로 마케팅하려는 목적을 가지고 요청되는 것이므로, 개선을 위한 정보나 의견을 제시하는 feedback과 맥락을 같이 하지만 제품 사용의 개인적인 경험을 통해 평가를 하는 review와는 차이가 있다. 따라서 정답은 (B)이다.

Paraphrasing 지문의 complete a brief survey
→ 정답의 Provide feedback

---

161 동의어

번역 두 번째 단락 3행의 "covered"와 의미가 가장 가까운 단어는?
(A) 설명되는
(B) 보장되는
(C) 계속되는
(D) 허용되는

해설 의미상 제품이 보증서로 '보장된다'는 뜻으로 쓰인 것이므로 정답은 (B) protected이다.

162-164 기사

홈 스타일 의류 라인 데뷔

마닐라 (9월 18일) – 현지 디자이너 마리테스 바우티스타는 필리핀의 수제 공예품에서 영감을 받아 전통 기법을 이용하는 지역 장인들에 의해 짜인 원단을 특징으로 하는 의류 브랜드인 홈 스타일을 선보였다.

162바우티스타는 어린 시절 어머니와 이모들로부터 기본적인 직조 기술을 처음 배웠고 마닐라 패션 디자인 스쿨에서 공부하면서 지식을 쌓아 올렸다. 그리고 나서 그녀는 트렌디 투데이에서 주니어 디자이너로 일하며 10년을 보냈다. 마침내, 그녀는 고향인 샌하신토로 돌아와 홈 스타일을 설립했다.

홈 스타일의 데뷔 컬렉션은 그 지역의 유명한 직조 기술과 디자인을 활용한 의류 및 헤어 액세서리를 포함한다. **163바우티스타 씨는 그녀가 사용하는 모든 직물을 현지 장인들로부터 구입한다.**

164현재 홈 스타일 상품은 엄선된 샌하신토 지역 매장에서만 구입할 수 있다. 하지만 바우티스타 씨는 더 큰 목표를 갖고 있다.

"저는 현지 생산을 유지하고 싶습니다."라고 바우티스타 씨는 말했다. "장인들에게도 좋은 일이고, 그것이 정통이지요. 하지만 **164'제품'이 지역에 머무르는 것을 원하지는 않습니다. 저는 우리 디자인을 전국, 어쩌면 전 세계에도 알리고 싶습니다."**

어휘 inspired 영감을 받은 craft 공예(품) feature 특징으로 하다 fabric 직물 woven 직조된 artisan 장인 practice 기법, 관행 weaving 직조 utilize 활용하다 textile 직물 craftspeople 장인 select 엄선된 authentic 정통의, 진짜의

---

162 세부 사항

번역 바우티스타 씨에게 직조를 소개한 사람은?
(A) 가족들
(B) 선생님들
(C) 수석 디자이너들
(D) 지역 장인들

해설 두 번째 단락의 첫 문장에서 바우티스타는 어린 시절 어머니와 이모들로부터 기본적인 직조 기술을 처음 배웠다(Bautista first learned basic weaving techniques from her mother and aunts in her youth)고 했으므로 (A)가 정답이다.

Paraphrasing 지문의 mother and aunts → 정답의 family

163 Not / True

번역 바우티스타 씨에 대해 명시된 것은?
(A) 마닐라에서 태어났다.
(B) 가까운 곳에서 자재를 구입한다.
(C) 많은 사업을 시작했다.
(D) 정기적으로 세계 여행을 한다.

해설 세 번째 단락의 두 번째 문장에서 바우티스타 씨는 그녀가 사용하는 모든 직물을 현지 장인들로부터 구입한다(Ms. Bautista purchases all the textiles she uses from local craftspeople)고 했으므로 (B)가 정답이다.

어휘 material 자재, 직물   nearby 인근의   source 공급자; 원천

Paraphrasing 지문의 purchases all the textiles ~ from local craftspeople → 정답의 buys materials from nearby sources

164 문장 삽입

번역 [1], [2], [3], [4]로 표시된 곳 중에서 다음 문장이 들어가기에 가장 적합한 위치는?

"하지만 바우티스타 씨는 더 큰 목표를 갖고 있다."
(A) [1]
(B) [2]
(C) [3]
(D) [4]

해설 제시된 문장의 접속부사 However가 문제 해결의 단서이다. 더 큰 목표를 갖고 있다는 문장 앞에 반전의 뜻을 가진 However를 사용했으므로, 그 앞에는 '큰 목표'와는 상반되는 내용이 와야 한다. 따라서 현재는 상품을 지역의 일부 매장에서만 구입할 수 있다(Currently ~ available only in select San Jacinto-area stores)며 아직은 제품의 유통 반경이 그다지 크지 않다고 언급하는 문장 뒤에 들어가야 적절하다. 또한 뒤따르는 단락에서 제품이 지역에 머무르는 것을 원치 않고, 디자인을 전국뿐 아니라 전 세계에도 알리고 싶다(I don't want the products to remain local. I want to bring our designs to the whole country-maybe even the world)는 바우티스타 씨의 큰 목표를 언급하고 있으므로 제시된 문장이 들어가기에 적절한 위치는 (D)이다.

165-167 웹페이지

| https://www.brandmarkproductsinc.com |
| 소개 | 제품 | 시작하기 | 문의 |

165우리 제품에 귀사의 로고를 넣고 유명해지세요!

165귀사의 로고나 회사 슬로건이 박힌 우리의 멋진 패션 의류로 귀사를 광고하는 것보다 더 좋은 방법은 없습니다. 귀사의 로고 파일을 제공해 주시면 브랜드마크 프로덕트 주식회사가 선정된 품목을 장식하여 영업일 기준 4일 이내에 주문품을 배송해 드립니다. 우리는 귀사의 주문품을 컬러 프린팅이나 최고 품질의 자수를 이용해 제작합니다.

당사는 25년간의 사업 경험을 통해 이름 인지도를 높이는 것과 관련해 중요한 사실을 밝혀냈습니다. 자주 166한쪽으로 치워 두거나 잃어버리는 물병과 열쇠고리 같은 물건들은 잊어버리세요. 귀사의 메시지는 당사의 고급 셔츠, 운동복 상의, 재킷 및 모자로 더욱 효과적이고 오래 남을 것입니다.

167주문하시려면 "시작하기" 탭을 사용하시거나 1-800-555-0155로 전화하셔서 고객 서비스 담당자와 통화하세요.

어휘 make one's mark 유명해지다, 성공하다   organization 조직   attractive 멋진, 매력적인   apparel 의류   feature 특별히 포함하다   adorn 장식하다   selected 선정된   business day 영업일, 평일   embroidery 자수   reveal 밝히다, 드러내다   recognition 인식   key chain 열쇠고리   frequently 자주   put aside (한쪽으로) 치우다, 무시하다   misplace 잃어버리다   effective 효과적인   long lasting 오래 지속되는   quality 품질 좋은   sweatshirt 운동복[추리닝] 상의   place an order 주문하다   representative 직원

165 추론 / 암시

번역 브랜드마크 프로덕트 주식회사에 대해 암시된 것은?
(A) 일부 제품의 생산을 중단했다.
(B) 대량 주문 시 할인을 제공한다.
(C) 운동복 제작을 전문으로 한다.
(D) 기업 홍보를 돕는다.

해설 웹페이지의 제목에 우리 제품에 귀사의 로고를 넣고 유명해지세요(Make your mark with your logo on our products!)라고 했고, 첫 단락의 첫 문장에서 귀사의 로고나 회사 슬로건이 박힌 우리의 멋진 패션 의류로 귀사를 광고하는 것보다 더 좋은 방법은 없다(There is no better way to advertise your organization ~ featuring your logo or company slogan)고 한 것으로 보아 브랜드마크 프로덕트 주식회사는 의류 제품에 기업들의 로고나 슬로건을 표시하는 방식으로 홍보를 지원하는 회사임을 알 수 있다. 따라서 정답은 (D)이다.

어휘 discontinue 중단하다   specialize in ~을 전문으로 하다   athletic 운동의   promote 홍보하다

Paraphrasing 지문의 advertise → 정답의 promote

166 동의어

번역 두 번째 단락 3행의 "put aside"와 의미가 가장 가까운 단어는?
(A) 저축된
(B) 기밀의
(C) 무시된
(D) 문을 닫은

해설 의미상 '한쪽으로 치워 두는' 물건, 즉 자주 사용하지 않고 신경 쓰지 않는 물건이라는 뜻으로 쓰인 것이므로 정답은 (C) ignored이다.

167 세부 사항

번역 웹페이지에 따르면, 고객 서비스에 연락해야 하는 이유는?
　(A) 주문에 관한 도움을 받으려고
　(B) 샘플 제품을 요청하려고
　(C) 약속을 잡으려고
　(D) 로고 디자인을 마무리하려고

해설 마지막 문장에서 주문하려면 "시작하기" 탭을 사용하거나 1-800-555-0155로 전화해 고객 서비스 담당자와 통화하라(To place an order, use ~ call 1-800-555-0155 to speak with a customer service representative)고 했으므로 (A)가 정답이다.

어휘 assistance 도움 finalize 마무리 짓다

> Paraphrasing　지문의 place an order
> → 정답의 get assistance with an order

168-171 웹페이지

https://www.clarrellestate.com.au/about

168소개	행사	사진	재단

168클라렐 에스테이트-발라튼 최고의 아트 센터에 오신 것을 환영합니다! 169이 사유지의 아름다운 토지는 60헥타르의 언덕이 많은 지형에 위치하고 있으며, 울창한 영국 정원과 유명한 건축가 오웬 바튼에 의해 설계된 인상적인 저택을 특징으로 합니다. 10년 전, 클라렐 재단은 이 사유지를 아트 센터로 바꾸기로 결정했습니다. 처음에, 재단은 클라렐 가의 예술 소장품을 강조하면서 대중에게 저택을 공개했습니다. 170지난 3년 동안, 이 건물의 입구 근처에 아트 스튜디오와 극장이 완비된 대규모의 다용도 단지가 건설되었습니다.

클라렐 에스테이트의 미술관과 정원은 일반인들에게 무료로 개방됩니다. 또한 극장은 뮤지컬 공연뿐 아니라 공개 강의를 주최하고, 스튜디오는 개별 예술가들의 엄선된 작품들을 전시합니다. 전체 일정표와 현재 예술가 명단, 극장 및 스튜디오 입장료에 관한 정보를 확인하시려면 행사 페이지를 참조하세요.

171클라렐 재단에 가입하셔서 회원 전용 특별 행사 및 공연 할인 혜택을 누리세요. 또한 회원에게는 개인 행사를 위해 정원을 예약할 수 있는 기회가 제공됩니다. 171회원이 되시려면 알리시아 지에게 aji@clarrellestate.com.au로 연락하세요.

어휘 foundation 재단 estate 사유지 premier 최고의, 제1의 exquisite 매우 아름다운 situated 위치한 hectare 헥타르 hilly 언덕이 많은 terrain 지형 feature ~을 특징으로 하다 lush 울창한, 푸르게 우거진 impressive 인상적인 manor 저택 noted 유명한 architect 건축가 transform 바꾸다, 변신시키다 initially 처음에 highlight 강조하다 multiuse 다용도 complex 단지 property 건물, 부동산 complete with ~이 완비된 free of charge 무료로 host 주최하다 as well as ~뿐만 아니라 showcase 전시하다 individual 각각의 curated 전문적으로 엄선한 admission fee 입장료

168 주제 / 목적

번역 웹페이지의 주안점은?
　(A) 명소에 대한 개요
　(B) 도시의 문화 축제
　(C) 지역 원예 동호회
　(D) 예술품 구매 기회

해설 페이지의 분류가 소개(About)이고, 첫 문장에서 클라렐 에스테이트-발라튼 최고의 아트 센터에 오신 것을 환영한다(Welcome to the Clarrell Estate-Ballarton's premier centre for the arts!)고 했으므로 이 웹페이지는 아트 센터라는 장소를 소개하기 위한 것임을 알 수 있다. 따라서 정답은 (A)이다.

어휘 overview 개요 attraction 명소

169 Not / True

번역 저택에 대해 명시된 것은?
　(A) 개인 파티에 이용할 수 있다.
　(B) 오래된 사유지의 일부이다.
　(C) 지역 음악가들의 콘서트를 주최한다.
　(D) 최근에 개조되었다.

해설 두 번째 문장에서 이 사유지의 아름다운 토지는 60헥타르의 언덕이 많은 지형에 위치하고 있으며, 울창한 영국 정원과 유명한 건축가 오웬 바튼이 설계한 인상적인 저택을 특징으로 한다(The exquisite grounds of the estate are situated ~ designed by noted architect Owen Barton)고 했고, 세 번째 문장에서 10년 전, 클라렐 재단은 이 사유지를 아트 센터로 바꾸기로 결정했다(Ten years ago, the Clarrell ~ transform the estate into an arts centre)고 했으므로 저택은 10년이 더 넘은 오래된 사유지의 일부라는 것을 알 수 있다. 따라서 (B)가 정답이다.

170 세부 사항

번역 웹페이지에 따르면, 지난 3년 동안 일어난 일은?
　(A) 새 건물이 건축되었다.
　(B) 예술 학교가 설립되었다.
　(C) 공원이 청소되었다.
　(D) 바튼 씨에 관한 영화가 제작되었다.

해설 첫 단락의 마지막 문장에서 지난 3년 동안 건물의 입구 근처에 아트 스튜디오와 극장이 완비된 대규모의 다용도 단지가 건설되었다(In the last three years, a large, multiuse complex was built ~ with art studios and a theatre)고 했으므로 (A)가 정답이다.

어휘 found 설립하다

> Paraphrasing　지문의 complex was built
> → 정답의 building has been constructed

171 세부 사항

번역 웹페이지에 따르면, 지 씨에게 이메일을 보내야 하는 이유는?
(A) 공연 입장권을 구입하려고
(B) 웹페이지 이용에 대한 도움을 구하려고
(C) 업데이트된 행사 일정표를 요청하려고
(D) 재단 회원권에 관해 문의하려고

해설 세 번째 단락의 첫 문장에서 클라렐 재단에 가입해 회원 전용 특별 행사 및 공연 할인 혜택을 누리라(Join the Clarrell Foundation ~ discounts on performances)면서 마지막 문장에서 회원이 되려면 알리시아 지에게 aji@clarrellestate.com.au로 연락하라(To become a member, contact Alicia Ji at aji@clarrellestate. com.au)고 했으므로 정답은 (D)이다.

어휘 inquire 문의하다

172-175 구인 광고

재무 이사

172팔리즈 재단은 선임 리더십 팀의 일원이 될 재무 이사를 모집합니다. 재단 이사장에게 직접 보고하는 관리직입니다. **173**재무 이사는 급여 관리자와 회계 책임자를 포함하여 7명으로 구성된 재무 부서를 관리합니다. 재무 이사는 회계 및 구매 시스템의 감독 및 유지 관리를 담당합니다. 이 직책에 있는 사람은 내부 통제 절차를 감시 관찰하고 법적 의무 준수를 책임집니다. 추가적인 책무에는 모든 회사 자금의 지출, 투자 및 관리와 재무 정책 및 관행 개발, 예산 준비, 그리고 이사회 보고서 작성이 포함됩니다.

175현직 임직원들에게 우선권이 주어질 것입니다. 그러나 뛰어난 자격을 갖춘 외부 지원자들의 지원이 권장됩니다. **174**관심 있는 분들은 4월 23일 금요일 오후 4시 30분까지 자격 조건을 기재한 이력서를 humanresources@pallizfoundation.org로 인사부에 제출해야 합니다.

어휘 foundation 재단 supervisory 감독[관리]의 payroll 급여 responsible for ~을 담당하는 oversight 감독 maintenance 유지 monitor 감시하다 internal 내부의 procedure 절차 ensure 확실하게 하다, 보장하다 compliance 준수 legal 법적인 obligation 의무 responsibility 책무, 직책 disbursement 지출 investment 투자 practice 관행 board of directors 이사회 party 당사자 qualification 자격 no later than 늦어도 ~까지, ~ 전에

172 세부 사항

번역 재무 이사는 누가 감독하는가?
(A) 재단 이사장
(B) 급여 관리자
(C) 회계 책임자
(D) 이사회

해설 첫 문장에서 팔리즈 재단은 선임 리더십 팀의 일원이 될 재무 이사를 모집한다(The Palliz Foundation seeks ~ senior leadership team)고 했고, 재단 이사장에게 직접 보고하는 관리직(This is a supervisory position reporting directly to the foundation president)이라고 설명하고 있다. 따라서 재무 이사의 관리자는 재단 이사장이므로 (A)가 정답이다.

173 세부 사항

번역 구인 광고에 포함되어 있는 직책 관련 정보는?
(A) 급여
(B) 일정
(C) 자격
(D) 직무

해설 첫 단락의 세 번째 문장에서 재무 이사는 급여 관리자와 회계 책임자를 포함하여 7명으로 구성된 재무 부서를 관리한다(The finance director manages ~ the payroll manager and accounting director)고 했고, 회계 및 구매 시스템의 감독 및 유지 관리를 담당한다(The finance director is responsible ~ purchasing systems)고 했다. 뒤이어 내부 통제 절차를 감시 관찰하고 법적 의무 준수를 책임진다(The person in this position monitors ~ compliance with legal obligations)고 덧붙이고 있다. 이는 구인 광고에서 모집하고 있는 직책인 재무 이사가 담당하게 될 업무에 대해 나열하고 있는 것이므로 (D)가 정답이다.

174 세부 사항

번역 지원자는 어떻게 이 직책에 지원할 수 있는가?
(A) 취업 박람회에서 부스를 방문함으로써
(B) 이력서를 인사과에 이메일로 보냄으로써
(C) 웹페이지에 이력서를 업로드함으로써
(D) 온라인 신청서를 작성함으로써

해설 마지막 문장에서 관심 있는 분들은 4월 23일 금요일 오후 4시 30분까지 자격 조건을 기재한 이력서를 humanresources@palliz-foundation.org로 인사부에 제출해야 한다(Interested parties should submit ~ no later than 4:30 P.M. on Friday, April 23)고 했으므로 (B)가 정답이다.

어휘 personnel office 인사과

> **Paraphrasing** 지문의 human resources department
> → 정답의 personnel office

175 문장 삽입

번역 [1], [2], [3], [4]로 표시된 곳 중에서 다음 문장이 들어가기에 가장 적합한 위치는?

"그러나 뛰어난 자격을 갖춘 외부 지원자들의 지원이 권장됩니다."
(A) [1]
(B) [2]
(C) [3]
(D) [4]

해설 제시된 문장의 접속부사 However가 문제 해결의 단서이다. 외부 지원자들의 지원이 권장된다는 문장 앞에 반전의 뜻을 가진 However를 사용했으므로, 그 앞에는 '외부 지원자의 지원 권장'과는 반대되는 내용이 와야 한다. 따라서 현직 임직원들에게 우선권이 주어진다(Preference will be given to current employees)는 문장 뒤에 들어가야 자연스러우므로 (D)가 정답이다.

어휘 qualified 자격을 갖춘 external 외부의 candidate 지원자

176-180 이메일 + 이메일

수신: 브리짓 모란디
발신: 메리베스 라이트
날짜: 3월 23일
제목: 환불 요청

안녕하세요, 브리짓.

177수자타 레디에게서 연락을 받으셨는지 궁금해요. 176그녀는 제가 화요일과 목요일에 가르치는 그림 수업에 등록했습니다. 179그녀는 다른 일이 생겨서 첫 주에만 참석할 수 있었습니다. 176투손 성인 학교 사무실에 있는 누군가에게 수강을 178중단할 수 있는지 문의했고, 수업료를 환불해 달라고 요청했다고 했습니다.

그녀는 환불을 아직 못 받았다고 하네요. 연락이 왔었나요?

메리베스 라이트

어휘 wonder 궁금하다   enroll in ~에 등록하다
commitment 해야 할 일, 약속   drop 중단하다   tuition 수업료

수신: 메리베스 라이트
발신: 브리짓 모란디
날짜: 3월 24일
제목: 답신: 환불 요청

안녕하세요, 메리베스.

이름은 익숙한데, 레디 씨는 저에게 직접 연락하지는 않았습니다. 사실, 그녀가 연락해야 할 사람은 제가 아닙니다. 저는 일정과 미술 수업을 위한 용품 주문만을 처리하거든요.

레디 씨가 누구와 통화했는지 모르겠습니다. **179투손 성인 학교 웹사이트의 환불 규정에 따르면, 환불은 수업이 시작되기 전에 요청되거나 수강을 중단해야 하는 문서화된 건강상의 이유가 있을 경우에만 승인됩니다.** 건강상의 이유로 인한 경우, 환불 금액은 이수한 수업의 수를 기준으로 합니다.

180레디 씨는 아마 이번 학기 대신 선생님의 두 번째 학기 수업에 참석할 수 있을 것입니다. 이것이 저의 제안입니다.

브리짓 모란디

어휘 familiar 익숙한   in touch with ~와 연락하는
personally 직접, 개인적으로   handle 처리하다   as well as
~와, ~뿐만 아니라   supplies 용품   grant 승인하다, 허락하다
documented 문서화된   semester 학기

176 추론 / 암시

번역 라이트 씨는 누구인 것 같은가?
(A) 일정 책임자
(B) 교감
(C) 미술관 소유주
(D) 성인 교육 교사

해설 첫 번째 이메일의 두 번째 문장에서 라이트 씨는 그녀(수자타 레디)는 제가 화요일과 목요일에 가르치는 그림 수업에 등록했다(She was enrolled in the painting class I teach on Tuesday and Thursday)고 했고, 네 번째 문장에서 그녀는 투손 성인 학교 사무실에 있는 누군가에게 수강을 중단할 수 있는지 문의했다(she asked ~ if she could drop the class)고 했다. 따라서 라이트 씨는 수자타 레디가 등록한 성인 학교에서 그림 수업을 가르치고 있다는 것을 알 수 있으므로 정답은 (D)이다.

어휘 coordinator 책임자, 관리자   vice 부[차석]의   principal 교장

177 세부 사항

번역 라이트 씨가 모란디 씨에게 이메일을 보낸 이유는?
(A) 초대를 거절하려고
(B) 해결책을 제안하려고
(C) 정보를 요청하려고
(D) 회의 일정을 다시 잡으려고

해설 첫 번째 이메일의 첫 문장에서 라이트 씨가 모란디 씨에게 수자타 레디에게서 연락을 받았는지 궁금하다(I was wondering if you have heard from Sujata Reddy)고 이메일을 쓴 목적을 밝히고 있다. 라이트 씨는 레디 씨가 모란디 씨에게 연락을 했는지에 대한 정보를 문의하려고 이메일을 쓴 것이므로 정답은 (C)이다.

어휘 decline 거절하다

178 동의어

번역 첫 번째 이메일의 첫 단락 4행의 "drop"과 의미가 가장 가까운 단어는?
(A) 미끄러지다
(B) 그만두다
(C) 낮추다
(D) 늦추다

해설 의미상 수강을 '중단하다'는 뜻으로 쓰인 것이므로 정답은 (B) quit 이다.

179 연계

번역 레디 씨는 왜 아직 수업료 환불을 받지 못한 것 같은가?
(A) 등록 사무소가 문을 닫았다.
(B) 환불 수표가 아직 우편으로 배달 중이다.
(C) 요청을 서면으로 제출하지 못했다.
(D) 이미 일부 수업에 참석했다.

해설 첫 번째 이메일의 세 번째 문장에서 라이트 씨가 그녀(레디 씨)는 다른 일이 생겨서 첫 주에만 수업에 참석할 수 있었다(She was only able to attend ~ commitment came up)고 했고, 두 번째 이메일의 두 번째 단락의 두 번째 문장에서 모란디 씨가 투손 성인 학교 웹사이트의 환불 규정에 따르면 환불은 수업이 시작되기 전에 요청되거나 수강을 중단해야 하는 문서화된 건강상의 이유가 있을 경우에만 승인된다(According to our refund policy on ~ documented health reason for dropping the class)고 했다. 따라서 레디 씨는 이미 수업에 참석했기 때문에 환불을 받을 수 없다는 것을 알 수 있으므로 (D)가 정답이다.

어휘 registration 등록   check 수표   in writing 서면으로

180 세부 사항

번역 모란디 씨는 레디 씨가 무엇을 할 수 있을 거라고 제안하는가?
(A) 이전에 지불한 수업료를 향후 수업을 듣는 데 사용한다.
(B) 다른 성인 학교에서 같은 수업을 찾는다.
(C) 수업의 절반에 참석해 학점을 취득한다.
(D) 교사에게 연락해 개인 과외를 계획한다.

해설 두 번째 이메일의 세 번째 단락 첫 문장에서 모란디 씨는 레디 씨가 아마 이번 학기 대신 선생님의 두 번째 학기 수업에 참석할 수 있을 것(Maybe Ms. Reddy can attend your second ~ instead of this semester's)이라고 했으므로 (A)가 정답이다.

어휘 previously 이전에 credit 학점 arrange for 계획을 짜다 tutoring 과외, 교습

> **Paraphrasing** 지문의 attend your second semester class → 정답의 take a future class

181-185 기사 + 편집자에게 보내는 편지

새로운 베이커리가 지역에 온다

오레베일 시 (10월 14일) - 크레슨스 베이커리가 캔턴 가와 리들리 가의 모퉁이에 곧 문을 열 예정이다. 이 지점은 이 전국적인 체인 브랜드의 우리 시 첫 번째 매장이 될 것이다. 모든 크레슨스 베이커리 매장과 마찬가지로, 이 지점도 주 7일로 운영될 것이다.

181이 근처에서 이와 유사한 사업체는 쿠퍼만 대학 캠퍼스에 있는 도넛 스테이션뿐이다. 크레슨스 베이커리는 그들을 대표하는 커피와 빵 제품 외에도 아침 샌드위치와 과일 주스를 제공할 예정이다. **182**이 업체는 앉아서 먹을 수 있는 음식점이 아닌 소형 시설을 열겠다는 자사의 개정된 사업 모델을 따르고 있다. 즉, 오레베일 시티 지점에서는 테이크아웃과 드라이브스루 서비스만 제공한다는 것을 의미한다.

베이커리는 캔턴 가의 가장 작은 공터에 들어설 것이다. 이 프로젝트에 대한 승인은 지역 주민들이 엇갈린 목소리를 냈던 공청회 이후에 이루어졌다.

184팩스턴 로에 거주하는 지나 홀튼은 동네에 새 베이커리가 생기는 것은 좋지만 리들리 가의 교통 혼잡이 걱정된다고 말했다. 그 증거로 그녀는 그곳의 혼잡한 교통을 찍은 사진들을 제시했다. **183**워포드 로에 거주하는 스티븐 루는 간단한 간식을 먹을 수 있는 편리한 장소가 있는 즐거움을 누릴 것이라고 말했다.

크레슨스 베이커리는 3월 초에 첫 고객들을 맞이할 예정이다.

어휘 chain 체인점 limit (지역의) 경계 operate 운영되다 in the vicinity 근처에서 in addition to ~이외에도, ~에 더하여 follow ~을 따르다, ~ 후에 일어나다 revised 개정된 compact 소형의 facility 시설 eatery 음식점 occupy 차지하다 vacant 비어 있는 lot 부지 approval 승인 public hearing 공청회 resident 주민 traffic congestion 교통 혼잡, 교통 체증 evidence 증거 present 제시하다 grab 급히[잠깐] ~을 먹다 slate (일정을) 계획하다

편집자님께,

오레베일 시에서 평생 거주한 주민으로서 크레슨스 베이커리에 대한 귀하의 보도에 감사드립니다. 안타깝게도 10월 14일자 기사는 일부 부정확한 정보를 포함하고 있습니다. **184**공청회 때 제가 공유한 사진들은 저희 집 앞의 교통 체증 상황을 포착한 것입니다. 또한, **185**시의 역사 보존 위원회의 일원으로서 저는 주로 베이커리의 건축 양식에 대해 우려했습니다. 크레슨스 베이커리의 초기 건물 디자인은 현대적이었습니다. **185**체인점이 주변의 오래된 건축물과 더 잘 어울리도록 외관을 수정하는 데 동의했다는 소식을 전하게 되어 기쁩니다.

지나 홀튼

어휘 lifelong 평생의 coverage 보도 contain 포함하다 inaccurate 부정확한 capture 포착하다 preservation 보존 primarily 주로 initial 초기의 contemporary 현대적인 modify 수정하다, 변경하다 exterior 외관 blend 섞이다 structure 건축물 surround 둘러싸다

181 추론 / 암시

번역 오레베일 시에 대해 암시된 것은?
(A) 개발이 가능한 땅이 거의 없다.
(B) 두 곳의 창고 구역이 있다.
(C) 대학의 본거지이다.
(D) 인구가 증가하고 있다.

해설 기사의 두 번째 단락 첫 문장에서 이 근처에서 이와 유사한 사업체는 쿠퍼만 대학 캠퍼스에 있는 도넛 스테이션뿐(The only similar business in the vicinity is the Donut Station on the Kupperman University campus)이라고 한 것으로 보아 오레베일 시에 쿠퍼만 대학 캠퍼스가 있다는 것을 짐작할 수 있다. 따라서 (C)가 정답이다.

어휘 little 거의 없는 district 구역 population 인구

182 세부 사항

번역 새로운 크레슨스 베이커리 지점이 차별화되는 점은?
(A) 역사적인 건축적 특징을 모사한다.
(B) 더 다양한 종류의 빵 제품을 제공한다.
(C) 고객을 위한 좌석을 제공하지 않는다.
(D) 도심 밖에 위치해 있다.

해설 기사의 두 번째 단락 세 번째 문장에서 이 업체(크레슨스 베이커리)는 앉아서 먹을 수 있는 음식점이 아닌 소형 시설을 열겠다는 자사의 개정된 사업 모델을 따르고 있다(The company is following its revised business model to open compact facilities rather than sit-down eateries)면서 즉, 오레베일 시티 지점에서는 테이크아웃과 드라이브스루 서비스만 제공한다는 의미(This means the Orevale City location will offer takeout and drive-through service only)라고 부연 설명했다. 따라서 새로운 크레슨스 베이커리 지점에는 앉아서 먹을 수 있는 좌석이 없다는 것을 알 수 있으므로 (C)가 정답이다.

어휘 replicate 모사[복제]하다 architectural 건축(상)의

183 추론 / 암시

번역 루 씨에 대해 암시된 것은?

(A) 홀튼 씨의 옆집 이웃이다.

(B) 크레슨스 베이커리를 애용할 계획이다.

(C) 최근에 오레베일 시로 이사했다.

(D) 역사 보존 단체의 일원이다.

해설 기사의 네 번째 단락 마지막 문장에서 워포드 로에 거주하는 스티븐 루는 간단한 간식을 먹을 수 있는 편리한 장소가 있는 즐거움을 누릴 것이라고 말했다(Wofford Drive resident Steven Lu said he would enjoy having a convenient place to grab a quick snack)고 했다. 따라서 루 씨는 새로 생기는 크레슨스 베이커리를 기꺼이 이용할 생각임을 알 수 있으므로 (B)가 정답이다.

어휘 neighbor 이웃 patronize 애용하다, 단골로 삼다

184 연계

번역 홀튼 씨가 차량 교통량 사진을 찍은 곳은?

(A) 캔턴 가

(B) 워포드 로

(C) 리들리 가

(D) 팩스턴 로

해설 기사의 네 번째 단락 첫 문장에서 팩스턴 로에 거주하는 지나 홀튼 (Gina Holton, who lives on Paxton Road)이라고 했고, 편집자에게 보내는 편지의 세 번째 문장에서 홀튼 씨는 공청회 때 제가 공유한 사진들은 저희 집 앞의 교통 체증 상황을 포착한 것(The photos that I shared during ~ traffic congestion in front of my house)이라고 했다. 따라서 홀튼 씨는 자신의 집이 위치한 팩스턴 로에서 사진을 찍었다는 것을 알 수 있으므로 (D)가 정답이다.

185 추론 / 암시

번역 편지에서 홀튼 씨에 대해 암시하는 것은?

(A) 건물 디자인이 변경되어 기쁘다.

(B) 자신의 베이커리 사업을 시작할 계획이다.

(C) 공청회에 참석하지 않았다.

(D) 신문사에 기사를 제출하기를 원한다.

해설 편지의 네 번째 문장에서 홀튼 씨는 시의 역사 보존 위원회의 일원으로서 주로 베이커리의 건축 양식에 대해 우려했다(as a member of the city's ~ concerned about the bakery's architecture)고 했고, 여섯 번째 문장에서 체인점이 주변의 오래된 건축물과 더 잘 어울리도록 외관을 수정하는 데 동의했다는 소식을 전하게 되어 기쁘다(I am pleased to report ~ the older structures surrounding it)고 했다. 따라서 홀튼 씨는 베이커리 체인점의 건물 디자인이 바뀌게 된 점에 만족하고 있음을 알 수 있으므로 (A)가 정답이다.

186-190 편지 + 기사 + 공지

브랜디 모티머
랙스커넥트 주식회사
위어 로 620
글래스고 G91 9HX

3월 11일

알리사 수실로
레프로이 가 29
글래스고 G3 7BQ

수실로 씨께,

아시다시피 랙스커넥트는 지난 1년간 글래스고 지역에서 서비스를 확대해 왔습니다. 당사의 새로운 광섬유 케이블 라인은 더 빠르고 믿을 만한 서비스를 제공하며 지상 배선의 필요성을 없애 줍니다. 시스템이 작동하기 위해서는 도시 전역에 인터넷 연결 장치를 설치해야 합니다. 공사 작업 1단계에는 시티 센터가 포함됩니다. **188**2단계에는 웨스트엔드가 포함됩니다. 2단계는 예상보다 오랜 시간이 걸렸지만 3단계는 보다 신속하게 진행할 수 있어서 일정을 맞출 수 있었습니다. 이제 귀하가 계신 지역에서 4단계를 시작할 준비가 되었습니다.

186, 189랙스커넥트는 레프로이 가 29번지에 위치한 귀하의 건물에 소형 인터넷 연결 허브를 설치하고자 합니다. 대로의 중심에 위치하고 있어서 귀하의 앞마당은 최적의 연결 지점이 될 것입니다. **186, 189**4월 10일까지 0141 496 0001로 전화하셔서 진행 가능 여부를 알려주시기 바랍니다. 감사합니다.

공익사업 자문 담당, 브랜디 모티머

어휘 expand 확장하다 fibre-optic cable 광섬유 전선 reliable 믿을 만한 eliminate 없애다 aboveground 지상의 wiring 배선 install 설치하다 throughout 전역에 phase 단계 involve 포함하다 expedite 신속히 진행하다 on schedule 일정대로 property 건물 optimal 최적의 proceed 진행하다 utilities (가스, 전기, 수도 등의) 공익사업

랙스커넥트 서비스 확장

글래스고 (3월 14일) - **188**웨스트엔드에서의 예상치 못한 지연이 있었던 이후, 랙스커넥트는 마침내 도시 전역에 광섬유 케이블을 설치하는 프로젝트의 최신 단계를 완료했습니다. **187, 188**사우스사이드의 주민들과 기업들은 이제 더 빠른 인터넷 서비스를 누리고 있습니다.

187프로젝트의 다음 단계를 위해 피니에스톤에서 랙스커넥트는 연결 허브를 위한 주요 위치를 확인했으며, 가능한 한 빨리 작업을 시작할 수 있도록 현재 주민과 주택 소유들에게 연락을 취하고 있습니다.

이러한 움직임은 올해 초 랙스커넥트가 네트워크를 확장하기 위해 3억 5천만 파운드를 투자했다는 발표에 따른 것입니다. 현지 공무원들은 이 프로젝트가 그들 지역에 새로운 사업과 소비를 가져다주기를 희망하고 있습니다.

어휘 power outage 정전 house 장소를 제공하다 headquarters 본사

어휘 unexpected 예상치 못한 latest 최신의 enjoy 누리다 identify 확인하다 key 주요한 reach out 연락하다 follow 따르다, 뒤이어 일어나다 invest 투자하다 official (고위) 공무원 spending 소비, 지출

임시 도로 폐쇄 안내

189, 190 레프로이 가 29번지의 공사로 도로 전체가 폐쇄될 예정임을 알려 드립니다. 폐쇄는 5월 31일 월요일부터 6월 8일 화요일까지 계속됩니다. 190 이 기간 동안, 자동차 통행은 레프로이 가에 거주하는 주민들에게만 한정됩니다.

어휘 temporary 임시의 closure 폐쇄 aware 알고 있는 automobile 자동차 limited to ~으로 한정되는

186 주제 / 목적

번역 편지의 주요 목적은?
(A) 인터넷 서비스 불량에 대해 사과하기 위해
(B) 건물주로부터 허가를 구하기 위해
(C) 지연에 대해 해명하기 위해
(D) 고객에게 인터넷 공급업체를 바꾸도록 설득하기 위해

해설 편지의 두 번째 단락 첫 문장에서 랙스커넥트는 레프로이 가 29번지에 위치한 귀하의 건물에 소형 인터넷 연결 허브를 설치하고자 한다(Raxconnect would like to place a small Internet connection hub ~ 29 Lefroy Street)고 했고, 세 번째 문장에서 4월 10일까지 0141 496 0001로 전화하셔서 진행 가능 여부를 알려주시기 바란다(Please call ~ whether we may proceed)고 했다. 따라서 건물 주인에게 공사 진행에 관한 허가를 구하려고 편지를 쓴 것이므로 (B)가 정답이다.

어휘 seek 구하다 permission 허가 property owner 건물주 explanation 해명, 설명 persuade 설득하다 switch 바꾸다

Paraphrasing 지문의 let us know whether we may proceed → 정답의 seek permission

187 추론 / 암시

번역 기사에서 피니에스톤에 대해 암시된 것은?
(A) 최근에 정전을 경험했다.
(B) 랙스커넥트의 본사가 있다.
(C) 하나의 연결 허브만 필요하다.
(D) 곧 인터넷 서비스가 업그레이드될 것이다.

해설 기사의 첫 단락 두 번째 문장에서 사우스사이드의 주민들과 기업들은 이제 더 빠른 인터넷 서비스를 누리고 있다(Residents and businesses ~ enjoying faster Internet service)고 했고, 두 번째 단락에서 프로젝트의 다음 단계를 위해 피니에스톤에서 랙스커넥트는 연결 허브를 위한 주요 위치를 확인했으며 가능한 한 빨리 작업을 시작할 수 있도록 현재 주민과 주택 소유자들에게 연락을 취하고 있다(For the next phase of the project, in Finnieston ~ work can begin as soon as possible)고 했다. 따라서 피니에스톤에서의 프로젝트가 끝나고 나면 앞서 프로젝트가 완료된 지역에서 그랬던 것처럼 인터넷 서비스가 향상될 것임을 알 수 있으므로 (D)가 정답이다.

188 연계

번역 랙스커넥트의 프로젝트 중 사우스사이드에서 진행된 단계는?
(A) 1단계
(B) 2단계
(C) 3단계
(D) 4단계

해설 편지의 첫 단락 다섯 번째 문장에서 2단계에는 웨스트엔드가 포함된다(Phase 2 involved West End)고 했고, 2단계는 예상보다 오랜 시간이 걸렸지만 3단계는 보다 신속하게 진행할 수 있어서 일정을 맞출 수 있었다(Although Phase 2 took longer ~ Phase 3 and get back on schedule)고 했다. 그리고 기사의 첫 문장에서 웨스트엔드에서의 예상치 못한 지연이 있었던 이후 랙스커넥트는 마침내 도시 전역에 광섬유 케이블을 설치하는 프로젝트의 최신 단계를 완료했다(After unexpected delays in West End ~ cable throughout the city)고 했고, 사우스사이드의 주민들과 기업들은 이제 더 빠른 인터넷 서비스를 즐기고 있다(Residents and businesses ~ enjoying faster Internet service)고 했다. 따라서 프로젝트 2단계는 웨스트엔드 지역, 최근 완료된 프로젝트 3단계는 사우스사이드 지역임을 알 수 있으므로 (C)가 정답이다.

189 연계

번역 수실로 씨에 대해 결론지을 수 있는 것은?
(A) 모티머 씨의 요청에 동의했다.
(B) 랙스커넥트의 직원이다.
(C) 글래스고의 다른 동네로 이사할 계획이다.
(D) 인터넷을 위한 비디오 콘텐츠를 제작한다.

해설 편지의 두 번째 단락 첫 문장에서 모티머 씨는 수실로 씨에게 랙스커넥트는 레프로이 가 29번지에 위치한 귀하의 건물에 소형 인터넷 연결 허브를 설치하고자 한다(Raxconnect would like to place a small Internet connection hub ~ 29 Lefroy Street)며 세 번째 문장에서 4월 10일까지 0141 496 0001로 전화하셔서 진행 가능 여부를 알려주시기 바란다(Please call us ~ whether we may proceed)고 했고, 공지의 첫 문장에서 레프로이 가 29번지의 공사로 도로 전체가 폐쇄될 예정임을 알린다(Please be aware that construction ~ the closure of the entire street)고 했다. 따라서 수실로 씨는 자신의 건물에서 공사를 진행하도록 모티머 씨의 요청을 수락했다는 것을 알 수 있으므로 (A)가 정답이다.

190 추론 / 암시

번역 공지에서 레프로이 가에 사는 사람들에 대해 암시하는 것은?
(A) 집으로 가는 셔틀 서비스를 이용할 수 있을 것이다.
(B) 일주일 동안 무료 인터넷 서비스를 받을 것이다.
(C) 랙스커넥트의 공사가 끝날 때 양식을 작성해 달라는 요청을 받을 것이다.
(D) 공사 기간 동안 도로를 이용할 수 있다.

TEST 6

공지의 첫 문장에서 레프로이 가 29번지의 공사로 도로 전체가 폐쇄될 예정임을 알린다(Please be aware that ~ the closure of the entire street)고 했고, 마지막 문장에서 이 기간 동안 자동차 통행은 레프로이 가에 거주하는 주민들에게만 한정된다(During that period, automobile access will be limited to residents who live on Lefroy Street)고 했다. 따라서 공사가 진행되는 동안 레프로이 가에 거주하는 주민들은 도로에서 자동차를 이용할 수 있다는 것을 알 수 있으므로 (D)가 정답이다.

191-195 보도 자료 + 이메일 + 후기

즉시 배포용

연락처: 케빈 오이세니치, kevin.o@albertandannies.com.au

굴와 (11월 2일) - **191,195**어제 고급 냉동 디저트 제조업체인 앨버트 앤 애니즈가 새로운 간식 몇 가지를 발표했다. **195**초콜릿 부스러기가 소용돌이치는 연한 맛과 진한 맛 초콜릿의 왈츠 같은 트리플 타임 초콜릿 아이스크림, 달콤한 비스킷이 혼합된 바닐라와 토피 아이스크림인 토피 스프리, 그리고 진짜 과일 조각이 들어간 라즈베리 셔벗이다. 신제품들은 11월 중순까지 호주 매장에 입고될 예정이다.

194이 회사는 25년 전에 각각 사장과 최고 경영자였던 앨버트와 애니 그룬던에 의해 설립되었다. **192**올해 초, 그들은 남아프리카 공화국 지부의 신설을 발표했다. 남아프리카 공화국 소매업체들은 12월 중순에 앨버트 앤 애니즈의 많은 제품들을 입수할 수 있을 것이다.

어휘 immediate 즉각적인 release 배포, 발표 gourmet 미식가(의), 고급 음식인 frozen 냉동의 unveil 발표[공개]하다 treat 간식 crumb 부스러기 swirl 소용돌이 infusion 혼합물 feature 특별히 포함하다 found 설립하다 respectively 각각 division 부서 retailer 소매업체

수신: 케빈 오이세니치 〈kevin.o@albertandannies.com.au〉
발신: 스카이 보타 〈sbotha@westerncapeeats.co.za〉
날짜: 11월 3일
제목: 인터뷰 요청

오이세니치 씨께,

저는 케이프타운 지역의 음식 애호가들을 위한 뉴스 사이트인 〈웨스턴 케이프 이츠〉의 기자입니다. **193,194**귀사의 제품에 대해 귀사의 창립자 중 한 분 또는 두 분을 인터뷰하고 이곳 남아프리카 공화국에서는 어떤 제품이 제공될지 알아보고 싶습니다. 저의 독자들은 무엇을 기대해야 할지 알고 싶어 합니다. 독자들은 또한 앨버트 앤 애니즈가 올해의 목재 범선 축제에서 홍보를 할 예정인지 알고 싶어 합니다. 주요 행사이기 때문에 대부분의 현지 업체들은 그곳에 부스를 대여합니다.

인터뷰는 전화 또는 화상 채팅으로 진행할 수 있습니다. 귀하의 답변을 기다리겠습니다.

스카이 보타

어휘 founder 창립자 be eager to ~을 하고 싶어 하다 promote 홍보하다 major 주요한 conduct (특정 활동을) 하다 look forward to ~을 고대하다

---

https://www.westerncapeeats.co.za/reviews

| 소개 | 소식 | 행사 | **후기** |

짐 사토, 12월 31일

남아프리카 공화국에 온 지 얼마 안 된 아이스크림 회사인 앨버트 앤 애니즈에 대해 알려준 귀사의 기사는 매년 열리는 목재 범선 축제에 제가 참석해야 할 이유를 하나 더 만들어 주었습니다. 앨버트 앤 애니즈 부스에서 몇몇 환상적인 아이스크림을 맛보게 되었습니다. **195**부스에서는 커피 트러플, 퍼지 민트, 그리고 초콜릿 프레첼 딜라이트의 세 가지 놀라운 맛을 제공했습니다. 기사에서 오이세니치 씨는 이것들이 남아프리카 공화국의 식료품점에 출시되는 첫 번째 맛이 될 것이며 시간이 지남에 따라 더 많은 맛들을 접할 수 있게 될 거라고 했습니다. 정말 기대됩니다!

어휘 sample 시식하다 sensational 환상적인 flavour 맛 state 말하다 roll out 출시하다 grocery outlet 식료품점

191 주제 / 목적

번역 보도 자료에 발표된 것은?
(A) 두 기업의 합병
(B) 기업 지도자들의 은퇴
(C) 제품군 확장
(D) 생산 공장의 이전

해설 보도 자료의 첫 문장에서 어제 고급 냉동 디저트 제조업체인 앨버트 앤 애니즈가 새로운 간식 몇 가지를 발표했다(Yesterday, Albert and Annie's, a leading maker of gourmet frozen desserts, unveiled several new treats)고 했으므로 (C)가 정답이다.

어휘 merger 합병 retirement 은퇴 expansion 확장 relocation 이전 plant 공장

192 추론 / 암시

번역 보도 자료에서 앨버트 앤 애니즈의 남아프리카 공화국 지부에 대해 알 수 있는 것은?
(A) 11월 중순에 문을 열 예정이다.
(B) 12월 중순까지 채용을 하지 않을 것이다.
(C) 곧 자체 웹사이트를 시작할 것이다.
(D) 소비자들에게 아이스크림을 직접 판매하지 않을 것이다.

해설 보도 자료의 두 번째 단락 두 번째 문장에서 올해 초, 그들(앨버트 앤 애니즈)은 남아프리카 공화국 지부의 신설을 발표했다(Earlier this year, they announced the opening of a South African division)고 했고, 남아프리카 공화국 소매업체들은 12월 중순에 앨버트 앤 애니즈의 많은 제품들을 입수할 수 있을 것(South African retailers will get access to a number of Albert and Annie's products in mid-December)이라고 했다. 따라서 앨버트 앤 애니즈는 남아프리카 공화국에서 소매업체를 통해 제품을 판매할 예정임을 알 수 있으므로 (D)가 정답이다.

어휘 launch 시작하다, 착수하다 directly 직접

193 세부 사항

번역 이메일에 따르면, 보타 씨의 독자들이 관심 있는 것은?
(A) 새로운 음식 맛보기
(B) 축제 부스 임대
(C) 개업
(D) 식품에 대한 후기 작성

해설 이메일의 두 번째 문장에서 보타 씨는 귀사의 제품에 대해 귀사의 창립자 중 한 분 또는 두 분을 인터뷰하고 이곳 남아프리카 공화국에서는 어떤 제품이 제공될지 알아보고 싶다(I would very much like to ~ will be available here in South Africa)면서, 저의 독자들은 무엇을 기대해야 할지 알고 싶어 한다(My readers are eager to know what to expect)고 했다. 따라서 보타 씨의 독자들은 어떤 아이스크림을 새로 맛보게 될지에 대해 기대하고 있는 것이므로 (A)가 정답이다.

어휘 be interested in ~에 관심이 있다

194 연계

번역 보타 씨에 대해 명시된 것은?
(A) 목재 범선 축제에 참석할 계획이다.
(B) 케이프타운 지역에서 자랐다.
(C) 그룬던 부부와 이야기하고 싶어 한다.
(D) 앨버트 앤 애니즈의 남아프리카 공화국 지부의 일자리에 지원했다.

해설 보도 자료의 두 번째 단락 첫 문장에서 이 회사는 25년 전에 각각 사장과 최고 경영자였던 앨버트와 애니 그룬던에 의해 설립되었다(The company was founded ~ president and CEO, respectively)고 했고, 이메일의 두 번째 문장에서 보타 씨는 귀사의 제품에 대해 귀사의 창립자 중 한 분 또는 두 분을 인터뷰하고 이곳 남아프리카 공화국에서는 어떤 제품이 제공될지 알아보고 싶다(I would very much like to interview ~ will be available here in South Africa)고 했다. 따라서 보타 씨는 앨버트 앤 애니즈의 창립자인 앨버트와 애니 그룬던 부부와 인터뷰를 하고 싶어 한다는 것을 알 수 있으므로 (C)가 정답이다.

어휘 attend 참석하다 apply for ~에 지원하다

195 연계

번역 축제에서 앨버트 앤 애니즈의 부스에 대해 결론지을 수 있는 것은?
(A) 오이세니치 씨가 직원으로 일했다.
(B) 사토 씨가 도착했을 때 커피 아이스크림이 없었다.
(C) 냉동 디저트를 특징으로 하는 부스 세 곳 중 하나였다.
(D) 회사의 최신 맛의 샘플을 제공하지 않았다.

해설 보도 자료의 첫 문장에서 어제 고급 냉동 디저트 제조업체인 앨버트 앤 애니즈가 새로운 간식 몇 가지를 발표했다(Yesterday, Albert and Annie's ~ unveiled several new treats)면서 초콜릿 부스러기가 소용돌이치는 연한 맛과 진한 맛 초콜릿의 왈츠 같은 트리플 타임 초콜릿 아이스크림, 달콤한 비스킷이 혼합된 바닐라와 토피 아이스크림인 토피 스프리, 그리고 진짜 과일 조각이 들어간 라즈베리 셔벗(Triple Time Chocolate ice cream ~ raspberry sorbet, featuring bits of real fruit)이라고 했고, 후기의 세 번째 문장에서 부스에서는 커피 트러플, 퍼지 민트, 그리고 초콜릿 프레첼 딜라이트의 세 가지 놀라운 맛을 제공했다(The booth offered three ~ Chocolate Pretzel Delight)고 했다. 따라서 부스에서는 새로 출시된 세 가지 맛 아이스크림은 제공하지 않았다는 것을 알 수 있으므로 (D)가 정답이다.

어휘 staff 직원으로 일하다

196-200 블로그 게시물 + 온라인 양식 + 온라인 양식

벤스 논프로핏 버스트 - 비영리 분야에서 일하는 사람들을 위한 자료처

보조금 받기

벤 파인만이 8월 18일에 게시함

보조금 신청서 작성은 정부 기관, 학교, 기업 또는 기타 단체가 제공하는 재정 지원을 위한 신청서 작성 기술입니다. 보조금을 향한 경쟁은 치열하며, 보조금 신청서 작성에 있어 평범함은 허용되지 않습니다. **196보조금 신청서 작성 기술을 향상시키기 위해 메도우 파크 대학의 크리스티나 길리엄이 가르치는 온라인 강좌를 수강하는 것을 고려해 보십시오.** 그녀의 '훌륭한 보조금 신청서 작성' 강좌는 4개의 90분 대화형 세션으로 나뉩니다. 이 강좌는 보조금 신청서 작성에 대한 기본 지식을 가진 이들을 위해 고안되었습니다. 이 월요일 저녁 수업은 11월 15일부터 12월 6일까지 진행됩니다. 자세한 내용과 등록을 원하시면 www.kristinagilliam.ca/course를 방문하십시오. **198결제 창에서 프로모션 코드 NPBURST를 이용하시면 350달러의 수업료에서 15퍼센트를 할인받을 수 있습니다. 이 코드는 9월 30일에 만료됩니다. 19710월 1일부터 최종 등록일인 11월 1일까지는 정가 등록만 가능합니다.**

어휘 nonprofit 비영리의 burst 한바탕, ~을 터뜨림 resource 자료처, 자원 sector 분야, 부문 grant 보조금, 지원금 art 기술 application 신청서 aid 지원 government 정부 entity 단체, 독립체 no room 여지가 없는 mediocrity 평범 divide 나누다 interactive 대화형의, 상호적인 registration 등록 promo 판촉용의 checkout 결제 창, 계산대 tuition 수업료 expire 만료되다 full-price 정가

www.kristinagilliam.ca/feedback

저의 '훌륭한 보조금 신청서 작성' 강좌에 참여해 주셔서 감사합니다. 잠시 시간을 내어 아래 양식을 작성하고 귀하의 경험에 대해 말씀해 주세요.

이름: 나탈리 발라드

지역: 위니펙

의견: 제가 수강한 다른 글쓰기 강좌들에 비해 비교적 짧았지만, '훌륭한 보조금 신청서 작성' 강좌는 괜찮은 개요를 제공해 주었습니다. 강사가 그녀의 경력 동안 기업들이 수백만 달러의 보조금을 받을 수 있도록 도움을 주었다는 것은 인상 깊었고, 제가 보조금 신청서 작가로 채용 될 경우 그녀를 자원으로 갖게 되어 기쁩니다. ¹⁹⁸운 좋게도 저는 등록 당시 벤스 논프로핏 버스트의 프로모션 코드를 사용했습니다. 그렇지 않았다면 수업료가 너무 비싸다고 생각했을 것입니다. ¹⁹⁹웹사이트에서는 길리엄 씨가 실질적인 신청서 작성 과정에 대해 구체적인 내용을 많이 포함할 것이라고 했지만, 그녀가 알려 주었던 것만큼은 아니었다는 인상을 받았습니다.

어휘 relatively 비교적 decent 괜찮은 overview 개요 impressed 인상 깊은, 감명받은 instructor 강사 register 등록하다 otherwise 그렇지 않으면 impression 인상, 느낌 specifics 세부 사항 process 과정

---

www.kristinagilliam.ca/feedback

저의 '훌륭한 보조금 신청서 작성' 강좌에 참여해 주셔서 감사합니다. 잠시 시간을 내어 아래 양식을 작성하고 귀하의 경험에 대해 말씀해 주세요.

이름: 폴 보이트

지역: 토론토

의견: 이 강좌는 전반적으로 훌륭했습니다. ²⁰⁰강사는 오든 인터내셔널의 설립자로서 그녀의 경험을 포함해 많은 귀중한 귀중한 식견을 공유해 주었습니다. 저는 보조금 신청서 작성 회사가 존재하는 지도 몰랐습니다! 현재 하고 있는 보조금 신청서 작성 일을 그만두게 되면 제 회사를 차릴지도 모르겠습니다. 이 강좌는 주로 보조금 기회를 조사하고 성공적인 보조금 신청서 샘플을 분석하는 데 중점을 두었습니다. ¹⁹⁹마지막 세션에서 우리 중 몇몇이 구체적인 글쓰기 요령을 요청했을 때, 길리엄 씨는 단순히 다른 자료를 참조하라고 안내해 주었습니다. 그녀의 웹사이트에 있는 강좌 설명은 그런 점에서 약간 오해의 소지가 있었습니다.

어휘 overall 전반적으로 a wealth of 많은, 풍부한 valuable 귀중한, 가치 있는 insight 식견, 통찰력 founder 설립자 realize 인식하다 mainly 주로 analyze 분석하다 specific 구체적인 refer (서적 등을) 참조하게 하다, 소개하다 description 설명 misleading 오해의 소지가 있는 in that regard 그 점에 있어서

---

196 주제 / 목적

번역 블로그 게시물의 목적은?
(A) 보조금 신청서 작성 요령 제공
(B) 학습 체험 추천
(C) 직원에 대한 집중 조명
(D) 웹사이트의 변경 사항 예고

해설 블로그 게시물의 세 번째 문장에서 보조금 신청서 작성 기술을 향상시키기 위해 메도우 파크 대학의 크리스티나 길리엄이 가르치는 온라인 강좌를 수강하는 것을 고려해 보라(To improve your grant-writing skills, consider ~ Meadow Park University)고 강좌를 추천하고 있으므로 (B)가 정답이다.

어휘 spotlight 집중 조명하다 preview 예고, 미리 보기

> Paraphrasing 지문의 taking an online course
> → 정답의 a learning experience

197 세부 사항

번역 파인만 씨에 따르면, 등록 기간은 언제 끝나는가?
(A) 9월 30일
(B) 10월 1일
(C) 11월 1일
(D) 12월 6일

해설 블로그 게시물의 마지막 문장에서 파인만 씨가 10월 1일부터 최종 등록일인 11월 1일까지는 정가 등록만 가능하다(On October 1, ~ the final registration day, November 1)고 했으므로 11월 1일이 등록 기간의 마지막 날임을 알 수 있다. 따라서 정답은 (C)이다.

198 연계

번역 발라드 씨에 대해 암시된 것은?
(A) 10월 1일 이전에 보조금 신청서 작성 강좌에 등록했다.
(B) 현재 보조금 신청서 작가로 일하고 있다.
(C) 이전에 길리엄 씨로부터 수업을 들었다.
(D) 파인만 씨의 블로그 게시물을 편집한다.

해설 블로그 게시물의 여덟 번째 문장에서 결제 창에서 프로모션 코드 NPBURST를 이용하면 350달러의 수업료에서 15퍼센트를 할인받을 수 있다(Use the promo code NPBURST at checkout to get 15 percent off the $350 tuition)면서 이 코드는 9월 30일에 만료된다(This code expires on September 30)고 했고, 첫 번째 온라인 양식의 세 번째 문장에서 발라드 씨는 운 좋게도 등록 당시 벤스 논프로핏 버스트의 프로모션 코드를 사용했다(Fortunately, I used Ben's Nonprofit Burst's promo code when I registered)고 했다. 따라서 발라드 씨는 10월이 되기 전에 강좌에 등록해 프로모션 코드를 사용하고 수업료를 할인받았다는 것을 알 수 있으므로 (A)가 정답이다.

어휘 previous 이전의 occasion 경우[때] edit 편집[교정]하다

199 연계

번역 발라드 씨와 보이트 씨에 대해 사실인 것은?
(A) 위니펙에서 함께 수업을 들었다.
(B) 파인만 씨와 인터뷰를 했다.
(C) 보조금 기회를 조사하는 방법을 배우기를 원한다.
(D) '훌륭한 보조금 신청서 작성' 강좌에서 같은 결점을 발견했다.

해설 첫 번째 온라인 양식의 마지막 문장에서 발라드 씨는 웹사이트에서는 길리엄 씨가 실질적인 신청서 작성 과정에 대해 구체적인 내용을 많이 포함할 것이라고 했지만, 그녀가 알려주었던 것만큼은 아니었다는 인상을 받았다(The Web site gave me the impression that Ms. Gilliam would include more specifics about the actual writing process than she did)고 했고, 두 번째 온라인 양식의 여섯 번째 문장에서 보이트 씨는 마지막 세션에서 우리 중 몇몇이 구체적인 글쓰기 요령을 요청했을 때 단순히 다른 자료를 참조하라고 안내해 주었다(When several of us ~ referred us to other resources)며 그녀의 웹사이트에 있는 강좌 설명은 그런 점에서 약간 오해의 소지가 있다(The course description ~ misleading in that regard)고 지적했다. 따라서 두 사람은 온라인에 있는 강좌 정보를 보고 기대했던 것과 실제 강좌 내용이 달랐다는 점을 공통적으로 지적했으므로 (D)가 정답이다.

어휘 weakness 결점, 약점

200 Not / True

번역 보이트 씨가 길리엄 씨에 대해 명시한 것은?
(A) 그녀는 토론토에 산다.
(B) 그녀는 보조금 신청서 작성 회사를 시작했다.
(C) 그녀는 파인만 씨를 위해 보조금 신청서를 작성했다.
(D) 그녀는 보조금 신청서 작성 설명서를 저술했다.

해설 두 번째 온라인 양식의 두 번째 문장에서 보이트 씨는 강사(길리엄 씨)는 오든 인터내셔널의 설립자로서 그녀의 경험을 포함해 많은 귀중한 식견을 공유해 주었다(The instructor shared ~ founder of Orden International)고 했고, 저는 보조금 신청서 작성 회사가 존재하는 지도 몰랐다(I never realized that grant-writing firms even existed!)고 언급했으므로 (B)가 정답이다.

어휘 author 작성하다, 저술하다   manual 설명서

> Paraphrasing   지문의 founder → 정답의 started a ~ firm

101 (C)	102 (B)	103 (C)	104 (A)	105 (D)
106 (C)	107 (A)	108 (A)	109 (A)	110 (D)
111 (C)	112 (D)	113 (C)	114 (D)	115 (C)
116 (B)	117 (A)	118 (A)	119 (B)	120 (D)
121 (D)	122 (B)	123 (C)	124 (D)	125 (A)
126 (A)	127 (C)	128 (B)	129 (C)	130 (D)
131 (B)	132 (A)	133 (C)	134 (B)	135 (A)
136 (D)	137 (C)	138 (B)	139 (D)	140 (A)
141 (D)	142 (B)	143 (C)	144 (C)	145 (A)
146 (D)	147 (C)	148 (D)	149 (A)	150 (D)
151 (A)	152 (C)	153 (C)	154 (B)	155 (A)
156 (C)	157 (C)	158 (B)	159 (D)	160 (B)
161 (D)	162 (C)	163 (B)	164 (C)	165 (A)
166 (D)	167 (A)	168 (B)	169 (A)	170 (C)
171 (C)	172 (D)	173 (B)	174 (C)	175 (B)
176 (C)	177 (A)	178 (B)	179 (D)	180 (A)
181 (A)	182 (D)	183 (C)	184 (B)	185 (C)
186 (B)	187 (A)	188 (A)	189 (B)	190 (D)
191 (B)	192 (C)	193 (D)	194 (D)	195 (B)
196 (C)	197 (A)	198 (A)	199 (D)	200 (B)

PART 5

101 명사 자리 _ 동사의 목적어

해설 빈칸은 동사 received의 목적어 자리이며, 빈칸 뒤 전치사구 of art supplies의 수식을 받고 있으므로 명사가 와야 한다. 따라서 '기부'라는 뜻의 명사 (C) donations가 정답이다.

번역 샌드빌 커뮤니티 센터는 미술 용품을 기부받았다.

어휘 supplies 물품

102 동사 자리 _ 수 일치

해설 The sales associates가 주어인 문장에 동사가 보이지 않으므로 빈칸은 동사 자리이다. 주어가 복수명사이므로 복수동사가 와야 한다. 따라서 (B) discuss가 정답이다.

번역 영업 사원들은 주간 회의에서 종종 잠재 고객 계정에 대해 논의한다.

어휘 sales associate 영업 사원 potential 잠재적인 account 계정

103 전치사 어휘

해설 빈칸 뒤에 장소를 나타내는 명사가 있고, 문맥상 '몰 옆에 호텔을 짓고 있다'는 의미가 되어야 적절하므로 '~ 옆에'를 뜻하는 위치 전치사 (C) next to가 정답이다.

번역 라벨리아 호텔은 윙게이트 몰 옆에 호텔을 짓고 있다.

104 인칭대명사의 격 _ 소유격

해설 빈칸에는 뒤에 온 명사구 official uniforms를 수식하는 소유격 인칭대명사가 들어가야 한다. 따라서 정답은 (A) their이다.

번역 이번 주 목요일부터 모든 테나코어 직원들은 공식 유니폼을 입어야 한다.

105 부사 자리 _ 동사 수식

해설 Mr. Kwon이 주어이고 guided가 동사이며, 빈칸은 주어와 동사 사이에서 동사 guided를 수식하는 부사 자리이다. 따라서 '능숙하게'라는 뜻의 부사인 (D) skillfully가 정답이다.

번역 권 씨는 까다로운 승인 과정 내내 제안서를 능숙하게 이끌었다.

어휘 proposal 제안서 approval 승인 process 과정

106 동사 어휘

해설 목적어 its staff 뒤의 to work를 목적격 보어로 취하고, '직원들이 원격으로 근무할 것을 권장한다'는 의미가 되어야 한다. 따라서 정답은 '권장[격려]하다'라는 의미의 (C) encourages이다. 'encourage 목적어 to부정사'로 암기해 두자.

번역 스탠브리지 회사는 직원들이 매주 하루나 이틀 정도 원격으로 근무할 것을 권장한다.

어휘 remotely 원격으로, 멀리서

107 명사 어휘

해설 to부정사 to allow의 목적어 자리에 들어가기에 적합한 명사 어휘를 고르는 문제이다. 앞에는 형용사 enough, 뒤에는 to부정사구(to fill out ~)의 수식을 받아 '서류를 작성할 충분한 시간을 허용하도록'이라는 의미가 되어야 자연스러우므로 '시간'이라는 뜻의 명사 (A) time이 정답이다.

번역 서류를 작성할 시간이 충분하도록 약속 시간 10분 전에 도착해 주세요.

어휘 fill out 작성하다

108 접속사 자리 _ 부사절 접속사

해설 빈칸 뒤에 주어와 동사를 갖춘 완전한 절이 왔으므로 부사절 접속사가 들어가야 한다. 문맥상 '만약 질문이 있으면'이라는 의미가 되어야 자연스러우므로 '만약 ~하면, ~할 경우'를 뜻하는 접속사 (A) If가 정답이다.

번역 업데이트된 계약에 대해 문의 사항이 있을 경우, 인사부에 연락하세요.

109 명사 자리 _ 동사의 주어

해설 빈칸은 동사 are의 주어 자리이고, 빈칸 앞에 정관사 The와 과거분사 printed가 있으므로 명사인 (A) advertisements가 정답이다.

번역 다가오는 뮤지컬의 인쇄 광고지는 극장 감독의 사무실에 보관되어 있다.

어휘 upcoming 다가오는

110 부사 어휘 _ 비교급

해설 동사구 should be stored를 수식하고 부정부사 no의 수식을 받아 '~보다 더 높이 보관되어서는 안 된다'는 의미가 되어야 자연스러우므로 '더 높이'를 뜻하는 비교급 부사 (D) higher이 정답이다.

번역 실험실 화학 약품은 눈높이보다 높은 곳과 높은 수납장 맨 위에 보관해서는 안 된다.

어휘 laboratory 실험실　chemicals 화학 약품　store 보관하다

111 형용사 자리 _ 수량 형용사

해설 빈칸은 뒤의 복수명사 company delivery vans를 수식하는 형용사 자리이고, '모든 회사 배달 승합차'라는 의미가 되어야 자연스러우므로 (C) all이 정답이다. (A) much는 뒤에 불가산 명사가 와야 하고, (B) total은 '총계의, 전부 합친'이라는 뜻이므로 문맥에 어울리지 않는다. (D) highly는 부사이므로 답이 될 수 없다.

번역 라일리의 차량 관리자에 따르면, 모든 회사 배달 승합차는 8월에 정비를 받을 예정이다.

어휘 fleet (회사의) 보유 차량; 함대　van 승합차　service 차를 정비하다

112 부사 자리 _ 동사 수식

해설 airlines가 주어이고 revise가 동사이며, 빈칸은 주어와 동사 사이에서 동사 revise를 수식하는 부사 자리이다. 따라서 '가끔'이라는 뜻의 부사인 (D) occasionally가 정답이다.

번역 항공사들이 가끔 위탁 수하물 정책을 개정하므로 승객들은 비행 전에 최신정보를 확인해야 한다.

어휘 passenger 승객

113 과거분사

해설 빈칸은 부정관사와 명사 사이에서 명사 stack을 수식하는 형용사 자리이므로 분사가 들어갈 수 있다. stack은 organize의 주체가 아니라 대상이므로 '정돈된 더미'라는 의미가 되어야 적절하다. 따라서 수동의 의미를 나타내는 (C) organized가 정답이다.

번역 퀸즈 랜딩 프로젝트의 계약서는 관리자의 책상 위에 정돈된 더미로 올려 놓아야 한다.

어휘 contract 계약(서)　stack 더미　supervisor 관리자

114 동사 어휘

해설 사이토 씨의 판매 전망이 너무 낙관적이라며 신뢰하지 못하고 있으므로 '이사들이 미심쩍어 한다'는 내용이 되어야 자연스럽다. 따라서 '의심하다'는 뜻의 동사 (D) suspect가 정답이다.

번역 일부 이사들은 사이토 씨의 판매 전망이 너무 낙관적이라고 미심쩍어 한다.

어휘 board 이사회　forecast 전망　optimistic 낙관적인　pause 잠시 멈추다　refuse 거절하다

115 명사절 _ that절

해설 빈칸 뒤에 주어와 동사를 갖춘 절이 왔으므로 접속사가 필요하다. 'be confident'와 함께 쓰여 'that 이하 내용을 확신하다'라는 뜻을 이루는 명사절 접속사 (C) that이 정답이다.

번역 코플러 씨는 새 관리자가 부서의 생산성을 향상시킬 것이라고 확신한다.

어휘 productivity 생산성

116 부사 어휘

해설 '너무 ~해서 …하다'라는 의미의 so ~ that절 구문으로, 과거분사 deteriorated를 수식하는 부사를 고르는 문제이다. '헛간이 너무 심하게 악화되어 회복되기 힘들다'는 내용이 되어야 하므로 '심하게'라는 뜻의 (B) badly가 정답이다.

번역 이스트우드 사유지의 나무 헛간은 너무 심하게 악화된 상태라서 회복될 가능성이 낮다.

어휘 barn 헛간　property 토지, 부동산　deteriorate 악화시키다　unlikely ~할 것 같지 않은　salvage 구조하다, 회복하다

117 전치사 어휘

해설 빈칸 뒤에 기간을 나타내는 명사구 its first month of operation이 있고, 문맥상 '운영 첫 달 동안'이라는 의미가 되어야 자연스러우므로 '~ 동안'을 뜻하는 (A) during이 정답이다.

번역 로즈빌 리조트는 운영 첫 달 동안 숙소를 할인 제공하고 있다.

어휘 accommodation 숙소　operation 운영

118 형용사 어휘

해설 새 휴대전화 모델의 '외관(look)'을 수식함과 동시에 빈칸 뒤의 '이전 모델(the previous one)'과도 자연스럽게 연결될 수 있어야 한다. '새 모델의 외관은 이전 모델과 비슷하지만'이라는 내용이 되어야 적절하므로 '~와 비슷한'을 뜻하는 (A) similar to가 정답이다.

번역 새로운 휴대전화 모델의 외관은 이전 모델과 비슷하지만 통화 품질은 훨씬 향상되었다.

어휘 involved in ~에 관련된　occupied by ~이 점유한

119 능동태 vs. 수동태

해설 동사 자리인 빈칸 뒤에 목적어가 아닌 전치사 to가 이끄는 전치사 구가 왔으므로 정답은 수동태인 (B) was promoted이다.

번역 시몬 보몬트 박사는 지난주에 브로더 테크놀로지의 연구 개발 책임자로 승진했다.

120 부사 자리 _ 형용사 수식

해설 빈칸은 부정관사와 형용사 사이에서 형용사 safe를 수식하는 부사 자리이므로 정답은 '환경적으로'라는 뜻의 부사 (D) environmentally이다.

번역 에너텍 산업은 환경적으로 안전한 리튬 정제 방법을 개발 중이다.

어휘 refine 정제하다 lithium 리튬

121 과거분사

해설 앞에 be동사가 있으므로 빈칸은 주어 the brake를 수식하는 주격 보어 자리이다. '브레이크가 걸려 있는지 확인하라'는 내용이 되어야 자연스러우므로 수동의 의미를 나타내는 과거분사 (D) engaged가 정답이다. 명사 (C) engagement는 주어 the brake와 동격 관계가 아니므로 답이 될 수 없다.

번역 모터에 시동을 걸기 전에 브레이크가 걸려 있는지 확인하세요.

어휘 engage (기계 부품 등을) 맞물리게 하다

122 명사 어휘 _ 복합명사

해설 빈칸은 동사 offers의 목적어 자리인데, 빈칸 앞에 명사 computer가 있으므로 computer와 함께 복합명사를 만들 수 있는 명사가 들어가야 한다. '컴퓨터 입문 수업을 제공한다'는 내용이 되어야 자연스러우므로 '수업'을 뜻하는 (B) lessons가 정답이다.

번역 헨더슨 기술 전문대학은 지역 사회 구성원들에게 무료로 컴퓨터 입문 수업을 제공한다.

어휘 introductory 입문의

123 동사 어휘

해설 the agency 이하는 선행사 the time을 수식하는 목적격 관계사절이므로 '시간'을 수식하기에 적절한 동사를 골라야 한다. '기록 검색에 걸리는 시간'이라는 의미가 되어야 자연스러우므로 '(시간이) 걸리다'를 뜻하는 (C) takes가 정답이다.

번역 기관이 기록을 검색하는 데 걸리는 시간에 대해서는 수수료가 부과되지 않습니다.

어휘 charge 청구하다 examine 검토하다, 조사하다 inspect 점검하다

124 관계대명사 _ 주격

해설 빈칸 이하(was built 80 years ago)는 선행사 The Durand Concert Hall을 수식하는 관계사절이다. 빈칸은 관계사절에서 동사 was built의 주어 역할을 하고 있으므로 주격 관계대명사인 (D) which가 정답이다.

번역 80년 전에 지어진 듀랜드 콘서트 홀은 완전히 개조되었다.

어휘 undergo (일 등을) 겪다 renovation 개조, 보수

125 부사 어휘

해설 빈칸 앞에 not이 있고, '아직 우리가 알지 못하는'이라는 의미가 되어야 자연스러우므로 not yet의 형태로 쓰여 '아직 ~않다'를 뜻하는 (A) yet이 정답이다.

번역 아직 우리가 알지 못하는 컴퓨터 코드에 결함이 있을 수 있다.

어휘 be aware of ~을 알다

126 부정대명사

해설 빈칸은 관계사절(who wishes to ~ Voltra Museum)의 수식을 받으며 동사 should fill out의 주어 역할을 하는 자리이므로 대명사 (A) Anyone과 (D) Those가 들어갈 수 있다. 관계사절의 동사는 선행사에 수를 일치시키는데 wishes는 단수 동사이므로 선행사 자리인 빈칸에는 단수를 나타내는 (A) Anyone이 정답이다. (C) Each other는 동사와 전치사의 목적어로 쓰이며, 주어 자리에는 쓸 수 없다.

번역 볼트라 박물관에 금전적인 기부를 하고 싶은 사람은 안내 책자 뒤에 있는 양식을 작성해야 한다.

어휘 monetary 금전의 fill out 작성하다

127 명사 어휘 _ 복합명사

해설 빈칸은 동사구 focus on의 목적어 자리인데, 앞에 명사 employee가 있으므로 employee와 함께 복합명사를 만들 수 있는 명사가 들어가야 한다. '채용뿐 아니라 직원 유지에도'라는 내용이 되어야 자연스러우므로 '유지'를 뜻하는 (C) retention이 정답이다.

번역 안정적인 인력을 추구하는 기업은 채용뿐 아니라 직원 유지에도 집중해야 한다.

어휘 stable 안정된 workforce 인력 recruitment 채용 coverage 범위 authentication 입증

128 전치사 자리

해설 빈칸 뒤의 명사구 a new user-friendly interface를 목적어로 취하는 전치사 자리로, '새로운 사용자 친화적인 인터페이스 덕분에'라는 의미가 되어야 자연스러우므로 '~ 때문에, ~ 덕분에'를 뜻하는 전치사 (B) Owing to가 정답이다.

번역 웹사이트의 새로운 사용자 친화적인 인터페이스 덕분에, 크레이머-리 회사는 고객 만족도가 향상되었다고 보고했다.

어휘 user-friendly 사용자 친화적인 subsequently 그 후에

129 전치사 자리

해설 빈칸은 뒤에 온 명사 interest를 목적어로 취하는 전치사 자리이다. '고객들의 관심에도 불구하고'라는 내용이 되어야 하므로 '~에도 불구하고'라는 의미의 전치사 (C) despite가 정답이다.

번역 윙거트 조리장은 많은 고객들의 관심에도 불구하고 앙투안스 피자의 두 번째 지점을 여는 것을 꺼린다.

어휘 reluctant 꺼리는

130 형용사 어휘

해설 명사 thinking을 수식하여 '창의적인 사고가 판매 증가에 도움이 되었다'는 내용이 되어야 자연스러우므로 '창의적인'이라는 뜻의 (D) Creative가 정답이다.

번역 블레이클리 씨의 마케팅팀의 창의적인 사고가 민디 오토바이의 판매를 증가시키는 데 도움이 되었다.

어휘 relative 상대적인 potential 잠재적인 distant 먼

PART 6

131-134 웹페이지

슬립커버

글렌 앤 메도우스 홈 굿즈에서 이제 여러분의 의자와 소파를 131**보호하기 위한** 다양한 종류의 실용적인 커버를 판매합니다. 우리의 슬립커버는 다양한 크기와 색상으로 제공됩니다. 가장 많이 사용되는 132**가구를** 위한 많은 옵션이 있습니다. 선택할 수 있는 아름다운 얼룩 방지 직물이 많이 있습니다. 133**그리고 매주 더 많은 옵션을 추가하고 있습니다.** 합성 소재의 사용이 걱정되신다면 내추럴 컬렉션에서 선택하시면 됩니다. 어떤 인테리어 디자인을 계획하시든지 글렌 앤 메도우스 슬립커버로 모든 방의 모습을 134**순식간에** 바꾸실 수 있습니다.

어휘 a selection of 다양한   heavily 많이, 심하게
stain-resistant 얼룩이 지지 않는   synthetic 합성의

---

131 to부정사의 형용사적 용법

해설 Glen and Meadows Home Goods가 주어, sells가 동사, a variety of practical covers가 목적어인 완전한 문장에서, 명사 covers를 수식하면서 빈칸 뒤의 your chairs and sofas를 목적어로 취할 수 있는 준동사가 필요하므로 (B) to protect가 정답이다. '의자와 소파를 보호하기 위한 실용적인 커버'라는 내용이 되므로 의미상으로도 자연스럽다.

132 명사 어휘

해설 앞 내용에서 의자와 소파를 보호하기 위한 커버를 다양한 크기와 색상으로 제공한다고 했으므로, 빈칸이 있는 문장에서 언급한 많은 옵션은 많은 종류의 커버를 뜻하고 이 커버의 용도는 의자와 소파 같은 가구를 보호하는 것임을 알 수 있다. 따라서 '많이 사용되는 가구를 위한'이라는 내용이 되어야 적절하므로 '가구'라는 뜻의 (A) furniture가 정답이다.

어휘 appliance 가전제품, 기기

133 문맥에 맞는 문장 고르기

해설 빈칸 앞에서 선택할 수 있는 얼룩 방지 직물이 많다고 했고, 빈칸 뒤에서 합성 소재의 사용이 걱정일 경우 사용할 수 있는 다른 옵션도 있다며 빈칸 앞뒤에서 모두 제품의 다양성을 일관적으로 강조하고 있다. 따라서 빈칸에도 다양한 제품의 구비를 강조할 수 있는 비슷한 내용이 들어가야 자연스러우므로 매주 더 많은 옵션을 추가하고 있다고 언급하고 있는 (C)가 정답이다.

번역 (A) 그것들은 자주 사용하면 잘 견디지 못합니다.
(B) 그것들은 우리 온라인 매장에서 더 이상 구매하실 수 없습니다.
(C) 그리고 매주 더 많은 옵션을 추가하고 있습니다.
(D) 우리는 그것들이 재미있고 착용하기 쉽다고 생각합니다.

어휘 hold up 견디다   frequent 빈번한

134 부사 자리 _ 동사 수식

해설 빈칸이 조동사 can과 동사원형 change 사이에 있으므로 동사를 수식하는 부사 자리이다. 따라서 정답은 (B) quickly이다.

135-138 이메일

수신: 전 직원 〈staff@kelseytech.co.uk〉
발신: 코세이 마스타니 〈kmasutani@kelseytech.co.uk〉
제목: 정보
날짜: 1월 26일

여러분 중 일부는 오늘 아침에 책상에 앉아 있는 동안 약간 135**불편함을** 느꼈을 수 있습니다. 우리 건물의 난방 장치 중 하나가 고장 났기 때문입니다. 안타깝게도, 수리팀은 목요일까지 문제를 해결하러 올 수 없습니다. 저층에 있는 열린 사무 공간이 온기가 조금밖에 없어 가장 영향을 많이 받는 구역입니다. 우리 인턴들이 그곳에 136**있어서** 다른 층에 있는 임시 사무 공간을 배정받게 될 것입니다. 137**따라서** 내일 아침에 도착하는 대로 인턴은 대체 업무 공간을 배정받기 위해 코너 씨에게 확인해야 합니다. 138**불편을 드려 죄송합니다.** 그동안 모두의 안전을 확보하고 이 문제를 빨리 해결할 테니 안심하십시오.

코세이 마스타니, 시설 관리자

어휘 crew 작업팀 level 층 affected 영향을 받는 assign 배정하다 alternative 대안의 assignment 배정 in the meantime 그동안 be assured that ~이니 안심하다 ensure 보장하다 resolve 해결하다

---

135 형용사 어휘

해설 뒤 문장에서 난방 장치가 고장 났다고 했으므로 빈칸이 있는 문장은 '약간 불편함을 느꼈을 수 있다'는 내용이 되어야 자연스럽다. 따라서 '불편한'이라는 뜻의 (A) uncomfortable이 정답이다.

어휘 prompt 즉각적인   overwhelmed 압도된

136 과거분사

해설 빈칸은 be동사 are과 함께 동사구를 이루는 자리로, 주어가 Our interns이고 빈칸 뒤에 목적어가 없으며 '우리 인턴들이 그곳에 있다'는 의미가 되어야 하므로 수동태로 쓰여 '(위치해) 있다'를 뜻하는 과거분사 (D) located가 정답이다.

137 접속부사

해설 앞 문장에는 인턴들이 임시 사무 공간을 배정받게 될 것이라고 했고, 뒤 문장에는 내일 아침에 도착하는 대로 인턴은 대체 업무 공간을 배정받기 위해 코너 씨에게 확인해야 한다고 했다. 두 문장이 인턴들은 임시 공간을 배정받아야 하므로 이를 위해 코너 씨를 찾으라는 인과관계를 나타내고 있으므로 '따라서'를 뜻하는 (C) Consequently가 정답이다.

어휘 however 그러나 likewise 마찬가지로 otherwise 그렇지 않으면

138 문맥에 맞는 문장 고르기

해설 난방 장치가 고장 났으나 바로 수리가 불가능하며, 이로 인해 인턴들은 업무 공간을 옮겨야 한다고 안내하는 글의 전체적인 내용상, 그에 따른 불편함에 대해 사과하는 내용의 문장이 연결되어야 자연스러우므로 (B)가 정답이다.

번역 (A) 인턴들은 6월이 되어야 여기 도착할 예정입니다.
    (B) 불편을 드려 죄송합니다.
    (C) 조만간 열린 사무 공간을 개조할 것입니다.
    (D) 난방기 유지는 때때로 많은 비용이 듭니다.

어휘 inconvenience 불편   maintenance 유지   costly 많은 돈이
    드는

139-142 안내 책자

사우더비 디자인즈

사우더비 디자인즈는 셰닝턴 지역의 소매 공간과 제품 전시를 디자인하
는 일류 기업입니다. 거의 30년 동안 사우더비 디자인즈는 수없이 많
은 상점들과 협업하여 그들의 소매 공간을 위해 아름다운 디자인을 **139
생산했습니다**. 우리는 **140심지어** 여러 박물관과 행사 제작사와도 협력
하여 마음을 사로잡는 현대적이고 매력적인 방문자 경험을 만들어냈습
니다. 소매 전시 디자인**141부터** 주요 문화 기관을 위한 프로젝트 완수에
이르기까지 사우더비 디자인즈는 귀하의 조직과 함께 귀하의 요구 사항
에 딱 맞는 완벽한 디자인 솔루션을 개발할 수 있습니다. **142오늘 연락
하셔서 귀사가 당면한 디자인 문제를 알려 주십시오**. 귀사에 도움이 될
솔루션을 개발할 수 있다고 자신합니다!

어휘 retail 소매   greater (도시가) 교외를 포함한   nearly 거의
decade 10년   collaborate with ~와 협업하다   countless
셀 수 없이 많은   captivating 매혹적인   streamlined 현대적인
inviting 매력적인   institution 기관

139 분사구문

해설 빈칸 앞에 완전한 절이 왔고, 접속사와 주어가 생략된 채 빈칸 뒤에
    명사구(beautiful designs ~)가 왔으므로 빈칸이 포함된 부분은
    분사구문이 되어야 한다. 빈칸 뒤에 목적어 beautiful designs가
    있으므로 능동의 의미를 나타내는 현재분사 (D) producing이 정답
    이다.

140 부사 어휘

해설 앞 문장에서 사우더비 디자인즈는 수많은 상점들과 협업했다고 했
    고, 빈칸이 있는 문장에서는 박물관과 행사 제작사와도 협력했다고
    했다. 따라서 사우더비 디자인즈가 상점 외에 뜻밖의 다른 기관 및
    업체들과도 함께 작업해 왔음을 강조하는 내용이 되어야 자연스러
    우므로 '심지어'라는 뜻의 부사 (A) even이 정답이다.

141 전치사 어휘

해설 빈칸 뒤에 나온 전치사 to가 핵심 단서이다. '소매 전시 디자인부터
    문화 기관을 위한 프로젝트 완수에 이르기까지'라는 내용이 되어야
    자연스러우므로 전치사 to와 함께 'from A to B'의 형태로 'A부터
    B까지'를 뜻하는 (D) From이 정답이다.

142 문맥에 맞는 문장 고르기

해설 빈칸 앞에서 요구 사항에 딱 맞는 완벽한 디자인 솔루션을 개발할
    수 있다고 했고, 빈칸 뒤에서 귀사에 도움이 될 솔루션을 개발할 수

있다고 자신한다며 앞뒤 문장 모두 잠재 고객을 향해 업체에서 제공
할 수 있는 서비스에 대해 홍보하고 있다. 따라서 빈칸에는 잠재 고
객에게 업체에 연락해 필요한 서비스에 대해 알려 달라고 권유하고
있는 (B)가 정답이다.

번역 (A) 우리는 그 당시 많은 디자이너와 예술가들과 함께 일했습니다.
    (B) 오늘 연락하셔서 귀사가 당면한 디자인 문제를 알려 주십
        시오.
    (C) 사실 우리는 작년에 처음으로 요금을 올렸습니다.
    (D) 그에 반해서, 우리의 사업은 지난 10년간 크게 성장했습니다.

어휘 challenge 문제   face 직면하다   rate 요금   in contrast 그에
    반해서   substantially 크게, 상당히

143-146 웹페이지

중앙 열차 서비스는 여행을 선물하는 일을 그 어느 때보다 **143더 쉽게** 해
줍니다. 우리의 기프트 카드는 특별한 사람에게 잊지 못할 여행을 선물
해 줄 수 있는 완벽한 방법입니다. 기차 여행은 승객들에게 걱정 없는 경
험을 제공할 수 있습니다. **144여행자들은 자유롭게 쉬면서 모험을 즐길
수 있습니다**. 놀라운 도시와 아름다운 국립공원을 즐겁게 방문하세요.

중앙 열차 서비스 기프트 카드는 **145만기가** 없습니다. 기프트 카드는 온
라인이나 주요 기차역에서 현금처럼 사용할 수 있습니다. 카드는 최대
500달러까지 구매할 수 있습니다. 추가 **146수수료는** 없습니다. 기프트
카드의 전액은 모든 승차권 구매에 적용될 수 있습니다.

어휘 unforgettable 잊지 못할   passenger 승객
worry-free 걱정 없는   redeem (상품권 등을) 현금으로 바꾸다
additional 추가의   apply 적용하다

143 비교급

해설 빈칸 뒤의 than ever가 문제 해결의 단서로, 빈칸에는 than과 함께
    쓰이는 비교급이 들어가야 한다. 따라서 정답은 (B) easier이다.

144 문맥에 맞는 문장 고르기

해설 빈칸 앞에서 기차 여행이 승객들에게 걱정 없는 경험을 제공할 수
    있다고 했으므로 빈칸에는 기차 여행객들이 편하게 여행을 즐길 수
    있다는 내용이 들어가야 자연스럽다. 따라서 여행자들은 자유롭게
    쉬면서 즐길 수 있다고 언급하고 있는 (C)가 정답이다.

번역 (A) 관광객들은 종종 파리와 런던을 방문합니다.
    (B) 좌석 선택을 변경하는 데에는 여러 가지 방법이 있습니다.
    (C) 여행자들은 자유롭게 쉬면서 모험을 즐길 수 있습니다.
    (D) 승객들은 개인 신분증을 지참하고 여행해야 합니다.

어휘 identification 신분증

145 동사 자리 _ 시제

해설 Central Train Service gift cards가 주어인 문장에 동사가 없으
    므로 빈칸은 동사 자리이다. 빈칸 뒤 문장들에서 기프트 카드에 대한
    일반적인 사실을 현재 시제로 설명하고 있으므로 빈칸에도 현재 시
    제 동사가 와야 한다. 따라서 정답은 (A) expire이다.

146 명사 어휘

해설 빈칸 앞에서 카드는 최대 500달러까지 구매할 수 있다고 했고, 빈칸 뒤에서 기프트 카드 전액은 모든 승차권 구매에 적용될 수 있다고 했으므로 빈칸에도 마찬가지로 기프트 카드의 금액과 관련된 내용이 연결되어야 자연스럽다. 따라서 '수수료'라는 뜻의 (D) fees가 정답이다.

어휘 instructions 설명(서), 안내(문)

PART 7

147-148 웹페이지

https://www.aci.com/childrens-oral-care/availableoptions

| **구매 가능 옵션** | 칫솔 | 구강 세정제 | 기타 제품 |

아르테미스 통합 산업(ACI)은 어린이와 성인을 위한 다양한 구강 위생 제품을 생산하는 우리나라의 선두 제조업체입니다. 우리의 베스트셀러 중에는 국내에서 가장 인기 있는 어린이 치약인 오라글리츠가 있습니다. **147(D)이 제품은 제품 우수상을 포함해 다양한 산업상을 수상했습니다.** **147(A)이 웹사이트에서 구입할 수 있는 것 외에도 오라글리츠는 전국의 슈퍼마켓과 약국, 건강식품 매장에서도 구매할 수 있습니다.**

오라글리츠에 관한 기본 사항		
맛	연령별 설계	**147(B)** 크기
복숭아	18개월~3세	5, 6 온스
딸기	3~4세	4, 5, 6 온스
바닐라	4~7세	4, 5 온스
148민트	**148**7세 이상	4, 6 온스

어휘 consolidated 통합된 leading 선두의, 선도하는 a range of 다양한 oral 구강의 hygiene 위생 toothpaste 치약 nationwide 전국의 ounce 온스(28.35g)

147 Not / True

번역 오라글리츠에 대해 언급되지 않은 것은?
(A) 다양한 곳에서 구입할 수 있다.
(B) 세 가지 크기로 나온다.
(C) 최근 매출이 증가하고 있다.
(D) 업계에서 높은 평가를 받고 있다.

해설 세 번째 문장에서 이 제품은 제품 우수상을 포함해 다양한 산업상을 수상했다(It has won ~ Product Excellence Prize)고 했으므로 (D), 네 번째 문장에서 이 웹사이트에서 구입할 수 있는 것 외에도 오라글리츠는 전국의 슈퍼마켓과 약국, 건강식품 매장에서도 구매할 수 있다(In addition to being ~ food stores nationwide)고 했으므로 (A), 표의 크기(Size) 항목에 4, 5, 6 온스(4, 5, and 6 ounce) 세 가지가 언급되었으므로 (B)는 사실이다. 오라글리츠의 매출액에 대한 언급은 없으므로 (C)가 정답이다.

어휘 regard 여기다[평가하다]

148 세부 사항

번역 8세 어린이에게 가장 좋은 오라글리츠의 맛은?
(A) 복숭아
(B) 딸기
(C) 바닐라
(D) 민트

해설 표의 마지막 줄에 7세 이상(7 years and up)을 위한 제품은 민트(Mint) 맛이라고 나와 있으므로 (D)가 정답이다.

149-150 이메일

수신: 파슨스 로 배포 목록
발신: 알프레도 모레노
날짜: 10월 12일
제목: 파슨스 로

149파슨스 로의 업체 여러분께:

1493월부터 메모리얼 대로와 할람 로 사이 구간의 파슨스 로가 확장될 예정입니다. 이 프로젝트로 중앙 회전 차선, 자전거 도로, 보행자 도로, 가로등이 추가될 것입니다. 또한, 물의 흐름을 개선하기 위해 측면 배수로가 추가될 것입니다.

파슨스 로 프로젝트는 올해 초에 할람 로와 잉그라함 가 사이 구간에서 수행된 작업과 연관됩니다. **150이 작업으로 여러분의 업체에 대한 접근성이 향상되고, 꽤 붐비기도 하는 파슨스 로의 보행자 안전이 제고될 것입니다.** 이 도로공사는 완료하는 데 3개월이 걸릴 것으로 예상됩니다. 자세한 정보를 원하시면 www.yorkcity.gov/parsons roadproject를 방문하십시오.

알프레도 모레노
지역 사회 관계 관리 담당
베서니 건설 엔지니어링

어휘 distribution 배포 widen 확장하다 boulevard 대로 lane 차선 pedestrian 보행자 gutter 배수로 flow 흐름

149 주제 / 목적

번역 이메일의 목적은?
(A) 지역 업체들에 곧 시행될 공사에 대해 알리려고
(B) 도로 개선 계획에 대한 의견을 요청하려고
(C) 새로운 신호등에 대해 업체에 조언하려고
(D) 정보 배포에 도움을 요청하려고

해설 이메일의 첫 줄에서 파슨스 로의 업체 여러분께(Dear Parsons Road Businesses)라고 수신인을 호칭하며, 첫 문장에서 3월부터 메모리얼 대로와 할람 로 사이 구간의 파슨스 로가 확장될 예정(Beginning in March ~ Memorial Boulevard and Hallam Road)이라고 공사 주변에 위치한 업체들에게 공사 일정에 대해 공지하고 있으므로 (A)가 정답이다.

Paraphrasing 지문의 Parsons Road will be widened
→ 정답의 upcoming construction

TEST 7

150 Not / True

번역 파슨스 로 프로젝트에 대해 명시된 것은?
(A) 세 번 지연되었다.
(B) 추가 자금이 필요하다.
(C) 10월 12일에 시작할 것으로 예상된다.
(D) 도로 주변을 걷는 일이 더 안전해질 것이다.

해설 두 번째 단락의 두 번째 문장에서 이 작업으로 여러분의 업체에 대한 접근성이 향상되고 꽤 붐비기도 하는 파슨스 로의 보행자 안전이 제고될 것(This work will improve access ~ which can be quite busy)이라고 했으므로 (D)가 정답이다.

어휘 delay 지연시키다 funding 자금

> **Paraphrasing** 지문의 increase pedestrian safety
> → 정답의 make walking near the road safer

151-152 문자 메시지

아킴 디알로 (오전 10시 47분)
안녕하세요, 니콜렛. **151당신의 이메일은 잘 되고 있나요?** 제가 방금 암호를 재설정했는데, 지금 네트워크에 연결이 안 되고 있어요. 저만 그런가요? 중요한 이메일을 하나라도 놓치고 싶지 않은데요.

니콜렛 코네 (오전 10시 49분)
아니요, 제 것도 안 되고 있어요.

아킴 디알로 (오전 10시 52분)
무슨 일인지 혹시 아시나요?

니콜렛 코네 (오전 10시 52분)
아니요, 하지만 제가 알아낼 수 있는 것이 있는지 볼게요.

니콜렛 코네 (오전 10시 58분)
방금 기술 지원팀에 확인했는데요. 공급업체와 관련된 세계적인 문제인 것 같아요.

아킴 디알로 (오전 10시 59분)
빨리 해결되면 좋겠네요. **152우리 고객은 기다려 주지 않아서, 요청에 즉시 답장하지 않으면 다른 납품업체로 갈 테니까요.**

니콜렛 코네 (오전 11시 2분)
맞아요. 소식이 들어오는 대로 알려 드리겠습니다.

어휘 resolve 해결하다 supplier 공급업체

151 세부 사항

번역 디알로 씨는 무엇을 할 수 없는가?
(A) 이메일 계정에 접속하기
(B) 인터넷 공급업체 찾기
(C) 이력서 정보 수정하기
(D) 기술 지원팀에 연락하기

해설 10시 47분에 디알로 씨가 코네 씨에게 당신의 이메일은 잘 되고 있는지(Is your e-mail working?)를 물으며, 방금 암호를 재설정했는데 지금 네트워크에 연결이 안 되고 있다(I just reset ~ to the network)고 했으므로 (A)가 정답이다.

어휘 locate ~을 찾아내다

152 의도 파악

번역 오전 11시 2분에 코네 씨가 "맞아요"라고 쓴 의도는?
(A) 납품업체가 불합리한 요구를 한다고 느낀다.
(B) 고객들이 참을성이 없다는 것을 이해한다.
(C) 회사에 새로운 서비스 공급업체가 필요하다고 생각한다.
(D) 곧 상황 업데이트를 받기를 기대한다.

해설 10시 59분에 디알로 씨가 우리 고객은 기다려 주지 않아서 요청에 즉시 답장하지 않으면 다른 납품업체로 갈 것(Our clients don't wait ~ move on to the next supplier)이라고 하자, 11시 2분에 코네 씨가 맞아요(That's true)라고 대답했다. 따라서 코네 씨는 고객이 조급하다는 디알로 씨의 말에 공감을 표현하려는 의도로 한 말이므로 (B)가 정답이다.

어휘 unreasonable 불합리한 impatient 조급한 status 상황, 상태

153-154 표지판

알립니다!

153일부 공원 방문객들이 예술 행위 또는 재미로 돌무더기를 일부러 쌓고 있습니다. 이렇게 허가 없이 쌓인 돌무더기들은 민감한 서식지에 지장을 주고 해당 구역의 자연미에 영향을 미칠 수 있으므로 **153공원 부지 내에서 이러한 행위를 자제해 주십시오.**

새로운 돌무더기는 또한 길 찾기 도구로서 쌓여 있는 바위 표식에 전통적으로 의존하는 등산객들을 위험에 빠뜨릴 수 있습니다. **154공원 관계자들만이 돌을 쌓을 수 있는 유일한 사람들이고, 길이 불분명할 수 있는 등산로에서는 전략적으로 그렇게 하기도 합니다.** 돌들이 쌓여 있는 것이 보일 경우 그대로 놔두시고, 직접 돌무더기를 만들어서 혼란을 일으키지 마십시오.

어휘 intentionally 일부러 stack 쌓다; 무더기 pile 무더기, 더미 amusement 재미 refrain from ~을 자제하다 unofficial 비공식적인 disrupt 지장을 주다 habitat 서식지 affect 영향을 미치다 endanger 위험에 빠뜨리다 traditionally 전통적으로 rely on ~에 의존하다 navigational 길 찾기의 official 관계자 strategically 전략적으로 trail 등산로 confusion 혼란

153 주제 / 목적

번역 표지판의 목적은?
(A) 역사적인 기념물에 대해 묘사하기 위해
(B) 등산객에게 위험한 등산로에 대해 경고하기 위해
(C) 방문객의 행동을 변화시키기 위해
(D) 건설 프로젝트에 도움을 요청하기 위해

해설 첫 문장에서 일부 공원 방문객들이 예술 행위 또는 재미로 돌무더기를 일부러 쌓고 있다(Some park visitors have been intentionally stacking ~ or for amusement)며, 두 번째 문장에서 공원 부지 내에서 이러한 행위를 자제해 달라(Please refrain from doing this on park grounds)고 당부하고 있으므로 (C)가 정답이다.

어휘 monument 기념물

154 세부 사항

번역 표지판에 따르면, 공원 관계자들이 하는 일은?
(A) 그룹 활동을 편성한다.
(B) 방향 표식을 만든다.
(C) 자원 허가증을 발급한다.
(D) 경치 좋은 전망을 볼 수 있게 해 준다.

해설 두 번째 단락의 두 번째 문장에서 공원 관계자들만이 돌을 쌓을 수 있는 유일한 사람들이고 길이 불분명할 수 있는 등산로에서는 전략적으로 그렇게 하기도 한다(Park officials are the only ones ~ the path may be unclear)고 했다. 따라서 공원 관계자들은 등산로에서 돌을 쌓아 길의 방향을 표시하는 일을 하기도 하므로 (B)가 정답이다.

어휘 coordinate 편성하다 directional 방향의 resource 자원 permit 허가증 grant 허락하다 scenic 경치 좋은 overlook 전망(이 좋은 곳)

155-157 기사

오린티, 웹사이트 업데이트를 설명하다

샌디에이고 (5월 2일)—155북아메리카 최대의 차 공급업체 중 한 곳인 오린티 주식회사는 최근 웹사이트에 최종 제품에 들어가는 모든 찻잎의 산지를 나열하는 페이지를 추가했다. 이 페이지는 이 회사가 자사의 차가 무농약 제품이라고 주장하는 것이 타당한지에 대한 최근의 공공 조사에 대응하여 제작되었다.

156"떠도는 소문은 현실을 반영하지 않습니다"라고 오린티 CEO인 지오반니 쇼가 화요일에 발표된 공개 성명에서 말했다. "우리는 당사의 엄격한 품질 기준을 충족하는 생산자들로부터만 찻잎을 조달합니다. 우리는 기준에 못 미치는 것에 결코 만족하지 않습니다."

157쇼 씨에 따르면, 이 회사는 또한 각각의 찻잎 묶음에 대한 생산자, 처리 날짜 및 기타 관련 데이터를 추적하는 소프트웨어를 사용하고 있다.

"이러한 수준의 세부 사항은 이를 위한 공간이 없다는 단순한 이유로 우리의 포장지에 표시되지 않습니다."라고 쇼 씨는 말했다. "우리는 투명성에 전념하고 있기 때문에 해당 정보는 당사의 웹사이트에서 확인할 수 있습니다."

인기 있는 블로그인 foodnews.org는 자사의 찻잎이 농약을 사용하지 않고 재배된다는 오린티의 주장에 처음으로 의문을 제기했다. 이 문제는 그 이후로 전국적인 관심을 끌었다.

어휘 purveyor 조달[공급] 회사 source 출처 end up 결국 ~하게 되다 scrutiny 정밀 조사 justify 타당함을 보여 주다 claim 주장하다 pesticide-free 무농약의 circulate 유포하다 reflect 반영하다 statement 성명 issue 발표하다 procure (어렵게) 입수하다 strict 엄격한 settle for ~에 만족하다 utilize 이용하다 track 추적하다 processing 처리 pertinent 관련 있는 batch 묶음 transparency 투명성 assertion 주장

155 세부 사항

번역 회사의 웹페이지에 새로 게시되는 것은?
(A) 재료의 산지
(B) 생산 공정 단계
(C) 일부 제품 테스트 결과
(D) 새로운 판매업체에 대한 평가 절차

해설 첫 문장에서 북미 최대의 차 공급업체 중 한 곳인 오린티 주식회사는 최근 웹사이트에 최종 제품에 들어가는 모든 찻잎의 산지를 나열하는 페이지를 추가했다(Orinti, Inc., one of North America's ~ tea leaves that end up in its final products)고 했으므로 (A)가 정답이다.

어휘 ingredient 재료 process 과정, 절차 evaluate 평가하다 vendor 판매 회사

> **Paraphrasing** 지문의 the sources of all the tea leaves that end up in its final products
> → 정답의 The origin of its ingredients

156 세부 사항

번역 쇼 씨는 왜 공개 성명을 발표했는가?
(A) 정책 변경을 발표하려고
(B) 실수에 대해 사과하려고
(C) 잘못된 정보를 바로잡으려고
(D) 새로운 지역 파트너를 공개하려고

해설 두 번째 단락의 첫 문장에서 "떠도는 소문은 현실을 반영하지 않습니다"라고 오린티 CEO인 지오반니 쇼가 화요일에 발표된 공개 성명에서 말했다("The rumors being circulated do not reflect reality". Orinti CEO Giovanni Shaw said in a public statement issued on Tuesday)고 했으므로 항간의 소문이 잘못된 것임을 지적하기 위해 공개 성명을 발표했다는 것을 알 수 있다. 따라서 (C)가 정답이다.

어휘 oversight 실수 misinformation 잘못된 정보 reveal 밝히다 regional 지역의

> **Paraphrasing** 지문의 The rumors ~ do not reflect reality
> → 정답의 correct some misinformation

157 추론 / 암시

번역 기사에서 오린티 주식회사에 대해 암시하는 것은?
(A) 몇 가지 포장 대안을 고려 중이다.
(B) 지도부를 교체하고 있다.
(C) 조리법을 기밀로 유지하기를 원한다.
(D) 전자 추적 시스템에서 정보를 얻는다.

해설 세 번째 단락의 첫 문장에서 쇼 씨에 따르면 이 회사는 각각의 찻잎 묶음에 대한 생산자, 처리 날짜 및 기타 관련 데이터를 추적하는 소프트웨어를 사용하고 있다(According to Mr. Shaw, the company also utilizes software that tracks the producer, the processing date, and other pertinent data for each batch of tea leaves)고 했으므로 전자 추적 시스템을 통해 생산 관련 정보를 확인하고 있음을 알 수 있다. 따라서 (D)가 정답이다.

어휘 alternative 대안 confidential 기밀의

> **Paraphrasing** 지문의 software that tracks ~
> → 정답의 an electronic tracking system

158-160 공지

목공 배우기

멀토니아 하드웨어 주식회사는 기본 목공에 대한 온라인 동영상 강좌를 제공하고 있습니다. 이 강좌는 재미있고 자신만의 속도로 완료할 수 있으며 무엇보다도 무료입니다! ¹⁶⁰**강좌는 사전에 녹화된 네 개의 섹션으로 나뉩니다.** 수강생은 원하는 만큼 많은 섹션을 수강 및 재수강할 수 있습니다. ¹⁶⁰섹션 1은 목공 장비, 공구 및 안전에 대한 소개입니다. ¹⁵⁸섹션 2는 다양한 유형의 목재와 적절한 용도에 대해 설명합니다. 섹션 3은 수납장 및 가구 수리의 기초를 소개합니다. 마지막 섹션은 목재 표면의 준비와 다양한 인기 있고 아름다운 마감 기술에 대해 설명합니다.

¹⁵⁹본 강좌는 다운로드할 수 있는 지침서와 수강생들을 숙련된 목공 장인과 연결해 주는 온라인 채팅 기능을 포함합니다. multoniahardware.com/tips/basicwoodworking에서 지금 바로 등록하세요.

어휘 woodworking 목공 pace 속도 divide 나누다 prerecorded 사전에 녹화된 appropriate 적절한 fundamental 기초 finishing 마감 instruction 지침 feature 기능 artisan 장인

158 추론 / 암시

번역 어느 섹션에서 프로젝트를 위한 목재를 선택하는 방법을 다룰 것 같은가?
(A) 섹션 1
(B) 섹션 2
(C) 섹션 3
(D) 섹션 4

해설 첫 단락의 다섯 번째 문장에서 섹션 2는 다양한 유형의 목재와 적절한 용도에 대해 설명한다(Section 2 describes various types of wood and their appropriate uses)고 했으므로, 섹션 2에서 용도에 따른 적절한 목재 선택법을 다룰 것임을 알 수 있다. 따라서 (B)가 정답이다.

159 세부 사항

번역 공지에 따르면, 수강생들은 강좌를 듣는 동안 어떻게 도움을 구할 수 있는가?
(A) 멀토니아 하드웨어에서 교재를 구입해서
(B) 다른 강좌 수강생에게 연락해서
(C) 멀토니아 하드웨어 지점을 방문해서
(D) 웹사이트를 통해 전문가에게 문의해서

해설 두 번째 단락의 첫 문장에서 본 강좌는 다운로드할 수 있는 지침서와 수강생들을 숙련된 목공 장인과 연결해 주는 온라인 채팅 기능을 포함한다(The course includes a downloadable instruction guide and an online chat feature ~ with an experienced woodworking artisan)고 했다. 따라서 온라인 채팅을 통해 목공 전문가에게 도움을 요청할 수 있으므로 (D)가 정답이다.

어휘 reach out 연락하다 expert 전문가

160 문장 삽입

번역 [1], [2], [3], [4]로 표시된 곳 중에서 다음 문장이 들어가기에 가장 적합한 위치는?

"수강생은 원하는 만큼 많은 섹션을 수강 및 재수강할 수 있습니다."
(A) [1]
(B) [2]
(C) [3]
(D) [4]

해설 제시된 문장은 섹션을 원하는 만큼 반복 수강할 수 있다며 섹션에 대한 전반적인 사항을 안내하고 있다. 따라서 강좌가 네 개의 섹션으로 나뉜다고 처음으로 강좌의 섹션에 대해 언급한 문장과 섹션 1은 목공 장비, 공구 및 안전에 대한 소개라며 각 섹션에 대한 세부 사항을 구체적으로 설명하고 있는 문장 사이에 들어가는 것이 글의 흐름상 자연스러우므로 (B)가 정답이다.

161-164 이메일

수신: 크리스틴 코에치 〈kcoetzee@rhyta.co.za〉
발신: 아니타 은구바네 〈angubane@clubfreshenup.co.za〉
제목: 클럽 프레신업 가입을 환영합니다.
날짜: 1월 12일

코에치 씨께,

클럽 프레신업에 가입해 주셔서 감사합니다. 앞으로 12개월 동안 웰빙을 향한 귀하의 계속되는 여정에 함께하게 되어 기쁩니다.

¹⁶¹**귀하의 클럽 프레신업 회원권으로 귀하는 매월 여섯 가지의 필수 건강 관리 및 미용 제품을 배송 받게 됩니다.** 각 배송물에는 매력적이고 재사용 가능한 용기에 담긴 다양한 개별 포장 제품이 들어 있습니다. 모든 배송물에는 제품 번호를 나열한 품목 표시 영수증이 첨부됩니다. 제품과 관련해 문의하실 때는 이 번호를 참고해 주십시오.

비타민부터 로션, 화장품까지 모든 것이 개인 선호도 설문지에 제공하신 여덟 가지 답변을 바탕으로 귀하만을 위해 선별될 것입니다. ¹⁶²**귀하께서 받으시는 모든 제품은 배송 날짜로부터 1년간 보증됩니다.** ^{163,164}**반품을 원하실 경우, 불만 이유를 적은 짧은 메모와 함께 미사용된 부분을 보내 주십시오.** ¹⁶⁴**수령 즉시 동등한 가치의 대체품을 보내 드리겠습니다.**

아니타 은구바네
클럽 프레신업 회원 서비스 전문가

어휘 entitle 자격[권리]을 주다 contain ~이 들어 있다 individually 개별적으로 accompany 동반하다 receipt 영수증, 수령 refer to ~을 참고하다 preference 선호(도) questionnaire 설문지 guarantee 보장하다 portion 부분 dissatisfaction 불만 alternative 대안

161 세부 사항

번역 클럽 프레신업 가입자가 매달 받게 되는 것은?
(A) 채식 요리 재료
(B) 피트니스 트레이닝 장비
(C) 가정용 청소용품
(D) 개인 위생 용품

해설 두 번째 단락의 첫 문장에서 귀하의 클럽 프레신업 회원권으로 귀하는 매월 여섯 가지의 필수 건강 관리 및 미용 제품을 배송 받게 된다(Your membership in Club Freshen-Up ~ health-care and beauty products)고 했으므로 (D)가 정답이다.

어휘 ingredient 재료 household 가정 supplies 용품

Paraphrasing 지문의 health-care and beauty products
→ 정답의 Personal care merchandise

162 세부 사항

번역 클럽 프레신업이 고객에게 제공하는 것은?
(A) 월례 상담
(B) 무료 배송
(C) 제품 보증
(D) 인쇄 카탈로그

해설 세 번째 단락의 두 번째 문장에서 귀하께서 받으시는 모든 제품은 배송 날짜로부터 1년간 보증된다(Every item you receive is guaranteed for one full year from the date of shipment)고 했으므로 (C)가 정답이다.

Paraphrasing 지문의 item → 정답의 product

163 세부 사항

번역 이메일에 따르면, 모든 제품 반품에 수반되어야 하는 것은?
(A) 원래 배송품
(B) 서면 설명
(C) 영수증 사본
(D) 선호도 설문지

해설 세 번째 단락의 세 번째 문장에서 반품을 원할 경우 불만의 이유를 적은 짧은 메모와 함께 미사용된 부분을 보내 달라(If you wish to return an item ~ the reason for your dissatisfaction)고 했으므로 (B)가 정답이다.

어휘 explanation 설명

Paraphrasing 지문의 a short note describing ~
→ 정답의 A written explanation

164 세부 사항

번역 클럽 프레신업이 제품 반품을 받을 경우 무엇을 할 것인가?
(A) 고객에게 향후 회비 할인 제공
(B) 구매 가격 환불
(C) 다른 제품으로 교체
(D) 향후 배송에 포함되는 제품 수 추가

해설 세 번째 단락의 세 번째 문장에서 반품을 원할 경우 불만의 이유를 적은 짧은 메모와 함께 미사용된 부분을 보내 달라(If you wish to return an item ~ your dissatisfaction)고 했고, 수령 즉시 동등한 가치의 대체품을 보내겠다(Upon receipt, we will send you an alternative of equal value)고 했다. 따라서 반품을 받을 경우 대체품으로 교체해 준다는 것이므로 (C)가 정답이다.

Paraphrasing 지문의 an alternative
→ 정답의 another product

165-167 편지

9월 9일

소라야 델가도
카레르 데 베르가라, 2, 08139
산 쿠가트 델 바예스
바르셀로나, 스페인

델가도 씨께,

이사회에서 귀하를 지중해 지역의 온대 리더십의 수상자로 선정하였음을 알려 드리기 위해 편지를 씁니다. **165**알레그리노 여행사에 대한 귀하의 공헌은 올해 우리 회사를 주목받게 하는 데 도움이 되었습니다. 귀하의 끈질긴 노력과 "새로운 길을 찾아라" 마케팅 계획 지휘, 그리고 광고의 전략적 개발 및 배치 덕분에 우리 여행사는 현재 유럽에서 가장 잘 알려진 브랜드 중 하나가 되었습니다.

166시상식은 11월 19일 코펜하겐에서 열리는 알레그리노 여행사의 다음 주주총회에서 열릴 예정입니다. 귀하께서 상을 수상하는 것 외에 그 회의에서 특별 연사가 되어 주실 것을 고려해 달라고 요청드리고 싶습니다. 시장 점유율을 높이고 서비스를 재구성하는 새로운 방법을 찾는 것에 대한 귀하의 통찰력은 주주들과 다른 직원들이 듣기에 정말 유용할 것이라고 믿습니다. 물론 코펜하겐 여행과 관련된 모든 경비는 회사에서 **167**부담할 것입니다. 수상을 수락하시고 최근 계획에 대해 연설해 주실 수 있을지 여부를 알려 주시기 바랍니다.

누르 다르위시, CEO
알레그리노 여행사

어휘 Mediterranean 지중해의 contribution 기여 on the radar 사람들의 관심을 끄는 relentless 끈질긴 initiative (목적 달성을 위한) 계획 strategic 전략적인 placement 배치 recognized 알려진 shareholder 주주 featured 특별히 포함된 insight 통찰력 boost 신장시키다 reframe 재구성하다 incredibly 믿을 수 없을 정도로 expense 비용 associated with ~와 관련된 cover (비용을) 대다

165 Not / True

번역 델가도 씨의 업적에 대해 명시된 것은?
(A) 회사에 대한 대중의 인식을 높였다.
(B) 직원들의 기여도에 대한 평가를 포함한다.
(C) 소비자 조사로부터 의견을 수집하는 일을 포함한다.
(D) 새로운 상을 개시하는 데 도움이 되었다.

해설 첫 단락의 두 번째 문장에서 델가도 씨에게 알레그리노 여행사에 대한 귀하의 공헌은 올해 우리 회사를 주목받게 하는 데 도움이 되었다(Your contributions to Allegrino Travel Agency helped place our company on the radar this year)고 했고, 귀하의 끈질긴 노력과 "새로운 길을 찾아라" 마케팅 계획 지휘, 그리고 광고의 전략적 개발 및 배치 덕분에 우리 여행사는 현재 유럽에서 가장 잘 알려진 브랜드 중 하나가 되었다(Due to your relentless work, your direction ~ one of the most recognized brands in Europe)고 했으므로 (A)가 정답이다.

어휘 awareness 인식 involve 포함[수반]하다 evaluate 평가하다
consumer 소비자 instrumental 도움이 되는

> Paraphrasing 지문의 place our company on the radar
> → 정답의 increased public awareness of
> her company

166 세부 사항

번역 델가도 씨가 요청받은 일은?
(A) 여행 계획 공유하기
(B) 동료에게 상 시상하기
(C) 주주가 되는 것 고려하기
(D) 회사 회의에서 연설하기

해설 두 번째 단락의 첫 문장에서 시상식은 11월 19일 코펜하겐에서 열리는 알레그리노 여행사의 다음 주주총회에서 열릴 예정(The award ceremony will be held at the next shareholders' meeting of Allegrino Travel Agency in Copenhagen on 19 November)이라고 했고, 두 번째 문장에서 델가도 씨에게 상을 수상하는 것 외에 그 회의에서 특별 연사가 되는 것을 고려해 달라고 요청하고 싶다(I would like to ask you to consider being a featured speaker at the meeting in addition to accepting your award)고 했으므로 (D)가 정답이다.

어휘 arrangements 계획, 준비 present 수여하다

> Paraphrasing 지문의 being a featured speaker
> → 정답의 Give a speech

167 동의어

번역 두 번째 단락 7행의 "covered"와 의미가 가장 가까운 단어는?
(A) 지급되는
(B) 숨겨진
(C) 보험에 든
(D) 지켜진

해설 의미상 여행 관련 경비를 회사에서 '부담한다'는 뜻으로 쓰인 것이므로 정답은 (A) paid이다.

168-171 문자 메시지

> **빈센트 베네딕트 (오전 9시 45분)**
> 안녕하세요. 저의 이웃인 라이언 씨에게서 당신의 연락처를 받았습니다. 어제 그녀의 집에서 일을 해 주셨어요. **168저희 집에 있는 콘센트를 옮겨 주실 수 있나 궁금합니다.**
>
> **맷 클레이튼 (오전 9시 55분)**
> 저희가 도와드릴 수 있습니다. 콘센트는 어디에 있나요? 그런데 제 사업 파트너인 데니스 보스워스를 이 메시지에 초대하겠습니다.
>
> **빈센트 베네딕트 (오전 9시 57분)**
> **169콘센트는 거실 바닥 근처에 있습니다. 그것을 위쪽으로 옮기고 싶어요.** 벽에 텔레비전 스크린을 설치할 건데 콘센트에 코드가 늘어져 있으면 보기 흉할 거예요.

> **맷 클레이튼 (오전 10시)**
> 알겠습니다. **169그런 종류의 일은 저희가 할 수 있습니다.**
>
> **빈센트 베네딕트 (오전 10시 2분)**
> 이런 작업은 비용이 얼마나 될까요?
>
> **맷 클레이튼 (오전 10시 3분)**
> **170그것은 아마 한두 시간 정도 작업일 겁니다. 저희는 시간당 50달러를 청구합니다.**
>
> **데니스 보스워스 (오전 10시 5분)**
> **170하지만 벽을 뜯고 나면 벽에서 파이프나 단열재 혹은 다른 배선을 발견할 수도 있습니다.**
>
> **빈센트 베네딕트 (오전 10시 8분)**
> 이해합니다. 알려 주셔서 감사합니다. 오셔서 필요한 작업을 확인하실 수 있을까요?
>
> **맷 클레이튼 (오전 10시 12분)**
> **171방문 일정을 잡으러 저희 사무실에서 전화로 연락을 드리도록 하겠습니다.**

어휘 power outlet 전기 콘센트 mount 설치하다 labor 노동 charge 청구하다 insulation 단열재 wiring 배선 get in touch with ~와 연락하다

168 주제 / 목적

번역 베네딕트 씨는 왜 클레이튼 씨에게 연락했는가?
(A) 일자리에 지원하려고
(B) 서비스를 요청하려고
(C) 수리에 대해 불평하려고
(D) 새 이웃을 환영하려고

해설 9시 45분에 베네딕트 씨가 클레이튼 씨에게 저희 집에 있는 콘센트를 옮겨 주실 수 있나 궁금하다(I was wondering if you ~ outlet in my house)고 했으므로 콘센트의 위치를 옮기는 작업을 요청하려고 연락했음을 알 수 있다. 따라서 정답은 (B)이다.

어휘 apply for ~에 지원하다

169 추론 / 암시

번역 클레이튼 씨의 직업은 무엇인 것 같은가?
(A) 전기 기사
(B) 조사관
(C) 배관공
(D) 판매사원

해설 9시 57분에 베네딕트 씨가 콘센트가 거실 바닥 근처에 있다(It's in my living room, near the floor)며 그것을 위쪽으로 옮기고 싶다(I want to move it up)고 했고, 10시에 클레이튼 씨가 그런 종류의 일은 저희가 할 수 있다(We can do this type of work for you)고 한 것으로 보아 클레이튼 씨는 전기 기술자임을 알 수 있다. 따라서 (A)가 정답이다.

170 의도 파악

번역 오전 10시 8분에 베네딕트 씨가 "이해합니다"라고 쓴 의도는?
(A) 방문 일정을 재조정할 것이다.
(B) 보스워스 씨와 후속 조치를 취할 것이다.
(C) 최종 비용이 견적과 다를 수 있다는 것을 알고 있다.
(D) 어떤 재료를 구입해야 하는지 알고 있다.

해설 10시 3분에 클레이튼 씨가 그것은 아마 한두 시간 정도 작업일 것 (That will probably ~ two hours of labor)이며 시간당 50달러를 청구한다(We charge $50 per hour)고 했고, 10시 5분에 보스워스 씨가 하지만 벽을 뜯고 나면 벽에서 파이프나 단열재 혹은 다른 배선을 발견할 수도 있다(However, we might ~ once we open it)고 덧붙이자 10시 8분에 베네딕트 씨가 이해한다(I understand)고 대답했다. 따라서 베네딕트 씨는 작업이 한두 시간 정도 소요될 것으로 예상하지만 상황에 따라 작업이 더 길어질 수 있고 그 결과 청구 금액이 달라질 수 있다는 점에 대해 인지했다는 의도로 한 말임을 알 수 있으므로 (C)가 정답이다.

어휘 follow up 후속 조치를 하다 vary 다르다 estimate 견적(액)

171 세부 사항

번역 베네딕트 씨가 다음에 예상할 수 있는 일은?
(A) 텔레비전 배송
(B) 일부 전선 제거
(C) 클레이튼 씨의 사무실에서 오는 전화
(D) 완료된 작업에 대한 청구서

해설 10시 12분에 클레이튼 씨가 방문 일정을 잡으러 저희 사무실에서 전화로 연락을 드리도록 하겠다(I will have someone ~ to schedule a visit)고 했으므로 (C)가 정답이다.

어휘 removal 제거 wire 전선 invoice 청구서

> **Paraphrasing** 지문의 get in touch ~ by phone
> → 정답의 A call

172-175 이메일

발신: 시타 제이 쿠마르
수신: 홈스테드 천연 제약 직원
제목: 소식
날짜: 10월 10일

제가 홈스테드 천연 제약회사에서 보낸 멋진 15년에 대해 모두에게 감사드립니다. 특히 지난 몇 년간 함께 일해 온 모든 동료와 멘토들에게 감사드립니다. 뿐만 아니라 **173,175제가 지휘한 프로젝트에서 일했던 분들에게는 안전하고 효과적인 약을 개발하기 위한 여러분의 헌신에 항상 감사했습니다.** 우리가 업계에서 함께 긍정적인 발전을 이룬 것이 자랑스럽습니다.

172,174저는 대가족과 가까이 있기 위해 인도로 돌아갈 예정입니다. 그러나 현장을 떠나지는 않을 것입니다. **172아이탈 리서치에서 업무를 맡아 천연 의약품을 만드는 일을 계속할 것입니다.**

행운을 빌겠습니다. 계속 승승장구하시길요!

시타 쿠마르

어휘 pharmaceutical 제약 (회사) grateful 감사하는 direct 지휘하다 commitment 헌신 effective 효과적인 extended family 대가족 field 현장

172 주제 / 목적

번역 이메일의 목적은?
(A) 전근을 요청하려고
(B) 일부 의약품에 대해 설명하려고
(C) 새 프로젝트에 대해 도움을 요청하려고
(D) 동료들에게 결정을 발표하려고

해설 두 번째 단락의 첫 문장에서 저는 대가족과 가까이 있기 위해 인도로 돌아갈 예정(I will be returning to India to be near my extended family)이라고 했고, 두 번째 단락의 세 번째 문장에서 아이탈 리서치에서 업무를 맡아 천연 의약품을 만드는 일을 계속할 것(I will be taking a job with Aithal Research ~ making natural pharmaceuticals)이라며 퇴사 및 새로운 직장에 대한 향후 계획을 알리고 있으므로 (D)가 정답이다.

어휘 transfer 전근 colleague 동료

173 추론 / 암시

번역 홈스테드 천연 제약회사에서 쿠마르 씨의 직책은 무엇인 것 같은가?
(A) 회계사
(B) 프로젝트 관리자
(C) 최고 경영자
(D) 행정 보조원

해설 세 번째 문장에서 쿠마르 씨가 제가 지휘한 프로젝트에서 일했던 분들에게는 안전하고 효과적인 약을 개발하기 위한 여러분의 헌신에 항상 감사했다(for those who worked on the projects that I directed ~ has always been appreciated)고 한 것으로 보아 약을 개발하는 프로젝트의 관리자였음을 짐작할 수 있다. 따라서 (B)가 정답이다.

어휘 administrative 행정의

174 Not / True

번역 쿠마르 씨에 대해 명시된 것은?
(A) 직장에서 은퇴한다.
(B) 자신의 회사를 차렸다.
(C) 친척들과 가까이 있으려고 이사한다.
(D) 아이탈 리서치에서 인턴십을 마쳤다.

해설 두 번째 단락의 첫 문장에서 쿠마르 씨가 저는 대가족과 가까이 있기 위해 인도로 돌아갈 예정(I will be returning to India to be near my extended family)이라고 했으므로 (C)가 정답이다.

어휘 relocate 이동하다

> **Paraphrasing** 지문의 to be near my extended family
> → 정답의 to be closer to her relatives

175 문장 삽입

번역 [1], [2], [3], [4]로 표시된 곳 중에서 다음 문장이 들어가기에 가장 적합한 위치는?

"우리가 업계에서 함께 긍정적인 발전을 이룬 것이 자랑스럽습니다."
(A) [1]
(B) [2]
(C) [3]
(D) [4]

해설 제시된 문장은 '업계에서 함께 발전을 이룬 것이 자랑스럽다'며 동료들과 함께 이룩한 성과에 대해 언급하고 있다. 따라서 신약 개발 프로젝트에 함께했던 팀원들의 헌신에 감사를 표하는 문장 뒤에 들어가야, 함께 헌신해 주어 감사하고 좋은 결과를 내어 자랑스럽다는 내용이 되어 글의 흐름이 자연스러우므로 (B)가 정답이다.

어휘 advance 발전

176-180 평론 + 이메일

〈부엌에서〉
후기 작성: 피터 고틀립

치 치엔은 식당이 어떻게 돌아가는지 알고 있다. 그녀의 새로운 책, 〈부엌에서: 식당 사업에서 번창하는 방법〉은 요리사들을 위한 합리적인 일정 수립부터 까다로운 손님들을 달래는 일에 이르기까지 업계의 어려운 문제를 다루는 것에 대해 식당 경영자들에게 능숙하게 조언한다. 책 전반에 걸쳐 치엔은 이해하기 쉬운 개념과 함께 간결하고 실용적인 제안을 제공한다. **176전반적으로 이 책은 식당의 일상적인 운영과 관련된 다양한 업무에 대한 다채로운 단편 정보들을 제공한다.**

치엔의 책은 그녀가 조사의 일환으로 식당 주인, 관리자, 그리고 고객들을 인터뷰했다는 점에서 다른 업계 안내서들 중에서도 특별하다. 그녀는 심지어 식사 경험에서 가장 중요하게 여기는 것이 무엇인지에 대해 제대로 **178알기** 위해 식당 평론을 쓰는 기자들과도 대화를 나눴다. **180나의 유일한 비평은 요리사의 역할이 식당의 성공에 결정적이므로 그들의 관점 또한 책에 포함되었어야 했다는 점이다.** 이 같은 지적 외에는 **177〈부엌에서〉는 통찰력 있고 유익한 읽을거리이다.**

어휘 thrive 번창하다 expertly 능숙하게 challenge 문제, 도전 reasonable 합리적인 appease 달래다 picky 까다로운 concise 간결한 practical 실용적인 snapshot 스냅샷; 짧막한 정보 task 업무 involved in ~에 관련된 get a good sense of ~을 잘 이해하고 있다 prize 소중히 여기다 criticism 비평, 비판 perspective 관점 crucial 중대한 caveat 경고, 주의 aside ~외에는 insightful 통찰력 있는 instructive 유익한

수신: editor@lakecountyherald.com
발신: qichien@rapidonline.com
날짜: 8월 5일
제목: 〈부엌에서〉

편집자님께,

귀하의 신문에서 피터 고틀립이 저의 최신 저서 〈부엌에서〉에 대해 쓴 평론을 읽게 되어 기뻤습니다. **179때때로 부정적일 때도 있지만 수년간 제 작품에 대해 그가 해 온 세심한 논평에 대해 감사하게 생각합니다.** 이번 경우에는, 제가 처음에 책을 위해 기자들과 인터뷰하는 것을 꺼렸기

때문에 그가 식당 평론가에 대한 챕터를 좋아했다는 점이 특히 기뻤습니다. 제가 좀 더 다양한 식견을 포함할 수도 있었다는 것은 사실이지만, **180안타깝게도 그가 가장 듣고 싶어하는 의견을 가진 사람들은 너무 바빠서 출판 마감일 전에 저와 대화를 나눌 수가 없었습니다.** 아마도 이 부분은 이 책의 개정판에서 다룰 수 있을 것 같습니다.

치 치엔

어휘 thoughtful 사려 깊은 negative 부정적인 reviewer 평론가 initially 처음에 reluctant 꺼리는 insight 통찰력 address (문제 등에 대해) 다루다

176 세부 사항

번역 치엔 씨의 저서의 주안점은?
(A) 요리사를 제대로 훈련시키는 방법
(B) 조리법을 개발하는 방법
(C) 식당을 경영하는 방법
(D) 매력적인 이야기를 쓰는 방법

해설 평론의 첫 단락 마지막 문장에서 전반적으로 이 책은 식당의 일상적인 운영과 관련된 다양한 업무에 대한 다채로운 단편 정보들을 제공한다(Overall, the book offers ~ the day-to-day operations of a restaurant)고 했으므로 (C)가 정답이다.

어휘 properly 제대로 engaging 매력적인

> Paraphrasing 지문의 operations of a restaurant
> → 정답의 manage a restaurant

177 Not / True

번역 고틀립 씨가 치엔 씨의 글에 대해 명시한 것은?
(A) 유익하다.
(B) 시대에 뒤쳐진다.
(C) 창의적이다.
(D) 정리가 잘 되어 있다.

해설 평론의 마지막 문장에서 고틀립 씨가 〈부엌에서〉는 통찰력 있고 유익한 읽을거리(In the Kitchen is an insightful and instructive read)라고 했으므로 (A)가 정답이다.

어휘 informative 유익한 outdated 구식인 imaginative 창의적인 organized 체계적인

> Paraphrasing 지문의 insightful and instructive
> → 정답의 informative

178 동의어

번역 평론에서, 두 번째 단락 3행의 "sense"와 의미가 가장 가까운 단어는?
(A) 지능
(B) 생각
(C) 기회
(D) 방향

해설 의미상 제대로 알기 위해, 즉 '지각'의 뜻으로 쓰인 것이므로 정답은
(B) idea이다.

179 추론 / 암시

번역 이메일에서 고틀립 씨에 대해 암시된 것은?
(A) 치엔 씨와 같은 회사에서 근무했었다.
(B) 외식 산업 회의에서 치엔 씨를 만났다.
(C) 한 책을 위해 치엔 씨가 그를 인터뷰했다.
(D) 치엔 씨의 다른 저서들에 대해 논평했다.

해설 이메일의 두 번째 문장에서 치엔 씨는 때때로 부정적일 때도 있지만
수년간 제 작품에 대해 그가 해 온 세심한 논평에 대해 감사하게 생
각한다(I have appreciated his thoughtful comments ~ even
if they are sometimes negative)고 했다. 따라서 고틀립 씨가 치
엔 씨의 이전 저서들에 대해서도 논평을 했다는 것을 알 수 있으므
로 (D)가 정답이다.

180 연계

번역 치엔 씨는 마감일 전에 어떤 사람들과 이야기할 수 없었는가?
(A) 요리사
(B) 식사 손님
(C) 기자
(D) 식당 주인

해설 평론의 두 번째 단락 세 번째 문장에서 고틀립 씨는 나의 유일한 비
평은 요리사의 역할이 식당의 성공에 결정적이므로 그들의 관점 또
한 책에 포함되었어야 했다는 점(My only criticism is ~ crucial
to a restaurant's success)이라고 했고, 이메일의 네 번째 문장
에서 치엔 씨는 안타깝게도 그가 가장 듣고 싶어하는 의견을 가진
사람들은 너무 바빠서 출판 마감일 전에 저와 대화를 나눌 수가 없
었다(unfortunately the people ~ the publishing deadline)고
했다. 고틀립 씨가 요리사의 관점이 책에서 빠져 있다고 한 것으로
보아 치엔 씨가 마감일 전에 대화를 나눌 수 없었던 사람들은 요리
사이므로 (A)가 정답이다.

181-185 이메일 + 문자 메시지

수신: 해리엇 트림블 〈htrimble@decobusinessdesign.com〉
발신: 칼 빈튼 〈karl.vinton@vintapparel.com〉
날짜: 5월 26일
제목: 빈트 어패럴 매장 배치
첨부: 🖇️매장 배치도

안녕하세요, 해리엇,

이번 최신 프로젝트에 당신이 참여할 수 있어서 기쁘며, **181우리는 당신
의 이전 작업에 매우 만족했습니다.** 다음은 시작하는 데 필요한 몇 가지
일반적인 지시 사항입니다.

매장의 다른 가구들 위로 보이도록 뒤쪽 벽에 빈트 어패럴 네온 사인을
충분히 높이 걸어 주세요. 네온 사인은 이미 발송되었고 다음 주 월요일
에 배달될 예정입니다.

**182직사각형 조명 기구들 또한 월요일에 도착할 것입니다. 측벽에 각
각 두 개씩 네 개가 있어야 합니다.** 옷을 진열하기 위한 받침대와 선반
은 이미 거기에 있습니다. 매장 중앙에 원형 선반 세 개를 배치하고 183
매장에 들어갈 때 왼쪽으로 선반 두 개를 놓아 주세요. 마지막으로 매장

에 들어갈 때 오른쪽에 계산대를 배치해 주세요.

더 자세한 내용이 포함된 배치 도면을 첨부했습니다.

칼 빈튼, 소유주

어휘 layout 배치 general 일반적인 instruction 지침
rectangular 직사각형의 light fixture 조명 기구 rack 받침대
shelving 선반 circular 원형의 cashier station 계산대

해리엇 트림블 (오전 8시 5분)
빈트 어패럴 현장에 들렀습니다. **184개업식이 빠르게 다가오고 있기 때
문에 6월 15일까지 모든 것을 준비해야 할 것입니다. 빈튼 씨는 7월 1
일 공식 행사에 대비하기 위해 6월 20일 주에 상품을 입고하기 시작해
야 한다고 강조했습니다.**

잭슨 오르테가 (오전 8시 6분)
할 수 있습니다.

해리엇 트림블 (오전 8시 7분)
**183,185그리고 배치 도면에 변경 사항도 있습니다. 183이제 선반 두
개가 있던 곳에 마네킹을 설치하고 선반을 측벽으로 옮길 것입니다.
185오늘 오후에 방문할 때 업데이트된 사본을 가지고 가겠습니다.**

어휘 stop by 들르다 job site 현장 in place 준비가 된
approach 다가오다 stress 강조하다 stock (상품을) 채우다
merchandise 상품

181 추론 / 암시

번역 빈튼 씨가 이메일에서 암시하는 것은?
(A) 트림블 씨와 전에 함께 일한 적이 있다.
(B) 빈트 어패럴의 새 지점에 네온 사인이 이미 배달되었다.
(C) 월요일에 매장을 시찰할 계획이다.
(D) 빈트 어패럴의 새 지점은 쇼핑 센터에 있다.

해설 이메일의 첫 문장에서 빈튼 씨가 트림블 씨에게 우리는 당신의 이
전 작업에 매우 만족했다(we were very pleased with your
previous work)고 한 것으로 보아 빈튼 씨는 트림블 씨와 함께 작
업한 적이 있다는 것을 짐작할 수 있다. 따라서 (A)가 정답이다.

어휘 inspect 시찰하다

182 세부 사항

번역 이메일에 따르면, 몇 개의 직사각형 조명 기구가 배달될 예정인가?
(A) 1
(B) 2
(C) 3
(D) 4

해설 이메일의 세 번째 단락 첫 문장에서 직사각형 조명 기구들이 월요
일에 도착할 것(The rectangular light fixtures will also arrive
on Monday)이고, 측벽에 각각 두 개씩 네 개가 있어야 한다(There
should be four—two for each of the side walls)고 했으므로
(D)가 정답이다.

183 연계

번역 마네킹은 어디에 설치될 예정인가?
(A) 뒤쪽 벽
(B) 매장 중앙
(C) 입구 왼쪽
(D) 계산대 오른쪽

해설 이메일의 세 번째 단락 네 번째 문장에서 매장에 들어갈 때 왼쪽으로 두 개의 선반을 놓아 달라(put the two shelving units along the left side as you enter the store)고 했고, 문자 메시지에서 8시 7분에 트림블 씨가 배치 도면에 변경 사항이 있다(there has been a change to the layout drawing)면서 이제 선반 두 개가 있던 곳에 마네킹을 설치하고 선반을 측벽으로 옮길 것(Now we are to install a mannequin ~ the shelving units to the side walls)이라고 했다. 따라서 마네킹은 원래 두 개의 선반을 놓기로 했던 매장 입구의 왼쪽에 설치되는 것이므로 (C)가 정답이다.

184 추론 / 암시

번역 트림블 씨가 암시하는 새로운 빈트 어패럴 지점의 개업식 날짜는?
(A) 5월 26일
(B) 6월 15일
(C) 6월 20일
(D) 7월 1일

해설 문자 메시지에서 8시 5분에 트림블 씨가 개업식이 빠르게 다가오고 있기 때문에 6월 15일까지 모든 것을 준비해야 할 것(We will have to ~ opening is fast approaching)이라면서 빈튼 씨는 7월 1일 공식 행사에 대비하기 위해 6월 20일 주에 상품을 입고하기 시작해야 한다고 강조했다(Mr. Vinton stressed that ~ the official event on July 1)고 했다. 따라서 빈튼 씨가 언급한 7월 1일에 있을 공식 행사는 개업식을 일컫는 것임을 알 수 있으므로 (D)가 정답이다.

185 세부 사항

번역 트림블 씨가 업데이트된 배치 도면으로 할 일은?
(A) 그녀의 사무실에 걸 것이다.
(B) 빈튼 씨와 함께 검토할 것이다.
(C) 오르테가 씨에게 가져갈 것이다.
(D) 빈트 어패럴에 우편으로 보낼 것이다.

해설 문자 메시지에서 8시 7분에 트림블 씨가 오르테가 씨에게 배치 도면에 변경 사항이 있다(there has been a change to the layout drawing)며 오늘 오후에 방문할 때 업데이트된 사본을 가지고 가겠다(I will bring an updated copy for you when I come over this afternoon)고 했으므로 (C)가 정답이다.

> **Paraphrasing** 지문의 bring → 정답의 take

186-190 웹페이지 + 이메일 + 이메일

포스퀘어 하우징은 밀튼빌 지역의 아파트들로 법인 주택을 제공합니다. 아파트는 가구가 완비되어 있고 무선 인터넷 서비스가 포함되어 있습니다. 아파트 내부의 평면도와 사진을 온라인으로 볼 수 있습니다.

센터 타워
밀튼빌 시내에 위치한 이 10층짜리 건물은 1층에 상점들이 있습니다. ¹⁹⁰센터 타워는 비먼 스퀘어의 남서쪽 모퉁이에 있고 옥상 정원을 특징으로 하며 ¹⁸⁶대중교통과 가깝습니다.

앙고라 플라자
밀튼빌 시내 가까이에 위치한 이 건물에는 셀프서비스 빨래방과 대형 주차장이 있습니다. 또한 ¹⁸⁶지하철역 두 곳과도 가깝습니다.

리젠트 아파트
밀튼빌에서 약 6마일 거리 외곽에 위치한 이 건물은 현장 비즈니스 센터를 갖추고 있고 ¹⁸⁶대중교통으로부터 도보 거리 이내에 있습니다.

시티뷰 가든스
시티뷰 가든스는 데이튼에 위치한 2층짜리 건물 네 동으로 이루어진 단지로 밀튼빌 시내에서 차로 약 20분 거리에 있습니다. ¹⁸⁷이 건물은 피트니스 센터와 수영장을 자랑하며 근린공원과 인접해 있습니다. ¹⁸⁶버스 노선이 그 동네를 지나는 경로를 운행합니다.

> **어휘** corporate 법인의 housing 주택 (공급) furnished 가구가 비치된 story 층 ground level 1층 feature 특징으로 삼다 public transportation 대중교통 laundromat 빨래방 approximately 약, 대략 on-site 현장의 within walking distance 걸어서 충분히 닿을 거리에 complex 단지 property 건물, 부동산 boast 자랑하다 adjacent to ~에 인접한

발신: gsteuber@wardertechnology.com
수신: info@foursquarehousing.com
날짜: 7월 12일
제목: 문의

포스퀘어 하우징,

저는 워더 테크놀로지 밀튼빌 지부의 인사부에서 근무하고 있습니다. 본사에서 임시로 근무할 외부 지역에서 오는 직원들이 사용할 수 있는 아파트를 찾고 있습니다.

밀튼빌에 두 달 이상 거주할 직원들을 위한 아파트가 필요합니다. ¹⁸⁷아파트에는 체육관과 수영장 같은 편의 시설이 있어야 합니다.

지나 스튜버

> **어휘** inquiry 문의 division (회사 등의) 부, 국 headquarters 본사 temporarily 임시로 amenities 편의 시설

발신: info@foursquarehousing.com
수신: gsteuber@wardertechnology.com
날짜: 7월 12일
제목: 요청하신 정보
첨부: 가격_임대.pdf

스튜버 씨께,

포스퀘어 하우징에 관심을 가져 주셔서 감사합니다. ¹⁸⁸8월 15일부터 이용 가능하며 귀하의 요건을 충족시킬 수 있는 방 두 개짜리 아파트가 있습니다. 이 아파트와 다른 아파트들의 가격표를 첨부했습니다. ¹⁸⁹이 아파트가 귀하의 요구에 맞는다고 동의하신다면 계약서를 보내 드리겠습니다.

186 Not / True

번역 웹사이트에 나열된 모든 아파트에 대해 사실인 것은?
(A) 밀튼빌 시내에 있다.
(B) 대중교통 근처에 있다.
(C) 수영장이 있다.
(D) 고층 건물에 있다.

해설 웹페이지에서 센터 타워(Center Tower)는 대중교통과 가깝다(is close to public transportation), 앙고라 플라자(Angora Plaza)는 지하철 역 두 곳과 가깝다(It is also close to two subway stations), 리젠트 아파트(Regent Apartments)는 대중교통으로부터 도보 거리 이내에 있다(is within walking distance of public transportation), 시티뷰 가든스(Cityview Gardens)는 버스 노선이 그 동네를 지나는 경로를 운행한다(A bus line operates a route through the neighborhood)고 했다. 따라서 웹사이트의 모든 아파트들은 대중교통 가까이에 위치하므로 (B)가 정답이다.

어휘 high-rise 고층의

187 연계

번역 스튜버 씨가 언급한 요건에 가장 적합한 아파트는?
(A) 센터 타워
(B) 앙고라 플라자
(C) 리젠트 아파트
(D) 시티뷰 가든스

해설 웹페이지의 시티뷰 가든스(Cityview Gardens) 항목 두 번째 문장에서 이 건물은 피트니스 센터와 수영장을 자랑한다(The property boasts a fitness center and a swimming pool)고 했고, 첫 번째 이메일의 마지막 문장에서 스튜버 씨는 아파트에는 체육관과 수영장 같은 편의 시설이 있어야 한다(The apartment should have amenities like a gym and a pool)고 했다. 따라서 스튜버 씨의 요청 사항에 가장 적합한 아파트는 시티뷰 가든스이므로 정답은 (D)이다.

188 세부 사항

번역 플래너리 씨에 따르면, 8월에 일어날 일은?
(A) 아파트 두 채가 이용 가능해질 것이다.
(B) 포스퀘어 하우징이 새 건물을 매입할 것이다.
(C) 워더 테크놀로지의 임대 기간이 끝날 것이다.
(D) 아파트 건물이 개조될 것이다.

해설 두 번째 이메일의 첫 단락 두 번째 문장에서 플래너리 씨가 8월 15일부터 이용 가능하며 귀하의 요건을 충족시킬 수 있는 방 두 개짜리

아파트가 있다(We have a two-bedroom apartment ~ meet your requirements)고 했고, 뒤이어 두 번째 단락의 첫 문장에서 비먼 스퀘어에 있는 귀사의 본사가 포스퀘어에서 소유한 아파트 옆에 있다는 것을 알려 드린다(I should point out ~ apartments owned by Foursquare)며 여기에 있는 아파트 한 채 또한 8월에 이용할 수 있게 될 예정(One apartment here will also become available in August)이라고 했다. 따라서 8월에는 총 두 채의 아파트가 이용 가능해지므로 (A)가 정답이다.

어휘 reach ~에 이르다

189 세부 사항

번역 플래너리 씨가 스튜버 씨에게 보낸다고 제안한 것은?
(A) 밀튼빌 지도
(B) 임대 계약서
(C) 아파트 사진
(D) 건물에 대한 거주자의 평가

해설 두 번째 이메일의 첫 단락 마지막 문장에서 플래너리 씨가 스튜버 씨에게 이 아파트가 귀하의 요구에 맞는다고 동의하신다면 계약서를 보내 드리겠다(If you agree ~ I can send a contract)고 했으므로 (B)가 정답이다.

190 연계

번역 플래너리 씨가 워더 테크놀로지의 본사에 대해 암시하는 것은?
(A) 밀튼빌에서 차로 20분 거리에 있다.
(B) 센터 타워 건물 옆에 있다.
(C) 리젠트 아파트와 같은 길에 있다.
(D) 대형 주차장이 있다.

해설 웹사이트의 센터 타워(Center Tower) 항목 두 번째 문장에서 센터 타워는 비먼 스퀘어의 남서쪽 모퉁이에 있다(Center Tower is on the southwest corner of Beeman Square)고 했고, 두 번째 이메일의 두 번째 단락 첫 문장에서 플래너리 씨가 스튜버 씨에게 비먼 스퀘어에 있는 귀사의 본사가 포스퀘어에서 소유한 아파트 옆에 있다는 것을 알려 드린다(I should point out ~ apartments owned by Foursquare)고 했다. 웹사이트에 나열된 아파트 중 비먼 스퀘어에 위치한 유일한 아파트는 센터 타워이므로, 플래너리 씨가 언급한 비먼 스퀘어에 있는 스튜버 씨의 회사 즉, 워더 테크놀로지 본사 옆에 있는 아파트는 센터 타워임을 알 수 있다. 따라서 정답은 (B)이다.

191-195 이메일 + 웹페이지 + 이메일

수신: 에버라스트 병원 간호부
발신: 그레첸 로버트슨
날짜: 2월 3일
제목: 데오나르도 시범 운행

사이버네틱 로보틱스 팀이 우리 병원에서 그들의 새 로봇 데오나르도를 테스트하는 동안 함께 일하는 데 동의해 주셔서 감사합니다. 아시다시피, 데오나르도는 간호사 여러분들이 더 많은 시간을 환자에게 집중할 수 있도록 하기 위해 개발되었습니다. 이것은 흥미로운 일입니다.

이제 한 달이 지나 **191사이버네틱 로보틱스에서 데오나르도와의 경험**

에 대해 듣고 싶어합니다. 다음 링크를 이용하여 온라인 설문 조사를 완료해 주세요. 192팀에서는 1월 28일에 있었던 주 정부 평가관들의 시찰 동안 데오나르도와 함께한 여러분의 경험에 대해 특히 알고 싶어합니다. 설문 조사의 마지막 부분에 로봇에 대한 추가 의견을 남길 수 있습니다.

www.cyberneticrobotics.com/survey/everlast/

그레첸 로버트슨
에버라스트 병원장

---

https://www.cyberneticrobotics.com/survey/everlast/01282

데오나르도는 함께 일하기 쉽습니다. 데오나르도에게 해야 할 일을 직접 말할 필요가 없어서 좋습니다. 우리 시스템에 환자 정보를 업데이트하면 데오나르도의 업무도 업데이트됩니다. 제 시간을 많이 잡아먹었던 사소한 일들을 데오나르도가 처리한다는 것을 알기 때문에 환자들에게 더 집중할 수 있었습니다. 192데오나르도는 최근의 주 정부 평가 동안 특히 도움이 되었는데, 우리가 할 필요 없도록 모든 간호사들을 위해 환자의 약을 전달해 주어서 우리는 환자 치료에 집중할 수 있었기 때문입니다. 조사관들로부터 긍정적인 평가를 받는 데 데오나르도가 도움이 되었다고 믿습니다.

데오나르도가 음성 명령에 응답할 수 있으면 좋겠습니다. 그리고 가끔, 움직일 때 바퀴가 삐걱거립니다. 하지만 194환자들이 데오나르도가 작동하는 것을 보는 것을 좋아하고, 모두들 데오나르도와 함께 사진 찍기를 원합니다. 사진을 찍을 수 있게 데오나르도가 가만히 서 있게 해 주실 수 있을까요?

란 듀이, 간호사

수신: 에버라스트 병원 간호부
발신: 그레첸 로버트슨
날짜: 2월 13일
제목: 데오나르도 사내 시범 운행

우리의 간호 로봇인 데오나르도를 도와주신 모든 분들께 감사드립니다. 우리 직원들이 이렇게 획기적인 일에 참여할 수 있어서 기쁩니다.

데오나르도와 직접 일하는 분들은 다음 주에는 데오나르도가 조금 다르게 행동할 거라고 예상할 수 있습니다. 몇 가지 새로운 업무를 수행하도록 프로그래밍될 예정입니다. 이전에 데오나르도는 업무 중간에 간호사실에서 대기했습니다. 194이제는 이 시간의 일부를 데오나르도와 함께 사진을 찍기 위해 포즈를 취하고 싶어하는 환자들과 상호작용하는 데 보내게 될 것입니다. 193데오나르도가 이러한 사교 모드에 있을 때 LED 얼굴의 눈이 작업 모드임을 나타내는 둥근 눈 대신 하트 모양이 될 것입니다.

마지막으로, 195병원에서 앞으로 몇 달 안에 병원의 다른 구역에서 작업할 두 대의 로봇을 추가로 구입할 예정입니다. 이 새로운 기술과 기꺼

이 함께 일해 주셔서 감사합니다. 로봇이 직원과 환자의 경험을 어떻게 더 향상시켜 줄지 알게 되기를 기대합니다.

그레첸 로버트슨
에버라스트 병원장

---

191 주제 / 목적

번역 첫 번째 이메일의 목적은?
(A) 곧 있을 시찰에 대해 설명하려고
(B) 간호사들에게 의견을 달라고 요청하려고
(C) 고용 기회를 발표하려고
(D) 로봇 작명에 대한 제안을 요청하려고

해설 첫 번째 이메일의 두 번째 단락 첫 문장에서 사이버네틱 로보틱스에서 데오나르도와의 경험에 대해 듣고 싶어 한다(Cybernetic Robotics ~ your experiences with Deonardo)며 다음 링크를 이용하여 온라인 설문 조사를 완료해 달라(Please use the following link to complete an online survey)고 요청하고 있다. 따라서 (B)가 정답이다.

어휘 invite 요청하다

192 연계

번역 데오나르도가 1월 28일에 수행한 업무는?
(A) 환자들의 건강 데이터를 분석했다.
(B) 환자들의 기록을 복사했다.
(C) 환자들에게 약을 가져다주었다.
(D) 환자들을 즐겁게 하기 위해 음악을 연주했다.

해설 첫 번째 이메일의 두 번째 단락 세 번째 문장에서 팀에서는 1월 28일에 있었던 주 정부 평가관들의 시찰 동안 데오나르도와 함께한 여러분의 경험에 대해 특히 알고 싶어 한다(The team especially wants to know ~ inspection on January 28)고 했고, 웹페이지의 다섯 번째 문장에서 데오나르도는 최근의 주 정부 평가 동안 특히 도움이 되었는데 모든 간호사들을 위해 환자의 약을 전달해 주었다(Deonardo was particularly helpful ~ we didn't have to)고 했다. 따라서 데오나르도는 주 정부의 시찰이 있던 1월 28일에 환자들에게 약을 가져다주었다는 것을 알 수 있으므로 (C)가 정답이다.

어휘 analyze 분석하다

Paraphrasing 지문의 delivered patients' medications
→ 정답의 brought medications to patients

193 Not / True

번역 두 번째 이메일에서 로버트슨 씨가 데오나르도에 대해 명시한 것은?
(A) 얼굴처럼 보이는 디스플레이가 있다.
(B) 의사들과 긴밀하게 협력한다.
(C) 환자들에게 식사를 가져다주기 시작할 것이다.
(D) 충전기가 특별하다.

해설 두 번째 이메일의 두 번째 단락 마지막 문장에서 로버트슨 씨는 데오나르도가 이러한 사교 모드에 있을 때 LED 얼굴의 눈이 작업 모드임을 나타내는 둥근 눈 대신 하트 모양이 될 것(When Deonardo is in this socializing mode ~ that it is in work mode)이라고 했다. 따라서 (A)가 정답이다.

어휘 closely 밀접하게 charging base 충전기

Paraphrasing	지문의 its LED face → 정답의 a display that looks like a face

194 연계

번역 로봇 회사가 적용한 것 같은 듀이 씨의 제안은?
(A) 로봇이 이제 환자들과 게임을 할 것이다.
(B) 로봇이 더 조용한 바퀴를 갖게 될 것이다.
(C) 로봇이 음성 명령에 응답할 것이다.
(D) 로봇이 이제 환자들과 사진을 찍을 수 있을 것이다.

해설 웹페이지의 두 번째 단락 세 번째 문장에서 듀이 씨가 환자들이 데오나르도가 작동하는 것을 보는 것을 좋아하고 모두들 데오나르도와 함께 사진 찍기를 원한다(patients like watching it work ~ take pictures with it)며 사진을 찍을 수 있게 데오나르도가 가만히 서 있게 해 줄 수 있는지(I wonder if you ~ still for pictures?)를 물었고, 두 번째 이메일의 두 번째 단락 네 번째 문장에서 이제 이 시간의 일부를 데오나르도와 함께 사진을 찍기 위해 포즈를 취하고 싶어하는 환자들과 상호 작용하는 데 보내게 될 것(Now, it will spend some ~ pose for pictures with it)이라고 했다. 따라서 로봇 회사에서 데오나르도가 환자들과 사진을 찍을 수 있게 해 달라는 듀이 씨의 제안을 받아들였다는 것을 알 수 있으므로 (D)가 정답이다.

어휘 apply 적용하다

195 세부 사항

번역 가까운 미래에 병원이 계획한 일은?
(A) 로봇 교체
(B) 추가 로봇 구입
(C) 로봇 광고
(D) 로봇 수리

해설 두 번째 이메일의 세 번째 단락 첫 문장에서 병원에서 앞으로 몇 달 안에 병원의 다른 구역에서 작업할 두 대의 로봇을 추가로 구입할 예정(the hospital will be purchasing two additional robots in the next few months to work in other areas of the hospital)이라고 했으므로 정답은 (B)이다.

Paraphrasing	지문의 purchasing two additional robots → 정답의 Buy more robots

196-200 이메일 + 광고 + 온라인 양식

수신: management_team@pfi.co.uk
발신: schakravarty@pfi.co.uk
제목: 연구 개발 책임자 채용

날짜: 7월 24일
첨부: 📎파일.txt

경영진 여러분께,

채용 위원회를 대표하여 새로운 연구 개발 책임자를 찾는 일이 거의 마무리되고 있음을 알려 드리게 되어 기쁩니다.

196적합한 후보자가 충족해야 하는 핵심 선발 기준인 제공되는 제품 품목들을 개선할 수 있는 검증된 능력, 소비자 취향에 대한 예리한 인식, 영양학에 대한 심도 있는 지식을 고려하여 후보를 알렉스 무링과 이네즈 푸엔테스로 좁혔습니다. 198어느 쪽이든 훌륭한 선택이 되겠지만 저는 푸엔테스 씨가 해당 역할에 더 적합하다고 생각합니다. 그녀는 무링 씨보다 경험이 다소 부족하지만 우리 회사의 요구에 부합하는 혁신적인 아이디어를 가지고 있습니다.

두 후보자의 이력서와 추천서를 첨부합니다. 197최종 인터뷰 날짜, 시간 및 장소는 해당 정보가 최종 결정되는 대로 다른 이메일로 보내 드리겠습니다. 여러분의 최종 채용 결정뿐만 아니라 이 면접에도 참여해 주실 것을 기대합니다.

수프리야 차크라바티, 채용 위원회 의장
프리미디언 식품 산업

어휘 on behalf of ~을 대표하여 selection 선발, 선택 criteria 기준 suitable 적합한 demonstrated 입증된 keen 예리한 awareness 인식 taste 취향 in-depth 깊이 있는 nutritional science 영양학 narrow 좁히다 pool 이용 가능 인력 suited 적합한 somewhat 다소 innovative 혁신적인 reference 추천서 forthcoming 다가오는 finalize 마무리짓다

프리미디언 식품 산업의 다가오는 행사들

198,20010월 7일 오전 10시에 프리미디언 식품 산업(PFI)의 연구 개발 책임자인 이네즈 푸엔테스 씨가 미래를 위한 식품 혁신이라는 제목의 워크숍을 진행합니다. 무엇보다도 그녀는 PFI가 최근에 파스타 제품을 재개발한 이유를 설명하고 새롭고 맛있는 방법으로 그것들을 준비하는 방법을 시연할 예정입니다.

푸엔테스 씨는 멕시코시티 과학기술 아카데미에서 식품 과학 학위를 받은 공인 영양학자입니다. 졸업하자마자 그녀는 이탈리아의 저명한 로마 요리 예술 학교에서 2년간의 인턴십을 수락했습니다. 199PFI의 경영진에 합류하기 전, 그녀는 캐나다 몬트리올에 본사를 둔 제스티 밀스에서 수석 제품 개발 관리자로 5년 동안 근무했습니다.

www.pfi.co.uk/events/register에서 이 무료 행사에 등록하시고, 온라인으로 참석하실지 또는 199버밍엄에 있는 저희 본사에 직접 참석하실지를 명시해 주세요.

어휘 facilitate 가능하게 [용이하게]하다 reformulate 다시 만들다 demonstrate 시연하다 novel 새로운 certified 공인의 nutritionist 영양학자 degree 학위 prestigious 명망 높은 culinary 요리의 executive 경영진 serve 근무하다 register 등록하다 specify 명시하다 in person 직접 corporate 기업의

196 주제 / 목적

번역 차크라바티 씨는 왜 이메일을 썼는가?
(A) 업무 경험을 설명하려고
(B) 새로운 제품군을 제안하려고
(C) 일부 입사 지원자에 대한 정보를 제공하려고
(D) 보류 중인 연구 프로젝트에 대한 의견을 제공하려고

해설 이메일의 두 번째 단락 첫 문장에서 적합한 후보가 충족해야 하는 핵심 선발 기준인 제공되는 제품 품목들을 개선할 수 있는 검증된 능력, 소비자 취향에 대한 예리한 인식, 영양학에 대한 심도 있는 지식을 고려하여 후보를 알렉스 무링과 이네즈 푸엔테스로 좁혔다(Given the key selection criteria ~ the applicant pool to Alex Mooring and Inez Fuentes)고 했으므로 (C)가 정답이다.

어휘 describe 설명하다 pending 미결의

197 세부 사항

번역 이메일에 따르면, 차크라바티 씨가 가까운 미래에 위원회 위원들에게 보낼 것은?
(A) 인터뷰 일정
(B) 원하는 리더십 기술 목록
(C) 소비자 설문 조사 분석
(D) 이력서 수정을 위한 팁 모음

해설 이메일의 세 번째 단락 두 번째 문장에서 차크라바티 씨가 최종 인터뷰 날짜, 시간 및 장소는 해당 정보가 최종 결정되는 대로 다른 이메일로 보내겠다(The dates, times ~ when that information is finalized)고 했으므로 (A)가 정답이다.

어휘 desired 원하는 analysis 분석 revise 수정하다

> **Paraphrasing** 지문의 dates, times → 정답의 schedule

198 연계

번역 경영진에 대해 결론지을 수 있는 것은?
(A) 차크라바티 씨의 추천에 동의했다.
(B) 최근에 더 많은 회원을 추가했다.
(C) 7월에 일자리를 위한 핵심 선발 기준을 개정했다.
(D) 추천서를 요청하기 위해 무링 씨에게 연락했다.

해설 이메일의 두 번째 단락 두 번째 문장에서 차크라바티 씨가 어느 쪽이든 훌륭한 선택이 되겠지만 저는 푸엔테스 씨가 해당 역할에 더 적합하다고 생각한다(While either makes for ~ Ms. Fuentes is better suited to the role)고 했고, 광고의 첫 문장에서 10월 7일 오전 10시에 프리미디언 식품 산업(PFI)의 연구 개발 책임자인 이네즈 푸엔테스 씨가 미래를 위한 식품 혁신이라는 제목의 워크숍을 진행한다(On 7 October at 10 A.M., Ms. Inez Fuentes ~ a workshop titled Food Innovation for the Future)고 했다. 따라서 차크라바티 씨가 추천한 후보인 푸엔테스 씨가 PFI의 연구 개발 책임자로 채용된 것을 알 수 있으므로 (A)가 정답이다.

199 추론 / 암시

번역 광고에 따르면, 푸엔테스 씨는 현재 어디에 살고 있을 것 같은가?
(A) 로마
(B) 몬트리올
(C) 멕시코시티
(D) 버밍엄

해설 광고의 두 번째 단락 세 번째 문장에서 푸엔테스 씨가 PFI의 경영진에 합류했다(joining PFI's executive team)고 했고, 마지막 문장에서 버밍엄에 있는 저희 본사(our corporate headquarters in Birmingham)라고 했으므로 현재 PFI의 경영진인 푸엔테스 씨는 PFI의 본사가 있는 버밍엄에 있을 것이라고 짐작할 수 있다. 따라서 (D)가 정답이다.

200 연계

번역 워크숍에 대해 암시된 것은?
(A) 주로 직접 참석하는 행사였다.
(B) 원래 예정보다 늦게 열렸다.
(C) 예산보다 비용이 더 들었다.
(D) 예상보다 참가자가 많았다.

해설 광고의 첫 문장에서 10월 7일 오전 10시에 프리미디언 식품 산업(PFI)의 연구 개발 책임자인 이네즈 푸엔테스 씨가 미래를 위한 식품 혁신이라는 제목의 워크숍을 진행한다(On 7 October at 10 A.M., Ms. Inez Fuentes ~ a workshop titled Food Innovation for the Future)고 했고, 온라인 양식의 첫 문장에서 아우어바흐 씨가 저는 10월 28일 푸엔테스 씨가 진행한 미래를 위한 식품 혁신 워크숍을 정말 즐겼다(I thoroughly enjoyed ~ on 28 October)고 했다. 따라서 워크숍은 원래 예정되었던 10월 7일보다 늦어진 28일에 열렸음을 알 수 있으므로 (B)가 정답이다.

어휘 budget 예산을 세우다 participant 참가자

101 (D)	**102** (B)	**103** (C)	**104** (B)	**105** (A)
106 (D)	**107** (C)	**108** (B)	**109** (A)	**110** (C)
111 (B)	**112** (C)	**113** (B)	**114** (B)	**115** (C)
116 (C)	**117** (D)	**118** (B)	**119** (B)	**120** (D)
121 (A)	**122** (C)	**123** (A)	**124** (A)	**125** (C)
126 (C)	**127** (A)	**128** (B)	**129** (C)	**130** (A)
131 (D)	**132** (B)	**133** (C)	**134** (B)	**135** (B)
136 (A)	**137** (D)	**138** (C)	**139** (D)	**140** (A)
141 (B)	**142** (A)	**143** (C)	**144** (B)	**145** (D)
146 (D)	**147** (D)	**148** (C)	**149** (9)	**150** (A)
151 (B)	**152** (A)	**153** (A)	**154** (D)	**155** (D)
156 (B)	**157** (D)	**158** (C)	**159** (D)	**160** (C)
161 (D)	**162** (C)	**163** (A)	**164** (D)	**165** (C)
166 (A)	**167** (B)	**168** (B)	**169** (C)	**170** (D)
171 (A)	**172** (A)	**173** (C)	**174** (D)	**175** (B)
176 (B)	**177** (A)	**178** (B)	**179** (A)	**180** (D)
181 (D)	**182** (C)	**183** (D)	**184** (C)	**185** (A)
186 (B)	**187** (A)	**188** (D)	**189** (C)	**190** (C)
191 (D)	**192** (A)	**193** (C)	**194** (B)	**195** (B)
196 (C)	**197** (B)	**198** (B)	**199** (A)	**200** (D)

PART 5

101 부사 어휘

해설 과거 시제 동사인 was awarded를 수식하여 '최근에 주어졌다'는 의미가 되어야 자연스러우므로 '최근에'를 뜻하는 (D) recently가 정답이다.

번역 그 건축 계약은 최근에 맨체스터의 종 건축에게 주어졌다.

어휘 award 주다   builder 건축업자, 건축 회사

102 형용사 자리

해설 문장의 동사가 현재 시제이므로 빈칸 뒤의 명사 Wednesday를 꾸미며 '매주 수요일에'라는 빈도를 나타내는 수식어구를 만들어야 적절하다. 따라서 '매, ~마다'라는 의미를 지닌 형용사 (B) every가 정답이다.

번역 매주 수요일 점심 특선 메뉴에는 작은 샐러드가 포함된다.

어휘 be included with ~에 포함되다   eventually 결국에

103 형용사 자리 _ 목적격 보어 _ 비교급

해설 빈칸은 5형식 동사 make의 목적격 보어 자리이며, 빈칸 앞에 비교급 강조 부사 much가 있으므로 빈칸에는 '훨씬 더 쉬운'이라는 의미를 완성하는 형용사의 비교급이 들어가야 한다. 따라서 (C) easier가 정답이다.

번역 맵소어 항공은 훨씬 더 쉽게 뒤로 젖힐 수 있도록 좌석을 다시 설계했다.

어휘 recline (의자 등받이가) 뒤로 넘어가다

104 전치사 어휘

해설 빈칸 뒤에 시간을 나타내는 명사구가 있고, 문맥상 '8시까지 방문할 수 있다'는 내용이 되어야 자연스러우므로 '~까지'라는 의미의 전치사 (B) until이 정답이다. 참고로, (A) since는 '(과거 시점) 이래로'를 의미하므로 현재완료 시제 동사가 있어야 답이 될 수 있다.

번역 직원들은 평일 저녁에 8시까지 회사 구내식당을 방문할 수 있다.

105 대명사 어휘

해설 빈칸은 to bring의 목적어 자리이고, 이력서 한 부(one copy)를 보냈지만 '또 다른 한 부'를 가져와야 한다는 의미가 되어야 하므로 부정대명사 (A) another가 정답이다.

번역 양 씨는 이력서 한 부를 보냈지만 면접 때 다른 한 부를 가져오라는 요청을 받았다.

106 명사 어휘 _ 복합명사

해설 빈칸은 동사 are submitted의 주어 자리이며, 빈칸 앞에 명사 payment와 함께 복합명사를 만들 수 있는 명사가 들어가야 한다. '지급 요청이 제출되고 나면'이라는 내용이 되어야 자연스러우므로 '요청'을 뜻하는 (D) requests가 정답이다.

번역 일단 지급 요청이 제출되고 나면 법인 지출이 승인되기까지 며칠이 소요된다.

어휘 payment 지급, 납부   corporate 법인의   expenditure 지출   debate 논쟁

107 과거분사

해설 빈칸은 be동사 다음에 들어갈 단어의 형태를 찾는 문제이다. 주어가 apron이고 빈칸 뒤에 목적어가 없으며, '앞치마가 애용되고 있다'는 수동의 의미가 되어야 자연스러우므로 수동태를 이루는 과거분사 (C) favored가 정답이다. '매우 좋아하는'이라는 의미의 형용사 (B) favorite은 문맥상 어울리지 않으므로 답이 될 수 없다.

번역 아웃소스드 키친 컴퍼니의 크로스백 앞치마는 전 세계 주방장들에 의해 애용되고 있다.

어휘 outsource (회사가 생산을) 외부에 위탁하다   apron 앞치마   favor 총애하다, 선호하다; 총애

108 동사 어휘

해설 빈칸은 to부정사에 들어가는 동사 자리이며, 빈칸 뒤의 명사 an agreement를 목적어로 취하는 타동사가 들어가야 한다. 문맥상 an agreement와 어울려 '합의에 도달하다'라는 의미가 되어야 자연스러우므로 '도달하다'라는 뜻의 (B) reach가 정답이다. 참고로, (A) arrive는 자동사이므로 목적어를 취할 수 없다.

번역　토스칼라 씨는 더 낮은 비용의 교체 부품에 대해 공급업체와 합의에
　　　도달할 수 있었다.

어휘　supplier 공급업체　replacement 교체　part 부품

109　명사 자리 _ 동사의 목적어

해설　빈칸은 동사 saw의 목적어 자리로, 앞에 부정관사 a가 있으므로 단
　　　수명사가 와야 한다. 따라서 '감소'라는 의미의 단수명사 (A) drop이
　　　정답이다.

번역　루시오르 슈즈는 생산 공정을 조정한 뒤 비용이 감소했다.

어휘　expense 비용　adjust 조정하다　process 과정

110　재귀대명사

해설　빈칸은 to limit의 목적어 자리이므로 목적어 역할을 할 수 있는 재
　　　귀대명사 (C) herself가 정답이다.

번역　에즐리 씨는 하루에 10분 휴식 두 번으로 제한하라는 요청을 받았다.

어휘　limit 제한하다

111　명사 어휘

해설　빈칸 앞의 형용사 detailed의 수식을 받아 문맥에 어울리는 명사
　　　를 고르는 문제이다. 호텔이 외진 곳에 있을 때 홈페이지에 제공되
　　　는 사항으로 '지도와 상세한 길 안내'가 적절하므로 '길 안내'를 의
　　　미하는 (B) directions가 정답이다. 참고로, '길 안내'를 의미하는
　　　directions는 항상 복수형으로 쓰인다.

번역　오키드 리지 호텔은 외진 곳에 있기 때문에 웹사이트는 지도와 상세
　　　한 길 안내를 포함하고 있다.

어휘　remote 외진　detailed 상세한　renovation 보수 공사
　　　setting 배경, 설정　appearance 외모, 외관

112　부사 자리 _ 동사 수식

해설　빈칸은 주어 Ms. Dolin과 동사 requested 사이에서 동사를 수식
　　　하는 부사 자리이다. 따라서 정답은 (C) specifically이다.

번역　돌린 씨는 파손을 피하기 위해 주문 번호 42번을 직접 배송해 달라고
　　　특별히 요청했다.

어휘　be hand delivered 직접 배송[전달]되다　breakage 파손
　　　specifically 특별히, 구체적으로

113　전치사 어휘

해설　동사구 is located 뒤에 장소를 나타내는 명사구 the northeast
　　　corner를 연결해 '북동쪽 모퉁이에 위치해 있다'는 의미를 나타내
　　　야 하므로 '~에(서)'를 의미하는 (B) at이 정답이다. (A) among(~
　　　중에)은 뒤에 셋 이상을 나타내는 복수명사를 취해야 하며, (C)
　　　into(~안으로)와 (D) to(~로)는 go나 move와 같은 움직임이나 방
　　　향성의 의미를 나타내는 동사와 주로 함께 쓰이므로 is located와
　　　어울리지 않는다.

번역　가희즈 마켓은 웰시 가와 질라 로의 북동쪽 모퉁이에 위치해 있다.

114　명사 자리 _ 동사의 주어

해설　빈칸은 복수동사 are의 주어 자리이므로 복수명사인 (B)
　　　Residents가 정답이다.

번역　해밀턴 카운티의 주민들은 복원된 수변 산책로를 기대하고 있다.

어휘　restored 복원된　waterfront (도시의) 물가[해안가]
　　　promenade 산책로　resident 주민, 거주자　reside 거주하다
　　　residential 거주의, 주택용의

115　관계대명사 _ 주격

해설　빈칸 이하는 선행사 regional factory leaders를 수식하는 관계사
　　　절이다. 선행사가 사람이고, 관계사절에서 동사 help의 주어 역할을
　　　하고 있으므로 주격 관계대명사인 (C) who가 정답이다.

번역　와케슈카 제조 협의회는 산업 표준을 세우는 것을 돕는 지역의 공장
　　　대표들로 구성되어 있다.

어휘　council 협의회　be made up of ~로 구성되어 있다　regional
　　　지역의　standard 표준, 기준

116　동사 어휘

해설　빈칸 뒤 '~에게'의 의미인 방향의 전치사 to와 어울리는 동사가 들
　　　어가야 한다. '문의는 후안 멘데스에게 보내져야 한다'는 의미가 되
　　　어야 적절하므로 '(~에게 우편물 등을) 보내다'라는 의미의 동사
　　　address의 수동태를 이루는 과거분사 (C) addressed가 정답이다.

번역　장기 광고 계약에 관한 문의는 영업부의 후안 멘데스에게 보내져야
　　　한다.

어휘　inquiry 문의　long-term 장기간의　advertising 광고
　　　obtain 획득하다

117　부사 어휘

해설　동사 participated를 수식하여 적절한 문맥을 완성하는 부사를 고
　　　르는 문제이다. '인턴들이 열심히 참여했다'는 내용이 되어야 자연스
　　　러우므로 '열심히'라는 의미의 (D) eagerly가 정답이다. '굉장히'의
　　　의미인 (A) tremendously는 주로 규모나 정도를 강조하는 부사이
　　　므로 동사 participated와 어울리지 않는다.

번역　바이오코어프스의 인턴들은 도시 저수지에서 물 샘플을 수집하고 분
　　　석하는 일에 열심히 참여했다.

어휘　participate in ~에 참여하다　collection 수집　analysis 분석
　　　reservoir 저수지　exponentially 기하급수적으로　severely
　　　심하게, 혹독히

118　형용사 자리 _ 주격 보어

해설　빈칸은 be동사 뒤 주격 보어 자리이고, 부사 too의 수식을 받고 있
　　　으므로 형용사가 들어가야 한다. 또한 '시스템이 너무 복잡하다'는
　　　의미가 되어야 자연스러우므로 '복잡한'이라는 의미의 형용사 (B)
　　　complex가 정답이다.

번역　멜로 씨는 밴티모어의 재고 추적 시스템이 너무 복잡하다고 주장
　　　했다.

어휘 argue 주장하다 inventory 재고 track 추적하다
complexity 복잡성

119 형용사 어휘

해설 빈칸은 명사 factor를 수식하는 형용사 자리이다. 일반적으로 '다년간의 업계 경험'은 '관리직에서의 성공'에 영향을 줄 수 있는 '매우 가치 있는 요소'이므로 '매우 가치 있는, 귀중한'이라는 의미의 (B) valuable이 정답이다.

번역 다년간의 업계 경험은 관리직에서의 성공을 예측하는 데 있어 가장 가치 있는 요소이다.

어휘 factor 요소 predict 예측하다 supervisory 관리의
temporary 임시의 purposeful 목적이 있는 respective
각각의

120 명사 자리 _ 동사의 목적어

해설 빈칸은 동사 sells의 목적어 역할을 하는 명사가 들어갈 자리이고, 빈칸 앞에 부정관사 a와 형용사 wide가 있으므로 명사인 (D) variety가 정답이다. 참고로, a (wide) variety of는 '(매우) 다양한'이라는 의미의 관용 표현이다.

번역 아이언 네일 하드웨어는 매우 다양한 주방 및 욕실 설치물을 판매한다.

어휘 fixture (붙박이) 설치물

121 부사 어휘

해설 문맥상 '스포츠 나우 숍에서만 독점적으로 판매된다'는 의미가 되어야 적절하므로 '독점적으로, 오로지 (~만)'라는 의미의 부사 (A) exclusively가 정답이다.

번역 인기 있는 제니 플렉스 운동화는 스포츠 나우 숍에서 독점 판매된다.

어휘 athletic shoes 운동화 eligibly 적임으로 extremely 극히
explicitly 명쾌하게

122 접속사 자리 _ 부사절 접속사

해설 빈칸 뒤에 주어와 동사를 갖춘 완전한 절이 왔으므로 부사절 접속사가 들어가야 한다. 따라서 '~에 반하여'라는 의미의 접속사 (C) whereas가 정답이다. 나머지는 모두 전치사이므로 오답이다.

번역 가장 최근에 문을 연 팔라스 파스타 하우스는 배달 전용 식당으로 운영되는 데 반해, 기존 지점에서는 식사 서비스를 계속 제공한다.

어휘 operate 운영하다 dine-in 식당에서 먹는 owing to ~ 때문에
apart from ~ 외에도

123 전치사 자리

해설 빈칸은 완전한 절 앞에서 명사구 three weeks를 연결하는 자리이므로 전치사가 들어가야 한다. 문맥상 '교육 수료 후 3주 안에'라는 내용이 되어야 적절하므로 '~ 안에, 이내에'를 의미하는 전치사 (A) Within이 정답이다. '~을 고려하면'이라는 의미의 전치사 (D)

Considering은 문맥에 맞지 않아 오답이다.

번역 교육을 마친 지 3주 안에 공장 작업자들의 효율성은 24퍼센트 향상되었다.

어휘 efficiency 효율성 further 더 멀리

124 명사 어휘

해설 유망한 유니폼 디자인으로 구성된 포트폴리오를 고객에게 제출했다고 했으므로, 고객의 '평가를 위해' 제출되었다는 의미가 되어야 적절하다. 따라서 '평가'를 의미하는 명사 (A) evaluation이 정답이다.

번역 유망한 유니폼 디자인의 포트폴리오가 평가를 위해 고객에게 제출되었다.

어휘 promising 유망한, 기대되는 description 묘사 inscription
(비석 등에) 새겨진 글, 비문 expectation 기대

125 동사 자리 _ 복합문제

해설 The sales representatives가 주어인 문장에 동사가 보이지 않으므로 빈칸은 동사 자리이다. 따라서 준동사 (A) to distribute는 답이 될 수 없다. 복수명사 주어에는 복수동사가 와야 하므로 (B) is distributing도 제외된다. 빈칸 뒤에 samples라는 목적어가 있으므로 능동태 동사가 필요하다. 따라서 (C) will be distributing이 정답이다.

번역 영업 사원들은 회사의 최신 의약품 샘플을 지역 전역에 있는 병원에 배포할 예정이다.

어휘 medication 약 distribute 배포하다 throughout 전역에 걸쳐,
도처에

126 형용사 어휘

해설 빈칸은 복합명사 emergency repairs를 수식하는 형용사 자리이다. '고비용의 긴급 수리'라는 의미가 되어야 자연스러우므로 '많은 비용이 드는'이라는 의미의 형용사 (C) costly가 정답이다.

번역 배송 차량에 대한 정기적인 정비 수행은 서비스 중단 및 고비용의 긴급 수리를 예방하는 데 도움이 된다.

어휘 maintenance 정비 prevent 예방하다 disruption 중단
annoyed 짜증이 난 damaged 손상된 steady 꾸준한

127 동사 어휘

해설 과거의 실패에도 불구하고 현재는 성공적인 사업체를 운영하고 있다고 했으므로 빈칸에는 포기하지 않고 계속했다는 내용이 들어가야 적절하다. 따라서 '끈기 있게 버티다, 굴하지 않고 꾸준히 하다'라는 의미의 동사 (A) persevered가 정답이다.

번역 과거의 사업 실패에도 불구하고 바라티 씨는 끈기 있게 버텼고 현재 성공적인 운송 사업을 운영하고 있다.

어휘 failure 실패 acknowledge 인정하다, 고마움을 표시하다
determine 결정하다 criticize 비판하다

128 부사 자리 _ 동사 수식

해설 빈칸은 자동사 spoke를 수식하는 자리이므로 부사가 들어가야 한다. '명확하게 말했다'는 의미가 되어야 자연스러우므로 '명확히'라는 의미의 부사 (B) distinctly가 정답이다.

번역 첸 씨의 말은 명확했고, 그의 자료는 정리가 매우 잘 되어 있었다.

어휘 material 자료   well organized 정리가 잘 된   distinct 뚜렷한, 뚜렷이 다른   distinctive 독특한   distinction 구별, 차이

129 접속사 자리 _ 부사절 접속사

해설 빈칸 뒤에 주어와 동사를 갖춘 완전한 절이 왔으므로 부사절 접속사가 들어가야 한다. 문맥상 '기차가 제때에 도착한다면'이라는 의미가 되어야 자연스러우므로 '~라면, ~라는 조건하에'를 의미하는 조건의 접속사 (C) provided that이 정답이다.

번역 기차가 제때에 도착한다면 마커스 씨는 시티 역에 오후 7시 13분에 도착할 예정이다.

130 동명사 _ 전치사의 목적어

해설 빈칸은 전치사 in의 목적어 자리이다. 빈칸 뒤에 목적어 their conclusions가 있으므로 목적어를 취할 수 있는 능동형의 동명사인 (A) formulating이 정답이다. (D) being formulated는 수동형이므로 답이 될 수 없다.

번역 보고서에서 연구원들은 그들이 결론을 내는 데 사용한 방법론을 설명했다.

어휘 methodology 방법론   formulate 만들어 내다

PART 6

131-134 정보

사인즈 프레스 플러스는 이 지역에서 가장 오래되고 가장 신뢰받는 간판 **131제조업체**입니다. 당사는 배너, 가게 간판, 심지어 차량 광고 랩핑까지 다양한 크기와 형태의 간판을 만듭니다. **132저희는 이 일을 30년 넘게 해 왔습니다.** 저희는 **133폭넓은** 경험을 이용하여 고객의 기업이 경쟁사보다 부각될 수 있는 간판을 디자인합니다. 귀하의 업체가 주목받도록 도움을 드릴 수 있습니다! 상담을 **134잡으시려면** 575-555-0161로 전화 주십시오.

어휘 wrap 랩핑, (둘러 감싼) 포장   enterprise 기업   stand out 부각되다, 눈에 띄다   notice 주목하다   consultation 상담

131 명사 자리 _ 복합명사

해설 be동사 is의 보어 역할로, 등위접속사 and로 연결된 최상급 형용사 oldest와 most trusted의 수식을 받아 '가장 오래되고 가장 신뢰받는 간판 제조업체'라는 의미의 복합명사를 만들 수 있는 (D) maker가 정답이다.

132 문맥에 맞는 문장 고르기

해설 빈칸 앞에서 회사가 다양한 크기와 형태의 간판을 만든다고 했는데, 갑자기 빈칸 뒤에는 폭넓은 경험을 이용해 간판을 디자인한다는 내용이 나왔다. 따라서 빈칸 뒤 문장과 자연스럽게 연결되려면 회사가 폭넓은 경험이 있다고 할 수 있을 만한 근거가 나와야 하므로, 빈칸에는 앞에서 언급된 다양한 간판을 제작하는 일을 this로 받아 이 일을 30여년간 해 왔다고 언급하는 문장이 들어가야 적절하다. 따라서 (B)가 정답이다.

번역 (A) 귀하의 주문은 신속하게 처리되었습니다.
(B) 저희는 이 일을 30년 넘게 해 왔습니다.
(C) 일부 회사들은 배송 트럭을 갖고 있습니다.
(D) 이 고객들은 마케팅 계획에 간판을 포함합니다.

어휘 give prompt attention 신속히[즉각] 처리[조치]하다

133 형용사 어휘

해설 명사 experience를 수식하여 '폭넓은 경험'이라는 의미가 되어야 적절하므로 '폭넓은, 광범위한'이라는 의미의 형용사 (C) extensive가 정답이다.

어휘 permanent 영구적인   rewarding 보람 있는   memorable 기억할 만한

134 동사 어휘

해설 a consultation을 목적어로 받아 '상담을 잡다'라는 내용이 되어야 자연스러우므로 '정하다, 준비하다'라는 의미의 구동사 (B) set up이 정답이다.

어휘 turn down 거절하다

135-138 기사

컵 채우기 날이 돌아온다

콜럼버스 (6월 16일)—전국적인 편의점 체인 아벨스 마켓이 지난 3년간 사라졌던 유명한 판촉 행사가 돌아온다고 발표했다. 6월 22일, 고객은 반값의 탄산음료를 받기 위해 행사에 참가하는 아벨스 마켓에 자신의 컵을 **135가져오면 된다.** 이 유통업체는 컵을 정의할 때 창의성을 강조하며 **136당사의** 소셜 미디어 계정에 탄산음료가 가득 담긴 꽃병 사진을 예시로 올렸다. **137매장의 탄산음료 기계 아래에 들어가는 용기는 무엇이든 사용할 수 있다.** 아벨스 마켓은 고객이 자신의 소셜 미디어 계정에 창의적인 컵의 사진을 게시하고 게시물에 회사를 언급할 것을 권장한다.

아벨스 마켓은 컵 채우기 날이 **138예전**처럼 연례 행사가 될지에 대해서는 언급하지 않았다.

어휘 nationwide 전국적인   convenience store 편의점   fountain drink (기계에서 나오는) 탄산 음료   retailer 유통업체   urge 강조하다, 촉구하다   creativity 창의성   define 정의하다   post 게시하다; 게시글   account 계정   state 언급하다

135 동사의 시제

해설 기사의 작성일은 6월 16일인 반면, 빈칸이 있는 문장에서는 6월 22일, 즉 미래의 일에 대해 언급하고 있다. 따라서 앞으로 할 수 있다는 가능성 및 해도 된다는 허가의 의미를 나타내는 조동사 can과 함께 쓰여 '아벨스 마켓에 컵을 가져오면 된다'는 의미를 만드는 (B) can bring이 정답이다.

136 인칭대명사의 격 _ 소유격

해설 빈칸이 있는 문장의 주어가 The retailer이고, 이 업체에서 컵에 대한 예시를 들며 꽃병 사진을 소셜 미디어 계정에 올렸다고 했으므로 해당 소셜 미디어 계정은 이 업체(The retailer)의 것임을 알 수 있다. 따라서 The retailer의 소유격인 (A) its가 정답이다.

137 문맥에 맞는 문장 고르기

해설 빈칸 앞에서 아벨스 마켓이 반값에 탄산음료를 받을 수 있는 판촉 행사에 가져올 컵에 대한 창의성을 강조하며 당사의 소셜 미디어 계정에 탄산음료를 담은 꽃병 사진을 예시로 올렸다고 했다. 따라서 빈칸에 컵에 대한 부연 설명이 들어가면 자연스러우므로, 탄산음료 기계 아래에 들어가는 용기는 무엇이든 된다고 언급하고 있는 (D)가 정답이다.

번역 (A) 회사는 온라인 광고 예산을 늘렸다.
(B) 아벨스 마켓은 더 이상 꽃병을 제공하지 않는다는 점을 참고하라.
(C) 컵 채우기 날은 한때 매우 인기 있는 행사였다.
(D) 매장의 탄산음료 기계 아래에 들어가는 용기는 무엇이든 사용할 수 있다.

어휘 no longer 더 이상 ~이 아닌 fit 맞다, 들어맞다

138 부사 어휘

해설 as it was에서 it과 was 사이에 들어가기에 적절한 부사 어휘를 고르는 문제이다. 글의 도입부에서 지난 3년간 사라졌던 판촉 행사가 돌아오는 것이라고 했으므로 '예전에 그랬던 것처럼 연례 행사가 될지'라는 내용이 되어야 자연스럽다. 따라서 '예전에'라는 의미의 부사 (C) previously가 정답이다.

어휘 smoothly 순조롭게 kindly 친절하게 constantly 끊임없이

139-142 웹페이지

카스타크 리크루팅: 우리가 하는 일

10년도 더 전에 사업을 시작한 이래로 당사는 온라인 일자리 등록 서비스를 139**통해** 셀 수 없이 많은 구직자들이 직장을 찾을 수 있도록 도와 왔습니다. 하지만 이것이 우리가 140**제공하는** 전부는 아닙니다. 우리는 또한 고용주들이 가능한 한 가장 짧은 시간 내에 공석을 채울 최적의 자격을 갖춘 지원자들을 찾을 수 있도록 돕습니다. 카스타크 리크루팅을 이용하는 대부분의 인사 담당자들은 우리 웹사이트에 채용 공고를 올린 후 2주 이내에 141**성공적으로** 새 직원을 채용합니다. 기업을 위한 카스타크 리크루팅의 서비스는 구독 기반이며 다수의 저렴한 맞춤형 요금제를 제공합니다. 142**요금은 각 회사의 사용 요구 사항에 따라 다양합니다.**

어휘 recruiting 채용 operation 사업 countless 셀 수 없이 많은, 무수한 job seeker 구직자 job opening 일자리 employer 고용주 qualified 자격을 갖춘 candidate 지원자 vacant 비어 있는 subscription 구독 numerous 많은 affordable 저렴한 customizable 맞춤형의

139 전치사 어휘

해설 문맥상 일자리 등록 서비스를 통해 직장을 찾도록 도와 왔다는 의미가 되어야 적절하므로 '~을 통해'라는 의미로 수단을 나타내는 (D) through가 정답이다.

어휘 versus ~ 대, ~와 대조적으로

140 동사 어휘

해설 앞 문장에서 구직자들의 구직을 돕는다며 제공하는 서비스에 대해서 언급했는데, 빈칸 뒤 문장에서도 고용주들의 직원 채용 또한 돕는다며 제공하는 서비스를 추가로 덧붙이고 있으므로 빈칸이 있는 문장은 '이것(구직자를 위한 서비스)이 우리가 제공하는 전부가 아니다'는 내용이 되어야 자연스럽다. 따라서 '제공하다'라는 의미의 (A) offer가 정답이다.

어휘 assess 평가하다 investigate 조사하다

141 부사 자리 _ 동사 수식

해설 Most human resources directors가 주어, who ~ Recruiting은 주어를 수식하는 관계사절이며, 빈칸은 주어와 동사 사이에서 동사 hire를 수식하는 부사 자리이다. 따라서 부사인 (B) successfully가 정답이다.

142 문맥에 맞는 문장 고르기

해설 빈칸 앞에서 기업을 위한 카스타크 리크루팅의 서비스는 다수의 저렴한 맞춤형 요금제로 제공된다고 소개하고 있으므로, 이 요금제에 대해 설명하는 내용이 뒤따라야 연결이 자연스럽다. 따라서 요금은 각 회사의 사용 요구 사항에 따라 다양하다고 언급하고 있는 (A)가 정답이다.

번역 (A) 요금은 각 회사의 사용 요구 사항에 따라 다양합니다.
(B) 우리의 데이터베이스에는 비슷한 직책이 많이 있습니다.
(C) 메시지를 개인별 맞춤 설정할 것을 권합니다.
(D) 당신이 이 지역에 온 것을 환영하게 되어 기쁩니다.

어휘 vary 다양하다 usage 사용 requirement 요구 사항 contain ~이 들어 있다 personalize (개인의 필요에) 맞추다

143-146 정보

의료 및 연구 임대 공간

브뤼셀 시의 에투알 센터는 일하기에 뛰어난 장소입니다. 센터의 이상적인 위치는 현장 직원들에게 공공 공원과 지역 편의 시설에 탁월한 접근성을 143**제공합니다.** 에투알 센터의 캠퍼스는 또한 최고의 의료 및 학술 기관들과 근접해 있습니다. 그 결과, 입주민들은 이 지역에 거주하고 근

무하는 뛰어난 144 **연구원들**과 관계를 육성하는 것이 얼마나 용이한지에 대해 말합니다. 145 **게다가** 에투알 센터의 캠퍼스 자체 내에서 큰 회의실, 여러 카페, 그리고 두 곳의 구내식당을 이용할 수 있습니다. 에투알 센터의 북쪽 타워는 현재 모두 임대되었지만, 곧 문을 열 예정인 남쪽 타워의 대부분은 여전히 임대가 가능합니다. 146 **공사는 10월 초에 끝날 것으로 예상됩니다.**

> 어휘 lease 임대차 계약 outstanding 뛰어난 ideal 이상적인 on-site 현장의 unbeatable 탁월한 amenity 생활 편의 시설 in proximity to ~에 근접한 institution 기관 consequently 그 결과 tenant 입주민, 세입자 nurture 양성하다 leading 뛰어난, 선도하는 occupied 공간이 사용 중인, 점유된

143 동사의 시제

해설 앞뒤 문맥에서 에투알 센터에 대해 현재 시제로 소개하고 있으므로, 빈칸이 있는 문장도 현재 시제로 '센터의 이상적인 위치는 탁월한 접근성을 제공한다'는 내용이 되어야 자연스럽다. 따라서 (A) affords가 정답이다.

어휘 afford 제공하다, 여유가 되다

144 명사 어휘

해설 빈칸 앞 문장은 에투알 센터가 의료 및 학술 기관들과 근접해 있다고 했고, 빈칸이 있는 문장은 '그 결과(Consequently)'로 시작했다. 따라서 앞 문장 내용에 따른 인과 관계가 형성되어야 하므로 '의료 및 학술 기관들이 가까이 있어 이곳에 거주하고 근무하는 연구원들과 관계 육성이 쉽다'는 내용이 되어야 적절하므로 '(과학) 연구원'을 의미하는 (B) scientists가 정답이다.

어휘 retailer 소매업체

145 접속부사

해설 앞 문장에서 에투알 센터의 캠퍼스가 의료 및 학술 기관들과 근접해 있어 연구원들과의 협력이 쉽다는 장점에 대해 언급했고, 뒤 문장에서도 역시 캠퍼스 내에서 이용할 수 있는 편의 시설들을 나열하며 장점을 언급했다. 따라서 '게다가, 또한'을 의미하는 (D) In addition이 정답이다.

어휘 in contrast 그에 반해 on one hand 한편으로는

146 문맥에 맞는 문장 고르기

해설 빈칸 앞에서 에투알 센터의 북쪽 타워는 현재 모두 임대되었지만 곧 문을 열 예정인 남쪽 타워의 대부분은 아직 임대가 가능하다고 했으므로, 남쪽 타워가 언제 문을 여는지에 대한 구체적인 정보가 뒤따라야 연결이 자연스럽다. 따라서 완공 일정에 대해 언급하고 있는 (D)가 정답이다.

번역 (A) 하지만 작년에 비해 채용이 감소했습니다.
　　 (B) 일부 기업들은 대신 지역 경제에 투자하고 있습니다.
　　 (C) 이 회사들이 프로그램에 합류할 수 있는 시간이 줄어들고 있습니다.
　　 (D) 공사는 10월 초에 끝날 것으로 예상됩니다.

어휘 compared with ~와 비교해 invest in ~에 투자하다 run out 줄어들다, 다 떨어지다

PART 7

147-148 광고

> **칼라 댄스 스튜디오가 문을 엽니다!**
>
> 3월 5일 토요일과 3월 6일 일요일 정오부터 오후 5시까지 홉킨스 베이에 있는 아름답고 넓은 스튜디오에서 열리는 개업식에 오세요.
>
> 147 **기념행사 동안 여러분은**
> * 147(A) **고도로 훈련받은 강사들과 어울리며 대화할 수 있습니다.**
> * 147(B) **즐겁고, 자유롭고, 느긋한 댄스 강좌를 즐길 수 있습니다.**
> * 147(C) **댄스 강좌 패키지 중 하나를 10퍼센트 할인받을 수 있습니다.**
>
> 우리는 춤이 누구에게나 도움이 된다고 믿기 때문에, 148 **초보자든 전문가든 상관없이 여러분에게 맞는 강좌가 있습니다!**
>
> 강좌 설명, 강사 프로필, 스튜디오로 오시는 길 등을 확인하시려면 온라인으로 www.calladancestudio.com을 방문하세요.

> 어휘 spacious 널찍한 bay 만 grand opening 개업식, 개장 mingle 어울리다 instructor 강사 easygoing 여유로운, 느긋한 expert 전문가 description 설명 directions 길 안내

147 Not / True

번역 기념행사 동안 방문객들이 할 수 있는 일이 아닌 것은?
　　 (A) 댄스 강사들을 만날 수 있다.
　　 (B) 댄스 강좌를 들을 수 있다.
　　 (C) 할인을 받을 수 있다.
　　 (D) 기프트 카드를 구입할 수 있다.

해설 두 번째 단락에서 기념행사 동안 할 수 있는 일(During the celebration, you can)을 안내하며 첫 항목에서 강사들과 어울리며 대화할 수 있다(mingle and chat with our highly trained instructors)고 했고, 두 번째 항목에서 댄스 강좌를 즐길 수 있다(enjoy fun, free, easygoing dance classes)고 했고, 세 번째 항목에서 댄스 강좌 패키지 중 하나를 10퍼센트 할인받을 수 있다(receive a 10 percent discount ~ lesson packages)고 했으므로 (A), (B), (C)는 모두 맞다. 기프트 카드에 대한 언급은 없으므로 (D)가 정답이다.

148 Not / True

번역 칼라 댄스 스튜디오에 대해 사실인 것은?
　　 (A) 여러 도시에 지점이 있다.
　　 (B) 댄스 강사를 위한 자격증을 교부한다.
　　 (C) 다양한 경험 수준에 따른 수업을 제공한다.
　　 (D) 개업식은 하루 동안 열린다.

해설 세 번째 단락에서 여러분이 초보자이든 전문가이든 상관없이 여러분에게 맞는 강좌가 있다(whether you are a beginner or an expert, we have a class for you!)고 했으므로 (C)가 정답이다.

어휘 multiple 여러, 다수의 certification 자격증 a range of 다양한

149-151 정보

> **자신감있게 여행하세요 – 심플 트립 방법!**
>
> 여행 계획에 한번 이상 비행기를 타는 일이 포함되나요? 심플 트립으로 시간은 절약하고 불편함은 피하세요. **149 여행 업계의 선두 기업들이 추천하고 수상 경력에 빛나는 심플 트립 앱이 공항에서 웹 체크인을 할 수 있게 해 주고, 현지 기상 조건과 출발 및 도착 시간 변경에 대한 최신 정보를 알려줍니다.**
>
> **151 앱 스토어에서 휴대 전화로 심플 트립을 다운로드하세요.** <u>그것은 계정을 설정하고 개별 맞춤 할 수 있도록 단계별로 안내합니다.</u> **150 심플 트립은 해커로부터 개인 정보를 숨겨 주는 다층 암호화를 통해 보안이 철저합니다.** 문서가 앱에 성공적으로 로딩되면 심플 트립은 보안 검색대와 체크인 키오스크, 탑승 게이트에서 스캔할 수 있는 디지털 통행권을 제공합니다.
>
> 티켓 카운터를 건너뛰고 앱을 통해 항공편에 체크인하세요. 목적지의 최신 입국 요건을 최신 상태로 유지하세요. 심플 트립으로 여행을 쉽고 편하게 즐기세요!
>
> ---
>
> 어휘 inconvenience 불편 keep up-to-date 최신 정보를 계속 알다 secure 보안의, 안전한 multiple 다수의 layer 층[단계] encryption 암호화 security 보안 bypass 건너뛰다 entry 입국, 출입 destination 목적지 breeze 식은 죽 먹기; 산들바람

149 추론 / 암시

번역 심플 트립 애플리케이션에 대해 암시된 것은?
(A) 앱을 위한 업데이트가 곧 공개될 것이다.
(B) 항공 여행에 중점을 두고 있다.
(C) 주요 공항에 대해서만 정보를 제공한다.
(D) 여행 전문가들이 개발했다.

해설 첫 단락의 세 번째 문장에서 여행 업계의 선두 기업들이 추천하고 수상 경력에 빛나는 심플 트립 앱이 공항에서 웹 체크인을 할 수 있게 해 주고 현지 기상 조건과 출발 및 도착 시간 변경에 대한 최신 정보를 알려 준다(Recommended by leading companies in the travel ~ changes to departure and arrival times)고 했다. 따라서 심플 트립 앱은 비행기로 이동하는 여행에 중점을 두는 앱임을 알 수 있으므로 (B)가 정답이다.

어휘 release 공개[발표]하다

150 세부 사항

번역 심플 트립의 사용 혜택은?
(A) 보안된 사용자 정보
(B) 항공사 좌석 업그레이드
(C) 항공사 요금 할인
(D) 무료 수하물

해설 두 번째 단락의 두 번째 문장에서 심플 트립은 해커로부터 개인 정보를 숨겨주는 다층 암호화를 통해 보안이 철저하다(Simple Trip is completely secure ~ information hidden from hackers)고 했으므로 (A)가 정답이다.

어휘 secure 보안의, 안전한 fare 요금 complimentary 무료의 check (수하물을) 부치다

151 문장 삽입

번역 [1], [2], [3], [4]로 표시된 곳 중에서 다음 문장이 들어가기에 가장 적합한 위치는?

"그것은 계정을 설정하고 개별 맞춤 할 수 있도록 단계별로 안내합니다."

(A) [1]
(B) [2]
(C) [3]
(D) [4]

해설 제시된 문장에서 그것이 계정을 설정하고 개별 맞춤 할 수 있도록 단계별로 안내한다고 언급했으므로, 앞 문장에는 그것(It)이 가리키는 단수명사가 있어야 한다. 또한, 계정 설정에 대한 안내는 보통 앱을 처음 다운로드하거나 처음 시작할 때 뒤따르는 단계이므로 앱 스토어에서 심플 트립 앱(It)을 다운로드하라는 문장 뒤에 들어가는 것이 글의 흐름상 자연스럽다. 따라서 (B)가 정답이다.

어휘 set up 설정하다 personalize (개인의 필요에) 맞추다, 개인화하다

152-153 문자 메시지

> **마누엘 카브레라 (오전 9시 18분)**
> 안녕하세요, 사라. **152 우리 고객인 포시스 씨가 그의 주방 색상 배합을 변경하고 싶어 해요. 153 지난 가을에 끝냈던 마로니 프로젝트의 사진을 보내줄 수 있나요?**
>
> **사라 베어드 (오전 9시 20분)**
> 물론이죠. 주방 사진만 보내 드리면 될까요?
>
> **마누엘 카브레라 (오전 9시 21분)**
> 주방과 거실 사진들로 보내 주세요.
>
> **사라 베어드 (오전 9시 22분)**
> 전송 중이에요. **153 2년 전에 했던 대커 가족의 주방 사진도 같이 보내 드렸어요.** 이때도 비슷한 스타일로 작업했었어요.
>
> **마누엘 카브레라 (오전 9시 23분)**
> 생각 잘하셨어요. 감사합니다!
>
> ---
>
> 어휘 color scheme 색상 배합 on one's way 가는 중인

152 추론 / 암시

번역 메시지 작성자들은 어떤 업종에서 종사할 것 같은가?
(A) 실내 장식
(B) 고급 식당
(C) 사진 촬영
(D) 가전제품 판매

해설 9시 18분에 카브레라 씨가 베어드 씨에게 우리 고객인 포시스 씨가 그의 주방을 위한 색상 배합을 변경하고 싶어 한다(Mr. Forsyth is changing his mind about the color scheme for his kitchen)고 하는 것으로 보아 두 사람은 실내 장식 업종에 종사하고 있음을 짐작할 수 있다. 따라서 (A)가 정답이다.

어휘 fine 고급의 appliance 가전제품

153 의도 파악

번역 오전 9시 23분에 카브레라 씨가 "생각 잘하셨어요"라고 쓴 의도는?
(A) 베어드 씨가 추가로 보낸 사진이 도움이 될 것이라고 기대한다.
(B) 고객이 새로운 색상 배합을 좋아할 것이라고 확신한다.
(C) 베어드 씨가 마로니 프로젝트에서 했던 작업에 감명 받았다.
(D) 대커 가족이 주방을 얼마나 마음에 들어 했는지 기억한다.

해설 9시 18분에 카브레라 씨가 지난 가을에 완수했던 마로니 프로젝트의 사진을 보내 달라(Can you send me the photos ~ last autumn?)고 요청했고, 9시 22분에 베어드 씨가 2년 전에 했던 대커 가족의 주방 사진들도 같이 보냈다(I have also included pictures ~ a couple of years ago)며 이때도 비슷한 스타일로 작업했다(We created a similar style for them)고 하자 9시 23분에 카브레라 씨가 생각 잘했다(Good thinking)고 대답했다. 따라서 카브레라 씨는 베어드 씨가 추가로 보내 주는 대커 가족의 주방 사진들이 도움이 되겠다는 생각으로 한 말임을 알 수 있으므로 정답은 (A)이다.

어휘 impressed 감명을 받은

154-155 공지

알립니다.

154, 155 이 다큐멘터리 영화에 나온 화자들의 견해는 그들만의 것이며 반드시 영화 제작자의 의견을 반영하는 것은 아닙니다. **155** 영화 제작자의 목표는 다양한 시각에서 주제를 보여 주는 것이었습니다. 화자들을 포함한 것이 그들의 관점을 지지하는 것은 아니며, 이 화자들이 대표하는 단체에 대한 영화 제작자의 지지를 의미하지도 않습니다.

어휘 view 견해 not necessarily 반드시 ~은 아닌 reflect 반영하다 filmmaker 영화 제작자 diverse 다양한 point of view 시각, 견해 inclusion 포함 constitute ~이 되다 endorsement (공개적인) 지지 perspective 시각, 관점 imply 의미하다, 나타내다 organization 단체 represent 대표하다

154 주제 / 목적

번역 공지의 목적은?
(A) 곧 개봉하는 영화에 대한 열기를 불러일으키려고
(B) 자선 단체에 대한 지지를 표현하려고
(C) 몇 가지 사실 오류에 대해 사과하려고
(D) 영화 제작자에 대한 억측을 막으려고

해설 첫 문장에서 이 다큐멘터리 영화에 나온 화자들이 밝힌 견해는 그들만의 것이며 반드시 영화 제작자의 의견을 반영하는 것은 아니다(The views expressed by the speakers ~ not necessarily reflect the opinions of the filmmakers)라고 언급한 것으로 보아, 공지는 관객들이 영화 제작자의 의도를 오해하는 일이 없도록 영화 제작자의 입장을 밝히기 위한 것임을 알 수 있다. 따라서 (D)가 정답이다.

어휘 generate 발생시키다, 만들어 내다 enthusiasm 열기, 열광 charitable 자선의 factual 사실에 기반을 둔 discourage 막다, 못하게 말리다 assumption 억측, 가정

155 추론 / 암시

번역 공지에서 영화 속 화자들에 대해 암시하는 것은?
(A) 같은 단체의 구성원들이다.
(B) 후속 인터뷰에 참여할 것이다.
(C) 영화 제작자로부터 모두 동일한 수수료를 받았다.
(D) 주제에 대해 다양한 의견을 내놓았다.

해설 첫 문장에서 이 다큐멘터리 영화에 나온 화자들이 밝힌 견해는 그들만의 것이며 반드시 영화 제작자의 의견을 반영하는 것은 아니다(The views expressed by the speakers ~ their own and do not necessarily reflect the opinions of the filmmakers)라고 했고, 두 번째 문장에서 영화 제작자의 목표는 다양한 시각에서 주제를 보여 주는 것이었다(The filmmakers' goal was to present the topic from diverse points of view)고 했다. 따라서 영화에 출연한 화자들이 다양한 견해를 언급했다는 것을 알 수 있으므로 (D)가 정답이다.

어휘 follow-up 후속의, 뒤따라 행하는

> Paraphrasing 지문의 diverse points of view
> → 정답의 different opinions

156-158 기사

센터 새로운 모험을 홍보하다

토론토 (5월 28일)—토론토 지구 우주 센터 이사회는 흥미로운 새 교육용 영화의 개봉을 발표했다. **156** 〈이 세상 밖으로〉라는 이름의 두 시간짜리 몰입 경험은 실시간 영상, 인터뷰, 그리고 최고 수준의 애니메이션을 통해 발사체와 사람 모두에 관련하여 향후 우주 임무에 무엇이 포함될 수 있는지를 설명한다.

158 〈이 세상 밖으로〉는 극장에 설치되어 현재 테스트와 세밀한 조정이 진행 중인 엔벨로프 시스템으로 선보일 예정이다. 이 시스템은 생생한 비주얼뿐 아니라 모든 방향으로부터 듣는 사람에게 **157** 전해지는 최상의 생동감 있는 사운드를 통해 감각을 즐겁게 해 줄 것을 약속한다.

성인 1인 요금 및 청소년, 가족, 학교 단체를 위한 특별 요금이 곧 발표될 예정이다. **158** 프로그램의 예상 공개 데뷔는 7월 1일이다.

어휘 tout 홍보하다 trustee 이사 immersive 몰입형의 footage (영화의 특정) 화면, 장면 first-rate 최고의, 1급의 involve 포함하다, 수반하다 with respect to ~에 관한 undergo 겪다 fine-tuning 세밀한[미세] 조정 delight 즐겁게 하다 vivid 생생한 superb 최고의 lifelike 생동감 있는, 실제 같은 project 전하다, 투영하다 youngster 청소년 anticipated 예상되는

156 Not / True

번역 〈이 세상 밖으로〉에 대해 명시된 것은?
(A) 여행 가이드가 필요하다.
(B) 애니메이션 비디오를 포함한다.
(C) 한 달 동안만 상영될 것이다.
(D) 학교 단체들에게만 공개된다.

해설 첫 단락의 두 번째 문장에서 〈이 세상 밖으로〉라는 두 시

짜리 몰입 경험은 실시간 영상, 인터뷰, 그리고 최고 수준의 애니메이션을 통해 발사체와 사람 모두에 관련하여 향후 우주 임무에 무엇이 포함될 수 있는지에 대해 설명한다(The two-hour immersive experience ~ with respect to both vehicles and people)고 했다. 따라서 〈이 세상 밖으로〉에 애니메이션 영상이 포함되어 있음을 알 수 있으므로 (B)가 정답이다.

> **Paraphrasing** 지문의 animation → 정답의 animated video

157 동의어

번역 두 번째 단락 6행의 "projected"와 의미가 가장 가까운 단어는?
(A) 계획된
(B) 제안된
(C) 계산된
(D) 전송된

해설 의미상 듣는 사람에게 사운드가 '전해지는'이라는 뜻으로 쓰인 것이므로 정답은 (D) transmitted이다.

158 Not / True

번역 엔벨로프 시스템에 대해 언급된 것은?
(A) 구축하는 데 비용이 많이 들었다.
(B) 비디오 녹화에 사용된다.
(C) 7월 1일까지 가동 준비가 될 것이다.
(D) 현재 토론토로 배송 중이다.

해설 두 번째 단락의 첫 문장에서 〈이 세상 밖으로〉는 극장에 설치되어 현재 테스트와 세밀한 조정이 진행 중인 엔벨로프 시스템으로 선보일 예정(Out of This World will be presented ~ testing and fine-tuning)이라고 했고, 세 번째 단락의 두 번째 문장에서 프로그램의 예상 공개 데뷔는 7월 1일(The anticipated public debut for the programme is 1 July)이라고 했다. 따라서 엔벨로프 시스템은 영화 개봉일인 7월 1일까지 가동 준비가 완료될 것임을 알 수 있으므로 (C)가 정답이다.

어휘 operational 가동[사용]할 준비가 갖춰진 currently 현재

159-160 이메일

수신: 헤일리 후아 〈hailey.hua@xmail.com〉
발신: 미들섹스 헤어 〈customersupport@middlesexhair.com〉
날짜: 3월 23일
제목: 다시 찾아 주세요.

후아 씨께,

오랫동안 만나 뵙지 못해 그립습니다! **¹⁵⁹앞으로 2주 이내에 예약하시면 모든 서비스에 대해 20퍼센트 할인을 받으실 수 있습니다.** 또한 **¹⁶⁰방문 당일 가족분의 헤어 커트를 예약하시면 가족분의 커트는 무료입니다.** 맞습니다. 고객님의 가족을 위한 무료 헤어 커트입니다! 저희는 고객님에게 미용실 그 이상이 되고 싶습니다. 저희는 고객님의 가족 전체를 위한 원스톱 헤어 관리 장소가 되기를 바랍니다.

스타일리스트와 서비스에 대해 알아보시려면 www.middlesexhair. com을 방문해 주세요. 고객님을 위한 예약 및 가족의 무료 헤어 커트는

저희 웹사이트에서 예약을 잡으시거나 문의 사항이 있으실 경우 555-0127로 바로 전화 주세요.

미들섹스 헤어 일동

어휘 entire 전체의 directly 바로, 곧장

159 세부 사항

번역 후아 씨가 미들섹스 헤어에서 20퍼센트 할인을 받을 수 있는 방법은?
(A) 쿠폰을 제시함으로써
(B) 새로운 고객을 소개함으로써
(C) 두 가지 이상의 서비스를 예약함으로써
(D) 2주 안에 예약을 잡음으로써

해설 두 번째 문장에서 후아 씨에게 앞으로 2주 이내에 예약하면 모든 서비스에 대해 20퍼센트 할인을 받을 수 있다(If you book an appointment ~ a 20 percent discount on all services)고 했으므로 (D)가 정답이다.

어휘 refer ~을 (…에게) 보내다

> **Paraphrasing** 지문의 book an appointment
> → 정답의 making an appointment

160 Not / True

번역 후아 씨의 가족 중 한 명이 받을 수 있다고 이메일에 명시된 것은?
(A) 미용실 웹사이트에 게시된 사진
(B) 후아 씨와 같은 혜택
(C) 무료 헤어 커트
(D) 새로운 지점 둘러보기

해설 세 번째 문장에서 후아 씨에게 방문 당일 가족분의 헤어 커트를 예약하면 가족분의 커트가 무료(if you book a haircut for a family member on the same day as your visit, their haircut will be free)라고 했으므로 (C)가 정답이다.

어휘 at no charge 무료의

> **Paraphrasing** 지문의 free → 정답의 at no charge

161-163 기사

라피도 항공사가 엔시노패스에 온다

엔시노패스 (3월 11일)—엔시노패스 공항 관계자는 라피도 항공이 올 여름 엔시노패스를 오가는 항공편을 제공하기 시작할 것이라고 발표했다. 라피도는 감마 에어와 서던 스카이라인과 함께 이 지역 공항에 서비스를 제공한다.

엔시노패스 시가 최근 몇 년간 성장함에 따라 엔시노패스 공항은 주에서 가장 작은 공항임에도 불구하고 항공 교통량이 증가해 왔다. **¹⁶¹엔시노패스로 가는 항공편이 자주 만석으로 예약되면서 여행객들은 종종 다른 지역의 공항을 이용해야만 했다.** 엔시노패스 공항과 시의회는 증가하는 수의 여행객을 더 잘 수용하기 위하여 더 많은 항공사를 지역에 유치하기 위해 노력해 왔다.

엔시노패스의 시장인 크리스 도노반은 "라피도 항공은 추가 항공사로서 우리의 최우선 선택이었습니다."라고 말했다. "162**라피도 항공은 저렴한 요금을 제공하고 정시 운행을 유지하며 안전 점검 기준을 뛰어넘는 것으로 알려져 있습니다.** 라피도 항공이 이곳 엔시노패스에서 우리와 함께하게 되어 기쁩니다. 이번 추가로 선택권은 늘어나고 거주자와 방문객 모두에게 항공 여행은 더욱 편리해질 것입니다."

163(B)**시와 공항 측은 또한 공항과 인근 주차 시설 간 셔틀버스 제공,** 163(D)**렌터카 부스 재정비,** 그리고 163(C)**공항 터미널의 증설도 협의 중이다.** 협상은 지역의 관광을 늘리기 위한 시의 장기 계획 중 일부이다.

라피도 항공의 엔시노패스와 서머셋 간 항공편은 7월 9일에 시작되며 같은 달 말에 더 많은 노선이 추가될 예정이다.

> 어휘 regional 지역의 state 주 to capacity (정원이) 꽉 차게 accommodate 수용하다 expansion 확충, 확장 fare 요금 on-time 정시에 surpass 뛰어넘다 inspection 점검 expand 확장하다 alike 둘 다 똑같이 in talks 협의[회담] 중인 surrounding 인근[주변]의 facility 시설 refurbish 재단장하다 negotiation 협상 route 노선

161 세부 사항

번역 엔시노패스 공항에 서비스를 제공할 더 많은 항공사는 왜 모집되고 있는가?
(A) 그 지역에 더 저렴한 항공편을 제공하기 위해
(B) 인근 공항의 불만에 대응하기 위해
(C) 운송 회사를 대신해 화물을 운반하기 위해
(D) 엔시노패스를 오가는 항공 여행을 개선하기 위해

해설 두 번째 단락의 두 번째 문장에서 엔시노패스로 가는 항공편이 자주 만석으로 예약되면서 여행객들은 종종 다른 지역의 공항을 이용해야만 했다(With flights to Encino Pass ~ had to use other regional airports)고 했고, 엔시노패스 공항과 시의회는 증가하는 수의 여행객을 더 잘 수용할 수 있도록 더 많은 항공사를 지역에 유치하기 위해 노력해 왔다(The Encino Pass Airport and the city council ~ increase in the number of travelers)고 했다. 따라서 엔시노패스 공항을 찾는 여행객들의 편의를 개선하기 위해 항공사를 유치 중임을 알 수 있으므로 (D)가 정답이다.

어휘 seek 찾다, 구하다 neighboring 인접한 cargo 화물 on behalf of ~을 대신하여

> Paraphrasing 지문의 to better accommodate the increase in the number of travelers
> → 정답의 To improve air travel

162 추론 / 암시

번역 라피도 항공에 대해 암시된 것은?
(A) 다른 항공사들에게 거래를 놓쳤다.
(B) 다른 항공사들보다 더 많은 항공편을 제공한다.
(C) 안전을 우선시한다는 평판을 갖고 있다.
(D) 주로 출장 여행객들이 이용한다.

해설 세 번째 단락의 두 번째 문장에서 라피도 항공은 저렴한 요금을 제공하고 정시 운행을 유지하며 안전 점검 기준을 뛰어넘는 것으로 알려져 있다(It is known for offering low fares, maintaining on-time schedules, and surpassing safety inspections)고 했으므로 라피도 항공이 점검 기준을 넘어설 정도로 안전을 중시하는 것으로 유명하다는 것을 알 수 있다. 따라서 (C)가 정답이다.

어휘 lose business 거래를 놓치다 reputation 평판 prioritize 우선시하다 primarily 주로

> Paraphrasing 지문의 surpassing safety inspections
> → 정답의 prioritizing safety

163 Not / True

번역 지역 관광을 늘리기 위한 시의 계획 중 일부로 언급되지 않은 것은?
(A) 주차 할인 제공
(B) 셔틀버스 서비스 제공
(C) 새로운 터미널 건설
(D) 렌터카 부스 개선

해설 네 번째 단락의 첫 문장에서 시와 공항 측은 또한 공항과 인근 주차 시설 간 셔틀버스 제공, 렌터카 부스 재정비, 공항 터미널 증설 등도 협의 중(The city and airport are also in talks to provide shuttle bus ~ and add another terminal to the airport)이라고 했다. 따라서 정답은 (A)이다.

> Paraphrasing 지문의 add another terminal
> → 보기 (C)의 Building a new terminal
> 지문의 refurbish the rental car booth
> → 보기 (D)의 Improving car rental booths

164-167 문자 메시지

> **케이시 윌러드 (오전 7시 43분)**
> 164**두 분 중 아무라도 오늘 아침에 출근하실 수 있을까요? 작업할 주문량이 너무 많은데 오늘 일하기로 되어 있던 지게차 기사 두 명이 전화로 병가를 냈어요.** 그래서 일하는 분이 한 명 밖에 없어요. 한두 명 더 있으면 정말 도움이 될 거예요. 발송 담당 직원들은 제품을 출고하는 게 빠르지 못해요.
>
> **카즈코 요네다 (오전 7시 46분)**
> 죄송합니다. 저도 그러고 싶지만 오늘은 다른 약속이 있습니다. 165**클라우디아 권에게 물어보시겠어요?** 그녀는 보통 시간이 되거든요.
>
> **케이시 윌러드 (오전 7시 47분)**
> 그녀는 주말 휴가를 내고 가족을 방문하러 포드 하버에 갔어요. 항상 초과 근무 수당을 벌 수 있는 기회를 반기는데 아쉽네요.
>
> **루카스 수아레즈 (오전 7시 51분)**
> 오전 10시쯤까지는 바쁘지만 그 이후에는 제가 갈 수 있습니다.
>
> **케이시 윌러드 (오전 7시 52분)**
> 고마워요, 루카스. 167**어떤 도움이라도 절실합니다!** 166,167**오늘 저녁 6시까지 트럭에 주문품을 싣지 못하면 월요일까지 배송을 나가지 못하거든요.**
>
> **루카스 수아레즈 (오전 7시 54분)**
> 알겠습니다. 167**최대한 빨리 가겠습니다.**

어휘 fill 이행하다 forklift 지게차 call in sick (전화로) 병가를 내다 shipping clerk 배송 담당 직원 commitment 약속한 일 flexible (시간이) 탄력적인, 유연한 harbor 항구 appreciate 환영하다, 고마워하다 opportunity 기회

164 주제 / 목적

번역 윌러드 씨는 왜 동료들에게 문자를 보냈는가?
    (A) 일부 작업자들이 예기치 않게 결근했다.
    (B) 발송 담당 직원들이 예정보다 빨리 일하고 있다.
    (C) 회사의 지게차 중 두 대에 기계적인 문제가 있다.
    (D) 너무 적은 수의 지게차 기사가 일하기로 예정되어 있었다.

해설 7시 43분에 윌러드 씨가 둘 중 아무라도 오늘 아침에 출근할 수 있는지(Can either of you come in to work this morning?) 물으며, 작업할 주문량이 너무 많은데 오늘 일하기로 되어 있던 지게차 기사 두 명이 병가를 냈다(We have a huge order ~ have called in sick)고 했다. 따라서 정답은 (A)이다.

어휘 unexpectedly 예기치 않게, 느닷없이 absent 결근한 mechanical 기계적인

> **Paraphrasing** 지문의 called in sick → 정답의 are ~ absent

165 세부 사항

번역 요네다 씨는 윌러드 씨에게 무엇을 하라고 제안하는가?
    (A) 장시간 근무하기
    (B) 추가 급여 제공하기
    (C) 다른 직원에게 연락하기
    (D) 임시직 근로자 데려오기

해설 7시 46분에 요네다 씨가 윌러드 씨에게 클라우디아 권에게 물어보라(Maybe try Claudia Kwon?)고 권하고 있으므로 (C)가 정답이다.

> **Paraphrasing** 지문의 try Claudia Kwon
> → 정답의 Contact another employee

166 세부 사항

번역 저녁 6시까지 일어나야 하는 일은?
    (A) 트럭에 짐을 실어야 한다.
    (B) 직원이 집에 가야 한다.
    (C) 지불을 받아야 한다.
    (D) 고객이 주문을 확인해야 한다.

해설 7시 52분에 윌러드 씨가 오늘 저녁 6시까지 트럭에 주문품을 싣지 못하면 월요일까지 배송을 나가지 못한다(If the order is not on the truck by 6 tonight, it won't go out for delivery until Monday)고 했으므로 정답은 (A)이다.

어휘 load (짐 등을) 싣다

> **Paraphrasing** 지문의 the order is ~ on the truck
> → 정답의 A truck must be loaded

167 의도 파악

번역 오전 7시 54분에 수아레즈 씨가 "알겠습니다"라고 쓴 의도는?
    (A) 주문을 취소할 것이다.
    (B) 상황을 이해한다.
    (C) 권 씨와 연락할 방법을 안다.
    (D) 트럭 열쇠를 받았다.

해설 7시 52분에 윌러드 씨가 어떤 도움이라도 절실하다(We need all the help we can get!)며 오늘 저녁 6시까지 트럭에 주문품을 싣지 못하면 월요일까지 배송을 나가지 못한다(If the order is not on ~ delivery until Monday)고 하자 7시 54분에 수아레즈 씨가 알겠다(Got it)며 최대한 빨리 가겠다(I'll be there as soon as I can)고 했다. 따라서 윌러드 씨가 말하는 긴급한 상황에 대해 이해한다는 의도로 한 말임을 알 수 있으므로 정답은 (B)이다.

168-171 기사

얌 앤 워크 푸드 투어스, 새 여행지를 추가하다

칼리지스테이션 (5월 15일)—6월 2일, 얌 앤 워크 푸드 투어스는 칼리지스테이션을 주 전체의 요리 관광지 목록에 추가할 예정이다.

"칼리지스테이션은 너무 오랫동안 요리 관광지에서 간과되어 왔습니다."라고 여행사 사주인 에드 로페즈는 말했다. 전직 요리사였던 로페즈는 한때 기자로 일했고 〈텍사스 비콘〉을 위해 요리에 대한 글을 썼다.

얌 앤 워크 푸드 투어스는 텍사스의 다른 9개 도시에서 당일 여행을 제공하며 방문객들을 식당, 빵집, 전문점으로 데려가 달콤하고 풍미 있는 음식을 맛보게 해 준다. 방문객들은 각 동네의 역사에 대한 정보도 알려주는 경험이 풍부한 가이드와 함께 도시를 산책한다. **169(B)로페즈 씨는 샌안토니오에서 일하기 전 그의 고향이자 그 뒤 다시 귀향한 칼리지스테이션에서 직접 관광 가이드 역할을 할 예정이다.**

168"처음부터 제 목표는 사람들이 좋은 음식을 발견하도록 돕는 것이었습니다."라고 로페즈 씨는 말했다.

169(A), 169(D)현지 여행 일정에는 주세피나즈 트라토리아, 유카탄 플레이트, 케랄라 케밥스, 스파이스 러브 스톱, 딜리셔스 도너츠 등 3시간 동안 5개의 목적지가 포함되어 있다. 170고객들은 특정한 음식 기호나 요구 사항이 있을 경우 개인 관광 일정을 잡을 수 있다.

지역 공무원들은 여행사가 지역에 들어오는 것에 대해 기대하고 있다.

171"얌 앤 워크 푸드 투어스가 우리를 그들의 여행지 목록에 추가하여 무척 기쁩니다."라고 칼리지스테이션 시장인 마리아 가르시아는 말했다. "그들의 존재는 분명 우리 지역의 요식업체에 긍정적인 영향을 미칠 것입니다."

표는 한 장에 50달러이다. 10주간의 관광 시즌은 7월 2일에 시작해서 9월 3일까지 계속된다. 관광은 일요일 오후 1시부터 4시까지 진행된다.

어휘 destination (여행) 목적지 statewide 주 전체의 culinary 요리의 overlook 간과하다 former 전의 cuisine 요리 outing 여행[견학], 나들이 specialty store (특산품을 파는) 전문점 sample 맛보다, 시식[시음]하다 savory 풍미 있는, 맛 좋은 treat 훌륭한 요리, 대접 experienced 경험이 풍부한 serve as ~의 역할을 하다 itinerary 여행 일정(표) time span 기간 specific 특정한 dietary 음식물의, 식이 요법의

TEST 8

preference 기호 thrilled 신이 난, 매우 좋아하는 presence 존재 have an impact on ~에 영향을 주다 establishment 시설, 기관

168 추론 / 암시

번역 로페즈 씨는 왜 얌 앤 워크 푸드 투어스를 시작했을 것 같은가?
(A) 관광을 주도한 경험을 활용하기 위해
(B) 음식에 대한 자신의 애정을 사람들과 공유하기 위해
(C) 현지 식당에 광고 기회를 제공하기 위해
(D) 집에서 더 가까이 근무할 수 있도록 하기 위해

해설 네 번째 단락에서 처음부터 제 목표는 사람들이 좋은 음식을 발견하도록 돕는 것이었다고 로페즈 씨가 말했다("From the beginning, my goal has been to help people discover great food," said Mr. Lopez)고 했으므로 로페즈 씨는 음식에 대한 자신의 열정을 사람들과 공유하려고 맛집 투어 서비스 업체를 시작했음을 알 수 있다. 따라서 정답은 (B)이다.

어휘 take advantage of ~을 이용[활용]하다

169 Not / True

번역 칼리지스테이션의 얌 앤 워크 푸드 투어스에 대해 명시되지 않은 것은?
(A) 세 시간 동안 지속될 것이다.
(B) 로페즈 씨가 주도할 것이다.
(C) 〈텍사스 비콘〉에 광고될 것이다.
(D) 방문객들을 다섯 개의 식당에 데려갈 것이다.

해설 세 번째 단락의 세 번째 문장에서 로페즈 씨는 샌안토니오에서 일하기 전 그의 고향이자 그 뒤 다시 귀향한 칼리지스테이션에서 직접 관광 가이드 역할을 할 예정(Mr. Lopez himself will serve ~ returning to the area)이라고 했으므로 (B), 다섯 번째 단락의 첫 문장에서 현지 여행 일정에는 주세피나즈 트라토리아, 유카탄 플레이트, 케랄라 케밥스, 스파이스 러브 스톱, 딜리셔스 도너츠 등 3시간 동안 5개의 목적지가 포함되어 있다(The local itinerary ~ Delicious Doughnuts)고 했으므로 (A)와 (D)는 기사에 언급된 사실이다. 광고에 대한 내용은 언급된 적이 없으므로 (C)가 정답이다.

170 Not / True

번역 개인 관광에 대해 명시된 것은?
(A) 참석하는 데 추가 비용이 든다.
(B) 모든 도시에서 제공되는 것은 아니다.
(C) 적어도 10주 전에 일정을 잡아야 한다.
(D) 특정 음식을 피하는 사람들을 위해 마련될 수 있다.

해설 다섯 번째 단락의 두 번째 문장에서 고객들은 특정 음식 기호나 요구 사항이 있을 경우 개인 관광 일정을 잡을 수 있다(Customers can schedule private tours if they have any specific dietary preferences or requirements)고 했으므로 정답은 (D)이다.

어휘 in advance 사전에 certain 특정한

171 Not / True

번역 가르시아 씨에 대해 사실인 것은?
(A) 관광 상품이 지역 업체에 좋을 것이라고 생각한다.
(B) 스파이스 러브 스톱을 소유하고 있다.
(C) 음식 관광에 참가한 적이 있다.
(D) 샌안토니오 출신이다.

해설 일곱 번째 단락의 첫 문장에서 얌 앤 워크 푸드 투어스가 우리를 그들의 여행지 목록에 추가하여 무척 기쁘다고 칼리지스테이션 시장인 마리아 가르시아는 말했다("We're thrilled to have Yum and Walk Food Tours add us to their list of destinations", said College Station Mayor Maria Garcia)고 했고, 뒤이어 그들의 존재는 분명 우리 지역의 요식업체에 긍정적인 영향을 미칠 것(Their presence is sure to have a positive impact on our area's dining establishments)이라고 덧붙였으므로 관광이 지역에 도움이 될 것으로 기대하고 있음을 알 수 있다. 따라서 (A)가 정답이다.

172-175 이메일

수신: 전 직원
발신: 재니스 카팔디
날짜: 10월 23일
제목: 손님

안녕하세요, 여러분.

저희는 조만간 성남전자에서 오는 직원 단체를 맞이할 예정입니다. **175**이들은 11월 10일에 도착해서 우리의 연구 및 생산 방식을 관찰하기 위해 일주일간 머물 것입니다. 방문객들이 이곳에 있는 동안 여러분 모두가 그들과 교류할 것을 권장합니다. 여러분의 작업 과정을 그들과 공유하고 그들의 질문에 답변해 주세요.

직원 단체의 임원들은 전자 제품 개발 및 제조 분야의 리더들입니다. **172**김성혜 박사는 연구 개발을 주도하고 있습니다. 그녀의 개별적인 기여는 자기장이 전기 장치 내 구성 요소의 효율성에 어떤 영향을 미치는지에 중점을 두고 있습니다. 그녀는 또한 다른 물리학자와 교수들로부터 전자기 현상을 설명하는 글의 작성과 편집 요청을 받아 왔습니다. 김 박사의 연구는 국제 전자 산업 전반에 영향을 미치고 있습니다. 그리고 **173**이진웅 성남전자 최고 생산 책임자는 서울 인근의 공장에서 제조 공정을 설계한 팀을 이끌고 있습니다. 이 씨의 팀이 개발한 수상 경력이 있는 기술은 비용 효율성과 품질을 모두 보장합니다.

17411월 10일 오후에 3층 회의실에서 손님들을 맞이할 환영회를 가질 예정입니다. 세부 내용은 행사 책임자를 맡고 있는 스튜어트 라크가 이 메일로 전 직원에게 전달할 것입니다. 참석할 계획을 세워 주세요. 문의 사항이 있으면 라크 씨와 저에게 연락하세요.

감사합니다.

재니스 카팔디, 운영 이사, 돌슬리 전자 주식회사

어휘 observe 관찰하다 production 생산 method 방법 interact 교류하다 executive 임원 field 분야 individual 개별의, 개인의 contribution 기여 magnetic field 자기장 influence 영향을 미치다 efficiency 효율성 component 요소 electrical 전기의 call on 요청하다 physicist 물리학자 electromagnetic 전자기의 phenomena 현상 influential 영향력 있는 head 이끌다 process 공정 cost-effectiveness 비용 효율성 specifics 세부 내용 coordinator 책임자, 진행자

172 추론 / 암시

번역 김 박사에 대해 암시된 것은?
(A) 물리학자이다.
(B) 보통 혼자 일한다.
(C) 대학에서 강의한다.
(D) 성남전자를 시작했다.

해설 두 번째 단락의 두 번째 문장에서 김성혜 박사는 연구 개발을 주도하고 있고(Dr. Sung-Hye Kim leads Research and Development), 그녀의 개별적인 기여는 자기장이 전기 장치 내 구성 요소의 효율성에 어떤 영향을 미치는지에 중점을 두고 있다(Her individual contributions ~ within electrical devices)고 했다. 또한 다른 물리학자와 교수들로부터 전자기 현상을 설명하는 글의 작성과 편집 요청을 받았다(She has also been called on ~ explain electromagnetic phenomena)고 했으므로 김 박사는 물리학자임을 알 수 있다. 따라서 정답은 (A)이다.

어휘 lecture 강의하다 launch (사업을) 시작하다, 착수하다

173 세부 사항

번역 이 씨가 담당하는 업무는?
(A) 판매 거래 협상
(B) 마케팅 전략 선택
(C) 제품 조립 공정 수립
(D) 인사부 관리

해설 두 번째 단락의 여섯 번째 문장에서 이진웅 성남전자 최고 생산 책임자는 서울 인근의 공장에서 제조 공정을 설계한 팀을 이끌고 있다(Jin-Woong Lee, chief production officer ~ at the plant near Seoul)고 했으므로 이 씨는 공장의 제조 공정 설계를 책임지고 있다는 것을 알 수 있다. 따라서 정답은 (C)이다.

어휘 be responsible for ~을 담당하다, 책임지다 negotiate 협상하다 strategy 전략 establish 수립하다, 설정하다

Paraphrasing 지문의 designed the manufacturing processes → 정답의 Establishing a product assembly process

174 추론 / 암시

번역 라크 씨는 이메일에 환영회에 대한 어떤 새로운 정보를 포함할 것 같은가?
(A) 목적
(B) 날짜
(C) 징소
(D) 시간

해설 세 번째 단락의 첫 문장에서 11월 10일 오후에 3층 회의실에서 손님들을 맞이할 환영회를 가질 예정(On the afternoon of November 10 ~ to welcome our guests)이라면서 세부 내용은 행사 책임자인 스튜어트 라크가 이메일로 전 직원에게 전달할 것(Specifics will be sent ~ the event's coordinator)이라고 했다. 환영회의 목적과 날짜, 장소는 이미 명시되어 있으므로 추가적인 세부 사항에는 시간이 포함될 것임을 짐작할 수 있다. 따라서 정답은 (D)이다.

175 문장 삽입

번역 [1], [2], [3], [4]로 표시된 곳 중에서 다음 문장이 들어가기에 가장 적합한 위치는?

"여러분의 작업 과정을 그들과 공유하고 그들의 질문에 답변해 주세요."
(A) [1]
(B) [2]
(C) [3]
(D) [4]

해설 제시된 문장에서 작업 과정을 그들과 공유하고 그들의 질문에 답변해 달라고 요청했으므로, 제시된 문장 앞에는 '그들(them, their)'이 지칭할 수 있는 사람 복수명사가 언급되어 있어야 하고, 어째서 그들과 작업을 공유하고 질문에 답변을 해야 하는지에 대한 상황이 제시되어야 적절하다. 따라서 성남전자에서 직원 단체(a group of employees)가 방문하여 우리의 연구 및 생산 방식을 관찰할 예정이라며 방문객들(visitors)이 머무는 동안 그들과 교류할 것을 권장한다는 문장 뒤에 들어가는 것이 글의 흐름상 자연스러우므로 (B)가 정답이다.

176-180 이메일 + 정책

발신: efeehan@rossfieldhotels.ie
수신: customerservice@parleganispublishing.com
179 날짜: 12월 15일
발송: 교재

고객 서비스 담당자님께:

176, 177, 179, 180 10월에 우리 회사는 직원들이 의무 사항인 식품 안전 자격증 공부를 할 수 있도록 〈식품 안전 과정 교재〉를 페이퍼백으로 60권 주문했습니다. 저는 방금 우리 관리자 중 한 명으로부터 귀사에서 이 교재를 영어 이외의 언어로도 제공한다고 들었습니다. 176, 179 영어 버전 20권을 돌려보내고 대신 폴란드어 10권과 포르투갈어 10권을 받을 수 있을까요? 신입 사원 중 일부가 이 중요한 정보를 모국어로 읽을 수 있으면 정말 감사하겠다고 했습니다.

제가 반품하기를 원하는 책들은 여전히 178 원래 포장 상태 그대로입니다. 빨리 상자에 담아 배송해 드릴 수도 있지만, 귀하의 승인과 서류

작업에 대한 안내를 기다리겠습니다.

엘라 피한
식품 서비스 책임자
로스필드 호텔

어휘 paperback 페이퍼백(종이 표지로 된 책) mandatory 의무적인 certification 자격(증) other than ~ 이외에 Polish 폴란드어 Portuguese 포르투갈어 instead 대신에 crucial 중요한 acknowledgement 승인, 인정 instruction 안내, 지시 paperwork 서류 작업

팔레가니스 출판사

반품 및 교환 정책

우리는 다음과 같은 조건하에 제품을 받습니다.

- 미표시, 미사용 물품은 구매일로부터 90일 이내에 반품 또는 교환이 가능합니다.
- ¹⁷⁹구매일로부터 30일 이상 지난 후 반품 또는 교환된 물품은 정가의 20퍼센트에 해당하는 재입고 수수료가 부과됩니다.
- ¹⁸⁰페이퍼백 책은 비닐로 포장된 열 권 묶음으로 나옵니다. 미개봉 묶음은 전액 환불 가능합니다. 개별 페이퍼백 책은 부분 환불을 받게 됩니다.
- 소프트웨어 제품 및 구독료는 환불되지 않습니다.
- 손상되거나 절판된 책에 대해서는 포인트가 발급되지 않습니다.

어휘 unmarked 표시가 없는 be subject to ~의 대상이다 restocking 재입고 cover price 정가 plastic-wrapped 비닐로 포장된 bundle 묶음 credit 금액, 돈 individual 개별의 partial 부분적인 subscription 구독 issue 발급[발행]하다 out-of-print 절판된

176 주제 / 목적

번역 피한 씨는 왜 팔레가니스 출판사에 글을 썼는가?
(A) 출판물에 대한 의견을 제공했다.
(B) 일부 교육 자료를 교환하기를 원한다.
(C) 잘못된 배송을 받았다.
(D) 손상된 책 몇 권을 반품해야 한다.

해설 이메일의 첫 문장에서 피한 씨가 10월에 우리 회사는 직원들이 의무 사항인 식품 안전 자격증 공부를 할 수 있도록 〈식품 안전 과정 교재〉를 페이퍼백으로 60권 주문했다(In October my company ordered 60 paperback ~ their mandatory food safety certification)고 했고, 영어 버전 20권을 돌려보내고 대신 폴란드어 10권과 포르투갈어 10권을 받을 수 있는지(May I send back twenty of the English ~ ten Portuguese books instead?)를 묻고 있다. 따라서 피한 씨는 주문했던 교재 중 일부를 교환하려는 목적으로 글을 쓴 것이므로 (B)가 정답이다.

어휘 publication 출판(물) incorrect 잘못된

Paraphrasing 지문의 send back ~ and get
→ 정답의 exchange

177 추론 / 암시

번역 로스필드 호텔에 대해 암시된 것은?
(A) 일부 직원들은 자격증을 취득해야 한다.
(B) 최근에 식품 서비스 관리자를 채용했다.
(C) 몇몇 유럽 국가에서 광고를 한다.
(D) 손님들 중 일부는 폴란드와 포르투갈에서 온다.

해설 이메일의 첫 문장에서 10월에 우리 회사는 직원들이 의무 사항인 식품 안전 자격증을 위한 공부를 할 수 있도록 〈식품 안전 과정 교재〉를 페이퍼백으로 60권 주문했다(In October my company ordered 60 paperback ~ their mandatory food safety certification)고 한 것으로 보아, 로스필드 호텔의 일부 직원들은 식품 안전 자격증을 의무적으로 취득해야 한다는 것을 알 수 있다. 따라서 정답은 (A)이다.

어휘 earn 취득하다 certificate 자격증

Paraphrasing 지문의 mandatory food safety certification
→ 정답의 must earn certificates

178 동의어

번역 이메일에서 두 번째 단락 1행의 "original"과 의미가 가장 가까운 단어는?
(A) 이상한
(B) 처음의
(C) 고대의
(D) 창의적인

해설 의미상 '원래의' 포장 상태 그대로라는 뜻으로 쓰인 것이므로 정답은 (B) initial이다.

179 연계

번역 로스필드 호텔은 12월에 무엇을 납부할 것 같은가?
(A) 재입고 수수료
(B) 구독료
(C) 만기가 지난 청구서
(D) 미사용 서비스에 대한 환불

해설 이메일을 작성한 날짜가 12월 15일(Date: 15 December)이고, 이메일의 첫 문장에서 10월에 우리 회사는 직원들이 의무 사항인 식품 안전 자격증 공부를 할 수 있도록 〈식품 안전 과정 교재〉를 페이퍼백으로 60권 주문했다(In October my company ordered 60 paperback ~ their mandatory food safety certification)고 했고, 영어 버전 20권을 돌려보내고 대신 폴란드어 10권과 포르투갈어 10권을 받을 수 있는지(May I send back twenty of the English ~ ten Portuguese books instead?)를 묻고 있다. 정책의 두 번째 항목에는 구매일로부터 30일 이상 지난 후 반품 또는 교환된 물품은 정가의 20퍼센트에 해당하는 재입고 수수료가 부과된다(Items returned or exchanged ~ 20% of the cover price)고 나와 있다. 10월에 주문한 물품에 대해 30일이 경과된 후인 12월에 교환을 요청하고 있으므로, 로스필드 호텔은 재입고 수수료를 지불해야 한다는 것을 알 수 있다. 따라서 정답은 (A)이다.

어휘 past-due 만기가 지난 invoice 청구서, 송장

180 연계

번역 〈식품 안전 과정 교재〉에 대해 언급된 것은?
(A) 전자 형식으로 이용 가능하다.
(B) 10월에 출판되었다.
(C) 곧 절판될 예정이다.
(D) 열 권 묶음으로 판매된다.

해설 이메일의 첫 문장에서 우리 회사는 〈식품 안전 과정 교재〉를 페이퍼백으로 60권 주문했다(my company ordered 60 paperback copies of the *Food Safety Course Book*)고 했고, 정책의 세 번째 항목에서 페이퍼백 책은 비닐로 포장된 열 권 묶음으로 나온다(Paperback books come in plastic-wrapped bundles of ten)고 했다. 호텔에서 주문한 〈식품 안전 과정 교재〉는 페이퍼백이라고 했으므로 열 권 묶음으로 포장되어 나온다는 것을 알 수 있다. 따라서 정답은 (D)이다.

어휘 electronic 전자의 format 형식 pack 묶음

> **Paraphrasing** 지문의 come in ~ bundles of ten
> → 정답의 sold in packs of ten

181-185 온라인 후기 + 메뉴

후기: 보빙워스의 피자　　　　　　**제출자: 제라드 랜디스**

★★★★☆

시내에 메이플 피자 하우스라는 새로운 피자 레스토랑이 있습니다. 놀랄 것도 없이 181그곳은 디저트 피자를 포함해 메이플 맛이 나는 다양한 시그니처 피자를 제공합니다. 나는 개인적으로 메이플 맛 피자를 전혀 좋아하지 않았지만, 183나머지 일행들은 메인 코스로 라지 사이즈 메이플 햄 피자를 즐겼습니다. 일행 다른 사람들은 메이플 호두 디저트 피자도 맛있게 먹어 치웠는데, 나한테는 너무 182달고 끈적거리는 파이 같은 맛이었습니다.

다행스럽게도 메뉴에는 메이플 맛이 나지 않는 피자도 몇몇 있었습니다. 나는 전통 치즈 피자를 주문했습니다. 그것은 아주 뜨겁게 제공되었고 맛이 있었습니다. 모두를 만족시킨 맛있는 메뉴 옵션이 있었기 때문에 메이플 피자 하우스에 별 5개 중 4개를 주며, 방문을 추천합니다.

어휘 flavoring 향료 flavored ~ 맛이 나는 party 일행, 단체 devour 먹어 치우다, 걸신 들린 듯 먹다 overly 너무 sticky 끈적한 traditional 전통의 piping hot 몹시 뜨거운 rate 평점을 매기다, 평가하다

메이플 피자 하우스
83 폭스 로, 보빙워스, CM2 9B
077 5014 0314
이제 신용카드 결제 가능합니다.

시그니처 메이플 피자 (레드 소스)	개인	183라지
치킨 메이플	4.5파운드	15파운드
183 **메이플 햄**	5파운드	183**17파운드**
파인애플	4파운드	14파운드

전통 피자 (184레드 소스 또는 화이트 소스 중 선택)		
치즈	4파운드	13파운드
채소	4파운드	13파운드
184 **미트볼**	4파운드	13파운드

185 **디저트 피자 (브라운 버터 소스)**	
시나몬 메이플	**11파운드**
메이플 호두	**11파운드**

모든 음료: 2파운드

어휘 lane 로, (좁은) 길 beverage 음료

181 세부 사항

번역 랜디스 씨는 식당의 메뉴에 대해 어떻게 생각하는가?
(A) 채식 옵션이 너무 적다.
(B) 식당의 이전 메뉴를 선호했다.
(C) 디저트 피자는 너무 비싸다.
(D) 시그니처 피자의 맛을 좋아하지 않는다.

해설 후기의 두 번째 문장에서 랜디스 씨는 식당에서 디저트 피자를 포함해 메이플 맛이 나는 다양한 시그니처 피자를 제공한다(it offers a number of signature pizzas with maple flavoring, including dessert pizzas)고 했고, 자신은 개인적으로 메이플 맛 피자를 전혀 좋아하지 않았다(I personally did not like the maple-flavored pizza at all)고 했다. 따라서 (D)가 정답이다.

어휘 care for 좋아하다

> **Paraphrasing** 지문의 like → 정답의 care for

182 동의어

번역 후기에서 첫 번째 단락 5행의 "sweet"와 의미가 가장 가까운 단어는?
(A) 중간의
(B) 기분 좋은
(C) 설탕 맛이 나는
(D) 사랑스러운

해설 의미상 '달고' 끈적거리는 맛이라는 뜻으로 쓰인 것이므로 정답은 (C) sugary이다.

183 연계

번역 랜디스 일행이 메인 코스로 주문한 피자는 얼마였는가?
(A) 5파운드
(B) 11파운드
(C) 13파운드
(D) 17파운드

해설 후기의 세 번째 문장에서 랜디스 씨가 일행들이 메인 코스로 라지 사이즈 메이플 햄 피자를 즐겼다(the rest of my party enjoyed a large maple-ham pizza as a main course)고 했고, 메뉴에 따르면 라지 사이즈(Large) 메이플 햄 피자(Maple ham)는 17파운드(£17)이다. 따라서 정답은 (D)이다.

184 세부 사항

번역 화이트 소스와 함께 제공되는 피자는?
(A) 메이플 햄
(B) 파인애플
(C) 미트볼
(D) 시나몬 메이플

해설 메뉴에 따르면 보기 중 미트볼 피자(Meatball)가 레드 소스 또는 화이트 소스 중 선택할(select red or white sauce) 수 있다고 나와 있으므로 (C)가 정답이다. (A) 메이플 햄과 (B) 파인애플 피자는 레드 소스로만 제공되고, 시나몬 메이플 피자는 브라운 버터 소스로 제공되므로 오답이다.

185 추론 / 암시

번역 식당에 대해 암시된 것은?
(A) 디저트 피자는 한 사이즈로만 준비된다.
(B) 현금으로만 결제가 가능하다.
(C) 집으로 배달을 한다.
(D) 더 큰 장소로 이전했다.

해설 메뉴에 따르면 디저트 피자(Dessert Pizzas)인 시나몬 메이플(Cinnamon maple)과 메이플 호두(Maple walnut)는 라지(Large) 사이즈로만 판매되고 있음을 알 수 있으므로 (A)가 정답이다.

186-190 웹페이지 + 문의 양식 + 이메일

---

https://www.northamcarparts.co.uk/home

| **홈** | 카탈로그 | 문의 양식 | 우리 소개 |

필요한 부품은 우리가 가지고 있습니다.

노섬 자동차 부품은 희귀하고 찾기 힘든 자동차 부품을 판매하는 선두 업체입니다. 몇 가지 예로 들자면, 자동차 변속기, 차체 및 프레임 부품, 스티어링 수리 도구 등 다양한 제품이 있습니다. 현재 창고에 준비되어 있는 상세한 부품 목록을 보시려면 온라인 카탈로그 페이지를 확인해 주세요. 저희는 빈티지 유럽 자동차를 전문으로 취급하지만, 미국산과 일본산 자동차를 위한 부품도 많이 있습니다. **188저희 카탈로그에서 필요한 제품을 찾지 못할 경우 문의 양식을 작성하시면, 필요한 부품을 찾으실 수 있도록 도와드리겠습니다!** **186저희가 받는 요청 건수가 증가하여 응답 시간이 현재 영업일 기준 2~4일임을 참고해 주십시오.**

부품은 영국, 프랑스, 벨기에, 또는 스페인의 모든 주소로 배송될 수 있습니다.

어휘 contact form 문의 양식 rare 드문 a selection of 다양한 transmission 변속기 steering-repair kit 조종 장치 수리 도구 to name a few 몇 가지 예로 들자면 detailed 상세한 warehouse 창고 specialise in ~을 전문으로 하다 plenty of 많은 fill out 작성하다 rise 증가

노섬 자동차 부품 문의 양식

연락처		차량 정보	
이름:	제럴드 알데군데	**제조업체:**	엑셀러
이메일:	carmanga55@saffronmail.de	**모델:**	드래곤파이어
전화번호:	+52 (164) 5559183	**연도:**	1988
주소:	카날스트라세 60 01067 드레스덴, 독일	**변속기:**	수동
날짜:	8월 6일	**드라이브:**	2WD

메시지:

188작년에 구입한 1988년식 엑셀러 드래곤파이어의 변속기 부품을 찾고 있습니다. 제가 이 부품을 찾지 못하고 있자 귀사를 통해 새로운 운전대를 찾은 친구가 저에게 귀사에 연락해 보라고 권했습니다. 이런 빈티지 영국 자동차 부품을 찾는 데 얼마를 청구하는지 궁금합니다. 또한 **190저는 귀사의 웹사이트에 독일이 배송지 명단에 없다는 것을 알았습니다. 현재 명단에 나와 있는 국가 이외의 지역으로 배송하기도 하나요?** 도움에 감사합니다! **187이 차를 작업하는 것은 멋진 경험이긴 하지만, 차를 도로에서 운전하고 싶은 마음이 간절합니다!**

어휘 manual 수동의 steering wheel (자동차의) 핸들 charge 청구하다 locate 찾다 destination 도착지 ship 배송하다, 수송하다 be eager to ~을 하고 싶어 하다

수신: 제럴드 알데군데 〈carmanga55@saffronmail.de〉
발신: 베서니 턴하우트 〈bturnhout@northamcarparts.co.uk〉
날짜: 8월 28일
제목: 배송 통지

알데군데 씨께,

189,190귀하의 물건은 8월 30일 늦어도 저녁 8시까지는 다음의 주소지에 도착할 예정입니다: 독일 드레스덴 카날스트라세 60, 01067. **189IHE 보험 배송 서비스를 통해 도착할 예정이므로 본인 또는 지정된 대리인이 물건을 받고 서명하기 위해 자리에 계셔야 합니다.** IHE에서 기사가 도착하기 전에 미리 연락을 드릴 것입니다. 기사가 자유롭게 출입할 수 있도록 도로에서 현관까지 가는 길에 장애물이 없는지 확인해 주십시오.

부품 마련에 도움이 될 노섬 자동차 부품을 선택해 주셔서 감사합니다!

베서니 턴하우트
노섬 자동차 부품 판매 담당자

어휘 no later than 늦어도 ~까지는, ~ 이전에 via 통하여 insured 보험에 가입된 designated 지정된 representative 대리인 present 있는 in advance 사전에 clear of ~이 없는 obstruction 장애물

186 세부 사항

번역 웹페이지에 따르면, 최근 노섬 자동차 부품에서 달라진 점은?
(A) 영업 시간
(B) 고객 문의 건수
(C) 창고 공간 용량
(D) 일본 자동차 부품 입수 가능성

해설 웹페이지의 첫 단락 여섯 번째 문장에서 자신들이 받는 요청 건수가 증가하여 응답 시간이 현재 영업일 기준 2~4일임을 참고해 달라(Please note ~ a rise in the number of requests we receive)고 했으므로, 노섬 자동차 부품에 들어오는 고객 문의가 예전보다 많아졌다는 것을 알 수 있다. 따라서 (B)가 정답이다.

어휘 inquiry 문의 availability 입수 가능성

Paraphrasing 지문의 requests → 정답의 customer inquiries

187 추론 / 암시

번역 문의 양식에서 알데군데 씨에 대해 암시된 것은?
(A) 차를 재건하는 일을 끝내고 싶어 한다.
(B) 새 핸들이 필요하다.
(C) 수년간 차를 소유해 왔다.
(D) 노섬 자동차 부품에서 일하는 친구가 있다.

해설 문의 양식의 마지막 문장에서 알데군데 씨가 이 차를 작업하는 것은 멋진 경험이긴 하지만 차를 도로에서 운전하고 싶은 마음이 간절하다(Working on this car has ~ get this thing on the road!)고 했다. 따라서 알데군데 씨는 차에 대한 정비를 어서 끝내고 주행하고 싶어 한다는 것을 알 수 있으므로 (A)가 정답이다.

188 연계

번역 알데군데 씨가 필요로 하는 부품에 대해 무엇이 사실일 것 같은가?
(A) 독일에서 제조되었다.
(B) 배송하는 데 영업일 기준 4일이 걸린다.
(C) 너무 커서 국제 운송이 어렵다.
(D) 노섬 자동차 부품의 카탈로그에 포함되어 있지 않다.

해설 웹페이지의 첫 단락 다섯 번째 문장에서 노섬 자동차 부품의 카탈로그에서 필요한 제품을 찾지 못할 경우 문의 양식을 작성하면 필요한 부품을 찾을 수 있도록 도와준다(If you do not see what you need ~ help you find the part you need!)고 했는데, 문의 양식의 첫 문장에서 알데군데 씨가 작년에 구입한 1988년식 엑셀러 드래곤파이어의 변속기 부품을 찾고 있다(I've been looking for a part ~ I purchased last year)며 문의 양식을 작성해 자동차의 부품을 구하고 있다고 문의하고 있다. 따라서 노섬 자동차 부품의 카탈로그에 알데군데 씨가 필요로 하는 부품이 기재되어 있지 않다는 것을 알 수 있으므로 정답은 (D)이다.

어휘 manufacture 제조하다 transport 운송하다

189 세부 사항

번역 이메일에 따르면, IHE가 제공하는 서비스는?
(A) 자동차 보험을 판매한다.
(B) 빈티지 자동차를 수리한다.
(C) 소포를 운송한다.
(D) 거리를 청소한다.

해설 이메일의 첫 문장에서 귀하의 물품이 8월 30일 늦어도 저녁 8시까지는 주소지에 도착할 예정(Your item will arrive on 30 August, ~ Germany)이라고 했고, IHE 보험 배송 서비스를 통해 도착할 예정(It will be arriving via the IHE insured delivery service)이라고 했다. 따라서 IHE는 물품 배송 서비스를 제공하는 업체이므로 (C)가 정답이다.

어휘 insurance 보험 transport 운송하다

Paraphrasing 지문의 delivery → 정답의 transports

190 연계

번역 노섬 자동차 부품에 대해 결론지을 수 있는 것은?
(A) 최근에 턴하우트 씨가 인수했다.
(B) 여러 국가에 창고를 가지고 있다.
(C) 웹페이지에 기재되지 않은 국가에 배송을 한다.
(D) 저녁 8시 이후에는 고객 문의에 응답하지 않는다.

해설 문의 양식의 네 번째 문장에서 알데군데 씨가 노섬 자동차 부품의 웹사이트에 독일이 배송지 명단에 없다는 것을 알았다(I noticed that ~ as a shipping destination)며 현재 명단에 나와 있는 국가 이외의 지역으로도 배송을 하는지(Do you ever ship ~ listed there?)를 문의했고, 이메일의 첫 문장에서 알데군데 씨에게 주문한 물품이 독일의 주소지에 도착할 예정(Your item will arrive ~ Dresden, Germany)이라고 했다. 따라서 웹페이지의 배송지 명단에 없는 독일로 알데군데 씨의 부품이 배송된 것이므로 (C)가 정답이다.

어휘 ship 배송[수송]하다

191-195 보도 자료 + 웹페이지 + 문자 메시지

RHC, 멈추지 않는 감동

즉시 배포용
연락처: 도라 수, +65 0555 1294

싱가포르 (8월 3일)—**191(D)5년 동안 사업을 이어가고 있는 레이더 홀딩스 코퍼레이션(RHC)**이 여섯 번째 건물 개조 프로젝트인 베이 커먼즈의 완료를 발표한다. **191(B), 191(C)부동산 중개인인 레이나 웡과 데릭 림이 설립한 이 회사는 산업용 건물을 아파트 단지로 전환하는 것을 전문으로 한다.**

"상업용 건물을 주거 공간으로 바꾸는 일에는 어려움이 있습니다."라고 웡 씨는 말했다. "하지만 우리는 새로운 건물을 짓는 대신 건물의 용도를 변경하는 데 전념하고 있습니다."

192이 같은 의지는 국가의 주택 공급에 대한 RHC의 기여에 칭찬을 아끼지 않은 싱가포르 주택도시개발부 장관 야미나 바다위의 최근 연설에서도 인용되었다.

193RHC는 4년 전 첫 전환 프로젝트인 칼랑 오버룩 아파트 단지를 완공했다. 이후 RHC는 아스텐 에스테이츠, 탐핀즈 타워, 레이크사이드 매너, 이슌 테라스, 그리고 현재 베이 커먼즈까지 다섯 건의 추가 프로젝트를 완공했다.

"베이 커먼즈는 당사의 이전 프로젝트로부터의 탈피를 의미합니다."라고 웡 씨는 말했다. "이 주택 단지는 주로 인근의 창이 기술학교 학생들을 위해 설계되었습니다." 그녀는 베이 커먼즈의 각 세대들이 현재 임대 또는 구매 가능하다고 덧붙였다.

어휘 impress 감동을 주다 immediate 즉각적인 release (신문 기사) 발표, 배포 found 설립하다 real estate agent 부동산 중개인 specialize in ~을 전문으로 하다 convert 전환하다 complex 단지 commercial 상업적인 residential

주거의 challenge 어려움, 도전 be committed to ~에 전념하다 repurpose 다른 용도에 맞게 고치다 commitment 의지, 헌신 cite 인용하다 minister 장관 applaud 칭찬하다 contribution 기여 housing supply 주택 공급 conversion 전환 represent 나타내다 departure 벗어남, (새로운) 시도 unit (공동 주택의) 한 세대[가구]

---

https://www.rayderholdingscorporation.com.sg/current-listings

| 우리 소개 | 현재 목록 | 소식 | 채용 |

레이더 홀딩스 코퍼레이션은 비어 있는 상업용 건물을 쾌적한 주거용 건축물로 바꿉니다. 아래는 현재 당사가 제공 중인 건물을 알파벳 순서로 나열한 것입니다.

아스텐 에스테이츠: 수영장, 피트니스 센터, 주차장이 있는 14세대 건물

베이 커먼즈: 공유 주방과 기타 휴게실이 있는 60개의 원룸 아파트

193**칼랑 오버룩:** 칼랑 강변에 위치한 40세대 아파트 단지

195**레이크사이드 매너:** 실내 수영장, 야외 테니스 및 농구 코트, 놀이터, 구내식당이 있는 28세대 건물

탐핀즈 타워: 수영장과 피트니스 룸이 있는 36세대 아파트 단지

이슌 테라스: 야외 체육 시설(테니스, 농구, 축구), 실내 수영장, 포획 후 방생하는 낚시터, 피크닉장을 갖춘 55세대 아파트 단지

자세한 내용 및 기타 문의 사항은 info@rayderholdingscorporation.com.sg로 연락하십시오.

어휘 vacant 비어 있는 property 부동산, 건물 pleasant 쾌적한 offering 제공품, 매물 alphabetical order 알파벳 순서 studio apartment 원룸 아파트 common room 휴게실 situated 위치해 있는 on-site 현장의 facility 시설 release 풀어 주다 query 문의

오늘 오전 9시 53분

안녕하세요, 고 씨. 194,195**다른 주민 한 분이 구내식당 카운터에서 당신의 지갑을 발견하고 여기 RHC 임대 사무소에 갖다 놓으셨습니다.** 194**오셔서 가져가시기 바랍니다.** 사무실은 오후 6시까지 열려 있습니다. 영업 시간 이후에는 0904 6802로 전화하시면 도와드릴 분이 계실 거예요.

알리시아 라자니, 임대 사무소장

어휘 fellow (같은 그룹이나 상황에 있는) 사람, 동료 resident 주민 drop off 갖다 놓다 leasing 임대 after-hours 영업[근무] 시간 이후, 퇴근 후

191 Not / True

번역 보도 자료에 따르면, RHC에 대해 사실인 것은?
(A) 국제적인 영향력이 있다.
(B) 작업 공간을 설계하는 것을 전문으로 한다.
(C) 두 명의 건설 엔지니어에 의해 설립되었다.
(D) 5년 동안 사업을 지속해 왔다.

해설 보도 자료의 첫 문장에서 5년 동안 사업을 이어가고 있는 레이더 홀딩스 코퍼레이션 (RHC)(In operation for five years, Rayder Holdings Corporation (RHC))이라고 소개했으므로 정답은 (D)이다. 국제적인 영향력에 대한 언급은 없으므로 (A)는 오답, 부동산 중개인인 레이나 웡과 데릭 림이 설립한 이 회사는 산업용 건물을 아파트 단지로 전환하는 것을 전문으로 한다(The company, founded by real estate agents ~ into apartment complexes)고 했으므로 (B)와 (C) 또한 오답이다.

어휘 presence 영향력, 존재

192 추론 / 암시

번역 보도 자료에서 바다위 씨에 대해 암시하는 것은?
(A) 그녀는 주택 공급 확장에 대한 RHC의 접근 방식을 높이 평가한다.
(B) 그녀는 RHC의 부동산 중 한 곳에 집을 갖고 있다.
(C) 그녀는 창이 기술학교에서 학생들에게 조언을 해 준다.
(D) 그녀는 림 씨를 자신의 고문으로 고용했다.

해설 보도 자료의 세 번째 단락에서 웡 씨의 의지는 국가의 주택 공급에 대한 RHC의 기여에 칭찬을 아끼지 않은 싱가포르 주택도시개발부 장관 야미나 바다위의 최근 연설에서 인용되었다(This commitment was ~ nation's housing supply)고 했으므로 (A)가 정답이다.

어휘 appreciate 높이 평가하다 approach 접근 방식 adviser 고문

> **Paraphrasing** 지문의 applauded → 정답의 appreciates

193 연계

번역 RHC가 건설한 첫 번째 단지에는 몇 세대가 있는가?
(A) 14
(B) 28
(C) 40
(D) 60

해설 보도 자료의 네 번째 단락 첫 문장에서 RHC는 4년 전 첫 전환 프로젝트인 칼랑 오버룩 아파트 단지를 완공했다(RHC completed its first ~ Kallang Overlook apartment complex)고 했고, 웹페이지의 세 번째 항목에 칼랑 오버룩은 칼랑 강변에 위치한 40세대 아파트 단지(Kallang Overlook : 40-unit apartment complex situated on the Kallang River)라고 나와 있다. 따라서 정답은 (C)이다.

194 주제 / 목적

번역 라자니 씨는 왜 고 씨에게 문자를 보냈는가?
(A) 그에게 새 이웃을 소개하려고
(B) 그의 지갑이 발견되었다는 것을 알리려고
(C) 정보에 대한 그의 요청에 응답하려고
(D) 임대 사무소의 영업 시간을 제공하려고

해설 문자 메시지의 두 번째 문장에서 라자니 씨가 고 씨에게 다른 주민 한 분이 구내식당 카운터에서 당신의 지갑을 발견하고 여기 RHC 임대 사무소에 맡겨 놓으셨다(A fellow resident found your wallet ~ at the RHC leasing office)며 오셔서 가져가시기 바란다(Please stop by to pick it up)고 했으므로 (B)가 정답이다.

195 연계

번역 고 씨는 어디에서 거주할 것 같은가?
(A) 아스텐 에스테이츠
(B) 레이크사이드 매너
(C) 탐핀즈 타워
(D) 이슌 테라스

해설 웹페이지의 네 번째 항목에 레이크사이드 매너는 실내 수영장, 야외 테니스 및 농구 코트, 놀이터, 구내식당이 있는 28세대 건물 (Lakeside Manor ~ on-site cafeteria)이라고 했고, 문자 메시지의 두 번째 문장에서 라자니 씨가 고 씨에게 주민이 구내식당 카운터에서 당신의 지갑을 발견하고 여기 RHC 임대 사무소에 맡겨 놓았다 (A fellow resident found your wallet ~ at the RHC leasing office)고 했다. 레이크사이드 매너는 웹페이지에 나열된 부동산 중 구내식당이 있는 유일한 곳이므로 (B)가 정답이다.

196-200 웹페이지 + 문자 메시지 + 온라인 후기

---

https://www.camsfurniture.ca/about_us

| **소개** | 카탈로그 | 후기 | 연락처 |

캠스 퍼니처는 50년 이상 오타와에서 터줏대감이었습니다. 뛰어난 고객 서비스에 집중함으로써 우리는 우리 매장에서 보내는 여러분의 시간이 쾌적하고 가치 있는 시간이 될 것을 보장합니다.

196 우리의 일상적인 사업 운영은 창업자인 캠 메어라의 장남 조지 메어라가 감독합니다. 조지는 그의 여동생 엘리스 메어라, 그리고 여러분이 필요로 하는 최고의 가구를 고를 수 있도록 도와줄 열정적인 판매 사원팀과 함께합니다. 우리의 거대한 쇼룸은 여러 유형의 주거 및 사무실 공간에 배치된 다양한 고품질 가구로 특색을 이루고 있습니다. 그리고 모든 최고의 가구 브랜드와 더불어 **199** 그린 디렉션 무역 박람회에서 입수한 독특하고 환경 친화적인 품목들을 취급하는 것을 자랑스럽게 생각합니다. 우리의 수석 구매 담당인 데비 사르노는 우리 매장을 위한 멋진 신제품을 선정하기 위해 이 행사에 매년 참석합니다.

198 우리는 집이나 업체가 오타와 시 경계 내에 있는 모든 고객에게 무료 배송 및 설치를 제공합니다.

어휘 fixture (같은 자리에) 오래 있어 온 사람[것], 터줏대감 exceptional 뛰어난 guarantee 보장하다 worthwhile 가치 있는 oversee 감독하다 eldest 가장 나이가 많은 enthusiastic 열정적인 sales associate 판매 사원 enormous 거대한 feature ~로 특색을 이루다 arrange 배치하다 carry 취급하다 environmentally friendly 환경 친화적인 source 얻다 complimentary 무료의 setup 설치 boundary 경계

린다 페이 (오후 1시 57분)
토비, 전 지금 캠스 퍼니처에 있어요. 우리 리셉션 구역을 위해 고르신 제품들이 훌륭하네요! **198** 판매원이 배송비와 설치비가 발생할 거라서 청구 금액이 예상보다 조금 더 나올 거라고 말했어요. **197** 작업팀이 금요일에 우리 사무실로 올 수 있으니, 월요일에 고객들이 도착하기 전에 모든 준비가 확실히 완료될 거예요.

토비 페센티 (오후 1시 59분)
좋아요! 비용이 약간 더 나오는 것은 문제가 되지 않을 겁니다. 예산은 충분합니다.

어휘 bill 청구서 charge 요금 crew 작업팀 definitely 확실히 in place 준비가 된, 제 자리에 있는

온라인 후기

7월 23일 오후 5시 32분에 린다 페이가 게시한 고객 후기

캠스 퍼니처의 직원들은 엄청나게 도움이 되고 전문적이에요. **199** 우리 회사의 리셉션 구역을 위해 친환경적인 가구를 구할 수 있어서 기뻤습니다. 가구는 정말 아름다워서 칭찬을 많이 받았어요. **200** 캠스의 배송팀은 가구가 정확하게 제대로 배치되도록 하기 위해 우리의 새 사무실 공간에서 시간을 추가로 더 보냈어요. 우리는 캠스 퍼니처에서 다시 쇼핑할 것을 기대합니다!

어휘 extraordinarily 엄청나게 eco-friendly 환경 친화적인 compliment 칭찬

196 추론 / 암시

번역 웹페이지에서 캠스 퍼니처에 대해 암시하는 것은?
(A) 현재 새로운 직원을 채용 중이다.
(B) 매장이 두 곳 있다.
(C) 가족 사업이다.
(D) 중고 가구를 전문으로 한다.

해설 웹페이지의 두 번째 단락 첫 문장에서 우리의 일상적인 사업 운영은 창업자인 캠 메어라의 장남 조지 메어라가 감독한다(Our daily business operations ~ son of founder Cam Meara)고 한 뒤, 조지는 그의 여동생 엘리스 메어라와 함께 한다(George is joined by his sister, Elise Meara)고 한 것으로 보아 캠스 퍼니처는 가족이 운영하는 사업체임을 알 수 있으므로 (C)가 정답이다.

어휘 specialize in ~을 전문으로 하다 used 중고의

> **Paraphrasing** 지문의 the eldest son of founder / his sister
> → 정답의 family

197 세부 사항

번역 문자 메시지에서 페이 씨가 월요일에 일어날 일이라고 언급하는 것은?
(A) 가구들이 배송될 것이다.
(B) 고객들이 방문할 것이다.
(C) 청구서가 전액 지불될 것이다.
(D) 리셉션 구역이 리모델링을 위해 폐쇄될 것이다.

해설 문자 메시지에서 1시 57분에 페이 씨가 작업팀이 금요일에 사무실로 올 수 있으니 월요일에 고객들이 도착하기 전에 모든 준비가 확실히 완료될 것(The crew can come out ~ our clients arrive on Monday)이라고 했다. 따라서 (B)가 정답이다.

> **Paraphrasing** 지문의 arrive → 정답의 visit

198 연계

번역 페이 씨의 회사에 대해 암시된 것은?
(A) 가격을 올렸다.
(B) 오타와 외곽에 위치해 있다.
(C) 인테리어 디자인 회사이다.
(D) 최근에 다른 조직과 합병했다.

해설 웹페이지의 마지막 문장에서 우리는 집이나 업체가 오타와 시 경계 내에 있는 모든 고객에게 무료 배송 및 설치를 제공한다(We offer complimentary delivery ~ the city of Ottawa)고 했고, 문자 메시지에서 1시 57분에 페이 씨가 판매원이 배송비와 설치비가 발생할 거라서 청구 금액이 예상보다 조금 더 나올 거라고 말했다(The salesperson told me ~ charge for delivery and setup)고 했다. 따라서 배송비와 설치비가 발생한다는 것으로 보아 페이 씨의 회사는 오타와 시 경계 내에 위치하고 있지 않다는 것을 알 수 있으므로 (B)가 정답이다.

어휘 merge 합병하다   organization 조직, 기관

Paraphrasing 지문의 spent extra time → 정답의 stayed for longer

199 연계

번역 페이 씨의 회사가 구입한 새 가구에 대해 결론지을 수 있는 것은?
(A) 사르노 씨가 조달했다.
(B) 환불 보증이 된다.
(C) 실내나 야외에서 사용할 수 있다.
(D) 페이 씨에게서 구입했다.

해설 웹페이지의 두 번째 단락 네 번째 문장에서 그린 디렉션 무역 박람회에서 입수한 환경 친화적인 품목들을 취급하는 것을 자랑스럽게 생각한다(we are proud to carry ~ the Green Directions Trade Fair)며 수석 구매 담당인 데비 사르노가 매장을 위한 멋진 신제품을 선정하기 위해 이 행사에 매년 참석한다(Our head buyer, Debbie Sarno, attends ~ new products for our store)고 했고, 온라인 후기의 두 번째 문장에서 페이 씨가 우리 회사의 리셉션 구역을 위해 친환경적인 가구를 구할 수 있어서 기뻤다(I was pleased ~ for our company's reception area)고 했다. 페이 씨의 회사가 구입한 가구가 친환경 가구라고 한 점으로 보아 캠스 퍼니처의 수석 구매 담당인 데비 사르노가 박람회에서 공수해 온 물건임을 알 수 있다. 따라서 (A)가 정답이다.

어휘 money-back guarantee 환불 보증

200 Not / True

번역 온라인 후기에서 페이 씨가 배송팀원들에 대해 명시하는 것은?
(A) 맞춤형 장비를 사용했다.
(B) 새 가구를 잘못 배치했다.
(C) 오래된 가구를 치워주겠다고 제안했다.
(D) 예상보다 더 오래 머물렀다.

해설 온라인 후기의 네 번째 문장에서 페이 씨가 캠스의 배송팀은 가구가 정확하게 제대로 배치되도록 하기 위해 우리의 새 사무실 공간에서 추가적인 시간을 보냈다(Cam's delivery team spent extra time ~ in exactly the right way)고 했으므로 (D)가 정답이다.

어휘 custom-made 맞춤형의   equipment 장비   incorrectly 잘못, 부정확하게   haul away 운반해 가다

실전 TEST 9

101 (A)	**102** (D)	**103** (C)	**104** (C)	**105** (B)
106 (A)	**107** (D)	**108** (C)	**109** (D)	**110** (A)
111 (D)	**112** (B)	**113** (D)	**114** (D)	**115** (C)
116 (A)	**117** (C)	**118** (B)	**119** (A)	**120** (C)
121 (A)	**122** (C)	**123** (B)	**124** (B)	**125** (D)
126 (D)	**127** (C)	**128** (A)	**129** (B)	**130** (B)
131 (D)	**132** (C)	**133** (D)	**134** (A)	**135** (C)
136 (B)	**137** (B)	**138** (A)	**139** (C)	**140** (D)
141 (A)	**142** (B)	**143** (B)	**144** (B)	**145** (C)
146 (A)	**147** (C)	**148** (D)	**149** (D)	**150** (C)
151 (B)	**152** (C)	**153** (A)	**154** (D)	**155** (B)
156 (C)	**157** (D)	**158** (C)	**159** (A)	**160** (D)
161 (B)	**162** (A)	**163** (B)	**164** (C)	**165** (A)
166 (D)	**167** (B)	**168** (A)	**169** (D)	**170** (D)
171 (B)	**172** (A)	**173** (A)	**174** (D)	**175** (D)
176 (C)	**177** (C)	**178** (D)	**179** (D)	**180** (B)
181 (B)	**182** (A)	**183** (B)	**184** (C)	**185** (D)
186 (D)	**187** (C)	**188** (B)	**189** (D)	**190** (C)
191 (C)	**192** (B)	**193** (C)	**194** (A)	**195** (B)
196 (A)	**197** (C)	**198** (D)	**199** (B)	**200** (B)

PART 5

101 전치사 어휘

해설 빈칸 뒤에 시각을 나타내는 명사구인 6:00 A.M.이 왔고, '아침 6시에'라는 의미가 되어야 하므로 시간 전치사인 (A) at이 정답이다.

번역 에디슨 딜리버리의 트럭은 매일 아침 6시 정각에 창고를 출발한다.

어휘 warehouse 창고 promptly 정확히 제 시간에

102 형용사 자리 _ 명사 수식 _ 과거분사

해설 빈칸은 부정관사와 명사 사이에 있으므로, 뒤의 명사 copy를 수식하는 형용사 또는 복합명사를 이루는 명사가 들어갈 수 있다. 문맥상 '서명이 된 사본'이라는 뜻이 되어야 자연스러우므로 명사를 수식하는 과거분사 (D) signed가 정답이다.

번역 아파트 임대 계약서에 서명이 된 사본이 본사로 배송되었다.

어휘 agreement 계약(서)

103 명사 자리 _ 동사의 주어

해설 빈칸은 동사 can be made의 주어 자리이므로 명사가 들어가야 한다. 따라서 명사 (C) Reservations가 정답이다.

번역 예약은 오전 6시 30분에서 오후 5시 30분 사이에 온라인에서 또는 고객 서비스로 전화 주시면 가능합니다.

104 부사 자리 _ 동사 수식

해설 접속사 and 앞 빈칸이 있는 절은 Ms. Shimabukuro가 주어, rose가 동사인 완전한 문장으로, 자동사 rise는 부사나 전치사구와 함께 쓰이며 목적어가 필요 없다. 따라서 빈칸에는 동사 rose를 수식하는 부사가 들어가야 하므로 (C) quickly가 정답이다.

번역 시마부쿠로 씨는 빠르게 승진하여 2년도 채 안 되어 관리자가 되었다.

어휘 rank 지위, 등급 quicken 빨라지다, 빠르게 하다

105 동사 어휘

해설 빈칸 앞 be동사와 함께 수동태를 이루는 과거분사 자리로, 뒤에 '보수 공사를 하기 위해'라는 내용이 이어지는 것으로 보아 박물관이 '문을 닫는다'는 의미가 되어야 적절하다. 따라서 '문을 닫은, 폐쇄된'이라는 의미를 가진 (B) closed가 정답이다.

번역 하이랜드 로봇 박물관은 추후 공지가 있을 때까지 보수를 위해 폐관될 예정이다.

어휘 renovation 보수, 수리 further 추가의 notice 공지

106 형용사 자리 _ 명사 수식

해설 빈칸은 소유격과 명사 사이에서 명사 athletes을 수식하는 형용사 자리이다. 따라서 '매우 좋아하는'이라는 의미의 형용사인 (A) favorite이 정답이다.

번역 홀리타운 아레나는 매 경기가 끝난 뒤 팬들이 좋아하는 운동선수를 만날 수 있는 장소를 지정한다.

어휘 designate 지정하다 athlete 운동선수

107 전치사 어휘

해설 빈칸 뒤에 넓은 장소를 나타내는 명사가 있고, '상업 지구에 설치될 때'라는 의미가 되어야 하므로 '~에'를 의미하는 (D) in이 정답이다.

번역 법률 서비스를 광고하는 옥외 광고판은 상업 지구에 설치될 때 가장 효과적이다.

어휘 billboard 옥외 광고판 legal 법률의 district 지구, 지역

108 형용사 어휘

해설 빈칸 뒤의 전치사 with와 어울려 쓸 수 있어야 하며, 문맥상 '도매 가격에 만족했다'는 내용이 되어야 자연스럽다. 따라서 be pleased with로 자주 쓰여 '~에 만족[흡족]하다'라는 의미를 나타내는 과거분사 (C) pleased가 정답이다.

번역 우에다 씨는 리스 국제 레스토랑 공급업체가 제공하는 도매 가격에 상당히 만족했다.

어휘 quite 상당히 wholesale 도매의 supplier 공급업체[자]

109 부사 자리 _ 준동사 수식

해설 빈칸이 없어도 완전한 문장을 이루고 있으므로 부사가 들어가면

된다. 따라서 앞에 있는 과거분사 written을 수식해 '전문가를 위해 특별히 작성된'이라는 의미를 만드는 '특별히'라는 뜻의 부사 (D) specifically가 정답이다.

번역 〈월간 지질학〉은 이 분야의 전문가들을 위해 특별히 작성된 기사로 구성된 전문 학술지이다.

어휘 geology 지질학   expert 전문가   field 분야   specify 명시하다

110 전치사 자리

해설 빈칸은 콤마 뒤에 오는 완전한 절에 명사구 the year-end sale을 연결하는 자리이므로 전치사가 들어가야 한다. 따라서 '~ 동안'이라는 의미의 전치사 (A) During이 정답이다.

번역 아서스 캠핑 용품의 연말 세일 기간 동안, 모든 겨울 품목은 25퍼센트 할인된다.

어휘 year-end 연말(의)   supplies 용품

111 형용사 자리 _ 명사 수식

해설 빈칸은 정관사와 명사 사이에서 명사 future를 수식하는 형용사 자리이다. 따라서 '가까운'이라는 뜻의 형용사 (D) near가 정답이다.

번역 가까운 미래에, 오크 대로와 프림로즈 가의 모퉁이에 철물점이 문을 열 예정이다.

어휘 hardware store 철물점

112 부정대명사

해설 동사 requested의 목적어 역할을 하는 that절에 주어가 없으므로 빈칸은 that절의 동사인 come의 주어 자리이다. 따라서 보기 중 유일하게 주어 역할을 할 수 있는 '어떤 사람, 누군가'라는 뜻의 부정대명사 (B) someone이 정답이다.

번역 카레니 씨는 기술 지원팀에서 누군가가 해리스버그 사무실로 즉시 와 줄 것을 요청했다.

어휘 immediately 즉시

113 부사 어휘

해설 빈칸 뒤의 형용사 unavailable을 수식하여 '잠시 이용이 불가능했다'는 내용이 되어야 적절하므로 '잠시'라는 뜻의 (D) briefly가 정답이다.

번역 시간 입력 시스템은 오늘 오후에 잠시 이용이 불가능했지만, 지금은 정상적으로 작동하고 있다.

어휘 entry 입력   function 작동하다   normally 정상적으로
directly 직접적으로   urgently 긴급히   precisely 정확히

114 동사 자리 _ 복합문제

해설 빈칸은 단수 주어 The upcoming career fair의 동사 자리로, 단수 동사가 와야 하므로 (A)와 (B)는 답이 될 수 없다. 또한 타동사 attend 뒤에 목적어가 아닌 전치사 by가 이끄는 전치사구가 왔으므로 정답은 수동태인 (D) will be attended이다.

번역 곧 있을 취업 박람회에는 100여 명의 고용주와 채용 대행업체가 참석할 예정이다.

어휘 upcoming 곧 있을   fair 박람회   recruiting 직원 채용

115 수량 형용사

해설 빈칸은 가산 단수명사 theater를 수식하는 형용사 자리이고, '각 상영관'이라는 의미가 되어야 자연스러우므로 '각각의'라는 뜻의 수량 형용사 (C) Each가 정답이다. (B) Much는 뒤에 불가산명사가 와야 하고, (D) All은 가산 복수명사 또는 불가산명사가 와야 한다.

번역 랜던 시네마의 각 상영관은 각기 다른 주제로 장식되어 있다.

어휘 decorate 장식하다   theme 주제, 테마

116 접속사 자리 _ 부사절 접속사

해설 빈칸 뒤에 주어와 동사를 갖춘 완전한 절이 왔으므로 부사절 접속사가 들어가야 하고, '아카데미가 새 플랫폼으로 전환하는 동안'이라는 의미가 되어야 자연스러우므로 '~하는 동안'이라는 뜻의 접속사 (A) while이 정답이다.

번역 살리나스 아카데미가 새로운 온라인 플랫폼으로 전환하는 동안 강좌 내용 변경이 중단되었다.

어휘 halt 중단하다   transition 전환하다   regarding ~에 관하여

117 부사 자리 _ 동사 수식

해설 빈칸은 조동사 will과 동사원형 help 사이에 있으므로 동사를 수식하는 부사 자리이다. 따라서 '직접'이라는 의미의 부사 (C) personally가 정답이다.

번역 브릭타운의 줄리안 트렌트 시장은 이번 주말 에반스 공원에 화초를 심는 것을 직접 도울 예정이다.

어휘 mayor 시장   plant 심다   personalize 개인화하다

118 형용사 어휘

해설 명사 pages를 수식하여 '(최신 정보로) 업데이트된 페이지로 교체해 달라'는 내용이 되어야 자연스러우므로 '최신의, 업데이트된'이라는 뜻의 (B) updated가 정답이다.

번역 직원 안내서의 28~35페이지를 업데이트된 페이지로 교체해 주세요.

어휘 handbook 안내서   careful 세심한   consistent 일관된
sizable 상당한

119 접속사 자리 _ 부사절 접속사

해설 빈칸 뒤에 있는 주어와 동사를 갖춘 완전한 절을 콤마 뒤의 절에 연결하는 자리이므로 부사절 접속사가 들어가야 한다. '인터넷 속도를 높여서 훨씬 빨리 다운로드할 수 있다'는 내용이 되어야 자연스러우므로 '~ 때문에, ~해서'라는 이유의 뜻을 나타내는 (A) Since가 정답이다.

번역 인터넷 속도를 높였기 때문에 대용량 문서를 훨씬 더 빠르게 다운로드할 수 있다.

어휘 provided (만약) ~라면

120 동사 자리 _ 태

해설 빈칸은 which 이하 명사절의 동사 자리이고, 빈칸 뒤에 타동사 send의 목적어가 아닌 전치사 to가 이끄는 전치사구가 왔으므로 수동태인 (C) should be sent가 정답이다.

번역 수석 그래픽 아티스트는 프리랜서가 제출한 사진 중 어떤 것을 크리에이티브 디렉터에게 보내야 할지 결정한다.

어휘 lead 수석   submit 제출하다

121 접속사 자리 _ 부사절 접속사

해설 빈칸 뒤 주어와 동사를 갖춘 완전한 절을 콤마 뒤의 절에 연결하는 자리이므로 부사절 접속사가 들어가야 하고, '호텔을 방문할 때마다'라는 내용이 되어야 자연스러우므로 '~할 때마다'라는 뜻의 (A) Whenever가 정답이다. 참고로, (B) Whichever도 '어느 쪽을 ~하든'이라는 의미로 양보의 부사절을 이끌 수 있지만, 뒤에 주어나 목적어가 빠진 불완전한 절이 온다.

번역 스타 호텔을 방문하실 때마다 활기찬 직원들이 환영받는 느낌을 받게 해 드립니다.

어휘 cheerful 활기찬, 쾌활한   nevertheless 그럼에도 불구하고   altogether 전체적으로 보아

122 부사 어휘

해설 빈칸 뒤 deciding to go to business school을 수식하여 '궁극적으로 경영대학원에 가기로 결정하기 전에'라는 의미가 되어야 자연스러우므로 '궁극적으로, 결국'이라는 뜻의 (C) ultimately가 정답이다.

번역 마틀루 씨는 경영대학원에 가기로 최종 결정하기 전에 법률 직종을 고려했다.

어휘 legal 법률의   strictly 엄격히   politely 정중히   slightly 약간

123 명사 자리 _ 주격 보어

해설 빈칸은 동사 is의 주격 보어 자리로, 빈칸 앞에 부정관사 a가 있고 뒤에 수식어 역할을 하는 분사구가 이어지고 있으므로 단수명사가 와야 한다. 문맥상 '한 세기 전으로 거슬러 올라가는 전통'이라는 내용이 되어야 자연스러우므로 '전통'이라는 뜻의 명사 (B) tradition이 정답이다.

번역 축제의 참석자들이 콘서트 홀의 잔디밭에서 피크닉 점심을 즐기는 것은 거의 한 세기 전으로 거슬러 올라가는 전통이다.

어휘 patron 이용객   date back ~까지 거슬러 올라가다   century 세기   traditionalist 전통주의자

124 동사 어휘

해설 빈칸은 주어 Many People의 동사 자리로, 빈칸 뒤 목적어 their online shopping carts와 잘 어울려야 한다. 문맥상 '배송료를 파악하고 나면 온라인 장바구니를 포기해 버린다'는 내용이 되어야 자연스러우므로 '버리다, 포기하다'라는 의미의 (B) abandon이 정답이다.

번역 많은 사람들이 배송료가 얼마가 될지 알게 되면 온라인 장바구니를 포기해 버린다.

어휘 shipping charge 배송료   eject 쫓아내다   resign 사직하다   discourage 단념시키다

125 명사 어휘

해설 관광 웹사이트에서 제공하는 정보의 종류에 대해 언급하고 있으므로 '지역의 인기 있는 명소'라는 의미가 되어야 적절하다. 따라서 '명소'를 뜻하는 (D) attractions가 정답이다.

번역 주에서 운영하는 관광 웹사이트는 지역의 많은 인기 있는 명소들에 대한 정보를 제공한다.

어휘 state 주   situation 상황   appeal 매력   demand 요구

126 지시대명사

해설 빈칸이 동사 should attend의 주어 자리이며, 문맥상 '조각품에 대해 더 알고자 하는 사람들'이라는 의미가 되어야 하므로 '사람들'을 뜻하는 대명사 (D) Those가 정답이다. 참고로, (B) Whoever는 접속사이므로 주절의 동사 should attend 외에 동사가 하나 더 있어야 하며, (C) Each other는 주어 역할을 하지 않으므로 오답이다.

번역 샤나 파비안의 조각품에 대해 더 알고자 하는 사람들은 5월 2일 디애나 갤러리에서 열리는 그녀의 강연에 참석해야 한다.

어휘 sculpture 조각품

127 부사 어휘

해설 합병이 몇 달간의 협상 끝에 해결되었다는 내용이므로 '마침내 해결되었다'는 의미가 되어야 적절하므로 '마침내'라는 뜻의 (C) finally가 정답이다.

번역 오즈나제와 텔루리스크 회사 사이의 합병은 몇 달간의 힘든 협상 끝에 마침내 해결되었다.

어휘 merger 합병   settle 해결하다   tough 힘든   negotiation 협상   instantly 즉시

128 전치사 자리

해설 빈칸 앞의 완전한 절에 명사구 two to three days를 연결하는 자리이므로 전치사가 들어가야 한다. 따라서 기간을 나타내는 명사와 함께 쓰여 '~ 이내에'를 뜻하는 전치사 (A) within이 정답이다.

번역 자동차 부품은 고객이 긴급 배송을 요청하지 않는 한 2~3일 이내에 배송됩니다.

어휘 part 부품   expedite 신속히 처리하다

129 형용사 어휘

해설 명사 colors를 수식하기에 적절한 형용사를 고르는 문제이다. 디자이너가 '매우 강렬한 색상'을 선택했다는 의미가 가장 자연스러우므로 '강렬한'이라는 뜻의 (B) intense가 정답이다.

번역 인테리어 디자이너는 로비 벽에 매우 강렬한 색상을 선택했다.

어휘 massive 거대한 direct 직접적인 sudden 갑작스러운

130 명사 어휘

해설 문맥상 '주기적인 간격으로 점검되어야 한다'는 내용이 되어야 자연스러우므로 '간격'을 뜻하는 (B) intervals가 정답이다.

번역 전문가들은 냉방 시스템이 주기적으로 서비스 기술자에 의해 점검될 것을 권장한다.

어휘 cooling 냉방 expanse 넓은 공간 classification 분류 detachment 분리

PART 6

131-134 이메일

수신: 로저 월 〈rogerwall@openemail.com〉
발신: 기예르모 토레스 〈gtorres@supplyflow.com〉
날짜: 5월 2일
제목: 답장: 배송 누락

월 씨께,

이것은 고객님께서 사무용품 4월 배송을 받지 못했다고 알려 주신 **131최근** 이메일에 대한 답변입니다. 고객님의 연간 구독은 최신 업데이트된 상태이고 고객님 측에서는 잘못된 것이 없음을 확인했습니다. 그러므로 이 오류는 **132저희** 측의 실수입니다. 저희가 새로운 배송 소프트웨어로 전환을 했는데, 일부 고객 정보가 제대로 옮겨지지 않았습니다. 이 문제는 해결되었으며 다시는 오류가 **133발생하지** 않을 것이니 안심하십시오.

익일 배송 서비스를 이용하여 고객님의 사무용품이 담긴 상자를 오늘 발송했습니다. **134내일 받으실 수 있을 겁니다.** 상자 안에는 기다려 주신 데 대한 감사의 표시도 찾으실 수 있을 겁니다.

더 궁금하신 점이나 우려 사항이 있으시면 주저하지 마시고 저에게 바로 연락 주십시오.

서플라이 플로우 주식회사, 고객 지원 담당, 기예르모 토레스

어휘 in response to ~에 답하여 verify 확인하다 subscription 구독 up-to-date 최신의 in order 제대로 된 oversight 실수, 간과 transition 전환하다 transfer 옮기다 rest assured that (~임을) 믿고 안심[확신]해도 된다 overnight shipping 익일 배송 complimentary 무료의, 칭찬의 token 표시, 징표 appreciation 감사 patience 인내심 hesitate 주저하다 directly 바로

131 형용사 어휘

해설 이메일의 제목에 따르면 이 글이 배송 누락이라는 이메일에 대한 답장임을 알 수 있으므로, 이 이메일은 4월 배송물을 받지 못했음을 알려 준 최근 이메일에 대한 답변이라는 내용이 되어야 자연스럽다. 따라서 '최근의'를 뜻하는 (D) recent가 정답이다.

어휘 constant 끊임없는 nearby 인근의

132 인칭대명사의 격 _ 소유격

해설 이 이메일은 서플라이 플로우의 직원인 토레스 씨가 고객인 월 씨에게 보낸 글로, 빈칸 앞 문장에서 고객인 월 씨의 연간 구독이 최신 업데이트된 상태이고 월 씨 측에는 잘못이 없음을 확인했다고 했으므로 이 오류는 서플라이 플로우 즉, 토레스 씨 회사 측의 실수라는 내용이 되어야 적합하다. 따라서 '우리 회사의, 당사의'를 뜻하는 (C) our가 정답이다.

133 동사 어휘

해설 문맥상 적절한 동사이면서 빈칸 뒤에 목적어가 없으므로 자동사가 들어가야 한다. 앞 문장에서 문제가 발생한 이유를 새로운 소프트웨어에 일부 고객 정보가 제대로 옮겨지지 않았기 때문이라고 설명하면서 이 문제가 해결되었다고 했으므로, 이러한 오류가 또다시 발생하지 않을 것이라고 안심시키는 내용이 되어야 자연스럽다. 따라서 '발생하다'를 뜻하는 자동사 (D) occur가 정답이다.

어휘 combine 결합하다 revise 수정하다 affect 영향을 미치다

134 문맥에 맞는 문장 고르기

해설 빈칸 앞에서 사무용품 상자(your box of office supplies)를 익일 배송(overnight shipping service)으로 오늘 발송했다고 했으므로, 배송 도착일이 내일임을 알 수 있다. 또한, 빈칸 뒤에는 상자 안에 담긴 또 다른 내용물에 대해서 언급하고 있으므로 빈칸에는 택배 수령과 관련된 내용이 와야 자연스럽다. 따라서 your box를 it으로 받아 내일 상자를 받을 수 있을 것이라고 언급하고 있는 (A)가 정답이다.

번역 (A) 내일 받으실 수 있을 겁니다.
(B) 이 주문은 처리하는 데 평소보다 더 오래 걸릴 것입니다.
(C) 그 상자는 매우 무겁습니다.
(D) 이 이메일에 첨부된 청구서를 검토해 주십시오.

어휘 process 처리하다 invoice 청구서 attached 첨부된

135-138 메모

수신: 타볼라 식품 유통업체 마케팅 부서
발신: 빅터 코티요
날짜: 3월 4일
제목: 정보

방금 우리 팀 폴더에 추가된 설문 조사 제안서를 확인하세요. 첫 번째 섹션에서는 **135소비자**에게 가장 좋아하는 채소의 등급을 매겨 달라고 요청합니다. 우리는 쇼핑객들이 신선하고 제철인 경우에만 특정 채소를 선호하는 것일 수 있다고 느꼈습니다. **136그래서** 그들이 어떤 냉동 채소를 가장 자주 사는지 그리고 왜 사는지에 대해서도 묻습니다. 또한, 음식 준비와 편리함에 대한 일련의 질문들도 **137삽입했습니다.** 이번 설문 조사를 통해 우리 고객이 원하는 바를 보다 잘 파악할 수 있을 것이라고 생각합니다. 모든 사항을 검토하시고 의견이 있으시면 신속히 회신 주시기 바랍니다. **138다음 주부터 설문지 배포를 시작하고자 합니다.**

어휘 distributor 유통업체 rate 등급을 매기다 particular 특정한 in season 제철인 frozen 냉동된 frequently 자주

preparation 준비 picture 상황의 이해, 제시 look over 검토하다 thought 의견, 생각

135 명사 어휘

해설 앞 문장에서 설문 조사에 대해 언급하면서 뒤 문장에서 쇼핑객들이 신선하고 제철인 특정 채소를 선호하는 것 같다고 한 것으로 보아 설문 조사의 대상이 쇼핑객임을 알 수 있다. 따라서 설문 조사의 첫 섹션에서 가장 좋아하는 채소 등급을 매겨 달라고 요청한 대상은 쇼핑객이므로, 쇼핑객과 동의어인 '소비자'라는 뜻의 (C) consumers가 정답이다.

어휘 executive 임원 merchant 상인

136 접속부사

해설 앞 문장에서 쇼핑객들이 신선하고 제철인 경우에만 특정 채소를 선호하는 것일 수 있다고 느꼈다고 했고, 뒤 문장에는 그들이 어떤 냉동 채소를 가장 자주 사는지 그리고 왜 사는지에 대해서도 묻는다고 했다. 두 문장이 쇼핑객들이 신선하고 제철인 채소를 선호한다고 파악하고 있기 때문에 냉동 채소를 살 때는 어떤 것을 왜 사는지에 대해서도 파악해 보겠다는 인과 관계를 나타내고 있으므로 '그러므로, 그래서'를 뜻하는 (B) Therefore가 정답이 된다.

어휘 in effect 실제로는 on occasion 가끔 nevertheless 그럼에도 불구하고

137 동사의 시제

해설 메모의 초반부에서 방금 팀 폴더에 추가된 설문 조사 제안서를 확인하라면서 설문 조사지의 내용을 현재 시제로 설명하고 있다. 따라서 설문 조사지 작성이 이미 완료되었으며, 음식 준비와 편리함에 대한 질문 또한 현재 설문 조사지에 삽입이 완료된 상태임을 알 수 있으므로 현재완료 시제인 (B) have inserted가 정답이다.

138 문맥에 맞는 문장 고르기

해설 앞 문장에서 설문 조사를 통해 기대되는 바를 언급하며 모든 사항을 검토하고 의견이 있을 경우 신속히 알려 달라고 당부하고 있으므로, 설문 조사를 곧 실시할 것이라는 내용이 이어져야 자연스럽다. 따라서 다음 주부터 설문지 배포를 시작하고자 한다고 언급하고 있는 (A)가 정답이다.

번역 (A) 다음 주부터 설문지 배포를 시작하고자 합니다.
(B) 우리는 우리의 고객이신 귀하께서 제공하시는 의견을 소중히 여깁니다.
(C) 높은 비용에도 불구하고, 우리 제품에 대한 수요는 증가했습니다.
(D) 우리 모두가 알다시피, 신선한 채소는 여러분에게 좋습니다.

어휘 distribute 배포하다 value 소중히 여기다 demand 수요

139-142 이메일

수신: vendors@grovecenterfleamarket.org
발신: alanc@spicebest.com
날짜: 10월 22일

제목: 주차 문제

판매업자 여러분께,

다음 달부터 그로브 센터 벼룩시장의 소유주들은 현장에 있는 주차 타워 이용에 매일 10달러의 균일 요금을 부과할 예정입니다. 이는 주간 벼룩 시장에 차를 가지고 오는 고객들이 더 이상 무료 주차를 누릴 수 없다는 것을 의미합니다. 저는 이것이 일부 쇼핑객들이 방문을 139**꺼리게 되어** 우리 사업에 지장을 줄 것을 우려합니다.

그로브 센터 벼룩시장의 위원장으로서, 저는 소유주들에게 요금을 면제하거나 감면할 것을 고려해 달라고 요청했습니다. 140**안타깝게도, 우리는 타협안을 찾지 못했습니다.** 가장 가까운 다른 대규모 주차 시설은 시청에 있으며, 우리 현장에서 큰 세 블록 정도 떨어져 있습니다. 노상 주차는 가능하지만 공간을 찾기가 141**어려울** 수 있습니다.

대안이 되는 142**해결책**에 대한 의견이 있으시면 모두에게 회신 부탁드립니다.

앨런 콜먼

어휘 vendor 판매업자, 행상인 flea market 벼룩시장 charge 부과하다 flat (가격이) 균일한 rate 요금 onsite 현장의 parking deck 주차 타워[건물] enjoy 누리다 hurt 지장을 주다 waive 면제하다 reduce 줄이다 large-scale 대규모의 facility 시설 alternative 대안이 되는

139 동사 어휘

해설 앞 문장에서 주차장 이용에 요금을 부과하기로 한 결정 때문에 고객들이 무료 주차를 이용할 수 없게 되었다고 했으므로, 이로 인해 '일부 쇼핑객들이 방문을 꺼리게 되어 사업에 지장을 줄까 봐 걱정된다'는 내용이 되어야 자연스럽다. 따라서 '사람 from ~ing'과 함께 쓰여 '~가 …하기를 꺼리게 하다, …하려는 의욕을 꺾다'라는 뜻을 나타내는 (C) discourage가 정답이다.

140 문맥에 맞는 문장 고르기

해설 앞 문장에서 소유주들에게 주차 요금을 면제하거나 감면할 것을 고려해 달라고 요청했다고 했는데, 뒤 문장에서 외부 주차 시설에 대해 안내하며 대안이 되는 해결책이 있으면 회신을 달라고 부탁하고 있는 것으로 보아 빈칸에는 요청 사항이 수용되지 않았다는 내용이 들어가야 연결이 자연스럽다. 따라서 타협안을 찾지 못했다고 언급하고 있는 (D)가 정답이다.

번역 (A) 그들의 사무실은 일요일에는 문을 열지 않습니다.
(B) 저는 그들에게 주차장을 확장해 달라고도 요청했습니다.
(C) 그럼에도 불구하고, 우리는 작년보다 더 많은 판매업자가 있습니다.
(D) 안타깝게도, 우리는 타협안을 찾지 못했습니다.

어휘 expand 확장하다 garage 주차장 compromise 타협(안)

141 형용사 어휘

해설 문맥상 길거리 주차는 가능하지만 '주차 공간을 찾기가 어렵다'는 내용이 되어야 적절하므로 '어려운, 힘든'을 뜻하는 (A) difficult가 정답이다.

어휘 pleasant 쾌적한 specific 구체적인

142 명사 자리 _ 전치사의 목적어

해설 형용사 alternative의 수식을 받아 전치사 on의 목적어 역할을 하는 명사 자리이다. solution은 가산명사이므로 앞에 한정사가 없을 경우 복수 형태로 와야 한다. 따라서 (B) solutions가 정답이다.

143-146 신문 기사

> 퀸즈빌 (11월 3일) - 지역의 두 번째 재활용 센터가 문을 연 덕분에 많은 지역 주민들에게 재활용이 더욱 쉬워졌다. "웨스트 퀸즈빌 주민에게 이제 재활용품을 가져다 놓을 수 있는 더 **143편리한** 장소가 생겼습니다." 라고 어제 열린 리본 커팅식에서 더스틴 라슨 시장은 말했다. "더 이상 시의 동쪽까지 갈 필요가 없습니다."
>
> **144행사에 참석한 사람들은 새로운 시설에 박수를 보냈다.** 하지만, 퀸즈빌 청정 연합의 아이다 아귀레는 재활용품의 도로변 수거를 없애기로 한 지역 의회의 결정을 비판했다. "**145만약** 선출된 공무원들이 재활용을 더 쉽게 만들기를 원한다면 도로변 수거를 재개해야 합니다."라고 전화 인터뷰에서 그녀는 말했다. 평일 오전 6시부터 오후 8시까지 문을 여는 대런 로 18번지의 새로운 시설은 혼합지와 일부 플라스틱만 수거한다. 알루미늄은 현재 **146받고 있지** 않다.

어휘 township 거주 지역, 읍 drop off 갖다 놓다 material 물질 mayor 시장 no longer 더 이상 ~이 아닌 travel (먼 곳까지) 가다 coalition 연합 criticize 비판하다 eliminate 없애다 curbside 도로변, 보도의 연석쪽 pickup 수거 recyclable 재활용품 resume 재개하다 elected 선출된 official (고위) 공무원 facility 시설 currently 현재

143 형용사 어휘

해설 앞 문장에서 두 번째 재활용 센터가 문을 연 덕분에 재활용이 더욱 쉬워졌다고 했으므로, '재활용품을 가져다 놓기에 더 쉽고 편리한 장소가 생겼다'는 내용이 되어야 자연스럽다. 따라서 '편리한'을 뜻하는 (B) convenient가 정답이다.

어휘 widespread 광범위한 ordinary 보통의 stable 안정된

144 문맥에 맞는 문장 고르기

해설 신문 기사 초반부에서 지역의 두 번째 재활용 센터의 개관 및 기념행사에 대해 언급하고 있고, 빈칸 뒤 문장에는 지역 의회의 결정을 비판하는 목소리도 있다는 내용을 '하지만(However)'이라는 역접 관계를 나타내는 접속부사로 연결했다. 따라서 빈칸에는 뒤 문장에 나온 비판의 목소리와는 상반되는 내용이 들어가야 적절하므로 개관식 행사에 참석한 사람들이 새로운 시설에 박수를 보냈다고 언급하고 있는 (B)가 정답이다.

번역 (A) 최근 쓰레기 매립지로 보내지는 가정 쓰레기의 비율이 감소했다.
　　(B) 행사에 참석한 사람들은 새로운 시설에 박수를 보냈다.
　　(C) 재활용 센터 두 곳 모두 직원들이 재활용품을 내리는 데 도움을 줄 수 있다.
　　(D) 웨스트 퀸즈빌에 있는 재활용 센터는 내년에 문을 연다.

어휘 household 가정의 landfill 쓰레기 매립지 applaud 박수를 치다 drop-off site 재활용 처리 센터 unload (짐을) 내리다

145 접속사 자리 _ 부사절 접속사

해설 빈칸 뒤에 주어와 동사를 갖춘 완전한 절이 왔으므로 접속사가 들어가야 하고, 문맥상 '만약 공무원들이 재활용을 더 쉽게 만들기를 원한다면'이라는 내용이 되어야 자연스러우므로 '만약 ~면'을 뜻하는 부사절 접속사 (C) if가 정답이다.

146 과거분사

해설 빈칸은 be동사 뒤에 적절한 보어를 골라 동사의 형태를 완성시켜야 하는 자리이다. 주어가 Aluminum이고 동사 accept는 타동사인데 빈칸 뒤에 목적어가 없으므로 수동태를 이루는 과거분사 (A) accepted가 정답이다.

PART 7

147-148 이메일

> 수신: 진 바수르
> 발신: 마일로 베일리
> 날짜: 2월 4일
> 제목: 정보
>
> 진에게,
>
> **148캐럴을 고용한 것은 옳은 결정이었다고 생각합니다.** 그녀는 우리 웹사이트의 디자인과 콘텐츠에 대한 훌륭한 아이디어를 가지고 있습니다. 그녀가 만든 새 사이트는 우리에게는 고객을 유치하는 데, 그리고 기존 고객에게는 필요한 정보를 얻는 데 도움이 될 것입니다.
>
> **147앞서 제안하신 사소한 변경 사항 외에도, 웹사이트에 회계 팁을 게시하고 일부 일화들을 공유할 블로그를 개설하는 것도 좋을 듯합니다.** **148캐럴과 함께 모여 앉아 서로의 생각을 공유할 필요가 있습니다.** 내일 아침 그녀의 일정이 비는데, 혹시 시간이 되시는지요?
>
> 마일로

어휘 attract 유치하다, 끌다 in addition to ~외에도, ~에 더하여 minor 작은 post 게시하다 anecdote 일화

147 주제 / 목적

번역 베일리 씨가 바수르 씨에게 이메일을 보낸 이유는?
　　(A) 제품에 대해 문의하기 위해
　　(B) 새로운 절차를 설명하기 위해
　　(C) 웹사이트 변경에 대해 논의하기 위해
　　(D) 새 고객에게 연락해 달라고 요청하기 위해

해설 두 번째 단락의 첫 문장에서 베일리 씨가 앞서 제안한 사소한 변경 사항 외에도, 웹사이트에 회계 팁을 게시하고 일부 일화들을 공유할 블로그를 개설하는 것도 좋을 듯하다(In addition to the minor changes ~ tips and share some anecdotes)며 웹사이트 개선안에 대해 논의하고 있으므로 정답은 (C)이다.

어휘 inquire 문의하다 process 절차[과정]

148 세부 사항

번역 베일리 씨가 하고 싶어 하는 것은?
(A) 일정 검토
(B) 추가 직원 채용
(C) 새 계정 개설
(D) 신입 직원과의 회의

해설 첫 문장에서 베일리 씨는 캐럴을 고용한 것은 옳은 결정이었다고 생각한다(I think we made the right decision in hiring Carol)고 했고, 두 번째 단락의 두 번째 문장에서 캐럴과 함께 모여 앉아 서로의 생각을 공유할 필요가 있다(We need to sit down with Carol to share our thoughts)고 했다. 따라서 캐럴은 새로 고용된 직원이며, 베일리 씨는 캐럴과 문제를 논의하기 위한 회의를 하고 싶어한다는 것을 알 수 있으므로 (D)가 정답이다.

149-150 영수증

그린 운동화
오리올 가 18502
시카고, 일리노이 주 60800
(312) 555-0132

8월 5일 오전 11시 27분
영수증 번호: 5926

루나웨이브 운동화
스타일: 플리트풋, 남성 사이즈 10   119달러

슈어삭스 면 러닝 양말
남성 사이즈 대   4.99달러

149쿨브리즈 티셔츠
남성 사이즈 중
149정가 14달러, 현재 15% 할인   11.90달러

소계   135.89달러
부가세 (6.25%)   8.49달러
합계   144.38달러

그린 운동화에서 쇼핑해 주셔서 감사합니다!
www.greensathletic.com에서 고객 설문지를 작성해 주시기 바랍니다.

모든 반품은 30일 이내에 이루어져야 합니다.
150반품을 하려면 영수증이 필요합니다.

어휘 athletic shoes 운동화 regularly 평상시에는, 보통은 subtotal 소계 sales tax 부가세 fill out 작성하다 required 필요한, 필수의

149 Not / True

번역 티셔츠에 대해 명시된 것은?
(A) 루나웨이브에서 만들었다.
(B) '대' 사이즈이다.
(C) 면으로 만들어졌다.
(D) 할인된 가격에 팔렸다.

해설 영수증의 중반부에 쿨브리즈 티셔츠(Coolbreeze T-shirt)가 정가

14달러(Regularly $14.00)인데 현재 15% 할인(now 15% off)해서 11.90달러($11.90)라고 나와 있으므로 (D)가 정답이다.

150 세부 사항

번역 고객이 물건을 반품하기 위해 해야 하는 일은?
(A) 온라인 양식 작성하기
(B) 6개월 이내에 물건 반납하기
(C) 매장 영수증 원본 제시하기
(D) 제품을 제조업체에 우편으로 발송하기

해설 마지막 문장에서 반품을 하려면 영수증이 필요하다(A receipt is required to make a return)고 했으므로 (C)가 정답이다.

어휘 complete 작성하다 manufacturer 제조업체

151-152 문자 메시지

모니카 블랑코 (오전 10시 43분)
안녕하세요, 캐리. 151이번 주 금요일에 일하세요? 제가 반일 근무를 하는데 혹시 저 대신 근무해 주실 수 있나 궁금해서요. 제 남동생의 생일 파티가 그날이거든요.

캐리 모건 (오전 11시 25분)
저도 반일 근무를 해요. 몇 시 근무 일정이죠?

모니카 블랑코 (오전 11시 37분)
오전 8시부터 정오까지요.

캐리 모건 (오전 11시 39분)
제가 할 수 있을 것 같네요. 사실 종일 근무해도 되거든요. 당신 다음 근무자가 저예요.

모니카 블랑코 (오전 11시 40분)
잘됐네요.

캐리 모건 (오전 11시 41분)
제가 지금 근무 중이거든요. 152조 씨를 보게 되면 제가 당신 근무와 제 근무를 같이 맡아도 괜찮은지 물어볼게요.

모니카 블랑코 (오전 11시 50분)
감사합니다!

어휘 shift 교대 근무 (시간) cover (자리를 비운 사람의 일을) 대신하다 as well as 또한, ~에 더하여 appreciate 고마워하다

151 의도 파악

번역 오전 11시 39분에 모건 씨가 "제가 할 수 있을 것 같네요"라고 쓴 의도는?
(A) 주말 행사 준비를 도울 수 있다.
(B) 금요일에 블랑코 씨의 근무를 대신할 수 있다.
(C) 파티를 위해 음식을 가져올 수 있다.
(D) 휴식 시간 동안 블랑코 씨와 만날 수 있다.

해설 10시 43분에 블랑코 씨가 모건 씨에게 이번 주 금요일에 일하는지(Are you working this Friday?)를 물으며 제가 반일 근무를 하는데 혹시 저 대신 근무해 주실 수 있나 궁금하다(I'm working a half shift, and I was wondering if you could cover it)고 한 데 대해, 11시 39분에 모건 씨가 제가 할 수 있을 것 같다(I might be able to)고 대답했다. 따라서 모건 씨는 금요일에 블랑코 씨 대신 근무해 줄 수 있다는 의도로 한 말이므로 (B)가 정답이다.

어휘 organize 준비하다

152 추론 / 암시

번역 조 씨는 누구인 것 같은가?
(A) 임시직 근로자
(B) 파티 기획자
(C) 상사
(D) 블랑코 씨의 친구

해설 11시 41분에 모건 씨가 블랑코 씨에게 조 씨를 보게 되면 제가 당신 근무와 제 근무를 같이 맡아도 괜찮은지 물어보겠다(When I see Mr. Cho, I'll ask him if it is OK to do your shift as well as mine)고 한 것으로 보아 조 씨는 모건 씨와 블랑코 씨의 근무를 관리하는 직장 상사임을 알 수 있다. 따라서 정답은 (C)이다.

어휘 temporary 임시의

153-154 메모

> 메모
>
> 수신: 모든 아비소마크 직원
> 발신: 유제니아 바호렉, 커뮤니케이션 차장
> 날짜: 1월 30일
> 답장: 당사 사보
>
> [153]쓰레기를 줄이기 위한 회사 전반적인 노력의 일환으로, 우리는 3월 1일부터 주간 사보의 인쇄판을 중단할 예정입니다. 그날 이후로 사보는 온라인 형식으로만 발간됩니다. 또한, [154]3월부터 사보의 직원 소식란을 위한 제출 기한이 매월 셋째 주 금요일에서 둘째 주 금요일로 변경됩니다. 이 변경 사항으로 마커스 큄비는 제출물을 처리하고 편집하는 데 필요한 시간을 갖게 될 것입니다. 제출 절차는 동일하게 유지되며, 마커스에게 직접 mquimby@avisomark.com으로 이메일을 보내시면 됩니다.

어휘 newsletter 소식지 company-wide 회사 전반[전체]의 effort 노력 reduce 줄이다 waste 쓰레기 discontinue 중단하다 effective 시행되는 forward 앞으로 submission 제출 process 처리하다; 절차

153 주제 / 목적

번역 메모가 쓰인 이유는?
(A) 최근 결정을 발표하기 위해
(B) 새로운 직원을 소개하기 위해
(C) 자원봉사 기회를 설명하기 위해
(D) 새로운 관행에 대한 의견을 요청하기 위해

해설 첫 문장에서 쓰레기를 줄이기 위한 회사 전반적인 노력의 일환으로 우리는 3월 1일부터 주간 사보의 인쇄판을 중단할 예정(As part of a company-wide effort ~ company newsletter, effective March 1)이라며, 사보에 대해 회사에서 결정한 내용을 직원들에게 알리고 있으므로 (A)가 정답이다.

어휘 describe 설명하다 invite 요청하다 practice 관행

154 세부 사항

번역 메모에 따르면, 직원들이 큄비 씨에게 이메일을 보내는 이유는?
(A) 개인 정보를 업데이트하려고
(B) 사보의 사본을 요청하려고
(C) 사보 형식에 대한 의견을 표명하려고
(D) 최신 소식을 제출하려고

해설 세 번째 문장에서 3월부터 사보의 직원 소식란을 위한 제출 기한이 변경된다(beginning in March, the submission deadline ~ will be changed)며, 이 변경 사항으로 마커스 큄비는 제출물을 처리하고 편집하는 데 필요한 시간을 갖게 될 것(This change will give Markus Quimby the time ~ and edit submissions)이라고 했고, 제출 절차는 동일하게 유지되며 마커스에게 직접 mquimby@avisomark.com으로 이메일을 보내면 된다(The submission process remains ~ at mquimby@avisomark.com)고 했다. 따라서 큄비 씨는 직원 소식란을 관리하는 사람이고, 직원들은 사보의 직원 소식란에 실릴 글을 큄비 씨에게 이메일로 제출하는 것이므로 (D)가 정답이다.

어휘 send in 제출하다

155-157 기사

> ### 스완지의 무인 버스?
>
> 스완지 (5월 12일) - [155]시 공무원과 지역 기업 대표들로 구성된 협력단이 일부 도시 노선을 위한 무인 버스 구입을 고려하고 있다. [155,157]스완지와 주변 지역의 교통 개선을 위한 방안을 찾도록 위임된 이 단체는 최근 무인 버스가 8킬로미터의 순환 노선을 하루 여러 차례 운행하는 스페인 말라가로 세 명의 회원을 보냈다.
>
> 협력단 회원인 개러스 엘리아스는 그가 알게 된 것에 대해 깊은 인상을 받았다. 안전과 교통 법규에 대한 우려에도 불구하고, [156]엘리아스 씨는 무인 버스가 특정한 경우에 한해서 이긴 하지만 머지않은 현실이 되고 있음을 알 수 있었다. "저는 무인 버스가 축제와 특별한 행사 기간 동안 특히 유용할 것이라고 봅니다."라고 그는 말했다. "무인 버스가 매일 도로 위에 있는 것이 상상이 되지는 않습니다."
>
> [157]교통 혁신 전문 엔지니어인 아니샤 디팍은 이번 여행에서 기술 컨설턴트 역할을 했다. 그녀는 모든 주행에서 데이터를 수집하면서 학습을 가능하게 해 주는 버스의 인공 지능 시스템의 복잡성에 강한 인상을 받았다.
>
> "인공 지능은 실제 상황에서 이 버스들이 아주 안전하도록 해 줍니다."라고 그녀는 말했다. "그럼에도 불구하고 비상 상황에 대비하여 항상 인간 운전자가 승차하는 것이 최선입니다."
>
> 무인 버스의 장점과 문제점을 논의하기 위해 공공 커뮤니티 포럼이 6월 2일로 예정되어 있다. 스완지 시 의회의 웹사이트 www.swanseatowncouncil.gov.uk를 방문하면 더 많은 것을 알아볼 수 있다.

어휘 driverless 운전자가 없는 consortium 협력단 government official 공무원, 관료 commission 위임하다, 의뢰하다 surrounding 주변의 loop 순환선, 고리 impressed 깊은 인상을 받은 regulation 규정 reality 현실 before long

머지않아 specific 특정한 particularly 특히 specialise in ~을 전문으로 하다 serve as ~로 일하다 strike 강한 인상[느낌]을 주다, 마음에 확 와닿게 하다 complexity 복잡함 artificial intelligence 인공 지능 nevertheless 그럼에도 불구하고 operator 운전자 on board 승차한 at all times 항상 in case of ~의 경우에, ~에 대비하여 forum 포럼, 토론회 drawback 문제점

155 주제 / 목적

번역 기사의 목적은?
(A) 새로운 기술의 작동 방식을 설명하려고
(B) 단체의 최근 활동에 대해 보고하려고
(C) 여행 포럼 참가자를 모집하려고
(D) 버스 일정 변경을 발표하려고

해설 첫 문장에서 시 공무원과 지역 기업 대표들로 구성된 협력단이 일부 도시 노선을 위한 무인 버스 구입을 고려하고 있다(A consortium of city government ~ buses for some city routes)고 했고, 스완지와 주변 지역의 교통 개선을 위한 방안을 찾도록 위임된 이 단체는 최근 무인 버스가 8킬로미터의 순환 노선을 하루에 여러 차례 운행하는 스페인 말라가로 세 명의 회원을 보냈다(Commissioned with exploring options ~ driverless buses run an eight-kilometre loop several times a day)며 협력단의 최근 활동에 대한 소식을 알리고 있으므로 (B)가 정답이다.

156 세부 사항

번역 엘리아스 씨가 무인 버스에 대해 나타내는 의견은?
(A) 어떠한 상황에서도 안전하지 않다.
(B) 무인 버스를 수용할 수 있도록 교통 법규가 개정되어야 한다.
(C) 제한적인 목적으로 실현 가능하다.
(D) 말라가에는 적합하지만 스완지에는 적합하지 않다.

해설 두 번째 단락의 두 번째 문장에서 엘리아스 씨는 무인 버스가 특정한 경우에 한해서이긴 하지만 머지않은 현실이 되고 있음을 알 수 있었다(Mr. Elias could see ~ reality before long, but only in specific cases)고 한 뒤, 무인 버스가 축제와 특별한 행사 기간 동안 특히 유용할 것으로 본다고 그(엘리아스 씨는) 말했다("I believe ~ useful during festivals and special events", he said)고 덧붙였으므로 (C)가 정답이다.

어휘 circumstance 상황, 환경 revise 개정하다 accommodate 수용하다 practical 실현 가능한; 실용적인 appropriate 적합한

> **Paraphrasing** 지문의 driverless buses ~ a reality before long, but only in specific cases → 정답의 They are practical for limited purposes

157 추론 / 암시

번역 디팍 씨에 대해 알 수 있는 것은?
(A) 최근에 스완지 시 의회에 선출되었다.
(B) 컴퓨터 시스템을 위한 데이터를 수집했다.
(C) 비상 회의 동안 메모를 했다.
(D) 컨설턴트로서 말라가에 출장을 갔다.

해설 첫 번째 단락의 두 번째 문장에서 스완지와 주변 지역의 교통 개선을 위한 방안을 찾도록 위임된 이 단체는 최근 무인 버스가 8킬로미터의 순환 노선을 하루에 여러 차례 운행하는 스페인 말라가로 세 명의 회원을 보냈다(Commissioned with exploring options ~ loop several times a day)고 했고, 세 번째 단락의 첫 문장에서 교통 혁신 전문 엔지니어인 아니샤 디팍은 이번 여행에서 기술 컨설턴트 역할을 했다(Anisha Deepak, an engineer ~ as a technical consultant on the trip)고 했다. 따라서 디팍은 단체에서 말라가로 보낸 세 명의 회원 중 한 명으로, 기술 컨설턴트 역할을 했다는 것을 알 수 있으므로 (D)가 정답이다.

어휘 elect 선출하다 take a note 메모[필기]하다

158-161 구인 광고

> 서울의 모브스 연구소에서 연구 개발 부서 내의 다른 과학자 팀과 협력하여 일할 협력 연구원을 찾고 있습니다.
>
> 모브스 연구소는 아시아, 유럽 및 북미의 사무실과 연구소에서 최첨단 의약품의 개발, 제조 및 판매에 참여하는 85,000명 이상의 직원을 보유하고 있습니다. **158연구 개발 부서는 세계적으로 사용되는 새롭고 효과적인 의약품을 만든다는 회사의 주요 목표 달성을 책임지고 있습니다.**
>
> <u>주요 직무:</u>
>
> - **159실험실 실험의 설계 및 수행**
> - **159철저한 데이터 분석 수행**
> - 상세 보고서 작성을 위한 협력
> - 특정 회의에서 연구 결과를 고객에게 내외부적으로 발표
>
> <u>직책 요건:</u>
>
> - 생물학 석사 학위
> - **160최소 5년 이상의 연구소 경력**
> - 뛰어난 구두 및 서면 소통 능력
>
> **161지원하려면 이력서와 자기소개서를 11월 10일까지 www.morveslaboratories.co.kr/careers에 제출하세요.**

어휘 laboratory 연구소, 실험실 seek 찾다, 구하다 associate 협력, 동료 collaboratively 협력하여 involved 참여하는, 관여하는 cutting-edge 최첨단(의) achieve 달성하다 primary 주요한 effective 효과적인 medication 약[약물] worldwide 전 세계적으로 function 기능 conduct 수행하다 experiment 실험 rigorous 철저한, 엄격한 analysis 분석 collaborate 협력하다 detailed 자세한 present 제시하다 findings 연구 결과 internally 내부적으로 externally 외부적으로 specific 특정한 master's degree 석사 학위 biology 생물학 oral 구두의 communication skill 의사소통 능력 cover letter 자기소개서

158 Not / True

번역 구인 광고에서 모브스 연구소에 대해 명시한 것은?
(A) 우수한 직원 복지를 제공한다.
(B) 인력 기반을 주로 유럽에 두고 있다.
(C) 주요 목적은 신약을 개발하는 것이다.
(D) 제품 유통을 위해 다른 회사와 제휴한다.

해설 두 번째 단락의 두 번째 문장에서 연구 개발 부서는 세계적으로 이용될 수 있는 새롭고 효과적인 의약품을 만든다는 회사(모브스 연구소)의 주요 목표 달성을 책임지고 있다(The Research and Development Division is responsible for ~ creating new and effective medications for worldwide use)고 했으므로 모브스 연구소는 효과적인 신약 개발을 주 목적으로 삼고 있다는 것을 알 수 있다. 따라서 (C)가 정답이다.

어휘 benefits 근로 복지 workforce 인력, 노동력 primarily 주로 partner 제휴하다 distribution 유통

> Paraphrasing   지문의 primary goal → 정답의 main purpose
> 지문의 creating new ~ medications
> → 정답의 develop new medicines

159 세부 사항

번역 해당 직책의 책무는?
(A) 실험에서 도출된 정보 분석
(B) 안전한 포장재 설계
(C) 제조 장비 운용
(D) 환자 문의에 대한 답변

해설 주요 직무의 첫 번째 항목이 실험실 실험의 설계 및 수행(Design and conduct laboratory experiments)이고, 두 번째 항목이 철저한 데이터 분석 수행(Perform rigorous data analysis)이므로 해당 직책의 책임은 실험을 진행하고 실험에서 나온 데이터를 분석하는 것임을 알 수 있다. 따라서 (A)가 정답이다.

어휘 analyze 분석하다 packaging 포장재 material 재질 patient 환자 inquiry 문의

> Paraphrasing   지문의 data → 정답의 information

160 세부 사항

번역 구인 광고에 따르면, 지원자가 갖추고 있어야 하는 것은?
(A) 의료 규정에 대한 지식
(B) 의학 학술지 편집에 관한 전문 지식
(C) 생물학 교수 관련 이력
(D) 연구소에서 일한 경험

해설 직책 요건의 두 번째 항목이 최소 5년 이상의 연구소 경력(At least five years of laboratory experience)이므로 (D)가 정답이다.

어휘 knowledge 지식 regulation 규정 expertise 전문 지식 journal 학술지, 저널 background 경력, 학력

161 세부 사항

번역 이 직책에 지원하는 방법은?
(A) 회사 사무실을 방문함으로써
(B) 온라인으로 이력서를 제출함으로써
(C) 채용 전문가에게 전화함으로써
(D) 현재 직원에게 이메일을 발송함으로써

해설 마지막 문장에서 지원하려면 이력서와 자기소개서를 11월 10일

까지 www.morveslaboratories.co.kr/careers에 제출하라 (To apply, submit a resume and cover letter to www.morveslaboratories.co.kr/careers by November 10)고 했으므로 (B)가 정답이다.

어휘 professional 전문가

162-164 이메일

수신: team@rosettipasta.com.au
발신: valentina_rosetti@rosettipasta.com.au
날짜: 8월 20일
제목: 업데이트

팀 여러분,

지난 몇 년간은 정말 정신없이 빨리 지나갔습니다. 5년 전 제가 수제 파스타를 팔기 시작했을 때, 제 집에 있는 주방보다 더 큰 공간이 필요하게 되리라고 전혀 예상하지 못했습니다. 상황이 얼마나 변했는지요! 이번 주에 우리 회사는 이곳 동부 호주의 지역 식품 유통업체에 제품을 공급하기 위한 계약을 따냈습니다.

162여러분이 없었더라면 이러한 성과는 분명히 가능하지 않았을 겁니다. 여러분 모두가 이런 엄청난 성장에 발맞추기 위해 열심히 일해 주셨고, 항상 쉬웠던 것은 아니었습니다. 164감사의 표시로, 저는 여러분 모두에게 보너스를 지급하기로 결정했습니다. 그것은 금요일 여러분의 계좌에서 확인 가능할 거예요.

163우리의 견고한 팀과 능률적인 생산 공정 덕분에 조만간 훨씬 더 많은 슈퍼마켓 진열대에 우리 제품이 놓이는 것을 보게 될 것이라고 낙관합니다. 미래는 밝습니다.

발렌티나 로제티
로제티 파스타 유한 회사, 최고 경영자

어휘 fast-paced 빨리 진행되는 space 공간 win 획득하다 supply 공급하다 regional 지역의 distributor 유통업체 eastern 동부의 achievement 성과, 성취 certainly 분명히 keep pace with ~와 보조를 맞추다 tremendous 엄청난 solid 견고한 streamlined 능률적인, 간소화된 process 공정 optimistic 낙관적인

162 주제 / 목적

번역 로제티 씨가 이메일을 보낸 이유는?
(A) 직원들에게 감사하기 위해
(B) 사업 계획을 제시하기 위해
(C) 연기를 발표하기 위해
(D) 프로젝트에 대한 지원을 요청하기 위해

해설 첫 단락에서 회사가 그동안 이뤄낸 업적에 대해 언급하며 두 번째 단락의 첫 문장에서 여러분이 없었더라면 이러한 성과는 분명히 가능하지 않았을 것(This achievement certainly would not have been possible without you)이라고 했다. 따라서 로제티 씨는 직원들의 노고에 감사하기 위해 이메일을 쓴 것이므로 (A)가 정답이다.

어휘 postponement 연기

163 세부 사항

번역 로제티 씨가 자신감을 표현하는 것은?
(A) 신제품 라인 개발
(B) 추가적인 기업 성장 가능성
(C) 광고 캠페인의 성공
(D) 노후한 기계의 교체 가능성

해설 세 번째 단락의 첫 문장에서 로제티 씨가 우리의 견고한 팀과 능률적인 생산 공정 덕분에 조만간 훨씬 더 많은 슈퍼마켓 진열대에 우리 제품이 놓이는 것을 보게 될 것이라고 낙관한다(With our solid team and our streamlined ~ more supermarket shelves soon)고 했으므로 정답은 (B)이다.

어휘 confidence 자신감　line 제품군, 제품의 종류　potential 가능성, 잠재력　machinery 기계(류)

164 문장 삽입

번역 [1], [2], [3], [4]로 표시된 곳 중에서 다음 문장이 들어가기에 가장 적합한 위치는?

"그것은 금요일 여러분의 계좌에서 확인 가능할 거예요."
(A) [1]
(B) [2]
(C) [3]
(D) [4]

해설 제시된 문장의 대명사 It이 문제 해결의 단서로, 앞 문장에 It으로 대신할 수 있는 단수명사가 있어야 하고 제시된 문장의 내용상 직원 계좌에서 확인할 만한 것이어야 한다. 따라서 감사의 표시로 여러분 모두에게 보너스(a bonus)를 지급하기로 결정했다고 언급하는 문장 뒤에 들어가면, a bonus를 it으로 받아 그것(보너스)이 계좌에서 확인 가능할 것이라는 내용이 자연스럽게 연결되므로 정답은 (C)이다.

165-167 이메일

수신: 시드 셰퍼드
발신: 회사 보안 팀
날짜: 7월 2일
제목: 신분증

셰퍼드 씨께:

165오늘 오전에 주신 새로운 실물 신분증 재발급에 대한 도움 요청을 받았습니다. 기존 명찰은 분실되었으므로 사용이 정지되었습니다. 교체 신분증을 받으려면 오전 7시에서 오후 5시 30분 사이에 폴센 홀에 있는 회사 보안실을 방문하세요. 정부에서 발급한 신분증을 제시해 주셔야 합니다.

그동안 회사의 새로운 실시 계획을 활용하실 수 있습니다. **166모든 직원의 모바일 기기에 설치된 회사 앱에는 이제 회사 주차장과 구내 건물에 출입 허가를 167얻는 데 사용되는 디지털 신분증이 포함되어 있습니다.** 앱에 있는 디지털 신분증을 이용하시려면 "ID 카드" 탭을 찾아보세요. 그런 다음 디지털 신분증을 스캔하여 모든 보안 구역에 들어가실 수 있습니다.

질문이 있으시거나 추가적인 도움이 필요하시면 863-555-0171로 회사 보안 팀에 전화 주세요.

감사합니다.

호퍼 테크놀로지 회사 보안 팀

어휘 corporate 회사[기업]의　security 보안　acquire 얻다　physical (온라인이나 디지털에 반하는) 실물의　identification badge 신분증　misplace 분실하다, 잃어버리다　deactivate 정지시키다, 비활성화시키다　replacement 교체[대체]물　be required to ~해야 한다　government-issued 정부 발급의　take advantage of ~을 활용[이용]하다　initiative 사업 계획　device 장치　gain 얻다　entry 출입　access 이용하다　secure 보안의, 안전한

165 주제 / 목적

번역 이메일의 목적은?
(A) 도움 요청에 대응하기 위해
(B) 신제품 판매를 촉진하기 위해
(C) 보안 문제를 당국에 알리기 위해
(D) 새로운 회사 정책을 발표하기 위해

해설 첫 문장에서 오늘 오전에 주신 새로운 실물 신분증 재발급에 대한 도움 요청을 받았다(We received your request ~ physical identification badge)고 했고 기존 명찰은 분실되었으므로 사용이 정지되었다(As your current badge ~ been deactivated)고 설명하며 교체 신분증을 받으려면 오전 7시에서 오후 5시 30분 사이에 폴센 홀에 있는 회사 보안실을 방문하라(To receive a replacement, visit the corporate security office in Paulsen Hall between 7 a.m. and 5:30 p.m)고 도움 요청에 대한 대응책을 제시하고 있으므로 정답은 (A)이다.

어휘 promote 촉진하다　alert 알리다　authorities 당국

> **Paraphrasing** 지문의 assistance → 정답의 help

166 추론 / 암시

번역 셰퍼드 씨에 대해 암시하는 것은?
(A) 이틀 전에 처음으로 회사 보안 팀에 연락했다.
(B) 회사 주차장을 이용하지 않는다.
(C) 폴센 홀이 어디에 있는지 모른다.
(D) 모바일 기기에 회사 앱을 설치했다.

해설 두 번째 단락의 두 번째 문장에서 모든 직원의 모바일 기기에 설치된 회사 앱에는 이제 회사 주차장과 구내 건물에 출입 허가를 얻는 데 사용되는 디지털 신분증이 포함되어 있다(The company app installed on all employees' mobile ~ corporate parking garage and campus buildings)고 했고, 셰퍼드 씨는 이 회사의 직원이므로 셰퍼드 씨의 모바일 기기에도 회사 앱이 설치되어 있을 것이라고 짐작할 수 있다. 따라서 (D)가 정답이다.

167 동의어

번역 두 번째 단락 3행의 "gain"과 의미가 가장 가까운 단어는?
(A) 이기다
(B) 얻다
(C) 모으다
(D) 늘리다

해설 의미상 출입 허가를 '얻다'라는 뜻으로 쓰인 것이므로 정답은 (B) obtain이다. 참고로, (A) win 또한 '따내다'의 의미가 있어 '얻다'와 비슷하게 느껴지지만, 계약서나 입찰 등과 같이 경쟁을 통해 얻어 내는 성과와 함께 쓰이므로 답이 될 수 없다.

168-171 온라인 채팅

> **마고 바셋 [오전 9시 16분]** 모두 안녕하세요. 신입 사원들을 위한 주간 뉴 애셋 점심 시리즈 일정은 어디까지 되어 가고 있죠?
>
> **스테판 루스 [오전 9시 18분]** 세션 주제를 마무리 지었습니다. 연사 한 명은 확정된 것 같습니다.
>
> **알반 미타트 [오전 9시 20분]** 맞습니다. **168**북부 교외 지사의 살리마 아부바카르가 시리즈의 첫 세션을 맡는 데 동의했습니다.
>
> **마고 바셋 [오전 9시 24분]** 잘됐네요. **168**우리가 계획한 대로 그녀가 6월 10일에 발표할 수 있나요?
>
> **알반 미타트 [오전 9시 26분]** **168**그렇습니다. 그리고 **169**그녀는 패널 토론이 자신의 주제인 재생 가능한 자원에 더 흥미로울 것이라고 제안했습니다. 토론은 그녀가 진행할 것이고요. 그녀가 패널로 제안한 직원 3명에게 이메일을 보냈습니다.
>
> **마고 바셋 [오전 9시 27분]** 좋은 생각이에요. 그리고 다른 세션들은요?
>
> **스테판 루스 [오전 9시 28분]** 그래서, **170**나머지 여섯 세션의 주제는 가상 화폐, 상품, 투자, 신생 기업, 부동산, 그리고 가상 인터페이스입니다. 이번 주말까지 이 세션의 연사들이 준비될 것으로 기대합니다.
>
> **마고 바셋 [오전 9시 31분]** 그리고 **171**세션은 모두 중부 지사에서 열릴 예정입니다.
>
> **스테판 루스 [오전 9시 32분]** 맞습니다. 7명의 신입 사원 중 4명이 중부 지사에 영구 배치됩니다. 나머지 신입 사원들은 필요한 교육을 위해 세션 당일에 그곳에 가 있을 예정이에요.

어휘 asset 자산 new hire 신입 사원 finalize 마무리 짓다 suburban 교외의 take on 맡다 engaging 흥미로운, 매력적인 renewable 재생 가능한 resource 자원 moderate (토론 진행을 위해) 사회를 보다 panelist 토론자 cryptocurrency 가상 화폐 commodity 상품 investment 투자 start-up 신생 기업 real estate 부동산 virtual 가상의 line up 준비[마련]하다 midtown 중간 지대 permanently 영구적으로 assign 배정하다 required 필요한, 필수의

168 추론 / 암시

번역 6월 10일에 열리는 뉴 애셋 점심 세션에 대해 암시하는 것은?
(A) 아부바카르 씨가 진행할 것이다.
(B) 미타트 씨가 소개할 것이다.
(C) 바셋 씨가 출연할 것이다.
(D) 가상화폐에 대한 정보를 포함할 것이다.

해설 9시 20분에 미타트 씨가 북부 교외 지사의 살리마 아부바카르가 시리즈의 첫 세션을 맡는 데 동의했다(Salima Abubakar ~ agreed to take on the first session of the series)고 했고, 9시 24분에 바셋 씨가 계획대로 그녀가 6월 10일에 발표할 수 있는지(Is she able to present on June 10 as we planned?)를 묻자 9시 26분에 미타트 씨가 그렇다(She is)고 대답했다. 따라서 아부바카르

씨가 6월 10일에 열리는 행사의 진행을 맡을 예정임을 알 수 있으므로 (A)가 정답이다.

어휘 feature 출연시키다

> Paraphrasing 지문의 take on the ~ session
> → 정답의 It will be led by

169 의도 파악

번역 오전 9시 27분에 바셋 씨가 "좋은 생각이에요"라고 쓴 의도는?
(A) 뉴 애셋 점심 시리즈에 참석하기를 열망한다.
(B) 아부바카르 씨의 아이디어에 찬성한다.
(C) 모든 세션 주제에 만족한다.
(D) 최근에 채용된 직원들을 만나기를 고대하고 있다.

해설 9시 26분에 미타트 씨가 그녀(아부바카르 씨)는 패널 토론이 자신의 주제인 재생 가능한 자원에 더 흥미로울 것이라고 제안했다(she suggested that a panel discussion might be more engaging for her topic, renewable resources)며 토론은 그녀가 진행할 것(She will moderate the discussion)이라고 하자 9시 27분에 바셋 씨가 좋은 생각이다(That sounds good)라고 호응했다. 따라서 바셋 씨는 패널 토론을 진행하겠다는 아부바카르 씨의 제안에 찬성하려는 의도로 한 말임을 알 수 있으므로 (B)가 정답이다.

어휘 be eager to ~하기를 열망하다 approve of ~에 찬성하다, ~을 승인하다

170 세부 사항

번역 아직 연사가 필요한 세션의 개수는?
(A) 1
(B) 3
(C) 4
(D) 6

해설 9시 28분에 루스 씨가 나머지 여섯 세션의 주제는 가상 화폐, 상품, 투자, 신생 기업, 부동산, 그리고 가상 인터페이스(the topics for the other six sessions ~ and virtual interfaces)라고 설명하면서, 이번 주말까지 이 세션들의 연사가 준비될 것으로 기대한다(I hope to have speakers ~ by the end of this week)고 했으므로 아직 연사가 정해지지 않은 세션은 6개임을 알 수 있다. 따라서 (D)가 정답이다.

171 Not / True

번역 뉴 애셋 점심 시리즈에 대해 사실인 것은?
(A) 직원 교육의 주요 구성 요소이다.
(B) 매주 같은 장소에서 열릴 예정이다.
(C) 패널 토론으로만 구성될 예정이다.
(D) 회사 외부에서 온 발표자가 포함될 것이다.

해설 9시 31분에 바셋 씨가 세션은 모두 중부 지사에서 열릴 예정(they'll all be held at the midtown office)이라고 했으므로 정답은 (B)이다.

어휘 component 요소 consist of ~로 구성되다 exclusively 오로지 ~만 presenter 발표자

172-175 기사

> ### 연구 결과 발표
>
> 갈웨이 (7월 1일) – 아일랜드 농경 협회의 에바 어반과 그녀의 연구팀은 목요일 갈웨이 교통부에 그들의 연구 결과를 발표했다. **172,173년의 연구 기간 동안 팀은 도로를 따라 나무와 관목 심기의 성공을 향상할 수 있는 방법을 연구하는 임무를 맡았다.**
>
> **173"새로 포장된 도로 옆의 땅은 종종 건설에 연계된 중장비로 단단하게 다져집니다."**라고 어반 씨는 말했다. "그 결과, 토양은 물이나 영양분을 잘 흡수할 수 없고, 이것은 새롭게 자라는 식물이 자리 잡는 것을 어렵게 만듭니다. 저희 팀은 고속 도로를 따라 다양한 실험 장소를 설치했고, 무엇이 효과적인지 알아내기 위해 나무 심기, 토양 갈기 및 개선하기의 다양한 조합을 시도했습니다."
>
> 정부의 후원을 받은 이 연구 프로젝트의 최종 결과는 50페이지 분량의 편람으로 편찬되었다. **174이 편람은 갈웨이 교통부를 위해 특별히 작성되었지만 이 책의 권장 사항은 전국의 지방 자치 단체에 의해 활용될 수 있다.**
>
> "각 챕터는 팀에서 식별한 10가지 모범 사례 중 하나에 대해 연구합니다."라고 어반 씨는 말했다. "이러한 기본 기술은 실시되는 위치에 관계없이 적용 가능합니다. 특정 위치에 따른 유일한 변수는 식물 선택인데, 식물 선택이 특정 지역에 따라 달라지기 때문입니다."
>
> **175이 연구가 전하는 또 다른 요점은 성공적인 식물 재배에는 통합적인 접근법이 필요하다는 것이다.** 다시 말해서, 한 가지 조치로는 충분하지 않다. 도로변 식물 심기를 개선하는 데는 현존하는 조건에 대한 철저한 평가뿐 아니라 관련된 특정 문제를 해결하기 위한 다양한 관리 실무가 필요하다.

어휘 findings 연구 결과 agronomy 농경학 association 협회 task 과업을 맡다 shrub 관목 planting (나무) 심기 paved (도로가) 포장된 compact (단단히) 다지다 heavy machinery 중장비 associated with ~와 관련된 soil 토양 absorb 흡수하다 nutrient 영양분 establish 자리 잡게 하다 set up 설치하다 experimental 실험의 plot 터, 대지 various 다양한 combination 조합 till (밭을) 갈다 amend 개정[수정]하다 determine 알아내다, 밝혀내다 work 효과가 있다 compile 편찬하다 handbook 편람, 안내서 specifically 특별히 apply 활용[이용]하다, 적용[응용]하다 municipal 지방 자치제의, 시의 practice 실행 relevant 적절한, 관련된 regardless of ~에 관계없이 implement 실시[시행]하다 site-specific 부지 고유의 variable 변수 selection 선택 depend upon ~에 달려 있다 geographic 지리적인 convey 전하다 integrated 통합적인 approach 접근법 thorough 철저한 assessment 평가 existing 현존하는 address 해결하다, 다루다 involved 관련된

172 세부 사항

번역 기사에서 다뤄진 연구의 주제는?
  (A) 도로변 초목 생태 유지하기
  (B) 고속 도로 노면 손상 방지
  (C) 토종 식물 사용 옹호
  (D) 운전자의 도로변 가시성 개선

해설 첫 단락의 두 번째 문장에서 3년의 연구 기간 동안 팀은 도로를 따라 나무와 관목 심기의 성공을 향상할 수 있는 방법을 연구하는 임무를

맡았다(During their three-year study, the team was tasked with researching ways to improve the success of tree and shrub plantings along roadways)고 했으므로 (A)가 정답이다.

어휘 vegetation 초목 prevent 막다 damage 손상 surface 표면 advocate 옹호하다 native 토종의 visibility 가시성

> Paraphrasing 지문의 tree and shrub → 정답의 vegetation

173 세부 사항

번역 어반 씨가 중장비를 언급한 이유는?
  (A) 식물이 일부 토양에서 잘 자라지 못하는 이유를 설명하려고
  (B) 도로가 더 효율적으로 건설될 수 있다고 주장하려고
  (C) 도로 유지 관리 작업팀이 어린 식물을 조심해서 다뤄야 한다고 제안하려고
  (D) 그녀의 연구팀이 사용한 장비를 설명하려고

해설 두 번째 단락의 첫 문장에서 새로 포장된 도로 옆의 땅은 종종 건설에 연계된 중장비로 단단하게 다져진다고 어반 씨가 말했다("The ground next to newly paved roads is often compacted by heavy machinery associated with construction," Ms. Urban said)고 했고, 뒤이어 그 결과 토양은 물이나 영양분을 잘 흡수할 수 없고 이것은 새롭게 자라는 식물이 자리 잡는 것을 어렵게 만든다(As a result, the soil can't absorb ~ difficult for new growth to establish itself)고 덧붙였으므로 정답은 (A)이다.

어휘 poorly 형편없이 argue 주장하다 efficiently 효율적으로 maintenance 유지 관리 crew 작업반

> Paraphrasing 지문의 difficult for new growth to establish itself → 정답의 grow poorly

174 Not / True

번역 기사에서 편람에 대해 명시된 것은?
  (A) 10페이지밖에 없다.
  (B) 대중에게 배포될 것이다.
  (C) 지역 논란의 주제였다.
  (D) 국가의 다른 지역에서 사용하기에 적합하다.

해설 세 번째 단락의 두 번째 문장에서 편람은 갈웨이 교통부를 위해 특별히 작성되었지만 이 책의 권장 사항은 전국의 지방 자치 단체에 의해 활용될 수 있다(Although the handbook was written specifically for the Galway Department of Transportation, its recommendations can be applied by municipal agencies throughout the country)며 다른 지역에서도 편람의 내용을 이용할 수 있다고 언급했으므로 (D)가 정답이다.

어휘 distribute 배포하다 subject 주제 dispute 논란, 분쟁 appropriate 적합한

> Paraphrasing 지문의 can be applied by municipal agencies → 정답의 appropriate for use in other parts

TEST 9

175 문장 삽입

[1], [2], [3], [4]로 표시된 곳 중에서 다음 문장이 들어가기에 가장 적합한 위치는?

"다시 말해서, 한 가지 조치로는 충분하지 않다."

(A) [1]

(B) [2]

(C) [3]

(D) [4]

해설 제시된 문장의 접속부사 In other words가 문제 해결의 단서이며, '다시 말해서'를 뜻하는 In other words는 앞에서 언급한 내용의 의미를 좀 더 명확히 하기 위해 다른 표현으로 바꿔 말할 때 쓰인다. 따라서 제시된 문장의 한 가지 조치로는 충분하지 않다는 내용과 동일한 내용의 문장 뒤에 들어가야 적절하므로, 성공적인 식물 재배에는 통합적 접근법이 필요하다고 언급하는 문장 뒤인 (D)가 정답이다.

176-180 청구서 + 기사

새벽하늘 출장 요리

호스슈 로 525
가든데일, PA 19061

청구서 날짜: 12월 6일   **청구서 번호:** 5688

176고객명	176모린 시바타	
회사	가든데일 지역 협회 (GNA)	
주소	스트로더 대로 4069, 가든데일, PA 19061	
전화번호	484-555-0152	이메일 mshibata@gardendalena.org
행사일	12월 15일	177잔액 기한 12월 13일

설명	수량	가격
소스를 곁들인 생채소 모듬 접시	5	125달러
닭꼬치구이 (쟁반)	5	150달러
퀴시 타르트 (쟁반)	5	175달러
180작은 초콜릿 케이크 (맞춤형 장식)	50	250달러
소계		700달러
보증금 (11월 25일 수령)		-200달러
177잔액		500달러

의견 및 특별 지시 사항:

176케이크 디자인에 대해 시바타 씨의 11월 30일 이메일을 참고하세요. GNA의 연례 축하연을 위한 것입니다.

어휘 dawn 새벽 catering 음식 공급 invoice 청구서 association 협회 balance 잔액 due (돈을) 지불해야 하는, 지불 기한인 description 설명 platter 접시 assorted 모듬의, 여러 가지의 raw 익히지 않은 dip (찍어 먹는) 소스 quantity 수량 skewer 꼬치 quiche 퀴시(계란 파이의 일종) custom 주문[맞춤] 제작 decorated 장식된 subtotal 소계 deposit 보증금 instruction 지시 사항 reception 축하[환영] 연회

가든데일 (12월 20일) – 178가든데일 지역 협회(GNA)는 지난 토요일 연례 축하연에서 칼라 푸게이트 시장에게 상을 수여했다. 푸게이트 시장은 새로운 레크리에이션 센터를 건설하려는 시의 계획에 대해 짧은 연설을 해 달라는 요청을 받았고, 그 후 웨스트사이드 파크 프로젝트에서 그녀의 역할에 감사하기 위한 특별 명판을 받았다. 마누엘 유엔 GNA 회장은 "푸게이트 시장은 작년에 있었던 공원을 위한 기금 모금 축제를 큰 성공으로 만드는 데 179중요한 역할을 했습니다."라고 말했다. 축제는 GNA가 예상했던 것보다 수천 달러를 더 모았다.

"기쁘고 놀라운 일이었습니다."라고 푸게이트 시장은 말했다. "우리는 공원 프로젝트라는 어려운 임무를 맡았지만, GNA와 지역 사회의 모든 사람들이 전체적으로 훌륭하게 해냈습니다."라고 시장은 말을 이었다.

GNA 축하연은 아름다운 장소를 제공해 준 가든데일 식물원에서 열렸다. 180음식은 새벽하늘 출장 요리에서 공급했으며 각 손님을 위해 GNA 로고로 장식된 개별 초콜릿 케이크가 포함되었다.

어휘 association 협회 honor (공적을 기려 훈장 작위 등을) 수여하다 mayor 시장 present 수여하다 plaque 명판 instrumental 중요한 fund-raising 모금 활동, 자금 마련 raise (자금 등을) 모으다 delightful 기분 좋은 mission 임무 at large 전체적으로 come through 해내다, 완수하다 admirably 훌륭하게, 감탄이 나올 정도로 botanical garden 식물원

---

176 추론 / 암시

번역 청구서에서 시바타 씨에 대해 암시하는 것은?

(A) 행사의 귀빈이 될 것이다.

(B) GNA에 출장 요리 주문에 대한 청구를 했다.

(C) GNA의 축하연의 준비 담당자이다.

(D) 일부 케이크를 직접 장식할 것이다.

해설 청구서 상단의 고객명에 모린 시바타(Customer name: Maureen Shibata)라고 나와 있고, 청구서 하단의 마지막 칸에 케이크 디자인에 대해 시바타 씨의 11월 30일 이메일을 참고하라(See November 30 e-mail from Ms. Shibata about cake designs)면서 GNA의 연례 축하연을 위한 것(This will be for the GNA's annual reception)이라고 했으므로 시바타 씨는 GNA의 축하연을 준비하는 담당자임을 짐작할 수 있다. 따라서 정답은 (C)이다.

어휘 guest of honor 귀빈 charge 청구하다 organizer 준비 담당자, 조직자

177 세부 사항

번역 GNA는 언제 새벽하늘 출장 요리에 500달러를 지불해야 했는가?

(A) 11월 30일

(B) 12월 6일

(C) 12월 13일

(D) 12월 15일

해설 청구서 상단에 잔액 기한(Balance due date)이 12월 13일(December 13)이라고 나와 있고, 하단에 잔액(BALANCE DUE)이 500달러($500.00)라고 나와 있다. 따라서 GNA는 잔액 500달러를 12월 13일까지 지불해야 하므로 (C)가 정답이다.

178 세부 사항

번역 기사에 따르면, 축하연에서 일어난 일은?

(A) 푸게이트 시장이 상을 받았다.

(B) 푸게이트 시장은 연설을 짧게 해 달라는 요청을 받았다.

(C) 푸게이트 시장은 청중들로부터 질문을 받았다.

(D) 푸게이트 시장은 GNA에 가입하라고 권유받았다.

해설 기사의 첫 문장에서 가든데일 지역 협회(GNA)는 지난 토요일 연례 축하연에서 칼라 푸게이트 시장에게 상을 수여했다(The Gardendale Neighborhood Association honored ~ reception last Saturday)고 했으므로 (A)가 정답이다.

> **Paraphrasing** 지문의 honored → 정답의 given an award

179 동의어

번역 기사의 첫 번째 단락 12행의 "instrumental"과 의미가 가장 가까운 단어는?

(A) 기계의

(B) 비공식의

(C) 음악의

(D) 중요한

해설 의미상 '중요한' 역할을 했다는 뜻으로 쓰인 것이므로 '중요한, 필수적인'이라는 의미의 (D) essential이 정답이다.

180 연계

번역 얼마나 많은 사람이 GNA 축하연에 참석했을 것 같은가?

(A) 5

(B) 50

(C) 100

(D) 200

해설 청구서의 중반부에 작은 초콜릿 케이크(Small chocolate cakes)가 50개(50) 주문되었다고 나와 있고, 기사의 마지막 문장에서 음식은 새벽하늘 출장 요리에서 공급했으며 각 손님을 위해 GNA 로고로 장식된 개별 초콜릿 케이크가 포함되었다(The food was provided by ~ cake for each guest decorated with the GNA logo)고 했다. 각 손님이 초콜릿 케이크를 하나씩 받았고, 케이크는 총 50개가 주문되었으므로 축하연에는 50명이 참석했다는 것을 알 수 있다. 따라서 정답은 (B)이다.

181-185 편지 + 이메일

치사카 게이밍 시스템즈

교토 시 나카교구, 니조 덴초, 410-1109

교토, 일본

토비 하이젠버거

라크 대로 1226

올버니, 뉴욕 12210

미국

5월 7일

제품 리콜:

CGS-P27 고속 게임 컴퓨터

하이젠버거 씨께,

[181]CGS-P27 고속 게임 컴퓨터가 리콜되었음을 알려 드립니다. 장치가 과열되어 사용할 수 없게 되었다는 보고를 받았습니다. 이 문제를 해결하기 위해 컴퓨터에 팬을 추가로 설치해야 합니다. [184]개인 고객 식별 번호인 PCI-70734를 이용하셔서 게임 시스템을 구입하신 매장에 반환하십시오. 그러면 귀하의 시스템이 제조업체로 보내져서 비용 없이 수리될 것입니다.

불편을 끼쳐 드려 죄송합니다.

부사장 고부 마쓰이

치사카 게이밍 시스템즈

어휘 recall 리콜 inform 알리다 unit (작은) 장치 overheating 과열 unusable 사용할 수가 없는 address 해결하다 fan 팬, 환풍기 identification 신원 확인 manufacturer 제조업체 expense 비용 vice president 부사장

수신: 버지니아 그레인저 〈v.granger@chisakagamingsystems.jp〉

발신: 제니퍼 킨케이드 〈jkinkaid@albancgm.com〉

날짜: 6월 12일

제목: 제품 리콜

그레인저 씨께,

[182]저희 소매점들은 예정대로 수리를 위해 귀사의 CGS-P27 고속 게임 컴퓨터를 반환받고 있습니다. 아시다시피, 게임 시스템의 소유자들은 2에서 3주 동안 시스템 없이 지내야 한다는 것을 알게 되면 기기 수리 맡기는 것을 꺼립니다. [184]오늘 하루에만 세 명의 고객(PCI-70734, PCI-17503, PCI-90022)이 시스템 수리받는 것을 거절했습니다.

좋은 소식은 귀사의 게임 시스템 사용자들의 고객 충성도가 매우 높다는 것입니다. 하지만 [185]리콜 이행률을 높일 수 있도록, 그리고 고객 관리 차원에서, 대체품 대여 [183]프로그램의 일환으로 저희에게 몇 가지 장치를 제공해 주시면 좋을 것 같습니다. 제가 이 사안에 대해 도울 방법이 있는지 알려주세요.

감사합니다!

제니퍼 킨케이드

알반 컴퓨터즈, 게임즈, 앤드 모어

어휘 retail store 소매점 accept 받아 주다 as arranged 예정대로 be reluctant to ~하기를 꺼리다 give up 넘겨주다[내주다] device 장치 decline 거절하다 loyal 충성스러운 compliance 이행, 준수 public relations 대민 관계, 홍보 gesture 의사 표시 loaner (수리하는 동안 빌려주는) 대체품 arrangement (처리) 방식

181 주제 / 목적

번역 마쓰이 씨가 편지를 보낸 이유는?

(A) 신제품을 광고하려고

(B) 고객에게 문제를 알리려고

(C) 환불이 지급되었는지 확인하려고

(D) 고객에게 업그레이드를 제공하려고

해설 편지의 첫 문장에서 마쓰이 씨가 CGS-P27 고속 게임 컴퓨터가 리콜되었음을 알린다(This is to inform you ~ has been recalled)고 했고, 장치가 과열되어 사용할 수 없게 되었다는 보고를 받았다(We have received reports ~ becoming unusable)며 이 문제를 해결하기 위해 컴퓨터에 팬을 추가로 설치해야 한다(To address this issue ~ installed in your computer)고 했으므로 고객에게 컴퓨터에 결함이 있다는 것을 알리려고 편지를 보냈음을 알 수 있다. 따라서 (B)가 정답이다.

어휘 alert (위험 등을) 알리다   issue 지급[발부]하다

> **Paraphrasing** 지문의 inform → 정답의 alert

182 추론 / 암시

번역 그레인저 씨가 일하는 회사는?
(A) 컴퓨터 제조업체
(B) 소매점
(C) 수리 회사
(D) 게임 대여 서비스

해설 이메일의 첫 문장에서 킨케이드 씨가 그레인저 씨에게 저희 소매점들은 예정대로 수리를 위해 귀사의 CGS-P27 고속 게임 컴퓨터를 반환받고 있다(Our retail stores has been accepting ~ for repairs as arranged)고 보고하고 있는 것으로 보아 그레인저는 CGS-P27 고속 게임 컴퓨터의 제조업체의 직원임을 짐작할 수 있다. 따라서 (A)가 정답이다.

183 동의어

번역 이메일의 두 번째 단락 3행의 "program"과 의미가 가장 가까운 단어는?
(A) 일정표
(B) 계획
(C) 방송
(D) 소프트웨어

해설 의미상 고객 관리를 위한 대체품 대여 '프로그램'이라는 뜻으로 쓰인 것이므로 정답은 '계획, 방식'을 뜻하는 (B) plan이다.

184 연계

번역 하이젠버거 씨에 대해 결론지을 수 있는 것은?
(A) 구매품에 만족하지 않았다.
(B) 선택 사항에 대해 논의하기 위해 그레인저 씨에게 전화했다.
(C) 수리를 위해 시스템을 맡기지 않았다.
(D) 2주간의 작업 완수 시간을 요청했다.

해설 편지의 네 번째 문장에서 하이젠버거 씨에게 개인 고객 식별 번호인 PCI-70734를 이용해 게임 시스템을 구입한 매장으로 반환하라(Please return the gaming system ~ identification number, PCI-70734)고 했고, 이메일의 첫 단락 세 번째 문장에서 오늘 하루에만 세 명의 고객(PCI-70734, PCI-17503, PCI-90022)이 시스템 수리받는 것을 거절했다(Today alone, three customers ~ systems repaired)고 했다. 하이젠버거 씨의 고객 번호가 PCI-70734이므로, 그가 수리를 위한 시스템 반납을 거절한 세 명의 고객 중 한 사람이라는 것을 알 수 있다. 따라서 정답

은 (C)이다.

어휘 bring in 제출하다   turnaround 작업을 완료해서 회송하는 데 걸리는 시간

> **Paraphrasing** 지문의 return → 정답의 bring ~ in

185 세부 사항

번역 킨케이드 씨가 이메일에서 요청한 것은?
(A) 무료 상품
(B) 시스템 업그레이드
(C) 컴퓨터 모니터
(D) 임시 대체품

해설 이메일의 두 번째 단락 두 번째 문장에서 킨케이드 씨가 리콜 이행률을 높일 수 있도록 그리고 고객 관리 차원에서 대체품 대여 프로그램의 일환으로 몇 가지 장치를 제공해 주면 좋을 것 같다(to increase compliance ~ as part of a loaner program)고 했으므로 (D)가 정답이다.

어휘 temporary 임시의   replacement 대체품, 대용품

186-190 이메일 + 웹페이지 + 웹페이지

수신: 마르셀라 와이리무 ⟨m.wairimu@theushindigroup.co.ke⟩
발신: 헨리 분야시 ⟨h.bunyasi@theushindigroup.co.ke⟩
날짜: 2월 3일
제목: 설문 조사

와이리무 씨께,

경영진에서 우리에게 고객들이 우리의 디지털 마케팅 서비스에 얼마나 만족하는지 알아볼 것을 요청했습니다. 이를 위해, **188 4월 한 달 동안 설문 조사를 실시할 예정입니다.**

186 설문 조사 설계 및 분석에 대한 당신의 전문 지식을 바탕으로 우리가 웹사이트에 광고하는 디지털 마케팅 서비스에 대한 평가를 포함한 고객 만족도 설문 조사를 개발해 주셨으면 합니다. 설문 조사는 여기 케냐에 있는 우리의 장기 고객들에게 각각 발송될 예정입니다. 2월 17일까지 초안을 준비하여 경영진이 검토할 수 있도록 보내 주시기 바랍니다. **187 당신과 저는 2월 23일 오후 2시에 있을 경영진 회의에서 초안을 발표할 것입니다.**

헨리 분야시

어휘 management 경영[운영]진   to that end 이를 위해, 그러기 위해서   conduct (특정 활동을) 하다   given ~을 고려해 볼 때   expertise 전문 지식   analysis 분석   evaluation 평가   draft 초안   distribute 배포하다   present 발표하다

https://www.theushindigroup.co.ke/services_survey

| 소개 | 서비스 | 계획 및 가격 | 회사 소식 |

188 만족도 설문조사
5월 1일

우신디 그룹에서는 최고 품질의 마케팅 서비스를 제공하기 위해 노력하고 있습니다. 이것이 저희가 오랜 고객분들께 당사의 디지털 마케팅 서비스에 대해 이 짧은 설문 조사를 완료해 주실 것을 부탁드리는 이유입니다. 귀하께서 제공하는 정보를 통해 저희는 개선 분야를 파악할 수 있습니다. 5월 19일까지 답변을 제출해 주십시오. 더 나은 서비스를 제공할 수 있도록 도와주셔서 감사합니다.

각 서비스에 해당하는 상자에 다음 값 중 하나를 기입해 주십시오.
1=매우 불만족, 2=불만족, 3=의견 없음, 4=만족, 5=매우 만족

디지털 마케팅 서비스

A. 소셜 미디어 광고 ☐
B. 서면 콘텐츠, 사진, 동영상을 포함한 콘텐츠 제작 ☐
190 C. 기존 및 잠재 고객 대상 이메일 마케팅 ☐
D. 웹 및 모바일 앱 개발 및 설계 ☐

고객명 (선택 사항): [＿＿＿＿＿＿＿＿＿＿＿＿＿＿＿＿]

어휘 strive 노력[분투]하다 complete 작성하다 identify 알아보다 improvement 개선 following 다음의 value 값, 가치 appropriate 적절한 dissatisfied 불만족스러운 creation 제작 existing 기존의 potential 잠재인

---

https://www.theushindigroup.co.ke/companynews

| 소개 | 서비스 | 계획 및 가격 | **회사 소식** |

서비스 개선 사항

189,190 고객 의견에 따라 우신디 그룹은 7월 15일에 새로운 이메일 마케팅 전략을 도입할 예정입니다.

우리는 새롭게 자동 전송 이메일에 중점을 둘 것입니다. 189 자동 전송 이메일은 고객의 행동에 따라 자동으로 발송되며 기존의 마케팅 이메일보다 훨씬 더 높은 응답률을 보입니다. 자동 전송 이메일은 기업이 비정기적인 구매자를 충성 고객으로 전환하는 데 도움을 줍니다.

우리는 이런 변화가 우리 고객사의 반복 구매 고객을 눈에 띄게 증가시킬 것으로 기대합니다. 우리의 서비스 가격은 동일하게 유지될 것입니다. 자세한 내용은 마케팅 계정 관리자에게 직접 연락하시거나, 0800 205 555로 우신디 그룹에 전화 또는 info@theushindigroup.co.ke로 이메일을 보내시면 됩니다.

어휘 introduce 도입하다 strategy 전략 triggered email 특정 이벤트 발생 시 자동 전송되는 이메일 automatically 자동으로 rate 비율, ~율 traditional 전통의 casual 비정기적인 loyal 충성스러운 anticipate 예상하다 result in (결과적으로) ~을 야기하다 noticeable 눈에 띄는 repeat customer 반복 구매 고객

---

186 Not / True

번역 이메일에서 와이리무 씨에 대해 언급된 것은?
(A) 그녀의 고객 중 한 명의 불만을 해결했다.
(B) 직원 설문지에 응답했다.
(C) 경영진의 일원이다.
(D) 설문 조사 개발에 대한 전문성이 높다.

해설 이메일의 두 번째 단락 첫 문장에서 와이리무 씨에게 설문 조사 설계 및 분석에 대한 당신의 전문 지식을 바탕으로 우리가 웹사이트에 광고하는 디지털 마케팅 서비스에 대한 평가를 포함한 고객 만족도 설문 조사를 개발해 주었으면 한다(Given your expertise in survey design and analysis ~ digital marketing services we advertise on our Web site)고 했으므로 (D)가 정답이다.

어휘 resolve 해결하다 complaint 불만 questionnaire 설문(지) skilled 전문적인, 숙련된

187 추론 / 암시

번역 2월 23일에 일어날 것 같은 일은?
(A) 우신디 그룹의 웹사이트가 업데이트될 것이다.
(B) 분야시 씨가 광고 예산을 검토할 것이다.
(C) 와이리무 씨가 오후에 회의에 참석할 것이다.
(D) 경영진이 정책 개정안에 투표할 것이다.

해설 이메일의 마지막 문장에서 분야시 씨가 와이리무 씨에게 당신과 저는 2월 23일 오후 2시에 있을 경영진 회의에서 초안을 발표할 것(You and I will present the draft at the management team's meeting on 23 February at 2:00 P.M.)이라고 했으므로, 2월 23일에 와이리무 씨는 분야시 씨와 함께 오후 회의에 참석해 발표를 하고 있을 것임을 알 수 있다. 따라서 정답은 (C)이다.

어휘 vote 투표하다 policy 정책 revision 개정

188 연계

번역 만족도 설문 조사에 대해 결론지을 수 있는 것은?
(A) 우편으로 발송되었다.
(B) 원래 일정대로 고객에게 배포되지 않았다.
(C) 경영진 회의 후에 수정되었다.
(D) 전 세계의 고객들에게 발송되었다.

해설 이메일의 첫 단락 두 번째 문장에서 4월 한 달 동안 설문 조사를 실시할 예정(we will conduct a survey during the month of April)이라고 했는데, 첫 번째 웹페이지의 제목에 따르면 만족도 설문 조사(Satisfaction Survey)가 5월 1일(1 May)에 실시되었으므로 설문 조사가 원래 일정대로 진행되지 않았음을 알 수 있다. 따라서 (B)가 정답이다.

어휘 distribute 배포하다 timetable 일정(표) revise 수정하다

189 주제 / 목적

번역 두 번째 웹페이지에 발표된 소식은?
(A) 서비스 요금이 곧 인상될 것이다.
(B) 마케팅 관리자가 교체되었다.
(C) 설문 조사가 월 단위로 실시될 것이다.
(D) 자동화된 고객 연락 시스템이 시작될 것이다.

해설 두 번째 웹페이지의 첫 문장에서 고객 의견에 따라 우신디 그룹은 7월 15일에 새로운 이메일 마케팅 전략을 도입할 예정(In response to customer feedback ~ a new e-mail marketing strategy on 15 July)이라고 했고, 두 번째 단락의 두 번째 문장에서 자동 전송 이메일은 고객의 행동에 따라 자동으로 발송되며 기존의 마케팅 이메일보다 훨씬 더 높은 응답률을 보인다(Triggered

e-mails are sent out ~ than traditional marketing e-mails)
고 하면서 새로운 자동 전송 이메일 시스템의 도입 소식을 전하고 있
으므로 (D)가 정답이다.

어휘　rate 요금　on a monthly basis 월 단위로　automated
자동화된　launch 시작하다

Paraphrasing　지문의 introduce → 정답의 launch

190 연계

번역　우신디 그룹이 설문 조사 응답을 바탕으로 변경할 디지털 마케팅 서
비스는?
(A) 서비스 A
(B) 서비스 B
(C) 서비스 C
(D) 서비스 D

해설　첫 번째 웹페이지의 설문 조사에서 디지털 마케팅 서비스 C는 기
존 및 잠재 고객 대상 이메일 마케팅을 하는 것(E-mail marketing
to existing and potential customers)이고, 두 번째 웹페이지
의 첫 문장에서 고객 의견에 따라 우신디 그룹은 7월 15일에 새로
운 이메일 마케팅 전략을 도입할 예정(In response to customer
feedback ~ a new e-mail marketing strategy on 15 July)이
라고 했다. 따라서 우신디 그룹은 설문 조사 응답을 바탕으로 고객을
대상으로 하는 이메일 마케팅 즉, 서비스 C를 새롭게 도입하는 것이
므로 (C)가 정답이다.

191-195 기사 + 웹페이지 + 웹페이지

루비오 감독을 기리다

머링턴 (7월 20일) - 페드로 루비오는 10년 전에 감독에서 은퇴했지만,
수상 경력이 있는 그의 영화들은 여전히 오늘날의 영화에 영향을 미치고
있다.

**191루비오의 어린 시절 집은 영화관 근처였는데, 거기서 그는 이 예술
장르에 빠져들었다. 그는 일주일에 몇 편씩 영화를 보았고, 때로는 같은
영화를 여러 번 보았다.**

다양한 장르에 대한 그의 폭넓은 익숙함은 그의 작품에 명백히 드러
난다. 영화는 로맨스 〈장미를 보내줘〉부터 공포물의 고전 〈그 집〉에 이
르기까지 다양하다.

**194루비오는 거의 40년간 감독을 한 뒤 65세의 나이에 영화 제작에서
은퇴했지만 여전히 바쁘다. 가장 최근에 그는 근처의 웨버튼 영화 학교
에서 초빙 강사로 일하고 있다.**

독자들은 머링턴 시네마가 8월 내내 루비오의 영화를 상영할 것이라는
소식을 듣고 기뻐할 것이다. 오랜 팬이든 혹은 루비오 영화를 본 적이 없
든, 여러분은 분명 머링턴 시네마에서 열리는 이 행사가 즐거울 것이다.

어휘　retire 은퇴하다　directing (영화) 감독, 연출　award-
winning 상을 받은　influence 영향을 미치다　multiple 다수의
extensive 광범위한　familiarity 익숙함　apparent 분명한
range from A to B 범위가 A에서 B까지 이르다　lecturer 강사
offering (영화, 책 등에 대해 사람들이 즐기도록) 제공된 것

https://www.merringtoncinema.com

| 홈 | 시간표 | 후기 | 연락처 |

나만의 영화 두 편을 고르세요.

**1928월에 우리는 칭송받는 페드로 루비오 감독의 생일을 기념하여 그의
영화들을 여러 편 상영할 것입니다. 여러분은 한 편의 가격으로 두 편의
영화 티켓을 구매할 수 있습니다! 193루비오는 감독 경력 초기에 아래
목록의 영화들을 제작했습니다.** 전체 영화 목록과 주간 상영 시간은 시
간표 페이지를 확인하세요.

〈지붕을 올려라〉, 코미디, 102분
건설 노동자들이 한 부유한 남자의 꿈의 집을 짓기 위해 최선을 다하는
동안 그의 형제는 그 프로젝트를 가로채려 애쓴다.

195〈다이아몬드 빗속으로〉, 공상 과학, 124분
**두 팀의 연구원들이 해왕성으로 항해하고 그들이 발견한 것을 지구로 전
송하려 애쓴다.**

〈주말과 추억〉, 드라마, 115분
한 무리의 오랜 친구들이 시골집에 모여 마지막으로 함께한 이후로 많은
것이 변했다는 것을 발견한다. 이 영화는 골드 드리머 상을 수상했다.

〈더 스트레인지 드라이브〉, 서부극, 107분
소몰이를 하는 카우보이들이 흥미롭고 색다른 이방인들을 잇따라 마주
친다.

어휘　feature 장편 영화　acclaimed 칭송[찬사]받는　complete
완전한, 전부의　viewing 상영　do one's best 최선을 다하다
wealthy 부유한　take over 탈취하다　Neptune 해왕성
findings 발견(물)　gather 모이다　cattle drive 소몰이
encounter 마주치다　unusual 색다른　stranger 낯선 사람

https://www.merringtoncinema.com/reviews

| 홈 | 시간표 | 후기 | 연락처 |

저는 최근에 페드로 루비오 감독에 관한 훌륭한 기사를 읽었습니다.
**194기사에는 그가 영화 제작에서 은퇴 이후 하고 있는 일에 대한 놀라
운 정보를 포함해 그의 작품과 삶에 대한 많은 정보가 있었습니다.** 기사
에는 또한 머링턴 시네마가 그의 영화를 상영할 것이라는 언급도 있었습
니다. 그래서 저는 영화관의 웹사이트에 가서 원 플러스 원 행사를 확인
했습니다. 저는 이것이 토요일을 보내기에 탁월한 방법이라고 생각해서
영화관에 갔습니다! 저는 두 편의 멋진 영화를 보았습니다. 195제가 본
영화 중 하나는 모르는 영화였는데, 우주에서 임무를 수행하는 과학자들
에 관한 것이었습니다. 정말 좋았어요!

저 같은 영화 팬들에게 머링턴 시네마의 판촉 행사는 완벽했습니다. 10
월에 메레데스 부이의 영화를 위한 비슷한 행사가 있을 예정으로 알고
있습니다. 다음에도 이런 멋진 행사를 꼭 이용할 생각입니다.

탈리아 박

어휘　contain ~이 들어 있다　deal 할인 (행사), 특가　mission
임무　promotion 판촉 (상품), 홍보　take advantage of ~을
이용[활용]하다

191 세부 사항

번역 기사에 따르면, 루비오 씨는 어떻게 영화에 관심을 갖게 되었는가?
(A) 가족이 영화 산업에 종사했다.
(B) 학교에서 영화 동아리에 참여했다.
(C) 어린 시절에 영화관을 자주 방문했다.
(D) 영화관에서 표를 파는 사람이었다.

해설 기사의 두 번째 단락 첫 문장에서 루비오의 어린 시절 집은 영화관 근처였는데 거기서 그는 이 예술 장르에 빠져들었다(Rubio's childhood home was near ~ fell in love with the art form)면서, 그는 일주일에 몇 편씩 영화를 보았고 때로는 같은 영화를 여러 번 보았다(He saw several movies ~ the same movie multiple times)고 했으므로 (C)가 정답이다.

어휘 participate in ~에 참여하다 frequently 자주 youth 어린 시절

> **Paraphrasing** 지문의 childhood → 정답의 youth

192 세부 사항

번역 첫 번째 웹페이지에 따르면, 머링턴 시네마가 판촉 행사를 하는 이유는?
(A) 최근에 개관하여 고객들을 유치하기를 원한다.
(B) 감독의 생일을 기념하는 것이다.
(C) 특정 영화를 상영하기 위해 영화 스튜디오와 제휴했다.
(D) 새로 업그레이드된 건물을 홍보하기를 원한다.

해설 첫 번째 웹페이지의 첫 문장에서 8월에 우리는 칭송받는 페드로 루비오 감독의 생일을 기념하여 그의 영화들을 여러 편 상영할 것(In August, we will celebrate ~ birthday by showing many of his movies)이라고 했으므로 (B)가 정답이다.

어휘 attract 유치하다, 끌다 partner with ~와 제휴하다 certain 특정한 premise 건물, 부지

193 세부 사항

번역 첫 번째 웹페이지에 따르면, 나열된 영화 네 편의 공통점은?
(A) 모두 120분 미만이다.
(B) 모두 우정에 초점을 맞춘다.
(C) 모두 루비오 씨의 초창기 영화이다.
(D) 모두 상을 받았다.

해설 첫 번째 웹페이지의 세 번째 문장에서 루비오는 감독 경력 초기에 아래 목록의 영화들을 제작했다(Rubio made the films listed below at the beginning of his directing career)고 했으므로 웹페이지에 나열된 영화 네 편의 공통점은 루비오 감독의 초창기 영화라는 것이다. 따라서 (C)가 정답이다.

어휘 in common 공통으로 focus on ~에 초점을 맞추다

> **Paraphrasing** 지문의 made the films ~ at the beginning → 정답의 are ~ early films

194 연계

번역 박 씨는 루비오 씨의 어떤 점에 놀라워했는가?
(A) 지역 영화 학교에서 가르치고 있다.
(B) 거의 40년 동안 영화를 감독했다.
(C) 여러 장르에서 일했다.
(D) 자신의 영화관을 개관했다.

해설 기사의 네 번째 단락 첫 문장에서 루비오는 거의 40년간 감독을 한 뒤 65세의 나이에 영화 제작에서 은퇴했지만 여전히 바쁘다(Rubio retired from filmmaking ~ he has kept busy)며 가장 최근에 그는 근처의 웨버튼 영화 학교에서 초빙 강사로 일하고 있다(Most recently, he has been working as a guest lecturer ~ Weberton Film School)고 했고, 두 번째 웹페이지의 두 번째 문장에서 박 씨는 기사에는 그가 영화 제작에서 은퇴한 이후 하고 있는 일에 대한 놀라운 정보를 포함해 그의 작품과 삶에 대한 많은 정보가 있었다(It contained a lot of information ~ since he retired from filmmaking)고 했다. 박 씨는 루비오 감독이 은퇴 후 하고 있는 일에 놀랐다고 했고, 기사에 따르면 그는 은퇴 후 영화 학교에서 강의를 하고 있다고 했으므로 (A)가 정답이다.

> **Paraphrasing** 지문의 working as a guest lecturer → 정답의 teaching

195 연계

번역 박 씨가 최근에 처음 본 영화는?
(A) 〈지붕을 올려라〉
(B) 〈다이아몬드 빗속으로〉
(C) 〈주말과 추억〉
(D) 〈더 스트레인지 드라이브〉

해설 첫 번째 웹페이지에 나열된 두 번째 영화 〈다이아몬드 빗속으로〉(Through a Diamond Rain)는 두 팀의 연구원들이 해왕성으로 항해하고 그들이 발견한 것을 지구로 전송하려 애쓴다(Two teams of researchers travel ~ send their findings back to Earth)는 내용이고, 두 번째 웹페이지의 첫 단락 일곱 번째 문장에서 박 씨는 제가 본 영화 중 하나는 모르는 영화였는데, 우주에서 임무를 수행하는 과학자들에 관한 것이었다(One of the films I saw ~ scientists on a mission in space)고 했다. 따라서 박 씨가 최근 처음 본 영화는 〈다이아몬드 빗속으로〉이므로 (B)가 정답이다.

196-200 정책 + 이메일 + 이메일

> **투고 정책**
>
> 〈언디나이어블〉은 신예 작가들의 단편 소설 및 비소설로 구성된 광고 지원 무료 문학 저널입니다. 처음으로 투고하는 사람들에게는 5달러의 수수료를 면제해 드립니다.
>
> - [198]이야기는 250에서 1,000 단어 사이어야 합니다 ([196]시는 받지 않습니다).
>
> - 삽화를 포함시키지 마세요. 모든 삽화는 사내에서 제작됩니다.
>
> - 여러분의 이야기를 이메일에 첨부해 submissions@undeniable. com으로 보내 주세요. 작품에 대한 간단한 줄거리와 함께 어떻게 〈언디나이어블〉을 알게 되었는지 알려 주세요.

- **199**출판이 승인되면 50달러의 사례금을 지불합니다.

- 이야기를 받게 될 경우, 여러분에게 계약서와 전자 송금을 설정하기 위한 양식을 보낼 것입니다.

어휘 submission 투고, 제출(물) undeniable 부정할 수 없는 ad-supported 광고를 보여 주고 무료로 제공하는 literary 문학의 journal 잡지, 학술지 fiction 소설 nonfiction 비소설 emerging 신예의, 신흥의 waive 면제하다 poetry 시 illustration 삽화 in-house 사내의 brief 간단한 synopsis 줄거리, 개요 honorarium 사례(금) upon ~할 때 acceptance 승인 publication 출판(물) transfer 송금

수신: submissions@undeniable.com
발신: len.sutherland@onyxmail.com
날짜: 3월 15일
제목: 자기소개서와 원고 제출물
첨부: ⓤ지의 여행

반갑습니다!

제 원고 제출물인 '지의 여행'은 패션업계에서 자신의 꿈을 실현하기 위해 장애를 극복하는 젊은 드레스 디자이너 토비 지에 중심을 두고 있습니다.

197저는 작년에 오리건 주 포틀랜드에 있는 아트만 학원의 작문 강사로부터 〈언디나이어블〉을 소개받았고, 그 이후 구독자가 되었습니다. **198**저는 특히 논픽션 코너를 좋아하며, 제가 가장 좋아하는 글 중 하나인 '웨이건 비치'는 제가 '지의 여행'을 쓰는 데 영감을 주었습니다. 저는 이 글이 이 섹션에 이상적으로 딱 맞을 거라고 믿습니다. '웨이건 비치'처럼 '지의 여행'은 희망과 인내의 실화입니다.

저와 같은 신인 작가들을 위한 포럼을 만들어 주시고 고려해 주셔서 감사합니다.

렌 서덜랜드

어휘 journey 여행 greetings 인사(말) center (~에) 중심을 두다 overcome 극복하다 obstacle 장애(물) realize 실현하다 instructor 강사 institute 학원, 기관 subscriber 구독자 particularly 특히 inspire 영감을 주다 fit 맞는 것, 적합한 것 perseverance 인내, 끈기 consideration 고려

수신: len.sutherland@onyxmail.com
발신: jerrybuckman@undeniable.com
날짜: 7월 2일
제목: 작가님의 원고 제출물

서덜랜드 씨께,

199작가님의 이야기 '지의 여행'은 6월 호에 많은 긍정적인 반응을 불러일으켰습니다. 축하합니다! 그리고 이야기 배치에 대한 작가님의 직감은 옳았습니다. 이 모든 것 때문에 우리는 작가님이 〈언디나이어블〉에 더 많은 이야기를 제출해 주시기를 희망하게 되었습니다. 추가 인센티브로 우리는 다음 달부터 사례금을 100달러로 인상할 예정입니다.

200구독자로서, 매달 다른 작가가 등장하는 스테이시 조던의 질의응답 칼럼에 익숙하실 것입니다. 작가님의 문학 훈련, 글쓰기 방법, 그리고 이

야기의 아이디어를 찾는 방법에 대한 몇 가지 질문에 대답해 주실 의향이 있으신지요? 만약 그렇다면, 작가님의 이메일 주소를 조던 씨에게 전달하겠습니다. 조던 씨가 가까운 시일 내에 연락할 것입니다.

제리 벅맨
부편집장

어휘 generate 발생시키다 a great deal of 많은 positive 긍정적인 issue (정기 간행물의) 호 instinct 본능, 직감 placement 배치 be familiar with ~에 익숙하다 feature 특별히 포함하다 be willing to 기꺼이 ~하다 method 방법 forward 전달하다 reach out 연락하다 associate 부[준]

196 Not / True

번역 정책에서 〈언디나이어블〉에 대해 명시하는 것은?
(A) 시를 받지 않는다.
(B) 광고가 없다.
(C) 작가들에게 그림을 제출할 것을 요구한다.
(D) 유명 작가들의 작품을 출판한다.

해설 〈언디나이어블〉의 투고 정책 안내문에서 첫 항목으로 나온 이야기 단어 수 지정 뒤에 추가로 시는 받지 않는다(no poetry, please)고 나와 있으므로 (A)가 정답이다.

어휘 author 작가

> Paraphrasing 지문의 no poetry
> → 정답의 not accept poems

197 세부 사항

번역 첫 번째 이메일에 따르면, 서덜랜드 씨는 어디에서 〈언디나이어블〉을 알게 되었는가?
(A) 공공 도서관
(B) 학교 서점
(C) 작문 강좌
(D) 옷 가게

해설 첫 번째 이메일의 두 번째 단락 첫 문장에서 서덜랜드 씨는 작년에 오리건 주 포틀랜드에 있는 아트만 학원의 작문 강사로부터 〈언디나이어블〉을 소개받았고 그 이후 구독자가 되었다(I was introduced to *Undeniable* last year by my writing instructor ~ since become a subscriber)고 했으므로 (C)가 정답이다.

198 연계

번역 '웨이건 비치'에 대해 결론지을 수 있는 것은?
(A) 오리건 주 포틀랜드에서 열린다.
(B) 출판용으로 받아들여지지 않았다.
(C) 서덜랜드 씨의 첫 글이다.
(D) 1,000단어를 넘지 않는다.

해설 정책 중 첫 항목에 이야기는 250에서 1,000단어 사이여야 한다(Stories must be between 250 and 1,000 words)고 했고, 첫 번째 이메일의 두 번째 단락 두 번째 문장에서 서덜랜드 씨는 〈언디

나이어블〉에 대해 언급하며 자신은 특히 논픽션 코너를 좋아하고 가장 좋아하는 글 중 하나인 '웨이건 비치'는 '지의 여행'을 쓰는 데 영감을 주었다(I particularly enjoy your Nonfiction Corner; one of my favorites was "Waygone Beach," which inspired me to write "Ji's Journey")고 했다. 따라서 '웨이건 비치'는 〈언디나이어블〉의 논픽션 코너에 수록된 글로 250에서 1,000단어 사이라는 것을 알 수 있으므로 (D)가 정답이다.

어휘   exceed 초과하다

Paraphrasing   지문의 between 250 and 1,000 words
→ 정답의 not exceed 1,000 words

199 연계

번역   서덜랜드 씨는 〈언디나이어블〉 6월 호에 실린 이야기에 대해 얼마를 받았는가?
(A) 5달러
(B) 50달러
(C) 100달러
(D) 250달러

해설   정책 중 네 번째 항목에 출판이 승인되면 50달러의 사례금을 지불한다(We pay a $50 ~ acceptance for publication)고 나와 있고, 두 번째 이메일의 첫 문장에서 서덜랜드 씨에게 작가님의 이야기 '지의 여행'이 6월 호에 많은 긍정적인 반응을 불러일으켰다(Your story, "Ji's Journey," generated ~ about the June issue)고 했다. 따라서 서덜랜드 씨의 글이 승인되어 6월 호에 실렸으므로 정답은 (B)이다.

200 추론 / 암시

번역   두 번째 이메일에서 조던 씨에 대해 암시하는 것은?
(A) 구독을 갱신할 계획이다.
(B) 〈언디나이어블〉을 위해 칼럼을 쓴다.
(C) 작문 수업을 가르친다.
(D) 작문 방식이 독특하다.

해설   두 번째 이메일의 두 번째 단락 첫 문장에서 〈언디나이어블〉의 구독자로서 매달 다른 작가가 등장하는 스테이시 조던의 질의응답 칼럼에 익숙하실 것(As a subscriber, you are likely familiar with Stacy Jordan's question-and-answer column ~ each month)이라고 한 것으로 보아 조던 씨는 〈언디나이어블〉에 칼럼을 기고하는 작가임을 알 수 있다. 따라서 (B)가 정답이다.

어휘   renew 갱신하다   subscription 구독   unusual 특이한
method 방식

TEST 9

기출 TEST 10

101 (B)	**102** (B)	**103** (C)	**104** (A)	**105** (B)
106 (B)	**107** (C)	**108** (C)	**109** (A)	**110** (D)
111 (C)	**112** (C)	**113** (B)	**114** (C)	**115** (B)
116 (B)	**117** (D)	**118** (B)	**119** (A)	**120** (D)
121 (A)	**122** (C)	**123** (A)	**124** (B)	**125** (C)
126 (D)	**127** (B)	**128** (C)	**129** (A)	**130** (B)
131 (A)	**132** (D)	**133** (B)	**134** (C)	**135** (D)
136 (B)	**137** (B)	**138** (C)	**139** (B)	**140** (C)
141 (B)	**142** (C)	**143** (D)	**144** (A)	**145** (C)
146 (A)	**147** (C)	**148** (A)	**149** (A)	**150** (B)
151 (B)	**152** (B)	**153** (A)	**154** (B)	**155** (C)
156 (A)	**157** (B)	**158** (D)	**159** (C)	**160** (D)
161 (C)	**162** (D)	**163** (B)	**164** (C)	**165** (D)
166 (C)	**167** (D)	**168** (A)	**169** (D)	**170** (C)
171 (D)	**172** (B)	**173** (B)	**174** (A)	**175** (C)
176 (B)	**177** (A)	**178** (D)	**179** (B)	**180** (D)
181 (D)	**182** (A)	**183** (B)	**184** (C)	**185** (D)
186 (C)	**187** (D)	**188** (A)	**189** (C)	**190** (D)
191 (D)	**192** (A)	**193** (C)	**194** (C)	**195** (D)
196 (C)	**197** (D)	**198** (B)	**199** (C)	**200** (A)

PART 5

101 to부정사의 부사적 용법

해설 빈칸 앞에 완전한 절이 있고 빈칸 뒤 the needs를 목적어로 취할 수 있어야 하므로 to부정사가 와야 한다. 문맥상 '고객의 욕구를 충족시키기 위해'라는 내용이 되면 자연스러우므로 '~하기 위해서'라는 목적의 의미를 지니는 (B) to meet이 정답이다.

번역 애버딘 은행은 고객의 요구를 충족시키기 위해 다양한 금융 서비스를 제공한다.

어휘 a range of 다양한 meet 충족시키다 need 요구

102 수량 형용사

해설 빈칸 뒤의 staff는 단·복수의 형태가 동일한 명사인데, 뒤에 복수동사 are가 왔으므로 이 문장에서 staff는 복수명사로 쓰였고 '모든 직원은 ~을 제공해야 한다'는 의미가 되어야 자연스러우므로 (B) All이 정답이다. (A) Every와 (C) Each는 뒤에 '가산 단수명사 + 단수동사'가 와야 하고, (D) Any는 가산 단·복수, 불가산명사와 함께 쓰일 수 있지만, 긍정문에 쓰이면 '어떤 ~라도'라는 뜻으로 막연한 대상을 지칭하므로 회사 전체 직원을 통칭하는 문맥에는 어울리지 않는다.

번역 전 직원은 백업 휴대 전화 번호와 이메일 주소를 제공하도록 요청받는다.

어휘 backup (비상시의) 대체, 여분

103 인칭대명사의 격 _ 소유격

해설 빈칸에는 뒤에 온 명사 ideas를 수식하는 소유격 인칭대명사가 들어가야 한다. 따라서 정답은 (C) his이다.

번역 오늘 란 씨는 회사의 회계 소프트웨어 개선을 위한 아이디어를 발표할 예정이다.

어휘 present 발표하다 improve 개선하다 accounting 회계

104 부사 어휘

해설 is enforced를 수식하여 적절한 문맥을 완성하는 부사를 고르는 문제이다. '엄격하게 시행되고 있다'는 의미가 되어야 자연스러우므로 '엄격히'라는 뜻의 (A) strictly가 정답이다.

번역 본사의 점심시간 1시간 정책은 엄격하게 시행되고 있으므로 늦게 돌아와서는 안 됩니다.

어휘 firm 회사 policy 정책 enforce (법률 등을) 시행하다 punctually 시간에 맞추어 bravely 용감하게

105 전치사 어휘

해설 빈칸에는 형용사 contingent와 함께 쓰여 '~에 달린'이라는 의미를 나타내는 전치사가 들어가야 한다. 따라서 정답은 (B) on이다.

번역 마르티노바 씨의 최고 재무 책임자 승진은 우리 경영 이사회의 승인 여부에 달려 있다.

어휘 board 이사회 be contingent on ~에 달려 있다 executive 경영진

106 부사 자리 _ 형용사 수식

해설 빈칸은 형용사 accessible을 수식하는 부사 자리이므로 정답은 '쉽게'라는 뜻의 부사 (B) easily이다.

번역 반도의 최남단 지역은 여행객들이 쉽게 접근할 수 없기 때문에 방문이 거의 없다.

어휘 peninsula 반도 southernmost 최남단의 portion 부분 rarely 좀처럼 ~하지 않는 accessible 접근 가능한

107 동사 어휘

해설 빈칸 뒤에 목적어가 두 개이므로 4형식 동사가 필요하고, '모든 고객에게 균일한 상담료를 부과한다'는 내용이 되어야 자연스러우므로 '~에게 …을 청구[부과]하다'를 의미하는 동사 (C) charges가 정답이다.

번역 바크니스 그룹은 모든 고객에게 균일한 상담료를 부과하여 미리 지불되도록 한다.

어휘 flat 균일한, 고정된 consultation 상담 in advance 미리

108 접속사 자리 _ 등위접속사

해설 소유격 their 뒤의 명사구 e-mail account와 time sheet을 연결해 줄 등위접속사가 필요하다. '이메일 계정 또는 근무 시간 기록표에 접속할 수 없다'는 내용이므로 '또는'을 의미하는 등위접속사 (C) or가 정답이다.

번역　8월 19일에 직원들은 이메일 계정이나 근무 시간 기록표에 접속할 수 없다.

어휘　time sheet 근무 시간 기록표

109　부사 어휘

해설　명사구 a reliable source of business를 수식하여 적절한 문맥을 완성하는 부사를 고르는 문제이다. '통상적으로, 믿을 수 있는 수입 원천이다'라는 의미가 되어야 자연스러우므로 '통상적으로, 일반적으로'라는 뜻의 (A) typically가 정답이다. 부사는 일반적으로 명사를 수식하지 않지만 명사구 앞에서 강조하는 역할을 할 수 있다.

번역　예약 없이 방문하는 고객은 통상적으로 오번 헤어 살롱의 믿을 수 있는 수입 원천이다.

어휘　walk-in 예약이 안 된　reliable 믿을 수 있는　source 원천　fairly 공정하게　sharply 날카롭게　evenly 고르게

110　부사 어휘

해설　recyclable을 수식하여 적절한 문맥을 완성하는 부사를 고르는 문제이다. '완전히 재활용될 것이다'는 의미가 되어야 자연스러우므로 '완전히'라는 뜻의 (D) fully가 정답이다.

번역　올해 말까지 쉐퍼의 식료품에 사용되는 모든 포장재는 완전히 재활용될 것이다.

어휘　packaging 포장(재)　recyclable 재활용할 수 있는　critically 비판적으로　initially 처음에　freshly 신선하게　fully 완전히

111　명사 자리 _ 전치사의 목적어

해설　전치사 with의 목적어 역할로 관사와 형용사 뒤에 명사가 와야 하므로 (C) experience가 정답이다.

번역　하이브룩 호텔 직원은 각 투숙객에게 특별한 경험을 제공하도록 교육받는다.

어휘　exceptional 탁월한

112　명사 자리 _ 전치사의 목적어

해설　빈칸은 전치사 in의 목적어 자리이므로 명사인 (C) appreciation이 정답이다. '~에 감사하여'라는 의미의 전치사구 in appreciation for는 알아 두면 좋다.

번역　도움에 감사하여 도서관의 도서 판매에 참가한 자원봉사자들에게 맞춤 제작된 티 머그잔이 주어졌다.

어휘　personalized 맞춤 제작된　appreciative 고마워하는　appreciation 감사

113　전치사 어휘

해설　빈칸 뒤의 기간 표현 the next two weeks와 어울려야 하며, 문맥상 '향후 2주 동안'이라는 내용이 되어야 자연스럽다. 따라서 기간 앞에서 '~ 동안'을 뜻하는 (B) over가 정답이다.

번역　직원들이 새로운 소프트웨어 사용법을 배워야 하기 때문에 향후 2주 동안 몇 가지 교육이 진행될 것이다.

114　부사 자리 _ 준동사 수식

해설　빈칸이 없어도 완전한 문장을 이루고 있으므로, 빈칸에는 앞에 나온 to부정사구 to take their seats를 수식하는 부사가 들어가면 된다. 따라서 정답은 '빨리'를 뜻하는 부사 (C) quickly이다.

번역　승무원들은 승객들에게 비행기 탑승 시 신속하게 자리에 앉아 달라고 요청했다.

어휘　flight attendant (비행기) 승무원　passenger 승객　board 탑승하다

115　동사의 시제

해설　문장의 맨 앞에 과거를 나타내는 시간 형용사 Last가 있어 '지난 7월'에 일어난 일에 대해 언급하고 있으므로 동사는 과거 시제가 되어야 한다. 따라서 (B) hosted가 정답이다.

번역　지난 7월 로하스 리퍼사는 성대한 개막 축하 행사를 주최했다.

116　전치사 어휘

해설　문맥상 '세 사람 중 한 명'이라는 의미가 되어야 적절하므로 '~의 (일부), ~ 중의'라는 부분의 의미를 나타내는 (B) of가 정답이다.

번역　김 씨는 회사의 경쟁력 상을 받은 세 사람 중 한 명이었다.

어휘　receive 받다　firm 회사　competitive edge 경쟁 우위, 경쟁력

117　명사 어휘

해설　전치사 for의 목적어 역할을 하는 명사 자리로, 빈칸 앞의 복합명사 production manager와 함께 쓰여 '생산 관리자직'이라는 의미의 복합명사를 만들 수 있는 '직책'이라는 뜻의 (D) position이 정답이다.

번역　주 제약회사의 생산 관리자직에 대한 면접이 오늘 시작된다.

어휘　pharmaceuticals 제약회사　participation 참여　outline 개요　arrangement 준비

118　전치사 어휘

해설　빈칸 뒤에 기간을 나타내는 명사 the summer가 있고, 문맥상 '여름 동안 일주일에 두 번'이라는 의미가 되어야 자연스러우므로 '~ 동안'을 뜻하는 (B) during이 정답이다.

번역　여름에는 역사적인 법원 견학이 일주일에 두 번 제공된다.

어휘　historic 역사적인　courthouse 법원

119　전치사 자리

해설　빈칸은 콤마 뒤에 오는 완전한 절에 명사구 the next few months를 연결하는 자리이므로 전치사가 들어가야 한다. 따라서 '~ 이내에'라는 의미의 전치사 (A) Within이 정답이다.

번역　앞으로 몇 달 이내에 어번디사는 뉴질랜드에 네 번째 제약 연구소를 열 예정이다.

어휘　pharmaceutical 제약의　laboratory 연구소, 실험실

120 명사 자리 _ 동사의 주어

해설 빈칸은 동사 organizes 앞 주어 자리이며, 빈칸 앞에 관사 The가 있으므로 명사가 와야 한다. 따라서 명사인 (D) coordinator가 정답이다.

번역 요하난사의 진행자는 모든 회의 장소로 물품을 배송하는 일을 주관한다.

어휘 organize 준비[조직]하다 supplies 물품 coordinate 조정하다 coordinator 진행자

121 동사 자리

해설 The owners가 주어인 문장에 동사가 보이지 않으므로 빈칸은 동사 자리이다. 따라서 '의도하다'라는 뜻의 동사인 (A) intend가 정답이다.

번역 로워크로프트 포슬린의 소유주들은 다음 달에 캐주얼 식기 세트의 생산을 시작할 계획이다.

어휘 dinnerware 식기류 intentional 의도적인 intentionally 의도적으로

122 형용사 어휘

해설 빈칸은 복합명사 vacation time을 수식하는 형용사 자리이다. '연장된 휴가 기간'이라는 의미가 되어야 자연스러우므로 '연장된'이라는 뜻의 (C) extended가 정답이다.

번역 마이코스 오토 메이커스는 장기근속 공장 직원들에게 연장된 휴가 기간을 승인해 주기로 동의했다.

어휘 grant 승인[허락]하다 exhausted 고갈된

123 부사 자리 _ 동사 수식

해설 The customer가 주어이고 believed가 동사이며, 빈칸은 동사 believed를 수식하는 부사 자리이다. 따라서 '실수로, 잘못으로'라는 뜻의 부사인 (A) mistakenly가 정답이다.

번역 그 고객은 그가 구입한 코트가 방수라고 잘못 믿었다.

어휘 waterproof 방수의

124 과거분사

해설 이 문장에서 come은 '(상품이) ~한 상태로 나오다'는 뜻의 2형식 동사로 쓰였으므로 빈칸은 주어 All cars를 수식하는 주격 보어 자리이다. 자동차는 '장치가 장착되는' 대상이고, '모든 차는 장치가 장착되어 나온다'는 내용이 되어야 자연스러우므로 수동의 의미를 나타내는 과거분사인 (B) equipped가 정답이다.

번역 로드웨이 모터스가 만든 모든 차는 운전자에게 안전벨트를 맬 것을 상기시켜주는 경보 장치가 장착되어 나온다.

어휘 buckle 버클로 잠그다

125 지시대명사

해설 빈칸은 전치사 as의 목적어 자리이고, 앞서 언급된 복수명사 The components를 반복해서 사용하는 것을 피하기 위해 쓰는 지시대명사 자리이므로 정답은 (C) those이다. CT640 식기 세척기의 부품과 이전 모델의 부품은 각각 다른 대상이므로, 정확히 동일한 대상을 지칭할 때 쓰는 인칭대명사 (B) them은 답이 될 수 없다.

번역 CT640 식기 세척기의 부품은 이전 모델의 부품과 대체로 동일하다.

어휘 component 부품 dishwasher 식기 세척기 largely 대체로

126 명사 자리 _ 복합명사

해설 전치사 for의 목적어 역할로 소유격 its와 형용사 innovative의 수식을 받아 '혁신적인 마케팅 전략'이라는 의미의 복합명사를 만들 수 있는 (D) strategies가 정답이다.

번역 나카토 그룹은 혁신적인 마케팅 전략으로 여러 업계 상을 수상했다.

어휘 industry 산업 innovative 혁신적인 strategize 전략을 짜다

127 분사 어휘

해설 빈칸은 최상급 부사 most widely의 수식을 받으면서 명사 book을 수식하는 형용사 자리이다. 보기는 모두 분사 형태로, 문맥상 '가장 널리 기대되는 책'이라는 내용이 되어야 자연스러우므로 '기대되는'이라는 의미의 (B) anticipated가 정답이다.

번역 크리트 핀통의 신작 추리 소설은 올해 가장 널리 기대되는 책이다.

어휘 estimate 추산[추정]하다 assume (사실일 것으로) 추정[상정]하다 predict 예측[예견]하다

128 접속사 자리 _ 부사절 접속사

해설 빈칸 뒤에 주어와 동사를 갖춘 완전한 절이 왔으므로 부사절 접속사가 들어가야 한다. 따라서 '~할 때'라는 의미의 접속사 (C) when이 정답이다.

번역 토비야르 건설 프로젝트가 예산 내에서 완공되자 지도부는 상당히 안도했다.

어휘 relieved 안도하는 budget 예산

129 전치사 자리

해설 빈칸은 쉼표 뒤 완전한 절에 명사구 two floors (of offices)를 연결하는 자리이므로 전치사가 들어가야 한다. 따라서 '~ 이외에도'라는 의미의 전치사구 (A) In addition to가 정답이다.

번역 사무실 두 개 층 외에도 이 건물은 여러 소매 공간을 제공한다.

어휘 retail 소매(업)

130 명사 어휘

해설 빈칸에 들어갈 명사는 전치사구 regarding construction noise and traffic delays(공사 소음 및 교통 지연에 대한)의 수식을 받으

면서, 내용상 프로젝트 관리자에게 전달될 수 있는 것이어야 한다. '공사 소음 및 교통 지연에 대한 우려'라는 문맥이 자연스러우므로 '우려, 걱정거리'라는 뜻의 (B) Concerns가 정답이다.

번역　공사 소음 및 교통 지연에 대한 우려는 프로젝트 관리자인 자스디 씨에게 전달해야 한다.

어휘　direct 보내다　material 자료　expansion 확장

PART 6

131-134 광고

RGBS 자동차 팀에 합류하세요.

RGBS 자동차는 ¹³¹현재 정규직 및 시간제 근로자를 채용 중입니다. 오늘 바로 지원하세요! ¹³²당신은 우리 생산 팀의 일원이 될 수 있습니다! 우리는 모든 종류의 자동차와 트럭에서 볼 수 ¹³³있는 첨단 제품을 만듭니다.

RGBS 자동차는 보수가 높고, 지속적인 교육과 승진 기회를 제공합니다. ¹³⁴휴가 일수 또한 후하게 제공합니다. 자세한 내용 확인 및 지원서 작성을 위해서는 www.rgbsautomotive.com을 방문하세요.

어휘　apply 지원하다　manufacturing 제조(업)　kind 종류
ongoing 진행 중인　promotion 승진　detail 세부 사항　fill out
작성하다　application 지원서

131 부사 어휘

해설　동사가 현재 진행 시제이므로 '현재 채용 중이다'라는 의미를 이루는 부사 (A) now가 정답이다.

132 인칭대명사 _ 주격

해설　해당 글은 구인 광고문으로 광고문을 읽을 만한 불특정 독자를 대상으로 하는 글이다. 광고를 읽고 있는 '당신'은 '우리 팀의 일원이 될 수 있다'는 의미가 되어야 적절하므로 (B) You가 정답이다.

133 주격 관계대명사 + 시제

해설　해당 문장에는 이미 동사(make)가 있으므로 빈칸 뒤의 과거분사 found는 앞에 나온 명사 products를 수식하는 관계사절과 함께 와야 한다. 본동사 make가 현재 시제이고 일반적인 사실을 언급하고 있으므로 현재 시제 동사와 함께 쓴 (B) that are가 정답이다. 참고로 주격 관계대명사와 be동사는 생략이 가능하므로 that are는 생략할 수 있다.

134 문맥에 맞는 문장 고르기

해설　빈칸 앞에서 RGBS 자동차는 보수가 높고 지속적인 교육과 승진 기회를 제공한다며 회사의 복지 혜택에 대해 설명하고 있으므로 비슷한 내용이 연결되어야 자연스럽다. 따라서 제공되는 휴가 일수에 대해 언급하고 있는 (C)가 정답이다.

번역　(A) 우리 회사는 경쟁이 치열한 산업입니다.
　　　(B) RGBS 자동차는 45년 전에 사업을 시작했습니다.
　　　(C) 휴가 일수 또한 후하게 제공합니다.
　　　(D) RGBS 자동차는 다양한 상품을 판매합니다.

어휘　competitive 경쟁을 하는　generous 후한　a selection of
엄선된, 다양한　merchandise 상품

135-138 회람

회람

수신: 마케팅 팀
발신: 알리사 제이콥스, 프로젝트 관리자
날짜: 9월 27일
제목: 회의 요약

다가오는 터보 오메가 2 스마트폰의 마케팅 캠페인에 대한 여러분의 세심한 작업에 다시 한번 감사드립니다. 어제 회의에서 ¹³⁵결정된 대로 우리의 목표는 11월 1일에 TV, 라디오, 소셜 미디어 광고를 시작하는 것입니다. 휴대폰 자체는 12월 1일까지 매장에 입고될 예정입니다. ¹³⁶이로써 우리에게는 소비자의 흥미를 불러일으킬 수 있는 한 달의 시간이 주어집니다.

¹³⁷곧 개리 카롤로가 보도 자료 초안을 작성하여 공유 드라이브에 게시하면 여러분 모두가 이 자료를 읽을 수 있을 것입니다. 수정에 관한 ¹³⁸제안이 있으면 일주일 내로 개리에게 이메일을 보내 주세요. 그는 다음 정기 회의에서 최종안을 발표할 것입니다. 그때 모든 미진한 부분을 매듭지을 것입니다.

어휘　wrap-up 마무리　upcoming 다가오는　launch 시작하다
draft 초안을 작성하다　press release 보도 자료　post 게시하다
present 발표하다　tie up 단단히 매다　loose end 미진한 부분

135 동사 어휘

해설　'~된 대로, ~되어 있듯이'라는 뜻으로 쓰이는 'as + p.p.' 구문의 과거분사 자리에 들어갈 동사 어휘를 고르는 문제이다. '어제 회의에서 결정된 대로'라는 의미가 되어야 자연스러우므로 (D) decided가 정답이다.

136 문맥에 맞는 문장 고르기

해설　빈칸 앞에서 목표는 11월 1일에 광고를 시작하는 것이고, 휴대폰은 12월 1일까지 매장에 입고 예정이라며 마케팅 캠페인의 일정에 대해 안내하고 있으므로 빈칸에도 이 일정과 관련된 내용이 이어져야 자연스럽다. 따라서 광고 시작일과 휴대폰 입고일 사이의 시간차를 This로 받아 한 달의 시간이 주어졌다고 언급하고 있는 (B)가 정답이다.

번역　(A) 근무가 끝날 때 전화기의 전원을 끌 것을 기억하세요.
　　　(B) 이로써 우리에게는 소비자의 흥미를 불러일으킬 수 있는 한 달의 시간이 주어집니다.
　　　(C) 필요할 경우 도매 가격 또한 조정 가능합니다.
　　　(D) 이러한 새로운 기능들은 터보 오메가 2의 판매를 확실히 증진시켜 줄 것입니다.

어휘　generate 발생시키다　consumer 소비자　excitement 흥분
wholesale 도매의　adjust 조정하다　feature 특징

137　부사 어휘

해설　빈칸에는 미래에 대한 일을 이야기할 때 쓰이는 조동사 will과 어울려 쓰이는 시간 부사가 들어가야 한다. 문맥상 '곧 개리 카롤로가 초안을 작성해 공유 드라이브에 게시하면 여러분 모두가 이 자료를 읽을 수 있을 것'이라는 의미가 되어야 하므로, 정답은 '곧'을 의미하는 시간 부사 (B) Soon이다.

138　명사 자리 _ 동사의 목적어

해설　빈칸은 동사 e-mail의 목적어로 쓰일 명사가 들어갈 자리이고, 빈칸 앞에 한정사 any가 있으므로 명사인 (C) suggestions가 정답이다.

139-142　제품 정보

코리옵시스 텍스타일즈 수제 실크 블라우스, 중간 사이즈, 45파운드

코리옵시스 텍스타일즈의 실크 블라우스는 빈티지 직물과 우리가 패치워크 방식으로 짜깁기한 기타 재활용 구성 요소들로 제작됩니다. **139우리의** 모든 옷은 수제품이기 때문에 각각은 유일무이합니다. **140정확한 복제가 불가능합니다.** 각 제품마다 내재된 독특한 변형이 코리옵시스 텍스타일즈 제품의 매력 중 일부입니다. 당신이 받은 블라우스는 스타일은 비슷하지만 사진과 똑같지는 않을 것입니다.

이 옷은 **141세심한 주의가 필요하다**는 점에 유의하십시오. 손세탁을 하거나 세탁망에 넣어 약한 강도로 찬물에 세탁할 것을 권장합니다. 사전 세척된 제품이기는 하지만 건조기 열로 인해 크기가 줄어들 수 있습니다. **142그러므로** 널어서 자연 건조하는 것이 중요합니다.

어휘　fabric 직물　component 구성 요소　sew 깁다, 바느질하다
patchwork 패치워크, 조각보 깁기　garment 옷　handcraft 손으로 만들다　one of a kind 단 하나뿐인 것　variation 변형
charm 매력　identical 동일한　gentle 가벼운[순한]　mesh bag 그물망　prewashed 판매 전에 세탁한　shrink 줄어들다

139　인칭대명사의 격 _ 소유격

해설　해당 글은 코리옵시스 텍스타일즈의 제품 정보로 빈칸 앞 문장에서 회사를 we(우리)라고 지칭하고 있고, 빈칸이 수식하는 '옷(garments)'은 이 회사 즉 '코리옵시스 텍스타일즈의 옷'을 의미하므로 we의 소유격인 (B) our가 정답이다.

140　문맥에 맞는 문장 고르기

해설　빈칸 앞에는 모든 옷이 수제품이라 유일무이하다고 했고 빈칸 뒤에는 각 제품의 독특한 변형이 제품의 매력이라고 했으므로 빈칸에는 제품의 독창성에 대한 내용이 들어가야 앞뒤 연결이 자연스럽다. 따라서 복제가 불가능하다며 제품의 독창성을 강조하고 있는 (C)가 정답이다.

번역　(A) 이는 편리한 반품 정책입니다.
　　　(B) 영수증을 항상 확인하십시오.
　　　(C) 정확한 복제가 불가능합니다.
　　　(D) 추가 배송료가 부과될 수 있습니다.

어휘　hassle-free 편리한　return policy 반품 정책　replicate 복제하다　charge 요금　apply 적용되다

141　형용사 어휘

해설　뒤 문장에서 옷을 손세탁 하거나 세탁망에 넣어 약한 강도로 찬물에 세탁할 것을 권장한다고 한 것으로 보아 옷이 '다루기 까다롭다'는 내용이 되어야 하므로 '다루기 까다로운, 세심한 주의를 요하는'이라는 뜻의 (B) delicate이 정답이다.

142　접속부사

해설　앞 문장에는 사전 세척된 제품이기는 하지만 건조기 열로 인해 크기가 줄어들 수 있다(dryer heat may cause it to shrink)고 했고, 뒤 문장에는 널어서 자연 건조(hung to air dry)하는 것이 중요하다고 했다. 두 문장이 건조기 열로 크기가 줄 수 있으므로 자연 건조해야 한다는 인과관계를 나타내고 있으므로 '그러므로, 따라서'를 뜻하는 (C) Therefore가 정답이다.

143-146　이메일

수신: 슈 장 〈sjiang@rowanatech.ca〉
발신: 맥스웰 바셰 〈mbaschet@mapleroadstorage.ca〉
날짜: 4월 4일
제목: 귀하의 계약
첨부: 장 계약서

장 씨께,

보관이 필요하신 일로 메이플 로드 보관소를 **143선택해 주셔서** 기쁩니다. 귀하께서 서명하신 계약서의 사본을 첨부해 드립니다. **144연락처 정보가 변경되면** 저희에게 알려 주십시오.

저희의 소개 프로그램에 대해 알고 계시나요? 추천해 주신 분이 저희와 계약을 맺을 경우 한 달치 무료 보관 서비스를 받으실 수 있습니다. 새로운 임차인 **145또한** 무료 한 달을 받게 됩니다. 이 프로그램 및 모든 특별 **146할인**에 대한 자세한 내용은 저희의 웹사이트 www.mapleroadstorage.ca에서 확인하실 수 있습니다.

맥스웰 바셰, 현장 관리자

어휘　storage 보관, 보관소　referral 소개　tenant 임차인

143　동사의 시제

해설　빈칸은 pleased 뒤에 that이 생략된 that절에서 주어 you의 동사 자리이다. 빈칸 뒤의 문장에서 귀하께서 서명하신 계약서(your signed contract) 사본을 첨부했다고 했으므로 주어인 you가 선택한 것도 이미 완료된 일임을 알 수 있다. 따라서 현재완료 시제인 (D) have chosen이 정답이다.

144 문맥에 맞는 문장 고르기

해설 앞 문장에서 자사를 선택해 주어 기쁘다고 했고 서명이 된 계약서 사본을 보낸다는 것으로 보아 이미 계약이 체결된 고객에게 확인 메일을 보내고 있음을 알 수 있다. 따라서 빈칸에는 연락처 변경 시 알려 달라며 계약 후 상황에 대한 요청 사항을 언급하고 있는 (A)가 들어가야 적절하므로 정답은 (A)이다.

번역 (A) 연락처 정보가 변경되면 저희에게 알려 주십시오.
　　(B) 이곳에서 즐겁게 근무하시기를 바랍니다.
　　(C) 가능한 한 빨리 답변 드리겠습니다.
　　(D) 하지만 사업 계약은 이해하기 어려울 수 있습니다.

145 부사 어휘

해설 앞 문장에서 추천해 준 사람이 계약을 맺을 경우 한 달 무료 서비스를 받을 수 있다고 했는데, 빈칸이 있는 문장에서 새로운 임차인도 무료 한 달을 받게 된다며 소개를 받은 사람도 같은 혜택이 주어짐을 알리고 있으므로 '또한'이라는 뜻의 (C) as well이 정답이다.

146 명사 어휘

해설 빈칸 앞 글에서 소개한 프로그램이 고객 추천 시 한 달 무료 서비스 제공과 같은 판촉에 대한 내용이므로, 빈칸에는 이 프로그램과 유사한 혜택과 관련된 어휘가 들어가야 한다. 따라서 special과 함께 쓰여 '특별 할인'이라는 의미를 이루는 (A) offers가 정답이다.

PART 7

147-148 공지

147카디널 가 프로젝트—업데이트

147평소와 달리 습하고 추운 날씨로 인해 리 로와 페투니아 로 사이에 있는 카디널 가의 도로 폐쇄가 늦봄까지 연장될 예정입니다. 공사는 계속될 것이지만 기상 조건이 개선되어야 비로소 카디널 가의 최종 도로 포장을 진행할 수 있습니다. 148카디널 가의 다리 건설이 완료되면 작업 인부들이 포장 공사를 시작할 것입니다. 질문이나 남기실 말씀이 있으시면 615-555-0184로 도시 계획과의 바이 응우옌에게 연락하십시오.

어휘 unusually 평소와 달리　closure 폐쇄　extend 연장하다
paving (도로) 포장　occur 발생하다　pavement 포장 (도로)

147 주제 / 목적

번역 공지의 목적은?
　　(A) 날씨 패턴의 변화에 대한 보고
　　(B) 새로운 우회로 공지
　　(C) 도로 공사 계획의 변경 사항 설명
　　(D) 도로 노후화의 원인 강조

해설 공지의 제목이 카디널 가 프로젝트 업데이트(Cardinal Street Project—Update)로 도로 공사의 진행 상황에 대한 새 소식을 알려 주고 있으며, 첫 문장에서 평소와 달리 습하고 추운 날씨로 인해

리 로와 페투니아 로 사이에 있는 카디널 가의 도로 폐쇄가 늦봄까지 연장될 예정(Because of unusually wet and cold weather ~ extended until late spring)이라고 했으므로 정답은 (C)이다.

어휘 detour route 우회로　deterioration 악화, 퇴보

148 Not / True

번역 카디널 가 프로젝트에 대해 명시된 것은?
　　(A) 다리 건설이 포함되어 있다.
　　(B) 응우옌 씨의 회사에서 작업 중이다.
　　(C) 도로 포장은 포함되어 있지 않다.
　　(D) 더운 날씨에는 완료될 수 없다.

해설 세 번째 문장에서 카디널 가의 다리 건설이 완료되면(once construction of the bridge ~ has been completed)이라고 명시되어 있으므로 (A)가 정답이다.

어휘 handle 처리하다　involve 포함[수반]하다

Paraphrasing　지문의 construction → 정답의 building

149-150 표지판

조지의 과수원 농장
알파인 로 2232

물건을 직접 고르세요! 150우리 과수원에 있는 과즙이 풍부한 복숭아 품종 다섯 가지 중에서 골라보세요! 149양동이는 무료로 제공됩니다.

150우리 시장에 들러 농장 직송의 신선한 과일로 만든 잼, 파이와 소스를 구입하세요.
피크닉 구역에서 즐길 수 있는 점심 식사도 판매합니다.

지정된 주차 구역은 앞에 있는 표지판을 따라 가세요.

수요일부터 금요일, 낮 12시부터 오후 5시까지
토요일 및 일요일, 오전 10시부터 오후 6시까지

어휘 orchard 과수원　variety 품종　bucket 양동이　stop by 들르다　farm-fresh 농장[산지] 직송의　ahead 앞에
designated 지정된

149 세부 사항

번역 조지의 과수원 농장에서 방문객들에게 제공하는 것은?
　　(A) 과일 채취를 위한 무료 양동이
　　(B) 맞춤형 피크닉 바구니
　　(C) 파이 및 잼 샘플
　　(D) 농장 투어

해설 세 번째 문장에서 양동이는 무료로 제공된다(Buckets provided at no cost)고 했으므로 (A)가 정답이다.

어휘 gathering 수집　customized 개개인의 요구에 맞춘

Paraphrasing　지문의 at no cost → 정답의 Free

150 추론 / 암시

번역 시장에 대해 암시된 것은?
(A) 새로운 주차 공간이 생겼다.
(B) 복숭아로 만든 제품을 판다.
(C) 새로운 운영진이 관리하고 있다.
(D) 일주일 내내 문을 연다.

해설 두 번째 문장에서 우리 과수원에 있는 복숭아 품종 중에서 고르라(Select from ~ peaches in our orchard!)고 했고, 네 번째 문장에서 우리 시장에 들러 농장 직송의 신선한 과일로 만든 잼, 파이와 소스를 구입하라(Stop by our market ~ made from farm-fresh fruit)고 했으므로 과수원에서는 복숭아를 재배하고 있고 시장에서는 이 복숭아로 제품을 만들어 팔고 있음을 알 수 있다. 따라서 정답은 (B)이다.

151-152 이메일

수신: 탄디웨 응송고 〈tngxongo@fancyandformal.co.uk〉
발신: 고객 서비스 〈service@homethings.co.uk〉
날짜: 10월 26일
제목: 퍼포머 보풀 롤러 (PL293 모델)

응송고 씨께,

151귀하에서 선택하신 퍼포머 보풀 롤러가 초강력 접착제 부족으로 인해 주문이 밀린 상태임을 알려 드리게 되어 송구스럽습니다. 3~4주 내로 새로운 물량의 선적이 있을 것으로 예상합니다. 하지만 기다리고 싶지 않으시다면 홈 씽즈에서 추가 비용 없이 익스트림2 보풀 롤러를 기꺼이 보내 드리겠습니다. **152**익스트림2 모델은 사용이 용이하도록 절취선이 있는 접착테이프가 들어 있으며 두 개의 리필이 제공됩니다. 퍼포머 모델과 마찬가지로 강력한 접착제로 대부분의 직물로부터 머리카락, 솜털, 보풀, 먼지 등을 효과적으로 제거합니다.

원래의 제품이 발송되기 전에 주문 내용을 변경하시면 주문하신 제품 대신 이 비슷한 제품이 배송되도록 요청하실 수 있습니다. 이해해 주셔서 감사합니다.

글렌 맥크레인
고객 서비스 담당자
홈 씽즈

어휘 lint 보풀 on back order 주문이 밀린 shortage 부족 adhesive 접착제 shipment 선적, 수송(품) perforated 절취선이 있는 sticky tape 접착테이프 ease 쉬움 effectively 효과적으로 fuzz 솜털 in place of ~ 대신에

151 주제 / 목적

번역 맥크레인 씨는 왜 이메일을 썼는가?
(A) 신제품을 강조하려고
(B) 지연에 대해 사과하려고
(C) 질문에 응답하려고
(D) 반품에 대한 상세 정보를 제공하려고

해설 첫 문장에서 귀하에서 선택하신 퍼포머 보풀 롤러가 초강력 접착제 부족으로 인해 주문이 밀린 상태임을 알려 드리게 되어 송구스럽다(I am sorry to inform ~ on back order because of a shortage of its ultra-strong adhesive)고 했으므로 정답은 (B)이다.

어휘 apologize 사과하다 delay 지연 respond 응답하다 detail 세부 사항

Paraphrasing   지문의 sorry ~ is on back order
→ 정답의 apologize for a delay

152 Not / True

번역 익스트림2 보풀 롤러에 대해 명시된 것은?
(A) 퍼포머 모델보다 저렴하다.
(B) 테이프가 추가로 제공된다.
(C) 퍼포머 모델보다 더 효과적이다.
(D) 높은 사용자 평가 등급을 받았다.

해설 네 번째 문장에서 익스트림2 모델은 절취선이 있는 접착테이프가 들어 있으며 두 개의 리필이 제공된다(The Extreme2 model includes ~ comes with two refills)고 했으므로 정답은 (B)이다.

Paraphrasing   지문의 two refills → 정답의 additional tape

153-154 문자 메시지

센 차이 (오후 6시 51분)
우리는 협상 회의에서 나와 지금 저녁 식사 중이에요. **153,154**게라치 씨가 우리 제안을 받아들이지 않았습니다.

마테오 미켈라치 (오후 6시 52분)
답답하네요. **153,154**우리가 만 유로를 추가로 제시하면 그가 팔 것 같나요? **153**여러분과 저는 이곳이 적당한 시설이라는 데 동의했습니다. 고객들에게 편리한 위치에 있고 들어오고 나가는 배송을 위한 고속 도로 접근성도 완벽하고 잠재적 세입자들도 이미 관심을 드러냈습니다.

센 차이 (오후 6시 53분)
그럴 것 같지는 않은데요. 하지만 다시 시도해 보겠습니다. 얼마까지 올릴 수 있나요?

마테오 미켈라치 (오후 6시 54분)
은행에서 우리에게 추가 2만 유로를 승인했습니다. 게라치 씨에게 만 유로를 더 제시하시고, 추가로 우리측 비용으로 건축 법규 위반 사항을 해결할 겁니다. 필요한 경우에만 2만 유로까지 올리세요.

센 차이 (오후 6시 55분)
최선을 다하겠습니다.

어휘 negotiation 협상 accept 받아들이다 frustrating 좌절감을 주는 facility 시설 incoming 들어오는 outgoing 나가는 potential 잠재적인 tenant 세입자 fix 해결하다 building code 건축 법규 violation 위반 expense 비용

153 추론 / 암시

번역 게라치 씨에 대해 암시된 것은?
(A) 건물을 소유하고 있다.
(B) 최근에 시설을 보수했다.
(C) 대출을 승인할 것이다.
(D) 미켈라치 씨와 만날 것이다.

해설 6시 51분에 차이 씨는 게라치 씨가 제안을 받아들이지 않았다(Mr. Geraci did not accept our offer)고 했고, 6시 52분에 미켈라치 씨는 우리가 만 유로를 추가로 제시하면 그가 팔 것 같은지(Do you think ~ he would sell?)를 물으며 여러분과 저는 이곳이 적당한 시설이라는 데 동의했다(You and I have agreed that this is the right facility)고 했다. 따라서 게라치 씨는 차이 씨와 미켈라치 씨가 매입하기를 원하는 건물의 소유주임을 알 수 있으므로 (A)가 정답이다.

어휘 own 소유하다 approve 승인하다 loan 대출

154 의도 파악

번역 오후 6시 53분에 차이 씨가 "그럴 것 같지는 않은데요"라고 쓴 의도는?
(A) 세입자를 유치하는 것이 어려울 것이라고 생각한다.
(B) 제안이 여전히 거절될 것이라고 믿는다.
(C) 배송을 준비하는 일이 쉬울 거라고 생각하지 않는다.
(D) 고객들이 위치를 찾는 데 어려움을 겪을 것이라고 생각한다.

해설 6시 51분에 차이 씨는 게라치 씨가 제안을 받아들이지 않았다(Mr. Geraci did not accept our offer)고 했고, 6시 52분에 미켈라치 씨가 우리가 만 유로를 추가로 제시하면 그가 팔 것 같은지(Do you think ~ he would sell?)를 묻자 6시 53분에 차이 씨가 그럴 것 같지는 않다(I can't see that happening)고 대답했다. 따라서 차이 씨는 추가 금액을 제시하더라도 게라치 씨가 제안을 수락할 것 같지 않다는 자신의 생각을 나타내려고 한 말이므로 (B)가 정답이다.

어휘 renter 세입자 attract 끌어들이다 reject 거절하다 doubt 믿지 않다, 의심하다 organize 준비하다

155-157 광고

블로섬 판매 시스템

블로섬 판매 시스템(BSS)은 세련되고 직관적인 포스(Point-Of-Sale) 장치로 사업 운영을 순조롭게 만들어 줍니다. 소규모 사업 소유주로서, 당신은 책임도 많고 평판도 쌓아야 합니다. BSS는 거래를 안전하고 원활하며 번거롭지 않도록 하는 데 필요한 모든 도구를 갖추고 있습니다.

귀하가 어디서 사업을 하든 맡아서 처리해 주는 시스템의 편리함을 누리세요. BSS는 상점, 전화 또는 온라인 판매에 상관없이 매일 24시간 기술 전문 지식으로 당신을 ¹⁵⁵지원하며 거래 절차를 간소화합니다. ¹⁵⁶우리의 혁신적인 장치를 통해 신용 카드용 마그네틱 줄이나 칩 리더기부터 수표용 디지털 스캐너, 인기 있는 모바일 앱 결제 서비스까지 다양한 결제 유형을 이용할 수 있으며, 잠재적인 판매 기회를 놓치지 않도록 보장합니다.

지금 바로 BSS에 등록하시고 무료 10일 체험판을 이용해 보세요. 등록하는 데 15분밖에 걸리지 않습니다. 승인이 나면, ¹⁵⁷휴대폰이나 태블릿에 연결되는 BSS 장치 구입 시 50달러를 할인해 드립니다. 931-555-0148로 전화하셔서 시연 일정을 잡으시고 BSS가 당신의 판매를 어떻게 활성화시킬 수 있는지 알아보세요!

어휘 breeze 식은 죽 먹기 sleek 세련된 intuitive 직관적인 point-of-sale 포스(판매 시점 관리) device 장치 reputation 평판 tool 도구 transaction 거래 seamless 원활한 hassle-free 번거롭지 않은 simplify 간소화하다 process

절차 back 지지[원조]하다 expertise 전문 지식 innovative 혁신적인 enable ~할 수 있게 하다 magnetic-stripe 마그네틱 줄 check 수표 potential 잠재적인 miss 놓치다 sign up 등록하다 trial 체험, 시험 registration 등록 demonstration 시연 bloom 번창하다

155 동의어

번역 두 번째 단락 3행의 "backing"과 의미가 가장 가까운 단어는?
(A) 편애하다
(B) 뒤바꾸다
(C) 지원하다
(D) 설립하다

해설 의미상 전문 지식으로 당신을 '지원한다'는 뜻으로 쓰인 것이므로 정답은 (C) supporting이다.

156 Not / True

번역 광고에서 언급되지 않은 결제 방법은?
(A) 현금
(B) 수표
(C) 신용 카드
(D) 모바일 앱

해설 두 번째 단락의 세 번째 문장에서 우리의 장치를 통해 신용 카드용 마그네틱 줄이나 칩 리더기부터 수표용 디지털 스캐너, 인기 있는 모바일 앱 결제 서비스까지 다양한 결제 유형을 이용할 수 있다(Our innovative devices ~ mobile app payment services)고 했다. 장치에서 지원하는 결제 수단으로 현금을 제외한 신용 카드, 수표, 모바일 앱이 언급되었으므로 (A)가 정답이다.

157 세부 사항

번역 BSS가 판매 촉진을 위해 제공하는 것은?
(A) 새로운 휴대폰
(B) 15일간의 무료 체험판
(C) 태블릿용 무료 장치
(D) 장비 할인

해설 세 번째 단락의 세 번째 문장에서 휴대폰이나 태블릿에 연결되는 BSS 장치 구입시 50달러를 할인해 드린다(save $50 on the purchase ~ your phone or tablet)고 했으므로 (D)가 정답이다.

Paraphrasing 지문의 save $50 on ~ device
→ 정답의 A discount on equipment

158-160 이메일

수신: cbrandt@prebleevents.com
발신: chsiao@yanvillefestival.com
날짜: 5월 15일
제목: 축제 지원

브란트 씨께,

얀빌 축제와 관련하여 연락 주셔서 감사합니다. ¹⁶⁰**우리는 주요 무대에 조명 장비 공급을 위해 브리머스 스테이징과 이미 계약을 맺었습니다.**

하지만 귀하의 회사인 프레블 이벤트에 대해 협력사들로부터 좋은 이야기를 들었습니다. ¹⁵⁸음식 공급 서비스를 제공하시나요? ^{158,159}배우와 무대 작업팀을 위해 음식을 관리해 줄 사람이 아직 없습니다. ¹⁵⁸이 일에 관심이 있으신지요? 알려 주시기 바랍니다.

세실리 샤오
얀빌 축제 부위원장

어휘 lighting 조명 · stage 무대 · catering 음식 공급 · stage crew 무대 작업팀 · vice-chair 부위원장

158 주제 / 목적

번역 샤오 씨가 이메일을 쓴 이유는?
(A) 주문 확인
(B) 가격 문의
(C) 보고서 제공
(D) 제안

해설 두 번째 단락의 첫 문장에서 음식 공급 서비스를 제공하는지(Do you provide catering services?)를 물었고, 배우와 무대 작업팀을 위해 음식을 관리해 줄 사람이 아직 없다(We do not have ~ stage crews)며 이 일에 관심이 있는지(Would you be interested in this work?)를 다시 묻는 것으로 보아 음식 공급 서비스의 제공을 제안하고자 이메일을 썼다는 것을 알 수 있다. 따라서 정답은 (D)이다.

159 추론 / 암시

번역 얀빌 축제의 주안점일 가능성이 높은 것은?
(A) 음악
(B) 도서
(C) 연극
(D) 패션

해설 두 번째 단락의 두 번째 문장에서 배우와 무대 작업팀을 위해 음식을 관리해 줄 사람이 아직 없다(We do not have ~ stage crews)고 했다. 배우와 무대 작업팀이 언급된 것으로 보아 얀빌 축제는 연극 축제임을 짐작할 수 있으므로 정답은 (C)이다.

160 문장 삽입

번역 [1], [2], [3], [4]로 표시된 곳 중에서 다음 문장이 들어가기에 가장 적합한 위치는?

"하지만 귀하의 회사인 프레블 이벤트에 대해 협력사들로부터 좋은 이야기를 들었습니다."

(A) [1]
(B) [2]
(C) [3]
(D) [4]

해설 제시된 문장에서 반전의 접속부사 However가 문제 해결의 단서이다. 이미 다른 업체와 계약을 체결했으나, 프레블 이벤트가 좋은 평판을 가진 것을 언급하며, 해당 업체에 다른 서비스를 제공할 기회를 제안하는 내용이 이어지는 것이 자연스러우므로 이미 다른 업체와 계약을 체결했다(We have already contracted with ~ for our main stages)는 내용 뒤인 (B)가 정답이다.

161-163 광고

크레이머즈 엠포리움
롤리 가 2323 · 휴스턴, TX 77021

¹⁶²사업을 시작한 지 25년 만에 저희 매장이 폐점합니다. 모든 것을 처분해야 합니다!

¹⁶¹냉장고에서 세탁기에 이르기까지, 여러분의 가정이나 사무실을 위한 수백 개의 신상 가전제품을 보유하고 있습니다. 대부분의 품목은 30% 할인됩니다. ¹⁶³배송은 50달러 균일 요금으로 저희 매장에서 60마일 이내에서 가능합니다. 오전 9시부터 오후 7시까지 매일 영업합니다.

기다리지 마세요! 상품이 빠르게 판매되고 있습니다!

어휘 emporium 상점 · appliance 가전제품 · mark down 할인을 하다 · flat 균일한 · merchandise 상품

161 추론 / 암시

번역 크레이머즈 엠포리움에서 구입할 수 있을 것 같은 것은?
(A) 컴퓨터
(B) 소파
(C) 식기세척기
(D) 식품

해설 두 번째 단락의 첫 문장에서 냉장고에서 세탁기에 이르기까지 여러분의 가정이나 사무실을 위한 수백 개의 신상 가전제품을 보유하고 있다(From refrigerators ~ new appliances for your home or office)고 했으므로 (C)가 정답이다.

162 세부 사항

번역 크레이머즈 엠포리움은 왜 상품을 할인가에 판매하는가?
(A) 곧 새로운 장소로 이전할 것이다.
(B) 특정 브랜드를 홍보하기를 원한다.
(C) 새로운 물품을 위한 공간을 만들어야 한다.
(D) 곧 폐업할 것이다.

해설 첫 문장에서 사업을 시작한 지 25년 만에 매장이 폐점한다(After 25 years ~ is closing)며 모든 것을 처분해야 한다(Everything must go!)고 했으므로 폐업으로 인해 물건을 처분하려는 목적으로 할인을 제공하고 있음을 알 수 있다. 따라서 정답은 (D)이다.

어휘 specific 특정한 · room 공간 · go out of business 폐업하다

Paraphrasing 지문의 is closing
→ 정답의 go out of business

163 Not / True

번역 배송에 대해 언급된 것은?
(A) 2개 이상 구매 시 무료이다.
(B) 특정 지역에서만 이용할 수 있다.
(C) 대형 품목에 한해서 된다.
(D) 물건의 가격에 포함되어 있다.

해설 두 번째 단락의 세 번째 문장에서 배송은 50달러 균일 요금으로 저희 매장에서 60마일 이내에서 가능하다(Delivery is available within 60 miles ~ $50.00)고 했으므로 (B)가 정답이다.

어휘 specific 특정한   limited 한정된

Paraphrasing	지문의 within 60 miles
	→ 정답의 only in a specific area

164-167 이메일

수신: 브루스 홀트
발신: 샤모니카 워커
날짜: 4월 9일
제목: 긴급, 기밀

브루스에게,

164새 회계 연도부터 이곳 블래넌 인더스트리즈의 모든 정규직 사원에게 퇴직 수당 변경 사항이 165적용됩니다. 그들은 더 이상 현금의 형태로 상응하는 퇴직금을 받지 않을 것입니다. 대신 퇴직금은 회사 주식의 형태로 지급되어 퇴직 포트폴리오에 예치될 것입니다.

우리의 현재 퇴직 관리 회사인 프록세이브 퓨처스는 퇴직 수당의 이러한 변화에 대해 통보를 받았습니다. **166이 회사는 해당 전환을 관리하고 블래넌 인더스트리즈 직원들에게 고객 지원을 계속 제공할 것입니다.** 문의 사항은 우리 인사부가 아닌 프록세이브 퓨처스의 피에르 데하네에게 전달되어야 합니다.

167유아 스즈키 인사부장과 함께 일하면서 그녀가 직원 복지 수당의 이러한 중대 변화에 대해 전 직원과 소통하는 데 있어 포함시켜야 할 정보를 제공하세요. 사장님께서 이번 전환과 관련된 모든 보고를 받고 싶다고 통보하셨습니다. 또한 저에게 계속 일간 재무 보고서를 보내 주세요.

샤모니카 워커 최고 재무 책임자
블래넌 인더스트리즈

어휘 immediate 즉각적인   confidential 기밀의   fiscal 회계의   retirement benefits 퇴직 수당   apply 적용하다   matching 어울리는, 걸맞은   form 형태   stock 주식   deposit 예치[예금]하다   transition 변화, 이행   direct 보내다   notify 통지하다   related to ~와 관련된

164 주제 / 목적

번역 이메일의 목적은?
(A) 거래에 대한 문의
(B) 회의 의제 계획
(C) 지침 제공
(D) 의견 요청

해설 첫 문장에서 새 회계 연도부터 이곳 블래넌 인더스트리즈의 모든 정규직 사원에게 퇴직 수당 변경 사항이 적용된다(Beginning with the new fiscal year ~ here at Blanen Industries)며 회사의 새로운 방침에 대해 안내하고 있으므로 (C)가 정답이다.

어휘 inquire 문의하다   transaction 거래   agenda 의제   instructions 지침, 설명

165 동의어

번역 첫 번째 단락 1행의 "applied"와 의미가 가장 가까운 단어는?
(A) 요청되다
(B) 지연되다
(C) 논의되다
(D) 시행되다

해설 변경 사항이 '적용된다' 즉 변화가 시작된다는 뜻으로 쓰인 것이므로 정답은 (D) implemented이다.

166 추론 / 암시

번역 프록세이브 퓨처스에 대해 암시된 것은?
(A) 직원들에게 보너스를 주고 있다.
(B) 직원들에게 회사 주식을 제공한다.
(C) 블래넌 인더스트리즈 직원들의 우려 사항을 처리할 것이다.
(D) 블래넌 인더스트리즈와 합병하고 있다.

해설 두 번째 단락의 두 번째 문장에서 프록세이브 퓨처스가 해당 전환을 관리하고 블래넌 인더스트리즈 직원들에게 고객 지원을 계속 제공할 것(The firm will manage ~ Blanen Industries employees)이라고 했고, 문의 사항은 우리 인사부가 아닌 프록세이브 퓨처스의 피에르 데하네에게 전달되어야 한다(Questions should be directed to ~ human resources department)고 했다. 따라서 프록세이브 퓨처스가 퇴직 수당 변경에 대한 블래넌 인더스트리즈 직원들의 우려나 문의에 대해 처리할 것임을 알 수 있다. 따라서 (C)가 정답이다.

어휘 share 주식, 지분   address 처리하다   merge 합병하다

167 세부 사항

번역 전 직원에게 정책 변경에 대해 통지하는 일은 누가 책임지는가?
(A) 홀트 씨
(B) 워커 씨
(C) 데하네 씨
(D) 스즈키 씨

해설 세 번째 단락의 첫 문장에서 유아 스즈키 인사부장과 함께 일하면서 그녀가 직원 복지 수당의 이러한 중대 변화에 대해 전 직원과 소통하는 데 있어 포함시켜야 할 정보를 제공하라(Please work with Yua Suzuki ~ her all-staff communication about this important change in employee benefits)고 했으므로 (D)가 정답이다.

168-171 온라인 채팅

모니카 지아 (오전 8시 27분)
안녕하세요, 유지 그리고 성호. 두 분 중 한 분이 오늘 이따가 저를 도와주실 수 있는지 궁금해요. 데자니 존스가 도울 예정이었지만 오늘 사무실에 없을 거라서요.
유지 사이토 (오전 8시 28분)
유감이네요. 그녀가 이유를 이야기했나요?
모니카 지아 (오전 8시 28분)
168감기 기운이 좀 있지만 집에서 고객들을 위한 데이터 분석 작업은 할 수 있을 거라고 했어요.
서성호 (오전 8시 29분)
그래서 데자니는 오늘 아예 안 오는 건가요?
모니카 지아 (오전 8시 31분)
네. 169,171데자니와 제가 내일 사무실 야유회를 위해 음식과 음료를 사러 윌리스 마켓에 갈 예정이었어요. 기억하시죠? 토요일 정오에 시립 공원에서요. 어쨌든, 데자니가 차가 있으니 가게에 우리를 태우고 가서 그녀의 신용 카드로 물품을 구입하려고 했어요. 두 분 다 차로 출근하시니까 한 분이 도움을 주실 수 있을 것 같아서요.
서성호 (오전 8시 32분)
171언제 가실 생각이었나요?
유지 사이토 (오전 8시 32분)
그럼요. 170제가 도와드릴 수 있고 제 신용 카드도 사용할 수 있어요.
모니카 지아 (오전 8시 33분)
2시쯤에요.
유지 사이토 (오전 8시 34분)
문제없어요. 그냥 제 사무실 자리로 오시면 제 차를 타고 가게로 가죠.
서성호 (오전 8시 35분)
다행이네요, 유지. 저는 오늘 오후에 회의가 여러 개 있어서 나갈 수 없을 것 같거든요.
모니카 지아 (오전 8시 35분)
고마워요, 유지. 이따 오후에 만나요.

어휘 analyses (analysis의 복수) 분석 supplies 물품 stop by 들르다 cubicle 칸막이 공간

168 세부 사항

번역 존스 씨는 오늘 왜 사무실에 없을 것인가?
(A) 몸이 안 좋다.
(B) 매주 금요일에 재택근무를 한다.
(C) 고객들과 만난다.
(D) 차가 고장 났다.

해설 8시 28분에 지아가 존스에 대해 감기 기운이 좀 있지만 집에서 고객들을 위한 데이터 분석 작업은 할 수 있을 거라고 했다(She said she had a slight cold ~ for her clients)고 전하고 있으므로 존스 씨는 감기가 걸려 출근하지 않았음을 알 수 있다. 따라서 정답은 (A)이다.

Paraphrasing	지문의 had a slight cold → 정답의 is feeling ill

169 세부 사항

번역 존스 씨가 전에 하기로 동의했던 것은?
(A) 지아 씨를 직장에 태워주기
(B) 야유회 장소 선택
(C) 새 칸막이 사무실로 이동
(D) 장보는 일 도와주기

해설 8시 31분에 지아 씨가 데자니(존스 씨)와 제가 내일 사무실 야유회를 위해 음식과 음료를 사러 윌리스 마켓에 갈 예정이었다(Dejani and I were going to ~ office picnic)고 했으므로 정답은 (D)이다.

Paraphrasing	지문의 buy food and beverages → 정답의 shopping

170 추론 / 암시

번역 야유회를 위한 음식과 음료를 구매할 것 같은 사람은?
(A) 지아 씨
(B) 존스 씨
(C) 사이토 씨
(D) 서 씨

해설 8시 32분에 사이토 씨가 제가 도울 수 있고 제 신용 카드도 사용할 수 있다(I can help, and we can use my credit card)고 한 것으로 보아, 사이토 씨가 지아 씨를 도와 야유회 장을 보고 자신의 신용 카드로 결제할 것임을 알 수 있다. 따라서 (C)가 정답이다.

171 의도 파악

번역 오전 8시 33분에 지아 씨가 "2시쯤에요"라고 쓴 의도는?
(A) 윌리스 마켓에서 적어도 두 명이 그녀를 도와줘야 한다.
(B) 시립 공원에서 열리는 행사 입장권을 두 장 예약했다.
(C) 약 2시간 뒤에 서 씨와 만날 계획이다.
(D) 오늘 오후 2시쯤 사무실에서 나가기를 원한다.

해설 8시 31분에 지아 씨가 데자니와 내일 사무실 야유회를 위해 음식과 음료를 사러 윌리스 마켓에 갈 예정이었다(Dejani and I were going to ~ office picnic)고 한 데 대해 8시 32분에 서 씨가 언제 갈 생각이었는지(When were you thinking of going?)를 묻자 8시 33분에 지아 씨가 2시쯤(Around two)이라고 대답했다. 따라서 지아 씨는 2시쯤에 사무실에서 장을 보러 출발할 생각임을 나타내려는 의도로 한 말이므로 (D)가 정답이다.

172-175 이메일

수신: 도로타 쿠차르스키 〈dkucharski@internationaltechnologicalsociety.org〉
발신: 루치아노 모레티 〈lmoretti@internationaltechnologicalsociety.org〉

날짜: 8월 8일
제목: 조사 결과

쿠차르스키 씨께,

172다음은 내년 6월에 있을 다음 173연례 기술 컨퍼런스의 개최 장소에 대해 제가 조사한 내용을 요약한 것입니다.

174로마에서 제가 찾은 최고의 선택은 호텔 알 폰테입니다. 이곳에서의 총 컨퍼런스 비용은 31,500유로입니다. 174참가자를 위한 개별 호텔 객실은 1박당 80유로입니다. 참석률이 높을 경우, 174인근의 호텔 밀비오에서 1박당 120유로로 참가자에게 숙소를 제공할 수 있습니다.

175제노바와 피렌체에 있는 호텔도 조사했지만 전체 컨퍼런스 비용에 있어 훨씬 더 싼 곳을 찾을 수 없었습니다. 이 도시들 중 한 곳에서 컨퍼런스를 개최하여 아끼는 금액은 기껏해야 500유로 정도입니다. 더 중요한 것은 이들 소규모 도시로 가는 데 드는 더 높은 항공료가 참가자들의 의욕을 저하시킬까 우려된다는 것입니다. 반면, 로마는 대부분의 유럽 도시에서 오는 저렴한 직항 항공편이 있습니다. 또한 부에노스 아이레스에서 오는 우리 동료들에게도 이편이 더 저렴할 것입니다.

호텔 알 폰테로 선택하기를 원하실 경우 호텔에서 제공하는 편의 시설 및 예상 비용에 대한 상세한 보고서를 제공해 드리겠습니다.

루치아노 모레티
국제 기술 협회 비서

어휘 summary 요약 individual 개별의 participant 참가자 attendance 참석률 house 수용하다 look into 조사하다 overall 전체적인 discourage 의욕을 꺾다 attendee 참석자 affordable 저렴한 pursue 추구하다 detailed 상세한 write-up 서면 보고서 anticipated 예상된 amenity 편의 시설

172 주제 / 목적

번역 이메일의 주요 목적은?
(A) 컨퍼런스 출장을 위한 예약
(B) 컨퍼런스 개최 가능 장소 비교
(C) 컨퍼런스 준비를 위한 예산 증액 요청
(D) 컨퍼런스 참석 비용 관련 문의

해설 첫 문장에서 다음은 내년 6월에 있을 다음 연례 기술 컨퍼런스의 개최 장소에 대해 제가 조사한 내용을 요약한 것(The following is a summary ~ conference in June of next year)이라고 했으므로 (B)가 정답이다.

어휘 venue 장소 organize 준비하다 inquire 문의하다

Paraphrasing 지문의 where to hold ~ conference
→ 정답의 venues for a conference

173 Not / True

번역 컨퍼런스에 대해 명시된 것은?
(A) 여행 업계 전문가를 위한 것이다.
(B) 매년 열린다.
(C) 보통 부에노스 아이레스에서 열린다.
(D) 8월에 열릴 것이다.

해설 첫 문장에서 컨퍼런스에 대해 언급하면서 연례 기술 컨퍼런스 (annual technology conference)라고 했으므로 정답은 (B)이다.

Paraphrasing 지문의 annual → 정답의 every year

174 Not / True

번역 호텔 밀비오에 관해 사실인 것은?
(A) 호텔 알 폰테보다 더 비싸다.
(B) 평소에 예약이 꽉 찬다.
(C) 제노바와 피렌체에 지점이 있다.
(D) 호텔 알 폰테보다 객실이 더 많다.

해설 두 번째 단락의 첫 문장에서 로마에서 제가 찾은 최고의 선택은 호텔 알 폰테(In Rome ~ Hotel Al Ponte)이고 참가자를 위한 개별 호텔 객실은 1박당 80유로(Individual hotel rooms would cost €80 per night for participants)라고 했는데, 같은 단락의 마지막 문장에서 인근의 호텔 밀비오에서 1박당 120유로로 참가자에게 숙소를 제공할 수 있다(we could also house participants in the nearby Hotel Milvio at €120 per night)고 했다. 따라서 호텔 밀비오는 호텔 알 폰테보다 1일 숙박비가 더 비싸다는 것을 알 수 있으므로 (A)가 정답이다.

175 문장 삽입

번역 [1], [2], [3], [4]로 표시된 곳 중에서 다음 문장이 들어가기에 가장 적합한 위치는?

"이 도시들 중 한 곳에서 컨퍼런스를 개최하여 아끼는 금액은 기껏해야 500유로 정도입니다."
(A) [1]
(B) [2]
(C) [3]
(D) [4]

해설 제시된 문장의 in one of those cities가 문제 해결의 단서이다. 컨퍼런스를 개최할 후보 도시에 대한 조사 결과를 언급하며 '이 도시들 중 한 곳'이라고 했으므로 주어진 문장 앞에 '이 도시들'이라고 언급한 도시들의 이름이 나열되어 있어야 한다. 따라서 제노바와 피렌체에 있는 호텔도 조사했다(I also looked into hotels in Genoa and Florence)는 문장 뒤인 (C)가 정답이다.

어휘 savings 절약 금액 at most 기껏해야

176-180 웹페이지 + 온라인 후기

https://www.centraluniversity.edu/nutrition/newsletter

| 홈 | 고객 서비스 | 구독 | 계정 | 로그인 |

〈센트럴 대학교 건강 소식지〉—영양과 건강을 위한 안내서

건강한 식사에 대한 조언은 TV 쇼에서부터 온라인 요리 포럼에 이르기까지 거의 모든 곳에서 구할 수 있습니다. 176당신이 접하는 조언이 과학적 증거를 기반으로 한 것인지를 알기는 종종 어렵습니다. 이것이 바로 〈센트럴 대학교 건강 소식지〉가 꼭 필요한 이유입니다. 이 소식지는

매달 센트럴 대학교 영양학부 연구원들의 연구 결과를 요약한 유익하고 이해하기 쉬운 기사를 177전달합니다. 예를 들어, 지난 4월호에서는 슈퍼마켓에서 판매되는 영양 보충제를 평가했습니다. 179뒷면에는 영양학부 학부장이 독자들의 질문에 답하는 전문가에게 질문하기 칼럼이 실립니다.

1년 구독료는 20달러이며 모든 이전 발행 호에 대한 온라인 이용이 포함됩니다. 또한 첫 구독 갱신 시 10% 할인 혜택을 제공합니다. 게다가 178구독자는 특별 보고서 및 비디오와 팟캐스트에 대한 링크가 포함된 무료 주간 "건강한 생활" 이메일 업데이트를 받습니다.

176시작하시려면 구독 페이지로 이동하셔서 안내를 따르세요.

어휘 nutrition 영양 encounter 접하다 evidence 증거 indispensable 필수적인 informative 유익한 summarize 요약하다 findings 조사 결과 issue (정기 간행물의) 호 evaluate 평가하다 nutritional 영양학적인 supplement 보충제 feature 특별히 포함하다 previous 이전의 subscription 구독 renewal 갱신 subscriber 구독자 instruction 지시

https://www.centraluniversity.edu/nutrition/newsletter/reviews

출판물: 〈센트럴 대학교 건강 소식지〉

★★★★★

후기 작성자: 아리 킴

게시 날짜: 8월 4일

178올해로 〈센트럴 대학교 건강 소식지〉를 2년째 구독하고 있으며 처음부터 끝까지 다 읽고 있습니다. 179특히 전문가에게 질문하기 칼럼이 인상적이고 항상 새로운 것을 배우고 있습니다. 예를 들어, 이번 달에 스텔라 부스 박사는 어떤 파스타가 가장 영양가가 높은지에 대한 질문에 놀라운 답변을 하셨습니다. 저는 콩을 재료로 한 파스타가 있는지조차 몰랐고 얼마나 많은 섬유질이 들어 있는지는 말할 것도 없습니다. 이 파스타를 먹어봤는데 다시는 일반 파스타로 돌아가지 않을 것입니다. 180저의 유일한 불만은 소식지가 고작 12페이지라는 것입니다!

어휘 review 논평하다 subscribe 구독하다 particularly 특히 impressed 감명받은 for instance 예를 들어 nutritious 영양가 있는 much less ~은 말할 것도 없다 fiber 섬유질 contain ~이 들어 있다 sole 유일한 complaint 불만

176 주제 / 목적

번역 웹페이지의 목적은?
(A) 가격 인상에 대한 이유 설명
(B) 출판물에 대한 독자 규모 증대
(C) 연구 프로젝트를 위한 지원자 모집
(D) 영양제 판매

해설 첫 단락에서 당신이 접하는 조언이 과학적 증거를 기반으로 한 것인지를 알기는 종종 어렵다(It's often difficult ~ scientific evidence)면서 이것이 바로 〈센트럴 대학교 건강 소식지〉가 꼭 필요한 이유(That's why ~ is indispensable)라고 잡지를 구독해야

하는 이유를 설득하며 잡지 구독에 따른 여러 혜택을 열거하고 있고, 마지막 문장에서 시작하시려면 구독 페이지로 이동하셔서 안내를 따르라(To get started ~ follow the instructions)며 구독을 독려하고 있으므로 (B)가 정답이다.

어휘 audience 독자[관람객] recruit 모집하다

177 동의어

번역 웹페이지에서 첫 번째 단락 4행의 "delivers"와 의미가 가장 가까운 단어는?
(A) 제시하다
(B) 수송하다
(C) 안내하다
(D) 청구하다

해설 의미상 소식지가 기사를 '전하다' 즉, '(메시지 등을) 전하다, 말하다'는 뜻으로 쓰인 것이므로 정답은 (A) presents이다.

178 연계

번역 킴 씨에 대해 사실인 것은?
(A) 보건 전문가이다.
(B) 20% 구독 할인을 받았다.
(C) TV 프로그램에서 영양 관련 조언을 얻는다.
(D) 센트럴 대학교에서 주간 이메일을 받는다.

해설 웹페이지의 두 번째 단락 마지막 문장에서 구독자는 무료 주간 "건강한 생활" 이메일 업데이트를 받는다(subscribers receive ~ e-mail update)고 했고, 온라인 후기의 첫 문장에서 킴 씨가 올해로 〈센트럴 대학교 건강 소식지〉를 2년째 구독하고 있다(This is my second year ~ Health Newsletter)고 했으므로 킴 씨는 구독자로서 무료 주간 이메일을 받고 있음을 알 수 있다. 따라서 정답은 (D)이다.

179 연계

번역 센트럴 대학교 영양학부에 대해 암시된 것은?
(A) 지역 교사들을 위한 수업 계획을 짠다.
(B) 부스 박사가 이끈다.
(C) 온라인 요리 수업을 제공한다.
(D) 연구원을 위한 일자리가 있다.

해설 웹페이지의 첫 단락 마지막 문장에서 뒷면에 영양학부 학부장이 독자들의 질문에 답하는 전문가에게 질문하기 칼럼이 실린다(The back page features ~ answers readers' questions)고 했고, 온라인 후기의 두 번째 문장에서 전문가에게 질문하기 칼럼이 인상적이고 항상 새로운 것을 배우고 있다(I'm particularly impressed ~ learn something new)며 이번 달에 스텔라 부스 박사는 어떤 파스타가 가장 영양가가 높은지에 대한 질문에 놀라운 답변을 했다(This month ~ most nutritious)고 했다. 영양학부 학부장이 전문가에게 질문하기 칼럼의 독자 질문에 답변을 한다고 했는데, 부스 박사가 답변을 했다고 했으므로 부스 박사가 영양학부의 학부장임을 알 수 있다. 따라서 (B)가 정답이다.

어휘 head ~을 이끌다[책임지다] job opening (직장의) 공석

180 세부 사항

번역 온라인 후기에 따르면, 소식지의 약점은?
(A) 한정된 범위의 주제
(B) 기사의 복잡성
(C) 사진의 부족
(D) 전체 길이

해설 온라인 후기의 마지막 문장에서 유일한 불만은 소식지가 고작 12페이지라는 것(My sole complaint is that the newsletter is only twelve pages long!)이라고 했으므로 (D)가 정답이다.

어휘 range 범위 complexity 복잡성 lack 부족 overall 전체적인 length 길이

181-185 청구서 + 이메일

브릿-리비전 편집 서비스 청구서

프리랜서 편집자: 리사 야마시타
청구일: 9월 30일
주소: 업살라 가 178 런던 E16 1DJ
연락처: (020) 7946 0612
lisa.yamashita@bluesun.co.uk
Stashcash ID: Lisa. Yamachita8

고객명	프로젝트 설명	완료일	시간
에디 켄트	대학 논문 편집	9월 5일	2시간
벤 갤러거	보조금 제안서 편집	9월 9일	10시간
184하이든 인테리어의 리디아 퀸	마케팅 서류 편집	9월 17일	8.5시간
위노나 로저스	저널 기사 편집	9월 22일	2시간
181토니 위더스	이력서 및 자기소개서 편집	9월 28일	2.5시간

어휘 invoice 청구서 description 설명 thesis 논문 grant 보조금 CV 이력서 cover letter 자기소개서

수신: 리사 야마시타 〈lisa.yamashita@bluesun.co.uk〉
발신: 클라우디오 아길라르 〈caguilar@britrevision.co.uk〉
185**날짜:** 10월 1일
제목: 당신의 최근 청구서

리사에게,

9월에 제출된 업무에 대한 청구서를 보내 주셔서 감사합니다. 당사의 독립 프리랜서 편집자로서 훌륭한 출발을 한 것에 대해 칭찬하고 싶습니다. 우리 고객들에게서는 당신 작업에 대한 긍정적인 이야기만 나왔습니다. 아시다시피, 182**우리는 당신이 근무 일과를 짜는 방식에 대해 지시하지 않습니다.** 대신, 브릿-리비전(BRV) 지침은 단순히 마감일을 준수하고 작업 품질을 유지할 것을 요구합니다. 당신은 둘 다 훌륭히 해내셨습니다.

183**그리고 당신이 켄트 씨를 위해 추가로 30분간 일한 것에 대한 비용도 지불할 것입니다.** 켄트 씨가 작성한 짧은 구두 프레젠테이션에 대해 전화상으로 자문을 해 주셨다고 그가 보고했습니다. 184**우리의 장기 기업 고객인 리디아 퀸을 위해 작업한 일에 대해서는 더 높은 시급을 지불**

했다는 것을 영수증에서 확인하실 수 있을 겁니다.

185**당신의 스태시캐시 계좌로 750파운드를 이체했습니다. 이 금액은 내일 아침까지 당신의 계좌에 표시될 것입니다.**

클라우디오 아길라르
브릿-리비전 편집 서비스 지급 계정 부서

어휘 render 제출하다 commend 칭찬하다 superb 훌륭한 independent 독립적인 dictate 지시하다 structure 편성하다 guideline 지침 maintain 유지하다 admirably 훌륭하게 oral 구두의 as for ～에 관해 말하자면 long-standing 오래된 corporate 기업의 rate 요금 initiate 시작하다 transfer 송금 appear 나타나다 accounts payable 지급 계정

181 추론 / 암시

번역 BRV 고객 중 누가 새 직장을 구하고 있는 것 같은가?
(A) 갤러거 씨
(B) 퀸 씨
(C) 로저스 씨
(D) 위더스 씨

해설 청구서의 표 마지막 열에 토니 위더스(Tony Withers)라는 고객이 이력서 및 자기소개서 편집(CV and cover letter editing) 서비스를 받았다고 나와 있는 것으로 보아 위더스 씨가 새 일자리를 구하고 있음을 짐작할 수 있다. 따라서 (D)가 정답이다.

182 추론 / 암시

번역 이메일에서 야마시타 씨에 대해 암시된 것은?
(A) 자신의 시간을 정할 수 있다.
(B) 매주 BRV 사무실을 방문한다.
(C) BRV를 위한 신규 고객을 찾아야 한다.
(D) 곧 승진할 자격이 될 것이다.

해설 이메일의 첫 단락 네 번째 문장에서 야마시타 씨에게 당신이 근무 일과를 짜는 방식에 대해 지시하지 않는다(we do not dictate how you structure your workday)고 했으므로 (A)가 정답이다.

어휘 be eligible for ～에 자격이 있다

183 Not / True

번역 이메일에 따르면, 야마시타 씨가 청구서에 포함시키지 않은 것은?
(A) 주소 변경
(B) 추가 작업
(C) 프로젝트 종료일
(D) 계좌 번호

해설 이메일의 두 번째 단락 첫 문장에서 야마시타 씨에게 당신이 켄트 씨를 위해 추가로 30분간 일한 것에 대한 비용도 지불할 것(Also, we will pay you ～ for Mr. Kent)이라며, 켄트 씨가 작성한 짧은 구두 프레젠테이션에 대해 전화상으로 자문을 해 주었다고 그가 보고했다(He reported ～ presentation that he created)고 했다. 따라서 야마시타 씨는 켄트 씨를 상대로 전화 자문을 해 준 일을 청구서에 기입하지 않았음을 알 수 있으므로 (B)가 정답이다.

번역 야마시타 씨는 어떤 프로젝트에 대해 시간당 가장 많이 받겠는가?
(A) 대학 논문
(B) 보조금 제안서
(C) 마케팅 서류
(D) 저널 기사

해설 청구서 표의 세 번째 열에 있는 하이든 인테리어의 리디아 퀸(Lydia Quinn of Hyden Interiors)은 마케팅 서류 편집(Marketing copy editing) 서비스를 받았고, 이메일의 두 번째 단락 세 번째 문장에서 우리의 장기 기업 고객인 리디아 퀸을 위해 작업한 일에 대해서는 더 높은 시급을 지불했다는 것을 영수증에서 확인할 수 있을 것(As for the work ~ at a higher hourly rate)이라고 했다. 따라서 야마시타 씨는 리디아 퀸의 마케팅 서류 편집에 대해 시급을 가장 많이 받았음을 알 수 있으므로 (C)가 정답이다.

185 세부 사항

번역 야마시타 씨는 언제 지급액을 수령할 것으로 예상할 수 있는가?
(A) 9월 28일
(B) 9월 30일
(C) 10월 1일
(D) 10월 2일

해설 이메일의 세 번째 단락에서 야마시타 씨에게 당신의 계좌로 750파운드를 이체했다(I have initiated ~ account)며 이 금액은 내일 아침까지 당신의 계좌에 표시될 것(The funds should appear ~ by tomorrow morning)이라고 했고, 이메일의 작성 날짜는 10월 1일(Date: 1 October)이라고 나와 있으므로 정답은 (D)이다.

186-190 이메일 + 설명문 + 이메일

수신: 신입 사원
발신: 헤미 아모스 〈hamos@motmanmotors.com〉
날짜: 6월 8일
제목: 모트만 모터스에 오신 것을 환영합니다.
첨부: ⑩ 정보

신입 사원 여러분,

환영합니다! 여러분 모두가 모트만 모터스와 함께하게 되어 매우 기쁩니다.

신입 사원 오리엔테이션은 6월 10일 오전 9시부터 낮 12시까지입니다. 아래 명시된 대로 우리 캠퍼스에 있는 핌즐러 빌딩의 각자 해당하는 방으로 출석해 주세요. 제가 각 방을 돌며 잠깐 신입 사원들을 만나겠습니다.

• 마케팅 및 고객 서비스: 두 그룹 모두 320호실로 출석하세요.
• **189엔지니어링: 215호실로 출석하세요.**
• 기술 서비스: 158호실로 출석하세요.

직원 대부분의 서류 작업이 마무리되었으므로 이 시점에서 **186모트만 모터스 포털 계정**이 최근 여러분께 보내 드린 직원 ID 번호를 이용하여 설정되고 여러분의 은행 계좌 정보가 계정에 입력되어 있는지 확인이 필요합니다. **187첨부된 설명서를 따라 마지막 단계를 완료해 주세요.**

15분 이상 걸리지 않을 것이며, **1876월 17일까지 해 줄 것을 요청합니다.** 질문이 있으면 망설이지 말고 연락하세요.

입사를 환영합니다!

헤미 아모스
모트만 모터스 인사부

어휘 thrilled 아주 흥분한 proper 적절한 indicate 나타내다 come around 들르다 briefly 잠시 report to ~로 출두하다 finalize 마무리 짓다 ensure 보장하다 identification 신원 확인 instruction 설명, 지시 hesitate 망설이다 reach out 연락하다

다음 단계를 따라 새 모트만 모터스 포털 계정을 만들고 활성화시켜 주세요. 시작하려면 https://motmanmotors.com/portal/activation로 가세요.

1. **188"새 사용자 등록" 페이지로 가서서 직원 ID 번호를 입력하세요.**
2. 이름과 주소가 뜰 것입니다. 이 정보가 정확한지 확인하세요.
3. '은행 계좌'라는 제목의 새 화면이 나타날 것입니다. 은행 계좌 정보를 입력하세요.
4. 마지막으로, 두 개의 보안 질문을 선택하고 답변을 제공하라는 요청을 받게 될 것입니다.

계정을 개설하는 즉시 계정이 활성화되고 급여 부서에서 알림을 받게 되며 지급 일정이 설정될 것입니다. 어려운 점이나 질문이 있는 경우 헤미 아모스 씨에게 hamos@motmanmotors.com으로 이메일을 보내세요.

어휘 activate 활성화하다 registration 등록 fill in 기입하다 security 보안 active 활성화된 payroll 급여 지급 alert 알리다

수신: 헤미 아모스 〈hamos@motmanmotors.com〉
발신: 카루나 디마아노 〈kdimaano@motmanmotors.com〉
날짜: 6월 9일
제목: 모트만 모터스 포털 문제

아모스 씨께,

어제 따뜻한 환영 이메일을 보내 주셔서 감사합니다.

188모트만 모터스 포털 계정을 설정하려고 하는데 제 직원 ID 번호에 문제가 있는 것 같습니다. 시스템에 정보를 입력할 때마다 오류 메시지가 뜹니다. 번호가 올바르지 않은 것 같습니다. 이 문제를 어떻게 해결해야 할지 알려 주시겠습니까?

질문이 하나 더 있습니다. **190오리엔테이션에 샌안토니오에 새로 온 사람들을 위한 정보가 포함될까요? 이 멋진 도시가 제공하는 모든 것들에 대한 탐험을 시작하려니 흥분됩니다.**

189내일 핌즐러 빌딩 215호실에서 만나 뵙기를 기대합니다.

감사합니다.

카루나 디마아노

어휘 address 해결하다 explore 탐험하다

186 세부 사항

번역 첫 번째 이메일에 따르면, 이전에 신입 사원들에게 발송된 것은?
(A) 광고
(B) 지원서
(C) 사원 ID 번호
(D) 사무실 단지로 가는 길 안내

해설 첫 이메일의 네 번째 단락 첫 문장에서 모트만 모터스 포털 계정이 최근 여러분께 보내 드린 직원 ID 번호를 이용하여 설정되고 여러분의 은행 계좌 정보가 계정에 입력되어 있는지 확인이 필요하다(we just need to ensure ~ information is entered there)고 했으므로 신입 사원들에게 직원 ID 번호가 발송되었음을 알 수 있다. 따라서 정답은 (C)이다.

어휘 application form 지원서, 신청서   direction 방향   complex 단지

> **Paraphrasing** 지문의 identification → 정답의 ID

187 세부 사항

번역 첫 번째 이메일에 따르면, 온라인 작업의 완료 마감일은?
(A) 6월 8일
(B) 6월 10일
(C) 6월 15일
(D) 6월 17일

해설 첫 이메일의 네 번째 단락 두 번째 문장에서 첨부된 설명서를 따라 마지막 단계를 완료해 달라(Please follow ~ complete this final step)며 6월 17일까지 해 줄 것을 요청한다(I ask that you do this by June 17)고 했으므로 정답은 (D)이다.

188 연계

번역 디마아노 씨는 어느 단계에서 문제를 겪고 있는가?
(A) 1단계
(B) 2단계
(C) 3단계
(D) 4단계

해설 설명문의 1단계에서 "새 사용자 등록" 페이지로 가서 직원 ID 번호를 입력하라(Go to ~ employee ID number)고 했는데, 두 번째 이메일의 두 번째 단락 첫 문장에서 디마아노 씨가 모트만 모터스 포털 계정을 설정하려고 하는데 제 직원 ID 번호에 문제가 있는 것 같다(I am trying ~ with my employee ID number)고 했으므로 디마아노 씨는 1단계의 직원 ID 번호 입력에 문제가 있음을 알 수 있다. 따라서 (A)가 정답이다.

189 연계

번역 디마아노 씨는 어느 부서에 입사하는가?
(A) 마케팅
(B) 고객 서비스
(C) 엔지니어링
(D) 기술 서비스

해설 첫 이메일의 세 번째 단락 두 번째 문장에서 엔지니어링 부서는 215호실로 출석하라(Engineering: report to room 215)고 했고, 두 번째 이메일의 마지막 문장에서 디마아노 씨가 내일 핌즐러 빌딩 215호실에서 만나 뵙기를 기대한다(I look forward ~ Pimzler Building)고 했으므로 디마아노 씨는 엔지니어링 팀에 합류할 것임을 알 수 있다. 따라서 (C)가 정답이다.

190 추론 / 암시

번역 두 번째 이메일에서, 디마아노 씨에 대해 암시된 것은?
(A) 대학을 막 졸업했다.
(B) 전에 아모스 씨를 만난 적이 있다.
(C) 건물을 찾는 일에 대해 걱정하고 있다.
(D) 최근에 샌안토니오로 이사했다.

해설 두 번째 이메일의 세 번째 단락 두 번째 문장에서 디마아노 씨가 오리엔테이션에 샌안토니오에 새로 온 사람들을 위한 정보가 포함되는지(Will the orientation ~ San Antonio?)를 물으며, 이 멋진 도시가 제공하는 모든 것들에 대한 탐험을 시작하려니 흥분된다(I am excited ~ city offers)고 한 것으로 보아 샌안토니오의 기존 거주자가 아님을 알 수 있다. 따라서 정답은 (D)이다.

어휘 graduate 졸업하다

191-195 이메일 + 청구서 + 회람

수신: 펠릭스 허먼 〈felixh@videogenieproductions.com〉
발신: 사프나 마타이 〈smathai@thehospitalequipmentco.com〉
날짜: 9월 17일
제목: 가편집본 영상 관련 참고 사항
첨부: @ 정보

허먼 씨께,

우리의 새 플루오로룩 이미저를 위한 정보 제공용 영상의 가편집본을 보내 주셔서 감사합니다. 지금까지 보기에는 훌륭한 것 같습니다. 플루오로룩이 최고의 의료 영상 장치인 이유를 명확히 보여줍니다. 최종 버전의 제작을 진행하기 전에 몇 가지 참고 사항이 있습니다.

- **191 20초: 병원 장비 회사의 역사에 대한 짧은 연대표를 삽입해 주시겠습니까? 이 이메일에 관련 정보를 첨부했습니다.**
- **192 1분: 이 장면에서 제어판의 상세 정보를 확인하는 것이 쉽지 않았습니다. 클로즈업 샷으로 교체해 주실 수 있을까요?**
- 2분: 의료 기술자가 환자의 위치를 잡아 주고 기계를 조정하는 장면이 너무 빨리 흘러갑니다. 이 부분의 속도를 늦출 수 있을까요?

9월 23일에 최종 버전을 볼 수 있기를 기대합니다. 늘 그렇듯이 비디오 지니 프로덕션에 계신 귀하와 귀하의 동료들의 훌륭한 작업에 감사드립니다.

194 프로젝트 관리자 사프나 마타이
병원 장비 회사

어휘 rough 대충 틀만 잡은; 초고   informational 정보를 제공하는   clearly 명확히   demonstrate 보여 주다   imaging device 영상 장치   insert 삽입하다   timeline 연대표   relevant 관련된   detail 세부 사항   sequence 장면, 순서   position ~의 자리를 잡다   patient 환자   adjust 조정하다

병원 장비 회사

청구서 9984

청구 날짜: 10월 25일

193(D) 설치 날짜: 10월 26일

195청구처:

올시티 병원

쇼어라인 가 3

클리어 레이크, 미네소타 55319

수량	품목 번호	설명	단가	총액
193(C)2	62630	플루오로룩 이미저	242,300달러	484,600달러
			193(B)배송 및 설치	2,350달러
			총액	486,950달러

어휘 invoice 청구서 billing 청구서 발부 installation 설치 bill 청구서를 보내다 quantity 수량 description 설명

회람

수신: 모든 병원 장비 회사 직원

발신: 마르시아 올리버, 영업 부사장

날짜: 10월 27일

답장: 수고하셨습니다!

플루오로룩 이미저의 성공적인 출시를 축하합니다! **195병원 장비 회사는 클리어 레이크에 있는 병원에 첫 판매를 개시했습니다.** 그리고 MDP 딜리버리에서 장비 두 대가 배송되었다고 알려왔습니다.

194특히 마타이 씨를 칭찬하고 싶습니다. 그녀는 우리가 여기까지 오는 데 중요한 역할을 했습니다. **195구입을 결정한 병원 관리자 파브리스 라몬테뉴 씨**는 자신의 결정이 정보 제공용 영상 때문이라고 했습니다. 그는 플루오로룩 이미저가 자신의 의료 기관에 왜 적합한 장치인가를 그 영상이 효과적으로 보여 주었다고 언급했습니다.

어휘 vice president 부사장 launch 출시 commend 칭찬하다 instrumental 중요한, 도움이 되는 administrator 관리자 credit B to A B를 A의 공이라고 말하다 remark 언급하다 effectively 효과적으로 institution 기관

---

191 세부 사항

번역 이메일에 첨부된 것은?

(A) 청구서에 대한 세부 정보

(B) 비디오 지니 프로덕션에 대한 후기

(C) 프로젝트 마감 일정

(D) 회사의 역사를 약술한 도표

해설 이메일의 두 번째 단락 첫 항목에서 20초 장면에 병원 장비 회사의 역사에 대한 짧은 연대표를 삽입해 줄 수 있는지(At 20 seconds ~ Hospital Equipment Company?) 물으며 이 이메일에 관련 정보를 첨부했다(I have attached ~ to this e-mail)고 했다. 따라서 정답은 (D)이다.

어휘 outline 개요를 서술하다

Paraphrasing 지문의 a timeline of the history ~ → 정답의 A graphic outlining a ~ history

192 세부 사항

번역 마타이 씨는 왜 1분째 장면을 교체하고 싶어하는가?

(A) 일부 내용이 명확하게 보이지 않는다.

(B) 일부 장비의 상표 표기가 잘못되었다.

(C) 해당 장면의 영상이 너무 빨리 움직인다.

(D) 의료 기술자가 너무 조용하게 말한다.

해설 이메일의 두 번째 단락 두 번째 항목에서 1분째 장면에서 제어판의 상세 정보를 확인하는 것이 쉽지 않았다(At 1 minute ~ in this scene)며 클로즈업 샷으로 교체해 줄 수 있는지(Could you replace ~ close-up shot?)를 묻고 있으므로 (A)가 정답이다.

어휘 visible 보이는 label 상표를 붙이다 incorrectly 부정확하게

Paraphrasing 지문의 had a hard time seeing the details → 정답의 Some content is not clearly visible.

193 Not / True

번역 플루오로룩 이미저에 대해 청구서에 명시된 것은?

(A) 할인가에 판매되었다.

(B) 배송이 무료였다.

(C) 구매자가 두 대를 주문했다.

(D) 10월 25일에 설치되었다.

해설 청구서의 표에 수량(Quantity)이 2대라고 나와 있으므로 정답은 (C)이다. 할인가에 대한 내용은 확인할 수 없으므로 (A)는 답이 될 수 없고, 배송 및 설치비(Delivery and Installation)는 2,350달러라고 나와 있으므로 (B)는 오답, 설치일은 10월 26일(Installation date: October 26)이라고 나와 있으므로 (D)도 오답이다.

어휘 free of charge 무료로 purchaser 구매자 install 설치하다

194 연계

번역 올리버 씨가 특별히 칭찬한 사람은 누구인가?

(A) 의료 기술자

(B) 병원 관리자

(C) 프로젝트 관리자

(D) 영상 제작자

해설 회람의 두 번째 단락 첫 문장에서 올리버 씨가 특히 마타이 씨를 칭찬하고 싶다(I would especially like to commend Ms. Mathai)고 했고, 이메일의 하단에 마타이 씨는 프로젝트 관리자(Ms. Sapna Mathai, Project Manager)라고 나와 있으므로 정답은 (C)이다.

195 연계

번역 라몬테뉴 씨는 어디에서 근무할 것 같은가?
(A) MDP 딜리버리
(B) 비디오 지니 프로덕션
(C) 병원 장비 회사
(D) 올시티 병원

해설 회람의 첫 단락 두 번째 문장에서 병원 장비 회사는 클리어 레이크에 있는 병원에 첫 판매를 개시했다(The hospital Equipment Company ~ Clear Lake)고 했고, 두 번째 단락의 세 번째 문장에서 파브리스 라몬테뉴 씨를 구입을 결정한 병원 관리자(The administrator ~ Mr. Fabrice Lamontagne)라고 했는데, 청구서의 청구처(Bill to)가 클리어 레이크에 있는 올시티 병원(All-City Hospital ~ Clear Lake)이라고 나와 있다. 따라서 라몬테뉴 씨는 클리어 레이크에 위치한 올시티 병원의 관리자임을 알 수 있으므로 정답은 (D)이다.

196-200 배송 전표 + 이메일 + 이메일

배송 전표

발신: 레이나 올리브 오일 회사
칼 타블라스 820
그라나다 18002, 스페인

수신: 베스트 프로덕츠 슈퍼마켓
중구 연해로 241
인천 22382, 대한민국

주문일: 11월 28일
주문 번호: SK6224

품목 번호	설명	수량
EVO160	750밀리리터 엑스트라버진 올리브유 표준 사이즈 손잡이 달린 유리병	15개
EVO161	1리터 엑스트라버진 올리브유 패밀리 사이즈 유리병	20개
EVO162	1.5리터 엑스트라버진 올리브유 셰프 사이즈 유리병	10개
197 EVO163	3리터 엑스트라버진 올리브유 대형사이즈 레이나 로고 양철통	5개
200 EVO001	50밀리리터 엑스트라버진 올리브유 12월 샘플 사이즈	2개

우리와 함께 이 계절을 기념하세요! 1월 31일까지 추가 주문 시 10% 할인됩니다.

어휘 description 설명 quantity 수량 cruet (기름·식초를 담는 양념병) bulk 대량 tin 통, 통조림

수신: 파블로 나달 〈pnadal@reinaoliveoilcompany.es〉
발신: 성민해 〈seongmh@bestproductssupermarket.co.kr〉
날짜: 12월 12일
제목: 주문 번호 SK6224

나달 씨께:

엑스트라버진 올리브유에 대한 최근 주문을 빠르게 처리해 주신 점 감사드립니다. 196안타깝게도 배송에 작은 문제가 있어 당신의 도움이 필요합니다. 파손되거나 누락된 것은 없었지만 1973리터짜리 대형 사이즈 컨테이너가 잘못 배송되었습니다.

이 제품들을 반송할 수 있도록 준비하려고 합니다. 어떻게 진행해야 하는지 알려 주세요.

감사합니다.

성민해
인수 및 유통, 베스트 프로덕츠 슈퍼마켓

어휘 fulfil 이행하다 shipment 배송 assistance 도움 damaged 파손된 missing 분실된 container 용기 arrange 준비하다 proceed 진행하다

수신: 성민해 〈seongmh@bestproductssupermarket.co.kr〉
발신: 파블로 나달 〈pnadal@reinaoliveoilcompany.es〉
날짜: 12월 14일
제목: 답장: 주문 번호 SK6224

성 씨께,

주문 번호 SK6224의 오류에 대해 사과드립니다. 귀하의 주문이 실수로 저희 전자 데이터베이스에 있는 다른 주문과 섞였다는 것을 파악했습니다. 198안타깝게도 저희는 창고에서 출하된 어떠한 물품도 재입고시킬 수 없습니다. 그러므로 추가 올리브유는 가지고 매장에서 판매하시면 될 것 같습니다. 또한, 199저희의 실수로 인한 것이므로 영업일 기준 5일에서 10일 이내에 추가 요금에 대한 환불을 받게 되실 것입니다.

저희는 현재 올리브 제철을 맞이하여 다음 주문에 대해 10% 할인을 제공하고 있습니다. 또한 20012월의 올리브 수확 축제 기간 동안에는 모든 배송물에 저희 회사의 클래식 올리브유 샘플이 포함되니 귀사의 쇼핑객들에게 무료로 배포해 주시기를 권해 드립니다.

저희는 베스트 프로덕츠 슈퍼마켓에 최상급 올리브유를 지속적으로 공급하기를 바랍니다.

파블로 나달
레이나 올리브 오일 회사 수출부 관리자

어휘 determine 알아내다 accidentally 실수로 combine 결합하다 restock 재입고하다 warehouse 창고 charge 요금 harvest 추수[수확] encourage 권장하다 with compliments 무료로

196 주제 / 목적

번역 첫 번째 이메일의 목적은?
(A) 주문하기
(B) 배송비 문의하기
(C) 배송 실수에 대해 논의하기
(D) 지불하기

해설 첫 번째 이메일의 첫 단락 두 번째 문장에서 안타깝게도 배송에 작은 문제가 있어 당신의 도움이 필요하다(Unfortunately, there is ~ need your assistance)고 했으므로 (C)가 정답이다.

어휘 inquire 문의하다

Paraphrasing 지문의 a ~ issue with the shipment
→ 정답의 a shipping mistake

TEST 10

197 연계

번역 성 씨가 언급하는 품목 번호는?
(A) EVO160
(B) EVO161
(C) EVO162
(D) EVO163

해설 첫 이메일의 첫 단락 세 번째 문장에서 성 씨가 3리터짜리 대형 사이즈 컨테이너가 잘못 배송되었다(the 3-litre bulk size containers were delivered in error)고 했고, 배송 전표의 표에 따르면 3리터짜리 엑스트라버진 올리브유 대형 사이즈(3-litre extra-virgin olive oil bulk size)의 품목 번호는 EVO163이라고 나와 있으므로 정답은 (D)이다.

198 추론 / 암시

번역 두 번째 이메일에서 레이나 올리브 오일 회사에 대해 암시한 것은?
(A) 신규 고객을 찾고 있다.
(B) 반품을 수락할 수 없다.
(C) 나달 씨의 소유이다.
(D) 올리브유 외에 다른 것도 유통한다.

해설 두 번째 이메일의 첫 단락 세 번째 문장에서 레이나 올리브 오일 회사의 파블로 나달이 안타깝게도 저희는 창고에서 출고된 어떠한 물품도 재입고시킬 수 없다(Unfortunately, we are unable to restock any items that have left our warehouse)고 했으므로 (B)가 정답이다.

> **Paraphrasing** 지문의 restock any items that have left our warehouse → 정답의 accept returns

199 세부 사항

번역 나달 씨가 성 씨를 위해 하겠다고 언급한 것은?
(A) 조사 착수
(B) 회사 안내책자 발송
(C) 환불 처리
(D) 수정된 청구서 발송

해설 두 번째 이메일의 첫 단락 마지막 문장에서 나달 씨가 성 씨에게 저희의 실수로 인한 것이므로 영업일 기준 5일에서 10일 이내에 추가 요금에 대한 환불을 받게 되실 것(you will receive a refund ~ because of our mistake)이라고 했으므로 정답은 (C)이다.

어휘 investigation 조사 arrange for 준비하다 revised 수정된 bill 청구서

200 연계

번역 품목 번호 EVO001이 배송에 포함된 이유는?
(A) 축제를 기념하고 축하하기 위해
(B) 회사의 신제품을 소개하기 위해
(C) 품절된 품목을 교체하기 위해
(D) 회사 데이터베이스의 문제를 해결하기 위해

해설 배송 전표의 표에 따르면 EVO001는 50밀리리터 올리브유 12월 샘플 사이즈(50-millilitre extra-virgin ~ sample size)라고 나와 있고, 두 번째 이메일의 두 번째 단락 두 번째 문장에서 12월의 올리브 수확 축제 기간 동안 모든 배송물에는 자사의 클래식 올리브유 샘플이 포함되어 있으니 귀사의 쇼핑객들에게 무료로 이 샘플들을 배포해 주기를 바란다(during our Olive Harvest Festival ~ with our compliments)고 했다. 따라서 EVO001은 올리브 수확 축제를 기념하기 위해 배송에 포함된 것이므로 (A)가 정답이다.

어휘 recognize 인정[기념]하다 out of stock 품절된 resolve 해결하다